W9-BVZ-347

Thomas Carlyle

THOMAS CARLYLE

A BIOGRAPHY

FRED KAPLAN

Cornell University Press

ITHACA, NEW YORK

Cornell University Press gratefully acknowledges a grant from the John Simon Guggenheim Memorial Foundation which helped to make possible the publication of this book.

First published 1983 by Cornell University Press.

Printed in the United States of America

The paper in this book is acid-free and meets the guidelines for permanence and durability of the Committee on Production Guidelines for Book Longevity of the Council on Library Resources.

Library of Congress Cataloging in Publication Data

Kaplan, Fred, 1937–
Thomas Carlyle : a biography.

Includes bibliographical references and index.
1. Carlyle, Thomas, 1795–1881—Biography. 2. Authors, Scottish—19th century—Biography. I. Title.
PR4433.K3 1983 824'.8 83-5364
ISBN 0-8014-1508-X

To Gloria

In a psychological point of view, it is perhaps questionable whether from birth and genealogy, how closely scrutinized soever, much insight is to be gained.—Thomas Carlyle, *Sartor Resartus*

The history of a man's childhood is the description of his parents and environment: This is his *in*articulate but highly important history . . . while of articulate he has yet none.—Thomas Carlyle, *The Life of John Sterling*

"I would," said Carlyle (answering the suggestion that he should write his autobiography), "as soon think of cutting my throat with my penknife when I get back home! —the biographers, too; if those gentlemen would let me alone I should be much obliged to them. I would say . . . Sweet friend, for Jesus' sake forbear!"—William Allingham, *A Diary*

One day [Carlyle] said, "As far as I can make out, the best portrait-painter who ever lived was one Cooper, in Cromwell's time. When painting Cromwell, Cromwell told him to put in the wart, and he did."—William Allingham, *A Diary*

Contents

Illustrations

proach, by its necessarily incomplete documentation, and by its author's personal intimacy with his subject. John Clubbe has recently reduced the four volumes of Froude's life and letters to one, primarily by eliminating the letters. Though Clubbe has preserved the virtues of Froude's seminal work, Froude's closeness to Carlyle and his own vested interest in some of the issues of Carlyle's life cannot, of course, be eliminated. David Alec Wilson produced in his six-volume biography a historical grotesquerie, a mass of undigested and unevaluated documentation whose main purpose was to prove that Carlyle was a saint and Froude a liar. Wilson's crusading assiduousness has provided us with a valuable but untrustworthy (and unreadable) repository of every document that he could collect relevant to redeeming Carlyle's reputation from Froude's "slander."

My interest has been in presenting the man who lived rather than engaging in discussion of his subsequent reputation. Accordingly, I have focused on primary material, both unpublished and published, and in every instance I have tried to secure the most authoritative and original text. Though I have read almost all the secondary material, from Victorian to contemporary, I have chosen to draw on this material only when it relates directly to my presentation of the life. Much valuable critical comment on Carlyle's works simply is not relevant to my scheme of presentation, and I hope that the authors of such studies will not feel slighted because of their necessary absence here. Those readers who are interested in the controversies and distortions that have burdened Carlyle scholarship can readily find them in numerous volumes in any adequate academic library. I intend my presentation of the life to speak for itself. Whatever his mistakes of insight and judgment, we need not apologize now for the exploitation of Carlyle by those whose insight and judgment were far inferior to his own. Whatever his failures, he was a man of compassion and humanity, whose life deserves our attention and our respect.

My major institutional debts are to the John Simon Guggenheim Memorial Foundation, New York, which kindly provided me with a fellowship, to Queens College, the City University of New York, which provided secretarial and duplication services, and to the Research Foundation of the City University of New York, which provided funds for travel in England and Scotland. I gratefully acknowledge their generous support. I am of course indebted to a large number of libraries and librarians for their cooperation in response to my visits and requests, and for permission to quote from unpublished materials. In particular I thank the Birmingham Public Library (England); the British Library; the Carlyle House, London, and the Arched House, Ecclefechan (the National Trust of England and the National Trust of Scotland); the Edinburgh University Library; the Library of the University of London; the London Library; the Masters and Fellows of Trinity College, Cambridge; the Trustees of the National Library of Scotland; the Victoria and Albert Museum; the Beinecke Rare Book and Manuscript Library, Yale University; the Henry E. Huntington Library and Art Gallery, San Marino, California; the Henry W. and Albert A. Berg Collection, the New York Public Library, Astor, Lenox and Tilden Foundations; the Houghton Library, Harvard University; the Paul Klapper Library, Queens College, the City University of New York; the Library of Bowdoin College; the Norman and Charlotte Strouse Collection of Thomas Carlyle, University Library, University of California, Santa Cruz; the Pierpont Morgan Library; and the Rare Book and Manuscript Library, Columbia University. Particularly helpful among librarians near and far were Rita Bottoms, Herbert Cahoon, C. P. Finlayson, Rosemary Graham, David M. Hamilton, Mimi Penchansky, Jean Preston, James S. Ritchie, Mary L. Robertson, Lola Szladits, and Marjorie G. Wynne. At Carlyle House, Chelsea, the former curators, Allan and Elizabeth Hay, and the current curator, Lt. Col. James Edgar, fetched and carried and opened and closed with enthusiasm. The current owners of Scotsbrig and Craigenputtoch, Thomas Blacklock and George and Renee Armour, were considerately hospitable, as was the Marquess of Northampton at Castle Ashby. Two substantial private collections of Carlyle letters were made available to me, the first by the kindness of Gordon N. Ray, the second by the kindness of the Marquess of Northampton; both have graciously provided permission for the publication of excerpts.

I am grateful to Georges Borchardt and Dorothy C. Young in New York and Richard Simon in London for their advice and for professional assistance. I am indebted to John Ackerman, an assiduous and talented manuscript editor, and Walter Lippincott, both of Cornell University Press. At Queens College, the City University of New York, Saul Novack has my warm thanks for his generous support throughout, as do William Hamovitch and Saul Cohen, all of whom have continually affirmed their commitment to scholars and scholarship. Ian Campbell of the University of Edinburgh provided assistance, hospitality, and friendship. I am grateful to Donald Hankey, architect, for his expert guidance at the Grange, Alresford; to Park and Jeanette Honan for hospitality in Birmingham; and to Ian Campbell, John Clubbe, K. J. Fielding, and Gloria Kaplan, for close, thoughtful readings of the manuscript. Among others whose assistance and support I acknowledge with thanks are the Honorable John A. Baring, Murray Baumgarten, Maier J. Benardete, Robert Colby, Vineta Colby, Robert

Day, Morris Dickstein, Horst Drescher, Martin Drury, Lillian Feder, Norman Fruman, Edward Geffner, Dolores Greenberg, Robert Greenberg, George Hendrick, Kenneth Heuer, Lois Hughson, Benjamin Kaplan, Julie Kaplan, Noah Kaplan, David Kleinbard, George Landow, Barbara Leavy, Peter Leavy, Allen Mandelbaum, Carlisle Moore, John Rosenberg, Clyde de L. Ryals, Charles Sanders, Mimi Silver, George Tennyson, Barney Triber, Gertrude Triber, Maureen Waters, Hugo Weisgall, Nathalie Weisgall, and Carl R. Woodring. To the latter I owe a unique debt of respect and affection; he is the "rigorous" teacher of "my youth" who for two decades has been a supporter and a friend. To a new friend, K. J. Fielding, to whose wise guidance and generous help this book owes much, I express my deep appreciation.

Fred Kaplan

Great Neck, New York

Thomas Carlyle

[1]

The Pursuer 1795–1816

In the quiet twilight the hoarse cawing of the rooks over Ecclefechan filled the young boy with sensations of mystery and beauty. The birds circled and returned to the Hill of Woodcockair two miles away, "mysterious to me . . . as the home of the rooks I saw flying overhead."[1] Ecclefechan in southwestern Scotland was the spot on earth his feelings and imagination most identified with throughout his life. Deeply a man of place, he hated wanderers and wandering, the nomadic obsession. In his mind and in his words he strained always to reproduce the movement of the rooks whose great circles gave form to mystery and established boundaries to the place he called home.

Born on December 4, 1795, in the Arched House, Ecclefechan, a building designed and constructed by his father and uncle, Thomas Carlyle soon discovered that his parents' world was circular, enclosing home, fields, family, meetinghouse, the rural arches of Christian Annandale, the interwoven community of Presbyterian Scotland. For generations the pattern had seemed to be permanent, but as he became a young adult it was his misfortune to find that his consciousness was the center of a circle that was collapsing. At its center was the new Victorian consciousness, crying like "an infant . . . in the night."

He was born long and lean to thickset parents. From the very beginning his fragility and his differentness made him a subject of concern. When he was two, however, the birth of a brother distracted parental attention, and in the years that followed he was able to explore Ecclefechan with other preschool children: the smoke and manure of a small market village; rural peace and isolation alternating with market-day sociability; the characters of the village—the beggar, the alcoholic, the blacksmith, the schoolmaster, the preacher. Soon, there were other brothers and sisters; and then the sight of death. His baby sister died in 1801. The coffinmaker went about his business; his mother wept. Later in the year, his uncle John died, his father's eldest brother. Before the funeral, the coverlid was lifted from "his pale, ghastly befilleted head," the sight of which horrified the young boy; he had seen "the King of Terrors."[2] He learned the rudiments of reading from his mother, arithmetic from his father, and when it was time he attended first a private school in Ecclefechan, and then, at age six, the nearby Hoddam parish school.[3] Noted for brightness but not for ruggedness, for eagerness to learn but not for social adaptability, he immediately became the pride of the schoolmaster, the special young person whom approving adults and jealous schoolmates label with the burden of differentness. For his parents, that quality had its rightful place in the circle of tradition. If their son was to be a man of learning, he would be a minister of the Lord; within their society the alternative for differentness was either madness or apostasy. For the young boy, there was worry, confusion, and resentment, some of which he expressed directly, much of which he repressed.[4]

Growing up in the shadow of the local meetinghouse, the young boy was taught to repress physical instincts. His parents' Burgher-Secession affiliation focused on the small, elite community that in his childhood built its own meetinghouse in Ecclefechan, found leadership in the Reverend John Johnstone, and became famous throughout Annandale for pious sincerity. Too young to attend worship, he followed the well-beaten path between his home and the meetinghouse both in his circular imagination and in the religious routines of his family. Hearing the frenzied barking of a neighbor's dog locked indoors, he took the familiar path to the open meetinghouse door and called out, " 'Matty, come home to Snap.' "[5] Once he reached the age where his behavior was deemed controllable, his attendance was required. Between the ages of five and eleven, he heard innumerable sermons from "the priestliest man I ever under any ecclesiastical guise was privileged to look upon."[6] It did not matter what theology the young boy was able to comprehend; he understood the essential message of his parents and his minister by example: "A man's 'religion' consists not of the many things he is in doubt of and tries to believe, but of the few he is assured of, and has no need of effort for believing."[7] The subliminal voice of his parents' community told him, among other things, that physical instincts came from the devil, not from God.

He sought two avenues of escape from the conflict that he began to feel between the restrictions of his parents' community and his own

Birthplace of Thomas Carlyle, Ecclefechan. Photograph by J. Patrick. By permission of the Edinburgh University Library.

instincts. In the changes of weather, he pursued the mysterious beauty of the Annandale countryside,[8] and soon he discovered the ancient remains of the Roman occupation. In his excited imagination the Anglo-Saxon tower of Repentance Hill became a physical representation of that heroic period that had witnessed the creation of the tribal designations of the nation. As a young man, he read Wordsworth, Southey, and the other Lake poets. When he raised his eyes, the sunlit view across the Solway Firth to the Cumberland Hills and the Lake Country took on an additional soft resonance.

The same glow that illuminated the natural landscape connected it with the world of the only human community he knew in his childhood years. Strategically located and large enough to maintain a number of rural industries, Ecclefechan provided the surrounding farmers with a busy market. The young boy explored its commercial life, curious about people and their activities, apparently a familiar observer, particularly on weekly market days and at the frequent cattle fairs. Ecclefechan drew cattlemen, traders, merchants, and entertainers from all over southern Scotland, as well as "the Italian with his mirrors and elaborate toys . . . from the Lake of Como, . . . Gamblers, Balladsingers, Beggars, dwarfs" mingling "their thousand voices with the bellowing of oxen and the din of buying and selling."[9] Still the town was small enough to retain a circular wholeness. The barter system predominated, wages were low, and cash was meager. The general agricultural depression and the stoicism of rural Calvinism combined to create a scarcity economy. Thomas saw his father's sympathy with the poor laborers, who in difficult years drank water from the brook at lunchtime instead of eating, too proud to complain, too embarrassed to draw attention to their plight. But James Carlyle "never meddled with Politics: he was not there to govern, but to be governed; could still *live,* and therefore did not *revolt.*"[10] While it was true that " 'the lot of a poor man was growing worse and worse,' " still "the precept reaches all the human clan / Submit to ev'ry ordinance of man."[11]

James Carlyle was shaped by neglect. Food had been a luxury and self-help a necessity in his small but noncohesive family. As an adult, he reacted against this boyhood isolation, working with his second wife, Thomas' mother, to make his own family into an intensely tight, self-sustaining unit. Whereas his father had been self-indulgent, lax, and undisciplined, James Carlyle became willful, purposeful, and defiant, "the strongest-minded man" his son ever knew.[12] His father had been indifferent to formal education, but James not only pushed his own children into literacy but propelled two of the sons into professional careers. His father farmed but did all work indifferently, for he felt that there was nothing sacred about labor. James Carlyle worked with full commitment. Thomas would recall that "we were all practically taught that *work* (temporal or spiritual) was the only thing we had to do; and incited always by precept and example to do it *well,*"[13] for "whosoever is not working is begging or stealing."[14] Whereas his grandfather cared little for religion, his father became a model of religious commitment.

It is doubtful that any single incident motivated James Carlyle's turn to religion. Instead, he felt a gradually increasing sense of the sinful nature of all men and the uselessness of all activities that interfered with the acceptance of oneself as a sinner who could be saved by God's grace. James Carlyle had ample evidence that he was a sinner, for he had inherited, among other qualities, the Carlyle family temper. As young men he and his brothers were notorious for their brawls, "among the best drinkers and best headsplitters at the annual fairs of the village. . . . Pithy, bitter-speaking bodies, and awfu' fighters."[15] His father had been "a fiery man; irascible,"[16] and like him James responded to provocation with a defense so prompt and thorough that it could hardly be distinguished from aggression. Thomas later attempted to justify his father's temper: "To me they were not and are not other than interesting and innocent [acts] scarcely ever, perhaps never, to be considered as *aggressions,* but always as *defences,* manful assertions of man's rights against man that would infringe them,—and victorious ones."[17]

Silhouettes of James and Margaret Carlyle. Reprinted from Thomas Carlyle, *Reminiscences,* edited by James Anthony Froude (London, 1881).

But there were countervailing models to the anarchic, uncontrollable temper. The tradition of the Covenanters was strong in Annandale, the Secession Church had been formed—"there was the Bible to read."[18] James Carlyle took as his model Robert Brand, a maternal uncle, from whom he "consciously and unconsciously . . . may have learned more . . . than from any other individual, . . . a just man and of wise insight . . . a rigorous Religionist . . . filled with a celestial Philosophy of the earthly Life." Though his father had read Anson's *Voyages* and the *Arabian Nights,* James himself would "not tolerate anything fictitious in books," sternly forbidding "his children to read the *Arabian Nights*—'those downright lies,' he called them."[19] Becoming "grimly religious," he attempted to live every moment of his life as if salvation, the most important aim of man's existence, were to be approached only through a complete fulfillment of the rules and spirit of the Burgher Seceder Church.

Each day James Carlyle read the Bible to himself and his family. Calvin he knew indirectly through the *Confession of Faith* and the catechisms, Knox through the covenant and through echoes of *The Book*

her children the conviction that her love was based on faith alone, a gift of God's grace which those whom God had chosen for his love could never lose, for "it was the Most High God that made Mothers and the sacred affection of children's hearts."[29] Much as he revered his father's authority, the deepest emotional attachment of his life was to his mother. She, not his wife or his father, was his ultimate dependency, and, both while she was alive and after her death, he conversed with her as with his other self.

Still, his mother could not prevent him from following the natural bent of his talent for learning. Nor could she check her husband's determination to encourage their eldest son's schooling, whatever the consequences. Unwilling to "part with him from her sight, still less trust him among the contaminations of a boarding-school," she vigorously argued against his going to Annan Academy; six miles distant, it was an alien world. James Carlyle simply said that his son would go, and on "26 May 1806, a bright sunny morning" that Thomas remembered all his life, he walked with his son to Annan.[30]

As Thomas left home, his mother extracted a reaffirmation of his promise that he would never fight. But she did not forbid him to fight back with his tongue, and he soon became expert at defending himself verbally, rapidly developing his talent for sarcastic retorts whose aggressive defensiveness became his most effective way of dealing with a hostile world. But at Annan Academy verbal skill was not a sufficient defense. Differentness was an incitement to aggression. In "Wotton" he depicted his schoolmates as cruel embodiments of "the rude, savage, natural man . . . dead to all voice of mercy or justice," who sensed that he felt "orphaned and alone." So "they flouted him, they beat him, they jeered and tweaked and tortured him by a thousand cunning arts, to all of which he could only answer with his tears; so that his very heart was black within him."[31]

The "defilement" ran the usual range of physical crudities that "rude, savage, natural" boys inflict on "inferiors, whether frogs, vagrant beggars, or weaker boys!"[32] The young boy felt demeaned, and the emotional trauma was deep. He struggled not only with savage insult but also with his mother's prohibition against fighting. At the end of his second or the beginning of his third year, he could take it no longer. If it was "disgraceful to be beaten . . . it was only a shade less disgraceful to have so much as fought." He felt the anxiety of separation from his mother, but he also felt the anxiety of victimization by his peers. Finally, he "revolted against them, and gave stroke for stroke." The beatings decreased. Though still harassed, "more cunningly, but not less effectually than before," the young Carlyle felt the pleasure that stems from catharsis: he had raised the battle to a different level. In his courageous fury, he had revealed his "genius" and superiority.[33]

Annan Academy specialized in training "large classes, at low cost, for University entrance at the age of fourteen," the basic subjects being French, Latin, arithmetic, algebra, and geography.[34] Classical studies extended beyond rudimentary Latin only as far as the Greek alphabet. Mathematics, which initially he found challenging and satisfying, soon became young Thomas' strongest academic subject. He was quick with French; indeed, he found modern languages attractive generally, and in the next decades taught himself Spanish, Italian, and German. By any standards, however, the education offered by Annan Academy was such that intellectually serious students were encouraged to rely heavily on the autodidacticism that has such a distinguished history in British culture. Indeed, Carlyle believed that whatever of importance he learned, he had not learned through formal schooling.

Initially, his intellectual bent earned the contempt of his contemporaries, further isolating him from companionship. He turned increasingly to books and began to read with time-consuming intensity. At the residence of a barrel-maker, where a number of Annan Academy boys boarded, he found an extensive lending library that included the novels and romances that his father had sternly prohibited the family from reading. Taught that romances were directly corrupting and that novels undermined a total commitment to religious facts, Thomas had been encouraged to carry with him, as both physical possession and moral commitment, *the* book of Ecclefechan, the Bible. Now, however, he had found an irresistible treasure house, from which he borrowed Smollett's *Roderick Random* and *Humphry Clinker*. In the next decade he read through Defoe, Fielding, Sterne, Congreve, and the *Arabian Nights*. Though he later developed a condescending attitude toward his contemporaries who wrote fiction, he always exempted those novelists he had first read as a youth. "To this day I know few writers equal to Smollett," he remarked at the age of sixty.[35] Such reading provided imaginative pleasure at a time before his ascetic moralism had hardened into an argument that would prevent him from enjoying fiction.

Fortunately, there suddenly rose before him another treasure of satisfaction, one that could be reconciled with the Bible and still provide some of the pleasures of reading secular literature. "One day in the street . . . I found a wandering Italian resting a board with" a "very bad" picture drawn on it, crying "images." Among the drawings was "a figure leaning on a pedestal with 'The Cloudcapt towers,' etc. Various passersby looked on, and a woman read aloud the verses, very badly, and then the name below, 'Shankespeare,' that was the way she gave it, 'Shankespeare.' " No one in his Ecclefechan household had ever read a word of Shakespeare, and the name was completely strange to the young boy's ears.[36] Soon he was avidly reading and rereading all the plays, enthralled by the imaginative, poetic depiction of man's worldly passions and philosophic perplexities. Shakespeare's realistic stoicism expressed truths that seemed compatible with the religious vision that was the foundation of his parents' piety. But, in addition, the linguistic and dramatic context gratified his senses and stimulated his imagination. He had found at an early age his lifelong favorite author—the author he would quote more than any other and use as his model for the writer as hero.

3.

The first two years at Annan Academy passed with excruciating slowness, the third more rapidly. Each weekend he walked (or rode, if the opportunity presented itself) to Ecclefechan and back on the road that passed Repentance Tower, Hoddam Hill, and Woodcockair.[37] The circle that was his world remained basically intact, though the flight of the rooks had begun to "circle downward to darkness." The family, of course, welcomed his weekly return. His mother felt the threat to their closeness created by his residence away, his academic studies, his gradual growing into adolescent problems. To his brothers and sisters, his weekend visits were special occasions, the return of the hero from the outside world, touched by its glamour but untainted by its corruption. These sabbatical weekends provided a loving embrace that compensated to some extent for the lonely weekdays, the visits sufficiently pleasurable to shape his lifelong pattern of frequent return from places far more distant than Annan. For "we Carlyles," Thomas wrote to his brother Alexander in 1820, "are a clannish people; because we have all something original in our formation, and find, therefore, less than common sympathy with others; so that we are constrained as it were to draw to one another, and to seek that friendship in our own blood which we do not find so readily elsewhere."[38]

Thomas bore the burdens and received the rewards of an eldest son. An older half-brother from his father's brief first marriage, a John Carlyle known as John of Cockermouth, had left the family to live with his deceased mother's parents, fading into unimportance from the moment of James Carlyle's remarriage. The next child, Alexander, born in 1797, had almost no formal education. Lacking his older brother's spark of early brilliance, "Sandy" or "Alick" found neither the initiative within himself nor the support from his family which might have given him opportunities for formal education. While his older brother performed precocious wonders to family applause, Alick became a farmer like his father. The third child was a daughter, who died within two years, the fourth a son who was to be, after his mother, Thomas' closest companion from his family. As a bright young student, John Aitken Carlyle took his brother as a model and followed him as best he could. The second daughter of the Carlyle family, born in 1803, survived the infancy that the first had not, but died of cancer of the bowels at the age of twenty-seven, her father's and her eldest brother's favorite, "the clearest, practically wisest little child. . . . My Father's life-*cloak* . . . his do-all, and necessary-of-life."[39] But to his youngest brother and three surviving younger sisters (James, born in 1805, Mary, Jean, and Janet, three, five, and eight years younger than the youngest son) Thomas soon became a deeply loved and heroic figure who bridged the world of Annandale and the world beyond.

By the beginning of 1808, his third year at the academy, Thomas began to reap the rewards of academic effort, the recognition of his superiority. Earlier, on one of his visits to the "grand schoolroom" during the particularly bitter first two years, James Carlyle had sat down by his son "and asked whether" he "was all well." Looking nervously at his schoolmates, Thomas had been relieved to see that they did not laugh.[40] But now his weekend progress reports increasingly glowed with confidence and self-satisfaction. His growing ability to express himself, inseparable from both his need to defend himself and his academic accomplishments, colored the accounts of his activities with which he entertained his parents. The more aggressively argumentative he became, the less eager most of his schoolmates were to tangle with him. His father, himself a sharp-tongued deflater of other people's pretensions, admired this same ability in his son. "Once, when . . . a pious old neighbor-woman who had come in was exciting herself in a theological controversy with the divinity student on some point or other, he broke out, 'Thou auld crack-brained enthusiastic, dost thou think to argue wi' our Tom?' "[41]

Soon the assumption that had been implicit in the decision to send him to Annan became explicit: he was to continue his education at the University of Edinburgh. Since his nine-year-old brother Alick showed no interest in school, there would be no family investment in *his* education. But in Tom's case the possibility that he would be a minister demanded support. Moreover, it would cost no more to go to the university than to attend Annan Academy. Carlyle later remembered that his father was "*always* GENEROUS to me in my school expenses; never by grudging look or word did he give me any pain."[42] The satisfaction of standing up to his schoolboy enemies was now increased by the knowledge that his life was about to enter a decisive, expansive phase. He passed the summer holidays at home and then, early in

November 1809, his parents put him under the charge of a carter who was taking bulk goods and another university-bound boy up to Edinburgh. Mother and father accompanied their son to the edge of town. It was still dark, the morning frosty. Margaret Carlyle gave him a two-volume Bible to keep him company the rest of the way. From a pass beyond Moffat, he had his last view of the highest Annandale landmark, Burnswark Hill; already he felt lonely. It took the travelers three days to make the eighty miles to Edinburgh. By the beginning of the second day, he had traveled farther from Annandale than his father was ever to do in his life.

4.

On the third afternoon, Edinburgh came into sight, the rock fortress of the old town an imposing image of a new world. Attempting to conceal his "sorrow" and "weariness," the young stranger felt a mixture of depression and excitement, "mysterious hopes and forecastings of what Edinburgh and the Student element would be."[43] The two boys took temporary lodging, then rushed out to see the sights of the city, scurrying up the Royal Mile to St. Giles, the Parliament, and the Castle. They looked at the "sublime Horse-Statue in Parliament Square." To his surprise, the experienced Tom Smail, an older Annan Academy graduate, pushed open a door behind which glowed Carlyle's introduction to the discordance of modern life: "an immense Hall, dimly lighted from the top of the walls, and . . . all in strange *chiaroscuro,* and filled with what I thought . . . a thousand or two of human creatures. . . . Some . . . in wig and black gown, some . . . in common clothes, . . . red-velvet figures, . . . Advocates pleading to Judges. . . . Certain wildly plangent lamentable kinds of sounds or echoes . . . pierced the universal noise of feet and voices."[44]

He soon made his way the short distance from his bleak lodgings in Simon Square to the university buildings, some narrow and grim with age, others disheveled by a temporarily suspended rebuilding from which the new quadrangle was to rise.[45] By the third day he had paid his library fee and registered for two classes, the first in intermediate Latin, which he had already mastered, the second in introductory Greek, of which he knew only the alphabet. Professor Christison taught Latin effectively, with a wide range of easy references to literature, history, and science; Professor Dunbar, conducting his large Greek class indifferently and inefficiently, did not allow Thomas even the hope that he might leave that class more knowledgeable than when he had entered. Observing his classmates, most of them poor, dirty, and anxious, he concluded that they had come to "the worst of all hitherto discovered Universities. . . . Right Education is, as nearly as may be, impossible: however, in degrees of wrongness there is no limit."[46] Within a week depression had overwhelmed his expectations of "a pure 'city of the mind,' glorious as the habitation of wisdom, and cloud-capt . . . with all earthly splendour."[47] "Eleven-hundred Christian striplings" had been "turned loose . . . in a square enclosure . . . with a small, ill-chosen Library . . . to tumble about as they listed, from three to seven years: certain persons, under the title of Professors, being stationed at the gates, to declare aloud that it was a University, and exact considerable admission-fees."[48]

He was abruptly made aware for the first time of the radical dislocation of the natural environment by the complexities of the modern city. Exploring the streets of the old town, he soon expanded his walks to the Royal Mile from Holyrood to the Castle, then across the drained marshes to Princes Street and the New Town, still under construction, whose Georgian luxuries made him ill at ease. Well-dressed cosmopolites strolled among expensive shops while he and his schoolmates lived in dirty, airless rooms, trying to make about twenty pounds last the six-month university session. Thomas immediately detested that from which he was excluded, and his keen eyes soon detected the degradation of a city rich with a variety of life, much of which was morally suspect and physically ugly, especially to one who was accustomed to the rural simplicity of Annandale. Years later, he would recall that Edinburgh was "a corrupt European city, full of smoke and sin."[49]

Though poor, Thomas was not impoverished. The twenty pounds on which he maintained himself from November to April represented at least one-fifth of his family's maximum cash income. With a steady supply of eggs, butter, and oatmeal brought from home by a carrier who regularly delivered supplies to university students from Annandale, his diet was similar to that of both his fellow students and his family in general. His room was narrow, dim, and spare; his clothes homespun and few—within the student world, then, he was distinguished only by his competence in Latin, his general unsociability, and his avid reading.

The friends of his first year were the books he borrowed from the college library. To the extent that he preferred to be alone, his student contemporaries apparently obliged him. Unhappy in his loneliness, he still felt proudly superior, his readiest defense against any overture of friendship being sarcasm and a retreat to his books. At the same time, he had suddenly become aware of the peculiarities of his Annandale accent and avoided speaking with any one he suspected might feel superior to him. As his autobiographical persona in *Sartor Resartus* remarks, "a keen and painful feeling of his own weakness, added to a certain gloomy consciousness of his real intrinsic superiority, rendered him at once suspicious and contemptuous of others."[50] The Bible that his mother had armed him with was his key to moral discriminations. Clearly he was nervous about sex and his own sexuality, later writing that his emotional training, though in "Wotton" he calls it "his principle," "forbade him to participate" in the "amusements, too often riotous and libertine," of his generally coarse colleagues, whose "impure influences," he often felt, "were contaminating and seducing him. Contaminate him they did, but seduce him they could not."[51] In short, the pattern established at Annan Academy had reasserted itself: reading, withdrawal, sarcasm. He was as unhappy his first year at Edinburgh as he had been at Annan.

Just as the lengthening spring days began to cheer him, the school year was over. Eagerly leaving Edinburgh, he saw his home again on a bright April morning, the memory of which remained vivid throughout his life: his father, dressed brightly in a red plaid, "walking out to try whether he would not happen to see me coming."[52] He stayed with his family for six months, granted the exemption from chores due a young man whose time had to be devoted to his studies for the ministry and whose health, after a winter in the noxious city, had to be fortified with nourishing food and frequent exercise. In November 1810 he returned to Edinburgh. His brothers and sisters cried at parting, and his parents reassured him of their love. His mother was particularly concerned about his spiritual well-being, for she knew that his restless mind had begun to question the claims of Christian miracles. He had asked her, " 'Did God Almighty come down and make wheelbarrows in a shop?' " In the summer night "she lay awake . . . for hours praying and weeping bitterly."[53] "Pale doubt, rising like a spectral shadow, was to be seen, distorting or obscuring the good and holy."[54]

Back in Edinburgh, he sensed that his previous isolation might have been self-imposed. The urban environment was still depressing, but at least it was familiar, and he had made a promising new acquaintance in Thomas Murray.[55] Three years older, more advanced in his studies and interested in literature, Murray was willing to befriend the provincial boy who had read unusually widely and could talk with enthusiastic assertiveness about interesting books and people. There were other opportunities for worthy companionship, for he was now sufficiently mature to begin to distinguish the people and situations that offered him opportunities from those that did not. He had grown to his full height in the past year, and now stood at a little under six feet; a thin, gangling adolescent with light blue eyes, clearing complexion, small, recessive top lip, and thrusting jaw.

The fifteen-year-old was attracted by the spectacle of the law courts, and fascinated by executions. He went to see a man "hanged for horse-stealing. He was a strong man, grimly silent. His body spun and twitched horribly." He could not rid his imagination of that scene. "At last I drew the horrible figure on paper as exactly as I could, and thenceforth it ceased to haunt me." He went to another execution: "an old woman who killed an infant, bastard of her son, and who had the reputation of a witch. She declared they *could not* hang her." He watched them put the rope around "the mere old wrinkled wretched bundle" and push her dangling into space, where she writhingly died, a testimonial to eternal facts. Three "footpads" or muggers assaulted him while he was walking; only his hat was damaged. A little later he saw three young "footpads" actually hanged.[56] The swift finality of such justice disturbed him. Was man dealing effectively with social problems? Or were these executions the will of God, eternal necessities enacted through the agency of man? Whose servant was "the King of Terrors"? He was morbidly fascinated by these hangings, whose images were as persistently painful as religious doubt and equally inseparable from his mother's unhappy tears.

In the schoolroom that second year, he felt less vulnerable emotionally. Bored students slept, yawned, scratched, and even read newspapers in Professor Dunbar's continuation of the Greek course. Active distaste kept him awake in Professor Ritchie's introductory class in logic, for the worldly minister taught a combination of mechanistic philosophy and elementary logic which seemed totally inconsistent with the religious beliefs of his parents. It was his first exposure to competent mechanism, the reduction of man and natural forces to a narrow series of positivistic rules that operate like a machine or a formula. But his first-year mathematics class with Professor John Leslie was a different matter. A fat, absent-minded eccentric who lectured with enthusiastic brilliance and taught mathematics, especially geometry, as part of a holistic system of natural forces, Leslie devoted particular attention to bright students who could keep up with him. The young man had finally found a teacher he could admire.

The truth of mathematics, according to Leslie, was based on "sensory data," universal mathematical truths directly related to the actual physical facts of experience.[57] In mathematics, ideal abstractions and human realities merged. The Common Sense school of philosophy that Leslie represented resisted the new analytic algebra, maintaining that synthetic geometry, based on Euclidean principles, "belonged to the general culture by virtue of its intellectual, moral, and aesthetic nature."[58] To the young Carlyle, such mathematics seemed part of a cohesive system rather than an isolated skill, consistent with the holistic obsession that was one of the chief characteristics of his parents' world.

There seemed no incompatibility between mathematics and preparation for the ministry, though in private the young man already doubted that his parents' ambition for him would be fulfilled. Suddenly mathematics dominated his academic interests, supplemented by his wide reading in literature, history, and science.

By the next session, when he enrolled in his newly found mentor's advanced mathematics course, he had already glimpsed the possibility that in mathematics he might find a vocation that would help him to support himself, either during his preparation for the ministry or as a substitute for it. With no shortage of beginning students to tutor in the subject, he appreciated the value of some small earnings. Mathematics was real, solid, specific. It appealed to his problem-solving enthusiasm. But it was also a system of both notation and description that cohered to the larger facts of the universe. In Leslie's mathematics one reasoned by comparison and analogy rather than by mechanical logic.[59] Thomas found such leaps of the mind exciting. Fifteen years later, in the exaggerated rhetoric of "Wotton," he captured the fantasy of the schoolboy mathematician who "gloried to track the footsteps of the mighty Newton . . . privileged to look from his high eminence, and to behold with thy own eyes the order of that stupendous fabric."[60]

By the summer of 1812 he had adjusted both to Edinburgh, where he stayed during much of the long vacation, and to his new view of himself. In addition to advanced mathematics, he had studied moral philosophy with the well-known proponent of the Scottish school of practical idealism, Thomas Brown, who had just succeeded the famous Dugald Stewart. To the boy from the Annandale countryside, "Missy Brown's" eloquence and enthusiasm seemed simplistic, his preciosity of manner both repellent and threatening. He remembered Brown's class as "unprofitable utterly & bewildering & dispiriting."[61] But now that he had mathematics and Leslie, he felt less bewildered by false systems. When he enrolled for his final-year courses in November, he reregistered in advanced mathematics, the common practice among serious mathematicians who wanted Leslie's guidance at the most sophisticated level the university could provide. He also enrolled in John Playfair's course in natural philosophy, or "Physics," which combined studies of the properties of the physical world with the mathematics that provided a symbolic language to describe them. He found that the distinguished elderly professor, whose mind and courtly manners had been formed in the rational glow of the previous century, hardly noticed him, though he worked hard, sometimes finding himself the only prepared student, sometimes the only student at all. When later in the term Playfair asked him to do a translation, he jumped at the opportunity to distinguish himself, only to feel rejected when the professor wrote a very lukewarm commendation of his work.[62] In Leslie's small class he felt appreciated.

5.

During 1812, his last year in the Arts Faculty, Carlyle continued to devote almost all his academic time to mathematics and most of his personal time to intensive reading. He carted armfuls of books, including a complete Shakespeare, back to his room. Resenting restrictions on borrowing, he considered the librarian an enemy, a prototype of the dry-as-dust categorizer whose professional mission was to prevent him from getting the books he wanted. Once secluded in the privacy of his room, he populated his imaginative world with literary characters and philosophical and scientific concepts.

This final year and a half as an arts student was, by comparison with his first years, his golden time. His talent and seriousness had been recognized immediately by Professor Leslie, retroactively by Professor Christison. Whatever economic perils the future might bring, he could still in good conscience accept his father's support. Though his lodgings were uncomfortable and the city unwholesome, he found himself growing used to the rhythmic movement between urban tensions and rural withdrawal. The city offered books, Annandale solitude; but he well knew that he was capable of making his own solitude wherever he went. Indeed, he sometimes feared that his studiousness would cut him off from other people, that his compulsion to avoid the infection of the city would deny him the city's advantages.

His successful summer in Edinburgh in 1812 apparently increased his confidence that he could balance his urban needs and his private compulsions. His face became familiar at the meetings of student debating clubs, whose affairs he found contemptible enough to parody but attractive enough to attend irregularly. He began to make a few friends, first Thomas Murray, then Robert Mitchell, a bright literature student also interested in mathematics who attended Professor Leslie's courses. During his final year, he found himself the key member of a small group of advanced students including, in addition to Murray and Mitchell, James Johnston, George Jeffrey, John Hill, and Clint Johnson. Loosely bound together by their intellectual concerns and their economic situations, these young men were eager to find sympathetic peers with whom they could share their amusements and anxieties. All of them seemed destined, at best, to making a bare living in the church or the schoolroom.

Thomas' habitual sarcasm seemed less offensive to these new friends than to those for whom he was a stranger with a dangerous verbal sting. What alienated others, his companions admired, seeing it as support for their belief that he was a young man of genius. His lively, ironic letters during the summers established his reputation for a literary distinction whose merits his friends hoped to appropriate. The virtue of his vices was such that they raised him to the level of Swift, nicknaming him "The Dean" or "The Doctor" and thereby implying that he too looked down from his high intellectual and moral standards on "the most pernicious race of little odious vermin that Nature ever suffered to crawl upon the surface of the earth."[63] But they were also aware that his aggressiveness was a defense against shyness and insecurity; that he could be marvelously entertaining; that he did not mean his sarcastic criticism to be taken as personal scorn; and that he was a victim of the same anxieties that plagued them.

Back at Ecclefechan for the summer of 1813, the young man of eighteen spent his time between "laziness" and "business," his mind on both Edinburgh gossip and his own future. Since he did not accompany his family to the meetinghouse each Sunday, his parents were soon aware that their eldest son no longer shared their conception of religious duties. But they assumed that he was still preparing to attend divinity school, preferably the Burgher Divinity Hall in Selkirk. Edinburgh, however, was infinitely preferable to Carlyle; there he had friends, associations, challenges; at Selkirk he would be a lonely novice, restricted by a parochial library. Since he doubted that he would actually complete the course anyway, he thought that it would make more sense to go to the Divinity Hall of the National Church in Edinburgh, where his personal life would be more rewarding and where he would have access to alternative academic and professional training. Soon he must begin to earn a living, and in Edinburgh he could find students, bide his time, and study mathematics.

In November 1813 he enrolled in three classes in Divinity Hall, soon finding that his professors were part of the clerical conspiracy to make religion spiritless and learning dull. Making haste quite slowly, he chose the slower of two curricular alternatives, six years of nonsupervised study after his residency with six annual appearances at Divinity Hall to present trial sermons. Although he did not look forward to leaving Edinburgh at the end of the academic year, the undemanding course of nonresidential study had a certain utility, for it allowed him to soften his father's sacrifices by earning his own living while postponing a vocational commitment. Simultaneously, he found ample time to pursue his real intellectual interests. In 1813, and for several years thereafter, he borrowed from the library books on electricity, poetry, drama, the essay, and fiction—from Benjamin Franklin to Cervantes. But it was "Geometry" that "shone before" him "as undoubtedly the *noblest* of all sciences." He "prosecuted it (or Mathematics generally) in all" his "best hours and moods."[64]

The city that he had once found repellent was now more attractive than any alternative. Though some of his friends had been forced to leave Edinburgh, he still had a wide acquaintance among his fellow students. Of all his friends, Thomas Murray, who lived in the same lodging house on South Richmond Street, most encouraged Carlyle's sharp tongue and satiric imagination. Murray enthusiastically trumpeted the merits both of a literary career and of an attractive Miss Merchant. With the latter the two young men played a purposefully dangerous game of collaboration and competition designed to provide flirtation without the risk of commitment. Like many of their country and class, they were aware that an early engagement and the ensuing family obligations posed grave risks to a successful career. Still, a powerful sexual tension led them to tempt one another and Miss Merchant on. When she took their game as serious courtship, however, Murray felt himself in danger. "I regret very much that I courted her acquaintance so much, for after having had some private walks with a female a person cannot break the connection for some time with any degree of propriety."[65] Safe in Annandale, Carlyle readily agreed that she was vain, affected, empty-headed, and that he had "already wasted too much time on her and those like her."[66]

Such affairs of the heart (and of the body) were much on the minds of young Carlyle and his friends. The most witty of his correspondents, John Hill, noting the contradiction between Thomas' pose as a "stoic, platonic, humdrum, bookworm sort of fellow" and the particular interest he took in Hill's "*affaires de coeur,*" counseled him "to fall in love. . . . You will be the better for it."[67] The next summer, Carlyle offered Murray advice that, apparently, was really intended for himself: "Do not get in love—if you can help it."[68] Aware of what it meant to be "*goatish*" and what it meant to be pure, Carlyle shrank from contamination, the strict standards of his parents forbidding masturbatory sex as well as fornication.[69] He never seems to have deviated from his parents' law. In some cases, however, there might be irresistible forces. He wrote to Robert Mitchell, his other confidant, that he should "Watch, watch . . . the passions and appetites and *lusts* [underscored twice] of the flesh."[70] Carlyle joked to Mitchell with some seriousness that a lecher would become "a wanderer on the face of the earth—every one that findeth him shall *geld* him!"[71] The irony of the biblical warning did not escape the son of a family in which the Bible was both literal fact and emotional necessity. The very physical desires that he and his friends were feeling would embarrass them unless brought under the strict control of utility and law. The warning to Murray contains a level of teasing anxiety, for Carlyle could also say that same year to Mitchell that "we must admit that physical causes *have* an influence on man."[72] An approach that did not take into account "the passions and appetites and *lusts*" could not possibly guide one successfully through the difficulties of adolescence.

The world in which Carlyle grew to manhood was, in fact, a blend of economic necessity and theological prohibition. The Ecclefechan household quietly lived with both, but in cosmopolitan Edinburgh the young man and his contemporaries more freely articulated their sense of the sinful world of which they were a part. Delicacy about the facts was not native to Carlyle. Rural farm life never disguised biological nature. Indeed, it provided him with a sense of physical realities which he sometimes expressed with a bluntness that his Victorian contemporaries found harsh. Years later, Carlyle found it possible to be as reticent as the next Victorian on certain matters, but for the young man of less than twenty the problem was how to accept his own sexuality and at the same time avoid the usual ways of expressing it physically. He learned to expend his energies in alternative ways, some challenging and rewarding, others tedious and dispiriting.

6.

When Carlyle left Edinburgh for Dumfries in June 1814 he had neither an arts degree nor a theological vocation. In March he had given a practice sermon on a topic and in circumstances that he hardly cared to remember. The degree itself was a mere formality, casually dispensed with in many cases by both students and their future employers.

At Dumfries he applied for the position of mathematics master at Annan Academy and, helped by a strong recommendation from Professor Leslie, he was granted an interview. The rector of Dumfries Academy, examining him on behalf of the directors at Annan, found him superior to the only other candidate and immediately offered him the job at £70 per annum. From the start, however, Carlyle anticipated that he would dislike teaching. Moreover, he had to face the irony that Annan Academy was where he had been unhappy for most of his schooldays, where he would have, at least at the beginning, "few or no acquaintance."[73]

Work, however, might be the antidote to loneliness and the appropriate channel for his energies. During the summer, while tutoring "two . . . boys learning Greek, Latin, and Mathematics," he anticipated that for the four months of the autumn term he "must lead the life of a *Mill-horse*."[74] But, despite the time spent in the classroom, he discovered that he still had the energy to pursue other interests. He chose a text and began to prepare the trial sermon he was scheduled to preach at Divinity Hall at Christmastime. Fortunately Robert Mitchell, who shared his mathematical interests and had chosen the same slow path to the ministry, lived close by, a tutor at Ruthwell-Manse, the home of a well-known minister and literary amateur, Henry Duncan, who was also a successful publisher and banker. It seemed natural that the two young men should work together in their preparation and accompany one another on the trip to Edinburgh. Without money or profession, they solaced themselves with amusing mathematical puzzles, Edinburgh gossip, and regular bouts of hard reading. Seizing one of the only opportunities available to an intellectual fish who is out of his water, Carlyle attempted to create his own stream, reading Defoe, Sterne, Byron, Tasso, Cervantes, Scott, Burns, Hume, and Horace, as well as minor poets, romancers, and historians. His talk and conversation flowed into a fullness of mixed references to literature, history, philosophy, and science. Moments spent away from study seemed precious time wasted.

In late December 1814 the two young men went up to Edinburgh to present their student sermons. Carlyle had chosen as text, "Before I was afflicted I went astray / but now have I kept Thy Word." The subject indicates the beginning of a nonclerical ministry, however, rather than the conclusion of a spiritual commitment. To some degree the choice of the text of this lost sermon is conventional, though less so than the choice of subject for his next sermon, "Is there such a thing as natural religion?"[75] To a considerable extent, however, both topics are characteristic of his lifelong interests, almost prescient of his future preoccupations. The sermon of 1814 was personal, emotional, autobiographical, though he described it fifty-two years afterward as " 'a very weak and flowery sentimental piece' "; that of 1815 was a dull exercise on a theological subject of contemporary interest.[76] The first sermon anticipates his later obsession with spiritual dedication, the second his later answer to the conventional question in his idea of "natural supernaturalism." Though the subject of the second sermon seems to hammer a dull nail into the coffin of his aborted ministerial career, the title of the first resonates with the personal voice of a young man who is deciding that he cannot fulfill the religious vocation for which his parents have intended him.

Except for the appearance at Divinity Hall, the visit to Edinburgh was mostly a revivifying vacation. Looking up old friends and enjoying their former haunts, the two young men pursued urban entertainment enthusiastically through most of December. Mitchell left first, Carlyle staying on through New Year. He purchased some books and experienced the "*warwhoops*" and the "*foul air*" of Hogmanay night in the capital, leaving Edinburgh "in the gayest humour in the world."[77] On the return journey, however, he felt his mood change as rapidly as the biting east wind increased his discomfort. He had gone through with his sermon, but as early as October he had told his friend that "my sentiments on the Clerical profession are like yours mostly of the unfavourable kind. Where would be the harm, should we both stop?"[78] The return to Annan was a return to bitter reality. Neither the meeting-house nor the schoolroom seemed the proper place for him.

He plunged back into work through the rest of the winter and the spring, increasingly restless, tormented by small irritants.[79] Ordinary noises began to disturb him, and his own sharp sarcasm alienated almost everyone he spoke to. His preference for solitude prompted him to think of himself as misanthropic. When he could not work, his irritability turned into a form of self-disgust, as if he harbored evil forces that he could not control. Despising his own depressions, he sought desperately for a way to control or accept them. For much of the spring, he "was seized with a certain, perverse, torpid, monotonous mental palsy—that incapacitates for everything." The weather was bad, and he was "pestered by melancholies, ph[l]egm, coughs and catarrhs."[80] Not even all of his reading was satisfying, particularly Hume's *Essays,* which forced him to confront the distance between his own intellectual openness and the closed system of Divinity Hall. It was a "pity" that Hume was "a Deist," he wrote to Thomas Murray, for "how much might his strong talents have accomplished in the cause of truth, when they did so much in that of error!"[81] But the young man felt increasingly unsure how to categorize himself other than as a Christian, which was sufficient to differentiate himself from Hume but not to satisfy the expectations of his parents.

In his moments of depression, he felt incapacitated "for every thing," including writing to friends, but once such moments had passed he rushed to apologize, fearful that he might lose the few friends he had.[82] Sometimes he emphasized that he had been too busy and other times too depressed, but by and large he was both. Continuing his teaching through the spring, he also read through a formidable list of authors, among them Dugald Stewart, Adam Smith, and Lord Kames. Meeting a friend on the road from Ecclefechan to Annan early in June, he spontaneously accompanied him to Dumfries to "witness the laying of the foundation stone of Burns' mausoleum," a poet whom he admired greatly and with whose neglect and suffering he identified.[83] Attracted by the "rumor that Francis Jeffrey Esqr was to be one of the pleaders" at the circuit-trials in Dumfries, he was disappointed when the well-known advocate did not appear. "If to these overpowering engagements," he told Thomas Murray, "you add the numberless fits of indolence—and the perpetual visitations of spleen, to which one is subjected in this dirty little uncomfortable planet of ours—I presume you will have a sufficient excuse for my silence."[84]

But he was beginning to find another way to speak. In his final year at Annan Academy he had inscribed a note in French in his schoolboy edition of Scott's *Rudiments of the French Language,* asking: "Why is the French language so universally studied? The English is more nervous, the Italian more musical. . . . The French . . . have said so often that their language was the best in the world that we English have at last admitted it—poor fools that we are!"[85] By 1809 he had taken the short step from pride in one's language to pride in one's use of that language. Thomas Murray, who also had literary aspirations, encouraged him to fantasy grandiose literary fame as the inevitable result of his talents if he would but dedicate himself to the necessary effort. To his student-friends it seemed inevitable that a young man who read so widely and spoke so effectively on literature and philosophy should himself have something significant to contribute. By the summer of 1814, Murray's enthusiasm for his friend's literary capabilities had become inseparable from self-appreciation, as if they were to become a tandem whose "juvenile epistles will be read—& probably applauded—by a generation unborn." Murray predicted "that the name of *Carlyle at least* will be inseparably connected with the literary history of the nineteenth century. This may be thought *great vanity* but the idea is exhilarating—generous ambition and perseverance will overcome every difficulty." Thomas was flattered but uneasy, for Murray hit too close to an ambition that he dared not admit readily. "What a foolish flattering creature tho[u] art! to talk of future eminence, and connection with the literary history of the Nineteenth century to such a one as me! . . . Yet think not that because I talk thus, I am careless about literary fame. No! Heaven knows that ever since I have [been] able to form a wish—*the wish of being known* has been the foremost."[86] That same year, writing in the margins of a book of Greek prose, he privately exhorted some heavenly benefactor: "Grant me that with a heart of independence . . . I may attain to literary fame."[87]

He had not yet told his parents that he doubted he would fulfill the vocation to which they had dedicated him. Of course, the ministry and a literary career were not necessarily incompatible, provided that his future literary achievements could be categorized as Christian and orthodox. He suspected that his father and mother would be quite pleased if their son became a modern version of John Owen, but he could no longer delude himself about this possibility. Whatever writing he would do, the development of his rational, skeptical intellect made it impossible that he could meet the standards of orthodoxy. The authors he most admired were not likely to provide models acceptable to his parents. In addition, from his earliest intellectual awakening he had sensed that his century would be one in which the most effective voices were those that confirmed not traditional orthodoxies but rich historical confusion and the emergence of new visions.

For the time being, however, the only alternative to earning his living as a minister was earning it as a schoolmaster, teaching mathematics and science. Geometry still fascinated him, and in the winter of 1814 he discovered that he could demonstrate both his mathematical and his literary skill by responding to articles on amateur mathematics that appeared in newspapers and journals, among them Henry Duncan's *Dumfries Courier.* Like modern acrostic puzzles, the geometry that Carlyle had learned at Edinburgh demanded ingenious solutions to problems of spatial relationships which could be put in realistic terms. For example, given a complex set of spatial factors, how could one be equidistant from all the trees in one's garden? Carlyle answered, "If Mr. N. is determined to be equi-distant from all his trees, he must go to—the centre of the earth." When another correspondent, referring sarcastically to "Master Thomas Carlyle, of Edinburgh," supplied an alternative solution, Carlyle made a humorous but aggressively satirical response that effectively inflated both the issue and the writer to the ridiculous. In the next issue an editorial remark took particular notice of the most literary of its mathematical contributors whose approach was termed "Carlyleian": perhaps the editor meant that the reaction was defensive, the defense satirical attack, and the language of attack rhetorical exaggeration. "I beg leave to add," Carlyle had responded, "that, should any further *anonymous* attempts at wit appear in your paper against me, I shall regard them 'as the wind that bloweth,' and suffer them quickly to 'fleet back' into the '*limbo of vanity*' whence they came." The sparring continued, and the real attraction was not the objective discussion of geometrical problems but the satiric jousting of intellectual rivals. Late in the month the editor "expressed regret for having to suppress Carlyle's 'severe retailiation.' " The young man of nineteen did not take criticism lightly.[88]

In June 1815 he returned to the *Courier* columns, which provided the opportunity to exercise further his literary skill. He had graduated from private to public letters, in which the response could be broader, with more play for unexpected variations of both temperament and knowledge. The *Courier* welcomed not only epistolary exchanges but essay-letters that attempted to present new ideas or information on topics that the editor judged of interest to his readers. Drawing upon

Benjamin Franklin's theories about electricity and lightning, Carlyle wrote two long letters about the cause and nature of thunder, which he signed "Ichneutes," the "Pursuer." No matter how insignificant or inaccurate the scientific information of the letters, they were clear revelations of a personality that had already found in both the subject and the signature crucial metaphors by which to express itself.

7.

During the summer of 1815 Carlyle was often depressed. The two letters on thunder and lightning were not the exhilarated, energetic expressions of someone "pos[s]essed—with the rage of writing. . . . The publication was purely the effect of *ennui,*" he confessed to Murray.[89] Sometimes he was able to lose himself in reading, but the wide range of his interests and his dissatisfaction with teaching continually reminded him of the instability of his position. Leaving Annan late in August for Ecclefechan, he felt increasingly unsettled about his future.

His father, dissatisfied with the depressed building trade, had returned to farming, his own father's occupation, moving the family to a farm called Mainhill, a few miles from Ecclefechan. The farmhouse was comfortable, the family busy settling in; however, though he did his best to disguise his feelings, Thomas could not share his parents' high spirits. He had "an Exegesis to write—but when—is another circumstance. To be serious . . . I am growing daily and hourly more lukewarm about this preaching business."[90] But he was expected in Edinburgh in December to deliver his second trial sermon. Not yet prepared to confront directly the real grounds of his disenchantment, he searched for an explanation for his alienation. The ministry had become an "overstocked" trade, he complained to Murray, in which one must fawn on inferiors with little "prospect of obtaining a livelihood at all."[91] Bored with his teaching, he returned to Annan in October in a bleak mood.

He arranged to deliver his trial sermon the day before Christmas 1815. He was fully aware that his audience's response to his discourse on whether there is "such a thing as Natural religion" would matter only to his immediate vanity. Through the summer and autumn he had prepared the sermon in English and then translated it into Latin. Though he found that he could write a formally perfect sermon, the enterprise was " 'weary, flat, stale, and unprofitable.' " But he was "engaged and must read it now."[92] He told no one except Mitchell that he had already decided to discontinue his study of divinity at the appropriate moment.

With Carlyle as passenger, the Glasgow Mail rolled out of Ecclefechan on the road to Moffat at the end of the third week of December 1816. Unhappily forced to listen to the affected speech of a finicky "*popinjay*" whose pretentions gave way the next day to the "bellowings of the distracted coachmen, and the outlandish warwhoops of two Irish Doctors," he impatiently felt the coach plod on through heavy snow. For much of the windy journey he observed the white countryside from the top of the coach. When the coach labored up hills, the passengers were all forced to dismount. Disgusted with the noise and frivolity at the crowded inn that night, he struck out on foot at four in the morning either to meet the coach later in the day or to stride into the capital at last on his own two feet. The wind had stopped. The moon shone across the white hills, "an Icelandic scene." Stumbling in the snow, once up to his chin, and attempting to follow the obliterated track, he finally got directions from a herdsman and soon found some indifferent company for the long walk. Leaving behind this "inoffensive companion" who seemed preoccupied with speculating on the "effects of snow upon human bodies," he hurried ahead alone and arrived early in the evening, "never . . . more happy at seeing Edinbr." The next day he presented his sermon, pleased to have disposed of it.[93]

Having returned to civilization after a year of provincial isolation, he intended to enjoy Edinburgh, but all his "old College cronies" had dispersed, mainly to provincial schoolrooms. Still, determined to make the best of his holiday, he walked vigorously over the familiar cityscape and sampled the pleasures of the bookstores. With the purchase of a few books, mostly on mathematics and physics, including Newton's *Principia Mathematica,* and some popular poetry, he prepared himself for the return to isolated Annan. One evening, while visiting the cousin whose parents he had lodged with while attending Annan Academy, he was introduced to a man he remembered having seen before, a native of Annan named Edward Irving, to whom the rest of the company seemed to defer. Irving and his companion, a schoolteacher, seemed condescending. He imagined that they were aware that he was poor and unknown whereas they were established and recognized. He was asked "a whole series of questions about Annan matters, social or domestic mostly; of which I knew little, and had less than no wish to speak." Intimately familiar with the town, the dark-haired, handsome inquisitor, with a disquieting, uncontrollable squint in his right eye, assaulted his new acquaintance with questions about recent births and deaths. Insulted and immensely angry, Carlyle finally exploded: "I have had no interest to inform myself about the births in Annan; and care not if the process of birth and generation there should cease and determine altogether!" Irving's companion remarked good-humoredly that such a development would soon put him out of business. Everyone laughed; the bad moment was over.[94]

Back in Annan, Carlyle kept company, outside of school hours, mainly with books and his correspondence with a few friends. For part of the winter he struggled with the *Principia*, but his skills were not quite sufficient.[95] He wanted "a theory of a man," he told his brother Jack, "a system of metaphysics, not for talk, but for adoption and belief; and here his mathematical logic afforded little help."[96] But he returned "to the study of Physics with more pleasure—after trying 'The Philosophy of Mind.' It is delightful, after wandering in the thick darkness of metaphysics—to behold again the fair face of truth. When *will* there arise a man who shall do for the science of mind—what Newton did for that of matter—establish its fundamental laws on the firm basis of induction—and discard forever those absurd theories—that so many dreamers have devised?—I believe this is a foolish question—for its answer is—never."[97]

Late in the spring of 1816 he became sick and was confined for weeks with an inflamed throat. He found it difficult to read. But his spirit and wit returned as the vacation approached. He consoled himself by telling Mitchell that "the Noble of Political society and the Noble of Nature are different persons, in nine cases out of ten."[98] The two of them belonged to the unfortunate majority. Mitchell had enthusiastically proposed that they escape their problems by going to France, which seemed a strange project to the sober Carlyle. "First, how are we to get to France; second, how are we to live in France; and third what good will living in France do us?"[99] He would prefer to be poor at home than in a strange place. But he did not want to stay in Annan and could return to Ecclefechan only as a visitor. In his isolation he felt that the circle of his parents' world was collapsing in on him, like a condensing star, with fire and heat and lightning. "What is to become of us, Mitchell? The period of our boyhood is past."[100]

[2]

The Heroic Self
1816–1821

Having selected Carlyle and Edward Irving as young men of the highest promise, their contemporaries pushed them toward one another as potential rivals for praise. Irving had preceded Carlyle at Annan Academy, and later at the university. Under the patronage of Professors Christison and Leslie, he left Edinburgh to gain time and experience as schoolmaster at Haddington, a short distance from the capital, while preparing himself for the ministry. When Carlyle returned to Annan in 1814, Irving, whom he "had heard much of . . . all along, how distinguished in studies, how splendidly successful as Teacher," seemed to be "illuminating and astonishing" everyone with his new teaching methods and compelling personality.[1]

As he labored at his detested teaching duties through the winter and spring of 1816, Carlyle thought that he was doing little more than spinning in place, struggling with painful difficulties of both vocation and spirit. In May, however, he received unexpected assistance from Professor Christison who was encouraged by Professor Leslie to recommend him for a teaching position at Kirkcaldy, a growing town of about four thousand.[2] Irving too had recently moved to Kirkcaldy, but Carlyle was assured that "Mr. Irving has the Academy, not the parish school . . . in a town and neighborhood so populous there is field enough for you both."[3] Flattered by such evidence of his former professors' continuing regard, he was also attracted by the advantage of being an hour's ferry ride across the Firth of Forth from Edinburgh. The Reverend John Martin, the town representative, assured him that there would be no duties except "those of teaching . . . Latin, French,

Arithmetic, Book-Keeping, Elements of Geometry, Navigation, Geography, Mensuration. Greek may be occasionally wanted."[4] But still, it was the detested teaching and, in addition, the sensitive young man would now have to confront Irving as an immediate presence. "I cannot say that I am violently taken with this offer. . . . I have written to them, that if they should like to wait, I could come to Edinr in Autumn, & talk with them about the place—& if they should not like to wait,—that there would be the end of the matter."[5]

The Kirkcaldy officials agreed to his suggestion, but a fortuitous meeting with Irving was the more important influence on Carlyle's decision to accept their offer. The sudden death of the wife of a man who had taught both boys at Annan Academy provided the occasion for their chance meeting in July. Home on holiday at the time, Irving came to comfort his former teacher and found his intense younger rival as well. " 'You are coming to Kirkcaldy to look about you in a month or two: you know I am there; my house and all that I can do for you is yours;—two Annandale people must not be strangers in Fife!' "[6] And so, late in August, Carlyle went to Kirkcaldy to be interviewed by John Martin, who informed the town council in September that "there is no doubt that his education in classical literature has been as thorough and complete as in Mathematical and Natural Science. . . . Indeed from the conversations I have had with him I am of opinion there are few young men of his standing who have directed their studies to a greater variety of objects or have acquired a more extensive range of knowledge."[7]

Having agreed to take the position, Carlyle returned to Annandale to spend the rest of the summer of 1816 with his family. His mother, unfortunately, was seriously ill from a "fever," which seemed to threaten "the extinction of her reason." It was the only time in his life Thomas had seen his stoical, withdrawn father cry.[8] Violent and uncontrollable, Margaret Carlyle hardly slept at all.[9] If the competent father found himself helpless, the elder children were shocked into numbness. "It was necessary to place her for a few weeks under restraint away from home," after which she returned somewhat calmer but apparently still sick.[10] Recuperation was slower than the son wished or than the family pretended. By September, she had become physically stable, "at the Church every sabbath since she came home behaving always very decently . . . she sleeps every night and hinders no person in sleep." But her behaviour was not yet completely normal.[11] She suffered the effects of a nervous breakdown for the good part of a year, not recovering until at least the summer of 1817.[12] Unable to depend on the rapid effect of drugs, the Carlyles had to bear as stoically as they could these protracted periods of suffering for the patient and for themselves. Time taught resignation. In the family view, such afflictions were mysterious visitations, a temporary withdrawal of God's grace. Apparently some Ecclefechan neighbors thought that Thomas' "apostasy" or "atheism" had caused his mother's breakdown and his father's misery, though many years later the explanation offered was that Margaret Carlyle's breakdown was the result of her "time of life" or menopause.[13] But, though her husband collapsed into tears and her children in shock, their faith in their mother and in God was not diminished by the experience. Anxiety within the family about physical and mental health did, however, increase, abruptly becoming a major concern. Such anxiety became a family motif, as if the Carlyles were keenly aware of some special fragility that made them vulnerable. Even the stoic father, soon after his wife's illness, took up the pattern in a letter to Thomas: "I thought to have written you myself this day and told all my thoughts about your health which is the foundation . . . of all our Earthly comfort."[14] Though they worried constantly about "Tom's" health, the concern within the family was pervasive.[15]

2.

For a moment Edinburgh flickered in the northern distance like a light of hope. Carlyle said good-bye to his family, wrote a brief farewell note to Mitchell, and parted from James Johnston on "a vile raw" November night in 1816. But the city that he had left so reluctantly two years earlier no longer fulfilled his expectations. The "fountain head of knowledge and good humour" now "seemed uninteresting," and its inhabitants' "pursuits very stale and unprofitable!"[16] Reform politics dominated political discussion while natural philosophy (physics) held the attention of academic circles. To Carlyle, both seemed mere expressions of fashion. The change, of course, had been in himself, not in Edinburgh. The buzz of passing fashions and small careers in the making constantly reminded him of his own narrow prospects. Still, it was late in November. On the other side of the Forth the "Burghers of Kirkcaldy" impatiently awaited their new employee's arrival. Though neither his mood nor his attitude promised a long career there,[17] he had no choice but to cross the water.

Carlyle and Edward Irving now began to work out the terms of their relationship. Less sociable than his new friend and convinced that he had no worldly future, Carlyle believed that he could survive mainly on correspondence and on "what can be derived from these poor old books, which we have or shall have made our own."[18] Irving was a sporadic reader, much more excited by people than by solitary study, and he urged his young friend to use his large personal library as if it were his own. Social life in Kirkcaldy, a narrow shipping and manufacturing town, was dull, except at the house of the Reverend John Martin, whose daughter Isabella was particularly attractive to Irving. But Irving desperately needed male companionship for those things that female society could not provide, especially in a culture that trained women poorly—if at all—for the role of intellectual and recreational companion. Like Carlyle, he wanted a friend with whom he could channel his vast resources of suppressed energy into useful social activity.

In Carlyle's fictive autobiographical fragment, written almost ten years later, Irving appears in the guise of Bernard Swane, Wotton's dearest friend, who "had forced his way into the privacy of this youthful misanthrope . . . and . . . had won his friendship." In this fictional portrait Carlyle effectively highlighted the differences between the two young Kirkcaldy teachers. One was sociable, optimistic, confident in his Christianity and in his own future, the other solitary, unsure of himself, ready to give up even the pretense of an orthodox Christian mission. They both argued for "the good and beautiful" in their different ways: "Bernard . . . in vehement, flowing, rhetorical pleadings; Wotton, in bitter sarcasms and with keenest intellect," the older man an embodiment of graceful spiritual exhortation, the younger of aggressive, intellectual harshness.[19] Their bond was that each recognized that they "both truly loved goodness."

In a way that such young men did not find awkward in that age, Carlyle and Irving began to depend on and to love one another. "He was as the sun in my firmament," Carlyle wrote almost forty years later, "where all else had become so wintry. His talk was so genial, cordial, freeflowing, hopeful & delightful to me; all my meetings with him stand out . . . as sunlit."[20] Though uncomfortable with Irving's histrionic pulpit oratory, Carlyle was sincerely impressed by Irving's desire to share the deep passion that he felt about matters of religion and morality. To Carlyle, his friend was "a man of noble faculties & qualities" who could be described adequately only in superlatives.[21] "Rarely could you find a person so superior to others, yet so beloved by them, so calculated to please at once the many and the few."[22]

To Carlyle, his friend's conviction seemed more endearing than his message convincing. Since the younger man increasingly doubted the actual truth of many Christian theological claims, the friends tacitly agreed to disagree. Still, Irving had a deep respect for the Burgher Seceder world of Carlyle's youth, having often visited Ecclefechan as a young boy, attracted by the pious sincerity of John Johnstone's preaching. He was therefore aware of the tensions that his friend felt as a result of his intellectual disaffiliation from the simple faith of his parents. As a result, Irving was sensitive to Carlyle's anxiety about his future vocation.

The two friends covered many subjects in their evening walks on the long Kirkcaldy beach, particularly mutual friends, Edinburgh gossip, and Kirkcaldy boredom, but Carlyle kept as quiet as he could about future prospects. In mid-March 1817 he went to Edinburgh to continue his *pro forma* registration at Divinity Hall for another year. He arrived to find that Dr. Ritchie was "too busily engaged . . . quarrelling with his students about the management of the library" and thus " 'not at home' when I called to enter myself;—'Good,' answered I; 'let the omen be fulfilled!' "[23] He wrote a long letter to his mother soon after his return, but said nothing about what had occurred on his visit. What he could tell some of his friends, he still could not tell his parents.

Whatever the state of his conscience, however, his outward life during the winter and spring was uneventful; the school did well; his own health was "uniformly good." He took pleasure in sharing his rooms with Alick, who came for a short visit. And he had neither good nor bad relations with the "natives" of Kirkcaldy.[24] But inwardly he brooded on his alienation from the community into which he had been born. Not only did he renounce the ministry, but he found that the combination of his doubts about the truth of Christian claims and his hostility to the practices of secular society left him without any affiliation at all. His new friend's concern for him was the pure gift of unexplainable love; his parents' had its base in natural feeling. But he had no grounds to believe that he could be accepted or loved in a society whose morality he detested and whose religious beliefs he doubted. Irving, who was surprisingly tolerant of religious insecurity, could look Hume and Gibbon in the face with impunity, but Carlyle could not. His books, those "friends that never fail me," were increasing his alienation, and he felt compelled to confront the counterclaims to Christian belief. Throughout the winter and spring he borrowed key works of eighteenth-century skepticism which his friend felt no need to read or read without his faith being in the least undermined. Impressed by what he had learned from his wide reading in mathematics, physics, and now astronomy, Carlyle was not prepared to admit the superior reality of religious to scientific "facts." His studies had taught him that the application of rational standards of proof to scientific matters produced clarity, the application of the same standards to religious matters, confusion. But, other than loose analogy and hortatory rhetoric, there seemed to be no agreed-upon standards by which to judge religious assertions.

Seeking enlightenment, he read Dr. Thomas Chalmers' widely praised *A Series of Discourses on the Christian Revelation, Viewed in Connection with the Modern Astronomy* (1817), only to conclude that "his best argument seems to be, that as it is in the scriptures, we have no business to think about it [at] all—an argument which was well enough known to be a panacea in cases of that nature."[25] Dr. Chalmers' straining of common sense provided sufficient proof that the confidence the young man believed inseparable from religious belief had already been irreparably undermined. Indeed, he believed that such confidence hardly existed at all anymore, except among the survivors of an older world. On the whole, the primary defenders of traditional Christian orthodoxy were either overcompensating for spiritual insecurity or defending churchly privilege. The acid common sense and intellectual power of Hume and Gibbon set standards for which he had the deepest respect, no matter how corrosive of traditional religious belief their logic and conclusions. Though he considered Hume and Gibbon atheists, whose denial of any God or providential power in the universe he instinctively rejected, he judged Dr. Chalmers a fool.

By temperament disdainful of modern social organizations, he desired to separate religion from its churches, to retain the Christian world view without sectarian Christian dogma. All churches, he concluded, are part of the inevitably recurring preemption of religious spirit by institutional organization. After a while there is always more organization than spirit, at which time a revolution or a reformation occurs. "Every 'true religion,' " he explained to Mitchell, "is propped & bolstered, & the hands of its rivals tied up; till by nursing and fattening it has become a bloated monster that human nature can no longer look upon—and men rise up & knock its brains out. Then there is great joy for a season; and forthwith a successor is elected, which undergoes the same treatment. . . . Such is the destiny of Churches by law established."[26]

His decision not to enroll again in Divinity Hall relieved some of the anxiety of his false position. Moreover, the return of warm weather, the prospect of summer vacation, and his friend's company combined to keep his spirits up. Irving's constant visits to John Martin's were slowly leading to an irrevocable attachment to Martin's daughter Isabella, but the two young teachers were still able to express their reserves of time and energy in long conversations and wide-ranging walks.[27] Often they roved through the woods until it was dark or made vigorous excursions to local sites of interest and neighboring cities, even to hear Dr. Chalmers, whom Irving admired. Noticing military tents on the Lomond Hills, on a bright Saturday, they hiked to the site of the trigonometrical survey, where Irving charmed the supercilious official into giving them a guided tour of the site. Through the theodolite, they saw "the Signal Column . . . on the top of Ben Lomond, sixty miles off, wavering and shivering like a bit of loose tape."[28] Carlyle's daily teaching still depressed him, but overall this was "a happy season"—a particularly golden summer.

3.

Rather than spend the entire summer in Annandale, Carlyle agreed to join Irving and his friends John Pears and James Brown on a walking tour through the Trossach Mountains northwest of Edinburgh. The four young teachers left Kirkcaldy on an overcast August evening, walking through the rain all the next day until the weather finally cleared. After breakfast in Callander, they were at the lovely Loch Katrine in a few hours. Enjoying his first taste of "grand and impressive . . . scenery," Carlyle was happy to be guided by Irving, who had been in the Trossachs before, who "could recommend everything," and who "was made (unjustly by us) quasi-responsible for everything."[29] Irving's leadership did not satisfy Brown, however, and tempers soon became strained. Pears sided with Irving, Carlyle with no one, though he was appealed to and flattered by Brown, who was jealous of Irving's leadership. "Had there not been at this point, by a kind of outward and legitimate reason . . . an actual division of routes, the folly might have lasted longer."[30] Having some business in Glasgow, Irving and Pears went toward Paisely while Carlyle and Brown proceeded to Loch Lomond, having agreed to meet the others in Glasgow. Carlyle apparently felt secure enough in Irving's friendship to accept the division; moreover, Brown proved a capable companion, and the landscape provided attractive compensation for any human loss. At the beginning of the tour, Carlyle had his first sight of an horizon glowing with industrial light and fire, the Carron Ironworks. At Greenock, he saw steamships puffing with mechanistic regularity.

After three particularly memorable days of "bright seas, bright skies" at Roseneath, the four were reunited on a "dusty, sunny Glasgow evening" and then separated again.[31] While Pears turned eastward to his own home, the others went south by the Falls of Clyde, stopping to see Robert Owen's social-industrial experiment at New Lanark, which they thought of little interest, and then continued to Annandale. Irving went to Annan and Carlyle continued on to Mainhill with Brown, who was surprised at his friend's rather abrupt change from light-hearted summer tourist to profoundly unhappy son of a sick mother. Apparently, Carlyle had said little or nothing about his mother's condition, but Brown could not help but notice his friend's unhappiness and soon left.

By late summer Margaret Carlyle was sufficiently recovered from the worst of her breakdown for Thomas to tell his parents that he had not and would never again enroll at Divinity Hall. While Ecclefechan gossiped "that James must be heartbroken because his son had fallen from Grace and become an athiest," the disappointed parents responded constructively. James Carlyle respected his son's "scruples."[32] It would be sinful for their son to profess a ministerial vocation to which he could not give full credence in his own conscience. Honest doubt more truly expressed the religious feeling of a sincere conscience than did the continuation in a religious vocation about whose underlying principles one had reservations. Through their tears Thomas' parents could discern the nobility of their son's character. "With the trustfulness of a Mother's heart," Margaret Carlyle confirmed her proud and sensitive son's belief that he was still the privileged recipient of her unchanging love.[33]

When he returned to his small room in Kirkcaldy in the fall of 1817, however, Carlyle felt even more restless; the energy of self-dissatisfaction had not been dissipated. Carrying on his activities as a schoolmaster "with all the regularity and *sang-froid* of a *mill-horse*," he increased his reading schedule, staying up late to absorb Hume, Gibbon, Smollett, Voltaire, Bacon, among dozens of other assorted writers on travel, history, science, and theology. To the young man, this was not simply reading but urgent life-and-death work intended to improve the mind. "A man's dignity in the great system of which he forms a part, is exactly proportional to his moral & intellectual acquirements."[34] Questions about what use all this reading might be sometimes surfaced. But he was in the process of developing a respect for intellectual activity which allowed him to read what he thought an "indecent" and "brutish" book like Matthew Lewis' Gothic extravaganza, *The Monk*.[35] He reasoned that intellectual curiosity, properly subordinated to general moral ends, was a moral act itself, the major sin not thought but sloth. Since his self-esteem and the reconciliation of his needs with his parents' values depended on his own estimation of his mental energy, he could say nothing more harsh of himself than that "my mind has on the whole been placid—sometimes almost stagnant."[36]

Geometry no longer seemed as interesting as it had. And he was preoccupied with other reading and with personal problems.[37] As a means to "the solution of problems," geometry depended "very much upon a certain slight of hand, that can be acquired, without great difficulty, by frequent practice." But he was not as sure as he "used to be that it is the best way of employing one's self," though he had no doubt that he was good at such tricks.[38] But mathematics was also "a powerful instrument which enables the mind of a man to grasp the universe & to elicit from it & demonstrate such laws," and Carlyle did not feel confident that he had or could master mathematics in this sense. "To see these truths . . . to *feel* them as one does the proportion of the sphere & cylinder! 'Tis a consummation devoutly to be wished—but not very likely ever to arrive."[39] It was becoming unmistakably clear to him that he preferred his other reading and his excursions with Irving to his pursuit of Newton. Perhaps he did not have the intellectual capability and determination in mathematics that might make Newtonian heights assailable. Crucial questions disturbed him. What, indeed, was the proper end of intellectual distinction, provided one could prevent oneself from being ripped apart by violent swings between ferocious discontent and intensive bouts of self-improvement? And how could this intellectual distinction become a formal entity that one could reveal to others and use to maintain oneself as an economic being? Through the spring and summer of 1818 he tried without success to answer these questions. A letter from Thomas Murray, who had been the first to encourage him to think of a literary career, reminded him of "the many joyful days which long ago, we spent together," but Carlyle responded that those were "sweet days of ignorance and airy hope! " Though he had once dreamed "of intellectual greatness, and of making me a name upon the earth," he now had abandoned hope for such renown. Indeed, he claimed he could "hardly care for" it, for he was completely committed to the improvement of his mind without regard for any reward or recognition. He recognized that this path cut him off from other men. Society was a conspiracy to enforce intellectual conformity, and most men were thus not the products of their own efforts to attain intellectual stature but the victims of both time and circumstance. "I now perceive more clearly than ever, that any man's opinions depend not on himself so much as on the age he lives in, or even the persons with whom he associates."[40]

Carlyle's situation, then, was a desperate one. He clearly saw that whatever his efforts to overcome the conspiracy of environment, he might succumb to the "narcotic atmosphere that surrounds him." If he could manage to escape, it would be at the price of the misery of solitude. Whatever his success or failure, the effort itself "forfeits sympathy, & procures hatred if he excell but a little the dull standard of his neighbors." There seemed no way that he could fight his way out of these emotional and intellectual dead ends. "There is before me a chequered and fluctuating scene," he told Thomas Murray, "where I see nothing clearly, but that a little time will finish it."[41] For the moment it was safer to renounce or at least disguise ambition, and to make whatever stand he could on some ideal principle, such as "the improvement of one's mind."

4.

In July 1818 Carlyle returned to Mainhill again, walking with Irving through the isolated "Peebles-Moffat moor country," a landscape they

Mainhill Farmhouse near Ecclefechan. Photograph by J. Patrick. By permission of the Edinburgh University Library.

would traverse many times in all kinds of weather—a series of journeys between home and the outside world which became in Carlyle's memory the ideal image of pastoral beauty. But that summer the visit to Mainhill was unusually brief. Having made arrangements earlier for a tour of the Cumberland Hills and Lakes during August, he was soon joined by James Johnston and Robert Mitchell. United for the first time in years, the three friends crossed the Solway to Whitehaven near St. Bee's Head, which "swelled gradually up" into the Cumberland Hills and could be seen from Woodcockair and Repentance Tower. It was Carlyle's first visit to England. Energetic hiking brought them to most of the sites that he had hoped to visit—Keswick, Buttermere, Derwentwater, Skiddaw, "Scawfell & Helvellyn"—a tour through country that had attracted him from boyhood on. They reached the peak of Skiddaw early one morning and later wandered in the churchyard at Grasmere.[42] The adventure seemed not a separation from home but a filling in of the sight-line that stretched from Hoddam Hill to Helvellyn. By the end of the month, he was on his way north to resume his teaching duties, his brother Alick accompanying him as far as Moffat. After walking on to Edinburgh, he stayed overnight with Irving's former assistant, saw Professor Leslie briefly, and then took the ferry across to Kirkcaldy, where his "prospects," he told his father, were "far from brilliant."[43]

During the summer a rival school had been formed by an enterprising newcomer who grasped the opportunity to benefit from Irving's imminent departure and Carlyle's apparent indifference to keeping his students. When he found that he had only twelve students left, Thomas wrote to ask his father's advice. The problem far exceeded the threat to the viability of his school. He would have no more than a little difficulty in getting his students back, but what was the point of continuing at the hated trade, which he could do with no more enthusiasm than beating "hemp" for a living? "The despicable wretchedness of teaching," he later complained to Thomas Murray, "can be known only to those who have tried it; and to Him who made the heart, and knows it all."[44] "When the Gods have determined to make a man ridiculously miserable, they make a schoolmaster of him." Might it not be better to live in Edinburgh on the proceeds from occasional private tutoring and his savings of about seventy pounds rather than to remain financially secure but miserable in Kirkcaldy? "In short I only wait for your advice," he assured his father, "till I give in my resignation against the beginning of December. I have thought of trying the law, & several other things, but I have not yet got correct informaton about any of them."[45]

The only certitude in all this confusion was that he would never teach again, other than as a private tutor. Family pride helped his parents to rationalize his decision: Why should he waste his brilliant intellect on ignorant students who could never understand *him*? And furthermore, if he remained a teacher, his need for sustaining social and intellectual relationships could never be fulfilled; he would be permanently alienated from "the kindly sympathies of life." Still, the question of what alternative to pursue remained completely, almost terrifyingly, open. But "Edinr is certainly my destination for the winter."[46]

What, however, was he to do in Edinburgh? Having vowed never to return to the work that had made him temporarily independent, he considered various alternatives and decided that for the time being he would study mineralogy (geology) as a postgraduate at the university. In the meantime, he could attempt to supplement his savings with private tutoring and look into the possibility of writing something salable for the Edinburgh booksellers. He was grateful when Mitchell, always eager to encourage his friend's literary career, obtained for him from Henry Duncan recommendations to two editors who might consider employing him. He attended classes, but predictably found the well-known Professor Jameson's lectures on geology insufferably dull, "one of those persons whose understanding is overburthened by their memory."[47] The vague prospect of a career in civil engineering turned completely flat when Professor Leslie advised him to go to America to "learn the engineer business."[48] He was not yet ready for exile, particularly across an ocean. "You will start, My dear Mother, at the sound of America. I too had much rather live in my own country; and lay my bones in the soil which covers those of my Fathers. Nor do I despair of getting a comfortable situation, for the exercise of my talents—somewhere within this sea-girt isle."[49] But to Mitchel he wrote, in February 1819, "What say you to that asylum or rather hiding-place for poverty and discontent, America?"[50] The joke had overtones of anxious seriousness.

Sensing changes and challenges within himself, Carlyle was on edge, his tolerance for self and others low. He dodged noisy locations and avaricious bedbugs until he finally located himself comfortably on Bristo Street. He did some occasional tutoring, but when a student's haggling over the fee offended him, he preferred pride to money. Professor Jameson's references to German geologists had given him the idea that he should learn German, thereby obtaining direct access to a culture about which Madame de Staël's book *De l'Allemagne,* which he had read in the autumn of 1817, had already provoked his curiosity.[51] He arranged to exchange French for German lessons with a former schoolfellow at Annan, "a pleasant & friendly creature" named Robert Jardine.[52] Through much of the winter of 1818–1819, he walked before breakfast, finished his German lesson by eleven, strolled for an hour, attended class or tutored in the afternoon, and read and walked again in the evening. Having given up the notion of geology as a profession, he thought of law as a substitute. But his nerves were being strained by these failures and self-deceptions. His mother feared that he was not reading the Bible each day, as he had promised. Assuring her that he occasionally read in his "favorite" book of Job, he did not have to tell her explicitly that he identified with the suffering of a man who, like himself, was trying to learn to live with confusion.[53]

He had come to Edinburgh not because he felt he could be happy or comfortable there but because none of his other alternatives provided an opportunity to express both his growing desire to decrease study and increase action and his need to find a vocation. "Till not very long ago," he wrote to James Johnston, "I imagined my whole duty to consist in thinking and enduring. It now appears that I ought not only to suffer but to act."[54] It seemed to him that the suffering caused by the interaction between personal confusion and cultural imperatives could be decreased by some commitment to and immersion in constructive work—an idea that had antecedents in Classical and Christian culture and that was expressed with special force in the rigorous work imperatives of the Calvinistic world from which Carlyle had emerged.

By late 1818, then, he began to transfer his emphasis from work as study to work as action, to search for a vocation. For reasons of conscience the ministry was not possible. Engineering and the prospect of America repelled him. The law was still a possibility. But the fact of the matter was that his longstanding, though partly suppressed, ambition for "literary fame" had coalesced into what he now freely acknowledged to himself and close friends: "I have thought of writing for Booksellers. . . . [Hold your laughter]; for *at times* I am serious in this matter." But "to live by authorship was never my intention. It is said not to be common at present."[55] Mitchell advised that he try to combine law and literature, after the model of Sir Walter Scott. Authorship as total vocation seemed impossible: "the road to subsistense, I do not mention fame, in that direction, is not very clear."[56] Irving strongly urged that he write for magazines like the *Edinburgh Review* and *Blackwood's,* exhorting his friend "to begin a new year by an effort continuous not for getting knowledge but for communicating it—that you may gain money & favor & opinion."[57] It was a vague, uncertain, but challenging possibility.

5.

Before they left Kirkcaldy in November 1818 Irving had introduced his friend to one of his former students, Margaret Gordon, a "fair-complexioned, softly elegant, softly grave, witty and comely type."[58] Nineteen-years-old at the time, she had lived for the past fourteen years with her aunt in Kirkcaldy. Her ancestry on both sides had some historical interest, but her father was deceased and her mother had remarried. Living in straitened circumstances as the adopted daughter of her widowed aunt, she had been trained in the academy in the usual subjects and conditioned into the frame of mind which encouraged her to improve her position through marriage. She fully appreciated that with family distinction but no money her future depended on a careful appreciation of character, compatibility, and practical opportunities in marriage.

Though half-committed to Isabella Martin, Irving had found his student so attractive that for a short while he thought of pursuing her himself, but was prevented by the formality with which Isabella and her father took his intentions by the autumn of 1818. His uncertain future made him a doubtful candidate for Margaret Gordon's hand in any case, and the prospects of his younger, less established friend would seem to have been nil. But although they had just moved to Edinburgh, the two men returned to Kirkcaldy for the Christmas holidays. Margaret's aunt had no objection to her adopted daughter having the advantages of whatever society Kirkcaldy offered, and Carlyle took the opportunity to see her. As he wrote to Johnston in February, the holidays "were the happiest, for many reasons which I cannot at this time explain, that for a long space have marked the tenor of my life."[59]

Margaret Gordon. Engraving from a watercolor miniature, about 1824. Reprinted from David Alec Wilson and David Wilson MacArthur, *Carlyle,* 6 vols. (London, 1923–1934), vol. 1.

Throughout 1819 and into the spring of 1820 he made the ferry ride to Kirkcaldy a number of times. It is not clear whether he declared himself as a serious suitor, but Margaret at no time indicated that her affection for him was of the kind and strength that could overcome practical difficulties.[60] She enjoyed her young friend's company only to the point that his visits became potentially misleading to him and compromising to herself. In the more controlled world of "Wotton Reinfred," Carlyle dramatized some of his feelings about Margaret in Jane Montagu, a character who combined characteristics of both Margaret Gordon and Jane Welsh. Finding Jane after a long separation, Wotton exclaims, "She did not love another! . . . She still loved him! And was she unfortunate? Did she need *his* help?" In the concluding scene of the unfinished novel, Jane confesses that her previous refusal to extend her love to him was the result of her complex relationship with her past, her aunt, and another man. Under such baneful influence, she has learned "only female accomplishments," though what she "most wanted was knowledge." Against her will, she has become the object of a marriage proposal from a villainous man whom her aunt encouraged, though her ambition is to become "a Corinna, a poetess, an intellectual woman!" Though he believed himself to be in love with Margaret, who "continued for perhaps some three years a figure hanging more or less in my fancy, on the usual romantic . . . terms," apparently she was not in love with him.[61]

His last visit occurred sometime in the late winter or early spring of 1820. Margaret's mother had recently remarried well, and her two daughters and their aunt gladly accepted her proposal that they all live together in her new London home. Unhappy that he was to lose even Margaret's proximity and bleak about his own prospects, Carlyle tried to walk the difficult line between the acknowledgment that he had nothing settled to offer and an expression of deep feeling that might extend their special relationship into a somehow brighter future. Both daughter and foster mother knew what was coming. The interview was short. Margaret's aunt remained with them throughout. The disappointed half-suitor returned to Edinburgh certain that his relationship with Margaret had less chance of success than even a due appreciation of the practical obstacles would have suggested.

He shortly retreated to Mainhill for the summer, where he unexpectedly received a letter from Margaret, who praised him for bearing gracefully the "short interview." Though she could be no more to him than a friend or a sister, she expressed confidence that his unusually gifted mind would allow him to overcome "rugged" barriers.[62] Responding immediately, he presumed the very relationship she had just denied and expressed his confusion about his own future at dramatic length. The impetuously intimate tone of the letter frightened her. She wrote to him again, defending her aunt, saying that her "regard for what was considered the interest of her charge . . . tempted her to look unkindly on you. She really esteems you."[63] But his wild letter had revealed that he was constitutionally incapable of corresponding in an acceptable way. He had immediately broken his promise "never to indulge those 'vain imaginations' which have made us both so unhappy. Yet tell me, do they not still require steady restraint? And would not I, by acceding to your request, encourage that 'weakness' it has been my object to remove?" As graciously as possible, she offered him parting advice:

> *Cultivate the milder dispositions of your heart, subdue the more extravagant visions of the brain. . . . Genius* will render you *great.* May *virtue* render you *beloved!* Remove the awful distance between you and ordinary men, by kind and gentle manners; deal mildly with their inferiority, and be convinced they will respect you as much, and like you more. Why conceal the real goodness that flows in your heart? . . . I give you not my address because I dare not promise to see you.[64]

They never spoke or corresponded again.

In July he learned that Irving had escorted Margaret from Paisely, where she had been staying for a holiday, on a two-week tour of "the Highlands by Inverary and Loch Lomond."[65] Though Irving's commitment to Isabella made him a safe escort, his delight in a companionship in which "there was such a hearty wish to give and receive gratification" was painful for his friend. As Margaret sailed to London, Carlyle tried to set up a summer routine at Mainhill, but he was frustrated and restless. By the autumn, he reported that "I hear not of Margaret, and know not if I ever shall," and lamented that "such beings are shadows, radiant shadows, that cross our path in this dark voyage; we gaze on them with rapture for a moment; and pass away—borne onward by the tide of Fate, never to behold them, never more."[66] He also had a few bitter, realistic moments in which he admitted that marriage was the most risky of ventures. If one makes a foolish choice, "the rest of one's life is the very gall of bitterness."[67]

6.

Shortly after he settled in Edinburgh in November 1818 Carlyle's health had begun to disturb him moderately, primarily because of recurrent stomach pains.[68] Sometimes he could not digest food; other times he felt constipated.[69] That his health should become a problem seemed both unwarrantedly punitive and at the same time consistent with his pervasive difficulties. He did feel somewhat better during the summer. Exercise, parental concern, and rural air were partial antidotes.[70]

In the summer of 1819 he was still asking, "with anxiety and fear," "what shall we do?"[71] The law seemed an acceptable answer for the moment. Soon the routine of the summer softened the bitterness of his conclusion that my "past is little else than a blank."[72] Encouraging his brothers and sisters in their studies, he supervised them, particularly his favorite Alick, who was attempting to improve his writing. Jack had already proved successful as a student and was soon to become the mathematics master at Annan Academy. Residing close by at Lockerbie, Jardine came once a week to exchange a German lesson for a French. Carlyle, however, made slow progress, creaking along laboriously with a dictionary.[73]

The surprising good news late that summer that Irving had been offered a month's trial as assistant to the famous Dr. Chalmers of Glasgow cheered him. It was a great opportunity. On the way to Glasgow in October, Irving came to Mainhill. The two friends walked in the brisk autumn air to Dryfe Water where Carlyle "set Irving on his road to Moffat and bid him good speed, on the top of a hill. . . . The blue sky was beautifully spotted with white clouds, which . . . the wind was beautifully chasing: 'Like *Life*!' I said, with a kind of emotion, on which Irving silently pressed my arm, with the hand near it or perhaps on it, and a moment after, with no word but his farewell and ours, strode swiftly away."[74]

Returning to Edinburgh in late fall, the roads across Tweedsmuir "very bad & the weather very wet," he "crossed this dismal region" with "melancholy, bitter recollections of the good which I had left; and forebodings of the evil I was likely to meet with."[75] By the new year, he warned his mother that his success in the law depended on circumstances that Providence "will regulate."[76] At the same time he confessed to Robert Mitchell that "Law, I fear, must be renounced: it is a shapeless mass of absurdity & chicane, and the ten years, which a barrister commonly spends in painful idleness before arriving at employment, is more than my physical or moral frame could endure."[77] The law would do him no good with Margaret Gordon. Science was "little else than a dry bead-roll of facts."[78] "I have even nearly lost all relish for mathematics."[79] Though he had been paid a few pounds for some hack-writing which he had done that winter, the prospect of a literary livelihood seemed non-existent. In desperation, he even considered going back to teaching. "It is true! I hate teaching . . . yet what can a solitary person do?"[80] The strain of his circumstances left him irritable, depressed, unable to eat regularly. Exerting himself intensely to maintain control over the continuing disintegration of his hopes and his constant unhappiness, his health began to show the strain.[81]

In Edinburgh in the autumn of 1819, he began to wonder if it would be possible for him to maintain a sound mind, a sound body, or even life itself. His vocationally aimless days of study and solitude felt "full of pain," his "best days . . . hurrying darkly and uselessly away. . . . I am altogether an unprofitable creature. Timid yet not humble, weak yet enthusiastic, . . . nature and education" had made him "unfit" to assert himself "among the thick-skinned inhabitants of this planet."[82] He now quite regularly took medicines for his stomach, particularly sulphate of magnesia, but assured his family that there was nothing wrong organically, that the "digestive apparatus" was simply unpredictable, responsive even to wet weather, sometimes quite satisfactory, other times refusing "to perform its functions."[83]

In late January 1820 he worked up the courage to submit to the editor of the *Edinburgh Review* a précis of a review-article by Marc Auguste Pictet on "interplanetary gravitation" which had appeared in *Bibliothèque Universelle.*[84] Leaving the brief piece with Francis Jeffrey's valet at his house in George Street, he permitted himself only slight hope. After a week, he had heard nothing. "Indeed I should not be surprised if it were not accepted: it was written on a very dry subject; and I was not at the time in my happiest mood for writing well. . . . I shall not take it greatly to heart. We can try again upon a more promising theme."[85] He did expect his brief letter to be answered and his manuscript returned, however, and "no answer, no return of MS., absolutely no notice taken . . . was a form of catastrophe more complete than even" he had "anticipated!" He constructed in his imagination "a pungent little Note, which might be written to the great man, with neatly cutting considerations offered him from the small unknown ditto."[86] So deep was the pain that he told only his brother Alick about it.[87] As a result of the recommendation that Henry Duncan had provided, however, he had the previous year gotten some small translation assignments from David Brewster, the editor of the *Edinburgh Encyclopaedia* and the *Edinburgh New Philosophical Journal.* Brewster now threw something additional his way, mere badly paid hackwork, brief factual accounts of various encyclopedia headings chosen by the accident of the alphabet.[88]

Though he made great efforts not to panic, Carlyle now recognized that he was threatened by some of the elements of mental breakdown. "Ever since the month of January last [1820], a train of ill-health, with its usual depression, aggravated by other privations and calamities too tedious to particularize, have pressed heavily upon me." He was the "victim of inquietude and despondency," he explained to Mitchell. His frame of mind matched the frozen Edinburgh winter, his wintry disenchantment claiming that "Edinburgh looks beautiful" only "in the imagination, because the heart, when we knew it of old, was as yet unwrung and ready to derive enjoyment from whatever came before it." Perhaps, as his brother Jack urged, he could recover his health at home, away from the "unwholesome city . . . and its selfish and unfeeling inhabitants," for, he told James Johnston, "after all, there is a world, even in Scotland, there is a world elsewhere."[89] But he hastened to reassure his family that he was not in as desperate a situation as they had imagined. Some days his stomach gave him no problem at all. Though he might feel depressed, bored, unable to work at one moment, at others he felt energetic, willful, determined to read and to write. Visiting Irving in Glasgow in April, he heard him preach and met Dr. Chalmers, who on a "cold vile smoky morning" over breakfast tried to persuade the young visitor that Christianity could be proved true by demonstrating its "visible fitness for human nature. . . . I listened respectfully, not with any real conviction, only with a clear sense of the geniality and goodness of the man."[90] He and Irving walked together as far as the Glasgow-Muirkirk road to Annandale. His friend "drew from" him "by degrees, in the softest manner, the confession that I did *not* think as he of Christian Religion, and that it was vain for me to expect I ever could or should."[91]

Early next morning he was alone at Muirkirk. Suddenly he remembered an incident that his father had witnessed there and "could never forget":

> On the platform of one of the furnaces, a . . . 'stoker' . . . was . . . throwing-in new fuel and ore, now poking the white-hot molten mass that was already in; a poor old maniac woman silently joined him and looked . . . after a while, his back being towards the furnace-mouth, he heard a strange thump or cracking puff; and turning suddenly the poor old maniac woman was not there; and, on advancing to the furnace-edge, he saw the figure of her, red-hot, semi-transparent, floating as ashes on the fearful element for some moments![92]

At Mainhill he carried on through the spring and summer with his encyclopedia articles and a brief review of a German book on magnetism. He acted as senior tutor in his correspondence with his brothers, whose intellectual interests were expanding. Soon he gave serious consideration to accepting a teaching position in York, which had been brought to his attention by a new acquaintance, the apothecary at York Asylum, Matthew Allen. The position was not offered to him. But in October 1820 he went to York to look into a tutoring position for which Allen had recommended him, and decided, "on personal inspection," that "the situation seemed scarcely preferable to manufacturing oakum in Botany-bay." Back in Edinburgh in November, he soon apologized to his mother for the ineffectual attempts he had made to "reward your truly maternal love and care of me." His own nervous suffering had sharpened his sympathy and identification with her fragile mental health. "I may say," he wrote to her in June, "I never till lately knew how to pity you as I ought. These nerves when they get deranged are the most terrific things imaginable. . . . No one can tell what you have endured already—Take care! take care!"[93] He assured her that though their religious "opinions" are "clothed in different garbs" they are "analogous at bottom."[94] Even their nervous systems had similarities. The admonition to "take care" was as much for himself as for her.

But there was one extraordinarily good sign during this difficult period. During the summer, after long months of slow progress, he had unexpectedly discovered not only that he understood the German books he was reading but that, for the first time in years, he felt especially energized by writers who spoke directly to his needs. "I have lived riotously with Schiller, Goethe, and the rest. They are the greatest men at present with me."[95] He still had no settled field of activity other than unremunerative literature, and thus had little idea what to do with this new enthusiasm. But he felt a stubbornness rising within him based on the conviction that, if he only persevered, his labors would be adequately rewarded. "I tell you, boy," he wrote to Alick, "that good times *are* in store for all of us: let us wait for them with stedfastness."[96] Some of this was, of course, bravado, intended both to reassure his family and to encourage himself. But such self-exhortation had a genuine power; he began to practice techniques of self-persuasion, as if through white-hot energy and indomitable will he could forge a new reality on the anvil of language.

Unfortunately, he could not shake free of his renewed conviction that his health was collapsing.[97] Worried about his mental state, Irving urged him to come to Glasgow for a long visit.[98] He accepted, though only for Christmas week 1820, but Irving was not to be silenced. As far as he was concerned, his friend's illness derived from the self-torment that resulted from the loss of spiritual communion and vocational commitment. "You altogether mistake at least *my* feeling if you think I have anything but the kindest sympathy in your case, in which sympathy I am sure there is nothing degrading, either to you or to me. . . . I feel for your condition as a brother would feel."[99]

But Carlyle felt degraded by his misfunctioning "bowels," for which he took "pills" and "castor-oil."[100] The harsh laxatives made matters worse, irritating the intestines and punishing the erring spirit that had allowed itself to become sick. Stimulated by an unsuitable regimen, the stomach began to initiate reactions of its own. Confused by the mysterious interaction between mind and body, he could no longer detect the real source of his pain. This "wicked rebellion of the intestines" insisted on constipation and flatulence as if it had an independent will of its own. When "the weary bowels had got cross again," he felt "bilious"—weak, tired, self-critical, and despairing.[101] "And do but think what a thing it is! that the etherial spirit of a man should be overpowered and hag-ridden by what? by two or three feet of sorry tripe full of——."[102] To his two brothers he revealed his obsessive fears and connected his misery to Edinburgh, "so lonely and desolate a place to me." For "when any thing affects the outward man, the inward gets so gloomy and desponding." He could not separate depression from stomach pain. "This disorder in the stomach. . . . There is nothing immediately dangerous to life in it; but . . . it chains down the fiercest spirit, and lays it prostrate in a dungeon built of the blackest materials which imagination can furnish."[103] He could not purge himself of what was wrong, dirty, fecal—what had to come out if he were to function effectively with himself and with other people. He warned Jack, who believed he "could endure . . . all . . . evils" if "it were give[n]" him "to attain such literary fame as" he predicted for his brother, that perhaps intellectual overwork was the source of his illness. "For God's sake be careful of your health! You know not what a jewel, how inestimable a thing it is."[104]

Clearer in his own mind about the nature of his illness, he began to feel a determination that he would not allow it to conquer him. "Languor and debility" could be overcome by some effort of the will. Lack of meaningful work and mission he believed to be "the *only thing* that can break my heart." Perhaps the misery of recent years was "temporary, the transition from youth to hardened manhood: in a year [or] two it may be all gone."[105] If he could have restorative sea breezes and "decent people" for company, he might begin to recover. Visiting Kirkcaldy in February 1821, he found that the fresh sea air had a salutary effect. Since his "stomach and bowels still" continued "lazy," he took laxatives "to keep *them* to their duty" and himself "from a state of weak discomfort." But he definitely felt better. There was still hope, he wrote to Jack early in 1821, that "I shall accomplish much, and among other things the long wished for results of gaining for myself some permanent employment, so that I may no longer wander about the earth a moping hypochondriac, the soul eating up itself for want of something else to act upon."[106]

[3]

The Phoenix
1821–1824

Desperately trying to convince himself and others that he was not sick, Carlyle went about his daily business through the winter and spring of 1821 as changeable in mood as the daily changes from mist at dawn to sun in the afternoon.[1] Each emotion had a discrete integrity that forced him to dramatize his feelings with passionate sincerity. He was obsessed with making a full sensory and spiritual response to what was in his mind and body at any given moment, despite his frequent self-reminders to keep his eye on eternity. The search for sustaining ways to express such immediate experience drained much of his energy.

Occasional attempts to write poetry could not deceive him into believing that he had any talent as a poet. Letters, reviews, a notebook journal, and other prose forms could best provide the spontaneous and meditative vehicle his emotional and philosophic expressiveness demanded. Soon, the idea of writing a book was a constant preoccupation; it would be a redeeming action, a channel for his energy and ambition which would relieve him of the tremendous burden of self-criticism. But what could he write about? No subject came to hand immediately. By the sping of 1821 he had convinced himself that he "must live by Literature, at all hazards," but the attempt would be not only economically precarious but also spiritually dangerous. What did it mean to live by literature? To be a writer he felt that he needed to say something that would have both the authority of traditional models and the originality of personal style. For the moment, he had neither. He had read widely in English and French literature, but from Shakespeare to Voltaire most of the models available to him embodied modern perplexities rather than new avenues of resolution and creativity. Shakespeare, Milton, and Pope were widely shared and well-known treasures rather than special personal discoveries. His own talent and sensibility made him an admirer but not an imitator of their poetic styles.

Dissatisfied with what seemed the limitations of his position, Carlyle sought a vehicle with both ascending and extending wings. Unfortunately, both Wordsworth and Coleridge seemed embodiments of the sublime and picturesque tradition, the latter with an unhealthy addition of abstract "moonshine." Eager to read Sir Walter Scott, he readily admitted that he found few memorable moments amid the general though entertaining triviality of Scott's work. Byron proved more exciting and relevant, but he was also more dangerous. The immoral edge of his anger cut too carelessly into the human fabric for the moral young Scotsman's comfort. Such poets "are like opium eaters; they raise their minds by brooding over and embellishing their sufferings, from one degree of fervid exaltation and dreamy greatness to another, till at length they run *amuck* entirely, and whoever meets them would do well to run them thro' the body."[2] During the summer of 1819 he had tried, while first learning German, to read Goethe. But his "unfortunate brain" felt "entirely desiccated with the labour of . . . scratching Teutonic characters"; his command of the language was insufficient to such demands.[3] He was impatient with much, but persevered with German and by the following spring was able to read Goethe's *Faustus.* Suddenly he was ecstatically enthusiastic, almost exalted. He had caught sight of a distant glow, a "new Heaven and new Earth which a slight study of German literature has revealed to me—or promises to reveal."[4]

Madame de Staël's *De l'Allemagne* had suggested to him that eighteenth-and nineteenth-century German culture might contain answers to questions that had not yet been resolved by the English and French. He thought that the language itself had the potential for repellent infelicities, "a frightful dialect for the stupid, the pedant and dullard sort," but "in the hands of the gifted does it become supremely good."[5] He advised Edward Irving "to persist in German. These people have some muscle in their frames."[6] Perseverance itself was a virtue; labor inevitably provided a reward. Soon enthusiasm led him to a broad, intuitive elevation of German literature over French. Invoking two authors as symbols of the difference between the cultures, he asked to be recommended "to Fichte rather than Voltaire."[7] Returning again to Goethe's *Wilhelm Meister,* he finished it on a night that he would "never forget. . . . It was in Edinburgh. I went out into the Town—there was a cold grey mist—the stars were visible. . . . I felt that in Goethe I had found the true wisdom."[8]

But of what did this "true wisdom" consist? Eager to find some grounds on which to affirm that he and his mother agreed on the highest principles and would "meet in that *upper country,*" he may have embraced Goethe's and Fichte's idealism because of its apparent similarity to the spiritual idealism of her world.[9] Goethe could hardly pass serious muster as a Christian. His European reputation was that of a humanist whose spiritual commitments flowed out of creative pilgrimage rather than authoritative theology. But this did not matter to Carlyle, whose orthodoxy had been left far behind. The vague "Christianity" that "seemed" to "live again" in Goethe was the Christianity of heightened spiritual sensitivity to the patterns of human experience. Immediately identifying with Goethe the man rather than with Goethe the philosopher, he warned Irving that if they were together he would talk of *Faustus* for hours, not because of its aesthetic attractions or its religious doctrine but because the pilgrimage of Faust is the very one that he himself has been experiencing.[10] Disappointed in almost every aspect of his life, Carlyle felt as if Goethe were reading his soul. Goethe had shown that a pilgrimage like Faust's could be accomplished. In his intense identification with Goethe, whom "I love and admire," Carlyle suddenly felt he had a new friend, almost a father, whose insights into the patterns of his own life seemed to express a comforting compassion.[11]

German literature and philosophy seemed fresh, inspiring, idealistic. Idealized by distance, Goethe's Weimar glittered like a hallowed and beautiful place, a sharp contrast to what seemed the spiritual wasteland of British and French culture. The old heaven and the old earth were withering. Impressed by what he learned about the handsome treatment of writers in Germany, Carlyle began to imagine a mythical Teutonic country in which the arts flourished under the patronage of enlightened leaders.

Like other Romantics who had read both Locke and Cobbett, he realized that his personal anxieties might mirror social conditions. He was skeptical, however, that the political, social, and economic organization of "old Earth" could be transformed into a "new Heaven." During the summer of 1819, agitation throughout England against the Corn laws and an unreformed Parliament had reached a bloody climax in the Peterloo Massacre at Manchester. Since Edinburgh did not have an extensive manufacturing industry, it only vibrated with secondary shocks, but in Glasgow the industrial workers threatened a revolution of their own. The young man observed the "great distress" of "the common people" in Edinburgh with as much contempt for the ruling class as sympathy for the workers.[12] Irving, despite his deep sympathies for the poor, wrote from Glasgow that he had nothing "to say in favour of Radicalism, for it is the very destitution of philosophy and religion and political economy." Carlyle thought "the danger . . . was small or imaginary and their grievances dreadfully real,"[13] but news of the Cato Street Conspiracy, a plan "to assassinate the cabinet," filled him with horror. Political "assassination," which had "long been a stranger to the British soil," offended the religious psychology that proclaimed that "the mighty changes" would come not from individual acts of worldly defiance but from individual acts of heavenly obedience. Rectification was in God's hands.

Byron and Shelley responded to the brutal events of 1819 with satirical condemnation of the government and inspired revolutionary propaganda. What the Romantic revolutionists urged, particularly armed rebellion, Carlyle feared would actually happen, though he thought that "some pity should be mingled with our abhorrence of the frantic conspirators. Well-founded complaints of poverty, one might almost say starvation, met with indifference or cold-blooded ridicule, . . . very naturally exasperate the ignorant minds of the governed, and impel them to enterprises of a desperate nature. . . . It is greatly to be dreaded that more formidable & better-concerted resistance will ensue."[14] In his sympathy for the plight of the working class, Carlyle recalled his father's story of the workers covertly drinking at the brook at lunchtime instead of eating, too proud to complain, too embarrassed to want to draw attention to their misery.[15] Still, as he surveyed the revolutionary potential of England and Scotland in 1820, his intuitive detestation of violent change demanded that he distinguish between legitimate grievances and undesirable solutions. His compassion for the suffering of the poor and the miserable was to increase, but so too was his fear of an attempt at renovation which would be more disastrous than the continuation of the horrid problem.

For the time being, however, he saw no reason to involve himself in these intractable public affairs. Who would listen to him anyway until he had provided himself with a secure platform from which to speak for peaceful change? He thought the present tensions might be harmoniously resolved through wise leadership. "In the mean time, what constitutes *our* wisest plan is to follow our private concerns as dilgently as we may, without mingling in civil broils—unless imperious necessity call us so to do."[16] As he searched for inspiration and confirmation of his distinctiveness, he was carried even further away from English affairs by his discovery of Goethe and German literature. The romantic idealist in him directed itself toward a "new Heaven and a new Earth"—a quest that, at least for now, had no public or social resonance.

2.

Returning to Edinburgh from his Christmas 1820 trip to Glasgow, Carlyle hastened to assure his family that his reports of ill health had been exaggerated. "I get low, very low, in spirits, when the clay house is out of repair."[17] Doing his best to convince himself that such depressions resulted from physical illness, he revealed some of the bases of his unhappiness when he advised Jack to avoid the isolation that studiousness often encourges, for "it is miserable to live alone, one gets envy and ill-will on hand, soreness and wasteness of hearth in prospect."[18] Before Christmas he had felt dreadfully bilious. "But I walked, and swallowed drugs, and walked and swallowed drugs again, till things have come back to their old level."[19] At best, he felt lonely and useless, depressed by the "raw weather and this unsociable place." Since he received some reviving warmth from the hearth at Mainhill, he kept his letters flowing, encouraging Alick to improve his education, urging Jack to reveal his heart to him. "Write any thing: I love to see the soul unveiled."[20] His new year's blessing for his family rose into the invocation of a prayer: "Yet let us be of cheer . . . that many new years, and far happier ones, may be in store for each of us."[21]

Confident that he could support himself through his writing, he plodded on with the encyclopedia articles for Brewster. There were now also some prospects for translation. Though he thought translation inferior to original work in compensation, self-esteem, and public recognition, he was eager to find steady literary employment of any honorable type. Baillie Waugh, the editor whose swaggering condescension he had instantly disliked when introducing himself two years before, asked him to support the *New Edinburgh Review* and soon sent him a book to review, Joanna Baillie's *Metrical Legends of Exalted Characters* (1821).[22] Through the winter and spring it seemed as if he had "tried about twenty plans . . . in the way of authorship; they have all failed; I have about twenty more to try."[23] Prospects seemed brighter, more hopeful, and Carlyle remained in comparatively good spirits, indulging his overbearing habit of sending long reading lists to friends and relations. He was still "weary & heavy laden, with very fickle health," but his entry into Edinburgh literary life and its rewards put him more at ease with himself and took some edge off his bitterness for the moment.[24] For "the literary world is going on much as it was wont: frisking Reviewers . . . a nameless throng, digging like moles at Encyclopedias, Journals, Monthly Reviews &c &c quite in the old stile."[25] He planned to spend much of the summer in Edinburgh, where work might come his way, though he still maintained, despite his good spirits, that he had "not been well for one day since last Autumn—sometimes very sick."[26]

Disturbed by his friend's complaints, Irving, for whom such "a miserable creature in his neighborhood is like a disease of his own," again attempted to help.[27] Arriving in Edinburgh late in May 1821 for the General Assembly of the church, Irving proposed that his friend accompany him to East Lothian where he intended to spend a few days with the recently widowed Grace Welsh and her daughter Jane, friends with whom he had been in contact since leaving Haddington in 1816. Traveling casually under a clear sky, the two friends appeared at sunset at the well-located, comfortable home of the widow and her nineteen-year-old daughter, whom Irving had tutored several years earlier. With a soft evening glow falling through the windows, the "finest" drawing room he had seen glowed with elegance and mysterious romantic sadness.

The stranger was welcome both for his friend's sake and for the enlivenment of a residence that both women found comfortable but boring. Dr. John Welsh, a competent, widely respected physician, had died of typhus fever less than two years before, leaving his wife to come to terms with loneliness and straitened circumstances. A sentimental and capricious woman, Grace Welsh was unable to organize her complex situation now that her dominant husband was dead. She was "a tall *aquiline* figure, of elegant carriage and air" who, in her severe widow's costume, seemed the embodiment of a middle-class hauteur that Carlyle had never encountered before.[28] She hovered uncertainly in an emotional shadowland where she was both her daughter's supporter and to some extent her rival.

Jane, the cherished only child of an assertive father, could not hide her feeling that the parent who had loved her most was gone. His death deprived her of the one authority figure she respected. His influence had sent her to school under Irving and James Brown; his confidence had elevated her sense of special merit. Since his death, she was in the process of confronting the likelihood that, despite her talent and education, marriage was the only institutional outlet for her energy. Though she joked that she would never marry, she had already recognized that her need for conventional security was at least as strong as her desire for special literary distinction. Though her ambition was to be learned and famous, she found herself devoting a great deal of time to parties, suitors, and excursions. But "the beautiful bright and earnest young lady" readily confessed to her visitor that she "was intent on literature as the highest aim in life, and felt imprisoned in the dull element which yielded her no commerce in that kind, and would not even yield her books to read."[29] To Jane, Haddington was "the bottom of the pit of dullness."[30]

Prodded by Irving, Carlyle spoke that evening of his own reading, writing, and literary ambitions, attempting to awaken Jane's interest in the "new Heaven and new Earth" of German literature. She listened intently, apparently almost as impressed by his learning as she was amused by his Annandale accent and country awkwardness. An excellent mimic and storyteller, she refrained that evening from exercising her natural bent for sarcasm. In the "red, dusky evening, the sky hanging huge and high, but dim as with dust or drought," the two men returned to the George Inn for the night, where Irving extracted from his friend the ready confession that he was attracted enough to Jane to take her very seriously indeed.[31] They stayed three more days, spending at least a few hours each evening in the Welsh's drawing room.

Back in Edinburgh, Carlyle's spirits were almost boisterous. He continued to complain about his health and life but in more general terms, for he was becoming increasingly capable of being happy while being miserable.[32] His imagination worked full force on Jane. "I came back so full of joy," he wrote to his brother Alick on the sixth of June, "that I have done nothing since but dream of [her]." "I have been busily engaged," he wrote to a friend six day's later, "in that important thing, Doing nothing."[33] Early in June he sent her an aggressive, intimate letter.

Sensing that her weakness was her intellectual vanity, he cast out German literature as a lure. He had the Romantic temerity to call the time he had spent with her at Haddington "those few Elysian hours," and closed the letter by admitting it was a "wonderful compound of pedagogy and sentimentality and absurdity."[34] With intuitive shrewdness, he urged her not to be "*very* cruel," encouraging her to maintain even "cruel" contact with him by assuring her that he would still "cherish" her in his imagination. He asked her to think of him as her "elder-Brother" if she could not accept his "impertinences." With this bewildering combination of attack and reassurance, the young man of twenty-six had dared what he had tried before only with Margaret Gordon: to attempt to establish an intimate relationship with a woman other than his mother.[35] He wrote, "Positively, I must see you soon—or I shall get into a very absurd state."[36]

Jane apparently concluded that he was in such a state already. His claim that he felt destined to know her better, "as if we had known each other from infancy upwards," coupled with his query about what her reaction would be to a visit from him to "Jane herself *professedly*," seemed an unacceptable exploitation of her agreement to receive from him only a reading list. At the end of June he received a parcel containing books that he had lent her. Eagerly opening it, he searched with "hysterical speed" for some personal word, shaking each volume to see if there were a letter between the pages. He found a note expressing

"Miss Welsh's 'compliments.' " To his disappointment, the one line was all he got, with his name misspelled. "Upon the whole, I suppose, you did well to treat me so," he wrote to her a few days later. "I had dreamed and hoped, indeed; but what right had *I* to hope, or even to wish?" When she coolly mentioned in her brief response on the sixth of July that she had "dismissed" her German teacher and was getting "on faster without him," he immediately wrote to announce that he had decided "*to set out in person to inspect and accelerate your progress in the German tongue,*" as if he had determined not to overlook even the slightest hint of encouragement. "Will you let me come? Will you be at home then? If you say No, if you *do not* say yes, it will dash the whole of this gay Spanish Castle to the ground. Can you *find in your heart* to do so? Can you? . . . *When* will you write to me? Tomorrow? Next day? If you knew *all,* you would sit down instantly."[37] Indeed, she did answer immediately, informing him that her mother "bids" her to say "that she is, at present, quite uncertain if we shall be at Haddington at the time you talk of visiting us." Nevertheless, he was welcome to call on her the next week at her cousin's in Edinburgh where she would be glad to listen to his "advice respecting" her "studies."[38]

3.

Carlyle's unsuitability as a suitor had been apparent from the beginning. With his constant complaints about his health, his rustic manners, and his lack of a practical vocation, he had little to recommend him except his "genius," his aggressive compliments, and his desire to serve. Cautious in most things, he now became reckless in his rhetoric while soberly recognizing that the son of a farmer could not present himself as a suitor to the daughter of a doctor unless he had more auspicious prospects. Shrewdly, he offered himself as a friend and mentor, not as a lover. Having for so long discharged his repressed sexuality in hard work, ill health, and vigorous exercise, he was readily capable of finding yet another outlet in intellectual discourse with an attractive and enthusiastic woman. But she knew that he found her desirable, and this fact stirred the depths and occasionally even excited the surface of this new relationship.

Jane Welsh could not imagine that such a man could become her husband, however. She was frightened of marriage because, among other reasons, she was frightened of sex. Reading Rousseau's *Julie, ou la nouvelle Héloise* (1761), she nervously boasted that "this Book this fatal Book has given me an idea of a love so *pure* (Yes you may laugh! but I repeat it) so pure, so constant, so disinterested, so exalted—that no love the men of this world can offer me will ever fill up the picture my imagination has drawn."[39] Not one of her current suitors met her high, asexual standard, a playful but defensive expression of her private recognition that the flirtatious games she had played with potential suitors since she was sixteen would ultimately lead to the sexual relations that were a part of marriage. When Carlyle saw her in Edinburgh briefly at the end of July, he could not have known that she not only had other men on her mind but that she nervously expected a marriage proposal from one of them—George Rennie. Certainly he realized that she did not consider him a serious suitor at all.

In August 1821 she sent him what she felt a weak attempt to translate some lines from Goethe, reminding him that he had not yet fulfilled his promise to send her copies of all his poems, unaware that he had written few and thought little of them. Fascinated with literature and eager to define herself in some role that would obtain recognition for her talent, she was vulnerable to a kind of literary lovemaking, provided it flattered her abilities and emphasized the improvement of her intellect. And Carlyle did everything he could to encourage her literary ambition. As he wrote to her in September 1821, literature "at once deepens and diversifies the happiness and the misery of our life."[40] Combining both personal and ideal interests, he urged her to believe that happiness was not the highest aim of human beings anyway but that isolation from kindred spirits led "to every species of wretchedness. . . . The heart that can taste of rapture must taste of torment also."[41] He knew the improvement of her education and the elevation of her ambition would inevitably separate her from others, and thought that if he could win her to his philosophy perhaps he could also reconcile her to his exclusive company. Suddenly realizing the intensity of Carlyle's pursuit, Grace Welsh ordered her daughter to end the correspondence.

Though Jane abhorred deception she continued to write to Carlyle, at the same time concealing both the extent of her pursuit by other suitors and the nature of her relationship with Edward Irving. Within a year after Irving had assumed the mathematics mastership in Haddington in 1810, he had been employed by Dr. Welsh as special tutor to his precocious ten-year-old daughter, who idolized her handsome eighteen-year-old teacher. Irving was fascinated by his "paragon of gifted young girls," and when he left in the summer of 1812 it was only because the Haddington authorities could not meet the salary offered him in Kirkcaldy.[42] Four years later, he already had an implied commitment to Isabella Martin, but it is certain that he had not forgotten Jane; perhaps he had even visited Haddington in the years since his departure. In 1817 he had discovered that the sixteen-year-old Jane was now a student at a finishing school in Edinburgh, and he took every opportunity to visit her at her cousin's home, where his attentions were favorably interpreted. Though he and Carlyle often traveled together from Kirkcaldy to the capital, Carlyle never learned that Irving had such a special friend in Edinburgh.

Whatever Irving's feeling for Jane when she had been his pupil, he now loved her and was not disappointed in his hope that she would return his feeling. Her preadolescent fantasy had suddenly matured; he whom she had idolized before she now "passionately loved."[43] But their relationship was doomed when it became clear by late 1820 that Irving would be held to the Martins' assumption that he had engaged himself to Isabella. With his honor, his reputation, and his clerical future at stake, he soon ceased to struggle with the inevitable. Immensely disappointed, Jane escaped into the sublimating heights of moral duty and urged him "to marry that other and preserve his honour from reproach."[44] He managed to accept his fate graciously enough to flirt with Margaret Gordon for a while between late 1818 and 1820, while attempting to retain with Jane the special emotional privileges of a suitor despite the impossibility of any commitment between them.

Drawing on the willful resources of a stubborn only child, Jane refused to brood on her disappointment or to keep the past alive.[45] Her father had died in the late summer of 1819, and, after the initial shock, she had attempted to find pupils to teach in Haddington. Feeling guilty about her father's death, the young lady felt that "we must kiss the rod even while we are writhing under the tortures which it inflicts."[46] Mother and daughter got on one another's nerves, both suffering from constant headaches and difficult menstrual periods. The memory of John Welsh prevented them from giving up their Haddington home, though it would have been the practical thing to do, since the lease still had some years to run. Their only cash income came from the rent of a small farming property called Craigenputtoch in southwestern Scotland. When Irving brought his friend to visit in May 1821, then, mother and daughter were nervous about both the distance between themselves and the uncertainty of the future. In addition, they realized that if it had not been for his commitment to Isabella Martin, Edward Irving would have entered their household on a very different footing.

During the summer of 1821 Carlyle wrote to Irving, whose emotions he had no glimpse of, that "I saw the fair pupil in Edinburgh. She is certainly the most—fit to read German of any creature I have met with."[47] Having impressed his German grammar and dictionary into pedagogic service, Carlyle assured his worried friend that there was no danger to Jane's moral and spiritual well-being in her studying German literature with him. Deprived of the relationship that he had yearned to have, Irving apprehensively saw her moving even further away from him, not so much into the arms of an old friend (his arms were open—but there seemed little chance that she would enter) as into an intellectual and literary world from which he felt excluded by both necessity and choice. He vividly imagined that by entering into Carlyle's world she would inevitably become the victim of its anxieties and confusions. "I could like to see her surrounded with a more sober set of companions than Rousseau (your friend), and Byron." The reading of "German poets" might "cut" her "off from . . . the wholesome intercourse of those amongst whom she is cast without being able to raise her to a better." Unfortunately, she already "contemplates the inferiority of others rather from the point of ridicule and contempt than from that of commiseration and relief" and "contracts in her own mind a degree of coldness and bitterness which suits ill with my conception of female character and a female's position in society."[48] Speaking from unhappy personal experience, Irving was as much sorry for himself as he was concerned about Jane. Unaware of the real grounds of his friend's opinions, Carlyle assured him that he should have "no fear of" the influence of German writers.[49]

Jane came to appreciate Thomas' excellence long before she concluded that his virtues necessitated her commitment to him. The aggressiveness of his interest, which both flattered her vanity and provoked her contempt, initially frightened her as well. Particularly since the death of her father, she at some level doubted that she was worthy of such intense love, expressing her insecurity as well as her fright in coy but serious statements that disclaimed any interest in marriage. George Rennie, from whom she would have welcomed a proposal, departed for Italy early in 1822, leaving her immensely disappointed and worried about his safety on the long winter voyage. To bolster her ego, she welcomed the attention of men, disguising as best she could her disappointment in Irving and in Rennie, and using a heightened sense of the ridiculous and a sharp tongue to defend herself against insecurities. At least for the time being, Carlyle was eager to serve as her target, if that was all he could be.[50]

When he called on her at her cousin's house in Edinburgh in November 1821, he was compelled to act the part of her mentor in German literature and to avoid personal subjects. Soon he urged her to correspond with him, despite her mother's prohibition. Unable to resist his appeals, which encouraged her to believe that she had a great future as an author, that she was the best German student imaginable, and that there was no harm in their correspondence since he meant only to be her friend, she allowed herself to be flattered by his claim that his "genius," without self-serving and worldly ambitions of its own, was at her disposal. At the end of December, both her patience and her control of the situation were low. "Oh Mr. Carlyle how I am plagued with you! Why will you not let me live at home in peace?"[51] The patent exaggeration of his seeming subservience affronted her own sense of unworthiness. At the same time his apparent disregard for fame and fortune angered her. After all, the one might give her pleasure, the other might give him means; to state contempt for the very success that would make it possible to become a serious suitor seemed a baffling wooing technique. If he thought so little of literary fame, how could he respect her own literary ambitions?[52]

But apparently she also recognized that she had been deeply stirred by elements in this new relationship. Corresponding with Thomas against her mother's wishes and without her knowledge, Jane admitted, "I am as nervous as if I were committing a murder."[53] Though she was confused, she was also excited. She concluded the year by inviting him to visit at Haddington when he had finished a new essay-review that he was writing and at least two dozen pages of the original book that he had been proclaiming to himself and to everyone else that he would start shortly. As an additional proviso she demanded that he learn to write a letter that would not anger her mother. Several weeks later she reminded him of a lesson in life which she was to relearn from him during their marriage, especially during his years of fame: "Patient suffering . . . is the first lesson to be learned by *one* of the parties in a Romantic Friendship."[54]

4.

With work to do, Carlyle found himself in the autumn of 1821 in better spirits than he had been for a long time; "dyspepsia . . . the queen of human ills" was no longer quite as onerous a consort.[55] Aided by "simple drugs," he could recognize a substantial improvement during the past year. He actually felt consoled by the thought that those who have a capacity to discuss their illnesses—among whom he classed himself—must conclude that they cannot be as ill as they had imagined. Noise bothered him a great deal, however, and he made the mistake of moving near the new Royal Circus, still under construction. But in late December 1821 he finally settled "between Edinburgh and Leith," with air and quiet and nothing but green fields "between me and the Forth," a spot almost as lovely as Mainhill, whose inhabitants he sorely missed.[56] From home came the news that Jack might come to Edinburgh next year to study medicine at the university, and that James Carlyle had been deeply moved when he received a pair of silver spectacles as a present from his eldest son.[57] Though Thomas confessed that he could never "return to the minister-office," he assured his mother that he would "lay aside vanities, be submissive &c," as she had counseled him.[58] He said nothing about Jane.

Finding his new lodgings comfortable, Carlyle took on an additional translation assignment and began to ponder possible subjects for his own book. In October Waugh had sent him a translation of Goethe's *Faustus* to review. Soon Brewster's request that he undertake a translation of Adrien Legendre's *Elements of Geometry* provided the opportunity to put his hard-won familiarity with mathematics to practical use. But, however much or little he did, he was perfectly capable at one moment of imagining that he was working himself to death and at another that he was an idle sinner. He was acutely conscious of the gap that separated what he was doing from "original composition," and in order to provoke himself to attempt the latter—or to justify his failure to begin "some Magnum Opus"—he described himself in an exaggerated rhetoric of strain and tension, of great aims, great obstacles, and heroic resolutions. "I *must* do something—or die, whichever I like better."[59] Tenacious about life, he heightened life by dramatizing with complete sincerity the intensity of his suffering, using his physical health as a metaphor for his spiritual condition. Irving warned him that the world was likely to take his claim of suffering and insufficiency literally.[60] Carlyle responded that such punishment would be well deserved, that he "[required] imperiously to be overhauled and severely castigated every way." He was unable to understand that others might see his suffering as self-inflicted, his complaints as self-indulgent.[61]

The outgoing, enthusiastic Irving also had an extraordinary capacity for self-dramatization, which he revealed in his preaching, his missionary work among the Glasgow poor, and his heightened rhetoric about his own and his nation's Christian destiny. In late autumn 1821 Carlyle was delighted to learn that Irving had been offered the opportunity to present himself for a month to the National Church of Scotland's Hatton Garden Chapel in London. There was the possibility of a permanent appointment. On a "dim," late December night, just before Christmas, they had a farewell meeting in the "Coffee-room of the Black Bull Hotel" in Edinburgh. Carlyle was sad, and Irving, who perhaps had already been to say goodby at Haddington, was nervous, "agitated with anxieties . . . doubtless with regrets as well."[62] Though he was to write and visit Jane over the next few years, he knew that his departure from Scotland would attenuate and perhaps sever the most cherished ties of his life. In a farewell gesture, Carlyle gave him "as road-companion" a bunch of the "best cigars" he ever had. Later he learned that Irving "had begun by losing every cigar of them,—left the whole bundle lying on our seat in the Stall of the Coffee-room."[63] They were never to be intimate again on anything like the old basis. Though Carlyle might never lose his friend, he had already lost his "friend's society."[64]

But the elders and the congregation of the Caledonian Chapel in London found in Irving precisely what they had been seeking. Impressed by his vigorous good looks, his Christian commitment, and his youthful energy, they made a generous offer which he shortly accepted. Soon to become a prophet in his new country, he was from the beginning someone whom others consulted, among them Isabella and Charles Buller, who asked his advice about the education of two of their sons. Never at a loss for instant enthusiasms, Irving immediately overwhelmed the Bullers with praise of Carlyle, proposing that the two boys be enrolled in the University of Edinburgh under his tutorship. During a trial period of half a year, the tutor, his students, and their parents (who would remain in London) might evaluate their fitness for one another and then either make a per annum arrangement or part company. The wealthy Bullers were prepared to offer £200 a year, more money than Carlyle had ever earned before, about twice as much as his father had ever earned in one year.

Much as he hated teaching, the prospect of tutoring on a well-paid regular basis with bright, companionable students hardly gave him pause. Writing immediately to Irving in London to accept the offer, he insisted only that he maintain his own lodgings rather than live in the Buller household. He consulted with no one. Certain that he did not want to do dull, energy-draining work, he had just the previous week turned down John Martin's offer of the editorship of a Dundee newspaper at "100 a-year, and a percentage." The thought of becoming even a well-paid servant in someone else's household was distasteful to Carlyle, but Irving quieted his fears. He had already alerted the Bullers, who were eager to be associated with a young man who had been praised as a genius with a brilliant literary future, that his friend "had seen little of life, and was disposed to be rather high in the humour, if not well used."[65] Warned that "the mother . . . is an excellent person" but "the sons likely to be more troublesome," Carlyle admitted that "the salary" of "two hundred a year, a round solid sum," is one "for which a man would submit to much."[66] Just how much would remain for the time being an open question. By temperament capable of defining "much" very narrowly, he also recognized that the advantages were overwhelming, the risks few.

Shortly after writing his acceptance to Irving, Carlyle in a burst of energy composed letters to his father, his mother, Alick, and Jack, offering to pay all expenses if the last would come to Edinburgh in the fall to study medicine. Two days later, he notified his "dear Friend" in Haddington that he had finished his review of *Faustus* and that "by the blessing of Heaven . . . I shall never be idle more." In the dramatic tone that he usually used to answer self-criticism, he pledged his unceasing labors to achieve something heroic in literature "or perish, as I ought, in trying it." His ongoing encyclopedia articles, however, hardly matched his high ambitions; he had no original work of his own to show her. But he could readily confess that he was lonely and at liberty. "In two weeks, I am with you; *unless* you declare I absolutely must not." As if it were a minor point or barely remembered, he added that he had been offered a tutoring position with many advantages, among them ample free time, the opportunity to travel, and a salary (exaggerated for this one time) of £250. As if he had not yet accepted the offer, he reasoned that these advantages "ought perhaps to induce me. Let me see you before I decide: it may not be so easy afterwards."[67]

Disturbed by his pledge in German, "All for Glory and her," Jane reminded him that both she and her mother disliked his "somewhat too ardent expressions of Friendship." If he could not write to her as if he were already married (to someone else, of course), then she advised him not to write to her at all. "One would almost believe the man fancies I have fallen in love with him, and entertain the splended project of rewarding his literary labours with myself." Frightened by his aggressiveness, she criticized him, sometimes cruelly, aware that both giving and receiving pain might create pleasure. She was less shocked to discover that she enjoyed such taunting than to find that Thomas revealed little interest in and sometimes even contempt for the practical efforts that might make him an acceptable suitor. His brief mention of what she considered "the most important topic" in his letter, the Buller offer, offended and perplexed her.[68] Perhaps he had not anticipated that his tactic would undermine his credibility and direct Jane's anger at him. Probably he had some idea that it would. Her anger might indeed be the beginning of a bond between them.

Later in the year, Irving insisted on giving Jane an unsolicited but perceptive analysis of her character. "You and I agree always when we meet with a person of power, but you do not go so far as I in exacting from them a good use of it. I do not wish it turned to arts of cruelty, which satire and ridicule and scorn are." Such people never have peace of mind and torture others in order to torture themselves. "Keep away these two things, the cruel treatment of another, and the deification of energy, and I will not be offended with the exercise of mental powers."[69] In the spring of 1822 he told her that he still loved her and that he was fighting a crucial battle as he attempted to channel his manly feelings toward her into "chaste affection," his love of Isabella Martin into marriage. Whatever advice he had for Jane was also a lament for an aborted relationship and a lost ideal. A willful, sarcastic, aggressive young lady with secular literary ambitions could hardly be a gracious recipient of his pietistic approval. Jane responded to his advice with the stern injunction that he must cease preaching to her if he wanted their relationship to continue at all.

5.

When Charles and Arthur Buller arrived in Edinburgh late in January 1822, Carlyle immediately took his two students "out on a walk, round by the foot of Salisbury Crags, up from Holyrood, by the Castle and Law-Courts, home again to George's Square." Years later, he could recollect "few more pleasant walks in [his] life!"[70] Perhaps he was reminded of the moment over twelve years earlier when he had arrived in Edinburgh for the first time and immediately dashed out to see the awesome sights of the city. From the beginning he apparently felt both sympathy and fondness for the two young boys. Spontaneously intelligent and broadly curious, the fifteen-year-old Charles seemed eager to appreciate the virtues of this handsome, experienced "genius"; Arthur, less intellectually alert than his elder brother, impressed Carlyle with his cheerful, trusting openness. Despite his aversion to teaching of any kind, Carlyle had been immensely fortunate. He now had a position in which he not only could support himself handsomely while still having ample time for literary work but also could feel genuine affection and respect for his students. They were to become "friends . . . till death parted" them.[71]

Despite Jane's warning that he would "repent" of it, Carlyle went to Haddington the first weekend in February 1822. The visit was a painful disaster. Both mother and daughter resented the brash appearance of a young man who did not qualify as a suitor and who was too aggressive to be welcomed as a friend. Grace Welsh believed that his temporary employment by the Bullers constituted no real improvement in his future prospects, and Jane, having just been disappointed by George Rennie, took out her own frustration on her tactless visitor. "After that unfortunate visit," Thomas felt that his connection with Jane "depended on a single hair" and trembled "lest some unguarded word . . . dissolve it forever."[72] Feeling "a perfect wreck," he begged her to continue their correspondence—even if only "one sentence from you"—in exchange for which he would pretend to be neither a lover nor a friend.[73] But, in a better mood, she teased, "You are not my *Friend*—you are not my *Lover*—In the name of wonder, Sir what *are* you?—Oh! I had forgot—'A wreck!'—'a perfect Wreck!!' "[74]

The correspondence between the "wreck" and "Dear Madame" continued, however, and suddenly, amid an exchange of reading lists, literary opinions, translations, even poems, Thomas found emphatic confirmation of what he had barely hinted at before: Jane had "dramatic genius," great literary talent! Should she write tragedies or comedies? After proposing the merits of the story of Boadicea for her consideration, he assured her that if that would not do he had "another Tragedy in store for" her.[75] Though Jane had only the faintest idea that he had determined to do everything in his power to persuade her to marry him, how might she have reacted had she been able to read his consoling advice to a friend whose engagement had just been broken:

> She was a person of genius . . . and much as I admire, not to say idolize, that characteristic in a . . . *sweetheart* . . . I confess I should pause before recommending it to any honest man in a wife. These women of genius, sir, are the very d——l, when you take them on a wrong tack. I know very well, that I myself—if ever I marry . . . am to have one of them for my helpmate; and I expect nothing but that our life will be the most turbulent, incongruous thing on earth—a mixture of honey and wormwood, the sweetest and the bitterest . . . the clearest sunshiny weather in nature, then whirlwinds and sleet and frost; the thunder and lightning and furious storms—all mingled together into the same season—and the sunshine always in the *smallest* quantity![76]

Now unwelcome in Haddington, except through the mediation of the postman, he did not write for a while, depressed by the "blue devils." But Jane was bored with the tedium of her conventional "fine lady" life, and she soon allowed the correspondence to be reinvigorated on a "dear Friend" basis. It was devoted mainly to literary matters, and Jane chided him good-humouredly for exaggerating the bleakness of his mood. His review of *Faustus* appeared in April 1822, and by early summer, eager to finish his translation of Legendre's *Geometry,* he increased his effort. He also went to "George-Square twice every day . . . to superintend the studies of the Bullers: I go down to bathe pretty regularly: I read & write . . . and teach and sleep & eat as quietly as I can."[77] But the habit of complaining had become so ingrained that he could claim that "the chief deformities in my life have arisen from that thrice-cursed stomach of mine!"[78] Still, he was depressed, in part because the prospect of continuing as a tutor, a translator, and a reviewer fell so far short of the achievement of writing something original.[79] Earlier in the year he had urged James Johnston, who had returned from Nova Scotia and was now despondently considering emigration to New Zealand, to "stay at home where your merits—slow in making themselves known anywhere—are at last appreciated by many."[80] Like so much of his advice to others, it was also self-encouragement. All through the spring of 1822 he had been reading Milton and histories of the Civil War in the hope of finding a "subject to write upon."[81] He began a notebook, mainly to jot down ideas inspired by his reading. The prospect of composing a sketch of the national character of civil-war England through a series of "mental portraits" of its chief leaders, among them Cromwell, Laud, Foxe, and Milton, initially excited him but came to nothing. Though he was not yet ready to deal with Cromwell, or Puritanism, or the Civil War—or even with himself in any sustained way—he was astounded by Milton's genius, particularly his eloquence and metaphorical talent.[82]

"Getting under way," as he was to call it in *Sartor Resartus,* was proving very difficult. "For the last three years" he had "lived as under an accursed spell," alternating between sarcastic defensiveness and harsh self-castigation.[83] "Wild passions without solacement, wild faculties without employment," had vexed and agitated him.[84] Unresolved conflicts had made him characteristically irritable and depressed. He feared the loss of his parents' love, the difficulty of creating a new reality to replace dead Christian myth, the verdict of the world that it might not provide work at which he could be happy. But by the summer of 1822 there seemed less reason for him to feel pervasively frightened. There had been ample demonstration that his family's love for him transcended material questions. His employment at the Bullers provided more cash and security than he had ever had before. His health, despite the regimen of castor oil and assorted purgatives, was as good as it had been in years. And finally, his pursuit of Jane, despite the problematical outcome, had avoided what had seemed certain failure, a testimony to his tenaciousness and to her genuine interest in him. Still, he felt restless and unhappy, and since he was angry at himself for being miserable and frightened, the mood could only intensify.

Going down Leith Walk on a blazing afternoon in August 1822, Carlyle realized that he had been mistaken all along in believing that "it was with Work alone, and not also with Folly and Sin, in myself and others, that I had been appointed to struggle."[85] The purpose of work was to create a visible structure that would articulate the quality of the inner spiritual life to ourselves and others. But it was his own "inarticulate Self-consciousness," "which only our Works can render articulate and decisively discernable," that needed to be discovered and affirmed.[86] The search did not depend on logic or reason. Since the struggle was not with external problems but with inner states, could he not choose through some effort of the will to create both himself and at the same time a work expressive of himself?

Having been unable to find emotional security in an act of traditional belief, he had been weakened into suspecting that the world belonged to the Devil, to matter and materialism. But if man is free, he is free to deny both doubt and logic, on the essential ground of his trust in his own feelings. Such a denial confirms that he has the freedom to deny whatever contradicts his spiritual needs. He will be free to reject the life-demeaning elements within himself and the external world. Such control over his own self-definition would enable him to defy whatever obstacles the world raised and to oppose any attempts, public or private, to define him in terms that contradicted his basic sense of himself. "And as I so thought," he wrote ten years later in *Sartor Resartus,* his fictionalized account of these experiences, "there rushed . . . a stream of fire over my whole soul; and I shook base Fear away from me forever. I was strong, of unknown strength; a spirit, almost a god."[87] What religious belief had lost, personal will could provide.

In the middle of August this demigod wrote to Jane, begging her to allow him to visit before he left for Annandale. Since he did not dare come without her permission, he would "submit implicitly" to her "wishes."[88] She refused. With that hope dashed, he made preparations to go south immediately, particularly to avoid George IV's impending visit to Edinburgh, which had galvanized the town into festive preparation. Vividly remembering the misery of the working class and the corrupt irresponsibility of the government, Carlyle was disgusted by the hypocritical concealment of ugly realities in the name of patriotic festivities. He was especially antagonized by a placard that urged everyone to wear their best clothes for the king's visit. Jane, in the meantime, came to Edinburgh, hardly disappointed that he had already left, more interested in following "the King as if my happiness here and hereafter depended on getting a sight of him—I heard and saw much,—dressed walked and rode till my limbs could scarce support me, but as to reading, writing, or thinking, no body had any time for that."[89]

Whatever his experiences at Leith Walk in early August, at the end of October he was neither a fire-eating hero of belief in the self nor a courageous noncomplainer overcoming all obstacles through self-acceptance. Seemingly, he had little to complain of. An offer from a bookseller to do a life of Milton for £150, an inquiry from an old acquaintance about his interest in a teaching position at Sandhurst, the imminent arrival of Jack in Edinburgh to study medicine, his success with both the Buller children and their parents, and an exchange of poems with Jane—all suggest that his situation had improved. But his description of himself at the end of October suggests that his habit of dramatizing moments of depression had not really changed: "I am very unhappy at present. I feel called upon by a voice of terror to *bestir myself* . . . and a thousand miserable causes—indecision, ignorance, dyspepsia . . . keep me rivetted to the spot . . . the weakest of the weak." Despite such posturing, however, he confessed that he "never was much more comfortable all my days."[90] He had just received a letter from Jane who not only admitted that "our meeting forms a memorable epoch in my history" but confirmed that his strategy of flattering her mind and talent touched a deep emotional chord. Describing the history of her emotional life since the death of her father, she admitted what he must already have guessed: John Welsh's death had made her "wretched beyond description," particularly because it removed the guide who had shown confidence in her talent and prompted her to high ambition, leaving her with an obligation that she doubted she could fulfill alone. "I wept to think, the mind he had cultivated with such anxious, unremitting pains was running to desolation." But "your eloquence awoke in my soul the slumbering admirations and ambitions that *His* first kindled there."[91]

On his twenty-seventh birthday, at the beginning of December 1822, Thomas piously condemned his own meager accomplishments and prayed that "the great Father of all give me strength to do better."[92] The letter, of course, was to his mother. To Jane, he sketched an outline of the epistolary novel he proposed that they coauthor—a novel in which he would take the part of a romantic youth saved from suicidal despair when he falls in love with the woman whose letters Jane was to write. "For a while you laugh at him, and torment him, but at length take pity on the poor fellow, and grow as serious as he is."[93] He wrote a brief sketch, "Cruthers and Johnson," in which the heroine resembles Jane and in which two male friends compete for the love of the same woman. In February he told her that he saw no incompatibility between a literary career and marriage; in fact, he confidently hoped that she would "be not only a shining ornament of literature, but what is even better, the happy and happy-making Wife of some gallant character that will know how to prize you."[94] Grace Welsh, who had kept them apart for so long, reluctantly permitted him to visit Haddington. By the spring, he was like a drug without which Jane could not rise. "Often at the end of the week my spirits and my industry begin to flag—but then comes one of Mr. Carlyle's brilliant letters that inspires me with new resolution, and brightens all my hopes and prospects with the golden hues of his own imagination—He is a very Ph[o]enix of a Friend!"[95]

6.

In the spring of 1823 Carlyle's German studies, which had been proceeding efficiently, suddenly took on a new dimension. Asked to write a short biographical sketch of Schiller for the *London Magazine,* he boldly proposed to an Edinburgh publisher that he also "undertake" a translation of Goethe's *Wilhelm Meister.* The opportunity to play a significant role in making German literature available to a wide British audience excited him. Reflecting on Schiller, Carlyle saw himself, and this Schiller of his imagination appealed to him more strongly than the Schiller of fact. Carlyle's Schiller also benefited from the love of pious parents, made a false start in the law, rejected fiction for history, and suffered all his life from a severe illness, the result of "unceasing toil and anxiety of mind." But "his spirit was too vigorous and ardent to yield. . . . His frame might be in pain, but his spirit retained its force, unextinguished."[96] Carlyle's own spirits raised by his plan to translate Goethe, he announced to Jane that "I purpose . . . translating *Meister* in spite of all its drawbacks. *Meister* will introduce us to its Author; for you must know that you and I are to go and live six months at Weimar, and learn philosophy and poetry from the great von Goethe himself."[97]

At this point, however, the Bullers, who previously had fit themselves into Carlyle's schedule, proposed a change. Having decided to leave Edinburgh for at least the summer, they took "a nine-months lease" on Kinnaird-House, a large furnished mansion in the isolated Tay Valley some twenty miles from Perth and about sixty-five miles north of Edinburgh.[98] The young tutor decided immediately that it was to his advantage to continue with his employers. He was reluctant to leave Jack's company and Jane's proximity, but his agreement provided opportunities to visit Edinburgh and Mainhill frequently. Furthermore, he had begun to believe that he could regain his health only by living in the country. Turning necessity (he must continue to support Jack and also lend Alick money to rent a farm of his own) into sustaining myth, he left Edinburgh willingly, having decided that "town life is growing every day more odious to me; my passion for the country sometimes almost rises to the height of a lover's for his mistress. . . . I am healthier than I was last year; and about to realize my favourite project of rustication."[99]

Like so many of his strategies for renewal, residence at Kinnaird-House initially seemed as if it might fulfill his expectations. Through the early summer he read and wrote, continuing to expand his article on Schiller and beginning his translation of *Wilhelm Meister*. Comfortable in a separate small cottage with a pleasant view, "as quiet as in the middle of [the] Sahara," he fulfilled his duty as a tutor in the morning, enjoyed vigorous exercise in the afternoon, and had most of the evening to himself.[100] The Bullers treated him kindly, allowing him to dine alone when it seemed that his restless sleep might be the result of subordinating his own requirements to the household schedule. He felt that if he were not actually improving in health he was at least "getting recon[ciled] to this thrice cursed stomach."[101] Deeply impressed by the beauty of the Highland countryside, he sometimes thought the advantages of pure air sufficient compensation for his adult company, which was largely restricted to Mrs. Buller, whom he found pleasant enough in her gossamer way, "full of whims" and "changes," and the senior Charles Buller, admirable in his simple, rugged common sense, a satisfactory companion on walks and rides.[102]

By autumn, however, Carlyle's health seemed worse, his stomach troublesome, his bowels flatulent. His insomnia equaled that of the previous spring, when he had tried to sleep with his fingers in his ears to muffle the common noises that often irritated him into total wakefulness. He recognized, however, that he was not organically ill. There was "not the slightest danger," for "no one ever dies of such disorders; the real object of dread is that of dwindling by degrees into a pitiful whining vale[tu]dinarian, which is far worse than death."[103] Not quite sure how to take his constant complaints, which both worried and unnerved them, the Bullers apparently agreed without objection to his spending at least February in Edinburgh, seeing his translation into the final stages of printing. Since the growth of his literary reputation flattered their household, they were eager to have him continue to tutor their sons and invited him to join them in Cornwall in May, provided they could be assured that his health would permit it.

To Carlyle's casual mention of the prospect of Cornwall in the spring, Jane ecstatically responded with travel news of her own. Their mutual friend Irving, who had married Isabella Martin in October, had invited her to visit him in London and planned to invite Carlyle also. Her letter radiated optimism and expectation, implying that this shared adventure would strengthen the bond between them.[104] Indeed, it seemed to Carlyle an irresistible opportunity. If he were willing to go south with the Bullers to Cornwall, then why not go on to London with Jane? And why could he not, Jane suggested, with his "genius," make vast sums in London as popular writers did?

Meanwhile, at Irving's insistence, Carlyle joined the newly married couple at Dunkeld in mid-October, after which they all returned to Kinnaird-House. Carlyle's presence seemed to gratify Irving considerably. Mrs. Irving stayed demurely in the background, fortunately unaware of Carlyle's opinion that she was "dead ugly," which Jane modified to "homely."[105] Irving expansively argued that Carlyle needed at least three months in London with them in order "to see the world, that so [he] might begin writing in good earnest."[106] But an invitation whose main claim was "that by conversing with Coleridge and the Opium eater [Thomas De Quincey], [he] should find out new channels for speculation, and soon learn to speak with tongues," did not have much appeal to a man who suspected that Irving's world was a hollow affectation.[107] Instinctively cautious, the younger man did not see how he could reconcile acceptance with his obligation to the Bullers. Furthermore, since he suspected the invitation of "savouring too much of patronage," he feared that the visit would undermine his independence. But Jane's decision had to be her own. He wrote that there was an "abundance of inducement"—the advantages of seeing "new forms of life" and "cultivated men."[108] He did not think she would find both her hosts attractive, particularly Isabella, whom "you will hardly like, but neither can you well dislike her. She *is* unbeautiful; has no enthusiasm, and few ideas that are not prosaic or conceited."[109] At the same time he observed that Irving loved Jane "as a sister," and concluded that, "on the whole, you must go." He offered to escort her there in May and back to Scotland at the end of the summer.

Carlyle was aware that the invitation expressed complex sentiments, but he had no conscious inkling of the private dialogue that still existed between his two friends. Disappointed by Carlyle's decision not to spend time in London, Jane was even more disappointed when a few weeks had passed without "a single line" from Irving. "I do not under[stand] him—sometimes I think he loves me almost half as well as you do," she wrote to Thomas, "and then again that I am nothing to him at all."[110] Disgusted with the slow progress of her studies, part of which she blamed on the painful headaches to which she had been subject for years, she increasingly thought of herself as "a very worthless concern," a dependent person fit only for "marrying and making puddings."[111] Her complaints about her health frightened Carlyle, but he immediately seized on them as a point of identity, convinced she could now better understand his "six long miserable years" of ill health.[112] His complaints intensified. Kinnaird-House, which had formerly seemed a place of revival, now depressed him. His high hopes that rustication would restore his health were gradually eroded by his nervous anxiety about his writing, against which he insisted on defining his worth as a human being.

Early in December 1823 he went to Edinburgh to consult with a well-known doctor who prescribed mercury and abstention from tobacco. Without his usual stimulant, he felt almost comatose, constantly "taking drugs," watching the wintry storms freeze and whiten the landscape, "unable either to think or write," despite the absolute quietness at Kinnaird.[113] But he slept soundly, "like a decent Christian." Engaging in the consoling warmth of a fantasy, he wondered if his mother would come to Cornwall with him and keep his cottage. Rural Kinnaird had failed to restore his health. If the prospect of spending time in rural Cornwall did not materialize, he might return to live at Mainhill, safe in the embrace of his family, where he had had his "healthiest days."[114] The Bullers had agreed that he would have three months leave before rejoining them in London in April. Kinnaird-House would be deserted by the beginning of February, and he would stay in Edinburgh and perhaps in Mainhill for as much of those three months as was necessary to see *Wilhelm Meister* through the press. "That done I go to London and Cornwall and France and the Lord knows whither."[115]

Whatever his outer prospects, he concluded the year with a startlingly bitter reverie, blaming his own worthlessness on his ill health. "Another hour and 1823 is with the years beyond the flood. What have I done to mark the course of it? Suffered . . . almost daily, grown sicker and sicker, alienated by my misery certain of my friends, . . . worn out . . . capabilities of enjoyment, reduced my world a *little* nearer the condition of a bare haggard desart, where peace and rest for me is none. . . . My curse seems deeper and blacker than that of any man. . . . How have I deserved this?"[116] He considered suicide, but he recognized that the temptation was rhetorical and naturally rejected it. It would be time enough to resort to such expedients when he had "*lost* the game, which I am as yet but losing." He assured himself, quite falsely, that if it were not for his bad health he "could snap [his] fingers in the face of all the world," reflecting in this moment of calculated expression on his family and his "duty of *not* breaking their hearts," for "love to my friends . . . is now almost the sole religion of my mind."[117] One of his characteristic reactions to good fortune was to increase his complaining. But he also had learned that the small family of the heart, which now included Jane, nourished a commitment to life and work that no amount of ill health could defeat.

By late November Jane was furious at Irving. Not having heard even "a word from the Orator," she began to believe that she had been ill used, especially since people had been saying that she was "dreadfully disappointed at his marriage!!!"[118] Carlyle still encouraged her, however, to think positively about the visit to London, perhaps because he himself now suspected that, despite the effect on his health, his "proper place" was not "in the country but in London or amid some great collection of men."[119] By the end of 1823 he had concluded an arrangement that was to bring him £180 for the first edition of *Meister* and the prospect of more. He soon finished the final section of his essay on Schiller, which had expanded into book length. Having arranged to receive proofs through the mail, he went south to Mainhill in mid-April. Finally, Jane received a letter from Irving shamefacedly acknowledging that the invitation had been revoked. "My dear Isabella . . . has succeeded in healing the wounds of my heart by her unexampled affection and tenderness; but am I hardly yet in a condition to expose them."[120] He had told his wife about his relationship with Jane, and this "dead ugly" lady did not want a dead-pretty lady visitor with whom her husband had once been in love. Irving told Carlyle that he could not have Jane as a visitor because they were changing houses, though he could still offer *him* hospitality. Carlyle told Jane this in an attempt to console her, thereby unwittingly revealing that Irving had lied and encouraging her to ask no further questions about why the invitation had been revoked. To Jane, the "Orator" was now "that stupendous Ass."

Winding up his affairs in Edinburgh in late May, Thomas arranged to have complimentary copies of *Meister* sent to family and friends. At Haddington to say good-bye, he counseled her to "be true to me and to yourself."[121] Waiting for his boat to sail, he wrote to her impetuously, for which she called him a "rash, headstrong Man" who had forgotten to "keep in mind" that "the continuance of our correspondence . . . depends upon your appearing as my friend and not my Lover."[122] But the artifice was only for the sake of her mother. Jane had accepted that in reality they were lovers beyond possibility of change or even redefinition. As his boat left the harbor in early June 1824 on the five-day voyage to London, he felt certain of this.

[4]

"Society's Brazen Doors" 1824–1826

The young man's last words from Edinburgh and his first from London were directed to his mother, whom he wrote three hours after he arrived, saying he was eager to "lose not a moment in relieving you from all your anxieties."[1] As his ship sailed up the Thames on Friday June 11, 1824, the sheer size and presence of the "monstrous capital" evoked from Carlyle the resolution that the fallen Babel would neither corrupt him nor break the charmed circle of family values. It was a bright warm morning and Carlyle had "a delightful view of the River & its ships in tens of thousands." As they "[wound] slowly thro' the forest of masts . . . up to [the] station at Tower wharf," he was astounded by what he saw. "One man seems as a drop in the ocean; you feel annihilated in the immensity of that heart of all the Earth."[2]

Within a few hours Carlyle was in Irving's drawing room in Pentonville, imagining that he would be "quite happy" there for the time that it would take to agree with the Bullers on the terms and place of his employment. The chief defect of "the great Nineveh of modern Europe" seemed "its vastness and expensiveness. You cannot stir in it without money, money, at every hand."[3] But Carlyle had little reason to be anxious. He had arrived in London with £180 from the translation of *Meister,* some savings from his salary, and the prospect of a fee for the publication in book form of his *Life of Schiller.* In addition, he had the moral support of his family, the assurance that his bond with Jane would not be broken, and the warm response of Irving, who had already trumpeted his friend's high qualities to his circle. Isabella Irving graciously offered him the hospitality that she would not extend to

Jane, and Carlyle, grateful to Irving for many kindnesses, responded warmly. He wrote to Jane, urging her to forgive their friend his weaknesses, for "true affection is so precious that any touch of it intermingled even with many other feelings in the bosom of an honest man is worth the keeping."[4]

Kitty Kirkpatrick. Photograph of a miniature. Reprinted from Wilson and MacArthur, vol. 1.

Soon after dinner a carriage appeared at Irving's door, its arrival marking Carlyle's initiation into the circle of Irving's admirers. An attractive, "strangely-complexioned young lady with soft brown eyes and floods of *bronze*-red hair" whom the Irvings addressed as " 'Dear Kitty' " was introduced to their visitor as Miss Kitty Aurora Kirkpatrick, Mrs. Buller's cousin. The amiable young lady had dropped in for only a moment "and soon went away," having first removed a loose nametag from one of the trunks that Carlyle had piled in the entranceway.[5] Both Isabella Buller and her sister Julia Strachey were Kitty's first cousins. James Achilles Kirkpatrick, Kitty's father and uncle to Isabella and Julia, had married an Indian princess while "resident at Hyderbad." In 1806 the immensely wealthy Anglo-Indian administrator, who emblazoned his person and possessions with Oriental splendor, had sent his young son and four-year-old daughter to live in England with their grandfather. James Kirkpatrick died before they touched English soil, however, and his children never saw their mother again.[6] By 1824 Kitty's closest living relations were her two cousins, one of whom employed Carlyle. Julia had married Edward Strachey, the son of another wealthy Anglo-Indian family, whose retirement from Indian service in 1819 had brought him to a comfortable town house on Fitzroy Square and a rambling country mansion at Shooter's Hill, near Greenwich. From the former he regularly walked to his work at the East India Company office where he shared responsibility for all communications to India with James Mill and Thomas Love Peacock.

Within days of Carlyle's arrival, he and Irving entered "the little winding avenue" at Shooter's Hill. "In a kind of open conservatory or verandah," he saw "the effulgent vision of 'dear Kitty,' busied among the roses, and almost buried under them, who, on sight of us, glided hastily in."[7] A half-dozen years later the vision contributed to his depiction in *Sartor Resartus* of Blumine, the "Rose-goddess," a "many-tinted, radiant Aurora" and "this fairest of Orient Light-bringers."[8] Carlyle was happy to discover that Mrs. Strachey was a sober, sweet woman, unlike her fashionable, irresolute sister, and he immediately admired her religious sincerity and quiet geniality. He visited Fitzroy Square and Shooter's Hill frequently during his first weeks in London, impressed with how lightly both the Stracheys and their cousin bore their wealth and position. Though he thought Edward Strachey's utilitarian and democratic principles desiccatingly secular, he was nevertheless attracted to his genial abruptness and earthy simplicity.

Delighted with the impression that his friend made, Irving was eager to polish his manner and stimulate his intellect. He brought him to Bedford Square to visit "the celebrated Mrs. Montagu," a tall, severe figure whom Carlyle could not like as much as she wished. He remembered her as "truly a remarkable and partly a high and tragical woman . . . with the remains of a certain queenly beauty, which she still took strict care of." She reigned over the confused household, which included her husband—a barrister and editor of Bacon—his children from three earlier marriages, and her own daughter from her first marriage.[9] Her coldness, no matter how much the product of a difficult life and trying responsibilities, seemed the outer armour of a woman who lived for herself rather than for others. The visitor from Scotland thought her aspirations outdistanced the limitations of her personality and vision, but he did appreciate that the household in Bedford Square had enthusiasm, high manners, and a suspicious over-eagerness to patronize intellectual achievement.

While Mrs. Buller indecisively pondered where to live, Carlyle diverted himself with visits to his new friends and long walks about the city whose variety and size astonished him.[10] Neither Ecclefechan nor Edinburgh had prepared him for London. Ecclefechan was still a visible emblem of traditional religious wholeness, and Edinburgh, under the gray pall of Presbyterian seriousness, seemed only a miniature token of the discontinuity that was so magnified in London. The "brick Babylon" threatened to "annihilate" individuality and to obscure with its thick darkness the overarching heaven that was still clearly visible in Scotland. "Hurrying along Cheapside . . . I looked up . . . and there stood Paul's . . . with its solemn dome and its guilded ball and cross gleaming in the evening sun, piercing up into the heaven . . . gigantic, beautiful, enduring: it seemed to frown with a rebuking pity on the vain scramble which it overlooked: at its feet were tomb-stones, above it was the everlasting sky."[11] At home in Mainhill, James Carlyle not only admired the descriptive power of his son's "account of St. Paul" but recognized the resonances of his favorite Puritan writers whose depiction of the relationship between time and eternity had become part of the drama of his family's life.[12]

Wary of the "vain scramble," the inexperienced visitor instinctively knew that in London the warping pressures of competition and survival pressed with an intensity that only the most stubborn could resist. Though attracted to the dynamics of the city, he found its fundamental structure repellent. Indeed, in its combination of illness and health, lassitude and energy, the town and the country, modern "tombstones" and the "everlasting sky," London seemed the inevitable product on a mass scale of the tensions of body, spirit, and culture which he had been experiencing for the past ten years. St. Paul's, which he saw "oft and from various points and never without new admiration," appeared the outward representation of those moments of confident epiphany in which he felt that the forces of health, resolution, and moral energy within him would indeed triumph.[13] He wrote to his family that he could hear reverberate through the nave of St. Paul's "Sounds of Death, Judgement and Eternity," a certain antidote to "that frivolous and fluctuating city."[14]

During his first weeks in London, Carlyle shrewdly combined his natural suspiciousness with youthful enthusiasm. More sparing than usual in his critical deflation of pretension, he had both sufficient presence of mind to protect himself from the blind enthusiasm that might overwhelm his individuality and enough reserve to spend more time looking and listening than he ordinarily did. Though he attempted to be fair in his judgments, his long-established prejudices asserted themselves, reinforcing his general opinion as to the fallen state of modern culture. In London there were no heroes, though there were some people who deserved praise, two of them fellow Scotsmen. His host he considered "about the worthiest man I have ever seen. To me he has certainly been friendly as few men are to any but a brother."[15] Even Isabella presented the "very model of a wife. . . . Her sole object" is "her husband's comfort, and that of his friends."[16] But it was Allan Cunningham, a minor poet, "not the cleverest, but the simplest, frankest, most modest," who proved his "greatest favourite."[17] Having been provided with an introduction to Thomas Campbell, whose verse he had long admired, Carlyle judged him to be one of those whom London pressures and inner weakness had bent into the contours of "a poor lite[rary] dandy . . . heartless conceited, shallow, sneering, pragmatical. There is no mystery in his looks; his eye glances, but it is with the empty vivacity of a Cockney Shopman." The "suffering & poverty" that he felt he too had been experiencing had "wasted [Campbell's] feelings, and made him callous and dissociable as *those old Nags,* which I once heard a Natural Historian describe, as animals that cared not for other horses."[18] Stimulated into a sociability more genial and far-ranging than he had even known, Carlyle could afford to critize Campbell for the very coldness of temperament which others had previously criticized in him.

Carlyle's new friends were determined that the young "genius," who did not seem to deserve his reputation for touchiness, should have the advantages of the best of London literary society. The result was a series of dinners and visits hosted by the Montagus, Stracheys, Bullers, and Irvings. He was quickly introduced to Henry Crabb Robinson, who had studied German at Weimar, to Charles Lamb, whose personality seemed even weaker than his essays, and to John Badams, an enthusiastic young chemist from Birmingham who had cured himself, so he claimed, of dyspepsia.

On a bright June morning in 1824, taken in tow by Mrs. Montagu and Irving, Carlyle went to Highgate to be introduced to Coleridge, the reigning deity of the Montagu household. Irving had already visited many times, for he was himself a prodigious talker and loved to "receive" what "Coleridge loved to impart." He regularly escorted his favorites to audiences with the "Sage of Highgate," including even Chalmers, who noticed that Coleridge's "conversation flowed in a mighty unremitting stream. . . . Irving drinks in the inspiration of every syllable that falls from him. There is a secret and, to me, unintelligible communion of spirit between them."[19]

In the summer sunlight, Carlyle followed along the garden paths as

Coleridge talked about "all conceivable and inconceivable things." Taken upstairs to the high second floor room "with a rearward view" over bright suburban gardens, he saw "country of the brightest green . . . handsome groves . . . crossed by roads and human traffic . . . heard only as a musical hum." In the distance "swam, under olive-tinted haze, the illimitable limitary ocean of London, with its domes and steeples definite in the sun, big Paul's and the many memories attached to it hanging high over all."[20] As Coleridge droned into his ears with a kind of nasal musicality, Carlyle had the distinct impression that this revered elderly man relied more on personal style than on persuasive substance: "a forest of thoughts; some true, many false, most part dubious, all of them ingenious in some degree, often in a high degree. But there is no method in his talk."[21]

With cruel incisiveness, Carlyle detected an ugly symmetry between his host's decrepit physical unattractiveness and his moral weakness. Coleridge's very presence awakened a deep emotional antagonism that Carlyle struggled to cover with ordinary civility. Though they talked of *Meister* and parted "very good friends," Carlyle found Coleridge's conversation unprofitable, even tedious, and his "promise" to visit him another evening was made for the sake of form. Carlyle admitted that the poet had "a kind, good soul, full of religion and affection, and poetry and animal magnetism," but felt that such hazy virtues could not compensate for his want of "*will*":

> He has no resolution, he shrinks from pain or labour in any of its shapes. His very attitude bespeaks this: he never straightens his knee joints, he stoops with his fat ill shapen shoulders, and in walking he does not tread but shovel and slide. . . . He is also always busied to keep by strong and frequent inhalations the water of his mouth from overflowing; and his eyes have a look of anxious impotence; he *would* do with all his heart, but he knows he dare not.[22]

At a time when he was looking for models of courage and strength, Carlyle concluded that Coleridge was a sterile man without the power to help himself or to help others, that his wisdom was a delusion even more pernicious in its effect than in its source. To those willing to suspend critical judgment and accept empty rhetoric, Coleridge seemed to offer spiritual leadership. But Carlyle believed that the old clothes of the past should not be taken out of the closet and spruced up when no alteration would make them fit the changed reality. And he could not recognize in Coleridge's nasal abstractions anything that resembled the "new Heaven and new Earth" that he had seen in Goethe and Schiller. Unlike the "Sage of Highgate," Carlyle tended to particularize the world and the mind in concrete, metaphoric, and personal terms. He might occasionally talk about Kant and Fichte, but he read and wrote about Schiller and Goethe. He could hardly recognize in Coleridge's metaphysical abstractions the German literature that he valued so highly, and he rejected the more vehemently the source of such radical distortions.

At first eager to learn from "this memorable man," Carlyle had listened for hours, astounded by a performance in which the speaker communicated "no meaning whatsoever to any individual of his hearers,—certain of whom . . . still kept eagerly listening in hope; the most had long before given up, and formed . . . secondary humming groups of their own."[23] The talk began anyplace and went noplace. Though Coleridge spoke for hours about the Church of England, he could not explain how it or any other church would be revived, and said only that all this would somehow be made clear in a major work that he "was about to write." As best he could, Carlyle pressed him to explain his remedy for the materialism and atheism that he too found so threatening a characteristic of modern Britain. Though Coleridge would suffer "no interruption," the question was apparently important enough to his own train of thought, however discontinuous, for him to attempt answers. But the younger man thought the answers either silly or incomprehensible, finding in the words of the "Sage" neither sense nor "sympathy for concrete human things either on the sunny or on the stormy side."[24] All that Carlyle had come to admire most—common sense, incisiveness, simplicity, independence, intellectual honesty, warm human sympathy—he felt that Coleridge lacked. The young man clearly sought to identify with the aura of greatness around a man who had a mission and the power to transform desire into works, but Coleridge was not that man. He was instead "the tragic story of a high endowment with an insufficient will."[25] Carlyle could pity him and occasionally respect his talents, but he fully agreed with and even admired the directness of the poet's self-judgment: " 'Ah, your tea is too cold, Mr. Coleridge!' mourned the good Mrs. Gillman once. . . . 'It's better than I deserve!' snuffled he, in a low hoarse murmur, partly courteous, chiefly pious. . . . 'It's better than I deserve!' "[26]

For Carlyle, Coleridge was a representation of fallen man, one who embodied many of the characteristics Carlyle had been taught to despise and which he constantly fought against within himself, particularly lassitude, dependency, and self-pity. That much of the world worshiped Coleridge proved the dangerous tendency of the fallen individual and the fallen society to create one another in their own image. Walking London's winding streets, Carlyle recognized that the city was the stock market of Britain, perhaps of all Europe, and thus the center for self-deceiving and corrupt transactions of the sort represented by Coleridge's unmanly life as Dr. Gillman's dependent. Still, his condemnation of Coleridge was brutally excessive, the words he chose revealing his own deepest anxieties: "a round fat oily yet impatient little man," "[a man] sunk inextricably in the depths of putrescent indolence," "an inspired ass," "the hulk of a huge ship [whose] mast and sails and rudder have rotted quite away," "a mass of richest spices, putrified into a dunghill." "He had been . . . decaying for years" was Carlyle's harsh epitaph on receiving the news of the poet's death in 1834.[27] Clearly, only some grave disappointment at the deepest level, some anxiety about the self at the core of his personality, could account for the vileness of this language. In responding to people like Coleridge, Carlyle revealed the deep emotional patterns instilled in him by his stern father and pietistic mother. He judged much of the world against their high standards, sometimes reshaping the reality to satisfy his own needs. Coleridge, in fact, was hardly as fallen as Carlyle judged him to be, just as Goethe was hardly as elevated as he imagined. Late in the month, his disappointing visit to the "Sage of Highgate" still fresh in his mind, he sent a copy of his translation of *Wilhelm Meister* and a letter to the "Sage of Weimar": "The hope of meeting you is still among my dreams. Many Saints have been expunged from my literary Calendar, since I first knew you; but your name still stands there, in characters more bright than ever."[28] The greater his disappointment in Coleridge, the more heavily he invested in Goethe.

By mid-June 1824, Mrs. Buller had finally come to a decision about Charles Buller's education. But, to Carlyle's disgust, it did not resolve the matter. The oft-discussed move to Cornwall was off, and six months residence in France and imminent enrollment at Cambridge were distinct possibilities. Rooms were engaged for Charles and his tutor at Kew-Green, "a pleasant village . . . close by the south bank of the Thames about six miles to the westward of London," but "*for a fortnight only!*"[29] Mrs. Buller's constant changes of mind seemed an imposition that no salary could justify. He moved to Kew-Green late in June but only after making clear to her "some fragments of my mind. . . . She fears me, but she loves no one."[30] Willing to dispense with Carlyle, Mrs. Buller apparently realized that he was willing to be dispensed with. Originally they had agreed that he would stay with them for six months, with a vague understanding that another six months might be agreed on later. But her son Charles particularly admired his tutor and had become personally attached to him. Carlyle, however, could no longer bear what seemed the senseless and self-indulgent whims of "essentially a cold race of people" who "live in the midst of fashion and external show" and "love no living creature."[31]

Despite his simmering anger, however, Carlyle managed to enjoy the village comforts of Kew-Green. On the first day, while it rained heavily, he wrote Jane, his "Beloved Enemy," a long account of what had transpired since he had left Scotland. The next day he visited Irving and wrote to his foster father in Weimar and his real parents at Mainhill. Though he regretted the distance from Shooter's Hill, the routine quickly asserted itself: studies with Charles, daily walks, visits to London, attendance at the "Bible Society" at Walthamstow, the last of which he described piously to his mother, assuring her he would read his Bible more regularly now that he was "settled."[32] But Mrs. Buller soon disturbed his routine with the demand that she "know *directly* whether I could go to France with them or not; that if I could not the Boy might be sent to prepare for Cambridge, and that if I could, we must instantly decamp for Royston a place in Hertfordshire about fifty miles off!"[33] Carlyle had no intention of going any further than London.

An unhappy Charles went to his parents to attempt mediation, but Carlyle had made up his mind irrevocably. He imagined a bill of particulars against Mrs. Buller, his crowning argument being that "after a week spent at Kew" his "health had begun to deteriorate rapidly." In short, the Bullers were "ruining my mind and body; I was selling the very quintessence of my spirit for two hundred pounds a years."[34] Actually, Carlyle had hardly complained about his health since arriving in London. His decision to quit the Bullers was based mainly on his feeling that he was demeaning himself by selling his "spirit" for cash and on his proud resentment of what he believed to be mistreatment. With careful economy and diligent free-lance work he could now live adequately for perhaps two years, and freedom from the restrictions of salaried employment would certainly enable him to benefit more substantially from his visit to England. He had chafed at the implied degradation of dependency, but now suddenly he was "once more free; and I must be a weak genius indeed," he wrote to his mother, "if I cannot find an honest living in the exercise of my faculties, independently of favour from any one."[35]

3.

Two weeks later, with a letter of introduction from Irving which claimed that he was "of the rarest genius and highest accomplishments," Carlyle unexpectedly found himself dashing northward by coach to Birmingham.[36] John Badams had persuaded him that under his strict regimen his health would be totally restored. Having given up his medical education in Edinburgh in 1813 after two years of study, Badams had become a self-taught and self-made "giant . . . in chemistry and physic" who owned and managed an extremely successful chemical factory. Diet, he believed, was the key to all stomach problems. He offered to teach this basic lesson to his new friend if he would spend six weeks with him under "strict regulation."[37] Not only did Badams seem "one of the most sensible, clever-headed" and "kindest . . . persons" he had "ever met," but he had also cured himself, after "four years of torment," of the very dyspepsia from which Carlyle suffered. That he had "utter contempt" for "all sorts of drugs" was a strong mark in his favor.[38]

His trust was not misplaced. An affectionate, attractive man, with sparkling blue eyes and a pale flushed complexion, Badams provided his guest with a comfortable, well-regulated household, active companionship, and the opportunity to explore industrial Birmingham. Carlyle enthusiastically agreed with his new friend that a careful regulation of food and a moderate use of drugs would do him a world of good and perhaps defeat his "curse!" Castor oil and exercise dominated the regimen, supplemented by small portions of soft food.[39] Soon the patient admitted that "the perpetual gnawing of pain with its confused irritation and obscuration of the soul" had left him; "but weariness and weakness and a passion for repose have succeeded."[40] The unexpected news soon after his arrival in Birmingham that his mother had been slightly ill made him momentarily hysterical: "But for you I should have felt myself utterly alone in this toilsome world; the idea of separation at this moment drives me to the borders of despair." Believing in Badams' regimen, he recommended to her the dietary part of it. Whatever trouble it might cause it would increase the chances that her children who needed her so much would have her with them for a longer time.[41]

Of course, Badams' medicines were no match for Carlyle's anxiety about his mother's ill health and his own pervasive sense of inadequacy. For the "hapless dyspeptical philosopher from the moors of Annandale," the pangs of self-disgust, the painful frustration of dreaming away his life and cursing as he read through trashy novels, overrode the beneficial effects of any restorative regimen.[42] Carlyle sometimes thought that he was "better than" he had "been for several years," but "scarcely a week passes without a relapse for a while into directly the opposite opinion."

Fortunately, the two men got on "lovingly together," despite Badams' tendency to exaggerate "his own achievements and purpose." The doctor and the "philosopher" discussed at length "all manner of subjects" on their walks and frequent riding excursions in Birmingham and the surrounding countryside.[43] Badams' horses rapidly carried them to Guy's Cliff, Warwick Castle, Sutton Coldfield, and Kenilworth, the latter on a three-day excursion "to the famous Ruin itself (*fresh* in the Scott Novels then)."[44] Observing the English countryside as a farmer's son, Carlyle compared the natural fertility of England with the harsh soil of Scotland. For the native of a severe land, the English countryside had a touch of paradise, and he could never look at it without reflecting on his father and two of his brothers struggling to make a living from the unproductive northern soil.[45] Carlyle had begun to discover that it was easier to appreciate home when he no longer lived there, that from a distance what was "unpleasant or repulsive is forgotten or softened down." He recognized that he was "fast becoming a *patriot* of the most decided stamp. Scornfully as I used to speak and think of Scotland in my hours of bitterness and irritation, I never fail to stand up manfully in defence of it thro' thick and thin, whenever a renegade Scot takes upon him to abuse it."[46]

Though there was much in Warwickshire to attract his sympathy and stir his emotions, Carlyle was sufficiently influenced by the eighteenth-century emphasis on the superiority of man's work to Nature's and by the Presbyterian elevation of the invisible over the visible world that he considered effusions about the sublimity of Nature unacceptable nonsense, perhaps even a kind of blasphemy. At the same time, however, he had a deep respect for the genius of place, for the literary or spiritual associations that a particular place contained. Warwickshire was Shakespeare country, and it was also the birthplace of Samuel Johnson, a man whom Carlyle increasingly admired. The intensity of his feeling when he "saw Lichfield yesterday and Dr. Sam's [Johnson's] house!" burst into an urgent call "for paper" so that he might express himself.[47] Late in September, on his way back to London, he passed quickly through Oxford, whose "domes and spires and minerets; its rows of shady trees, and still, monastic edifices, venerable in their antique richness and intricate seclusion," impressed him less than Stratford. Through his literary eyes he looked at Stratford as he imagined Shakespeare must have seen it as a boy.

That "an ugly black canal" had been brought even into Shakespeare's birthplace could not help but remind him of the new industrial riches of which Birmingham was the center, the funace-roaring, fire-and-coal-belching embodiment of capitalism's triumphant power.[48] Deeply impressed by the fiery spectacle, he accepted the general claim that the workers made a fair day's wages and more for a fair day's labor. His imagination was preoccupied both with the wealth that industrial activity produced ("it is in a spot like this that one sees the sources of British power") and the sheer visual excitement of constant explosions of heat and fire.[49] Three years before, when he had seen the glow of the ironworks at Carron and the steamer on the lake at Greenock, he could not have imagined that they were the first tentative extensions of a revolution that had already transformed the landscape and the life of large parts of England.

Carlyle kept in touch with the Irving circle while he was in Birmingham, spending several tedious hours with a small contingent of Scotch Presbyterians whom Irving was attempting to revitalize. But in general he preferred quiet reading, desultory sightseeing, and visits to interesting shops. One day in a bookstore run by "a smirking little dumpy Unitarian Bookseller," he found a "completely hostile criticism" of his translation of *Wilhelm Meister,* which was particularly harsh in its criticism of his Scotticisms (he later discovered that the reviewer was De Quincey).[50] Somewhat shaken, Carlyle totally dismissed the anonymous author's criticism, reminding himself that favorable reviews were appearing and that the book had become somewhat fashionable in London. Having learned months before that printers and booksellers sometimes collaborated to cheat authors by falsely reporting the number of volumes printed and sold, he suddenly became convinced that the publisher of *Meister* had cheated him "out of 500 copies."[51]

Between contempt for booksellers and general lassitude, he felt increasingly concerned about his health. At the end of August Irving urged his return to London. For a moment Caryle hesitated, indulging the fantasy that he could restore his health only by returning to the countryside, perhaps by underwriting a farm for Alick in Annandale and living there as the resident writer and scholar of a happy rural household. But late in September 1824 he headed south toward London, intending to collect the necessary books to finish his revision of Schiller for publication. An appointment in Dover, where he had agreed to join his friends for "a watering party," drew him at a leisurely pace through the rich autumnal Kent countryside.[52] Arriving on a bright October evening, he found that the Irvings, Kitty Kirkpatrick, and the Stracheys treated him as the resident invalid of genius, flattering him with heavy doses of sympathy and sociability. For much of three weeks, initially as a guest with the Irvings in Kitty's rented house and later in separate lodgings with the Irvings, he worked for a few hours in the morning on *Schiller* and took the sea air and refreshing waters for much of the rest of the day.[53] Dover, a clean and attractive old town so close to France that one could see it on a clear day, delighted his imagination and evoked his wonder.[54]

Though Carlyle had already decided that he had nothing more to learn from Irving, he still loved the genuine goodness-of-heart that neither his friend's sentimental Christian affectations nor his continual self-deceptions could completely obscure. Quite rapidly, however, he came to detest Irving's relationship with his newborn child, Edward. In Carlyle's eyes, Irving, who was constantly involved in the infant's care, was a ludicrous "dry-nurse" who not only refused to recognize the distinction between male and female roles in caring for a baby but actually had the blindness to argue that his involvement was selfless. Thinking of his own father's manly aloofness, Carlyle considered Irving's constant attention to the child destructive and unmanly. The Irvings seemed pagans worshiping at the feet of a baby-idol; they "could not be more attentive to the infant Lama, were they high priestess and priest of Thibet."[55] Laughing at Irving amidst some loving tears, Carlyle had nothing but a bitter—and revealing—contempt for the child. "It is a feeble, shapeless slut of a thing, as all children of six weeks are," he wrote to Jane, who had additional reasons for resenting Irving's domestic idyll. She responded with disgust. "Kiss 'Him' for me—I would not do it myself for five guineas. Young children are such nasty little beasts!"[56]

Jane would have been equally unenthusiastic about the company with whom Carlyle took afternoon walks at Dover—the dour Isabella on one arm and the "little-black-eyed, auburn-haired" Kitty on the other.[57] Mrs. Strachey would not completely dismiss the notion that the dyspeptic "genius" from Annandale would find a compatible opposite in the wealthy "daughter of Asiatic pomp and dreamy indolence."[58] Whatever the Irving circle's knowledge of his relationship with Jane, it was clear that there had been no public engagement. Moreover, Carlyle did not speak or act like a man who expected to marry a particular woman in the foreseeable future. Kitty, and perhaps Mrs. Strachey too, probably harbored the hope that something would come of the relationship between a charming woman who was "sole mistress of herself and fifty thousand pounds" and a handsome, lean, cranky, but brilliant young man eight years her elder to whom she obviously was attracted.[59] "I was told," Kitty is reported to have said years later, that since he "had made no name for himself . . . any such idea could not be thought of for a moment. . . . What could I do, with everyone against it?"[60]

Carlyle did not, of course, in any sense believe it possible to exchange Jane for Kitty. Much as he admired Kitty, he clearly considered her with the excluding eyes of a Scots sectarian whose strong sense of birth, place, and mission meant that an alliance with an exotic representative of Anglo-Indian wealth could be no more than a momentary fantasy. Such flirtations effectively highlighted the broad range of mutual need and involvement already established between himself and Jane. His comic threat to "shake hands with you for good . . . if you marry any of these fritters of perfumery and small sarcasm" was only an amiable prelude to his expression of passionate commitment, a recognition of her need to be guided by his dominant genius and his need to shape her into a woman who would be dependent upon him. For "Nature meant you for more serious things, and . . . you will yet attain them. O that I had power to form you and form your destiny according to my image of what you should be! O that I were a sovereign and a sage!—O that I were not a fool! What have I ever done for you, I often ask . . . I have loved you three-fourths for my own sake."[61] Jane's answer made her feelings about Kitty clear. "Miss Kitty Kirkpatrick—Lord what an ugly name! 'Good Kitty!' Oh! pretty dear delightful Kitty! I am not a bit jealous of her—not I indeed—Hindoo Princess tho' she be! Only you may as well never let me hear you mention her name again."[62] But she also made clear not only that she would never marry "a fine gentleman," but that she would marry "one warmhearted, highminded *dearest* Friend" of genius if only the practical obstacles could be overcome. He could have no doubt whom she meant.

Despite her request, Jane did hear Kitty's name again. Edward Strachey enthusiastically proposed a quick visit to Paris. Carlyle declined, but Mrs. Strachey was eager to have her husband chaperone the two young people and urged Carlyle to go. When would he have another such opportunity to see France? After several changes of mind he was finally persuaded by Mrs. Strachey, "the little fidgetty, higgle-haggling, good-hearted, logic-chopping Mr. Strachey and . . . the fair Princess whose name I must *not* mention," assuring Jane that he was "as it were half forced to accompany them."[63] The next day, having crossed the channel in bright weather, he found himself hurrying through the French countryside with Kitty and Strachey in the private carriage of the "Hindoo Princess." On a "brilliant October afternoon," the travelers first sighted the French capital, "a huge bowl, or deepish *saucer* of seven miles in diameter, not a breath of smoke or dimness anywhere, every roof and dome and spire and chimney-top clearly visible, and the skylights sparkling like diamonds."[64] It was the finest view of a town that he had ever seen.

4

Responsive to the vigor of the bustling city, Carlyle tried to absorb the vivid particularity of places and people that were characteristically French. But he also looked at Paris with the skeptical eyes of a Scots Presbyterian for whom a sensual and self-indulgent emphasis on the external necessarily implied a neglect of the internal matters of conscience and spirit. Though he could not prevent his prejudices from limiting his experiences, he had come with sufficient fascination to find Paris "vastly entertaining," a special exhibition that he was at liberty to enjoy. The first evening he sat "in the still dusk" of the Place Vendôme, smoking a cigar. He had "roved about the Boulevards with his friends in a happy humour," pleased with the unexpected opportunity that had suddenly brought him to a place whose history had been so much a part of his education. Whereas Strachey butchered the language with comical Anglo-French phrases, Carlyle drew on his reading knowledge of French to make himself adequately understood, despite the Scots overlay on his accent. When French soldiers suddenly entered the Place Vendôme, beating "drums fiercely" and arranging the administration of the city for the night, he reflected that soldiers hardly differed from one country to another: "All the world is of kin, whether it all agree or not!" "Rat-at-tat-ta, rat-at-tat-ta they went along, waking the echoes, the drummers seemingly delighted with their own performance, the people charmed."[65]

In the end, however, he concluded that, at least between France and England, the differences were more important than the similarities. The France that he knew from literature he had already condemned, for it seemed the destructive avatar of eighteenth-century materialism and rationalism at its worst. Rousseau appeared a mad exhibitionist whose confessions he feared, Voltaire a shallow destroyer of belief and stability. He felt hesitant respect for Napoleon's achievements; a man who could drill a nation of "fops and pastry-cooks" into an effective military force could never be completely dismissed. From Luther to Goethe the cultural heritage of Protestant Germany embodied peasant integrity, common sense, and spiritual aspirations, whereas in Roman Catholic France religion was bankrupt, literature secular, and "eating, everlasting eating," an obsession.

Carlyle's Protestant values were offended that the French could not "live without artificial excitements, without *sensations agréables.*" He called their city a "vanity fair" and said that their houses were "not homes, but places where they sleep and dress."

> They live in *cafés* and promenades and theatres; and ten thousand dice are set a-rattling every night in every quarter of their city. Every thing seems . . . addressed to the eye not the touch. Their shops and houses are like toy-boxes; every apartment is tricked out with mirrors and expanded into infinitude by their illusion. . . . The people's character seems like their shops and faces; gilding and rouge without; hollowness and rottenness within.

Much of the general life of Paris seemed a distorting mirror purposely manipulated to disguise and evade the eternal facts that, for Carlyle, ultimately governed all the activities of men.

> One Sunday evening [I] went out to the Champ de Mars . . . covered with people, its dusky half-grass, half gravelled extent . . . almost hidden with the multitude. And what . . . had they to recreate themselves with that blessed Sabbath evening? A balloon was to go up, and the men were there holding it down by ropes during its inflation in great numbers. . . . I saw it go up to the great delight of the Parisian populace. They shouted, yelled, clapped their hands, strained their necks, opened their eyes and mouths, and gave every evidence of intense satisfaction. . . . That was the amusement of the Parisian populace that blessed Sabbath evening.[66]

Despite its widespread corruption, England showed genuine national concern for Christian values and moral standards, whereas France seemed mainly a nation of image-worshipers and sensation-seekers.

As long as he could keep in touch with the sources of his strength, however, Carlyle did not feel threatened by the corruptions of Paris any more than by those of London, where St. Paul's dome dramatically reminded him that eternal truths dominate transient frivolities for those who lift their eyes beyond their immediate physical needs. Even among the "jugglers and quacks and cooks and barbers and dandies and gulls and sharpers" of Paris, one was constantly made aware that more serious and permanent realities govern man's ultimate value. Thus he reported that one day he "turned aside into a small mansion with the name of *Morgue*" where "lay the naked body of an old grey-headed artisan whom misery had driven to drown himself in the river! . . . His lean horny hands with their long ragged nails were lying by his sides . . . this poor outcast stretched in silence and darkness forever." He "gazed upon the wretch for a quarter of an hour. . . . To live in Paris for a fortnight is a treat; to live in it continually would be a martyrdom."[67] Carlyle took full advantage of his fortnight.

Though Kitty established a comparatively sedentary routine, the two men constantly mingled with the rich life of the city. Dominated by tall, tenement-like buildings, the dirty, crowded capital reminded him of Edinburgh, though the overwhelming press of street-business in this "Vanity-fair of the universe" seemed totally unique—the exterior world garishly occupied, the internal world readily deserted.[68] To a man who valued family, privacy, and the life of the conscience, it appeared that the Parisians had reversed the natural order and created a grand guignol.[69] The narrow streets stank, but the monuments and museums were "wonders of the earth." The primary human panorama, however, spilled from the streets into the gallery, which was one day invaded by "wild Savoyards," rapidly clearing the way for Charles X, who appeared with a group of courtiers whom Carlyle thought "very ugly people." Louis XVIII had just died, and the new king was still a curiosity. Carlyle could not bring himself to join the half hearted cheer for the insecure "poor gentleman" who, like Paris, seemed hardly royal in position or spirit.[70]

Since Carlyle had not had time to solicit introductions before leaving England, French literary circles were closed to him. He had read widely in eighteenth-century French literature, but he knew almost nothing about more recent developments and hardly cared to pursue what he thought to be a barren literary spirit. He was aware, however, that Paris was Europe's most important center of scientific inquiry, and began to explore this aspect of the city's intellectual life. He attended the famous Baron Georges Cuvier's "introductory lecture, on comparative anatomy," and came away much impressed.[71] Thinking that Jack might want to study medicine in Paris, he inquired about medical programs and hospital opportunities and visited the famous charity-hospital, the Hôtel Dieu, where he was astonished to learn that the broad support of "anatomie pathologique" made cadavers freely available for dissection. He overcame his normal shyness to introduce himself to Legendre, whose *Geometrie* he had translated. Grateful to his young Scots translator, the French mathematician took him to a meeting of the Royal Institute of Science, where Carlyle heard François Magendie, an influential pioneer in understanding the nervous system, give "a paper on the fifth pair of nerves" and saw a large number of distinguished scientists, including Laplace, Lacroix, Poisson, Chaptal, and Thénard.[72]

Rather than pursue intellectual interests, however, Carlyle spent most of his time absorbing the general atmosphere of the French capital, later claiming that all his experiences in Paris, except to the extent that "its old aspects and localities" helped him "in writing of the *Revolution,*" belonged "under the head of amusement."[73] Most evenings he dined at the Palais Royal, "titillated and horrified" by what he termed the "chosen abode of vanity and vice."[74] On his last night in Paris he saw Napoleon's favorite actor in a performance of Voltaire's *Oedipus,* a play whose relevance to his own life probably eluded him. He was impressed, however, when "all the people standing up" raised "a vehement shout of approval" at the recitation of "*C'est nos craintes qui ont formé les cieux.*"[75] Back in Dover on November 7, 1824, he wrote to Mainhill that he had "seen many strange things, which may people my imagination with interesting forms, and perhaps yield some materials for reflexion and improvement." On the whole he did not "regret this jaunt," on which he had spent no more than five pounds; it was a great deal of experience at very little cost.[76]

5

Though he remained in London another four months, he gradually concluded not only that the conditions of "this enormous Babel" were unsatisfactory, but that the excitements of any large city were contrary to the needs of his nervous system.[77] Fortunately, his agreement to board with the Irvings, whose "brat" idolatry repelled him, was superseded by their decision to take on a well-paying boarder who could make them a definite commitment. Though he found his own lodgings at a quiet, comfortable home just a short distance from Irving, Carlyle was determined to create a permanent residence of his own. Having "lived too long in tents, a wandering Bedouin," he felt that he "ought to settle somewhere," not among the Scots in London but in some community in the North.[78] He broached to Alick his old idea that they rent a farm in Scotland, Alick plowing the soil while he tilled literary fields. He suggested that his parents find another farm—one whose land required less work than that of Mainhill—and said that he would join them, contributing through his literary earnings and regaining his long-lost health. Clearly Carlyle was homesick, with the particular urgency of a man who has resolved that rootedness of place is essential to health, happiness, and productivity.

Nothing came of his relationship with Kitty, but he continued to see the Stracheys and the Montagus regularly, and even met the Bullers again. They offered to employ him as a tutor for Arthur, but their conditions could by no means overcome his distaste for such work. Crab Robinson entertained him, lending him German books, and Bryan Procter (a young poet, writing under the name of Barry Cornwall, who had married Mrs. Montagu's daughter) and Allan Cunningham were frequent companions. Thomas Campbell seemed more responsive than previously, probably because he was less concerned that the young man from Scotland would ask professional favors. Irving was still frequent company, but Carlyle now observed his friend's affectations with a sober, loving regret. One day, recognizing Irving's "broad hat . . . on the road down to Battle-Bridge . . . amid the tide of passengers, and his little child sitting on his arm," he asked himself, " 'Why should *I* hurry up; they are parted from me, the old days are no more!' "[79] He was lonely for Jane, but he did not consider moving close to Haddington. Indeed, such a move would be impractical, for he knew that if he could solve his two immediate problems, obtaining a satisfactory residence and a reasonable expectation of income, then his home would automatically become Jane's as well. He actually took the step of mentioning to his family that he was considering marriage.

The London that he had come to in search of intellectual stimulation seemed particularly destitute of inspiring literary figures in the spring of 1825. He wrote to Jane that "Coleridge is sunk inextricably in the depths of putrescent indolence. Southey and Wordsworth have retired far from the din of this monstrous city. So has Thomas Moore. Whom have we left? The drawf Opium-Eater (my Critic in the London Magazine)." Hazlitt was in France, Leigh Hunt in Pisa. "The very best" of those left "are ill-natured weaklings . . . only *things* for writing articles."[80] Such declamatory condemnations have the ring of a man who clearly recognizes what has passed but not yet glimpsed what is to come. Byron, Shelley, and Keats, the best of his own generation, were dead. The new generation was still too young to have established itself in London or on the English literary scene. And as for Carlyle himself, he readily admitted that he had accomplished little. Increasingly, Irving's claim that in London he could find kindred souls and fertile soil for the flowering of his genius seemed unfounded. Even the cost of living was not balanced by compensating advantages, "the very expense of it [was] almost enough to drive" him away, whereas "two guineas a week" were sufficient "to keep a decent roof" over his head in his "Fatherland."[81] "With regret, and . . . the hope of often seeing [London] again," he was ready to leave, for he was convinced that in Scotland he would not only make better use of his remaining funds but also regain his health. Jack assured him that he was "perfectly right in resolving to leave London. . . . It must be very bad for your health . . . and so lonely at the same time. . . . Come home to Scotland again, where you will be sure of finding true friends to welcome you."[82]

By the beginning of 1825 his certainty that he would return to Scotland had merged with his desire to establish a permanent home with Jane. He had proposed that he solve his economic problem by undertaking a translation of the complete works of Schiller, but Jane responded that his assumption of such a stultifying, unoriginal task would substantially erode her commitment to his "genius." He drew back, writing her that since "literature is the *wine* of life; it will not, cannot, be its *food.*" But how was he to make his living if translating, as food, was unacceptable?[83] His answer was that he should return to the "nature" from which he had departed. Might it not be possible to have food, wine, and health in some rural paradise? Jane immediately responded that such a notion was ridiculous. Life on a farm would be tedious, aggravating his tendency to cut himself off from others and thereby intensifying his depression and his satirical nature. Mindful of her own lonely tedium in Haddington, she could not contemplate a marriage that would further diminish her contacts with stimulating people and places.[84] To show her contempt for "turning Farmer," she mockingly proposed that he devote himself to improving the land on

Craigenputtoch, the isolated sheep farm that she had inherited from her father.[85] But Carlyle took her little "joke" seriously, immediately writing to urge that she "say, Yes!" not only to the farm but to accompanying him there as his wife.[86]

"Speak, then, my Angel! How say you? Will you be mine, mine?" he wrote, but she immediately responded that whereas she loved him she was "not *in love* with" him.[87] The project of "keeping house at Craigenputtock," which was in southwestern Scotland some twenty miles from Dumfries, seemed insane, but then the prospect of keeping house with him anyplace disturbed her considerably.[88] She still had strong emotional reservations. Under the weight of her sense of failure and inadequacy, her own literary aspirations had been flattened into a thin, secondary concern. Repeated efforts to write had come to nothing, except the realization that each new try would prove as fruitless as the one before. Since Carlyle's enthusiastic attempts to help her be something more than a housewife were motivated in part by his desire to keep her dependent on him until a more durable attachment could be forged, he had no hesitation now in substituting for his exaggerated praise of her literary talents a new idealization of her as "mistress of a house" and "the model of wives . . . that highest destination of even the noblest woman."[89] Having already reached the conclusion that she would not have an independent career, Jane now hoped that he would provide the contact with genius that would compensate for her own failure and keep her close to the excitement of the literary life.

But she also felt compelled to ask herself if she loved him in the way that a woman hopes to love the man she marries. Her practical objections to his proposal were serious: she did not want to decrease her standard of living, and the thought of a rural isolation worse than that of Haddington was impossibly burdensome. But her most important consideration was one which she only now confessed—she did not want to marry him because she neither loved him in a romantic way nor felt toward him the sexual attraction that she had always imagined she would feel toward the man who would become her husband. Indeed, the very fact that she had sufficient prudence to raise practical objections seemed to her sufficient evidence that she was not possessed by romantic passion in this unusual affair. Still, she admitted her disappointment that her deepest, most intuitive resource was not being activated, for her heart was "capable . . . of a love to which *no* deprivation would be a sacrifice."[90]

Jane granted that the concept of the ideal lover might be a romantic fiction, but recognized that its power was nevertheless such that reality had to be measured against it. He had asked her to act as if he fulfilled that ideal and awakened within her the excitement that would permit her to throw caution of every kind aside. Not only could she not do that but she felt compelled to make bluntly clear the disparity between her feelings for that romantic fiction on the one hand and the reality that he presented on the other. Would he desist from pressuring her now if she assured him his eventual success was "most *probable,*" though she would "marry" him tomorrow rather than give him up?[91]

He recognized that his own temperament and situation encouraged more desperate resolutions than did hers, and was relieved that she had not accepted his impulsive proposal that they marry immediately. Instead of expressing resentment at her confession, Carlyle complimented her on her sincerity. If there was anger, he buried it deeply, content to let time decide whether the sexual attraction between them was sufficient to a happy marriage. Perhaps he silently demurred from her assumption that such an attraction was crucial. Certainly he had not seen that romantic passion played much of a role in his parents' marriage. Moreover, having learned not to express his sexuality directly, he had concluded that romantic and physical desires, even those that seem to provide initial motivation for marriage, usually decline rapidly under the pressures of familiarity, children, and hard work. Had he placed as much importance on romantic love within marriage as did Jane, he might have worried whether his state of mind would allow his "unhealthy" body to perform effectively in a sexual relationship, but he no longer had even the slightest reason to doubt that they would and should marry, whatever the problems. And by mid-February she confessed that she listened to his "voice as to the dictates of a second conscience," and blushed at the mention of his name like a conventional young lady who is in the embarrassing and irreversible condition of being "*half engaged.*"[92]

By this time Caryle had begun to consider practical ways to deal with his grand obsession, the recovery of his health. He was convinced that he suffered from a disease of the nervous system, and believed that if he could give up drugs, carefully regulate his diet, and exercise moderately in a healthy environment he might indeed be well again. Dating his illness from 1818, he pondered the possibility that his seven "years of pain" were part of a higher plan in which suffering was "a sort of blessing in disguise" which had kept him "clear" of degrading sexual and economic temptations. Why should he not now enjoy seven "fat" years? His economic future actually seemed less a threat than his health. He felt secure enough to dismiss a scheme whereby he would superintend the education of a few pupils in Edinburgh and to reject a reasonable offer from the publisher of *Schiller* that he do a life of Voltaire. Instead, he had decided to do "a *series* of translations from the German" for an Edinburgh publisher, which would be more practical since he planned to live in Scotland for the time being.[93]

From London, he went first to Birmingham to reinforce the "Badamian Code," which he continued to follow. There, at the beginning of March, he learned that his brother and father had acted on his request and rented a farm high on a bluff known as Repentance Hill or Hoddam Hill.[94] While still dallying in Birmingham, Carlyle received a charming portable writing desk. He assumed that it was from Mrs. Strachey, who had given him a gold pencil before he left London, but in fact it was from Kitty Kirkpatrick. Badams, who had to rush back to London on business, offered him the gift of "a little fiery corn-fed indefatigable Welsh pony."[95] Moved by the tokens and tears of regret extended by his English friends, Carlyle looked with suspicious eyes on "icy Edinburgh" and the "coldness" of his "true but hard and forbidding fatherland." He was determined to "try once more," to "seek for friendship in" his "own country as for hidden treasure." But if he could not find it, he resolved that he would "stay no longer there."[96] Soon he had "arrived once more" in his "Father's house."[97]

6.

Much of the year at Hoddam Hill was "like a second boyhood."[98] Aware that he had much to repent of, he was also aware that he had much for which to be thankful, particularly the constant love of those who would never reject him, whatever his worldly or spiritual state. Repentance Tower, the Anglo-Saxon or Celtic border tower that dominated the bluff, was "a fit memorial for reflecting sinners," a visible reminder of the values that the Carlyle family lived by and of the inseparable connection between divine grace and God's chosen people.[99] The affection of his adoring family showed itself immediately in an enthusiastic welcome. Within a week, he visited Edinburgh and then Haddington. He had not seen Jane for almost a year.

At the end of May 1825, accompanied by Alick, his sister Jean, and his mother, who were to remain with him, he settled into his little farmhouse. For Thomas, the return to the ministering arms of his mother fulfilled a long-held fantasy. At times he had thought that his ill health was a punishment for some crime repugnant to family and God. But if he would "become a good child . . . the old knave will cease to flog me."[100] Not surprisingly, his health improved, partly through renunciation of anxiety-creating ambitions, partly through acceptance of his condition as a patient. Though he did his best to recreate the timeless experiences of childhood, his adult responsibilities sometimes pulled him back, particularly his failure to progress in fulfilling his agreement with his Edinburgh publisher to have his translations from German novels ready by November. Believing that he needed this holiday from excessive self-demands, he anticipated that, though ambition seemed "dead within" him for the moment, such contentment could not last. It was as if he had temporarily "fallen into a deep sleep," in a time of enchantment. "Am I twenty years younger than I counted; again a little heedless boy, that I can so live from one hour to the other?"[101] He sensed that he would never again have the opportunity to be his mother's child in quite this way. He took long rides, on an Irish horse, galloping into the wind with the conviction that he might dash out of himself the demons that occasionally threatened to repossess him; he smoked a great deal, ate simply, had long talks with his brothers (Jack was home for the summer), and constantly gazed at Repentance Tower and the magnificent view of the Cumberland peaks, immersing his aching spirit in the rural world of family solace.

But, under no illusion that he could remain in provincial isolation once he was healthy again, he confessed that "this is no scene for the healthy Philosopher whatever it may be for the sick."[102] Though he sometimes imagined that permanent residence in the countryside might be best for him, especially if he could have his family with him forever, he could not deceive himself into believing that such a yearning was anything more than a regressive fantasy. The patient would indeed leave the "Hospital" at the appropriate time, for "Life cannot be an Idyll any more than it can be an Epic; it is a despicable system of Book-keeping by Double Entry."[103] Though the entry in one column usually cancelled the entry in the other, the year at Hoddam Hill was an exception to this rule.

With only £200, however, he could not afford to let ambition rest for very long. In April 1825 he had met with David Brewster, a habitual organizer of joint literary ventures who had plans for a new journal in which Carlyle would be the editor responsible for literary contributions. But, though the project was kept alive through the year, it never had life of its own. His agreement to provide three volumes of translations of German romances might add something to his income. By late fall, though, he disappointed his publisher with the news that he would not keep his November deadline. With books procured from a number of sources in Edinburgh, London, and Germany, he finally got to work in the winter, translating Richter, Musaeus, Fouqué, Tieck, and Hoffmann. Once started, he eagerly pushed on, the act of translating having set his own creative juices flowing, directing him toward some "undertaking of more pith and moment." Something original, he felt, lay "deep and crude, if it lies at all, within [his] soul."[104] His first shallow effort to pull it out produced the notion that he would write a novel. It was probably the initial conception of what would become two years later the aborted "Wotton Reinfred." Riding early in November "round by *the* Smithy and Hoddam Kirk," he was thinkng of his "*Kunstwerk*" when "my cursed beast, knowing that I was studying . . . whirled round at full gallop down a steep place, and had my fair person dislodged from his back and trailed some yards upon the base highway in the twinkling of an eye! . . . What a termination for my *novel!* But the time will come, must come!"[105]

Early in the summer he had invited Jane to visit Hoddam and Mainhill, a visit to which Grace Welsh gave her reluctant consent. From Templand, fourteen miles away, where she and her mother were visiting, Jane traveled to Hoddam early in September 1825. Her ostensible purpose was to "pay" his "Mother a visit," the necessary ritual in which the daughter-in-law-to-be was to be given the blessing of the prospective mother-in-law.[106] The visit proved a success. Margaret Carlyle had signaled in advance that she would accept her son's choice. Sensitive to the potential incompatibility between Haddington gentry and Annandale farmers, Carlyle did his best to emphasize the noble simplicity of his family, while Jane tried to dramatize the conviction that the good heart transcends superficial differences. Both realized that in their class-conscious society they would be vulnerable to the allegation that he was marrying above his station, she below. The next spring, he responded to her suggestion that they live with his parents by saying that she could never adapt to "the rugged peas*t* element and way of life," though she "was *not* afraid of it."[107] His idea that they live in Haddington frightened her not only because she found the place infinitely tedious, but also because she felt awkward bringing the son of a farmer to live in the house of the daughter of a doctor.[108]

Over forty years later this single year at Hoddam Hill was remembered as the one in which he "had conquered all [his] skepticisms, agonising doubtings, fearful wrestlings with the foul and vile and soul-murdering Mud-Gods of [his] Epoch . . . and was emerging, free in spirit, into the eternal blue of ether."[109] Unquestionably, certain of his general attitudes had been affected by his reading of Goethe, "the first of the moderns," whose pioneering example in traveling life's "steep rocky road" gave him emotional comfort and some security.[110] But for Carlyle all theological positions were unacceptable, except the general belief that the just power that governs the universe can be seen in most human beings, manifesting itself in attitudes and actions that may or may not be incorporated into conventional religious institutions. Since such heretical thoughts were painful to his family, he did what he could to conceal from them his strong doubts about much of basic Christian belief in miracle, in Christ as the son of God (rather than as divine in the way that all men are), and even in personal immortality.

In his own evolving religious views, he substituted for Christian theology his personal belief that the universe is a spiritual structure illumined by the divine force within man and the cosmos which promises ultimate justice and potential salvation through work and struggle. No church and no theology seemed to him credible or helpful. As long as he remained true to himself, his work, and his belief in cosmic justice, he could reject weak dependency and the world's corruptions. Later he referred to what had happened to him during his year at Hoddam Hill as a "conversion," its emotional force sufficiently strong for him to feel thereafter that any and all of the movements and philosophies of the next decades, "Puseyisms, Ritualisms, Metaphysical controversies and cobwebberies . . . Universal Suffrages . . . Nigger Emancipations, Sluggard-and-Scoundrel Protection Societies," had no attraction for him.[111] He felt impregnable to their influence, except insofar as human tragedy evoked his human sympathy. To some extent he had accomplished what he wanted more than anything else: to "become independent of the world" in a way that would permit him to triumph over the weakness of his nervous system, the anxieties of ill health and thwarted vocation, and even such seeming finalities as death.[112] He felt deeply relieved and occasionally exalted.

7.

The Irving circle had tightened around Jane in July, however, and forced her to reveal to her fiancé that she had once been in love with his friend. In the mid-summer of 1825, Mrs. Montagu, whom Carlyle had encouraged to extend friendship to Jane, had taken up the relationship with a cool vengeance. With a sharp nose for amatory crosscurrents, she combined intuition with a few facts and concluded not only that Jane had once been in love with Irving but that she probably still loved him. Claiming that her action was based upon her own unhappy experiences, she urged Jane to confess to her intended, for "there must be no Blue-beard's closet in which the skeleton may one day be discovered."[113] Jane now felt that she had no choice but to tell him immediately, before less than helpful friends told him themselves. Openly admitting that she had deceived him about her feelings for Irving, she confessed that she had "loved him—must I say it—*once* passionately loved him."[114]

Carlyle took shrewd advantage of her confession, using it to bring them closer to the frankness that he believed necessary if their relationship were to continue. He assured her, "You exaggerate this matter greatly: it is an evil, but it may be borne."[115] He would not hesitate to admire her frankness and forgive her completely, if she in return forgave his weaknesses now and in the future. "As I am, take me or refuse me: but not as I *am not;* for *this* will not and cannot come to good."[116] Did she understand the irremediable extent of his misery and would she marry him nevertheless? At best it would sometimes effect the mood of their marriage, at worst it might give the marriage characteristics intolerable to ordinary women. "You know me not; no living mortal knows me. . . . I can no longer love. . . . Am I not poor and sick and helpless and estranged from all men? I lie upon the thorny couch of pain, my pillow is the iron pillow of despair: I can rest on them in silence, but that is all that I can do. Think of it, Jane! I can never make you happy. Leave me, then!"[117] Her feelings of guilt had been intensified by a delay in the receipt of his letter, and she was now not at all inclined to withdraw from their relationship, or even to accept his claim that he could "no longer love." She would not believe it, uncertain whether or not this alleged despair also took direct physical form. Eager to mend matters, she assured herself and him: "This is a mere delusion my Darling: you *can* love,—will, shall love; not Jane Welsh, perhaps, but your Wife you will love."[118] Her response perfectly suited his need. If she insisted on taking him on hope, then what followed was her responsibility.

At the end of January 1826 Carlyle thought that they would be married within the year. Before a date could be determined, however, there were two crucial matters to resolve—where they would live and what living arrangements would be made for Grace Welsh. The latter problem had to be disposed of before Jane's conscience would permit her to set a precise date for the marriage. Grace Welsh's hostility to the marriage was based in part on economic anxiety. Her husband had left very little, and thus the marriage was a significant step into the unknown not only for the bride and groom but also for the bride's mother. Her antagonism was allayed somewhat, however, when Jane insisted on turning over to her the annual rent (about £200 a year) from Craigenputtoch, which James Welsh had left directly to his daughter.

During the late winter and spring of 1826 both parties explored solutions. Jane rejected Carlyle's suggestion that they live in Annandale, since her mother could not be happy there. She wrote that her mother had been "looking forward to my marriage with a more tranquil mind, in the hope that our separation is to be in a great measure nominal,—that by living wheresoever my Husband lives she may at least have every moment of my society which he can spare."[119] Since Grace Welsh had decided to vacate the Haddington house, Carlyle proposed that the married couple occupy it for a year, unaware that the cash from its sale was necessary to cover current expenses. Having suggested a suburb of Edinburgh and then changed his mind, he responded to Jane's accusation that he was indecisive with the flat denial that there was any inconsistency in his proposals. Assuming the paternal role, he lectured her on her comparative immaturity. He again offered to release her, which she again declined, gently warning him that it would "take many caresses to atone for" such manipulations.[120] She loved him—"tenderly, devotedly as ever Woman loved." But "I may not put my Mother away from me even for *your* sake."[121] But she had accepted the stark territorial imperative in his claim that "the moment I am master of a house, the first use I turn it to will be to slam the door of it on the face of nauseous intrusions of all sorts which it can exclude; my prospective cottage would be calculated for different objects than your Mother's."[122]

Despite the fact that his proposal that they marry within six months depended upon settling this problem, he responded with brutal frankness to her argument that after careful preparations the three of them might be able to live together. He did not believe that Grace Welsh could live like "a second *wife* to her daughter's husband!"[123] And since she could never fulfill such a role, he could not enter into such an arrangement. Though Jane already knew very well what its basic tenets were, he took the opportunity to detail the marital credo that ruled their relationship thereafter:

> *The Man should bear rule in the house and not the Woman.* This is an eternal axiom, the Law of Nature h[erself w]hich no mortal departs from unpunished. . . . I must not and I cannot live in a house of which I am not head. . . . It is the nature of a man that if he be controuled by any thing but his own Reason, he feels himself degraded. . . . It is the nature of a woman again (for she is essentially *passive* not *active*) to cling to the man for support and direction, to comply with his humours, and feel pleasure in doing so, simply because they are his; to reverence while she loves him, to conquer him not by her force but by her weakness . . . to command him by obeying him.[124]

But still the matter of where the couple would reside remained to be settled. Carlyle firmly recommended either Edinburgh or Haddington. Edinburgh might be better, since he needed work for both income and self-satisfaction. He did not believe that marriage would make him any happier than he already was, whereas "if regular labour and diligent pursuit of duty" did "not make" him "happy," he would "be unhappy in Heaven itself."[125] Reminding her of his poverty, he proudly proclaimed that though he would accept whatever gift her mother offered he would neither request nor expect anything. Nervous about the future, eager to avoid recriminations afterward, he again made the facile offer that they "forget the whole negociation, and live in peace and hope together as . . . before."[126] This problem of where they would live seemed to drag on forever in a kind of hostile stalemate. Anticipating some of the conflicts of the future, he urged Jane not to forget that "this is an engagement for Eternal Union, not a paction, as it were between foes, for an Armed Neutrality!"[127] Late in May 1826, however, Grace Welsh took the decisive step. She rented a small house on Comely Bank in a northwestern suburb of Edinburgh. The two women would make it habitable during the summer and the couple would occupy it soon after their October wedding at Templand. But Grace Welsh, who had paid the £32 rent for the first year, would live permanently at Templand. She wrote conciliatorily to her future son-in-law that "this long perplexing emigration of ours now draws to a close. May God grant that it may draw us *all* together in the bonds of love and happiness with every good wish for your welfare. Believe me in affection what you w*d* wish the Mother of your Jane to be."[128]

Though the waiting seemed like "purgatory," the two nervous young people had used it, instinctively, to build a kind of fail-safe system in which elaborate commitments to understand and to forgive guarded against the marriage foundering on physical and other incompatibilities. And, at last, the "hottest and droughtiest summer" Carlyle had "ever seen" was finally over.[129] Early in October 1826 he received "the last Speech and *marrying* words of that unfortunate young woman Jane Baillie *Welsh*" and sent in response his "last blessing as a Lover . . . my last letter to Jane Welsh: my first blessing as a Husband, my first kiss to Jane Carlyle is at hand! O my darling! I will always love thee."[130] Soon after the middle of the month he rode up to Templand with Jack, the only representative of the Carlyle family at what both bride and groom wished to be as private a wedding as possible. Thomas was strongly mindful of his mother's command that he write to her "in *two days*."[131] They were married on the morning of the seventeenth and, unescorted by family or servants, arrived on the same day at Comely Bank to spend the first night of a marriage that was to endure for just a few months short of forty years.

[5]

"Jenny Spinner"
1826–1828

Carlyle awakened on his wedding morning in a "sullen" mood, "sick with sleeplessness, quite nervous, *billus,* splenetic and all the rest of it."[1] He was immensely grateful to Jane, who had "mercifully dealt with" him, ordering "another bed to be made in the adjoining room," to which he might retire whenever he felt it necessary.[2] Under compelling orders from his mother to write and to tell "the very worst," he remonstrated, "You should not have ordered me to write in *two days,* but after *three weeks.*"[3] Jane respected Margaret Carlyle's stipulation that she not read the letter, and, with astonishing frankness, the son made clear to the mother that the experience had been a failure. Five days later he wrote to Jack, saying that he desperately wanted to speak to him "about many things, *ut cum fratre, ut cum medico* [both as a brother and as a doctor]." He said he was still "in a maze, scarce knowing the right hand from the left in the path I have to walk."[4] The problem apparently was in the "outward man," some lack of physical responsiveness so private it could not be detailed even in such candid communications to his mother and brother, the two people with whom up to that point he had been most intimate.

In his eyes it was a failure not of love but of a body that would not do love's bidding, the result of ill health and confusion. He had made his excuses in advance, and Jane had openly wondered whether she was in love with him as a wife should be with a husband. Clearly, Puritan inhibitions and Romantic idealizations were in the seven-foot wide bed with two sexual innocents. Fragile evidence suggests that though they were able to express affection with whispers and embraces, their sexual relationship did not provide physical satisfaction to either of them,[5] despite the efforts made during the first half-dozen or so years of the marriage. Whispers and embraces indicate that their affection did take physical form, but the account of the abysmal marriage night, the early retreat to separate beds and rooms, the vehement distaste for children, the constant pressure of ill health, and the general tone of physical repression provide convincing circumstantial support for the claim that sexual intercourse played little or no role in the routine of their relationship during almost forty years of marriage.

Exhausted after his sleepless night, Thomas passed the next day in a daze, solaced only by Jane's forced good spirits. He slept well the second night, probably because his wife did not think it desirable to put additional strain on the relationship and did not feel up to experiencing again the tensions of the first night. Better rested, he felt that yesterday's pervasive darkness was "now becoming somewhat *grey*, and promising ere long to be quite sunshiny and bright."[6] But still, he had not recovered his senses and felt terribly depressed. As if purposely to intensify his physical and psychological anguish, he made a vow to give up tobacco the day after his wedding, terming it "a piece of abstinence that afflicts me not a little."[7] Perhaps he imagined that doing so would improve his health, though it is just as likely that at some level the decision was an expression of penance for sexual failure.

Carlyle did not seem to know precisely what was expected of him. He thought that Jack, who had at least read medical textbooks, would be like "a lamp in a dark place," capable of explaining physiological details. He himself could not "explain matters yet; but by and by I doubt not I shall see it all. Meanwhile tell my Mother that I do believe I shall get *hefted* [adjusted] to my new situation, and then be one of the happiest men alive."[8] He had Jack pass the message along to Margaret Carlyle that on Jane's "express request" he was to "read a sermon, and a Chapter with commentary, at least every Sabbath evening to" his "household." In addition, Jack was to tell her that they were "taking seats in church, and design to live soberly and devoutly as beseems us."[9]

It is doubtful that even Margaret Carlyle could have given credence to her son's claim that he might shortly be "one of the happiest men alive," though she would have been pleased that he had made such a claim and would have trusted in divine providence to improve his situation. The plan to attend church was no more than rhetoric to please his mother and to assuage his own guilt. Both as son and husband, Carlyle felt guilty that he had disappointed others in crucial ways. But his promise to imitate the pious rituals of his parents was kept for a short time at best, mainly because his detestation of hypocrisy was stronger than his dutiful intentions and because he manifested his loyalty to his parents' religion in other ways. Jane, who had neither family pressure nor internal motives for attending church or saying prayers, hoped to make her husband happier by pleasing his mother. The notion that he would soon be one of the happiest men alive was also for his mother's ears only. To his brother, he made his miserable situation clear: "Why am I not happy then? Alas Jack *I am billus:* I have to swallow salts and oil: the physic leaves me pensive yet quiet in heart and on the whole happy enough; but next day comes a burning stomach, and a heart full of bitterness and gloom."[10]

Carlyle's complaints about his health, which had been muted for a long time, now increased under the pressure of adjusting to the demands of marriage and to life away from the comforting family circle. "Certainly at this moment I should be among the happiest of men," he wrote to Jack in late October, "if I were not among the unhealthiest."[11] He immediately returned to "drug-taking," particularly castor oil and epsom salts. As his feeling of weakness, irritability, and dislocation increased, his anxiety "to be well" only intensified his preoccupation with his illness. He was to some extent aware of his hypochondriacal intensification of his physical pain. He told his mother, "Were it not that I am so over-anxious to be *well,* I should not let my *illness* discompose me."[12] At the end of the first month of his marriage he again wrote his mother, saying that he sought to relieve "the suspense in which I know well you are living with regard to me." He would tell her " 'the very worst.' " "Tho' this is now the fourth week of my marriage, I am by no means 'come to', . . . as you would say, or yet 'hefted' [adjusted] to my new *gang* [way of life]. The consequence is considerable irregularity in regard to health, and of course to spirits and life generally."[13] In order to deal with his recalcitrant stomach and bowels he had gone on the "starving system," a remedy that only weakened him further. But he urged his mother not to exaggerate his condition, assuring her that he was, in fact, no worse than he had been other critical times in his life.

Carlyle tried to write, but immediately burned in disgust what he had written. Though his outer four walls were reasonably impervious to "naseous intrusions," the inner walls of his stomach and psyche were being assaulted by tensions that caused him immense pain. Jane ministered to him as best she could, fussing over his diet and arranging the routines of the household to suit his needs. The cure of his illness had to precede the satisfactory performance of marital duties. Hiding her disappointment, she exaggerated her optimism to compensate for his gloom. To some extent, Carlyle took her cheerfulness at face value. His ill health was an acceptable excuse for sexual clumsiness and failure, and her compensatory optimism encouraged him to blame himself less.

Whatever his own condition, he assured Jack that "on the whole this wife of mine surpasses my hopes: she is so tolerant, so kind, so cheerful, so devoted to me! O that I were worthy of her!"[14] He repeated the same message to his mother, assuring her Jane was not to blame. Indeed, "I am astonished at the affection she bears me, and the patience with which she listens to my doleful forebodings and turns them all into gay hopes." Margaret Carlyle could only be gratified by her son's claim that Jane knew her traditional role as wife and demonstrated that she had learned the lesson of female subservience. "In *every* thing great and little she gives me entirely my own way."[15] The alacrity with which Jane fulfilled her role, even under these difficult circumstances, suggests that to whatever extent her performance was purposefully willed, it may also have been, to some considerable extent, psychologically natural. Perhaps her subservience to her husband expressed some of the guilt she felt at having survived her cherished father. To her "dear new Mother" she wrote that "I wished to send you glad tidings of great joy; that your son was well and happy beside me. . . . But alas! . . . we are still, some of us in the slough of Despond—Nevertheless . . . with all its drawbacks our lot is far from unhappy. We love each other; have done ill to no one; and one of us at least is full of hope. . . . It is not impossible, nay highly probable that we shall yet have great cause to rejoice."[16]

2.

Early in December 1826 Carlyle confided to his private notebook both his bewilderment about his married state and his determination to get on with his work: "Married! Married' *Aber still davon!* But of that no words—and of a thousand other things. I am for business."[17] The substitution of private German for public English reveals the depth of his personal anguish. Though he wanted to get on with "business," he was frustrated by not having an immediate project at hand and angry at himself for his inability to get words down on paper. For the time being, his notebook was a solace. The very act of writing provided emotional relief, and his entries in the next few months exceeded in length those of the previous four years. A line of Goethe's spoke to him with autobiographical intensity. The unhappy man is one "who is possessed by some *idea* which he cannot convert into an *action,* or still more which restrains and withdraws him from action." Aristotle also came to mind: "The end of man is an *Action* not a *Thought.*" "How many eulogies of Activity, and Nothing acted!" On the same day, he quoted the German Romantic writer Ludwig Tieck: "My whole life has been a continued night-mare: and my awakening will be in Hell."[18] The selections from his readings exemplified his own confusions; they were dreams that embodied his frustration, myths that spoke about the ambiguities of marriage and sex: "Adam is fabled by the Talmudists to have had a wife before Eve: she was called Lilis . . . and their progeny was all manner of terrestial, aquatic and aërial—Devils!"[19]

Within a few days he was assuring his mother that he was feeling better, "getting more and more habituated to [his] new condition of life."[20] Aware of her tendency to exaggerate, he was eager to communicate any signs of improvement as quickly as possible. Indeed, he was less nervous, frenetic, and dismal, mainly because he and Jane had worked out an emotional *modus vivendi.* He recognized that "the philosophy of the heart is far better than that of the understanding" and that it was his wife, "among the best women that the world contains," who through her love had taught him that love could soften even his pain and transcend the limitations of his personality.[21] Jane had quickly and quietly accepted the value of a marital love that did not depend on sexual satisfactions.

Carlyle grasped an essential point of his own situation when he wrote to Alick, then seriously considering marriage to a young Annandale lady, "I am inclined to think true affection on the part of the *wife* is perhaps even more essential than on that of the husband."[22] No matter how frequently he affirmed his love for Jane, he believed that the dynamics of their relationship, and probably of all marriages, were such that the wife must have the emotional resources to accept whatever demands, many of them unspoken, the husband made. Jane herself seemed to interpret her husband's failures as the necessary correlatives of his genius, a view that strengthened her in her unusual capability not only to accept her husband's particular failures but also to tolerate the disagreeable aspects of his personality. At this stage in their marriage she was genuinely hopeful that a combination of her compassion and the world's recognition and rewards would enable her husband to overcome the ills that afflicted his mind and body. Carlyle himself rarely tired of repeating his belief that it was possible for him to regain his health. But, at the same time, he occasionally confided to such friends as Badams and to his notebook that he was determined to accept the possibility that he would never be healthy again.

For the moment, however, long-range salvation was less important than "some suitable employment." The doctor of the family, just beginning his own leisurely search for medical employment, confirmed Jane's opinion that "when he falls upon some work we shall be still happier."[23] Marriage itself, Carlyle quickly agreed, was not the cause of his problems of health or temperament. It was, in fact, a "necessity." His mood was light enough to welcome his old friend Thomas Murray "with the right hand of old Friendship into this Land of Matrimony."[24] But for now Carlyle had no work to do.

Though "some sort of occupation" seemed better than none at all, he was reluctant to return to the most obvious and readily available work, translation.[25] His proposal to translate all of Schiller had been rejected. He had no ready market for articles, no commissions for reviews. Finally, it seemed unlikely that Brewster's proposal that he edit a new magazine would come to anything and, in any case, Carlyle was disinclined to involve himself with tedious editorial duties. Yet, for want of anything else to do, he played with the possibility, outlining in his notebook, perhaps for Brewster's consideration, a detailed prospectus for a magazine—a miscellany of biographical sketches, essays on literature, morals, and manners, book reviews, and information about modern science.[26] Although he really wanted to begin a book of his own ("it would do far more for me than any mere publishing or editorial engagement"),[27] he confessed to Mrs. Montagu that he felt "too helpless and undetermined" to begin the kind of artistic and inventive occupation that would close the gap between his intentions and his achievements. That he found modern literature uninviting and modern writers despicable was hardly sufficient excuse for his own inability to "speak out" the urgent things "that are lying in me, and giving me no sleep till they are spoken!"[28]

Before the old year was out he thought he had found a vehicle for those urgent voices. He proudly announced to his mother, "I fairly began—a Book!"—at the same time apologizing for the startling fact that it was "only a *novel*."[29] At New Years he gave her a biography of a well-known missionary and translator of the Bible, telling her: "While reading it, believe that *your* son also is a kind of missionary in his way; not to the Heathen of India, but to the British Heathen, an innumerable class, whom he would gladly do something to convert, if . . . his perplexities and manifold infirmities would give him leave!"[30] But since Margaret Carlyle saw novels, even Goethe's *Wilhelm Meister,* as dubious vehicles for communicating any kind of truth, he needed to emphasize that his would be a moral and didactic work whose religious qualities would make it possible for it to be read even in Annandale. He reminded her that the missionary urge and the voice of God could fulfill themselves in diverse ways. He was aware that the evidence that he was triumphing over his "manifold infirmities" would outweigh his mother's doubts, and felt certain that she had sufficient confidence in him to forego most questions and to take his word as to the moral quality of his conception.

Now that he was working steadily, Carlyle was happier than he had been since moving to Edinburgh. For about two months he kept diligently at his novel, drawing on his experiences in an attempt to create a didactic fable, modeled on the example of Goethe's *Wilhelm Meister,* in which a young hero searches for transcendent wisdom. Margaret Carlyle, Edward Irving, Margaret Gordon, and Jane Welsh contributed substantially to their fictional counterparts, as Carlyle mixed autobiography and moral fiction to reveal the rather abstract patterns, psychological and intellectual, of his modern hero-in-the-making. Even Coleridge appeared in a transparent parody. Carlyle drew on his experiences in London and his wide reading in German literature to depict Wotton as a young man caught between the claims of the world and the claims of the spirit. Still at it in the middle of February, he boasted to his mother, "I have begun another Book, which if I had rightly finished I would not give a fig for them all! It is to be a curious book this; but I hope a good and even moral one! It proceeds slowly, yet constantly day after day."[31]

Even this slow pace, however, soon decreased. Carlyle's sheer effort of will faltered before his growing sense that the formidable problems that interrupted his progress would not easily be overcome. He took advantage of a publisher's suggestion that he translate Goethe's memoirs to be "knocked . . . sadly ajar" and admitted that "poor Reinfred has been living not growing for the last three weeks." So uncompelling was "Wotton" that, though he claimed he had "not abandoned the *Book,*" he assured the publisher of the proposed translation that "the fittest of all times to commence the undertaking would be the present." Since "Wotton" was a private matter, knowledge of which he was at pains to keep within the family, he did not have to confess its existence to anyone else. Instead, to give the matter a sense of urgency, he told the publisher he was willing to "postpone" a different "Literary Engagement . . . the joint Editorship of a new Periodical," which in fact existed only as a prospectus in his notebook.[32] He could expect reasonable payment for any translation, whereas "Wotton" was an artistic speculation, whose progress became less promising as the days went by.

In March, however, Hunt and Clarke withdrew their interest, wary of a market that had become increasingly soft and had led Tait to postpone publication of *German Romance.* Carlyle returned to "Wotton" at least twice in the spring. The first time, "though making but sorry progress," he was "determined to persevere to a conclusion"; the second try ended when, at the beginning of June, he had the good fortune to have "a new enterprize" on hand which allowed him to admit that "Poor Wotton has prospered but indifferently . . . tho' daily on the anvil; the metal is too unmalleable, often indeed quite cold, and the arm and the hammer have so little pith!"[33] He does not seem to have engaged in much speculation about what prevented him from continuing with the manuscript. Jane, to whom he read each portion as soon as it was completed, had given him no end of encouragement. Visions of success in a literary form with which she identified, and to which she had at one time committed herself, prompted her to think highly of her husband's effort. "Poor Wotton! Dear Wotton! He was growing such an angel of a Hero," she wrote to Jack. "But—Sir Thomas has given me his hand 'it shall be *done.*' "[34]

3.

In the final passage of the uncompleted "Wotton," Jane Montagu tells her eager but baffled suitor that "early next spring we moved northwards, and, after a short residence among these fells, still farther northwards into Scotland, to the spot you know so well! Dear Land!"[35] Almost as soon as they had settled in Edinburgh, within six months of their marriage, Carlyle seriously proposed the he and Jane leave for the "Dear Land," mainly because he could not liberate himself from the fantasy that his ill health could be cured only by living in the countryside.[36] It made no difference that he lived in a pleasant almost rural suburb of Edinburgh, or that, since the anguishing first month of his marriage and the start of work on "Wotton," his complaints about ill health had been subordinated to other preoccupations. He wanted pure air. He also wanted to move closer to his family and to strengthen the family circle. "Father and Mother and all that we cared for in the world, within a half-day's journey!"[37]

Suddenly in March 1827 he had the unexpected opportunity to indulge this fantasy in the particular form he had proposed to Jane before their marriage. Craigenputtoch, Grace Welsh's only source of income, was being mistreated by a careless tenant who was constantly in arrears with the rent. Carlyle suggested that the "blackguard" be terminated and that Alick, eager for a farm of his own, combine his capital with Thomas' in an arrangement in which Alick would run the farm, with assistance from his family, while Thomas and Jane enjoyed the benefits of healthful, quiet country life.

Though life in Craigenputtoch might be cheaper than in Edinburgh, Carlyle had no special need to reduce his expenses at this time. Jane had calculated that she could manage the household on £2 a week, excluding the annual rent of £32 which Mrs. Welsh had paid in advance as a present to the newlyweds. If her figures were correct, the couple had sufficient funds (Carlyle had finally been paid by Tait for *German Romance* early in the new year) for at least another year or perhaps two at their present standard of living. Jane's mother, living modestly with her own father at Templand, desired but did not need to have her rent paid in full and on time by her Craigenputtoch tenant.

And would it be of any economic advantage to Carlyle to be that new tenant? Sooner rather than later, beyond the grace period of a year or two, he would have to earn his living as a writer wherever he resided, which could very well have continued to be Edinburgh or could have been almost anyplace else, including London. Actually, though his initial urge to move to Craigenputtoch was impulsive, the final decision, a telling combination of accident and plan, was a second or even a third choice.

At the end of March he informed Alick that both he and Jane were committed to "the scheme." He granted that "town-life" at Comely Bank had fewer "annoyances" than life in the city itself, but added: "Many a time do I regret the liberty and safe seclusion which the country affords one . . . nay which I had attained not so long ago on the top of Repentance Hill."[38] Given to an idealizing nostalgia, he sought to recreate what he imagined had been his before his marriage, incorporating Jane into his own pastoral vision. Her response was completely supportive, though the active impulse was entirely his. Remembering her father's sacrifice to repurchase the farm, she resented its mistreatment and argued that the present tenant should be evicted, whether they occupied it or not. But she did not have any enthusiasm for Craigenputtoch, agreeing only out of loving compliance to her husband's wishes.

Just before the middle of April 1827, Carlyle parted from his wife for the first time and met Alick at Scotsbrig, from which they traveled the thirty-four miles to Craigenputtoch. The farm was in even worse condition than Alick had reported. Grace Welsh, responsive to her dead husband's investment in the farm of his ancestors, with a "heart full sore" now asserted that the tenant must be evicted, that she "would sooner live on potato[e]s . . . than that such an unprincipled dirty wretch should find footing upon it."[39] Carlyle proposed that Alick take possession of the farm at the end of May and institute reforms and repairs, building an additional small house for himself and repairing the main house for Jane and Thomas to occupy on Whitsunday of May 1828. Aware that much could happen in the interim, Jane quietly accepted the plan, recognizing that the price of her union was the subordination of her preferences to her husband's needs. She did not accept the reasoning that had produced his decision, for she was aware that his health had "not improved since we married" and was "almost certain" that "it [would] never improve." Though Carlyle kept sufficient balance to admit that he did not "look for an Arcadia" at Craigenputtoch, his vision of their life there still gushed with self-deceiving sentimentality: "We shall sit under our bramble and our saugh-tree . . . and none to make us afraid; and my little wife will be there forever beside me, and I shall be well and blessed, and the latter end of that man will be better than the beginning."[40] Jane could hardly enter into the spirit of this fantasy.

Despite the initial confusions of their marital relationship, the lines of power had been drawn clearly enough for Jane to work toward amelioration rather than opposition. It was particularly baffling to her that, even as their Edinburgh circle was expanding and her husband's professional opportunities increasing, they should have to defer to the *chance* that residence at Craigenputtoch, the very suggestion of which she had termed madness two years before, would improve Thomas' health. Years later Carlyle claimed what his letters of the time deny, stating not only that Comely Bank was "a gloomy intricate abode to me" but also that they were "as lonely as two wood-doves in their nest for the first year or so; very lonely, and with outlooks very bad" and consequently "went to Craigenputtoch, May 1828, as to the *cheaper* & healthier, and advisable kind of place."[41] To go to Craigenputtoch because he felt lonely in Edinburgh was hardly a rational act, and when the decision was tentatively made early in the spring of 1827 finances were not a consideration at all. By June they were even more secure, for he had been commissioned to write an article for the prestigious, well-paying *Edinburgh Review.*

Carlyle's London friends had continued to serve him well, though this time it was not Irving but the placid, amiable Bryan Procter, Mrs. Montagu's son-in-law, who late in January 1827 sent him a sealed letter of introduction to the editor of the *Edinburgh Review.* More than twenty years older than Carlyle, Francis Jeffrey straddled literature and politics. A celebrity in Edinburgh and increasingly well known in the literary and political circles of London, he had made his reputation as a successful lawyer and influential advocate of Whig politics and philosophy. As cofounder and editor of one of Britain's two major literary reviews, he could publicize his party's views through his own contributions and by carefully selecting the other materials that he published. At the same time, he was responsible for keeping the *Review* entertaining and challenging, a balance between sober Whig respectability and literary excitement which people would be eager to read. The recommendation from Procter guaranteed that now Carlyle would at least be noticed by the man who, for whatever the reason, had made no response at all when, six years earlier, Carlyle had delivered his article on Pictet to Jeffrey's home on George Street. Carlyle, of course, had known the editor's name since he first became aware of the *Edinburgh Review,* and had recognized his face ever since his first days in Edinburgh. Reading Jeffrey's essay on Byron in 1814, Carlyle had written that "none but a man of keen penetration, and deep research could

Francis Jeffrey. Painting by Colvin Smith. By permission of the National Galleries of Scotland, Edinburgh.

have written such a thing."[42] Even then, however, he had regretted that Jeffrey spent so much of his time on politics and so little on literature.

On an evening in early February, not long after he received Procter's letter, Carlyle went to see this "extra-ordinary man," who still lived in the house on George Street. "The little man received me in his kindest style; talked with me for an hour, tho' very busy, on all possible things; and really proved himself by much the most agreeable citizen of Edinburgh that I had ever met with."[43] Courtly, affectionate, and with a keen eye for young men of talent, Jeffrey cheerfully questioned the highly recommended Carlyle on his activities and ambitions.[44] The older man found little to interest him in Carlyle's immersion in German literature, but he ascribed this slightly off-putting eccentricity to youthful impetuosity and, in the best tradition of Whig civility, decided that he could tolerate Carlyle's obsession with Goethe. Carlyle confided to his mother that Jeffrey "invited me repeatedly to come to the 'Court' any morning, and he would introduce me to various people, among others to Sir Walter Scott. . . . He also spoke about writing in his Review; but I told him he must first read the *German Romance* to see what manner of man I was, and then we might determine if I could suit him. We parted in the friendliest style, mutually tolerant of each other."[45]

The differences of temperament and philosophy were in fact so great that, despite Jeffrey's intense efforts and Carlyle's initial willingness, their friendship could not last long; the one bond between them, mutual recognition that Jeffrey must help Carlyle as best he could, was too slight. Jeffrey, of course, made friends easily; it was in his nature and in the nature of his professional activities. Carlyle did not. He recognized from the first what Jeffrey would learn only gradually: ultimately he would press demands that Jeffrey would not be able to fulfill, making their relationship untenable in Carlyle's eyes, though Jeffrey himself would never make their relationship dependent upon Carlyle rigorously fulfilling his expectations.[46]

In his initial conversation with Jeffrey, Carlyle made no attempt to soften his views or his character, sensing that however their relationship developed, it must do so despite the differences between them. He recognized that Jeffrey immediately thought of him as "an enthusiast, distracted nearly, but amiable in . . . direction." To Carlyle, Jeffrey seemed "a man of the kindliest and richest nature, which the perverse utilitarianism of the time has all his life been striving vainly to spoil."[47] Jeffrey had said, "We must give you a lift!" and, despite his distaste for Jeffrey's politics and philosophy, Carlyle could not easily reject such an offer.[48] Thus, in May 1827, Carlyle "resolutely buckled" himself up "and set forth to the Parliament House for the purpose of seeing . . . the little jewel of Advocates." "I accosted him, and with a little explanation, was cheerfully recognised. 'The Article? Where is the Article?' seemed to be the gist of his talk to me; for he was to all appearance anxious that I would undertake the task of Germanizing the public, and ready enough to let me do it" as long as "I did not treat the whole Earth not yet Germanized as a 'parcel of blockheads'; which surely seemed a fair enough request."[49] Though he had never read a word that Carlyle had written, Jeffrey urged him to contribute to the *Review,* apparently having decided that if German literature were the young man's enthusiasm, it would be best to encourage him to write on that subject. He had no fear that Carlyle would succeed in "Germanizing" even a small corner of the earth, except perhaps the narrow Carlyle drawing room, which Jane, who was studying German again, somewhat proudly remarked "might now pass for a Sanctuary to Goethe."[50]

They walked together to the older man's lodgings, discussing "these matters." Though the June 1827 issue, already in the press, could not accommodate a substantial article introducing the reading public to German literature in general, there was space for "some little short paper." "Two days after, having revolved the thing," Carlyle met with Jeffrey again and engaged to do a brief essay on Jean Paul Richter for immediate publication and a long paper on German literature for the fall issue. At the same time, Jeffrey invited Carlyle to join him in his town activities at will and to visit him for long discussions at his new country house, Craigcrook, only a short walk from Comely Bank. Carlyle could hardly restrain his excitement.[51]

Carlyle's brief essay, ostensibly a review of a new life of Richter written in German, was an impressive debut, one that Jeffrey and some of the readers of the *Edinburgh Review* recognized as an occasion. Procter's high recommendation and the editor's generous gamble had been resoundingly confirmed, though some of the essay's implications were less than reassuring. Carlyle's extravagant claim for Richter's greatness could hardly be challenged by a reading public to whom his works were basically unknown, but the boldness of the claim implied a certain parochialism and insular ignorance among readers like Jeffrey, who prided themselves on the sufficiency of their educations and their culture. Carlyle, of course, was incapable of writing anything but disguised autobiography, and his Richter was thus, to a considerable extent, a self-projection. He claimed for Richter the perogatives of genius, originality, and independence of style and mind: "Genius has privileges of its own; it selects an orbit for itself; and be this never so eccentric, if it is indeed a celestial orbit, we mere stargazers must at last compose ourselves; must cease to cavil at it, and begin to observe it, and calculate its laws."[52] Jeffrey and other readers must have suspected that Carlyle was speaking as much for himself as for Richter.

The Whig reading public and Jeffrey, himself a competent versifier, could not readily accept Carlyle's claim that "a true work of art requires to be *fused* in the mind of its creator, and, as it were, poured forth (from his imagination, though not from his pen) at one simultaneous gush."[53] In addition, Carlyle's dismissal of the value of conventional biography implied that he did not share the Whig predilection for quantitative lives-and-letters or for well-laundered, official accounts of both greater and lesser men. While searching in the Advocate's Library for books, he had responded to the well-meant advice of "an *entire* blockhead" that he "cultivate the field of Biography" by assuring him that he would not; biography as a literary form would have to be substantially redefined before it could be a vehicle for his own genius.[54]

Carlyle, however, was more certain than his audience that "genius will reconcile men to much" and that Richter (and perhaps writers of similar originality) would eventually "be considered not a strange crack-brained mixture of enthusiast and buffoon, but a man of infinite humour, sensibility, force and penetration." In Richter's case, genius was a success story: "His writings procured him friends and fame; and at length a wife and a settled provision."[55] The very qualities, however, that had helped Richter attain such rewards, particularly his originality of style, were those that Jeffrey feared might make "friends and fame" less accessible to Carlyle. The final sentence of the essay, influenced by Richter's style but even more a product of Carlyle's own fascination with extended metaphor, concrete imagery, and rhetorical syntax, was both strange and challenging to an English audience: "In the moral desert of vulgar Literature, with its sandy wastes, and parched, bitter and too often poisonous shrubs, the Writings of this man will rise in their irregular luxuriance, like a cluster of date-trees, with its greensward and well of water, to refresh the pilgrim, in the sultry solitude, with nourishment and shade."[56] Some readers took unhappy notice that this was an uninvited pilgrim wandering in their wasteland.

Jeffrey, however, would not allow the pilgrim to wander away without support. Returning late in July from a visit to Templand, Scotsbrig, and Craigenputtoch, the Carlyles found they had a doubly valuable friend. Not only was he willing to support Carlyle, but at the same time he wanted both Thomas and Jane to become his regular social companions. Recognizing that they were both, to different degrees and for different reasons, somewhat shy and proud, he was not in the least embarrassed to pressure them. His meeting with Jane in June had been successful, characteristic of the fifty-year-old man's delight in female company. Forced to be quiet more often than not in her husband's presence, Jane responded immediately to Jeffrey's courtly compliments and his eagerness to hear her speak. "He became, in a sort," Carlyle wrote years later, "her would-be openly declared friend and quasi-lover; as was his way in such cases. He had much the habit of flirting about with women, especially pretty women, much more the both pretty and clever; all in a weakish, mostly dramatic, and wholly theoretic way."[57] His friendship with Jane encouraged Jeffrey to do even more for Carlyle, and he began to stop by at Comely Bank in the autumn to visit Jane on his way home to Craigcrook. Carlyle wrote that "Jeffrey's acquaintanceship seemed, and was for the time, an immense acquisition to me; and everybody regarded it as my highest good fortune."[58]

4·

Jane thought it would be a shame to settle for Craigenputtoch just when Edinburgh's attractions were expanding, partly through Jeffrey's assistance. His friendship, Carlyle later wrote, made the couple feel "as if no longer cut off and isolated, but fairly admitted, or like to be admitted, and taken in tow, by the world and its actualities."[59]

Soon after the return from Annandale and Dumfriesshire, Carlyle had dined with the notorious Edinburgh literary celebrity John Wilson. He had first seen this distinguished-looking eccentric walking on Princes Street in 1814. Carlyle's almost photographic memory for visual portraits had fixed the image of "a very tall strong-built and impetuous looking young man, age perhaps about 28, with a profusion of blond hair, with large flashing countenance of the statuesque sort, flashing pair of blue eyes, which were fixed as if on something far off . . . impetuously striding along, regarding nobody to right or left."[60] Under the pseudonym "Christopher North," Wilson dominated the pages of the Tory *Blackwood's Magazine,* chief rival of the *Edinburgh Review,* with his exuberant wit and satirical bonhomie. He was "alive to all high interests and noble objects" and to "any germ of talent or aspiration he might notice in that kind, among his pupils," and eloquently defied those who doubted that he was intellectually or morally qualified for the chair of moral philosophy at the university.[61] Ambrose Tavern was his favorite pulpit, whiskey punch his constant companion. For ten years Edinburgh had echoed with wild stories about Wilson, some of them exaggerated, gradually transforming him into a representative type—the "man of fine gifts and possibilities, who had recklessly squandered them all."[62]

An engaging talker with a compulsion to entertain, Wilson dominated his evening with Carlyle. Unlike Coleridge, Wilson was not a monologuist. He could create the illusion that he was responding to his listeners, primarily because he was able to manipulate them so effectively, constantly modulating his performance in regard to their response.

A marvelous public entertainer both in person and in print, Wilson applied his vivaciousness to personalities and anecdotes, using his learning as a footnote to his wit. He seemed to have neither ideas nor earnestness: "On serious speculative points he glided almost immediately into the sentimental; on practical or personal points, into the realm of quiz."[63] Fourteen glasses of whiskey punch had no more effect on him "than if you had poured them into an iron pump, which only kept volcanically talking all the same." Only toward morning, when the sun came up and the party considered dispersing, could one "perhaps notice that his complexion seemed as if getting half-perceptibly something of a grey-blue tinge intermingled; that the snuffy lip had a still more off-hand defiant look;—and, on the whole, that internally the temper was getting visibly a shade fiercer."[64] Wilson and Carlyle walked together as far as their common route took them, Wilson still talkative and convivial, Carlyle impressed with both Wilson's talent and his charm.

In fact, Carlyle hoped that he and Wilson would become friends. They met a number of times during the next year, sometimes fortuitously, often by arrangement, including Carlyle's attendance at one of Wilson's lectures and a visit by Wilson to the Carlyle home at Comely Bank. The earnest Victorian-in-the-making found himself curiously attracted to the Regency wit in decline, but Wilson did little to encourage Carlyle in his hope that they would see more of one another. He was essentially a private man whose very public mask was a guard against personal intimacies.

Wilson was also a shrewd judge of character, and he probably surmised that an attempt at friendship between himself and this aggressive young man would inevitably disappoint them both. In a short time, Carlyle concluded that Wilson was a wounded man whose excesses were compensation for frustrations, failures, and inconsistencies that could no longer be resolved, that this "big volcano of a man" was an unhappy Byronic figure, a grandiose ego, admirably talented but deluded into believing that he could be both Radical and Tory, provocateur and authority, wastrel and genius. "He hung together only like the whirlwind, like the smoke-cloud, by law of gravitation and impact."[65] Moving in a different direction, the Carlyles did not see Wilson again after the spring of 1828.

In November 1827 Carlyle met De Quincey, but again the relationship failed to prosper, mainly because Carlyle found more to pity than to admire in this man whose gentle sensibility was his only bulwark against desperate poverty and illness. Aware that he had written a critical review of Carlyle's translation of *Wilhelm Meister,* though unaware that Carlyle had found some of the review just and none of it offensive, De Quincey "grew pale as ashes" when Carlyle entered. "But we soon recovered him again," Carlyle recalled, "and kept him in flowing talk to a late hour. He is one of the smallest men you ever in your life beheld"—and such an ingenious, courteous speaker that Jane later remarked, " 'What wouldn't one give to have him in a Box, and take him out to talk!' "[66] He had "a most gentle and sensible face, only that the teeth are destroyed by opium. . . . It might soften a very hard heart to see him so courteous, yet so weak and poor; retiring *home* with his two children to a miserable lodging-house, and writing all day for the King of Donkies, the Proprietor of the Saturday Post."[67] Having used a word that he had recently coined, "*I-ety,*" meaning extreme egotism, to describe his new "acquaintance . . . almost . . . friend," Carlyle was pleased when De Quincey accepted his invitation to visit one Wednesday night in late November, and sat up "till midnight" with the other company. He agreed with Jack, who was on his way to Munich, that De Quincey is "an innocent man," unlike Wilson, "and . . . extremely *washable* away."[68] He tempered his genuine sympathy for De Quincey's misfortunes with the judgment that they were to some extent self-created, and apparently decided that it was better to have been De Quincey's acquaintance than to be his friend.

In contrast, the relationship with Jeffrey continued to intensify, their temperamental differences for the moment proving unimportant. Carlyle had perhaps been both attracted to and suspicious of the strong Byronic element in Wilson's personality, recognizing that for many years he himself had struggled painfully to control his Byronic side, the impulsive and sardonically isolated critic of himself and of humankind. There was nothing of Byron in Jeffrey, however; he was a practical, sober man who believed that the rules and regulations of good conduct and humane behavior should govern each man's sense of himself and his relationship with society. He took to Carlyle partly because he felt that here was a talent that, with proper regulation and cultivation, would make an important contribution to society.

Though Jeffrey had not yet gauged the extent of Carlyle's stubbornness or appreciated his idiosyncratic radicalism, he had correctly anticipated Carlyle's strong commitment to tradition and continuity. He did not have to read Carlyle's letter to Jack in the late summer to know that Carlyle believed that "culture is and continues the one greatest blessing which can fall to the lot of any man."[69] This commitment was a reaction against Radical-Toryism, another version of Byronic Romanticism, and an anticipation of the Victorian emphasis on "culture" rather than "anarchy." Carlyle believed that "light goes quicker than warmth: hence every new intellectual revolution, seems at first destructive to morality."[70] And Jeffrey had no doubt that, however original or even revolutionary some of Carlyle's attitudes might seem, all his efforts sprang from a constructive moral consciousness that fostered basically the same public standards of behavior as did his own. Emotionally, Byron and Wilson were anarchists; they advocated and practiced heterodox moral conduct. Carlyle and Jeffrey, though they would take very different paths, shared an ultimate vision of orthodox social stability.

In September 1827 Carlyle appealed to his new friend for practical assistance. A professorship had suddenly become available at London University, providing Carlyle's imagination with a serious alternative to Craigenputtoch. Jeffrey had recently helped Jack with money to spend a postgraduate year in Munich, and Carlyle hoped that Jeffrey would now help him by supplying a recommendation for the position in London. Jane found the prospect of a move to London particularly exciting. Carlyle believed that his own merits and Jeffrey's help ensured him a reasonable chance of appointment to a professorship in either English literature or moral philosophy. He was less aware than both Jeffrey and his London friends that his temperament and his opinions made him an unlikely candidate at a new university founded expressly to provide secular education compatible with the tenets of Whig rationalism and utilitarianism. Irving responded to his request for advice with guarded approval, since he himself disapproved of the university's basic irreligiosity. With some embarrassment, Jane attempted to explain to Mrs. Montagu, whose husband might have some influence on the decision, that Carlyle was not as inconsistent and contradictory as his sudden preference for the professorship over Craigenputtoch might make him seem. "Both," she claimed, "are solutions (by different methods) of the problem of living." Jane herself preferred to remain in Edinburgh, for "our dear little home here grows more attractive every day; all the conveniences both of town and country lie around it; and we have as good society as the place (indeed perhaps any place) affords."[71] Her second choice was London, her third Craigenputtoch, but her husband had now added the economic argument to his case for leaving Edinburgh. He maintained that either with a professional income in London or on reduced expenses at Craigenputtoch "one should be equally independent as to income: in the one case being placed *below* the necessity of *writing* for bread, in the other raised *above* it."[72]

When he had made his arrangements with Alick in the spring of 1827, this economic argument had not played an important role. But by early fall 1827 it was clear that Carlyle was willing, with a repressed, self-protective eagerness, to forego considerations of health and family for a settled position that conveyed distinction and salary, whether in London or anyplace in Britain, including Edinburgh. To assuage Alick's potential disappointment and his own anxiety, he feigned indifference and pessimism as he waited for Jeffrey to return to town and for Irving and Henry Duncan to respond to his requests for advice.[73] In a few days he learned that Henry Duncan felt that he could not recommend his young friend, whom he had helped before and desired to help again, unless he had assurances that Carlyle would teach a moral philosophy based on "a sincere faith in Christianity." Carlyle's awkward attempt to reconcile his beliefs with Duncan's Christianity was not successful, and Duncan responded, unhappily, that "your Christianity is not the Christianity of the Bible,—nor, I trust, of the 19*th* Century."[74] Duncan was apparently unaware that his sectarian standard was hardly relevant to a university whose founding principles and current trustees attempted to minimize religious qualifications of any sort. To the extent that Carlyle was aware of the university's materialistic principles he chose to ignore their incompatibility with his own spiritual beliefs as long as his appointment remained a possibility.

Jeffrey, however, did his best to deflate his new friend's hopes. With tactful honesty he told Carlyle that, despite his own influence and Carlyle's merit, his efforts on the young man's behalf were likely to fail. Jeffrey told Carlyle that he was seen as "a *sectary* in taste and literature, . . . inspired by some of the zeal by which sectaries are distinguished—a zeal, that is, to magnify the distinguishing doctrines of your sect, and rather to aggravate than reconcile the differences which divide them from the votaries of the Establishment, and I confess I doubt whether the patrons of the new University either will or ought to appoint such a person to such a charge."[75] Though Jeffrey had no doubt that "in all *other* respects" Carlyle "was qualified for the situation" and that he could recommend him "as a man of virtue, temper, genius, and learning," he also had to admit that Carlyle had damaged his academic qualifications through his close association with German literature and with what the readers of his article on Richter had begun to call the "mystic school."

Carlyle attempted to defend himself, straining against the charge and its consequences. Whereas he previously had counted the exoticism attached to his name an advantage, he now felt its disadvantage strongly enough to argue that there was nothing perjoratively "foreign" in his association with the "mystic school," which, in his view, existed only as a journalistic simplification. In the privacy of his notebook Carlyle wrote that every true poet must be a mystic in the sense of perceiving the highest spiritual truths, but in the "great" article on German literature which he was writing for the *Edinburgh Review* during September, he devoted considerable space to the admission that "there is in the German mind a tendency to mysticism" which should be "carefully guarded against." "It is a fault," he wrote, for mystics usually "either know not clearly their own meaning, or at least cannot put it forth in formulas of thought, whereby others, with whatever difficulty, may apprehend it."[76]

Though Jeffrey pressed Carlyle's qualifications on Henry Brougham and the other tough-minded Whigs whose power was making London University a reality, they were clearly not impressed. Somewhat naively, Carlyle sent Brougham a copy of "The State of German Literature," which, despite its clarifications about the mystic school, could only have confirmed Brougham's opinion that Carlyle was not the person for the position. In fact, as Jeffrey informed Carlyle, the position would probably be offered to Thomas Campbell, but only after some political fence-mending had been completed. This information enabled Carlyle to salvage much of his ego by emphasizing to himself and to others that the university had decided "to postpone the appointment of Moral Philosophy altogether."[77] Since Jeffrey "could not press the business" further, Craigenputtoch seemed an ever more likely destination.

Undoubtedly, Carlyle's enthusiasm for Craigenputtoch varied, reflecting his uncertainty as to the soundness of his motives. The lure of the isolated moors touched a real need, but one that was potentially regressive—a variant of the painful self-isolation he had suffered in the anxious years when he struggled to choose a vocation and to transcend his social inhibitions. Then too, Edinburgh life had its definite attractions, and turning his back on them might confirm some of his Edinburgh friends and Irving's London circle in their opinion that he was intractable, unassistable, and, indeed, "sectarian." Some of them also would feel personally hurt that he had elected to leave them. Indeed, though he attempted to disguise the depth of his disappointment, Jeffrey took Carlyle's decision to leave Edinburgh almost as personal rejection.

5.

During the winter of 1827–1828 and through the spring, his brother Jack in Munich sent many letters describing the "marvels of that strange land." Germany was much on Carlyle's mind both as a subject for his literary efforts and as a place to visit. "Mrs. C. and I have some thoughts of going thither next winter ourselves!" he wrote to David Hope.[78] "The State of German Literature" had appeared in October 1827 and was widely read, thereby establishing the prominence of his name among those interested in foreign literature. Through Procter's recommendation and Mrs. Montagu's intervention, William Fraser, who had recently visited the venerable Goethe at Weimar, solicited Carlyle to write for his journal, *The Foreign Review.*[79] Late in November Carlyle sent him an article on the German playwright Zacharias Werner, which appeared in the January 1828 issue, followed by two more articles, "Goethe's Helena" for April publication and "Goethe" for July publication, both finished at Comely Bank. The latter was an attempt to summarize the importance for modern European literature of a man who "was once an Unbeliever, and now . . . is a Believer; and he believes, moreover, not by denying his unbelief, but by following it out; not by stopping short, still less turning back, in his inquiries, but by resolutely prosecuting them."[80]

The fantasy of visiting Weimar as a winter refuge stayed alive for the next few years. But the news that Reverend Chalmers, now professor of moral philosophy at St. Andrews University, had decided to resign that position immediately dispersed thoughts of Weimar and got Carlyle busy pursuing this new prospect late in December 1827. He consulted with Jeffrey and other friends, and by the middle of January 1828 he had presented his formal candidacy. Not that Jeffrey or anyone else was particularly encouraging. John Martin of Kirkcaldy, who years before had recommended Carlyle to the Kirkcaldy school board, was doubtful, and Jeffrey frankly stated that merit would not determine the choice—the appointment was to be purely political. Nevertheless, Carlyle immediately solicited recommendations. He claimed that "between writing Wotton Reinfred in the Dunscore Moors, and teaching Moral Philosophy at St. Andrews, I would not at this moment make a choice, but rather leave Destiny to make it for me."[81] He wrote a flattering letter to Procter, eager to have his recommendation, and received commitments from David Brewster, John Leslie, Wilson, Irving, Buller, and Jeffrey. On the one hand, it was to be destiny's decision; on the other, Carlyle would try to give destiny a bit of a push.

The alternatives clearly involved more than financial considerations. He had £300 in the bank, plus interest due on the money.[82] If he were to go to Craigenputtoch, then he must certainly make plans for "a visit to Germany for the study of music and painting . . . and . . . six months (in an excursion from the Craig) at Weimar itself." Jack, after all, had already shown that it could be done on very little money. He wrote to Goethe, whom he assumed to be his trump card in this game of recommendations, and forthrightly asked him to support his candidacy. "The qualifications required, or at least expected, are not so much any profound scientific acquaintance with Philosophy properly so called, as a general character for intelligence, integrity, and literary attainment. . . . To the Electors personally I am altogether a stranger."[83] To his mother, who had visited Edinburgh for the first time during the last weeks in December and into the new year, he emphasized his independent strength of mind on the matter, though to Alick he actually confessed that, "on the whole, I think there is a chance."[84] He remained optimistic for a few months. But the impressive letters, all duly forwarded to the electors, did him no good and by March "the whole matter" had "evaporated." Goethe's letter arrived too late to help, but still served as a gratifying testimonial of the idol's high opinion of a man who "rests on an original foundation and has the power to develop in himself the essentials of what is good and beautiful."[85]

Though Jeffrey probably knew, certainly from experience if not as fact, that the appointment had been accounted for "long before [Carlyle] made any application," he did his best in a hopeless enterprise and pleaded with Carlyle not to "run away to Dumfriesshire, though this Temple of Glory and Science should for the present be shut."[86] Carlyle admitted that Edinburgh was "growing more and more a sort of home," but at the same time he felt that a trap was closing around him—" 'The *Prison* called *Life!*' "[87] In Craigenputtoch he could stretch his resources a little further and not have to write as quickly for money. More important, he might enjoy better health there. At other times, however, he admitted that the advantages of Craigenputtoch did not weigh very heavily in the balance. He was still trying to keep his options open.

Late in March 1828 he left Jane at Templand, where her aunt was dying, and went to Scotsbrig and then Craigenputtoch, where it seemed to him that the renovations and repairs were proceeding too slowly. Jane's aunt died early in April and, returning to Comely Bank from the funeral, the Carlyles discovered that the house had been let in their absence. Though there was something of accident in this there was also a purposeful passivity, for surely they must have suspected the possibility of what had now occurred. Almost with triumph, as if it were testimony that he had kept faith with his family, Carlyle announced to Alick, "The most important thing I had to say, is that *certainly* we *are* coming down to the Craig at Whitsunday first!" The letting of the house in their absence "of itself was sufficient to decide us."[88] To his mother, whose company he had enjoyed during his March visit, he wrote that they were coming down "to *neighbor*" her, and extended his blessing: "All good be with you, both now and forever! I am always, My Dear Mother's Son—Thomas Carlyle."[89]

Carlyle's Edinburgh friends, particularly Jeffrey, could hardly believe that it had actually come to this. Carlyle himself "had many doubts and misgivings about removing thither for the present" and took refuge in the thought that "no rational alternative remains."[90] He tried to convince Jack, who had doubts about the wisdom of the move, that there would be substantial benefits in the change. But Jack, with the cool judgment that distance brings, implied that the "sort of chance" that had produced this decision might not be chance at all. Jeffrey could not be brought to approve of the decision, but did all he could to speed the Carlyles on their chosen way by putting them up for a few days at Craigcrook while their luggage and household goods were in transit. He and others promised to visit Craigenputtoch shortly, no matter how inconvenient the journey.

[6]

"My Wild Moorland Home"
1828–1831

Life at Craigenputtoch, where the Carlyles ostensibly resided for six years, was no more isolated or lonely than rural life in general. Winter was the hardest period of the year, the warmer months alive with revivifying outdoor activities, visitors, and visiting. While a farm in Dumfriesshire might seem incompatible with the literary life to the urbane Jeffrey immediately and to Carlyle after a time, Jeffrey could not fully appreciate how much Carlyle was still the son of country parents nor could he understand the intensity of his emotional ties to the family circle. He had broken many sectarian restrictions but his return to the countryside represented, among other things, an attempt to strengthen these emotional bonds. And Dumfries, fourteen miles away, to which there were twice weekly visits for mail and other necessities, Templand, about the same distance, Scotsbrig about thirty miles, even Edinburgh, were all readily accessible except in the most brutal weeks of winter. Alick and his sister Mary "as a rule dined with us every Sunday, where was usually good talk or reading," and James and Margaret Carlyle, Grace Welsh, all of Carlyle's sisters and brothers, including Jack when he finally returned from Germany in the spring, repeatedly visited for days and even weeks at a time.[1] And though there were no educated companions close by, peasant neighbors and their Craigenputtoch servants, of whom there were six at the beginning—including an indoor maid, a dairy woman, an outdoor farm woman, a farmhand, and a young sheepherder, mostly under Alick's management naturally—created a daily atmosphere of human substance, populating a quiet world with lonely people.

Craigenputtoch. Photograph by J. Patrick. By permission of the Edinburgh University Library.

From the outset, Carlyle intended to relieve the isolation of life at Craigenputtoch with long excursions to Edinburgh, London, and even Weimar during the difficult winter months, not to speak of summer visits in various directions. The visit to Weimar never occurred. Of the six years at Craigenputtoch, two winters were spent in more social locations, a nine-month visit to London in 1831–1832 and a four-month residence in Edinburgh in the winter and spring of 1833. The move to Craigenputtoch had had a temporary cast from the beginning. When he left for London in the summer of 1831, Carlyle was eager to consider alternatives and had already at some intuitive level made up his mind that his country interlude was over. The London experience confirmed his intuition.

With Carlyle, Jeffrey good-humoredly but seriously complained, everything had to be in the grand gesture, exaggerated, immensely serious. "But you will never persuade anybody that the regulation of life is such a mighty laborious business as you would make it, or that it is not better to go lightly through it, with the first creed that comes to hand, than to spend the better part of it in an anxious verification of its articles."[2] Urging him to write, Jeffrey teasingly reminded him of the practical facts of life, unable to allow his affection for his friend to overwhelm completely the sting of Carlyle's implied rejection of their shared world of finely tuned mutual interests which could only be advanced through cooperation and compromise. Made uneasy by Carlyle's self-assertiveness, Jeffrey tried to increase Jane's identification with his own attitude by tactfully drawing to her attention what she already knew, that Carlyle as a "man of energy who expects to make discoveries . . . and to acquire dominion over them" was more likely to be hard on a wife who desired to be happy than was a man like himself who believed that an easygoing passivity would produce harmonious relations between people.[3] Carlyle's parents' voices, never hesitating to remind him from childhood on that life is indeed "a mighty laborious business" in preparation for eternity, had provided him with a "first creed" that he could not reject, no matter how much Jeffrey contradicted it, no matter how he himself transformed it. Jeffrey's message, that "you have no mission upon earth . . . half so important as to be innocently happy," could only be dismissed by Carlyle as sheer nonsense at best.

Before leaving Craigcrook in May 1828 Carlyle had agreed, at Jeffrey's request, to do a review-article on Burns immediately and an article on Tasso for later publication. He was in the enviable position of having an editor who solicited him on topics that were known to interest him and who paid him handsomely. While Jane was making her peace, as best she could, with her new place of residence, Carlyle finally got to work in what he affectionately called his "Devil's Den" on the first of the two essays.[4] While Jane was ill in August, her husband was "very busy," taking exercise on his horse and hurrying with his essay on Burns in order to meet Jeffrey's lightly imposed deadline. Aware that he was obliged to him for his kindness as an editor, Carlyle was grateful but uneasy that Jeffrey had recently offered to lend him money, suggesting he could use it as he wished (though preferably to facilitate a return to Edinburgh). Carlyle was morbidly afraid of being in debt to anyone, and had already chastised his brother John for too freely accepting the hospitality of Baron David D'Eichthal in Munich. Not to stand completely on one's own two feet economically was to lose one's independence and manhood. But at least, he noted, "Jeffrey *shall* have his *Article* at the appointed time. That wonderful little man is expected here very soon. . . . He takes no little interest in us; writes often, and half hates half loves me with the utmost sincerity."[5]

Early in October 1828 Jeffrey arrived at Craigenputtoch with his wife and his daughter Charlotte, as well as his "lapdog and maid." The "Duke," as Jane affectionately called him, walked with his family through the mud of the uncompleted road and was greeted with the honor and affection due a kind family friend. Around a roaring fire in the sitting room Jeffrey was at his conversational best, talking "from morning till night, nay till morning again."[6] In his own house, surrounded by a world that he believed secure and a reflection of his own values, Carlyle was at his most sociable, appreciating the effort that Jeffrey had made and the sincerity of his commitment to his friends.[7]

While the good weather lasted, through the summer and fall of 1828, visitors came: William Graham, Carlyle's old Glasgow friend who lived in the region, Henry Inglis, a young and solicitous admirer who asked Carlyle for guidance and advice on life and letters, Jane's uncles and aunts, and even Grace Welsh, who was constantly ill in minor but troublesome ways and irked by her obligations to her irritable, elderly father. Late in November, James Carlyle spent a week at Craigenputtoch with his two sons, daughters, and daughter-in-law.[8] The presence of such visitors seemed to confirm Carlyle's beleaguered assertion that he and his wife could sustain a productive and balanced life at Craigenputtoch. Jeffrey's constant plea that the Carlyle's return to civilization was undercut by the very acts of friendship which brought him and others to visit.

The most persuasive outer voices, those of Carlyle's family, had a vested interest, of course, in the couple's remaining. Much of the capital for Alick's livelihood had come from his admired older brother, whose support and company he could spare only at great loss. Constant visits to Scotsbrig intensified for parents and son the value of their closeness. Indeed, by the next winter Jane quietly complained that her husband rarely seemed even to think of inviting her on those visits, as if he felt the bonds of marriage did not quite equal family ties in importance.[9] Jack's "rage for travelling," like a disease that needs cure, though it angered his eldest brother and deeply worried his mother, united the family in the earnest plea that he give up this foreign folly and return to Annandale.[10] "My first thought each morning," he wrote from Vienna, "is about my 'two homes' in Scotland, and the far-off friends who still love me in spite of all my follies." Feeling guilty for, among other things, his long absence from the family circle, Jack pledged to his mother that he would "not be led astray into vice by the temptations around" him. "The first thing I do on waking . . . is to read two chapters of the Bible according to the promise I made you at parting."[11] By inference, his medical skills were also needed at home, where the family was brought even closer together by the eldest daughter's serious illness.[12]

But the inner voice also spoke loudly. Carlyle's introspective Protestant self-consciousness created a special drama of the inner life which proudly assumed that the central concern of man was to come to terms in his own conscience with his emotions, beliefs, and aspirations. If "space is a mode of our Sense," then Craigenputtoch, whatever its external physical appearance, should be no more than an extension of the moral and imaginative strength of its inhabitants. And if "Time" also is a "mode of our Sense," a proposition that Carlyle admitted he was attracted to without quite understanding it, then "this solid world, after all, is but an air-image; our *Me* is the only reality, 'and all is Godlike or God.' "[13] This was an attitude toward Craigenputtoch that Jeffrey was unlikely to understand or to sympathize with. In a moment of self-flattery, Carlyle affirmed his mistaken belief that "this position at Craigenputtoch [is] quite an original one for a Philosopher and lover of Literature." He quite aptly identified his feelings with his reading of one of the quintessential English Puritan public myths. We are, "as it were, a sort of Crusoe's Island, where the whole happiness or sorrow depends on the Islander himself."[14]

When Jeffrey left after his three-day visit in October, expecting to receive the revised proofs of Carlyle's article on Burns shortly, he had gotten the Carlyles' promise that they would soon return his visit. As the Jeffreys were deparing, Carlyle "sorrowfully" said to them that they were carrying "off our little temporary paradise."[15] No doubt Jeffrey hoped that a winter at Craigenputtoch would encourage his friend to seek a more permanent paradise someplace else. Editor and author actually had been on their best behavior throughout the visit, alert to the strain placed on their relationship by a difference of opinion as to whether an earlier draft of Carlyle's article on Burns needed shortening and revision. Jeffrey had found it "distressingly long . . . and . . . *diffuse*." He conceded that the "noble strain of sentiment, and kind and lofty feelings, and much beauty and felicity of diction" outweighed the mystical "jargon" and the straining to defend dubious positions with exaggerated rhetoric. But he wished "to God" that Carlyle would "fling away these affectations, and be contented to write like [his] famous countrymen of all ages."[16] The material that would print to sixty pages had to be reduced to forty-eight, and Jeffrey, mainly by eliminating quotations from Burns's poetry in the early section, sent back the proofs of a shortened manuscript.

Though first inclined to withdraw the article, Carlyle shortly thought better of it. Disguising his "indignation," he wrote to Jeffrey in a manner that the editor thought "frank and goodnatured," assenting to the "proposed mutilation." Carlyle sent the proofs back in "a kind of publishable state" but with the "private persuasion" that "probably I shall not soon write another for that quarter."[17] Ten years later, when the essay was republished by the author himself, he did not reinsert the deleted material.

The Carlyles protected themselves with an effective routine during the first winter in Craigenputtoch. Though they continued their visits to Dumfries, Scotsbrig, and Templand, except during impassable conditions when "we bolt the door against Frost, and utterly defy him with blazing fires," Carlyle found satisfaction and self-sufficiency in his long day's work on various essays for Jeffrey and for the *Foreign Review.* Rapid exercise either cutting trees or galloping on his horse late in the day, learning Spanish and reading *Don Quixote* in the evenings with Jane, and conversations with Alick and Mary at night kept him alert.[18] "The stillness of these moors" seemed preternatural. Though the "solitude . . . is not to be equalled out of Sahara itself," he boasted that his wife "too is happy, and contented with me, and her solitude," though the cold got into her bones and she developed mysterious coughs, sniffles, and weaknesses.[19] His own health seemed "better . . . not worse," though still not good enough for him to consider himself normal.[20]

Though they could not escape to Weimar, perhaps a variant of Weimar could come to them. They urged De Quincey to visit, entertaining themselves with a proposal to De Quincey that they found "a sort of Colony here, to be called the 'Misanthropic Society' . . . each to have his own cottage . . . so that each might feel himself strictly an individual . . . but the whole Settlement to meet weekly over coffee; and . . . hurl forth their defiance, pity, expostulation, over the whole universe civil, literary, and religious." If De Quincey would "come hither, and be king over us; *then* indeed . . . the 'Bog School' might snap its fingers at the 'Lake School' itself, and hope to be one day recognised of all men." What was missing, then, were the Edinburgh Wednesday nights at home.[21] They were not to be overvalued, however, and Jane, with little besides make-work to do, still hardly complained. Her commitment to her husband was unswerving. While at Templand on a Christmas visit she thought about him "every hour every moment," wondering if he were restless at night, "wandering about 'on on' smoking and killing mice. . . . I love you and admire you like—like anything." By early March 1829 the hills were "all gleaming like Strombolis or Aetnas, with the burning of heath," and Jack had returned from Vienna, welcomed as eagerly as the warm weather.[22]

Though mid-winter "biliousness" had attacked Carlyle briefly, mainly because of the pressure he felt to write more review-articles, he had recovered sufficiently to write during the spring on Voltaire and Novalis for the *Foreign Review* and on "Signs of the Times" for the *Edinburgh Review,* the more widely circulated and better-paying of the two journals. He had retreated from his half-vow never to submit to Jeffrey again. More effective than any of his previous articles, disguised neither as review nor as literary analysis, "Signs of the Times" focused directly on contemporary England and the modern Englishman, without (much to Jeffrey's approval) any ostensible references to the German pantheon and foreign philosophies. Ironically, Jeffrey preferred Carlyle's Romantic organicism, which directly attacked the mechanism of the Whig and utilitarian world view, to the "desperate darkness of wilful and audacious mystics."[23]

In a strikingly calm, controlled, and precise manner Carlyle argued for a balance between the dynamical and mechanical in an age in which the mechanical was now dominant and in which the spiritual basis of the most important achievements of Western culture had been obscured by substituting external machinery, institutional structures like government and mass media, for underlying "spiritual Truth." Fascination with material and mechanical surfaces—with "physical power"—threatened to perpetuate the self-delusion that refused to admit that ultimately spiritual truth was the basis of all power and that "self-denial [was] the parent of all virtue."[24] Carlyle thought political revolutions such as the French made a positive contribution in rejecting the regressive and mechanical political structures of the eighteenth century. But political freedom was not enough, and revolutions that did not lead toward individual *inner* reformations had failed to do their most important work. With an optimism that Whig circles would find redemptive, Carlyle maintained that the widespread signs of unhappiness, discontent, and turmoil were evidence that "doubtless this age also is advancing." Later, he would emphasize the assumption that things would have to get a lot worse before they got better, a position too millennial and apocalyptic for sober editors and politicians. "Nay, after all, our spiritual maladies are . . . chains of our own forging, and which ourselves also can rend asunder."[25]

2.

Such Romantic Protestantism, unfortunately, had its tragic mirror image in Edward Irving's public preaching, which in June 1829, the very month that "Signs of the Times" was published, attracted large crowds in Annandale and Dumfriesshire. Irving had recently, in fact, published a hortatory apocalyptic pamphlet, the title of which, *The Signs of the Times,* he took from the New Testament.[26] Carlyle had seen Irving the previous May before leaving Edinburgh, and was uneasy on his account. He was certain that the notoriety created by the frenetic excesses of preaching and prophecy in which his old friend was indulging would put him even more out of favor with the authorities and the established church.[27] Though larger than life to his admirers, Irving put Walter Scott "in mind of the devil disguised as an angel of light, so ill did that horrible obliquity of vision [Irving's squint] harmonize with the dark tranquil features . . . resembling that of our Saviour in Italian pictures, with the hair carefully arranged in the same manner."[28] Irving

Edward Irving. From a drawing by A. Robertson. Reprinted from A. L. Drummond, *Edward Irving and His Circle* (London, n.d.).

had already become the center of a group of organized religious enthusiasts, separate from the National Church of Scotland, who believed that they had been granted special prophetic powers and that the day of judgment was imminent. His eloquent public harangues on sinfulness and the need for immediate redemption were fascinating entertainments for the curious, and their rhetoric had the power to move the simple. Irving's public mystique had increased even further as the result of a "horrible accident at Kirkcaldy" where "the kirk [church] fell and killed eight and twenty persons," which in James Carlyle's eyes was the result of Irving going " 'up and down the country . . . *screaching* like a wild bear.' "[29]

Irving stopped at Craigenputtoch in June 1829, dining with other clergymen and Carlyle at the home of the local parish minister. He stayed two nights, wandering through "the safe green solitudes" in the "beautiful summer weather" with Thomas, Jane, and John Carlyle.[30] One day later Thomas accompanied his old friend to Dunscore, heard him preach one of his more restrained, though "flowingly" sincere, sermons, and said good-bye to him the next day at Auldgirth Bridge, where Irving caught the coach to Glasgow.

Carlyle saw Jeffrey again early in August in Dumfries.[31] Tired of many things and suffering from a general deterioration of health, Jeffrey had just resigned as editor of the *Edinburgh Review* and was about to assume a full-time political career. He had been flattered at his recent unanimous election as dean of the Faculty of Advocates. Whatever Carlyle's reservations about Jeffrey as an editor, he now felt uneasy, since the latter said nothing about the attitude of the new editor, Macvey Napier, toward Carlyle's work or about the proposal that Carlyle had made that he write an article on Luther, who was much on his mind. Napier seemed in no rush to ensure Carlyle's contributions. In the meantime, William Fraser of the *Foreign Review* pressed Carlyle to commit himself on Luther and other subjects. Fraser was even hospitable to Jack, who much needed the money, publishing his brief reviews of German travel and medical books and accepting his article on animal magnetism. Leaving Dumfries in the evening after a heavy downpour, the friends parted, after a pleasurable reunion, with the agreement that the Carlyles would come to Edinburgh in October and stay at Craigcrook.

Three weeks in Edinburgh and Haddington, much of it spent with the Jeffreys at Craigcrook, invigorated the Carlyles after a quiet summer. If not a small celebrity in his own right, Carlyle was at least sufficiently well known to attract even more attention than during his last months at Comely Bank and, since he did not complain, he probably enjoyed the attention and the social whirl. Though Jeffrey's hospitality was faultless, his tolerance of Carlyle's mannerisms and opinions broad, the visit ended less comfortably than it had begun, probably, as Carlyle later speculated, because he and Jane had stayed too long. Jeffrey's health was not of the best. The two men tended to argue, which was their usual method of communication. But the maintenance of the dialectic within the bounds of friendship depended heavily on Jeffrey's amiability and paternal tolerance, both of which had decreased somewhat. Jeffrey, in Carlyle's eyes intellectually shallow and spiritually mechanical, seemed always to address him as if he were speaking to a jury in a situation in which the value of an assertion depended on whether or not he could convince "fifteen clear-headed men" that it was true.[32] Carlyle found such an approach to life somewhat insulting and depressing.

Returning to Craigenputtoch late in October 1829, "after nightfall amid the clammy yellow leaves, and desolate rains," Jane attempted to put a good face on a less than promising winter.[33] But in fact this second winter and the ensuing events were devastatingly miserable for both the Carlyles. The particularly harsh weather shattered the equanimity that Jane had felt in the face of the elements the previous year.[34] The snow dazzled her eyes in the sunlight. "Oh for a sight of the green fields again or even the black peat-moss—anything rather than this wide waste of blinding snow! The only time when I can endure to look out (*going* out is not [to] be dreamt of) is by moonlight, when the enclosure before the house is literally filled with hares—and then the scene is really very picturesque—the little dark forms skipping and bounding over the white ground so witch-like!"[35] Utilizing his unexpected practical bent, Carlyle devised an improved form of removable spiked snowshoe for horses.[36] He seemed more proud of this invention than of his literary work, which went badly. Both of them felt sick that winter, Jane actually in bed much of the time, Carlyle on his feet but melancholy with complaints, partly the result of the distressing deaths and depressing funerals within a week of one another of an aunt and an uncle, laid in their graves "thro' the storm and snow" in "a wild and sad-looking scene." Jane's grandfather had a stroke. Mrs. Welsh hurt her back.[37]

In these distressing circumstances, invitations to Edinburgh friends like John Wilson were mere formalities, vain gestures that brought no visitors from the distance. The family circle lost an important member when Jack left Scotsbrig for Birmingham and London, encouraged to explore the possibility of opening a practice in rural Warwickshire or in Birmingham itself. His company was sorely missed, especially since he was the only family member with whom the Carlyles could talk about matters beyond the world of Annandale. Smoothing his brother's way into the London circle whose company he had once enjoyed may have left Carlyle less than content with his own position at Craigenputtoch. Letters came during this first year at Craigenputtoch from long-familiar London and Birmingham addresses. Mrs. Montagu, warmer in her letters than in person, shrewdly implied a contrast between the activities of London and the Carlyles' social isolation. She assured Jane, "The most popular person in London is the best listener—and I have served such an apprenticeship under Coleridge, that I shall advertize myself at so much an hour—to you I shall listen *gratis* when I am so happy as to hear your most welcome voice."[38]

By the middle of June it was apparent that the twenty-seven-year-old Margaret Carlyle was ill with cancer of the digestive organs. In Dumfries, where the family had brought her for more readily available medical attention, "the Doctor, who was unwearied in his assiduities, formed a worse opinion at every new examination." It was clear that she was terminally ill, "the whole of the lower bowel . . . in a state of decay, and the bowels generally as it were already dead." On Monday, June 21, Alick returned from Dumfries, depressed and pessimistic. Late Tuesday afternoon it was apparent that she was dying. About eight at night a messenger was sent on the four-hour ride to alert her brothers at Craigenputtoch to come immediately. Surrounded by "sympathizing relatives" and attended by the minister, she responded to her mother's plea for forgiveness "if she had ever done her anything wrong . . . 'Oh no, no, Mother, never, never,' earnestly, yet quietly and without tears. . . . About a quarter past ten . . . she . . . threw her head on the pillow, looking out with her usual look; but her eyes quickly grew bright and intense, the breath broke into long sighs, and in about two minutes, a slight quiver in the under lip gave token that the fight was fought, and the wearied spirit at its goal."[39] Alick and Thomas were awakened at about midnight by the knocking of the messenger. They left immediately for Dumfries, hoping to see their sister one last time. He would never forget "that solstice night with its singing birds and sad thoughts."[40] When they arrived at about four in the morning they "found her dead." Riding home at sunset, he was "so broken by emotions & fatigues . . . on getting into the *quite* solitary woods" that he "burst into loud weeping." He "lifted up" his "voice and wept, for perhaps ten or 20 minutes,—never the like *since*."[41] Even in the middle of July, her eldest brother was still dreaming of her almost nightly. In an attempt to protect himself from the pain created by the death of someone he loved, he tried to numb his feelings. If there were an afterlife they would meet again; if not, not; it was all in the hands of some divine force whose mystery would have to be respected. He wrote to Jack, who had decided not to return from London for the time being, that he did not feel "sorrow, for what is Life but a continual Dying?"[42]

But months before his sister's death he had complained to his distant brother, "O Jack, Jack I was never more tired, in my opinion, these seven years. I awoke at five—and swallowed" castor oil.[43] He worked regularly throughout the winter, but spent too many painful moments worrying about the value of his work and anxiously waiting for books to come from his correspondents in Edinburgh and London. "Writing is a dreadful Labour," he wrote, "yet not so dreadful as Idleness."[44] Ill at ease with the new editor of the *Edinburgh Review,* he could not have been surprised when Jeffrey confided that Napier "is more alarmed at your mystical propensities even than I am." The older man kindly offered to act as an intermediary, assuring him that Napier "is anxious to avail himself of your talents."[45] It was only partly true. Napier wanted little to do with him on German subjects; on other subjects, he was willing to give consideration only if the topics were cleared before submission. But when Carlyle suggested Napoleon as a topic, Napier turned him down; he was even more disinterested in Luther, whose complete works Carlyle was avidly reading and who seemed to him the most important modern European. Carlyle was further depressed by a shortage of ready cash; all his money was invested in the farm, which paid a disappointingly low return on both the capital and Alick's labor. Another article on Richter, written the previous fall, appeared in the *Foreign Review,* but the payment was slight and slow in coming.

In March 1830 the well-to-do Jeffrey had generously offered Carlyle a stipend of £100 per annum: "You would be more comfortable if you had more money, and I would be *much* more comfortable, and more happy, if you would take a little of mine."[46] But Carlyle could not accept the money, and blamed, to some extent, "a state of society . . . in which a man would rather be shot thro' the heart, twenty-times, than do both himself and his neighbor a *real ease!* How separate Pride from the natural necessary feeling of Self? It is ill to do; yet may be done."[47] If so, he could not effectively do it. But his own labors were not producing income. Still hoping to do an article on Luther for the *Edinburgh Review,* he entered into an agreement, through Fraser, to write a four-volume history of German literature at £100 per volume for a series on world literature being put out by a London publisher. He worked at this project in fretful spurts throughout the depressing winter of 1829–1830, hampered by the difficulty of getting books and by his own lack of interest in the undertaking. Though by the late spring the publisher had broken the contract, Carlyle stubbornly maintained that he did not regret the time he had put into it. In London Jack tried in vain to interest John Murray, the well-known publisher of Byron. Jeffrey offered to read the manuscript to see what he could do, but returned it with the judgment that no one would publish it, primarily because Carlyle had devoted too much space to early German literature. The general opinion was that the small market for books on things German had dried up.

The previous autumn the young writer had claimed that he had come to Craigenputtoch for "one reason" only: "That I might not have to write for bread; might not be tempted to tell lies for money."[48] But, in fact, he could not help but recognize that that was in fact precisely what he was doing, whether for an unreliable London book publisher or for the detestable periodicals. He was increasingly disgusted with himself for not undertaking some original work that would justify the sacrifices made in order to live at Craigenputtoch. Queried about a life of Goethe, he declined; instead he daydreamed about next winter in Weimar where he would write a life of Luther for independent publication rather than for a popularizing cabinet series of great men's lives for which a marginal London publisher had solicited him. "That Book of the great German Lion . . . shall be the best Book I have ever written."[49] Anticipating at the beginning what was to be his obsession in the end, he offered in response to the request that he write a life of Luther to do "the best single" one-volume biography of "the brave Fritz," Frederick the Great, and have it ready within a year.[50] Though he published some old odds and ends and had a new outlet in *Fraser's Magazine,* run by William Fraser's brother James, he was still short of ready cash. But what he most regretted was that he did not yet have a book of his own. Though he defended Craigenputtoch to Mrs. Montagu as a place where a man who has given up the foolish notion of happiness can indeed have many basic advantages, he excused his long silence with a poignant admission: "I meant to send you some outline of our way of life in this solitude, which were a Patmos, only that no Revelation is yet forthcoming."[51]

3.

Throughout the summer and autumn of 1830 Carlyle was an author in search of a book, unaware for the moment that what he sought was already in the process of arriving. In August he wrote to Goethe, his spiritual father-confessor, "When I look at the wonderful Chaos within me, full of natural Supernaturalism, and all manner of Antidiluvian . . . fragments; and how the Universe is daily growing more mysterious . . . I see not well what is to come of it all."[52] But he thought of himself as an artist whose time had come to create some work that embodied the "inspired function" of the artist as "Priest and Prophet," a depiction of the state of the human community which would dramatize the decline of spiritual values, communal harmony, and moral sensitivity while at the same time directing the world toward countervailing modes of mind and behavior. He confessed that "except writing from the heart and if possible to the heart, Life has no other business for me, no other pleasure."[53] He also wanted to create a book that would demonstrate his conviction that "the moral nature of man is deeper than his intellectual; things planted down into the former may grow as if forever."[54]

Carlyle was convinced that he could now see reality more clearly than ever before. His protracted apprenticeship had made him sensitive to the phases of life, the time for growth and the time for fruition. His parents had trained him to regard time and space as less than spirit and eternity. Scotland had taught him that physical survival under adverse circumstances could be managed without loss of spiritual and artistic vision. Margaret's tragic death brought his eyes upward from the wintry earth to the high summer stars; his intense pain was a vehicle for connecting earth and heaven, for asserting that in the mysteries that denied mechanism there was a central role for renunciation and continual struggle. In what seemed almost an optical miracle, the strength of his vision had increased so that he could see clearly what heretofore had been invisible or obscured in visible things. Thus, when he learned of Edward Irving's intensifying difficulties with the church, he hoped that the Scotch Kirk would expel him. The two friends might then join forces in a new church, "to see the world as it here lies visible and is, . . . [to] fight together, for God's *true* cause, even to the death! With one such man I feel as if I could defy the Earth."[55] Such a battle cry, if its rhetoric can be separated from the anguish of his sympathy with his friend's then desperate situation, suggests that by the late summer he had had enough for the time being of stoic acceptance and of solitary work.

Aware that there were as many redefinitions of "God's Truth," including Irving's and his own, as there were philosophies, economic interests, political values, and religious visions in a rapidly changing world whose traditional harmony had been shattered, he was only a little surprised when, in mid-July 1830, he received a packet of assorted material from the "Saint-Simonian Society" in Paris. Gustave D'Eichthal, a disciple of the French Utopian socialist who had preached social equality, equitable distribution of wealth, worker solidarity, and rule by the naturally meritorious, provided Carlyle with a number of books and pamphlets, among them Saint-Simon's bible for a new religion, *Nouveau Christianisme.* D'Eichthal, the most talented of Saint-Simon's young followers (who to Carlyle's delight turned out to be the nephew of the Baron David D'Eichthal, who had assisted Jack two years before in Vienna) had read "Signs of the Times." The Saint-Simonians thought they had found a kindred soul in England and, to some extent, they were right. Carlyle was flattered that they had read his essay and been impressed by it sufficiently to send him material and to hope that he would become the chief Saint-Simonian of England, using his influence and energy to spread the message of a new Christianity.

Certainly, the Saint-Simonians' assumption was understandable, for they knew nothing about Carlyle's personality and his general unwillingness to associate himself with groups in any but a tangential way. He saw himself, indeed, as an artist, not an organizer. By temperament he was not capable of being a disciple. But he did find their ideas attractive on the whole, not because they were original but because they agreed so strikingly with his own. The corrupt inefficiency and insufficiency of the current ruling class; the unacceptable exploitation of the agricultural and industrial poor; the need for structures of association between human beings based on spiritual rather than on class values; and the general sense that European society was on the verge of momentous changes, revolutions of the spirit as well as of the body politic—all were assumptions that Carlyle immediately recognized he held in common with these strange Frenchmen whose "gay" capital city he had been in five years before without any notion "that among the *Palais-Royals* and *Cafés et deux Billards* . . . there was an Apostolic Society, cherishing within it a New Religion."[56]

But much as he agreed that the eighteenth century was one of "Denial, of Irreligion and Destruction; to which a new period of Affirmation, of Religion, must succeed, if Society is to be reconstituted," he could not accept, could not even understand how the Saint-Simonians could accept, the key point of Saint-Simonian doctrine: that "God has returned to France in Saint-Simon, and France will announce the new God to the world."[57] To Carlyle, the Saint-Simonian analysis of what was wrong, like his own, even somewhat like Irving's, was "scientific," by which he meant accurate: mechanistic philosophy, utilitarian principles, corrupt social and economic arrangements were destroying spiritual values and communal well-being. But the Saint-Simonian prescription—a revival of Christianity, with Saint-Simon as a latter-day Jesus Christ—seemed, like Irving's revivalism, sheer folly. He could not understand how the moral precepts and the social doctrine of the Saint-Simonians could be called a religion, since there seemed to be no "SYMBOL OF SYMBOLIC REPRESENTATION" of divinity.[58] How could there be a religion without a god? And dead institutions certainly could not be revived. Old clothes could not be put on a new man. But the assertion that human beings must unite in a religious brotherhood seemed like an echo of his own mind. Despite Goethe's almost immediate advice that he keep his distance from these Saint-Simonians, Carlyle encouraged the correspondence. By December 1830 he had actually translated Saint-Simon's *Nouveau Christianisme* into English—an act of respect for his new friends.

Jeffrey, who had made an unexpected visit to Craigenputtoch in September, thought Carlyle's "Saint-Simonian" ideas about property and social equity nonsensical radicalism of which he had a "horror." Like the patient father of a bright but misguided son, he explained at length the grounds of his position. "It is only by protecting and assuring the right of *property*" that civilization has advanced from barbarism, incessant brutishness, and constant "animal subsistence."

> Your very rich man after all spends almost all his income on the poor, and except a very little *waste* of food among the servants and horses, is a mere distributor of his rents among industrious and frugal workmen. But if you ever touch his overgrown wealth . . . there is no stopping till *all* private accumulation or property is divided and made common, and with it all the advantages of working by large capitals destroyed. But this is as tiresome as mysticism.[59]

With the recent Whig elevation to ministerial power in London, Jeffrey had been offered and had accepted the position of Lord Advocate for Scotland, the government's chief administrator of Scottish affairs. He was about to be elected a member of Parliament. Carlyle, with one eye on the Saint-Simonians (and particularly on the revolution that had recently ended Bourbon rule in France) and the other on his own struggle to write an original book on the true sources of power, thought that power indeed came from other sources and did not share Jeffrey's view that the subject was "tiresome."

He had other contradictory experiences fresh in his mind, including Alick's failure to make a go of Craigenputtoch. It now appeared inevitable that "he could not keep this Farm any longer than Whitsunday" 1831. Alick could not afford to continue to work a farm whose proceeds were less than his minimal subsistence costs and his £200 per annum rent. The outlook was "nothing but loss and embarrassment on all hands."[60] The fault, Carlyle believed, was not in his brother but in the ruinously high rents for farms, "some thirty per cent too high."[61] That the three categories of workers he most respected and believed to be the bedrock of society—the craftsman, the farmer, and the artist—could not make a reasonable living out of their hard labor given the present constitution of society seemed to him sufficient evidence for his conclusion that "the perversities and misarrangements moral and physical of this best of all stages of Society are rising to a head; and one day, see it who may, the whole concern will be blown up to Heaven and fall thence to Tartarus, and a new and fairer era will rise in its room."[62]

If people would recognize that under the aspect of eternity no one has anything but temporary occupancy of property, a moral renovation would follow which would so soundly reject materialism and mechanism that indeed the issue of economic and social equity would inevitably be quietly resolved. He was quite clear what his own attitude would be on the matter: "I have no *Property* in anything whatsoever; except perhaps (if I am a virtuous man) in my own Free-will: of my Body I have only a life-rent; of all that is without my Skin only an accidental Possession."[63] His basic attitude toward what seemed a blind overemphasis on reform of the machinery of society, an approach that culminated in the Reform Bill of 1832, expressed itself in his commitment to "radical *inward* Reform."[64] Though he sometimes took positions on specific reforms of the machine (he was quietly in favor at this time of Catholic emancipation and also the Reform Bill) and in later years himself had suggestions to make, his radical but religious rhetoric sometimes allowed sharply different people and groups to imagine that he was in agreement with them, from utilitarian radicals on the one hand to Tory conservatives on the other.

With these issues much on his mind, "musing amid the pale sunshine" of October 1830, Carlyle wrote what he had at first intended to be an article. It soon seemed too long unless it were divided into two sections; and now, as he continued to write "with impetuosity" at "the strangest of all things," it appeared "as if it would swell into a Book." He told Jack it was "a very singular piece" that "glances from Heaven to Earth & back again in a strange satirical frenzy."[65] He called it "Teufelsdreck" (Devil's-shit) after its main character. He wrote assiduously each day until the afternoon and then walked contemplatively "in this meek pale sunshine . . . in this grave-like silence" in which "there is something ghostly; were it not that our meadows are of peat-bog and not of asphodel, and our hearts too full of earthly passions and cares, you might fancy it the abode of spirits, not of men."[66] Comparing London, "the noisiest, busiest spot on the Earth," with the private silence of Craigenputtoch, he felt a surge of confidence in himself and in his work: he had been right to come to Craigenputtoch, since "here, truly is the place for thinking . . . since I came hither I have seen into various things."[67] "Nevertheless" he had firmly made up his mind that "we are coming to London," perhaps this winter, depending on the progress of this book and whether or not he could earn sufficient funds from articles.[68]

By early November he had written to Fraser about publishing "Teufelsdreck" as two articles. The need for ready cash had overwhelmed his somewhat declining interest in expanding the material and the manuscript was soon on its way to London. He discussed with Napier the possibility of an article on Byron, which the editor declined. Encouraged by Jeffrey and unwilling to lose him as a contributor, however, Napier commissioned Carlyle to do a long review-article on a multivolume survey and translation of German poetry, which he sent off by late January with the suggestion that he write an essay on Jeremy Bentham. Carlyle felt deeply antagonistic to Bentham's rationalism and felt that he could write well on the subject, for like "the Devil" who "forever says No," "Bentham is a denyer, he *denies* with a loud and universally convincing voice: his fault is that he can *affirm* nothing, except that money is pleasant in the purse and food in the stomach, and that by this simplest of all Beliefs he can reorganise Society."[69] Having become aware that a too-exclusive identification of his name with German subjects might be damaging, he made it unmistakably clear to Napier that he wished to write on English subjects and confided to Jack that "there is no Periodical so steady [as the *Edinburgh Review*], the salary fair, the vehicle respectable."[70] In the meantime, he tried to dispose of sections of the uncompleted "History of German Literature" as separate articles, and shortly had the good fortune to place the chapter on the *Nibelungenlied* with John Bowring of the relatively new *Westminister Review.*

In the two months or more that had elapsed since he had sent Fraser the manuscript of his long "Teufelsdreck" article, Carlyle had changed his mind again about the structure and length most appropriate to his concept and decided that it must be a full-length book. Angry that *Fraser's Magazine* paid poorly and had a small circulation, particularly in comparison with the *Edinburgh,* he did not see why he should waste what he had tentaively called "Thoughts on Clothes" when, extended to book length, it might "produce some desirable impression on the world." He told Jack that if he had sufficient money, he would go to London immediately "and *see* what I could *see.*"[71] Since he did not, he would wait until he had completed his book.

Managing to survive in London on money borrowed from Badams and some meager income from writing, Jack acted as his brother's agent and retrieved the manuscript from Fraser, in complete agreement that a revised version of "Thoughts on Clothes" "would doubtless produce a great impression at present." Jack showed it to Irving, who agreed that "the first part seemed too long & too German" and "that there was perhaps too little action in proportion to the machinery employed . . . that you seemed to have poured out the rich flood of your own thoughts, without caring whether the reader might feel it possible to keep pace with you."[72] More than anything else, they both urged Carlyle to come to London, though Jack stressed Irving's argument that "one cannot make any thing by honest writing of books, but only by writing for Reviews."[73] But in London there would be a responsive forum for his talents, including his old students Charles and Arthur Buller, William Glen, a new friend of Jack's, and John Mill, James "India House" Mill's son, the author of those interesting Saint-Simonian articles on the spirit of the age which had caught Carlyle's attention when they began in the *Examiner* early in January. Sketching the rich variety and depth of London social and intellectual life, with accounts of old friends and new acquaintances, Jack assured his brother that, despite the degradation of literary life and the literary professionals who "are all hidebound and their thoughts . . . low and grovelling," he "would soon collect a number of young people who are striving after better things & without any guidance."[74] By March 1831 his own needs and such encouragement had had their effect. Having already frequently discussed leaving, the Carlyles now resolved that their new moral imperative demanded a new forum, "as if . . . I *ought* not to lie so buried in these times."[75]

To some extent the fulfillment of the resolution depended on money. Alick's prospects for the next year were dim. He had just married, and would shortly make Carlyle an uncle for the first time. While looking out for another farm, he might stay on at Craigenputtoch simply as a resident. As for Carlyle's own investment in the farm, some of it had been lost and what remained might best go toward helping Alick make a start somewhere else. Mary, who had married in December, had gone to live with her husband at Scotsbrig, at Margaret Carlyle's urging. The eldest son was actually "vexed" at his mother. Jack, feeling quite guilty about how much his own dependency had contributed to his eldest brother's situation and about his strong inclination not to practice medicine, considered becoming an army doctor. Carlyle asked him whether, while attempting to find a publisher for his book, he could earn enough to support himself by giving lectures, like Teufelsdreck, "on Things-in-General." Jack had nothing of his own to spare his eldest brother, but he urged him to come to London, "convinced . . . that every man of talent who has anything to say is sure of finding people to listen to him whatever dialect he may speak in."[76]

Snowbound for much of February 1831, Carlyle was restless until late in the month when his manuscript was returned. He began to revise and lengthen it, extending the biographical section dealing with the fictional professor's life and amplifying the sections on religion and society. By mid-March he thought he had the revised "First & Second Chapters down *perfect*."[77] He felt confident enough both in his working method and in the result to compliment himself and his mother by drawing on one of the favorite family metaphors, " 'it'll no loup out again'!"[78] He hoped to be done by June, though only about one-third of the manuscript was completed. Aware that he had more confidence in the writer and the work than in the reading public, he exhorted himself to push on toward completion, whether it would sell or not. "The buying and reading of it does not depend on me."[79] As Alick began to dispose of his stock, his eldest brother expanded his manuscript, writing daily in the fine June weather, and prepared his mother for the changes that were planned. The farm looked particularly lovely as he was preparing to leave it. But, he told Margaret Carlyle, he had to leave for the sake of his work. "I would desire nothing better could I fly away with the whole premises, and set them down somewhere about Highgate or Pimlico; and there find work."[80] His only stipulation to Jack about sleeping quarters in London was that there be "no Bugs and no noises about *midnight,* for I am pretty invincible when once fairly sealed. The horrors of nerves are somewhat laid in me, I think; yet the memory of them is frightfully vivid."[81] Probably his temporary sense of good health had more to do with his having overcome the "one true wretchedness, the Want of Work."[82] Anticipating the Victorian ethos for which he was to be such an effective spokesman, he found a temporary cure for many ills in losing himself in "action," though often the hardest work was getting himself to work at all.

4.

With the product of the most sustained and gratifying period of writing he had experienced, Carlyle left Craigenputtoch on August 4, 1831, "very high in the humour, and defiant both of the Devil and the World," assuring his mother that his spiritual interests and values were identical with hers. Jane cried herself to sleep when the sounds of the carriage wheels "could no longer be heard."[83] When and whether she would join him depended on his estimation of his prospects after a few weeks or a month. This was an exploratory visit, not a commitment to stay. He took the boat overnight to Liverpool, where he spent the weekend at the home of Jane's uncle, observing the bustling "dismembered aggregate of streets and sandpits."[84] He arrived by coach on Tuesday, not at the Angel Inn in Islington, where Jack was waiting for him, but on the opposite side of town, for "there are men in Liverpool who will *book* you to go by any coach you like, and to enter London at any place and any hour you like; and then *send* you thither by any Coach or combination of Coaches *they* like."

After a happy reunion with his brother, he went immediately to see Jeffrey, who advised that the first publisher he try be John Murray. Carlyle had already heard the rumor that Murray was "a dilatory, imperative, unmanageable sort of fellow," inclined to cooperate with the powerful and not so much as provide "a civil or even definite answer" to anyone else.[85] Still, since he had a note from the influential Lord Advocate which stated that its bearer was "a genius and would likely become eminent," Murray was well worth a try. On his second attempt that same day he found the publisher in. After some discussion—in which the author indicated that he was pressed for time and "anxious that his decision should be given soon"—he agreed to deliver his manuscript the next day.[86] Murray promised an answer by the following Wednesday.

More likely than not, Murray, "a tall squinting man; not of the wisest aspect," would have published his long essay on clothes had Carlyle been more clever in his use of Jeffrey's influence and in his own handling of the negotiations.[87] Having immediately confessed to Murray that he was in London only because he was in a great rush to dispose of the manuscript, he should not have been surprised that the publisher became even more dilatory than he might ordinarily have been. Macvey Napier had warned the young author that widespread preoccupation with political reform made this an "unpropitious period for the disposal of literary wares," but Carlyle nevertheless rushed like an over-eager seller into a wary buyer's market.[88] Though he did take Napier's warning seriously, especially since it was seconded by others, his strategy for approaching and convincing a publisher did not in the least reflect any concession to these conditions. He wrote to Goethe that "the whole world here is dancing a Tarantula Dance of Political Reform, and has no ear left for Literature." Nevertheless, he assured Goethe that he would do his "utmost" to get the work published, for it "was meant to be a 'word spo[ken] in season.' "[89] Jeffrey himself was optimistic, with good reason, that Murray would agree to publish, though he had not yet himself read any of the manuscript. One of the most successful of current London publishers, Murray seemed less interested in literature than in politics and less interested in literary judgments than in diplomacy and courtesies. Jeffrey's influence, combined with the argument that the book represented a radical though eccentric word "spoken in season," might have been sufficient to commit Murray to the volume.

On the following Wednesday Carlyle found the publisher out, the "Dog of a Bookseller gone to the country."[90] After haranguing the clerk, who suggested that his employer would write to the eager author shortly, he left his card and insisted that he would return in the morning. Though warned that Murray had a reputation for "procrastination; but also for honorableness, even munificence," the impatient author, his Annandale accent and excited manner demanding attention, attempted to confront the publisher the next day. He

> was first denied to me, then showed his broad one-eyed face, and with fair speeches signified that his family were all ill, and he had been called into the country; and my Manuscript—lay still unopened! I reminded him, not without emphasis, of the engagement made, and how I had nothing else to do here, but see that matter brought to an end: to all which he pleaded

> hard in extenuation, and for 'two or three days' farther allowance. I made him *name* a new day: 'Saturday first'; then I am to return and hear how the matter stands. I begin to fear this Blockhead will spin me out into still longer delays.[91]

More expert at dealing with people and situations than with literary judgments, Murray probably sensed both Carlyle's vulnerability and his antagonism. His insistence that he have an answer in three days must have struck the publisher as both presumptuous and ludicrous, though it did not in the least ruffle his good manners or, for the moment, influence the decision—angry authors, after all, were of much less concern than influential patrons. When Carlyle appeared at Murray's office on Albemarle Street on Saturday, the publisher "as usual was not in; but an answer for me: my poor Teufelsdreck wrapped in new paper, with a Letter stuck under the pack thread! I took with a silent fury, and walked off."[92] Though he initially must have assumed that it was a rejection, he shortly discovered that it was no more than another delay in which Murray admitted that he had not yet read the manuscript, since "all his Literary friends were out of town" and "he himself occupied with a sick family . . . but that if I would let him keep it for a month, he would *then* be able to say a word, and by God's blessing a favorable one." Walking through Regent Street, the manuscript under his arm, he "looked in upon James Fraser," who offered to publish the book if the author would pay "*him* a sum not exceeding £150 sterling."[93] As much depressed as angry, "yet in the mildest terms taking leave of Fraser," Carlyle walked back to his lodgings, carrying "Teufk" openly in his hand, "*not* like a gentleman."[94]

With a letter of introduction which Napier had provided, he went the same day to Longman, Rees, & Co., who agreed to look at the manuscript and return it within two days, "honest, rugged, punctual-looking people" who "will keep their word; but their chance of *declining* seems to me a hundred to one."[95] His assessment was correct; the manuscript was promptly returned, " 'notwithstanding the high ability.' "[96] He now turned to Jeffrey, who had offered to read the manuscript, though Carlyle felt that his friend's intense involvement with politics would not allow him the "leisure" to be of assistance. Though he had sufficient ready cash, the £100 would last the year and no more, whether in London, Edinburgh, or Craigenputtoch. The time was rapidly approaching when he and Jane must make a decision about their residence. Each desperately missed the other, Jane being particularly vulnerable in her isolation at Craigenputtoch, where friends' efforts to entertain her were almost as dispiriting as Alick's arriving drunk to take her home from a visit to Templand. Carlyle had based his hope that he and Jane would spend a secure winter in London on his expectation of an immediate publication contract for "Teufelsdreck,"—something that now seemed all but impossible. And he was quite right to think that Jeffrey's and Montagu's efforts to get him a government position would come to nothing.

Jeffrey's response to his manuscript did nothing to lift the author's spirits. Having read about twenty-eight pages, the advocate found it tough going, but he "very much admired the scene of the sleeping City."[97] He asked for more time and promised to write to Murray, who probably had thought himself off the hook when he returned from the country to find that the impetuous author had declined to leave the manuscript for the month. Jeffrey now arranged to meet with the publisher to settle it one way or another. Stubbornly responding to delay with a defensive retreat of his own, Carlyle had decided for the moment that, if no publisher would provide him with a profit for the book, since it was so important to have the timely word spoken in season when it had a chance of attracting attention, he would agree to forgo *all* payments or royalties. Within the month, Jeffrey had worked two wonders. Through his introduction and recommendation, Jack was offered the position of traveling physician to the Countess of Clare, an Irish Catholic "of rank and wealth" in her middle thirties who had recently separated from her husband. His salary was to be a handsome £300 per annum.[98] And, as Carlyle wrote to Jane, who had already accepted her husband's invitation that she join him in London for the winter, whether he published or not, Jeffrey had elicited from Murray an offer to "print a small edition (750 Copies) of *Dreck,* on the half-profits system (that is I getting *nothing,* but also *giving* nothing) after which the sole Copyright of the Book is to be mine."[99] Murray probably had read little or none of the manuscript, responding entirely to Jeffrey's pressure and deferring to the widespread opinion that his prospective author was a genius of great originality.

Though granting that these conditions were much better than having to pay anything out of his own rather bare pocket, the young author went immediately to see if another publisher, Colburn and Bentley, might offer better terms. Unlike Longman, Colburn did not even have to glance at the manuscript in order to come to a decision. Receiving an unequivocable denial of interest that night, Carlyle immediately wrote to Murray "to accede to" terms that had been offered and suggested November as "the best season" for bringing it out.[100] Though contemptuous of Murray, "the slipperiest, lamest, most confused unbusinesslike man I have seen," he met with him the next week, settled the agreement, and was sent off by the publisher to deliver the manuscript "to his printer."[101] Acknowledging that Jeffrey's efforts had been successful, he admitted to Jane that he felt somewhat guilty that he had "a certain despicable tendency to think crabbedly of the poor Duke," whose company seemed less attractive, mainly because, against all reason, he felt "merely as if he were not kind enough to *me.* Is he not kinder than most other men are? Shame on me!"[102] Jeffrey having already done him considerable good, Carlyle now concluded that, given their differences, "it becomes more and more clear to me that we shall never do any good together." He confessed to Jane, with resonances of Margaret Gordon's advice to him over ten years before, that he needed her help so that he might learn "to be a little softer, to be a little merciful to *all* men." Such stubborn and willful contempt for others could not be excused on the grounds of poverty and ill health. "Why should a man . . . let Satan have dominion over him?"[103]

Within a week Carlyle was self-destructively furious at Murray again. The publisher had somehow learned that the manuscript had been rejected by Longman and perhaps had also discovered that Carlyle had approached Colburn and Bentley just a few days before he and Carlyle concluded their own arrangements. Since there was now solid evidence that his competitors had turned it down, perhaps on the basis of a substantive evaluation of the manuscript's quality and salability, Murray felt it necessary to protect both his pride and his investment by soliciting an expert literary opinion from a disinterested party. Consulting only with Jack, who supported and reinforced his brother's response, Carlyle sharply answered Murray's new stipulation by defending his own conduct as needing no defense, and concluded: "If you mean the Bargain, which I had understood myself to have made with you, unmade, you have only to cause your Printer who is now working on my Ms., to return the same without damage or delay, and consider the business as finished."[104]

Murray may not have been surprised at the response. Indeed, he may have anticipated, without regret, that the author might prefer self-assertion to negotiation. He had no reason to publish the manuscript other than to please Jeffrey and to gamble that at some future time Carlyle's "genius" would provide profits—a risk that he had no special need to undertake. Carlyle wrote brazenly to Jane, "I shall give Murray perhaps another chance, if he be eager for it," but did not consult Jeffrey, from whom the publisher may have expected to hear on Carlyle's behalf.[105] Such a negotiation might have been resolved in Carlyle's favor. Murray had a keen sense of the value of having the Lord Advocate obliged to him, and Jeffrey undoubtedly would have done his best to help. Instead, the author offered "cheerfully" to release Muray "from all engagement . . . with me. . . . The rather as it seems reasonable . . . to expect some higher renumeration for a work that has cost me so much effort, were it once fairly examined."[106] If Murray wanted an expert opinion on the manuscript, then Carlyle now wanted the payment that he believed his labors deserved anyway. If Murray wanted to create tests, then he wanted a monetary reward for passing them. Carlyle, of course, had already almost given up on the possibility of publication: "Dreck cannot be disposed of in London at this time."[107]

Bitter that he had been made to cool his heels in the anterooms of power, he immediately demanded that Murray open up new negotiations with a fixed timetable that would allow him to judge "whether the limited extent of my time will allow me to wait yours" (Carlyle had, of course, already committed himself to stay in London through the winter). "If not, pray have the goodness to cause my Papers be returned with the least possible delay."[108] The publisher must have marveled at how touchy and unwise a man he was dealing with. Had Carlyle politely insisted that a bargain was a bargain and sent Jeffrey around to smooth the troubled waters, the result might have been entirely different. Though he soon persuaded himself that the inhospitable political climate and reform obsession had made it impossible for him to publish his manuscript in 1831–1832, his personality in fact had more to do with the failure of his single best opportunity than did any external causes. Like a shrewd diplomatist, Murray did not return Carlyle's manuscript to him immediately but sent it to an "expert" reader, who revealed the mixed nature of his literary intelligence by asking whether the work was a translation and at the same time praising the author's talent and knowledge. The reader, probably John Lockhart, the editor of the *Quarterly Review,* chose to say nothing about the book's revolutionary style and message. But, like Jeffrey on another, more friendly level, he concluded what Murray must have taken some mischievious satisfaction in reading and passing along to Carlyle at the beginning of October 1831: "The Author has no great tact: his wit is frequently heavy; and reminds one of the German Baron who took to leaping on tables, and answered that he was learning to be lively."[109]

It was all Murray's fault, the supportive Jane assured Margaret Carlyle. He "has lost heart lest it do not take with the public and so like a stupid ass as he is has sent back the manuscript."[110] In some of the later editions of *Sartor Resartus,* the title that he gave the manuscript before it was finally printed two years later, Carlyle perversely included this letter of evaluation, as if it were a medal of honor or purple heart, a dramatization of his victory over repressive external forces. In the meantime, within a few days of Jane's eagerly awaited arrival in London and Jack's departure for the Continent with his generous employer, he put the manuscript away in a drawer. Though there seemed no hope "of place or promotion" for him in London, except perhaps by lecturing, he still felt "disposed to believe" that he "ought to lift up" his "voice among this benighted multitude."[111] He soon took the manuscript out of the drawer again to circulate it among those new friends whose stimulation and companionship he had been eagerly pursuing since his arrival.

[7]

London Doubts 1831–1832

A few hours before Carlyle left Craigenputtoch in August 1831 a package of presents from Goethe arrived, from which he snatched two of the master's books to read on the steamer to Liverpool. The two men had exchanged gifts and letters regularly since that drowsy late afternoon seven years before when Carlyle had been exhilarated to learn not only that the great man had read his translation of *Wilhelm Meister* but that he thought the translator a disciple well worth assisting. With paternal concern, Goethe had extended the terms of the relationship from the professional to the personal, also including Jane, who hastened to improve her German, in his affections. Indeed the Sage of Weimar, disappointed in his own son, sometimes seemed preoccupied with his British progeny. Poems, books, jewelry, and even a lock of Jane's hair accompanied their regular correspondence, whose adulation flattered Goethe and whose existence assured the young writer that someone outside his family and close friends had the highest confidence in his future.

It was in part because he had discovered Goethe that Carlyle so easily found the strength to reject Jeffrey and Coleridge. Carlyle needed a literary father, an articulate embodiment on an international scale of the virtues that he himself was trying to emulate. James Carlyle and Goethe were contemporaries. Whereas one was uneducated and anonymous, the other was a writer and famous; together they were an effective representation of all Carlyle's values. For a crucial ten-year period, during which he struggled to find a vocation, an identity, a livelihood, and a mate, Carlyle obsessively read, wrote about, and championed

German literature and its most famous writer, "a wise and great man" who "understands me."[1] In a sense, he became the truest of sons, a disciple. At a time when the basic foundations of life seemed to shake beneath him, when the horrid fate of expatriation to America seemed one of his few real alternatives, he found in this new world of German culture a master to whom he could apprentice himself, a father to whom he could become a son.

Germany and Goethe had an additional advantage: they were far away. The young man might not have found them as attractive in the flesh as in the imagination. Throughout the 1820s he often had expressed his desire to visit, but just a year before the old poet's death he made it clear that there never had been any real reason to go: "Weimar is not distant, but near and friendly, a familiar City of the Mind," a construct of the imagination.[2] For Carlyle, Goethe was an antidote to Voltaire and skepticism, something he needed at a time when his faith in his own father's world was wavering. Despite the respect between James Carlyle and his son, there could be no question in the son's mind that his psychological and intellectual problems were simply beyond his father's comprehension. But these same things were the very process of Goethe's life.

Carlyle could not mistake their shared identity as father models. In fact, he even saw a physical resemblance between the two men. James Carlyle had a "noble head; very large; the upper part of it strikingly like that of the Poet Goethe."[3] It is as if Carlyle were creating a portrait or a bust—he was fascinated by such images—in which the two faces became one. But the essential difference was that Goethe had lived through the painful period of uncertainty about self and society which the young man thought he was now experiencing. Goethe had somehow traveled to the other shore, to calmness, purpose, and wisdom, transformed into a "true Poet . . . the Seer; whose eye has been gifted to discern the godlike Mystery of God's Universe, and decipher some new lines of its celestial writing; we can still call him a *Vates* and Seer; for he *sees* into this greatest of secrets."[4] Moreover, the drama of Goethe's life had been played on an international stage with which Carlyle desired to identify himself, for "there is certainly no German, since the days of Luther, whose life can occupy so large a space in the intellectual history of that people."[5] But "so closely are all European communities connected, that the phases of mind in any one country . . . are but modified repetitions of its phases in every other."[6] The "City of the Mind" rarely recognizes national borders.

Before leaving Edinburgh for Craigenputtoch in the spring of 1828, Carlyle had received from Goethe, among other presents and commissions, two medals that he was instructed to deliver to Sir Walter Scott.

With this commission Goethe was attempting to pay his respects to the celebrated novelist and at the same time to provide an occasion for the unknown Carlyle to meet the well-known writer. But Scott was out-of-town when Carlyle called and he never responded to the somewhat sycophantic letter that accompanied the medals, in which the young writer requested advice from the man he addressed as "my native Sovereign whom I have so often . . . wished that I had claim to see and know in private and near at hand."[7] Though Scott's failure to respond was probably accidental, Carlyle resented what he imagined to be a purposeful slight.

In October 1831, soon after Carlyle arrived in London, Scott, "old and sick," left London for Naples in a last futile effort to recover his health. Carlyle wrote, "To me he is and has been an object of very minor interest for many many years; the Novel-wright of his time, its favourite child, and *therefore* an almost worthless one." His qualification resulted from his brooding awareness that there is "something in his deep recognition of the worth of the Past, perhaps better than anything he has *expressed* about it: into which I do not yet fully see."[8] His private opinion of Scott's actual achievement remained unswervingly low; compared to Goethe he was a lightweight entertainer. Though even Goethe seemed sometimes to oscillate between high wisdom and transparent foolishness, Carlyle never doubted that anyone other than his mother and father had more influenced his life. Soon after arriving in London, he informed his "much honored Friend" that fifteen of his British "friends" had sent him a testimonial letter and an engraved seal, which they expected would arrive toward the end of August 1831, in time for his eighty-first birthday celebration. His own feeling was deeper than respect. "Figure me and mine as thinking of you, loving you . . . with wishes as warm as loving hearts can feel."[9]

The publication in London and Germany of the letter and seal, which Carlyle had intended to keep private, provoked John Wilson to claim that Carlyle preferred a foreign "sovereign" to a native one both for the advantage of novelty and as an expression of a temperament so original that it was also perverse. Eager to remove the taint of foreignness, which had attached itself to his growing reputation and which remained despite efforts to disengage himself, he looked around for English subjects to write on but found that Luther remained the figure who most attracted him. He devoted only a brief moment to attempting to sell his unpublished "History of German Literature" to Longman, for it was immediately clear that it would have no buyers in London or anyplace else in Britain. But the manuscript that he did spend great effort on trying to sell during the first month and more of his stay in London was one whose physical setting, exotic title, exaggerated style, and "mystic" philosophy did nothing to sever the connection that people made between Carlyle and Germany. The fact that he had decided to emphasize his Englishness in the future in no way removed the foreign stigma that his eager pro-German evangelism had created.

But, in fact, Carlyle now felt that he no longer needed any "sovereign" at all, whether native or foreign; he was beginning to feel that he was something of a sovereign himself. This personal ascendency in no way implied that he intended to renounce his former commitments, however. In an essay that he wrote in the autumn and that Napier published in December 1831, he took care to describe the "characteristics" of modern society in terms that kept the English reader's attention focused on the home front. Nevertheless, he reminded his readers that the answer to the ills of the time had already appeared "in the higher Literature of Germany," in which, "for him that can read it," there is "the beginning of a new revelation of the Godlike."[10] Goethe had provided him with the key to that revelation, but in *Sartor Resartus* and his new essays he felt that he had risen to the strength of voice and personality which made him an independent force, a presence of power and originality with a message so important, whatever the Germanic influence, that it deserved an audience of its own. He already had a small audience, including some people prominent in the literary society of London and Edinburgh. But he now wanted an audience whose dedication would transform auditors into actors, listeners into disciples.

Early in the summer of 1831, when urging his older brother to come to London, Jack had evoked the tone of discipleship. He believed that his brother's published "little fragments" revealed "a clear and fearless liberty that I find in no other English author of these times. You are not chained in any den, like Irving, plunging and floundering. You have not dreaded to explore the thick darkness with perfect freedom, and having come through it all and know it all your light is only the more constant and serene on that very account." Jack in effect claimed that his brother had almost arrived at that position of wisdom on the far side of despair which Goethe, the great model, had revealed to them in his own life as the goal for mankind. "You may depend upon it you will meet response from many hearts even in these times of Mammon."[11] He only needed the experience of living among men in the center of their activities in order to direct his words accurately to the heart of the matter. London was the place for that.

His other dedicated convert, also a frustrated writer who now identified her ambitions with his acts, was his wife. While he plunged into the "wild wondrous chaotic den of Discords" in search of supporting voices, she dreamt that a young man was proposing marriage to her. She asked him if he believed in " 'every opinion that Carlyle has put down in Teufelsdreck?' " When he answered yes, she gave him her hand and said "that is so far good." Her own temporary hagiography was absolutely clear. "Since five this morning I have been reading Meister the only Book besides Teufelsdreck and the Bible which I mean to keep always by me."[12]

For some years, Carlyle had been recommending Goethe and God to his countrymen. His certainty that London contained the highest concentration of ignorance on spiritual and moral matters was confirmed both by what he experienced in the first weeks of his visit and by his need to believe that a "missionary" to the English was what the English needed. He had reason to hope people would listen to his message, that disciples would gather round him, eager to hear truth. Jack had assured him that this would be so, and Irving had urged him to come to London and "purify" the literary world. Toward the end of September 1831, he boasted to his mother that he had found "various well disposed men" who seemed desirous of learning from him. Certain that his mother would understand that he meant no blasphemy, he confided that he had a mission and compared himself to Christ. Invoking the language of religious service which was a bond between mother and son, he rather successfully persuaded himself that what he would or would not do was in God's hands. Margaret Carlyle was his best audience for such expressions. "My poor performances in the writing way are better known here than I expected: clearly enough also there *is* want of instruction and light . . . as probably for eighteen hundred years there has not been: if *I* have any light to give, then let me give it."[13]

2.

But Carlyle wished to do nothing rash or precipitate; the dispensation of light could blind the source as well as illumine the object. Though radiant in his imagination, he felt the need to be cautious in action. Amid so much uncertainty he did his best to resist making practical and emotional commitments that the future might render untenable. Whatever "light" he had to give might in confused times be misinterpreted or misused by others and even by himself. London vibrated with the currents of Reform Bill agitation and a thousand and one schemes for the transformation of man and society. It was an atmosphere in which the variety of opinions and sects threatened to make any one position simply another sideshow in the large circus of activity. His common sense told him to go slowly on such delicate matters. He did his best to remind himself to be a listener as well as a speaker for, more than anything else, he needed the satisfaction of communication with other men. Aware of some of his own limitations, he worried that the blinding aggressiveness of the missionary role would prevent him from realizing an open exchange of ideas and affections, that his exhortatory and satirical tone would repel people from the substance of his message. His own passion, which might attract some, would inevitably alienate others; his sense of mission was so intense that it threatened to absorb him in the very dangers that he wished to combat. There was the danger of becoming like Edward Irving, who believed he was giving light to the world, but for whom "dark mad times seem coming."[14]

When Carlyle awakened at Shooter's Hill on a "beautiful morning" in the middle of August 1831, he was in the process of learning that the old loving circle had "drifted quite to leeward."[15] Mrs. Montagu was compulsively eager to see Jane, but she seemed shrill, domineering, cold. She had argued with Jack over his reluctance to share her harsh opinion of Badams, through whose bankruptcy the Montagus had lost money. Badams himself, whom Carlyle visited at his home in the suburb of Enfield, had become irresolute and alcoholic. The Bullers, who were at their country seat in Cornwall, invited the Carlyles to visit. But it was only young Charles, who was rapidly becoming an effective spokesman for positions so extreme that even his radical family disapproved, for whom Carlyle felt any regard. At Shooter's Hill, Mrs. Strachey seemed pale, withered, like a flower frozen in ice, though her husband was "as talkative and full of vivacity as ever."[16] Kitty Kirkpatrick, he learned, had married and was already a mother.

Acceding graciously to inevitable changes, Carlyle was, however, not prepared to accept that the one friend he had thought would never change had changed radically. As a friend "Irving alone stands true."[17] But in all other respects Irving seemed to be standing on thin ice. Within a few weeks of their reunion in London, Carlyle became aware not only that Irving's popularity had diminished to the narrow confines of his own congregation but that Irving and some of his supporters believed he was "working miracles," even if of an unspecified sort. This pretense shocked Carlyle, who believed that miracles had their foundation and their manifestation in the natural. Irving had already been expelled from the National Church of Scotland for preaching that Christ performed his ministry on earth in a human form with human limitations, a position that Carlyle thought quite sensible. Where should one look for a miracle if not in the ordinary, the supernatural in the natural? Fortunately, Irving's own church in London had no mandate to renounce its preacher, but his charismatic presence had begun to polarize the congregation.

Always fearful that his friend would go too far, Carlyle was soon shocked by the realization of his worst anticipations. At the beginning of October, Irving had insisted on giving a farewell blessing in his church for Jack, " 'the brother that was going to foreign lands.' "[18] The tone of the proceeding seemed suspect; though moving, it was also mawkish, strained, and slightly surreal. Carlyle had already heard that there had been occasional outbursts of uncontrolled babbling and screaming at Irving's church. He reported to his mother that suddenly, during regular service and with Irving's encouragement, "hysterical women, and crackbrained enthusiasts," were uttering "confused Stuff, mostly 'Ohs' and 'Ahs' and absurd interjections about 'the Body of Jesus'; they also pretend to 'work miracles,' and have raised more than one weak bedrid woman, and cured people of 'Nerves,' or as they themselves say, 'cast Devils out of them.' " He wrote that "poor Irving" considered all of this "as the 'work of the Spirit' " and boasted "at great length," that it made "*his* Church the peculiarly blessed of Heaven."[19]

Suddenly the whole city seemed to echo with astonishment and ridicule at the news that Irving's regular services were dominated by "the tongues." Additional sessions were held in private homes, one of which the Carlyles, not yet fully aware of what had happened during the previous days, innocently attended when they arrived on a social call.

> We found [Irving's] house all decked out for a 'meeting'. . . . As we talked a moment with Irving who had come down to us, there rose a shriek in the upper story of the house, and presently he exclaimed: '*There* is one prophecying; come and hear her!' we hesitated to go, but he forced us up into a back-room, and there we could hear the wretched creature raving like one possessed; *hoo*ing and *ha*-ing, and talking *as* sensibly as one would do with a pint of brandy in his stomach. . . . Nothing so shocking and altogether unspeakably deplorable was it ever my lot to hear. Poor Jane was on the verge of fainting.[20]

As Carlyle anticipated, the adverse publicity made the preacher even more stubbornly certain that God's spirit was speaking through strange tongues and inspired voices. Carlyle believed that Irving had taken leave of his senses, but he did not know what he could do to help. He thought to write a letter "to him . . . but gave it up again as hopeless." In "despair of being able to accomplish anything," he felt somewhat guilty that he did not even try. Though he made efforts later, his premonition that they would do no good, other than to salve his own conscience, turned out to be correct. Deeply pained by his friend's disaster, which was more hurtful to everyone because Irving thought it a victory, Carlyle could only "hope that he is not utterly lost, but only gone astray for a time."[21]

Irving stuck to his new vision, convinced that he had found "Thy Word." Shortly forced to leave his church, he created a dissenting chapel, the headquarters of the new "Catholic Apostolic Church," whose dominion by an inspired board of enthusiasts inevitably transformed the spiritual leader into the servant of the congregation. To outsiders it seemed that Irving had been divested of spiritual authority and priestly leadership. In Carlyle's eyes, the master had become the prisoner of his disciples, a man who performed their will rather than expressing his own.

The collapse of the Irving circle gave Carlyle an additional impetus to strike out in search of new friends. Though he insisted to Murray that he had come to London only to arrange for the publication of *Sartor,* his desire to experience the variety and excitement that were unequalled anyplace else in Britain was equally important. With Irving, he went to dine at the home of Henry Drummond, a wealthy banker whose belief in the imminent arrival of the millennium was so strong that he became a lay pillar of Irving's new Church. With Jack, he visited Badams, returning there again with Jane late in October. Twice he was the reluctant overnight guest of the inebriated Charles Lamb, whose "fibre of genius shining thro' positive delirium and crackbrainedness" did not make him less intolerable to Carlyle, who genuinely believed Lamb "to be in some considerable degree *insane.*"[22] During the second visit, the querulous Lamb mocked Jane's evening bowl of oatmeal and (uninvited) dipped his spoon in and tasted "the Stuff." Jane responded that " 'your astonishment at my porridge cannot exceed my surprise at your manners,' and had her bowl removed." Lamb, now "a confirmed shameless drunkard" who "*asks* vehemently for gin-and-water in strangers' houses," elicited hardly a dram of compassion from Carlyle: "Poor Lamb! Poor England where such a despicable abortion is named genius." At the time he knew nothing about Lamb's tragic personal history.[23] In August, Carlyle renewed contact with his fellow Scotsman Alan Cunningham, whose unpretentiousness both Carlyles liked. That same month he met the elderly William Godwin, the philosophical novelist and champion of women's rights. Godwin was connected with Shelley through his daughter and with Romantic radicalism through his own writings, but the evening was one of tame trivia—a "jingle of pianos" and hours of card playing. Carlyle had a few minutes of conversation with the "little thickset man, with bushy eyebrows," and wanted more. Godwin appeared gratified by something Carlyle said, "seems beginning to talk, when they force him up to—play whist, and I only see him for the rest of the night!"[24]

Dressed in a new London suit, which Jeffrey had teased Jane about, and with a letter of admission from the Lord Advocate, Carlyle visited the House of Commons, which he found surprisingly small and, predictably, crowded with foolish talk.[25] "Vain hope to make mankind happy by Politics! . . . Reform one man (reform thy own inner man), it is more than scheming out reforms for a nation."[26] Politicians and booksellers seemed allies in ignorance, men who were masters of "puffing," or advertising themselves and their wares in false terms to a society that was increasingly unable and unwilling to tell the false from the true.[27] The view from his lodgings in Tavistock Square, rented from Edward Irving's brother, George, embodied the ironic oppositions. "I look . . . over" the roofs of houses "and see the top of St. Pancras' Steeple, with its silent carved-work and stone cross, and the beautiful dappled August sky stre[t]ching out above it. Downwards into the street stands one object at which I know not whether to laugh or cry: it is a huge sign bearing these words: 'the cheapest shop in the world for Combs and Brushes'; and, alas, the *window is shut,* and this cheapest Shopkeeper has bankraped and gone out of sight!"[28]

Jeffrey and the Whigs he thought of as poor shopkeepers who would also shortly go out of business. In addition, he was personally angry at the Lord Advocate, to whom he owed £60, certain that the influential politician was doing less than he might both to get *Sartor* published and to introduce its author to people of interest and distinction. "I take his friendship for me, as I have all along done, to be perhaps three part palabra, and one part half-sentiment, half goodwill." Though he wanted nothing more, he claimed, than to repay the debt and to get Jane's picture out of his unworthy "hands," he still kept in close touch with the "Duke" as long as there was some chance that Murray might publish *Sartor*.[29] Until Jane arrived in London, Carlyle made frequent use of Jeffrey's free mailing privileges as a member of Parliament. So common a practice was this that the good-natured advocate, irritable with ill health and the various demands made on him, mumbled one day that he was being made into a mere post office. Naturally it was irksome to be visited for one's franking privilege rather than for oneself.

While the arrangement with Murray seemed to prosper, Carlyle proposed that Jane join him for the winter in London, where he intended to read galleys and supervise his book through the press. When the arrangement collapsed, he admitted that he did not want to spend the winter at Craigenputtoch under any conditions. Jane was eager to come to London, which she had never seen, but she wisely insisted that her husband must take responsibility for the decision. Whatever the outcome, she would be better protected from recriminations if her own desires were subordinated to his needs. Early in September 1831, after the decision had been made, she revealed what had been on her mind for the past few years. "At Craigenputtoch we have always had a secret suspicion that we were quite wrong—removed out of the sphere of human activity fully as much thro' cowardice as superior wisdom—(am I not right in regard to you as well as myself) and thus all our doings are without heart and our sufferings without dignity—With a goal before me I feel I could leap sixbar gates."[30]

To some extent, then, they had both been aware all along that Craigenputtoch was not necessary for reasons of health or finance. It had been a place in which to hide and recover from wounds, a refuge whose ministrations they might need again in the future, "a safe haven (tho but a desert island) in stress of weather."[31] Heretofore Carlyle had not had the will, the courage, or the belief in himself to face "society." He and Jane constantly emphasized that he had done some of his best work, including *Sartor,* at Craigenputtoch. But as the years went by they both, with different emphases, cast ever-darker shadows of unhappiness and isolation on the Craigenputtoch period, so much so that in his later, always brief visits Carlyle found more and more unbearable the depressing isolation of a place that only Jane hates "even more than I do."[32] But the practical Carlyle, who plunged eagerly into the London maelstrom, was still uncertain that this visit could be extended into a permanent residence, particularly with the collapse of the arrangement with Murray and the unlikelihood of finding any regular employment.

In the meanwhile he lost no time in looking for kindred spirits who would listen and respond to his message and his presence. Delighted to discover that he had a reputation, though not an entirely favorable one, he found that he could extend his literary acquaintance almost at will, provided that he took initiatives and searched out those whose works or reputations suggested that a relationship would be beneficial. One of the most promising young men was William Glen, a young Scotsman studying law in London, whose talents and idealism Jack had described in glowing terms and whose adulation of Carlyle and his message brought him eagerly to the visitor's lodgings in the middle of August 1831. Though Carlyle quickly perceived that there were dangerously unstable elements in his young admirer's personality, he seemed "an authentic 'young man of genius,' full of fire and love . . . hovering as yet between light and darkness." He was sure that Jane would approve of him "were it only on this one ground, that he is my Disciple, by far the best I have ever had."[33] William Empson eagerly promised to introduce him to two other sympathetic souls, one of whom, Sarah Austin, the wife of the distinguished legal expert John Austin, had found such wonders in German literature that she spent much of her time translating various German works into English. The other was John Stuart Mill, a good friend of Sarah's and the centerpiece of a group of young men whose Whig-Radical connections had made them the restless heirs of a secular utilitarianism that, even to Mill, sometimes seemed a less than satisfactory formula for the future. Not yet sure that he had anything important to say to his contemporaries, Mill listened eagerly to all voices, particularly to fresh ones, for he was predisposed by training and personality to hear every side of an argument.

Carlyle, however, had no doubt that he had something important to say, especially to men like Glen and Mill. He was both lonely and passionately hopeful, aware that there was a void within him which needed to be filled with companionship, whatever the price he must pay for the experience. For the first time matters of health and economy seemed unimportant; the inevitable separation from the charmed circle of his family was not too heavy a loss in comparison to the advantages to be gained. Moreover, he had never felt or looked better. Though thirty-six, in an era when middle age often appeared distressingly early, his surprisingly youthful, energetic, and idiosyncratically handsome figure—almost six feet tall, full shock of light brown hair, intent blue-gray eyes, an aquiline, clean-shaven face anchored by a confident jaw that balanced a recessive upper lip—impressively embodied a personality that for all its inner struggles seemed to his London contemporaries bright with genius. Goethe's disciple was eager to become, in his own way, a master himself.

By the beginning of September, he had summoned his premier disciple from Craigenputtoch. Unwilling to be separated any longer, Carlyle set her to work to dispose of Craigenputtoch for the winter and to prepare herself and her luggage for the voyage. For him to return to help with packing and transporting clothes, books, and produce (butter and oatmeal from Scotsbrig) seemed impractical. But with a mania for particulars and a compulsive need to control details and minimize costs, he gave her travel instructions "with a vengeance," unaware that as the day for departure drew closer the nervous tension and fatigue that had accumulated during almost six weeks of separation threatened to undermine her health completely.[34] She had missed him dreadfully. Worse, she had found it difficult to sleep, had unpleasant dreams, ate sparingly, and felt constantly exhausted and ill tempered.

The prospect of living in London excited Jane immensely, for it was the realization of a fantasy that had remained with her since Irving had withdrawn his invitation in 1824. But her rapid expenditure of energy in moments of high nervous hope propelled her toward an end while at the same time depleting the means to accomplish it. Aware of her plight, delegations from Scotsbrig came to assist, intent on relieving her loneliness. She appreciated such attempts to help, but without her husband and in an unstable mood she could not avoid venting some of her willfulness and barely repressed anxiety on her visitors and on her mother. Early in September she had a distressingly unpleasant ten days at Templand, when her mother got on her nerves in ways that she could not control. Blithely ignorant of the disparity between her whims and Jane's emotional needs, unable to understand that a farewell party was inappropriate for a daughter on the verge of collapse, Grace Welsh made her daughter bitterly aware that she would get no help from her mother.

Jane, insecure in her role as wife, worried in a jokingly repressed way that her husband would take "up with . . . other women" (the separated husband and wife teased one another with assurances on the matter which could only increase the tension). In her anxiety to complete the work that would end their separation, she overexerted herself.[35] Indeed, Carlyle's assurances that she had nothing to fear from anyone else increased the pressure on Jane to conform to *his* definition of her role and needs. Thus, his belief that she was an indefatigable worker, once she had begun a task, led her to conclude that she had best keep any doubts about managing the move to herself. Of course, his notion that she flourished under the pressure of work and duty never led him to the realization that her well-being might have benefited from some regular occupation other than housekeeping. He was asking her to do much more than discharge household tasks and supervise domestic services, however. The marriage was premised not only on her recognition of her husband's genius but also on her total identification with his mission and his values. "I perceive that of all women my own Jeannie is the wife for me: that in her true bosom (once she were a Mystic) a Man's head is worthy to lie. Be a Mystic, Dearest; that is, stand with me on this everlasting basis, and keep thy arms around me."[36] Though she had hardly a "Mystic" bone in her body (whatever that might mean), it seemed clear that any faltering in her commitment was potentially disastrous.

The last urgent plea she had received from her husband before leaving Craigenputtoch was that she "take every care of" herself; "there is more than thy own that thou carriest with thee."[37] Though he had constantly urged her to be careful of her health, while at the same time creating a situation that taxed her strength, the final injunction has a special tenderness that in later years helped to support the family tradition that Jane was pregnant at this time. Had she indeed been pregnant, conception would have to have occurred sometime in the spring and she would not yet have been noticeably unfit for hard work and a difficult journey. And her miscarriage would have occurred either on the trip or soon after her arrival in London: had she carried the child longer than the four or five months between June and November 1831, a miscarriage would have precipitated an illness much more serious than the almost chronic but still minor sicknesses that troubled her throughout the autumn and winter. In fact, the alleged pregnancy seems highly unlikely. Neither Jane's letters nor those of other family members contain even an ambiguous reference to it. She could of course have disguised a two or three months' pregnancy, but would have had to tell her husband about it in order for him to refer to her condition in his mid-September letter. And, finally, the idea that there could have been a pregnancy that the couple was aware of implies that Carlyle promoted a situation in which Jane was compelled to work extraordinarly hard under great pressure, to leave a reasonably comfortable home close by her own mother and her husband's family, to make an arduous journey to a city that she had never visited and in which she knew no doctor (Jack would be in Italy), and to give birth to a child while in fragile health and living in crowded lodgings. It is unlikely if not impossible that Thomas would have knowingly subjected Jane to this.

Jane arrived in London at the end of September 1831. Within a few days her headache had declined, and soon her nerves had calmed sufficiently for her to make visits. Carlyle had already warned her that it might be necessary to search for new rooms because bedbugs had recently made an ominous appearance in the Tavistock Square lodgings. They shortly moved into comfortable rooms in a house run by a family, one of whose daughters, Eliza Miles, immediately worshiped Jane. They had a large drawing room and a small bedroom "in an airy and remarkably quiet street," and Carlyle was glad to report that the honest proprietors "assure us they *very seldom see* a bug."[38]

Carlyle was delighted to have his wife with him again. Though he commented to Alick that his health was "tolerable," much the same as it had been for years, he assured his mother that "My health has improved since the Wife came to look after me; I am about beginning to write something, and can hope to spend the winter profitably and pleasantly enough."[39] Jane, however, was shocked to see the changes in Irving, his graying hair and tired features. She dashed over to visit Mrs. Montagu, who warned her to "prepare yourself for an old woman, sallow and severe . . . not cold-hearted, but schooled into the suppression of her feelings—I say this lest you should think I receive you coldly."[40] She could not immediately see Jeffrey, who was ill. Her husband was particularly eager to introduce her to two of his most promising new friends, Sarah Austin and John Mill. Within a short time Anne Procter, Mrs. Montagu's daughter, was Jane's "most intimate acquaintance," Sarah Austin "the best woman I have yet found here," and Mr. Mill of "all the literary people that come about us the one I like best."[41]

4

Mill's kindness, intelligence, and responsiveness endeared him to Carlyle from the start. Writing to Jane, Carlyle characterized his new friend as "a slender rather tall and elegant youth, with small clear roman-nosed face, two small earnestly-smiling eyes: modest, remarkably gifted with precision of utterance; enthusiastic, yet lucid, calm; not a great, yet distinctly a gifted and amiable youth."[42] Sarah Austin, whose "warm blue eyes (almost hectically intense)" illuminated "an eagerness, a warmth in her whole manner and look, which has in it something feverish," had brought the two men together early in September.[43] Each was attentive to the other's recent essays, and each brought preconceived notions to the meeting.[44] Mill had suspected that Carlyle's outlook was limited to the excesses of Germanic mysticism which his own commitment to practical reform and philosophical analysis found so empty and repellent. He was pleased, therefore, to discover that Carlyle was more than the sum of his writings, that he had the force of intellect and personality to make an important contribution to a discussion of contemporary problems. The younger man immediately granted that Carlyle did not seem "so entirely the reflexion or shadow of the great German writers" as he had been inclined to consider him. This strange but welcome visitor from provincial Scotland "had had his eyes unsealed" and "sees the aspects of things with his own eyes." Impressed by Carlyle's "liberality & tolerance," Mill was delighted that this new friend, who seemed to him "a great hunter-out of acquaintances," had found him through the agency of the articles he had written in the *Examiner,* "the only substantial good I have yet derived from writing those papers."[45]

Though by personality disciplined, passive, and responsive, trained by the rigors of his father's system to feel more comfortable with structures than with revolutions, Mill at this time was emphasizing the need for total change in public matters and trying to keep an open mind and explore new relationships in his personal life. For some years he had been more than uneasy with the rigid utilitarianism that his father, Jeremy Bentham's most prominent disciple, had imposed on him. He was also dissatisfied with the limited provisions of the controversial Reform Bill and, like Carlyle, believed that only reform so radical that it would create a new society could resolve contemporary social ills. The previous summer Mill had met Harriet Taylor, the wife of a well-to-do merchant, whose beauty and talent so struck him that he immediately began the relationship that was to fulfill his early training in Radical politics and personal self-effacement even as it struck a path away from the emotional restrictions of his father's world.

Mill initially found Carlyle interesting, distinctive, and attractive. Carlyle found Mill, six years his junior, almost as promising in person as he had appeared in his articles on the Saint-Simonians and the spirit of the age, which he had read while at Craigenputtoch. In the first enthusiasm of their meeting, he felt that Mill was a man he could love, though he was aware that this expectation was based more on hope than on experience. He was well aware of Mill's limitations, and he carefully distinguished between being gifted and being great.

After the two men breakfasted together the next week at Empson's, Mill began to schedule introductions for Carlyle and to advance his literary prospects. To Carlyle's delight, Mill arranged for him to meet the most amiable and impressive of the Saint-Simonians, Gustave D'Eichthal.[46] Though he eventually gave his translation of *Noveau Christianisme* to D'Eichthal in the hope that he would make use of it, Carlyle was already sufficiently disenchanted with the political eccentricity and intellectual naiveté of the Saint-Simonians to agree with Jack, who had attended their meetings in Paris, that they are "an upholstery aggregation, not a Promethean creation; therefore cannot live long."[47] But D'Eichthal was even more personally responsive than Mill. He immediately became a favorite with both Carlyles, particularly Jane, who could not help contrasting the delight of being hostess to Mill and D'Eichthal with so many lonely tea hours at Craigenputtoch. Like her husband, she initially assumed that Mill's alert attention to Carlyle's words meant that he agreed at least with his basic principles, an impression that Mill unwittingly helped to create. By personality, his habit was to wait, to listen, and to learn, and also to disagree with an impersonal politeness, more often by asking a question than by making a statement. Even Jane, and certainly Thomas, readily mistook much of Mill's politeness for agreement, especially since there was much that they did agree on in their analysis of the contemporary scene.

Throughout the winter and into the spring of 1831–1832, they continued to meet regularly at the British Museum, at Carlyle's lodgings, and at India House, where Mill was following in his father's footsteps, eventually to inherit one of the three key positions that had been filled by James Mill, Thomas Peacock, and Edward Strachey. As the weeks passed, each became increasingly aware of the distances that remained between them. Carlyle was more hopeful and enthusiastic than Mill, and perhaps more in need of disciples than Mill of a master, but still he was keen enough to de-elevate him to the status of a "partial disciple" by December 1831. But their differences of opinion, as yet not formulated in any dramatic way, hardly prevented him from finding Mill as great a "favourite" as Glen, who worshiped him unconditionally.[48] And as the winter drew to an end, with significant changes in prospect, Thomas told Jack that "of male favourites Mill stands at the top."[49] He saw no reason why his increasing reservations about Mill, due mainly to his growing recognition of their differences of personality and philosophy, should in any way decrease the warmth of their personal contact. There was no question in either of their minds that they liked one another and that indeed Mill thought highly enough of Carlyle to listen carefully to him, to respect his judgments and attitudes, and even on occasion to imitate his style.

5.

But in October 1831 Carlyle's general expectations were high: the vacationing London literati were returning to town; Jane had joined him; new friends and old, whatever the nuances of the relationships, provided a fertile ground for social and intellectual stimulation; and there was still reason to hope that "there is work in abundance for me here."[50] But what kind of work, he asked himself. Irving's tragedy dramatized the dangers of an ill-chosen task and an unsound approach. Though moved by George Irving's tearful pleas to help his brother, Carlyle saw a moral irony in what had happened: "The punishment was not unjust; that he who believed without inquiry, should now believe against all light."[51] He hesitantly considered and then declined the possibility of himself addressing the public as a lecturer, partly because he had not had the forethought to prepare some lectures while at Craigenputtoch, partly because he did not feel that he could face up to such an overtly public role. It would take a calm, independent courage to make a success at telling Londoners what they did not want to hear. Moreover, his inquiries had given him the impression that those friends whose support he would need had doubts as well. Lecturing was mainly the province of political and religious "quacks," and it seemed foolhardy, without absolute confidence in his ability to triumph, to identify himself with a form of expression that might lead to guilt by association. He thought it best to postpone such a project at least until the next year, after he had carefully prepared some lectures. If he were to "speak aloud," it would be "in defiance of all men and things."[52] "On the whole, this London is the most *twilight* intellectual city you could *meet* with: a meaner more utterly despicable view of man and his interests . . . you could nowhere fall in with."[53] He concluded that the main hope was in people like Mill, who also looked to the future; and that public lectures would hardly prove an effective forum for serious debate on the necessity of radical change.

By early October 1831 he had two new writing projects in hand, an aborted essay on a minor German dramatist that he labeled a "dud" and locked away, and a review-essay for the *Edinburgh Review* of Thomas Hope's *An Essay on the Origin and Prospect of Man* and Friedrich Schlegel's *Philosophical Lectures.* Though he made it clear to Napier that there were other topics that he preferred to write on, particularly Luther, Johnson, and the "position of the Author in our System of Society," he apparently felt in no position to reject Napier's suggestion that he devote an essay to Hope.[54] Napier had not ruled out Luther, but his stipulation that his contributor not exceed "six-and-thirty pages" and his general tone of discouragement had convinced Carlyle that his precarious relationship with the *Review* might not survive any attempt to assert his own preferences.[55] He needed the work, the sense of worth and usefulness that came from writing; he needed the money; and he wanted the wide exposure that publication in the *Edinburgh Review* provided.

Conceding that he "might have something to say upon . . . Hope's Book on *Man,*" he was determined to turn necessity into opportunity. "Works of that sort are a characteristic of our era." Though he had only seen a copy in the British Museum, which had led him to conclude that it was "perhaps the absurdest Book ever printed in any time or place," he quickly decided that such work represented "the highest culminating-point of the Mechanical Spirit of this age; as it were, the *reductio ad absurdum* of that whole most melancholy Doctrine."[56] He immediately set about the surprisingly difficult task of locating a copy he could use at home. In the meantime, his essay "German Literature of the Fourteenth and Fifteenth Centuries" appeared in the *Foreign Quarterly Review.* By early November, he was working daily on the new piece, which, though ostensibly a review of a German book, would hardly mention Germany or German literature at all. He hoped to have it ready for December publication.

Not having done any sustained writing since the previous spring, Carlyle found it difficult to get started. It was not until the end of November that he had a title, "Characteristics," and "six pages perfectly ready, the rest vague enough in my head."[57] Pressing on with it in his cramped, temporary writing space, while Jane either kept absolutely quiet or went out on errands and visits, he celebrated his thirty-seventh birthday with the expectation that he would be done in about two weeks. He flatly refused Alick's offer to repay some of the money that he believed he owed his older brother, urging him to use all his resources to stock his new farm. His major hope was that "happier days were beginning" for Alick. His major disappointment was his estrangement from Irving, whom he now dared not visit, since "his home . . . is more a Bedlam than a home," the "strait waistcoat" an imminent danger.[58] *Sartor* had been frequently and now finally refused but Carlyle stiffened his lip; even if Napier should fail to encourage his contributions, there would be sufficient commissions for essays to keep him in meager but adequate funds.

"Characteristics" was an extraordinarily revealing and influential essay of about twenty-five pages. Carlyle thought of it as "a sort of second *Signs* of the *Times*"; Napier, though he published it, said that on first reading he found it "inscrutable." Its author would not have been surprised if Napier had found it inscrutable even on second reading and beyond. The editor's respect for genius clearly did not include the perception or the ideological sympathy necessary to crack what Carlyle now admitted was a kind of code language that he had been creating for some years in order to obscure a personality and a message for which many were as yet unprepared, while at the same time striking an identifiable theme and chord for the sympathetic and the initiated. Aware that his elliptical and "aphoristic style" ran the genuine danger of "being abstruse," he himself feared that "it might be too *scrutable;* for it indicates decisively enough that Society . . . is utterly condemned to destruction, and even now beginning its long travail-throes of Newbirth."[59] The controversial prose style that he devised for his published essays, so different from the style of his private letters, was to some extent an extension of his lifelong strategy of evading or obscuring crucial problems or questions—a strategy that he had learned in his relationship with his mother. It now seemed the appropriate garment for a radical message that even in disguised form was likely to provoke pained and painful responses.

Carlyle had tended to stand aloof from and devalue what he saw as overreactions to difficult political and social conditions. But the intensification of revolutionary activity, swirling around the seemingly endless Reform Bill debates, alarmed him: "A second edition of the French Revolution is distinctly within the range of chances." There had been "riots" at "Coventry, at Worcester &c,"[60] and the cholera, which had just arrived in England and was rumored to be spreading rapidly, increased the tensions in a country in which even controlled imaginations had begun to envision the probability of some national catastrophe. In Carlyle's opinion, the burning of ricks and the riots of unemployed factory workers in response to economic depression and political disenfranchisement were not the real basis of the current revolutionary threat. He was convinced that domestic tranquillity could readily be reestablished by any government that accepted its primary responsibility to provide all willing workers an adequate livelihood through fair employment and to guarantee a reasonably secure future for the working class. He did not believe that a violent revolution would occur in England, partly because he anticipated that even the worst of governments would accept this responsibility, partly because he had a deep appreciation of the stubborn patience of the English working class. Still, to the extent that revolution is the turbulent manifestation of the divine power's refusal to continue to tolerate a corrupt, false, and stultified society, Carlyle believed that revolution was not only desirable but inevitable in England. If this were indeed God's world, then there was no reason to feel fear, though he felt anger and resentment at corruption, even on the brink of or in the midst of the purging fire. "Twenty choleras and 20 Revolutions" should not "terrify" him. "The crash of the whole Solar and Stellar System could only kill you once."[61]

But the threatening uncertainties of life demanded a complex, psychologically comprehensive defense against death and disorder. Out of his experience with physical illness, Carlyle constructed a metaphor for the psychological, social, and spiritual illness that he considered characteristic of the modern world. He dimly remembered the time before he was aware of his body as either healthy or ill, when "health and sickness were foreign traditions." But such a season could not last; the conditions of society prevent the continuation of personal harmony and wholeness. The society, uncertain of itself and divided on the most important matters, imposes self-consciousness on everyone who is not protected by some narrow fundamentalism or some vegetable-like sluggishness of mind. "The beginning of Inquiry," which for Carlyle had come in his teens, "is Disease," and all systematic knowledge in science and philosophy is the self-conscious attempt to put right or at least to cope with "the feeling of something being wrong."[62] But, he believed, "it is in Society that man first feels what he is; first becomes what he can be."[63] Society is, in fact, the collective individual. Whatever illness he himself feels, then, both results from and contributes to the illness of society as a whole. Like a person, society is alive and "vital," or self-conscious and ill.

Through late November and into December 1831, as he worked on his essay, the import of his perception became more and more clear: the self is contained in the mind, not the mind in the self. There is no way to "rise above the mind," which contains everything. Metaphysical and rational attempts to understand man and nature were futile efforts to limit rather than to open and expand man's capability to live and to experience reality. All systematic critical thought was by definition skeptical, rational, negative. And no belief or conviction could come "out of Negation."[64] The conscious mind, attempting to transcend itself, constantly denied and rejected the true nature of the mind, attempting to impose self-consciousness on an essentially unconscious force. He now saw what no one in Western culture had seen quite as clearly before: the strongest force within man is Nature, which is unconscious, mysterious, spontaneous, and "the sign of health is Unconsciousness. . . . The true force is an unconscious one." For "boundless as is the domain of man, it is but a small fractional proportion of it that he rules with Consciousness and by Forethought . . . the mechanical, small; the great is ever, in one sense or other, the vital; it is essentially the mysterious, and only the surface of it can be understood."[65]

Deep in man's unconsciousness, Carlyle believed, lie the roots of life, concealed in "Darkness" by a beneficent Nature that will not try us constantly with death and pain. Nature creates a balance "of Light and Darkness, the Light resting on the Darkness. . . . Everywhere there is Dualism, Equipoise; a perpetual Contradiction dwells in us: 'where shall I place myself to escape from my own shadow?' "[66] If the mind, which defines its possessor, could be accepted in its true nature—mysterious, spontaneous, unconscious, in vital touch with both light and darkness—then man would be defined by how he accepts and manifests the battle between Faith and Doubt in all his activities. In modern society, the balance between Faith and Doubt had been tipped in favor of Doubt, the disease of inquiry so widespread that it threatened to triumph and destroy the desirable dialectic between Light and Darkness. Our first fall, then, had been out of paradise into conflict, and "Evil . . . must ever exist while man exists"; but our second fall, which led us into diseased, pervasive self-consciousness, was our loss of Faith that the conflict would end in a victory for "Good."[67]

Despite this grim diagnosis, Carlyle had no doubt that the battle had not yet been lost. He himself was a living embodiment of the inevitable victory of Faith. He saw signs of the coming "Morning" in the patterns of history, which he sensed he would want to explore in depth, particularly the Reformation, the French Revolution, and the new urban and industrial conditions. His flair for assertive poetic metaphor was itself an act of optimism. "Deep and sad as is our feeling that we stand yet in the bodeful Night: equally deep, indestructible is our assurance that the Morning will not fail. Nay, already, as we look round, streaks of a dayspring are in the east," where the "higher Literature of Germany" contained "the beginning of a new revelation of the Godlike."[68] The age of Miracles is always the present; the signs of the turbulent times pointed toward clearing away the confusions of the past. The "Conscious or Mechanical" would be rejected, and "the principle of life . . . [would] then withdraw into its inner sanctuaries . . . deeper than ever into that domain of the Unconscious, by nature infinite and inexhaustible; and creatively work there. From that mystic region, and from that alone, all wonders, all Poesies, and Religions, and Social Systems have proceeded."[69] God, then, was in man; and the Artist—for "Literature is but a branch of Religion"—is the man who creates representations of God, the mysterious, the infinite, and the Good, from his deepest unconsciousness, as an act of Faith, and Light, and Love. He felt that it was his task as an artist to create beyond fears and doubts. Anticipating a metaphor that the Victorians were to use widely, Carlyle compared himself and his contemporaries to "Soldiers, fighting in a foreign land; that understand not the plan of the campaign, and have no need to understand it; seeing well what is at our hand to be done. Let us do it like Soldiers; with submission, with courage, with a heroic joy."[70]

6.

By mid-December 1831 the essay had gone off to the bewildered Napier, who may have understood more than he was willing to admit. Though neither the tone nor the message were particularly suitable for the *Edinburgh Review,* there was a general recognition, shared even by horrified Whigs, that some kind of "genius" was at work in the clotted prose, wild predictions, revolutionary expectations, and egomaniacal claims. Carlyle ended the year in a buoyant mood. The weather was dreadful (the mud, smoke, and damp even "nastier" than at Craigenputtoch); Jane's health was a problem; and their future in London increasingly uncertain. Still, by the end of December, he was well into an essay on Samuel Johnson, which he conceived of as a sort of biographical "sketch" that he had wanted to try for some time. "Two or Three Magazine men [particularly Fraser] are chirping to me with open arms; even offering to raise their prices!"[71] But, despite feeling "totally *above* the reptile word of Authors here," he and Jane anticipated that they would leave London in the next few months and return to Scotland.[72]

Indeed, there was "abundance of work" and Carlyle felt "in working tune."[73] Such work, however, could be done anyplace. Carlyle missed his family. He had not found enough disciples in London. And he was almost always eager to believe that he would be better off someplace else. Jane enjoyed London social life and her new friends, but she had suffered a series of colds and weakening influenzas. Lodgings were uncomfortable for both of them, and they would need to have quarters of their own, if they were to stay. But they saw no hope of that in the overcrowded and often expensive London housing market. Furthermore, it seemed out of the question that Carlyle could obtain regular employment other than as a free-lance writer. Toward the end of the year, then, he and Jane decided that they would return to Craigenputtoch, though both of them recognized that it would be only a temporary stop on their way back to Edinburgh or London. It was another year before Carlyle realized that, despite all his dissatisfaction with the "brick Babylon" and its inferior modern building materials, it was in London that he would have to construct his permanent "temporary" home. For the time being, however, permanently leaving Scotland and his family seemed too painful to do without being certain that it was necessary.

Meanwhile, he did a brief translation from Goethe's *Autobiography* for Holcroft's *Monthly Magazine*. Fraser, under duress, finally paid him for an article on Schiller, Goethe, and Madame de Staël and eagerly offered to publish his review-article-in-progress on Croker's edition of Boswell's *Johnson*. Even James Tait from Edinburgh consulted him on plans for a new "radical or mystic-radical Magazine," leaving Carlyle to assume that he would be offered the editorship and become a major contributor as well. Edward Bulwer solicited a contribution to his *New Monthly Magazine*. Disappointingly, negotiations for the publication of his uncompleted history of German literature at the payment of £300 stopped just short of final agreement.

Despite his cultivation of a stoic exterior, Carlyle was a man who hated partings, mourned change, and created a melancholy inner poetry whose highest strain was elegiac remembrance of all those loved and loving things and people that were no more. His own birthday in December 1831 and the turn into the new year sharply reminded him of the age of his parents. Though he did not have particular premonitions about either of them, he anticipated that at some time in the future he and his brothers and sisters would have to confront the actual fact of their deaths. Writing the first section of his essay on Johnson, which was published separately under the title "Biography," he perceived that one could find the true poetry of human reality in the patterns of men's actual lives, that the factual life cycle is itself the most meaningful pattern for generalizations about the interaction between the vital spirit of life and its physical environment. As he felt the past move away from him, his preoccupation with it increased, "for the Past is all holy to us; the Dead are all holy."[74] History might be the true poetry; in the lives of great men we might find ourselves writ large. Boswell, despite his weaknesses of personality, had the greatness to recognize Johnson's greatness, to "Hero-worship," to become the disciple of a man whose moral and religious strength based on faith in divine order made him a worthy father. To a man with fathers much on his mind, the most touching incident in Johnson's life was when, fifty years after his father's death, he stood in the rain—his head bared, tears trickling down his face—at the very spot in the Uttoxeter marketplace where, as a young boy, he had disobeyed his parent.

Naturally, then, the crimes of impiety and rebellion against parental authority preoccupied Carlyle. The question of how a son could atone for such acts, which Johnson asked himself, reverberated in his thoughts. He was sadly aware that the forces that demanded the rejection of the old, despite one's love for those who embodied the past, were beyond the control, even the manipulation, of the children of the new society. He could only assure his own mother and father that he loved them deeply, believing that the best that was within him had come from them and their nurturing. He wrote to his mother at the beginning of the third week in January 1832 that "I esteem it . . . the greatest of all earthly blessings that I was born of parents who were *religious,* who from the first studied to open my eyes to the Highest."[75] Unhappy to learn that his "Father was again afflicted with his old complaint of cold," he urgently advised warm clothes and staying indoors, "especially when the Sun is not shining. . . . Tell my Father that I love and honour him."[76] Two days later, he received a letter from his sister, which Jane brought up to him with tears in her eyes. Early in the morning on January 22, the day on which he had sent his love, his father had died.

On the one hand, the shock was sudden, precipitate; on the other, he had prepared himself for it for many years, aware at some level that the continuity between his and his father's life could not be broken as long as either of them lived. Carlyle now assumed the role of head of the family. His own coming of age had been slow and circuitous, and his father's death thus marked a major step forward; the childless man of thirty-six had become a surrogate father himself. From London, he immediately wrote to Jack in Rome to break the news. To his younger brother Jamie, the only Carlyle son living in Scotsbrig, he urged that he "*ought*" to conduct prayer services every Sabbath evening "in our Father's house . . . in so far as your views will allow."[77] To his mother, he sent words of comfort, couched in the language to which she could best respond: "Whoso trusteth in Him has obtained the victory over Death: the King of Terrors is no longer terrible."[78]

But the "King of Terrors" could not be so readily dismissed. Carlyle assured his family that his father's noble and industrious life deprived death of some of its sting. The rhetoric of pietistic comfort, though hardly ever credible to Carlyle himself, took on a ring of certainty when he evoked it for his mother. But he was not straining his own personal beliefs when he told her that "I have long continually meditated on Death, till, by God's grace, it has grown transparent for me, and holy and great rather than terrific."[79] In the case of personal loss, however, such transcendence was not easily achieved, as Jack recognized, for "you are suffering much. . . . There is a heavy sadness . . . and a tone of defiance."[80] In such moments of personal stress, he assuaged his pain with characteristic howls of defiance, as if courage were self-authenticating; and he attempted to memorialize the dead and the past in writing or in thought, as if the precious moments from the past could be kept alive in the present.

Jack, however, counseled his mother to rely on "fortitude and resignation." The doctor had written at length to Thomas, just prior to his father's death, of his own doubts about God and the providential nature of the universe. His eldest brother had advised him to have faith, and to demonstrate that faith in action, which would relieve all doubt, evoking the example of his own years of suffering. But the stress brought Jack's early family training to the fore, and he wrote his mother that "the only consolation . . . is that we are in the hands of God and that he chastiseth those whom he loveth. . . . Why should we grieve at all if there were no seed of unbelief in us? . . . It is the evil spirit of doubting that dwells in us."[81] The answer to the pain and mystery of death, then, was perfect belief.

Thomas did not disagree with his brother. But for him resignation and coming to terms with his father's death were inseparable from some action that would both memorialize his father's life and provide the release that he felt in creating and recreating the past. Putting aside his essay-in-progress on Samuel Johnson, he isolated himself from everyone but Jane, with whom he took contemplative walks and had long, melancholy conversations about his father and hers as well. In death, the two fathers seemed to their children remarkably alike in both the nobleness and self-sacrifice of their lives. In the middle of the fourth week of January, he began to write his memoir of James Carlyle. Living in the past for the next five days, he felt that for the first time he saw clearly and wholly the patterns and the significance of his father's life. The memoir became a resonant monologue about the son's sense of the meaning and the mission of his own life and its relation to what his father had been and done. On Friday, while James Carlyle was being buried in the churchyard in Ecclefechan, Thomas stayed alone in the house and remarked, as he continued to write, that "my Father is now in his grave; sleeping by the side of his loved ones: his face to the East, under the Hope of meeting the Lord when He shall come to Judgment—when the Times shall be fulfilled. Mysterious Life! Yes, there is a God in man."[82] On Sunday night he finished the memoir. His mother's words of comfort, " 'It is God that has done it; be still, my dear children,' " brought the first stages of an uneasy quietness and peace to the family heart.[83] But it was not until he had put down on paper the past that he cherished and the emotions that seemed sacredly enveloped in the contours first of his father's life and now of his own that the eldest son could return to making his way in the world.

[8]

"My China Row Chelsea" 1832–1834

As eagerly as he had come to London, Carlyle now made preparations to leave. His old fantasy that rural life was good for his health had again asserted itself. He imagined that he and Jane would make Craigenputtoch more a hearth and less an exile by cultivating small domestic matters and taking "a greater interest in the people there."[1] Suffering from nervous exhaustion when she arrived in London, Jane had been plagued by recurrent headaches, menstrual cramps, heavy bleeding, and nasal and bronchial afflictions that ranged from minor colds to aching influenzas. It was all the more powerful a sign of her unhappiness at giving up London social life that she felt even more low and dismal as the time for departure approached in March 1832. She would hardly admit to herself, let alone to others, how depressed she felt. But her husband confidently believed that he was doing the right thing. As he wound up his affairs, he assumed for both of them that we "are glad to have come to London, and glad to leave it."[2] Among other things, the sight of Irving descending either to Bedlam or to excommunication—or to both—could be borne better from the distance. Visiting immediately after the news of James Carlyle's death, his old friend had insisted on comforting him with prayers and attitudes that Carlyle found mawkishly repulsive, an affront to his father's calm manliness. Yet, clearly, Irving was sincere. Such sickness, unlike Jane's, was beyond cure.

Despite the unhealthiness of the London literary climate, the Carlyles appreciated the healthy friends they had, for "there *is* actually some reasonable conversation to be come at . . . amid the mass of Stupidity and Falsehood,"[3] he wrote to his mother. Jeffrey was the best of those he could not tolerate, Fraser, his eager and contemptible publisher, the worst; on the one side appeared the light frothiness of the Regency inheritance, on the other the grubby materialism of literature as a business. Carlyle already wore his seriousness like a Victorian dark

Thomas Carlyle. Steel engraving from sketch by Daniel Maclise, 1832. Reprinted from Wilson and MacArthur, vol. 2, frontispiece.

coat. "Nothing in this world is to me more mournful, distressing and in the end intolerable, than mirth not based on Earnestness (for it is false mirth); than wit, pretending to be wit, and yet not based on wisdom."[4] Fraser he dealt with peremptorily, driving a hard bargain for his essay on Johnson, which he had divided into two parts. That Fraser had been willing to publish him when all others refused did not at all moderate his proud demand that he be paid at least what he imagined he could get from some other publisher. In February 1832, at the same time as he allowed the artist Daniel Maclise to sketch his portrait for a series of brief biographies of writers which would appear in *Fraser's Magazine,* he was pleased to receive Napier's positive response to his proposal that he write an article on Ebenezer Elliott's recently published *Corn-Law Rhymes.*

Maclise's sketch he thought completely inaccurate, "except in the coat and boots, and hair of the head."[5] Like so much of London life, it was a misrepresentation, its depiction of a rather dandyish-looking young man in a pose of relaxed indifference mistaking the surface affectation for the inner reality. The sketch had robbed him of his earnestness, and for the visitor from Scotland it was the exciting interplay of earnestness and mirth which provided the context essential to men who wished to find comfort and inspiration in one another's company. The sincerity and the seriousness of personality without which nothing worthwhile could be accomplished did not seem to him in the least incompatible with bold imagination, sweetness of character, wild humor, and verbal wit. Carlyle found these qualities in his conversations with Mill, D'Eichthal, Sarah Austin, Crabb Robinson, who had returned from Rome, Charles Buller, whose ill health shortly took him out of town, and even with Glen, in whom he could not help noticing increasing signs of mental disorder. But the rest of the brotherhood were a small and even wavering group, the worst a "wholly miserable" lot "of whom one can say nothing, except it were a prayer for them."[6]

Among his new friends in the literary brotherhood was Leigh Hunt. Carlyle already had one foot on the road back to Scotland when he received, at Hunt's request through the young, unknown John Forster, a copy of the latest book by the veteran Romantic turned journalist who had been Shelley's friend. Hunt and his wife Marianne provided congenial company for a series of visits throughout February and into March. But Carlyle never had any doubt that Hunt was incapable of the kind of earnestness and moral sincerity that he admired and ultimately insisted upon as a condition of friendship. Like Jeffrey, Hunt sparkled on the surface with bright eyes and glittering wit. A generous, affectionate man who lived for the moment, he was eager to enjoy comforts that his precarious livelihood frequently denied him and unwilling to let weighty matters of the common sort dampen his high spirits and love of conversation. Despite a series of bankruptcies, illnesses, and toilsome enslavements to journalism, nothing could "persuade him that Man is born for another object here than *to be happy.*"[7] To the sober Carlyle, Hunt was a phenomenon to be remarked on and marveled at but never to be elevated as a model or emulated as a man. Still, he saw in Hunt a nobleness of spirit which seemed somehow innocent and childlike, as if Hunt's growth had been arrested at some adolescent stage of lovable irresponsibility. "Poor Hunt! nowhere or never an ignoble man!"[8] But Carlyle was certain that he could never have any communion of spirit with a man for whom happiness was the end and purpose of life; he valued Hunt, and they made efforts to be friends, but the relationship hardly gave him pause in his preparations for departure.

While he and Jane were at Dumfries, on their way to Craigenputtoch, Carlyle learned that Goethe had died. He took the event calmly, though solemnly, as if the death of his "spiritual father" provided an exclamation point to the death of his physical father. Whatever tears he had shed for James Carlyle, he was dry-eyed about Goethe, who had lived for him less as a man than as an embodiment of his own hope for the future. His highest obligation to Goethe was to fulfill that hope. Goethe was "not to be mourned over, but to be viewed with reverence, with solemn awe. 'How beautifully sinks that summer sun! So dies a Hero; glorious; to be worshipped!' "[9] Now that necessity demanded, Carlyle felt he was ready to function as a father himself, the eldest son serving as the head of the family, the disciple of Goethe and German literature ready to stand on his own feet. Arriving at Craigenputtoch, which seemed a peaceful purgatory, a moment of pause between two actions, he thought it important that he pay his last respects to his mentor. Besides, he had as many as three separate requests from editors to provide a brief prose eulogy on Goethe's death. Stalling Napier, who expected momentarily to receive the completed essay on the *Corn-Law Rhymes,* he quickly composed his memorial for a short-lived magazine edited by Edward Bulwer, and then atoned for his lie to Napier by rushing to complete the promised essay. With the onset of fine spring weather, he enjoyed frequent gallops. He also tussled with a longer essay that he had agreed to do on Goethe, to settle the score and finally put the word "finish" to his long years of debt.[10]

Though he recognized that Jane's life at Craigenputtoch was "but a dull one," he managed to convince himself that "she seems to desire no other; has, in many things, pronounced the word *Entsagen* [renunciation]," as if she were but a projection of the doctrine of selflessness which he believed Goethe had taught him to be the highest principle of disinterested conduct. Like a creator of a fiction who is unaware of the personal resonances of his own verbal creations, he responded to her occasional expressions of boredom by telling her "many times" that "there is *much* for her to do, if she were trained to it: her whole Sex to deliver from the bondage to Frivolity Dollhood and Imbecillity into the freedom of Valour and Womanhood."[11] Unwilling, even unable, to challenge the self-serving assumptions that underlay his advice and his definition of womanhood, Jane more often than not gave every appearance of accepting her husband's and her own position, especially since it was clear that their eventual deliverance from Craigenputtoch depended completely on his decisions. She continued "the strangest shadowy existence," in which everything but daily necessities was "all a dream of the absent and distant, of things past and to come."[12]

In the meantime, Carlyle had finally completed the essay on Goethe's works and seemed now in comparatively good spirits. As the spring and summer of 1832 passed, the question of the definition and role of the writer in contemporary society hovered constantly in the back of his mind. He was eager to do an essay on authorship that would be an exercise in self-definition as well as in cultural analysis. But he hesitated to put pen to paper, partly because Napier seemed disinterested, mostly because he sensed that to publish his private thoughts on the matter at this time would be to challenge his limited tolerance for public exposure. He would not risk emphasizing the gap between his idealized model and his own modest achievements. To his private journal he confided the extremity of his self-definition: "Authors are martyrs—witnesses for the truth—or else nothing. Money cannot make or unmake them. They are made or unmade, commanded and held back by God Almighty alone, whose inspiration it is that giveth them understanding."[13] Margaret Carlyle's expectation that her son would be a priest of the church resonated as he transformed his chosen profession into a new priesthood, Presbyterian election combining with Romantic elevation of the artist. Authors, he wrote, "are truly the Church; and peace will never be till they are recognised as such and sanctioned and solemnly obligated to the functions thereof,—say this time two hundred years . . . and no Church Reform but only a Church New-creation can be of any avail."[14]

To Mill, his most faithful London correspondent, he maintained a semblance of modesty, aware that his religious fervor, even if in unorthodox approaches, might drive a wider wedge between them. London news and then packets of books from Mill's well-stocked personal library were almost as welcome as the delicate but obsessively involving dialogue the two men held on their roles as authors. Attracted to Carlyle, but wary if not frightened of what seemed his shamanism, Mill protected himself by increasing the distance between them, elevating his friend and denigrating himself. He argued sincerely, and accurately, that Carlyle was an artist, he himself an interpreter of artists; the former was a creator, the latter a mediator between the creator and his audience. His own value, he believed, resided in his capability both to understand the artist and to communicate the artist's message to the world in prosaic but understandable ways. As his own self-sacrificing relationship with Harriet Taylor intensified, he took a back seat to no one in emphasizing his inferiority to higher creatures. "And it is thus that I may be, and therefore ought to be," he wrote to Carlyle (humbled by his admiration for his friend's widely praised essay on Johnson), "not useless as an auxiliary even to you, though I am sensible that I can never give back to you the value of what I receive."[15] Somewhat embarrassed by the explicitness of Mill's praise, Carlyle half-heartedly attempted to downplay an evaluation with which he basically agreed. It was easy for him to recommend Mill to Leigh Hunt as "one of the best, clearest-headed and clearest-hearted young men now living in London."[16]

Their own distance from London and their friends soon made the Carlyles feel lonely and restless. The peaceful but purgatorial summer was certain to be followed by an unhappy winter if they remained isolated. Apparently Jane, frequently ill and quietly depressed, had little to say other than to affirm her passivity on such matters. She took a bitter but resigned pleasure in remarking that she had the remains of a fine woman, the "mischievous creature" of some years ago "sober enough now—a long succession of bad days and sleepness nights have ef[f]ectually tamed her."[17] Her husband, on the contrary, felt an almost explosively willful energy, "a boundless appetite for reading," bulwarked by what he called " 'desperate hope': . . . I feel a kind of defiant assurance that much shall yet be well with me, the rather as I care little *whether or not*."[18] Seemingly unconcerned, for the moment, about his own health, he worried slightly about Jane's, particularly when she went to nurse her mother, who during the autumn became ill with an unspecified "nervous disability" whose symptoms anticipated Jane's during her own nervous illnesses years later.

Though he had worked hard—writing an obituary and a long essay on Goethe, an aborted article on Byron, the piece on the *Corn-Law Rhymes,* and then reading through the complete works of Diderot for an essay that he finished in October—he did not see why he could not work equally hard, if he chose, in a more socially and intellectually stimulating place. By midsummer he had convinced Jane that he would go mad without more people to talk to. "The solitude here, generally very irksome, is threatening to get injurious, to get intolerable."[19] But the "beautiful autumn days" passed tranquilly enough, primarily because they had by then already decided to spend the winter in Edinburgh. Now possessing more than sufficient funds, he even considered the possibility of publishing *Sartor* at his own expense. Jane shortly wrote to her cousin Eliza to look for a house or flat for them with three crucial qualities—"first it must be free of bugs, secondly of *extraordinary* noises—and lastly of a high rent."[20] As soon as he had finished writing on Diderot, he began to clear the way for the move. Certain to return, but only for the next summer, Carlyle was beginning to accept the prospect that in the future he would be a city dweller.

He was somewhat tired from his crowded schedule of reading and writing and thought he would mainly look around and read while in Edinburgh. He had an unwavering contempt of writing for periodicals, except as financial necessity demanded, and, unsatisfied by the unpublished *Sartor,* was again ambitious to write a major work of his own. Fascinated by the history of the National Church of Scotland, which was richly interwoven with his own life and the history of his nation, he determined to read everything he could find on the subject. His interest in France and the French Revolution was also intense. "If among your modern French Books," he told Mill, "you can spare me any that really illustrate the late condition of that country (under *any* of its aspects) they were highly welcome. . . . Any tolerable History of the Revolution. . . . I am very curious about France. Indeed I thank Heaven I have still a boundless curiosity about all human *things.*"[21] In the autumn and winter, and through the next year, Mill, who was an intense Francophile and a close student of French culture and history, eagerly lent him whatever he had, on occasion even buying for his own library books he thought Carlyle might need. Though Carlyle could only partly realize it, he had begun to focus on a great and challenging theme. The writing of his essay on Diderot; his recent contacts with the Saint-Simonians; his response to the current political agitation and Reform Bill rhetoric; his friendship with Mill; his own reading and writing on France, including his essay on Voltaire, and his visit to Paris in 1824; and, not least, his fascination with both personal and public images of fire, electricity, and revolution—all were beginning to draw together, beaming intensely, like a torchlight, on the French Revolution, revealing it as the key event of modern times.

The Carlyles ate their usual plain Christmas dinner at Craigenputtoch. Their departure was briefly delayed, first by Grace Welsh's illness and then by the death of Walter Welsh, Jane's maternal grandfather. But on New Year's Day 1833 Carlyle rode through "a world of frost-mist and snow-*slush* being almost superstitiously determined to see [his] Mother once more" before he left.[22] They spent the night talking quietly by the fire, surrounded by "despondency," made bearable by "love" and "sacred duty." By the end of the first week of the new year he was in Edinburgh, in rented rooms, at least "till the beginning of April."[23]

2.

His four months in Edinburgh helped him to conclude that he could live neither there nor in Craigenputtoch. Indeed, there was some doubt in his mind that he could live in Britain at all. Countless shipfuls of emigrants, fleeing overpopulation and underemployment, sailed westward with a regularity that both frightened and attracted him. The fear that his own survival might demand emigration heightened his identification with these victims of scarcity. Faced with the threat of violent revolution, England had decided to experiment with political revolution. To Carlyle, a reformed Parliament meant democracy, but democracy was in effect "*no* Government." In an overpopulated country with a scarcity economy, how could semi-anarchy work?[24] The explosive pressure of scarcity, he concluded, could be alleviated only by emigration, which, if England had wise captains, would become an organized government program, its additional virtue being that it would create flourishing outposts of Anglo-Saxon culture in distant regions of the world.[25]

Since he had gone directly from London to Craigenputtoch the previous year, Carlyle now could not help but measure the English against the Scottish capital. Edinburgh seemed stagnant and provincial, a village compared to the cosmopolitan bustle of the "brick Babylon." With the passage of the Reform Bill the previous June even political tension had slackened into mumbling and whispered exhaustion. Always more contained, puritan, and middle-class than London, Edinburgh seemed to have no intellectual vigor. Its sedateness goaded the enthusiastic visitor into both immediate dissatisfaction and an intensely argumentative frame of mind. Old Edinburgh friends found him irritable. He almost always seemed eager to talk, even if only to shock others, in extreme ways about subjects they would just as soon have let alone. Of his Edinburgh acquaintances the only one who seemed somewhat "earnest" was Sir William Hamilton, a well-read and optimistic middle-aged man who had some small importance as a philosopher.[26] He was "finely social and human," with a "courageous trust in humanity." An athletic man, he took long walks with Carlyle, who was happy in his awareness that Sir William genuinely liked him.[27] Jeffrey, who spent much of January socializing with the Carlyles, urged Carlyle not to "fancy that people repel you" and even claimed that his young friend was becoming more "tolerant" of his "fellow sinners."[28]

The disenchantment with Edinburgh was increased by the fact that Jane, who loved the city and felt at home in it, was ill with colds and influenza for much of the time. Initially attended by an elderly, old-fashioned doctor for whom she had great respect, she imagined that she would soon be well, especially since the doctor accurately reported that, organically, there was nothing wrong with her. "Sick and heartless" much of the time, she also seemed to have "a kind of seated dyspepsia," which Carlyle thought was much like his own. As in so many marriages, the stronger personality seemed to be transforming the weaker into a mirror image of itself.[29] Though the "old Doctor" continued to come, he confessed "his inability to help her much."[30] A visit from her Liverpool cousin, who was young and affectionate, and from her mother, who at fifty-one suddenly looked strikingly older, did not raise her spirits. Both Carlyles were aware how far behind them was the younger generation, how close to themselves and to death the older.

Still, they had no difficulty in carrying on with a leisurely schedule of rest, quiet mornings, regular visits, and constant reading. More than anything else, the availability of books justified the stay in Edinburgh. Carlyle regularly went to the Advocate's Library and the College Library, reading whatever of interest he could find on the history of the Scottish church and on the French Revolution. As before, he supplemented his reading with the books he borrowed from Mill, whose collection included items on the Revolution which could not be found in any other library in Britain. Aware that Mill himself had vague plans to write on the Revolution, Carlyle urged him to have his say, but Mill claimed that he lacked the self-confidence to undertake a major work at this time. Miserably depressed, Mill imagined that Carlyle was in high spirits. He responded to Carlyle's enthusiastic assurances of love with the self-deprecating confession that he felt himself incapable of loving, that he envied his friend's exhilaration, faith, and affectionate personality. Since Carlyle's letters to Mill tended to be exhortative, Mill wanted to believe that those high moments of affirmation, which seemed to bask in the supernatural glow of the natural, represented Carlyle's general frame of mind.

In reality, Carlyle's correspondence with his London friends was his only escape from an almost unrelievedly bleak humor. Edinburgh was depressed, economically, spiritually, and intellectually. Most everyone and everything seemed stupid, even contemptible, and Carlyle did little to conceal his attitude. Jane's ill health of course undercut domestic cheerfulness. He counseled his younger sister, who had set her heart on marrying a young man the family had doubts about, that she would have to live permanently with the consequences of her action. His own health seemed stable but unsatisfactory, as if dyspepsia were to be his normal condition, though at this time it appeared he suffered, at worst, from a somewhat sensitive stomach. He did take strength from the one "great Truth, . . . that the Supernatural differs not from the Natural."[31] But it was a truth that Edinburgh neither corroborated nor supported in any particular way.

On a "beautiful spring day; the season of hope," he affirmed that it is "beautiful that *I*, here and now, am alive!"[32] But even in good spirits, he found the question of where to live a formidable problem. He had done an essay on Count Cagliostro while in Edinburgh and now contemplated writing something connected with his reading on the French Revolution. Since he now realized that he actually could *not* afford to publish *Sartor* at his own expense, he thought that he might persuade Fraser to publish it as a series of articles. Though his prospects for magazine publication were undoubtedly less promising than in previous years, where the couple lived was not a question of money. With economic depression, it cost no more to live in Edinburgh than at Craigenputtoch. But further residence in Edinburgh, except insofar as it increased the availability of books, now seemed irrelevant to his work.

Thus, early in May 1833, they sent their possessions back to Craigenputtoch and reserved seats on the Thornhill coach. Aware that her habit was always to be too early, her husband's to be too late, Jane did everything possible to hurry them toward the depot, but they arrived to see the coach "vanishing at the far end of Princes Street!"[33] They returned to their lodgings and hid, departing on the next coach two days later. Jane had a fearful headache, and by the time they arrived at Templand she had developed influenza, from which her mother was suffering as well. A week later, however, they were finally home. As they drove up to the house, Jane was heartbroken to see that the proud grove of trees her father had planted so many years ago had burned to the ground, destroyed by an accidental fire that the indifferent tenant had failed to stop.

Fortunately, Carlyle's plan to have Fraser publish "Thoughts on Clothes" under a new title in serial parts worked, providing about £80 and fifty-eight bound author's copies at a time when he had no prospects beyond the publication of "Count Cagliostro" in *Fraser's* summer issue. From November 1833 to August 1834, the much maligned Fraser, as dependable as ever, ran the installments of *Sartor Resartus* despite the almost uniformly negative comments, not to speak of cancellations, from bewildered readers. In the meantime, Carlyle fidgeted through what he thought of as "months of suffering and painful indolence" at Craigenputtoch.[34] While the absence of commissions had grave practical consequences, it also provided him the opportunity to feel deeply how frustrated he was as a writer. "The chief desire of my mind," he exclaimed to Jack, "has again become to *write* a masterpiece." Fortunately, his supply of books was augmented substantially when he was given access to a sizable private library about ten miles away. The man who throughout his life resented what seemed the conspiracy of institutions and librarians to prevent free access to books was grateful for this opportunity; Barjarg Library was "really a very great favour."[35] He believed the highest good any government could do was to establish a public library in every village and city. Whatever his dismal frame of mind, especially as the winter came on, at least reading was "like a kind of manuring compost," without which he could not survive, let alone grow.[36]

Late in August, a completely unexpected and unknown visitor, bearing a note of introduction from Mill through Gustave D'Eichthal, "found the house amid desolate heathery hills." Ralph Waldo Emerson later described his host as "tall and gaunt, with a cliff-like brow," a man who was "clinging to his northern accent with evident relish; full of lively anecdote, and with a streaming humour which floated everything he looked upon."[37] Impressed by Emerson's gentleness and flattered that the American had made a pilgrimage to Scotland to see him, Carlyle insisted that his guest stay overnight to give them at least that much opportunity to get to know one another. Eager for companionship, Carlyle was at his entertaining best. He impressed Emerson with his wide range of literary and philosophic knowledge and with the broad motifs of his nonsectarian spiritualism. Emerson, who recently had lost his wife and his own sectarian commitment, responded favorably to Carlyle's personality and to his emphasis on renunciation, spiritual timelessness, and the search for spiritual heroes in modern culture. Like Mill, Emerson felt that Carlyle was a charismatic presence whose power for spiritual good overrode particular differences of personality and belief.

When Emerson left the next day, an unusual friendship had begun. Its great sustaining factors were that it was conducted primarily through the mails and that Emerson worked so diligently for Carlyle. No matter how wavering the Englishman's opinion of his American friend's intellectual and political positions, Carlyle could never forget that Emerson had come to visit him in the wilderness and then worked in practical ways on his behalf. He recognized immediately that, for all their similarities, the crucial difference was one of personality. The very element that he himself lacked was the element Carlyle loved most in his new friend: "What I loved in the man," he reported to Mill, "was his health, his unity with himself; all people and all things seemed to find their quite peaceable adjustment with him, not a proud domineering one, as after doubtful *contest,* but a spontaneous-looking, peaceable, even humble one."[38] Whether or not Carlyle saw Emerson plain, he clearly recognized a contrast against which he could better understand himself.

Much to Carlyle's disappointment, however, the guest whom he expected did not come. Though Mill had for a time planned to visit Scotland during late September or October, his commitment to Harriet Taylor transcended any other obligations and the much-anticipated visit to Carlyle suddenly disappeared into the distance. He wrote to Carlyle from Paris, apologizing with the vague claim that he had been taken abroad by an inescapable high duty. Harriet, who was then in the first stage of a trial separation from her husband—a separation complicated by the difficult problem of the disposition of the children—had found a trip to Paris to be a temporary but successful evasion of her agreement not to see Mill during this period. From Paris, where he did some research errands for him, and then from London again late in November, Mill assured Carlyle that he could spend the winter in the French capital at a reasonable cost. But when Carlyle hinted that London was likely to be his eventual destination, Mill eagerly asserted that only there would he find a small but growing band of sympathetic hearts whose companionship would make him happy.

Knowing little of Mill's private affairs, Carlyle tactfully curbed his own imagination. Like Emerson, Mill seemed the best kind of disciple: one with sufficient strength of reputation and mind to have credibility. It did not seem sensible to ask awkward questions about his relationship with Mrs. Taylor. In the meantime, Mill sent books, encouraged him to write on a subject that he himself had long planned to write on, and discretely questioned his grandiose, prophetic view of history as well as the effectiveness of his ironic style. Carlyle readily defended his notion that a "right *History* (that impossible thing I mean by History) of the French Revolution were the grand Poem of our Time." His ironic style he felt less comfortable in defending, except as a reflection of his "unreasonable temper," his isolation from his audience, and the "genuine feeling of the ludicrous" which underlay his "gloom." Recognizing that the knife of irony cuts two ways, into his audience *and* into himself, he believed, "I could have been the merriest of men, *had* I *not* been the sickest & saddest." By September 1833, Carlyle had in fact already decided that he could be the great poet of history and the Revolution. Mill's role was to help him with books and information; Carlyle urged Mill to write to him "as to your elder Brother."[39]

By now it was also clear that he could fulfill his mission best in London.[40] And, the matter of work aside, Carlyle had a deep emotional need to see the city again. Whatever the practical difficulties, he had begun to believe that they could be overcome as readily there as at Craigenputtoch, away from the solitude of "the everlasting skies and the everlasting moors; the hum of the world all mute as Death."[41] To Carlyle, Craigenputtoch now seemed an inhuman paradise in which frustration and madness were more likely than fulfillment and peace. It was "a place we never knew good in," he later confessed to Jack, "except what we gained as at the sword's point . . . a place I care not if I never see again!"[42] Whatever his own health, he now believed that his mind and his spirit, that part of himself he most valued, had a greater opportunity for harmony in London, which was the center of all activity, than anyplace else. When the alternative of a position at the astronomical observatory in Edinburgh arose in December, he was furiously bitter at Jeffrey for not supporting him but also relieved that the trap of financial security had not compelled him to live where he did not want to.

The strongest hold on him in Scotland was his family, "the little circle of my own kindred."[43] But at Craigenputtoch life "is but a kind of Life-in-Death . . . one sits as in the Belly of some Trojan Horse . . . neck and heels crushed together. Let us burst it, in the name of God," he urged Jack.[44] He was on the verge of making the break, no matter how painful, when, late in February 1834, their servant quietly announced that she would leave them at the beginning of summer, regardless of their plans. Their long-deliberated and deeply felt desire to move to London had become so strong that suddenly the decision to do so existed as if it had already been made long before. After a few minutes' meditation, they said to one another: "Why not *bolt,* out of all these rocky despicabilities . . . and peat-moss, and isolation, and exasperation, and confusion, and go at once to London?"[45] He dreaded to tell his mother. "I will say who knows but you [Jack] and I may yet bring her up to London to pass her old days waited on by both of us!" Whatever would happen, "go whither she may, she will have her Bible with her and her Faith in God."[46] For him, it seemed his last chance to free himself and redeem his life as an artist and as a missionary.

As they made their plans for Thomas to go in advance to search for a house, he did his best to control the guilt and unhappiness of his departure, which all the Carlyles knew would be permanent. He communed with himself, seeking relief: "May God direct us and go with us! My poor mother! But once for all one must cut himself loose though his heart bleed; it is better than perennial torpor which ends in death." He planted flowers in the garden without the expectation of seeing them in the spring. "It is a bodeful, *huge* feeling I have, like one to be delivered from a Bastille; and who says, delivered? or cast out?" By March he felt strong enough to accept the pain. "Many things are sad to me: the saddest is to forsake my poor mother; for it is a kind of *forsaking,* though she, too, sees well the necessity of it. May He to whom she ever looks not forsake her!"[47] At the beginning of the second week in May, with Alick and Jamie standing silently at the pier, he took the ferry from Annan, and left behind, with a wave of his hat and with "something like a tear" trembling in his eyes, a family and a promise that whatever the distance between them they would never in truth be parted.[48] On first sighting London again, he hummed the defiant words of a ballad that his mother had frequently sung to him when he was a boy.[49]

3.

"What if I should go to America myself?" he had asked Jack back in December.[50] But now he was in London, where so much—perhaps even the final opportunity to avoid emigration—depended on whether or not he could make a success of his new project, "like a rising from the grave . . . like an issuing from the Bastille."[51] Behind him were "six of the strangest years . . . that ever fell to the lot of any mortal." But he was not growing "younger or stronger by waiting."[52] In front of him, as he entered London humming that magic childhood song, was the difficulty of finding a place for them to live, then of finding something for them to live on, at least after the initial year. He had £200 in cash, enough to sustain the immediate future, and the prospect of additional income from the publication of "The Diamond Necklace" and a series of articles or a book on the French Revolution would keep despair away, provided that expenses could be kept down. The key was the rental of a suitable house.

With Leigh Hunt's convivial assistance, the choice was narrowed, after three weeks of leg-aching effort in Kensington, Knightsbridge, and Chelsea, to a house on Brompton Road and one on Cheyne Row. Having exhausted himself, and all other reasonable prospects as well, Carlyle detailed the comparative advantages and disadvantages to Jane, coming down slightly on the side of the house in Chelsea, but with the proviso that no decision need be made until she herself arrived. When, almost a year before, Hunt had touted the attractions of his new location in Chelsea on Upper Cheyne Row, they had seemed somewhat the less for Hunt's very presence there. But Carlyle's fear that the Hunts would be "intrusive" was contained by the striking advantages of a comparatively spacious, high-ceilinged, "excellent Old House with a garden on a tree-lined street within a short walk of the river." Located in a quiet and unfashionable part of town, it was available at the strikingly low rent of £35 per annum.

Cheyne Row, Chelsea. Etching. Reprinted from *New Letters and Memorials of Jane Welsh Carlyle,* edited by A. Carlyle (London, 1903).

When Jane arrived early in June, her "little canary-bird" Chico in tow, she was again suffering from a severe headache. After a few days of dashing about London "in all manner of miscellaneous conveyances" to look at house prospects, he and Jane found that the virtues of the house at 5 Cheyne Row triumphed. Among its advantages were village-like quietness within a half-hour walk or a ten-minute ride of the center of London and a prevailing west wind that blew urban pollution away from them. In addition, the house seemed free of the bugs that Jane so feared. With Bessy Barnet, whom Mrs. Montagu, with typical spite, accused of having been Badams' mistress but in whom the Carlyles had great confidence and could treat "not as a servant but as a friend," they moved in on June 10, 1834, never to live anyplace else for the rest of their lives.[53] Thomas informed his mother that "it is pronounced '*Chainie* Row': a fine, quiet old street of about 20 houses, with huge old trees opposite us in front, and then a most silent—brick wall. The river is near, and very gay"[54]

Despite the gaity of this lively London springtime, Carlyle was keenly aware that he had begun a solemn and risky adventure on which depended not only his livelihood but the credibility of his role as an artist. The book that he began writing in September occupied his energies for the next three years, the one volume that he had imagined he would finish by the spring of 1835 expanding into three. "In general, except when writing, I never feel myself that I am *alive*."[55] More than anything else, he wanted to write a a masterpiece, an achievement that would be a work of art rather than a work of expository logic or historical fact.[56] His own knowledge had been grounded in a series of revelatory experiences which told him that his strength as a man and as a writer was in his vision of the supernatural within the natural, the patterns of providence within the facts of history. Having already isolated the decisive conflux of events in modern European history, he now thought it inevitable that he would forge himself as an artist on the hot crucible of that most explosive and significant of events. If he could deal effectively with both the drama and the meaning of the French Revolution, he would make a contribution that, either now or later, the world would have to notice, for the patterns of the Revolution, after all, were woven into the living fabric of contemporary society.[57]

From London, where he enjoyed the help of Mill and where vast numbers of books were available, he could see Paris and France more clearly than from Craigenputtoch. Modern European man had had his clothes burned off by the fires of the Revolution; he could be seen in his nakedness without the outworn symbols of the past, struggling in his contemporary affairs to find new garments, new symbols to express his changed condition. Within art and the power of language, Carlyle felt, were the resources to create the purgative drama that would once and for all persuade society that the old could never be revived and that the new was in the process of being born. Since belief systems and the institutions that clothed them were at issue, it was not a matter of thought and logic, but of feeling and faith. The only kind of writing that could deal persuasively with the central issues, Carlyle believed, was a literature grounded in "Reality." In the facts of history the artist could discern the ultimate reality of the supernatural, just as he could also see God in man.

The object of the artist, then, was to seize the facts with the transforming power of fire, Carlyle's favorite metaphor for creativity, and in the case of the Revolution to seize fire with fire, a double conflagration that promised both the flames that would destroy the old and those out of which the new would be born. Any history that aimed to present the objective facts foundered on the delusion that external reality had some absolute, identifiable quality. Actually, the limitations of the subjective vision inevitably determined, even for the so-called objective historian, that which he was capable of seeing. For Carlyle, whatever objectivity there was resided in the universal and providential laws that man glimpsed only with the eye of poetry and religion. These laws were not even accessible to logic and intellect, and, once perceived, they taught that ultimate trust had to be placed in the visionary capability of extraordinary men.

Such visionary artists could find the larger patterns of truth within historical facts, patterns whose ultimate proof lay in the intuitive acceptance of the subjective unconscious and the unfathomable, mysterious nature of all life. For man lives by the "Inward Sense," and the most important facts of history are ultimately "of the spiritual kind."[58] Whatever man seizes upon and indeed creates in the external world is a product of his moral being, which has mysterious depths that cannot be confined within the narrow limitations of logical definition and objective history. The spiritual mystery and power of the universe are independent of specific belief systems and their institutions, independent even of Christianity. For Carlyle, the important aim was to find some spiritual ideal on which to base human institutions and conduct, an ideal that could provide the sustaining spark for a society in which evil men and devils would have their due. To find a "a *genuine* ideal," as the Scottish Kirk had done, was the essential work of mankind. Though such ideals would last only a time and then lose their power ("each generation has its own faith, more or less; and laughs at the faith of its predecessor,—most unwisely"), the historical events in which such ideals are embodied must be studied and appreciated.[59] For, if it were a *genuine* ideal, it would retain its power to influence the future.

For Carlyle, history had in effect become the "sanction" of the seer and the prophet, for it enabled him to address the realities of the present and the future while discussing the "realities" of the past. For the Romantic artist, sanction came from personal rebellion; for the new Victorian seer, sanction was grounded in social involvement, through history, among other channels. Until 1834, Carlyle felt he had "absolutely no permission to speak!"[60] But the sustaining energy that came from his new certainty that the ultimate poetry was within history gave him the courage to believe that by writing a history of the French Revolution he could make the contribution that would authenticate the new role he had chosen for himself.

All around him there were his "*enfans perdus* [lost children]," including Mill and Charles Buller and other young, idealistic Radicals.[61] He not only wished them well but hoped to bring them in from the wilderness, not to the shelter of the old institutions, which he believed were dead or dying, but to the enterprise of creating new structures whose clothes and symbols would be vital and alive. Though the Radicals claimed to be atheists, "the true Atheist" was the Whig, who "worships . . . nothing but Respectability." The Tory was "an Idolator," worshiping a variety of gods that the French Revolution had destroyed. But the Radical is "a wild heathen Iconoclast" who "has an *infinite* hope" and who looks toward the future.[62] To the extent that they could not see the unconscious, mysterious nature of the larger reality, the Radicals constantly lost their way in the effort, misapplying much of their energy and idealism.

But Carlyle could identify with their energy, their youth, and their hope for the future, and he could mildly, but nevertheless unvaryingly, disagree with any efforts to identify him with their programs. The Radical encouragement of secular atheism was the "saddest of counter-perversities: the denial that Man or the World has any Father but Death." But "whoever recognises the infinite nature of Duty believes in a God, against his own Consciousness," as if God or what that word represents is an ineradicable, unconscious, mysterious force that must manifest itself in good men, despite their intellectual claims. Toward atheism he felt "dissent and sympathy, nothing more," certainly not disdain or condemnation.[63] But, unlike the Radicals, whose good works and loving personalities, at least in the case of Charles Buller, brought them within the definition of God's influence, he would place more emphasis on self-improvement than on other-improvement, on "the working out of what was best and purest" in oneself.[64]

With Leigh Hunt, who had little respect for marriage as an institution, Carlyle argued that it was the duty of man to maintain as best he could whatever moderately satisfactory institutions he had until he could replace them with something better. The instinct to conserve was strong. But, like the Radicals, he believed that there was nothing worse than attempting to perpetuate institutions that had outlived their usefulness, that were, in fact, only pretending to be alive, usually for some self-serving purpose, one of whose results was to prevent the birth of the new. The king had best be seen to be naked if there were to be any chance of creating more life-inspiring clothes for the future. Those institutions that perpetuated misery, promoted anarchy, denied individual responsibility, and depended on machines and materialism undermined the intuitive spirituality within man and deprived the people of hope for the future. They were already tinder about to burst into consuming fire. It would be best to help such fires to burn, which one could do simply by recognizing the reality. The role of the artist and the prophet was to invoke the language that would dramatize the flames. "IMPOSTURE is in flames, Imposture is burnt up: one red sea of Fire, wild-billowing, enwraps the World; with its fire-tongue licks at the very Stars." For the moment he was capable of believing that the French Revolution had begun "the End of the dominion of IMPOSTURE."[65]

[9]

Fire and Friends 1834–1837

Soon after Carlyle published *The French Revolution* in June 1837, "little Queen Victory" came to the throne. One year later, pressured by a visitor from Scotland, Carlyle reluctantly watched the coronation procession wind through the London streets from the palace at Pimlico to Westminster Abbey. Among the huge crowds that lined the coronation route were many men who romanticized the seventeen-year-old queen.[1] But Carlyle had been educated in a sterner world, and he would never share the sentimental optimism with which Queen Victoria's accession inflated the liberal imaginations of so many of her young subjects.

Three years later the queen took a consort. Walking through a pouring February rain on his way to a literary breakfast, Carlyle accidentally saw the marriage procession, his shrewd eyes at once piercing the various mists: "I wish her marriage all prosperity," he wrote to his mother, "but it is her business, not mine. She has many enemies among the Tories, who report all kinds of spiteful things about her; she seems also to have abundance of obstinate temper, and no great overplus of sense: I see too clearly great misery lying in store for her, if she live some years; and Prince Albert, I can tell him, has got no sinecure by the end."[2] To Carlyle, the new queen seemed the appropriate embodiment of the worst qualities of the country as a whole. In his most gloomy moments, he imagined that the script had been written and the cast chosen by a vengeful heaven that would not for long tolerate selfishness, hypocrisy, and stupidity.

Whatever his gloomy prediction for the public future, he had himself passed an excruciatingly difficult three years since his return to London. The change from the rocky silence of Craigenputtoch to the flat tumult of London seemed almost surreal. During the first months, he adjusted to a different landscape by superimposing other scenes and thoughts. Many of his walks were solitary, often by choice, sometimes of necessity.[3] There was company enough, but its quality was not satisfying.[4]

Like other Victorians, Carlyle dreamt of a perfect fellowship, the family extended and improved. Though far from an optimist, he had retained through the lonely Craigenputtoch years a desire for some "higher cooperation," a noble fellowship.[5] The Scottish wasteland had become impossible, among others reasons precisely because it both intensified and denied the fulfillment of this desire. Now that he was living in London it seemed possible to hope that such a fellowship would become a reality. But, since his formative education had taught him to be selective, his critical assessment of the value of others continually undermined the urge for fellowship. Indeed, the discriminating knife had an even sharper edge, for it had been honed on the Presbyterian doctrine of the elect. "The good are *thin-sown* everywhere, and perhaps not thicker here than elsewhere, tho' there are *more* to choose from," he reminded his family.[6] Without being fully aware of it, Carlyle found himself in the paradoxical position of harboring a vision of companionship, of idealized utopian fellowship, which was incompatible with his emotional need for exclusivity. Only his family could provide such fellowship, a trusted circle of good hearts all committed to God and honesty. But they were miles away in Scotland, and Jack in even more distant Italy.

The one true friend he had made outside his family and marriage was frustratingly close and impossibly distant. Since arriving in London, Carlyle had made four attempts to visit Edward Irving, concerned by the rumors of his isolation and illness. Fearful of Carlyle's influence and jealous of her husband's company, Isabella Irving, along with her fellow Irvingites, carefully controlled access to her saint in his Newman Street "Pagoda." They had good reason for their caution. The prisoner of their mutual illusions was dreadfully sick. With "an insuppressible indignation" that mixed with "pity," Carlyle finally forced admission, but, despite his attempt to be alone with his friend, Isabella would not leave the room. He wrote to Jack, "I never in my time was concerned in another such despicability as I was forced to suspect her of." And as for Irving, "He complains of biliousness, of a pain at his right short-rib; has a short thick cough which comes on at the smallest irritation."[7] The outcome seemed all too clear.

John Badams had died the previous September, but the "tragedy" of his decline had been apparent over a number of years. The news of his death had been a shock, but when Carlyle learned of it in January 1834 it seemed the distant echo of an event already months past. Irving, however, seemed to be dying in front of him. And if Badams was "among the men" he "loved most in the world," Irving had been like a second self, a twin brother.[8] In his frustration, Carlyle fantasied that he would snatch away his "old best Friend" from the madness and fanaticism of his followers "to save him from Death and the Grave!" But he had neither the resolution nor the power to do anything more than visit him "again soon and often."[9]

By September 1834 Irving was somewhat on his feet, and even rode over to Cheyne Row for a brief visit. Carlyle, who urged him to rest, was pleased that he soon went into the country to try to recuperate. Irving visited again in October, ill but composed. In the twenty minutes that he stayed, saying farewell before his departure for Glasgow, he managed to convey his love to his friends and his deep sense of "affectionate" seriousness. He looked around the room and commented that Jane had "always a little bower of elegance round her be where she will."[10] "Darkness at hand, & the weather damp," Carlyle "watched till [Irving] turned the first corner . . . and . . . vanished . . . altogr."[11] He died in Glasgow at the end of the first week in December.

No matter how expected the death, Carlyle was deeply shocked, as if part of himself had been destroyed. Asked to write a memorial essay, he set to work on the "melancholy" task.[12] By the middle of December, he had produced the brief eulogy that Fraser soon published. But the impact of his friend's death was not exorcised by the printed words. The plain facts, and the blame, as Carlyle saw them, could not be made a matter of public discussion at that time. And the personal dimension of the relationship between himself, his wife, and his dear friend seemed too close and too private to permit anything but a formal eulogy. Not until the death of Jane, which reawakened his ache of over thirty years earlier, did he feel compelled to write his detailed reminiscence of Edward Irving, instructing that it not be published until after his own death.

But, in private, Carlyle did ask who and what were responsible for his friend's "early death." The answer to the question was like a warning to himself. "This mad City (for it is mad as Bedlam, nine-tenths of it) killed him; he might have lived prosperous and strong in Scotland, but there was in him a quality which the influences here took fatal hold of."[13] The fatal weakness was an innocent pride, a failure of privacy and asceticism, a view of God and man which allowed society and aspiration to substitute public illusions for personal realities. Irving had not honed his mind on skepticism, his personality on disappointment.

In the end, he lacked the hard common sense that said no to popular delusions, whatever their rationalizing rhetoric. He was too eager to lead, too unwilling to be lonely. Having come to the modern Babylon, he had allowed himself to be deceived into believing that one could have its public applause without being its spokesman and its victim. Carlyle commemorated New Year's Day 1835 by writing in his private journal that he was now "friendless here or as good as that."[14]

But there was no lack of things to do; the autumn had been lovely, the weather "finer" than he had ever experienced before. Visitors came to Cheyne Row, sufficient to the needs of a man who was struggling with a new book and who now, after the death of Irving, made even more of a point to distinguish between acquaintances and friends. During the autumn holidays the town had been quiet. Though he complained of being "too solitary," he took advantage of the lull to get on with his work and to savor quiet evenings of reading.[15] Though Mrs. Hunt soon irritated Jane with her constant attempts to borrow household items, Hunt himself kept his distance, to Carlyle's pleasant surprise (though, in fact, he may have been even a little affronted that Hunt visited so infrequently). The sensitive Hunt apparently overread Carlyle's self-protective messages, but he also found his new neighbor's stern pronouncements about the nature and purpose of life an implied criticism of his own values. Henry Taylor, a civil servant at the Colonial Office and the author of a popular verse idyll, "a good man, whose *laugh* reminds me of poor Irving's," soon became a regular companion, promising to introduce Carlyle to Southey and Wordsworth when they were in town.[16] Carlyle wrote Jack that the couple saw Allan Cunningham "pretty often."[17] And, late in November, he went to a massive Radical meeting with Charles Buller, which he found great entertainment, though "it was bitter earnest with them." Carlyle foresaw murderous violence if the Radicals attempted revolution.

His relationship with Mill was at a standstill, though there was no personal hostility between them. Despite dinners together and occasional walks, the friendship did not deepen. It seemed to Carlyle that Mill had reached the limit of his responsiveness. He was involved with Harriet Taylor in a way that absorbed his emotional energy, and his friends worried where that relationship with "Mrs. (Platonica) Taylor" would take him.[18] In August, the Carlyles had gone to what seemed a slightly awkward dinner at Mrs. Taylor's home. They had met not only John Taylor, "an obtuse most joyous-natured man, the pink of social hospitality," but also the primary influence on the small circle that Harriet Taylor flourished in, the Unitarian minister William Fox, "a little thickset bush-locked man of five-and-forty," whom Carlyle thought as empty intellectually as his Unitarianism was bankrupt spiritually.

Carlyle, however, was more disturbed by the disappointment of his own prospects than by Mill's coldness. The former was remediable, the latter a matter of personality, about which he could do nothing. His £200 would not last for more than a year. Whatever bargain he might enter into with Fraser or some other publisher for his new book was not likely to produce any immediate cash. It had even to be doubted that the sales thereafter, assuming that he had it ready by the next spring and available for sale in the fall, would amount to anything at all, let alone allow him to carry on for another year in London or anyplace else. The opportunity to do a "fluff" article or two for Fraser repelled him and there were no other offers of a concrete sort. His essay "The Diamond Necklace," which he had brought with him to London, had no takers yet. And, at the moment, *Sartor Resartus* was without commercial value. Indeed, the reception of its serial publication had lowered his worth to Fraser, and the bound copies that he had sent to various people had produced only two responses, one from an Irishman, who praised it highly and asked that he be sent anything by this extraordinary writer, the other from Emerson, who soon offered to help publish it as a book for the first time anyplace. Moreover, at dinner at the Taylors', he had learned that he must now dismiss the one hope that he had been keeping quietly in mind. For over a year Mill and his friends had been planning a new Radical journal, explicitly declaring that they expected substantial and frequent contributions from Carlyle and intimating that he might be considered for the editorship. The possibility had been much on Carlyle's mind, but, to no one's surprise but his own, he was not offered the position. That he indeed imagined that he could have been chosen by a committee of London Radicals and that he could have made an effective editor of their journal is characteristic of his capability to deceive himself while under economic stress. Fortunately, this was the last time in which he indulged the expectation that he would be offered a position for which, in reality, he was unsuited.

When Carlyle began writing *The French Revolution* in September 1834, he encouraged himself with the delusion that he would be done by March 1835. Extensive reading in histories and memoirs of the period had filled almost two years of his imagination. The floor of his shelfless study was crowded with the books he had borrowed and bought. During the warm days of late summer and early autumn, he took occasional quiet walks to the British Museum, usually smoking a cigar, and returning with a few hours' worth of references and "museum headache." At the beginning of the first week of September, he wrote a letter to his mother, as if it were necessary before starting any great enterprise to confess to and consult her. The very nature and structure of the book he had in mind could not readily fit the theology of his mother's world. As in all such efforts, he was thus even more needful of her support.[19]

Within the week he had actually begun. Some days later, "after two weeks of blotching," he had "produced—two clean pages!" By the beginning of October, having completed three short chapters, he was both thrilled by the high challenge of writing "an Epic Poem of the Revolution" and frightened by the originality of what he was doing. "I am alone," he told Jack, "without models, without *limits*."[20] He wanted to write impressionistic and apocalyptic history, to creat a "flame-picture" of the most important revolution in modern times. He quickly saw that even the distinctiveness of his previous style would be insufficient both to his own personal passion and to the emotional and spiritual explosiveness of the issues with which he was dealing. He would have to create a prose supple, passionate, and fiery enough to embody the spirit of the Revolution itself and to dramatize his own vision of God's intercession in human history. He imagined himself writing at white-hot intensity for about nine months in order to complete the task, as if to take longer would be to burn himself out. By temperament, he was not made for the long haul.

As the weeks passed, he made steady progress toward the "Taking of the Bastille." The London winter darkened around him, but his mind's eye filled with bright images of creative and destructive flames. In the middle of October, looking out of his "back top-windows," he noticed a strange red glow in the sky, so prominent that it was clearly a major fire. Fascinated by the spectacle of the Houses of Parliament burning, Carlyle joined the huge crowd that watched the "low confused mass of houses" crumble to the ground. The sight was impressive, but it disappointed the expectations of some of the onlookers. Voices complained that it did not " 'make a *good* fire!' 'Come now,' they said at times when something flamed up, 'that's not so bad tho'!"[21] After two hours of delight in the fiery destruction of this symbol of the corrupt past, he returned home. At about the same time, he received a letter from his brother which illumined his imagination even more brightly. Early in September, Jack had observed a dramatic eruption of Mount Vesuvius, "frequent loud noises like thunder, . . . frequent flashes of forked lightning which appeared to dart with the smoke and vapour from the clear atmosphere."[22]

Carlyle's realization of the magnitude of his project, however, soon dashed his expectation that he would be finished by March. In December, confessing that he was making only slow "progress," he admitted the possibility that the book would be in two volumes rather than one. By the new year he was thinking of "*three* now," aware that the section he hoped to finish by the middle of January and that he would designate "the first *volume*" was no more than one-third the complete book.[23] Confronting for the first time the challenge of a long project, he groaned under the strain. Committed to the principle that one establishes one's worth through the intensity and dignity of work, he insisted on dramatizing in grandiloquent terms the Herculean severity of his labors. When not writing, he was miserable and self-deprecating; when writing, he was miserable and self-glorifying. It was "the hardest work" he had had for a long time.[24] He needed encouragement, and found it mainly in self-exhortation. The task was both joy and pain, the book both friend and enemy.

He saw developing under his pen a very personal, passionate, and partial narrative. But Jane commented that what he had done so far seemed more readable than *Sartor,* and this encouraged him. He tried to put financial matters out of his mind. Though Fraser had agreed to publish the book, and indeed had already advertised it as forthcoming, it was under the half-profits system, in which the publisher returned nothing to the author until all the publisher's expenses had been met by sales. Thereafter, the profit was divided equally.

Carlyle, who had just had a birthday, felt more vigorous and healthy than at any previous time in his life, "a young brisk man—turned of forty! In my mind I feel quite young yet; and *growing,* as when I was eighteen: this is the greatest blessing." If he could not live by literature, he assured his mother, he would "fling" it away "and seek bread *otherwise:* there is bread to be had elsewhere."[25] In the meantime, he felt confident that it was going to be "a tolerable enough Book." That it would also be "a queer Book, yes a *very* queer Book," did not daunt him in the least.

He showed small sections of the first volume-in-progress to Mill, who, despite his preoccupation with Harriet Taylor, was still Carlyle's closest London friend. Undoubtedly Mill had an influence on the book Carlyle was writing and a stake in it beyond that of anyone but Carlyle himself. Mill had first suggested the topic and, over a number of years, he had provided information and encouragement. Indeed, through his discussions with Carlyle, he had actually helped shape the imaginative contours that the work was taking. Apparently his response to fragments of the first volume had been positive. He was at least as much if not more knowledgeable than Carlyle about the facts and literature of the Revolution, and in February 1835 he offered to read the complete manuscript of volume one and to make comments in writing that might be incorporated as footnotes. Carlyle thought it a good idea.

On the night of Friday, March 6, there was a knock at the door. Mill appeared distraught, "an innocent young creature, with rich auburn hair and gentle pathetic expression, beautiful to contemplate."[26] He semicoherently asked Jane to go out to comfort someone waiting in the carriage. For a moment it seemed that a discreet private relationship was about to be made public and adulterous. If this were the case, Carlyle was certain that the blame was Harriet's. But Carlyle's moral disapproval was less important emotionally than his concern that the ambitious, intemperate, and theatrical Mrs. Taylor would damage his friend and destroy their friendship. Carlyle hoped that he could maintain a polite distance between himself and Harriet Taylor while at the same time maintaining his friendship with Mill, but the more room Mill made in his life for Harriet the less he had for Carlyle. Mill seemed to the Carlyles an innocent, flawed logican blinded by a "shrewd" married "woman, with a taste for coquetry," who had taken "possession" of him "and wrapped him up like a cocoon."[27] They were momentarily relieved to discover, then, that he had *not* come "to take solemn leave of us . . . before setting out for the Devil" with "his Platonic inamorata."[28]

Forcing the words out of himself, "the very picture of despair," Mill managed to communicate to the Carlyles what seemed almost inconceivable: that Carlyle's "poor manuscript, all except some four tattered leaves, was annihilated!" Having been mistaken by a servant for wastepaper, it had been put into the fire, where it made an ironic blaze of its own. Precisely where the fire blazed was—and remains—unclear. Mill immediately assured the Carlyles that he himself was completely to blame. For whatever the reason—perhaps Mill's emphasis on his own responsibility, perhaps something he inadvertently said, perhaps indeed some remark made by Harriet to Jane outside in the carriage—Carlyle years later told Mill's sister that "my opinion really was, that night when your Brother came to us pale and agitated, as I have seldom seen any mortal, that Mrs. Taylor's house and some trifling neglect there had been the cause of the catastrophe." He assured Harriet Mill, who had just seen her brother to his grave, that he himself had nothing to do with the fact that "that poor story of the burnt Manuscript had ever oozed out." But, despite her opinion to the contrary, he was certain that the "trifling neglect" had been at Mrs. Taylor's. "Whether permission had been *asked* to show Mrs. Taylor the M.S. I don't the least know; but that it did not the least *need* to be asked in the relation she had then to us and him, I do well know."[29]

If the accident did occur at Mrs. Taylor's, it was most likely the result of leaving the manuscript beside her bed where it was mistaken for scrap paper and either tossed into a fire or used as kindling in the morning. Mill's account, supported by his sister, was that the "misfortune arose from" his "own inadvertence, in having given your papers amongst waste paper for kitchen use" at his home in Westminster. His sister claimed to "remember our search, and my dear brother's extreme distress, and I fancy, though of this I do not feel so sure, that some pages were found."[30] The accusation that Mrs. Taylor purposely destroyed the manuscript, which is unlikely, has not been substantiated. That Mill would have been eager to protect Mrs. Taylor and take the blame himself, if there had been any need to do so, would have been as clear to Carlyle as it is to modern readers. Given his need to elevate Harriet into a deity and lower himself into a worshiper, Mill would have found the sacrifice demanded by such a situation fulfilling and even pleasurable. But whatever the facts, the events had an ironic appropriateness for these particular people. Mill and Harriet Taylor had had their already inflamed nervous systems fired by the anguish of the kind of accident that seemed inherent in their situation. And Carlyle, convinced that "rebellion" is a "barren thing," but writing a book whose main thrust was to affirm the necessity of violent revolution, his mind obsessed with images of fire, had "seen" his manuscript go up in flames.[31]

By the time Mill left at midnight, the strain of keeping up their outward spirits for his sake had brought both Carlyles to the edge of nervous collapse. For them, the outlook was a bleak one. It seemed doubtful that the loss could be repaired, that he could or should go on with the book. During a restless, painful night, he felt "something cutting or hard grasping me round the heart." He dreamt of his "father and sister Margaret alive; yet all defaced with the sleepy stagnancy . . . of the grave, and again dying as in some strange rude country."[32] But he managed through the night to absorb the pain into the "sweet consolation" of his parents' faith, into the "grace and duty of being spiritually minded."[33]

In the morning he decided that he would try again. Except for the oft-handled, heavily interlineated, and now destroyed manuscript, the book existed only in Carlyle's memory. The cost of having a secretary write out another copy was beyond the writer's means, even if he had thought of it, and there is no hint that he did. Since it was his practice to immerse himself in the materials through constant reading and thinking and then to write as quickly and as passionately as he could, throwing unsatisfactory efforts into the fireplace, there were no surviving earlier drafts, whether full or fragmentary. There was hardly anything in the way even of supplementary notes. But he had been chastened, not destroyed. "I was as a little Schoolboy, who had laboriously written out his *Copy* as he could, and was shewing it not without satisfaction to the Master: but . . . the Master had suddenly torn it, saying: 'No, boy, thou must go and write it better.' "[34] Remembering that he had thought highly of what he had written, he could solace himself with the explanation that this was not accident but a check on pride.

Mill, of course, took a less providential and more immediately practical approach. Would Carlyle at least allow him to "repair . . . the loss . . . of time and labour—that is of income?" Mill was immensely relieved when Carlyle accepted, though the £200 that he sent initially was returned with firm orders that £100 was adequate and fair. Aware that his friend could easily afford such reparations, Carlyle worried about Mill's conscience almost as much as he did about his own practical circumstance. Also, the story, if it got out, could help no one and might harm Mill. His own state of mind and his resolution to rewrite might be undermined if the loss became known before he had convinced himself (and consequently others) that he could act on his intention. The only way he could do that was to have done it.

Early on Saturday morning, determined to go on, he began to write to Jack a full account of what had happened. Jane cautioned him. Who would be served by communicating the misfortune, even to his brother, until he were well under way and calm in his mind about eventual success? They agreed that members of the family should be told later, perhaps by the end of the month, when he could write that they need not grieve for a loss that had already been grieved for and that had been restored. Omitting all details, he wrote to Fraser that because of an accident the book would be ready for press at a date much later than they had expected. Even to Emerson he suppressed the name of the "Kind Friend" whose carelessness had resulted in the manuscript being "torn up as wastepaper." To his family, later, he did not disguise Mill's role in the misfortune.

Carlyle was eager to reestablish trust between them and shortly offered to let Mill read the manuscript of the first section of the second volume, "The Feast of Pikes," which he had almost completed at the time that he loaned out the manuscript of the first volume. "For the sake of retributive justice," Mill preferred to "wear the badge of" his "untrustworthiness. If however you would give me the pleasure of reading it give it to Mrs. Taylor—in her custody no harm could come to it—and I can read it aloud to her as I did much of the other—for it had not only the *one* reader you mentioned but a second as good."[35] In the weeks after the accident, however, Mill avoided visiting or meeting his friend, a harbinger of the alienation to come, made inevitable by his commitment to Harriet and aggravated by what had happened. Carlyle's opinion of Mill and Harriet Taylor was not for public ears, but he did not mute it when he wrote to his brother: "He is a pure-minded clear man every way; but with the strangest, unluckiest, Utilitarian husk round him, which he will never cast off . . . all these people look forever at some *theory of a thing,* never at any *thing.* Poor Mill's Platonica is . . . little likely to help him . . . I for my share can see no wholesomeness in the witchery of the woman."[36] Therafter, the new sections of the manuscript, as well as the rewritten ones, remained in Carlyle's hands until they went to the printer.

Before the end of March 1835 he had finished the first section of volume two and returned to rewrite volume one from the beginning. Unfortunately, it seemed to him the hardest task he had ever undertaken. He had an ideal image of the value of what he had written, and the new material did not seem as good, at least initially. The task seemed to be touched by bitterness, as if he could taste the burnt leaves in his mouth, smell the acrid fragments of time and life which had been lost. After a brief spurt of energetic rewriting, he found himself unable to go on. For a few weeks he collapsed onto the couch in the living room and read the "trashiest heap of novels" available.[37] Within three weeks or so he was ready to try again. Though he made slow progress, aware of the burden and frustration of redoing what had been done before rather than going ahead with new material, he was soon able to quote Frederick the Great, who after an important defeat remarked that " ' another time we will do better.' "[38] By the end of April, the second chapter had been "done again . . . and the Third goes along much more sweetly."[39] Again there was a lull, however, in which gloomy thoughts about his own and Europe's future darkened his spirits. He threw his "poor ill-starred *French Revolution,*" which seemed "a mass of unformed rubbish," into a locked drawer.

Determined not to judge himself harshly if he could not complete the book, he attempted to find value in what he had already done and to accept the possibility of failure in this particular task. He would never regret having come to "the boundless confusion of London" where he had seen "the real faces and lives of my fellow mortals, stupid or wise so unspeakably instructive to me." But "if I *never* write it, why it will never be written." The act seemed inseparable from "much that is coming to crisis with me," a crisis that he felt desirable and ultimately redemptive. He felt neither despairing nor rebellious. "I feel rather," he wrote to Jack, "as if quite possibly I might be about *bursting* the accursed enchantment that has held me all my weary days in *nameless* thraldom; and actually beginning to be alive!"[40]

In the middle of July, after about five weeks of rest, he suddenly pressed forward again, for "that wretched burnt Manuscript must . . . be replaced," though the "whole business" had gotten "inexpressibly ugly."[41] He could bear even the choking London summer if only he could complete the first volume shortly. By the end of the first week in September, he expected to "*be done with that burnt manuscript* . . . in three or four days."[42] The triumphant moment came at the middle of the month, the end of the "hottest summer" he was ever to spend in the "brick wilderness." With "a kind of passion to see green fields again," he shortly went by himself to visit his family in Scotland, where in October he saw Halley's comet flame across the sky.[43] He had not visited them for almost a year and a half.

By the beginning of November he was back at his desk in Cheyne Row, pressing on with his book. At Christmastime he remembered Edward Irving's prayer, "May the worst of our years be over."[44] For the first time since the previous March he was working on new material. Though he had reason to be dispirited, "enchanted to this sad Book," he finished the second volume by the end of April 1836.[45] By July he had only "a hundred pages more" to write, which went on through the fall "about as ill as anybody could wish."[46] By November he was "within *forty-five* pages of the end."[47] His target was New Year's Day 1837, with publication in March, two years to the month later than he had originally hoped. He recognized that it "is a wild savage Book, itself a kind of French Revolution" that "has come out of my own soul; born in blackness, whirl-wind and sorrow." He did not expect it to have much success. At ten o'clock in the evening of January 12 he finished, "ready both to weep and to pray."[48] Instead, he went out for a walk in the darkness.

3.

With the death of Edward Irving an epoch had come to an end for Carlyle. The friends of his youth were gone. Though he was pained by the news of Robert Mitchell's death in 1836 and by James Johnston's in 1837, such losses confirmed his sense that he was now far distanced from both the people and the places of his early years, his family, of course, excepted. In fact, his love of Scotland was not love for a nation in general but a love of principle—fatherland, thrift, Presbyterianism—and of the few specific places that were inseparably associated with his family and his childhood memories. With *The French Revolution* finally completed, he dramatically threatened that it was "London or else the Back-woods, of America or Craigenputtock!"[49] But the threat of Craigenputtoch was rhetorical; not only was he determined not to live there, but "the less I *hear* about that detestable place," he confessed to Jack, "the thankfuller I shall be." He "would fly to Newfoundland sooner than go back."[50] Actually, he felt reasonably certain that his only destination in Scotland was to end where he had begun, with the people he loved who were gradually gathering together in a narrow place. "One night," in the summer of

1837, "late," he "rode through the village where" he "was born. . . . The old kirkyard tree . . . was nestling itself softly against the great twilight in the north. A star or two looked out, and the old graves were all there, and my father's and my sister; and God was above us all. I really . . . have no words to speak."[51]

But his need for living company and conversation was greater than he usually admitted. Though he idealized fellowship, he often simply needed to avoid loneliness and, given an audience of one or more, he frequently exploded into aggressive monologues, as if it were necessary to grasp the companionable moments in order to provide a balance for the solitary years. London was a place where he could always find people with whom to talk. And in the small world of literary London he was a man of whom others were aware. Whatever his eccentricities, he seemed accomplished enough to have a reputation and young enough to be thought to have a future: his Scots accent, spirited rhetoric, knowledge of European literatures, and emotional outspokenness made him attractively distinctive. Those who knew he was working on an account of the French Revolution anticipated an important book. He was eager to meet the remnants of the greater and lesser Romantics, while at the same time keeping his eye open for the young men who would be the next generation of notables; as such, he found himself a kind of bridge between the past and the future—old enough to be a mature figure but young enough to be a man of the new generation.

In the winter of 1834–1835, Henry Taylor fulfilled his promise to introduce him to Southey and Wordsworth. Widely acquainted with the literary celebrities of the day, Taylor delighted in making small parties for friends and acquaintances at which he brought together the "most brisk, and . . . the . . . best gifted." Since his bachelor lodgings were too cramped for entertaining, he frequently made use of the home of his cousin, whom Carlyle thought "one of the finest old women ever discovered."[52] One evening, "in bad wet weather," he walked to Miss Fenwick's house near St. James's Park where he joined Taylor and Southey, who were taking their after-dinner wine. Carlyle recalled Southey as "a lean gray-white-headed man, of dusky complexion" with large nose, *no* chin . . . care-lined brow . . . *vehement* hazel eyes." His "grand spiritual feature" seemed his "irritability . . . his grand bodily . . . leanness and long legs: a nervous female might shriek when he rises for the first time, and stretches to such unexpected length—like a lean pair of tongs!"[53]

Carlyle was delighted with Southey's company and gratified that the poet also enjoyed the time they spent together. They discussed a wide range of shared interests, including their attitude to De Quincey, with whom Southey was furious for having made indiscreet comments on the private lives of the Lake Poets in a series of articles he was currently publishing. Southey was still touchy about the old relationship between himself, the recently dead Coleridge, and their respective wives—so much so that he demanded that Carlyle tell De Quincey that he is "one of the greatest scoundrels living" and ought to be given "a sound beating." Carlyle unavailingly protested that he had not seen the "poor soul" for seven years and had no expectation of ever seeing him again.[54] In the next few years, he was to see Southey again at Taylor's and even at Cheyne Row, where the poet visited in 1838. Once they spoke about Shelley, whom neither of them admired, either "for talent or conduct." He was, Carlyle wrote, "a kind of ghastly object; colourless, pallid, tuneless, without health or warmth of vigour; the sound of him shrieky, frosty, as if a *ghost* were trying to 'sing' to us."[55] Years later, writing a brief memoir of Southey, Carlyle unwittingly stressed the bond of identification which he felt with him, describing that very excitable man, to whom "a deep mute monition of Conscience had spoken," as if he were describing himself: " 'You are capable of running mad, if you don't take care. Acquire *habitudes;* stick firm as adamant to them at all times, and work, continually work!' "[56] When *The French Revolution* was published in 1837, Southey was among the first to praise it extravagantly.

In contrast to Southey, Wordsworth was for the most part indifferent to Carlyle, both on the two occasions when they met that same winter and at a number of other meetings in the next few years. Relations between the two men were cordial, but Wordsworth kept aloof. Carlyle was only a partial admirer of his poetry, and his moderate expectations were not disappointed; the old man's conversation seemed boring, "mere . . . platitudes," as if he had "fallen into the garrulity of age, and is not what he was."[57] Carlyle thought him a man of prose rather than poetry, but did remark "a tint of naturalness, of sincere insight," whose "fine shrewdness" and calm self-absorption reduced him to "a *small* genuine man" who could not bear to hear anyone else praised,[58] partly because he had "been much spoiled; king of his country, unrecognized, and then adulated."[59] So overly proud was Wordsworth of his poetic achievements that he seemed to Carlyle to be "impatient that even Shakespear should be admired: 'so much out of my own pocket.' "[60] And so self-absorbed was Wordsworth that he seemed uninterested in anyone else, as signified by the "handful of numb unresponsive fingers" he offered in shaking hands.[61] At a breakfast in honor of the poet, Carlyle listened to the famous man's "good, frank . . . sonorous . . . business-like" voice speak with innocent naturalness of dry mechanical matters. He was "a little disappointing, but not much."[62]

When their paths crossed at various dinner parties, the two men occasionally spoke quietly together, usually "upon the subject of great poets," Wordsworth gradually revealing that he judged himself the greatest of all. On one occasion, Wordsworth, whose talents as pen-portraitist reminded Carlyle of his father's, described scenes and personalities that he had witnessed as a young man in revolutionary France which evoked certain aspects of the Revolution which Carlyle's reading had not provided. Another evening, from a great distance at a large dinner, Carlyle watched the poet, who had terribly weak and sensitive eyes, sit "beautifully screened in the shadow of" a "vertical green circle" that he had created by imposing between himself and the harsh light a screen that he always carried to such dinners. He sat "silent, in rock-like indifference, slowly but steadily gnawing some portion of what I judged to be raisins, with his eye and attention placidly fixed on these and these alone."[63] In 1842 Wordsworth published the sonnet "In Allusion To Various Recent Histories And Notices Of The French Revolution," which in no uncertain terms condemned Carlyle's notion that history is an avenging arrow from God and violent revolution an inevitable part of progress. Carlyle's opinion of Wordsworth hardly changed thereafter.[64]

In March and April 1835, Francis Jeffrey, "grown wizened and old, body and mind," visited frequently. Unable to come to terms with the failure of the relationship, Jeffrey blamed Carlyle's stubbornness and nervous sensitivity. Carlyle's unwillingness to be practical had made it impossible for his friends to help him, Jeffrey tried to argue to his favorite, Jane, but "got only a scorching (of hot language) for his pains; and notice that *he* was not the man who knew best about Carlyle." But Carlyle felt pity for Jeffrey's decrepitude and insecurity. "On Sloane Street," he wrote to his mother, they saw "a poor but decent-looking middle-aged woman, fallen down dead! . . . A Policeman and a quick-shifting crowd were round the spot; and there the poor woman lay, nobody knowing who she was: as we came back, four other Policemen were bearing the body to . . . lie . . . till it should be claimed. . . . Life is always 'fearful and wonderful'; Death always hovering nigh."[65] Mill had also begun to fade into the gallery of faces from the past. He was continually ill in the next few years and spent a good deal of the time abroad, hoping to improve his health. "He seemed . . . to be withering or withered. . . . His eyes go twinkling and jerking with wild lights and twitches, his head is bald, his face brown and dry."[66] Many of his friends thought he would die shortly. The intensification of his affair with Harriet Taylor took him even further away. Though they were still to have some pleasant Sunday walks and country excursions together, the two friends saw less of each other. Carlyle believed that the infrequency of their meetings was not his fault, and to a certain extent he was right. Differences of personality and difficult personal choices for Mill inevitably dissolved what had been from the beginning a somewhat fragile friendship.

But it was to Mill that Carlyle owed his introduction to the man who became his most cherished friend for most of the next decade. He accidentally met John Sterling at Mill's India House office in February 1835, later describing him as "a loose . . . thin figure," a little under six feet, with light complexion and dark-blonde hair, who was "carelessly and copiously talking."[67] Like older and younger brother, he and Sterling rambled westward to Knightsbridge, delighting in each other's conversation, "arguing copiously, but *except* in opinion not disagreeing."[68] Apparently Sterling immediately trusted Carlyle's ability not only to respect opposition but to feel deep affection for someone whose virtues transcended their differences on particular issues. That Sterling had a deep streak of earnestness and youthful innocence endeared him immensely to a man who valued sincerity more than anything else. Having already heard good things about him from Mill and others, Carlyle was pleased to discover that a man who had been praised from a distance fulfilled his expectations in person.

Carlyle, however, was aware of Sterling's unsuccessful efforts to find a satisfying role for himself in the confusing drama of modern life. As a young Cambridge graduate, he had in 1830 taken part with a number of Cambridge friends in an abortive attempt to further the cause of the Spanish republicans in exile. A few years later, soon after his marriage, Sterling had attempted to still his doubts about vocation, God, and personal health by going to run a family-owned plantation in the West Indies. Despite the benefit to his delicate health, the restless young man soon found his balmy paradise unbearably boring and shortly returned to England. He had met Coleridge as early as 1827, and between the time of his return to England in 1832 and 1834 he was a constant visitor at the Grove. Believing the master's claim that the salvation of men of talent and of English culture depended on the revitalization of the Church of England, Sterling took orders and committed himself to the pastoral obligations of the curateship of rural Herstmonceaux under the auspices of "his old tutor and friend, the Reverend Julius Hare."[69] He had already written a stiff, sincere, and thinly veiled autobiographical novel called *Arthur Coningsby,* which the Carlyles had read at Craigenputtoch in the spring of 1833. Since Sterling was also ambitious to write poems and to mingle with and influence the art and thought of his age, Carlyle concluded that his temporary commitment to the church was "a clerical aberration," one that reflected the baneful influence of the Sage of

John Sterling. Steel engraving from a drawing, c. 1840. Reprinted from Thomas Carlyle, *Centenary Edition, The Life of John Sterling* (London, 1897).

Highgate. Sterling fulfilled his clerical duties for eight months but was in the process of withdrawing from this commitment when he met Carlyle in February 1835.

Within the next months, the Carlyles saw "a good deal" of Sterling, who suddenly became a familiar and cherished figure at Cheyne Row, "very clever, and true and kindhearted."[70] The intimacy was furthered when he took up residence in London in the fall. Some of Sterling's friends, among them Frederick Denison Maurice, came along with him. Though Carlyle bewailed that "Coleridge is the Father of all these," he was delighted to have them.[71] In addition, Sterling had an impressive family whose members immediately expanded their circle to include John's new friends. Carlyle missed the family he had left behind; Jane thought of herself almost as an orphan. In a short time, John's "Mother and Jane" were "about 'sweering [*sic*] an eternal friendship.' "[72] His father, Edward Sterling, was an argumentative, boisterous newspaperman whose pronouncements as the editor of the influential *Times* had gained him the nickname "The Thunderer." Carlyle had met him at Sarah Austin's home in Bayswater the previous year, and he soon joined his wife as a regular visitor to Cheyne Row, where he lavished his affection on Jane in particular. To the Carlyles, he soon became "Signor Hurricane, the good Father and Thunderer."[73]

Another treasure who came to Carlyle indirectly through Mill was Godefroy Cavaignac, a young Frenchman "with a sense of irresistible power & indomitable will."[74] "Intense in everything," he was a volatile republican whose opposition to Louis Philippe had brought him to exile in England. In the spring of 1836 he eagerly visited the man Mill and others had said so much about and who was writing a substantial work on the revolution in which Cavaignac's parents had participated and suffered. The relationship between the idealistic Frenchman and both the Carlyles became intense, sustained with happy feelings on all sides until he returned to France under the terms of a general amnesty in 1840. He was a Romantic as well as an idealistic revolutionary, whose escape from political imprisonment in France brought him to the Carlyle household glowing, especially in Jane's eyes, with "that sort of dark, half-savage beauty with which one would paint a fallen angel . . . who fears neither Heaven nor Earth."[75] Jane found this Byronic idealist, "who *defies* all men and *honours* all women," immensely attractive. By the late spring of 1836 he was a regular visitor.

Despite his long-standing prejudice against the French, Carlyle concluded that this was "a courageous energetic man. . . . The best Frenchman by many degrees whom I have met with."[76] Carlyle immediately discovered, as he did with Sterling, that Cavaignac's nobility of character made differences of opinion irrelevant to the delight they could take in one another's company. For he was "very pleasant to converse with, walk with, or see drop in on an evening, and lead you or follow you far and wide over the world of intellect and humanly recorded fact."[77] Though he wished that the Frenchman would "speak a little plainer, or learn to speak English" less "obscurely," his heavy accent apparently hardly impeded their frequent discussions of modern

France and the book that Carlyle was working on.[78] He provided a partial replacement for Mill as a highly informed participant in the shaping of Carlyle's ideas. But he also provided a window into the interior of the French mind. Carlyle's argumentative discussions with Cavaignac helped him to develop his own ideas about the meaning of the Revolution.[79] Carlyle sensed from the beginning that it would not be a long-term relationship. "With strange *English* in his mouth" (Carlyle conveniently forgot, and conveniently remembered when it suited him, how strange his own Annandale accent sounded in English ears), Cavaignac reminded Carlyle that this "honest and artless" Frenchman and he had come from irreconcilable places and were passing in different directions. "Let him pass in peace, for the time our two roads lie in sight of each other!"[80]

Late in November 1836 "a notable Literary woman," Harriet Martineau, made the first of her many visits to Cheyne Row.[81] While on a literary tour in America the previous year, she had carried as "her constant companion" a copy of *Sartor Resartus,* probably the first American edition, which had been published the previous month through the agency of Emerson. Their common American friends imagined that Carlyle would want to meet such "a rare being," a woman who "needs only to be known to be loved."[82] To Carlyle, she seemed a "strange visitor" but a pleasant one, whose reputation as a "Poetess Political Economist" and as an outspoken, "ill-favoured" woman did not in the least prevent him from appreciating her intelligence and liveliness.[83] Her Unitarianism was not in her favor, but it seemed a minor flaw in a thirty-five-year-old, self-supporting spinster who maintained herself by a prolific output of popular works on political economy, travel, social observation, history, poetry, and even fiction. She had the additional liability of a serious physical defect, for she was as "deaf as a Post" and had to be spoken to "through an ear-trumpet."[84] Carlyle later wrote that "to admire her literary genius," a reputation based more on assiduous work than on talent, "or even her solidity of common sense, was never possible . . . but she had a sharp eye, an imperturbable self-possession, and in all things a swiftness of positive decision, which, joined to her evident loyalty of *intention,* and her frank, guileless, easy ways, we both liked."[85]

In other words, she was a decisive, intelligent, hard-working woman who liked and admired the Carlyles and could be counted on to do her best for them. Particularly fond of Thomas, she apparently leaned her ear trumpet to his Scots accent devotedly enough to suspend for a time his reservations about her liberalism and Unitarianism, her advocacy of Negro emancipation, and her admiration of her brother, who was a controversial proponent of Christ as man rather than as God. The

Carlyles frequently went to parties at her small house in Westminster, and they entertained Harriet on their evenings at home and during impromptu visits, pleased that the terms they had set for their household and their friends were completely acceptable to her.

4.

One distant friend, however, had been urging an exclusivity of friendship and a practical step that would remove him from these new friends and from Britain altogether. As soon as Carlyle moved to London, he announced to Emerson that his move was not a betrayal of rural ideas and transcendental values but a necessary practical step. He needed to earn a living and to find a community of men whom he could live among. Emerson had a simple solution to the problem which he thought infinitely preferable to residence in London. He suggested that Carlyle come to America for six months or a year; if he liked it and found the rewards sufficient, he might become a permanent resident. Emerson assured him, quite correctly if with some exaggeration, that his American brothers were more eager than the English to recognize his genius and provide a supportive environment for his work. With his fingers to the pulse of much of American literary life, Emerson touted the miracle of the prophet he had met at Craigenputtoch to the young men of New England. Carlyle's letters were handed round in Emerson's circle, and his published writings, particularly *Sartor,* were avidly absorbed by a generation which found his rugged, emotional style an embodiment of their own glorification of Romantic independence. In Carlyle's spiritual message they discovered a manifestation in the whirlwind of what they had begun to call transcendentalism. George Ripley, one of Emerson's friends, was "convinced" that Carlyle was "an actual Incarnation, and not merely a Presence and a Force."[86]

Carlyle had sufficient perspective on himself and his culture to find such praise embarrassing. Nevertheless, with the disastrous burning of his manuscript only a few months behind him and his economic future still precarious, he took some pleasure in passing these words along, with his own qualifications, to family and friends. If his aura was not quite as angelic as George Ripley painted it, his future was not necessarily quite as dark as it seemed. Ripley sounded out Carlyle's interest in a professorship of German at the recently founded Lowell Institute. Emerson, saner though also unstinting in his praise, had more practical proposals to offer. In late 1834 he urged him "to come & found a new Academy that shall be church & school & parnassus, as a true Poet's house should be."[87] Having expressed to Emerson his fear that he might eventually end up in "the Western Woods," Carlyle for the next three years found himself indulging in an elaborate fantasy that had advantages for both himself and his friend. It was an immense relief and emotional satisfaction while he worked on *The French Revolution* to be courted by his American friends. He was wanted there. Also, he could, when discussing his own potential as an emigrant to the new land, deal more effectively with the Carlyle family's growing but bitter realization that Alick would most likely emigrate to America. He dried his mother's tears with the speculation that the entire family might emigrate, the whole clan simply transport itself to a better country, with Margaret Carlyle in some magic way being transported from her hearth at Scotsbrig to some fantasy farmhouse in the new world.

Eager to have his friend beside him, for both his own sake and that of his country, Emerson anticipated the glowing reception that Carlyle would have in America as a lecturer and a teacher. Carlyle, who had earlier regretted that he had not prepared himself to make his living as a lecturer, now felt he could not be available for lecturing anywhere until he had finished his book. Though he sometimes thought about lecturing, by February 1835 he admitted that it was not "yet with any seriousness." After the burning of the manuscript in March, his resolution to rewrite it was accompanied by a renewed fear that America might be his destination. He assured Emerson that he did not share the idealistic apotheosis of that new country: "I should rather fancy America mainly a new Commercial England, with a fuller pantry: little more or little less."[88] But Emerson's call was not only a practical one, though he continually played on that tune: the other song he offered was the harmony of love between brothers, Carlyle and Emerson, England and America. With his mind set on visions of a small community of the spiritually elite, he anticipated welcoming his friend into his home, where they might live together or very close to one another in a special fraternity of love. At moments, Carlyle seriously responded to Emerson's affection, as if that visit, even if it were to be no more than a visit, were imminent.

But he would never set a date. At the same time that he advised Alick to go to America, a journey that seemed "inevitable for thousands and millions of European men," he himself felt more and more that he should remain in England, though he would hardly admit this to Emerson.[89] Carlyle's decision rested on practical matters. If he could earn a living, he would stay. Though his funds were low, they were not depleted. His savings, the £100 from Mill, and the prospect of some payment for an article or two would be almost enough to sustain him until the publication of his book. In reserve were loans from his well-paid brother Jack, who tried unsuccessfully to persuade Thomas to accept from him what the older brother had provided when he needed it. It also occurred to Carlyle that he might actually find employment of some kind other than literary. Indeed, he even engaged his old but not completely admired friend Basil Montagu in a serious discussion about a clerkship in Montagu's office. But he dismissed the prospect, admiring "the *faith* of Montague—wishing *me* for his Clerk; thinking the Polar Bear . . . might be safely trusted tending Rabbits!"[90] In a moment of discouragement at the beginning of 1836, he even wrote to propose himself for a professorship of astromony which had become available at Glasgow. Fortunately, nothing came of it.

To Emerson, it seemed that Carlyle's visit was momentarily delayed but still imminent, necessary for both practical and fraternal reasons. Convinced of his friend's genius, he in the meantime devoted a considerable amount of time and energy to spreading his written words, the next best thing to having him there in person. Though he had reservations about the difficulties if not the infelicities of Carlyle's style, Emerson thought *Sartor* a major book, its author a man who deserved recognition and support. In late winter 1835, he asked Carlyle for fifty to one hundred copies of the bound serial version. Fraser would supply no more than four copies, convinced that it was folly to invest one more penny in a book that had yielded him no profit and much criticism. But, on the power of 150 subscription pledges from Emerson and his friends, a Boston publisher agreed to an edition of 500 copies, which was published in April 1836 and completely sold out by September. A second edition followed almost immediately, and its sales were just as brisk.

Carlyle's American friends had done for him what his English friends either could not or would not do. The American public was actually reading Carlyle. Emerson's inexperience in business and in publishing meant that the author did not profit at all from these two editions, but this situation was rectified with the publication of an American edition of *The French Revolution,* which Emerson funded at his own risk and "for the benefit of the author," with the cooperation of another Boston publisher, C. C. Little and James Brown.[91] Since the market was there, it is doubtful that Emerson ran any real financial risk in the matter, but it was a sign of his commitment to his friend that he was willing to supply the capital as well as to devote his own time at no recompense. Although Carlyle became a little too used to such assistance from Emerson, occasionally forgetting how much he owed his American friend, he generally did remember that "you" became "an Accountant for my sake. At bottom this money was all yours; not a penny of it belonged to me by any law except that of helpful Friendship."[92] Despite the steady sales of *The French Revolution* in both England and America, it was from America that profits came first, the arrangement with Fraser being much less advantageous than that with Little & Brown. In August 1838, when the first £50 that he earned from the book arrived "from across three thousand miles of salt water, from kind hands that we never saw," Jane cried briefly; Thomas sent a small present of cash to his mother, for "the 'kitlin ought to bring the auld cat a mouse' . . . an American mouse!"[93]

If Emerson had two wishes on behalf of Carlyle—to help him with the promotion of his books and to welcome him to America—he made the latter less and less likely to the extent that he accomplished the former. The more money that Carlyle received through Emerson's efforts, the less motivation he had to earn his livelihood in a foreign land. And soon there were other sources of income. If he had managed to resist the lure of "Yankee" dollars during the most difficult period of his writing career, there seemed no reason to expect that he would succumb to either practical advantage or the call of friendship and make the difficult journey once it could not be argued as a matter of necessity. "To be in a *home* is to me almost as essential as to be in a *skin*, I cannot sleep, cannot live at all quietly till my environment have grown habitual to me,—made itself into a kind of *habit* or *skin* for me."[94] Emerson had hoped that Carlyle would come to America out of desire; by 1837 it had gradually dawned on him that he would come only out of necessity, and that need no longer existed. "I do believe," Carlyle tried to assure his increasingly dubious friend, that "if I live long, I shall get to Concord one day."[95] By the summer of 1840, however, even the ever-optimistic Emerson continued this dialogue about a future visit only to nourish his own hopes: "I have heard so oft of your projected trip to America, that my ear would now be dull & my faith cold, but that I wish it so much."[96]

5.

Having imagined at various times in his life that his health was shattered, Carlyle was moderately surprised to realize that he had little cause to complain about his body between 1834 and 1841. Allan Cunningham remarked that when a man reaches middle age his previous physical complaints usually diminish or disappear, a generalization to which Carlyle responded with specific self-recognition. There seemed no reason to believe that he would not "live long." By March 1839, he actually thought himself "to be growing healthier, in spite of much . . . sickness and depression."[97] Except for one bad bout of influenza, the sickness was mainly upset stomach, the old problem of flatulence, and constipation. Occasionally he had an earache and a stuffed ear, a suitable affliction for a man who was always hyperconscious about his difficulty sleeping and who found the noise of modern society a manifestation of its unwillingness to listen to the meaningful cosmic silences. But even the self-pitying patient could not help but recognize that since coming to London the physical pain had become either less intense or more bearable. It was certainly less frequent, something a man could live with and would not die of.

Still, he kept a sensitive emotional thermometer always in his mouth. Though he recognized that the "Influenza, a dirty, feverish kind of cold," had external, physical origins, he attributed the condition of his stomach to a strained and tired nervous system.[98] With the success of *The French Revolution,* he had less reason to worry himself into illness. Soon he admitted to Emerson that his American fantasy was a "day-dream" of escape, some vision of rest.[99] The source of illness was in his psyche, not his body. "It is one's own mind that is wrong."[100] His bodily health was ruggedly strong; "the foundations of this lean frame of mine must be as tough as wire."[101] He advised Emerson that his complaints should be understood as "*weariness* merely."[102] But, since his physical well-being depended on how effectively he controlled his anxiety, he had a heightened sense of the struggle of dealing with what he believed by definition was an overly sensitive nervous system. His profession itself seemed one that was hard on his nerves. The nervous systems of thinkers and writers, he told Mill, were sometimes just "*too weak* for the work."[103] Whenever he played with the notion of an alternative occupation it was with the conviction that he would be emotionally more stable if he could escape such strains. Other people, including his wife and some of his friends, supported the claim that he was temperamentally unsuited to the career he had chosen. On the one hand, there was the traditional notion of the inspired writer who created a harmonious balance between his personal and professional needs, between temperament, social life, and career; on the other, there was the Romantic counter-definition of the writer as the restless, deeply committed, and suffering victim of his own genius, whose nervous system and social needs would have to be sacrificed to the lonely, draining demands of his art. "Let no woman who values peace of soul ever dream of marrying an author," his wife concluded.[104]

Perhaps the very recognition that much of his past illness had emotional causes helped him to find the strength to incorporate into his conscious life the conviction that the unconscious was the dominating force in determining health. Of course he was aware that this was an interpretation of the origin of illness that might cause resentment if applied to sick friends. In fact, he did his best to be tactful in relating to three real invalids whose welfare was dear to him, John Stuart Mill, John Sterling, and his own wife. After Sterling's death he did not hesitate to say that Sterling's illness was only the "last ounce which broke the camel's back. I take it, in this as in other cases known to me, ill-health was not the primary cause but rather the ultimate one, the summing-up of innumerable far deeper conscious and unconscious causes,—the cause which *could* boldly show itself on the surface, and give the casting vote."[105] In all three cases, his awareness of the likely outcome probably helped him to get additional perspective on his own condition at one time or another. But it did not lessen his dismay in the face of their suffering or decrease his frustration at his inability to help them.

Mill's case had the most favorable conclusion. Early in 1836 he was so "sickly and weak" that Carlyle was "obliged to go to see *him*."[106] A year later, he was still "in the same weakly state," but Carlyle had concluded that it was " 'a disease of the mind' " produced, at least in part, by the tensions that "his Platonic love and he" were generating as they struggled with the possibility of a divorce and the difficulties of their future together.[107] Mill had good reason for a renewal of "those long fits of depression" of previous years.[108] Despite his frequent trips to warmer climates on the Continent, he found that his health troubles were resolved only over the long period of time that coincided with the resolution of his emotional difficulties. But by 1841, there were "so few *intersections*" between the two friends—their "orbits running in a perverse concentric way"—that Mill's recovery was less and less a personal benefit to Carlyle.[109]

Unfortunately, the friend who replaced Mill in Carlyle's affections during these years was already mortally ill with tuberculosis when they first met. It did not help Sterling in the least for Carlyle to urge, "Let us both get well! I do hold it in my own case, a kind of disgrace and crime to be sick."[110] Sterling attempted to lead an active literary life in London, but by 1837 he was a doomed invalid, forced to spend some considerable part of each year in the comparative warmth of southwest England or on the Continent. From the beginning of their friendship, his death had seemed only a matter of time; from about 1840 it occurred to even the most optimistic of Sterling's family and friends that that time was short.

Jane's case, naturally, was the most baffling and serious for Carlyle. As his own health improved, hers declined.[111] As Carlyle lost his conviction that he was in ill health, Jane apparently caught the idea of his rejected germs. She, too, at frank moments, ascribed her frequent sickness to "a bad nervous system, keeping me in a state of greater or less physical suffering."[112] Her susceptibility to physical illness was frequent and devastating. Whether or not London life would agree with her had been on the Carlyles' minds from the beginning, for they both remembered how frequently she had been ill during their visit in 1831–1832. The first winter of their residence went well, but by the late summer of 1835 Jane felt "very poorly," having "suffered much from the summer."[113]

Usually, however, the summer was the season she enjoyed most, so much so that in later years she actually refused to leave London to accompany her husband on his flights north during the warm months. She always "grows better with the hot weather; I always worse," Carlyle wrote in 1839.[114] She usually gathers "vigour as the sun mounts,—like any flower of the field!"[115] Indeed, the matter of her health aside, Jane soon began to feel that life in London was preferable to life anyplace else. Her husband's eccentricities of personality would remain the same wherever they lived. But in London she had friends, stimulation, opportunities; whatever the disadvantages, she was certain that they were far fewer than the benefits. If health were to be considered, there was no reason to believe that she would be healthier in any of the alternatives that were being discussed. Since she had frequently been ill at Craigenputtoch, she had no reason to imagine that the London winters rather than her own special susceptibility were responsible for her frequent illnesses.

As soon as Carlyle left for Scotland in late September 1835, however, she felt well again. But she had a disastrous winter in 1837, "miserably ill . . . Influenza for the *third* time . . . in great misery."[116] There were many deaths from influenza that winter, and for a time it was feared that Jane might not survive. The couple was therefore reassured when they were told that "nothing organic had gone wrong."[117] She knew that neither Scotland nor her husband had restorative powers, and insisted on remaining in London when he went north that summer. To her delight, she found herself feeling surprisingly well, and apparently noticed that her recurrent illnesses were less frequent and less intense when she was relieved of the strain of attending to her husband's needs. Not that she wanted to give him up altogether, but she appreciated the advantages of these summer separations. Late in August 1838 he left for a long visit in the north, leaving Jane, who now had a social circle of her own, to revel in good company and comparative freedom. "I have not had a single headache these three weeks," she wrote her husband in September.[118]

Despite such moments of rejuvenation, her health declined steadily over the years. Except for the most serious bouts of influenza, and a mental as well as a physical collapse in later years, her health was never so bad that she could not function and never so good that she could function without tiredness, pain, and frequent long spells in bed. First precaution and then illness forced her to spend the cold months indoors. Hardly a winter passed without an initial siege and then a number of serious relapses. Sickness exhausted her, and exhaustion made her even more vulnerable, particularly because she found it difficult to sleep. The sources of her illnesses are obscure. Like her mother, who occasionally came to nurse her during these years, she seems to have been subject from childhood on to migraine headaches and heavy menstrual bleeding. When she was seriously ill in the spring and summer of 1836, Carlyle told his doctor brother that her "ailment is being *sick* far too often (I mean as women are sick)."[119] Despite her distaste for her mother's company, she actually fled to Templand that summer, partly to escape from Jack, who was visiting at Cheyne Row. She got along with him almost as badly as she got along with her mother, but she particularly objected to his medical opinion that her illnesses were psychosomatic. Reasonably well trained in his profession, Jack had the opportunity to observe and diagnose this patient's problems over a long period of time. In his opinion, her health would show a remarkable improvement if she found some occupation and purpose that would relieve her of the need and the opportunity to be constantly concerned with her health. At moments, observing his wife's condition, Carlyle apparently agreed.

But Jane's health was a touchy subject. Aware that her immediate difficulties might be alleviated by the advantages of a warm climate, Carlyle was still sufficiently self-absorbed to reject Jack's urgent invitations that they visit him in Italy during the winter, though "my poor sick Wife might perhaps profit by it."[120] Occasionally, in the bleak London weather, he daydreamed about the sunny lands that he had never seen, but such a voyage seemed an extravagant expenditure, both of money and time. Jane herself was a poor traveler, who suffered excruciatingly from seasickness. Though he himself bore the physical part of travel well, he usually found it psychologically tiring and just not the thing to do as a matter of principle. Jack's expectation that the brothers might vacation together in Rome or Munich or Geneva or Paris always began in hope and ended in disappointment. Carlyle had reason to go to Scotland. But he could think of no reason to go anyplace else, except as an expression of a kind of restlessness that he did not admire. There were infinite realms to voyage through within the mind and soul, on the wings of reading, meditation, and writing.

Even if Thomas agreed that Jane would be less frequently ill if she could occupy herself more regularly with some sustaining work, there remained the definitions of role and personality, in part enforced by society, which they had gone to some lengths to make a central part of their relationship. A career for Jane? It had been ruled out long ago. Aware of his wife's abilities, especially as a letter-writer, he could not help but suspect that she compared her talents with those of successful women writers such as Harriet Martineau. One such writer, Geraldine Jewsbury, was soon to become her closest female friend. But there were reasons why such a career was not, he believed, either in her interest or in his. He was uncomfortably aware of what they both had lost. "It is a pity, and perhaps not a pity, that so lively a pen did not turn itself to writing of Books? My *coagitor* too might become a distinguished female. Nay, after all, who knows? But perhaps we are better as we are. 'Probably just as well.' "[121]

[10]

A Public Man
1837–1841

From his windows at Cheyne Row Carlyle saw an unusually heavy snowfall descending on the London streets in late December 1836, blanketing the city in a distinctive silence, "the wheel-vehicles making no noise . . . many persons drunk . . . and a few others . . . tripping along muffled in cloaks, with blue noses."[1] The printer had just begun setting type for *The French Revolution,* of which only the brief final chapter remained to be written. Anticipating the imminent publication of his essays "Mirabeau" and "The Diamond Necklace," the reprinting in America of *Sartor,* and the publication by June of *The French Revolution,* he told his mother that "with the commencement of the year, there is going to be quite an *explosion!*"[2] It would have to be bright to pierce the London fog which was "like a sea of ink." In January, people had "to light candles at noon, coaches have torch-bearers running at the horses' heads."[3]

He believed that his moment was about to come, that the wager of the last years would be collected either as honorable work without public result or as general recognition of his achievement. He could not, however, count on financial reward, and, burdened with the anxiety of continuing economic insecurity and a chronically sick wife, he needed additional money. He had long flirted with the idea of gaining bread and influence by lecturing, and thus, when Harriet Martineau, Henry Taylor, and two new friends, Jane and Thomas Wilson, came to him in the December silence and suggested that they arrange a lecture series for him in the spring, he responded positively. When a suitable hall was unavailable at the most likely place, the "Lecturing prospect" seemed "to have ended . . . for this year."[4] But he set his friends to work again with the insistence that he did not care where he lectured as long as he had an appropriate audience.

By the beginning of March 1837, it had been settled that, starting in the first week of May, he would speak between three and four in the afternoon, two days each week, until his six lectures were completed.[5] Since he was busy with the proofs of his new book, he doubted that he would have time to prepare written lectures, but he did not want to risk the dullness of a formal presentation anyway. He recognized that he was at his best when he felt most tense, and thus thought it appropriate to heighten the risk. He would, however, make certain that he had prepared the subject matter carefully. Since he had so little time, it struck him that he could make effective use of his unpublished history of German literature. He had spent years studying the subject and had some published articles—even an unpublished text—with which to refresh his memory. He had made some effort to dissociate himself from an exclusive identification with German literature, and the success of that effort, which he expected to be crowned by the publication of *The French Revolution,* encouraged him to feel that he could now lecture on German literature without increasing his public identification with a foreign culture.

While he worked, friends visited regularly. Cavaignac came every ten days or so and Harriet Martineau frequently stopped by. Sterling's health made his visits infrequent, but his parents and soon one of his brothers associated with the Carlyles with a family-like intensity. Henry Taylor and Allan Cunningham could not be kept away. Hunt maintained his distance, but his distance was not far; there were sufficient goings and comings between the two households to give some vigor to the relationship for a few years. The Wilsons, a brother and a spinster sister particularly interested in literature, were supportive. The Bullers kept in touch, particularly through Charles; so, too, did the Montagus, though the distance of recent years was never really closed. Through a new friend, Count Carlo Pepoli, an exiled Italian professor, Jane became excited about Italy and began to learn the language. Erasmus Darwin had first come to Cheyne Row in the spring of 1835 and had found Carlyle "looking very much like any other Scotchman except that he wore a green hat the size of a small umbrella." (Carlyle had a penchant for what was then thought to be exotic headgear; though it made him instantly identifiable on the streets, it proved a constant embarrassment to his wife.) Jane "kept up one unceasing chatter for nearly an hour, discoursing about Craigputtock and everything else in the world."[6] The shy, semi-invalided brother of Charles Darwin (the naturalist soon met Carlyle and at first found him unsympathetic, an antipathy vigorously returned when *Origin of Species* was published) enjoyed an independent income and the conviction that his neurasthenia prevented him from doing anything much with his life. By 1837

Erasmus Darwin. Photograph, June 8, 1856. Courtesy of the Rare Book and Manuscript Library, Columbia University.

Erasmus had become a constant visitor, like an elder brother or uncle to Jane, who found him a marvelous audience and a faithful chauffeur. As in so many instances, visitors who came to see Carlyle more often than not found themselves, quite happily, spending much of their time with Jane.

With the corrected proofs of *The French Revolution* in the printer's hands by early April, Carlyle could concentrate his full potential for nervousness on the first of the approaching lectures. He had almost no experience as a public speaker. Supported by his friends, who recognized the financial necessity of a sizable audience, he became as anxious as Jane and other intimates to have it over with. There was little expectation that he would perform well by conventional standards. Already exhausted by his work on his book, he felt that the last thing he needed was the strain of some detestable public performance at which the rich and the idle would come to stare. Yet he was bolstered by the conviction that he had something important to say. The wide distribution of the prospectus and the response to public advertisements made it clear that he could expect a sizable paying audience, and why should he object to earning £100 or more in this way? The work seemed honorable enough, though it was a nervous ordeal.

The six lectures were moderately successful. Henry Taylor found that Carlyle's nervousness made him "dreadfully nervous in listening to him," and expressed "the greatest relief" when he was done.[7] But the lectures were "well attended" by an audience that Carlyle termed "pretty . . . mostly of quality."[8] Curiosity-seekers, cultural enthusiasts, and the well-to-do, who either found it *de rigueur* to attend such affairs or had been alerted to the peculiarities of the speaker, were apparently entertained by his nervous mannerisms. Under such circumstances, public suffering merited public applause and widespread support. Scattered in the audience were friends and disciples, some of them young men who found the message as exciting as the presentation was nerve-racking. Jane, like her husband, simply wanted it to be over. At the end of the first lecture, the exhausted speaker solaced himself with the thought that "it was not a *break-down;* this is all that can be said of it: the next will be better we hope."[9] Margaret Carlyle wept that her son had gotten the first of his lectures "honorably done" and read and reread the account in the *Times.*[10]

Carlyle had already praised the high virtues of Teutonic culture and personality to the English public in his essays. But the lectures were an opportunity to elaborate on variations that might both instruct and entertain and that were likely to prove palatable because of the speaker's insistence that the glories of English or Anglo-Saxon culture were basically Teutonic, not Celtic. He pointed out that "valour" and "intellect" were the most striking characteristics of the German "race," the race that, in his view, encompassed all of northern Europe. He argued that the spread of English culture around the globe demonstrated the superiority of Teutonic virtues, and suggested that "the breed has been in some cases even improved by crossing and transplanting,—as in the instances of the English and Americans."[11] He believed that the triumph of Teutonic spiritual courage was embodied in the life and message of Martin Luther, whose Protestantism underlay that of the great English and Scotch reformers. Carlyle reminded his audience, even if only by implication, that the strength and energy of Britain derived from this tradition. His presence as a speaker and a personality enforced the point that his words conveyed. If he seemed nervous, eccentric, somewhat foreign, even extravagant, he was still clearly on their side and one of them. It was Britain he was praising. Both the *Times* and *Spectator* reported favorably, the latter wishing "all success to his ingenious, instructive, and interesting prelections."[12]

When he left for Scotland toward the end of June 1837, the desperately tired author, who actually believed that the writing of his book "amid such sickness, poverty, and despair . . . had really all but killed" him, not only had made himself £120 richer but also had done much to provide advance publicity for his new book.[13] The result had not been intentional, but the publicity for the lectures put forward his name and his "genius" in a manner that insured additional attention to *The French Revolution.* At one level, whatever the fortunes of his public career, he already felt that he was seeing beyond external shadows and material limitations. "Verily this whole world grows magical and hyper-magical to me."[14] But his livelihood depended on lecturing or publishing or both. In fact, his credibility lecturing, from which there was money to be earned, depended to some extent on his achievement as a writer, from which profit could not be expected.

A few weeks after arriving at Scotsbrig, where family solicitousness soothed his spirit and reminded him that there he would always find love and respect, Carlyle had the first review in hand. Its publication in the *London and Westminster Review* had been carefully arranged by Carlyle, Mill, and James Fraser, who had provided early proof sheets. Eager to help his friend and to continue to make amends for the accident of two years before, Mill lavished the highest praise on this "most original book," saying that "every idea and sentiment is given out exactly as it is thought and felt, fresh from the soul of the writer, and in such language . . . as is most capable of representing it in the form in which it exists there." In his attempt to anticipate criticism, Mill made distinctiveness the highest virtue, and urged that the book "needs to be read with" a "catholic spirit." For "this is not so much a history, as an epic poem . . . the history of the French Revolution, and the poetry of it, both in one; and on the whole no work of greater genius, either historical or poetical, has been produced in this country for many years."[15] Mill suggested to his readers that his strong recommendation of the book was even the stronger because he was not generally in sympathy with Carlyle's style and political views. Carlyle, appreciating Mill's clever ploy to disarm possible critics, patiently waited to see if that criticism would come. Fortunately, when it came, it was not very damaging, mostly because it proved so emotionally and obsessively hostile that it tended to provoke both suspicion about its soundness and lively interest in the book itself. The book's detractors turned out to be its best publicists.

Also, there was substantial praise, especially from the young Victorians who were then coming into their own. Though the two men had not yet met, Dickens, whose *Pickwick Papers* Carlyle was reading that same summer, thought the book marvelous. Browning, Forster, and Tennyson were immediate enthusiasts. But Carlyle's interests were served most practically by William Makepeace Thackeray, a young journalist and artist whose friends had intersected with Carlyle's own even before the two men met in the spring of 1837. Charles Buller and John Sterling had shared a Cambridge late adolescence with the "half-monstrous Cornish giant; kind of painter, Cambridge man, and Paris Newspaper Correspondent" who had read the almost legendary Scotsman's essays as they became known to his personal circle and his professional world.[16] Both Carlyle and Thackeray were contributors to *Fraser's;* their pictures appeared together in the composite of "The Fraserians" which Daniel Maclise painted in 1835. Unlike Buller and Sterling, Thackeray had to make his own living, having only his pen and sketchbook to provide funds for a family that would soon include three daughters and a mentally ill wife who needed constant care. Knowledgeable and in need, he jumped at the request to review *The French Revolution* for the *Times,* for the sake of both his own reputation and Carlyle's. Jane, who saw a copy in proof, warned her husband that it was "so small a *ting*" that "he cannot boast of having . . . '*served Thacker*[*a*]*y*' however he may have '*served Carlyle.*' "[17] Early in August, the *Times* arrived at Scotsbrig, where Carlyle intercepted it on "a sunny monday morning" as he and Jamie were escorting Alick back to Ecclefechan. "They made me take place under the shade of the . . . beech-trees," he wrote to Jane, "and read it all over to them, amid considerable laughter and applause. One is obliged to men in these circumstances who say even with bluster and platitude greater than Thackeray's, Behold this man is not an ass."[18]

Whatever his reservations about Thackeray's tone, he appreciated the publicity that the favorable review would create. Though he described Carlyle's style as "prose run mad," Thackeray had extravagant praise for the suitability of the prose to the subject matter, the power and the fascination of the "gloomy rough Rembrandt-kind of reality . . . of historic painting," and the writer's "absolute freedom from

CANT." Carlyle could hardly find it a "small *ting*" to have it said in the *Times* that his book "possesses genius, if any book ever did." Thackeray's political message, however, may have been less to his liking, not because it was inconsistent with his own views but because it seemed to lack the emotional tenderness and the religious dimension of his own concern for the threat of violence. Thackeray lacked Carlyle's poetic and religious view of history, and his paraphrase of the author's warning about the excesses of republicanism and the dangerous revolutionary situation in England and Europe seemed to suggest that realistic good sense and political shrewdness were the highest grounds of analysis. Radicalism, immoderation, hunger were, for Thackeray, enemies of order rather than the necessary prerequisites for the new order that the "world-revolution" was in the process of creating.

As with all books, the temptation to dissociate it from the reality it described was a strong one: the crucial criticism was that the prose had become mad, barbarous, and Germanic—the same objection that Sterling had made at length to Carlyle in 1835 about the style of *Sartor.* Carlyle's defense had been that in a world crumbling into chaos a revolutionary style that helped to dramatize the fall of such classical and Johnsonian illusions of order was not only appropriate but necessary. The discussion with Sterling had expanded into a substantive exploration of what was for the younger man the critical issue, whether or not Carlyle believed in a personal god compatible with Anglican or any other kind of Christianity. The discussions of *The French Revolution,* however, generally tended to aestheticize the book. It was an epic poem, to be responded to as poetry, much as one might respond to *Paradise Lost:* the issue was the quality of the poetry rather than the truth of the theology or the politics.

Jane, who toured southwestern England with the Sterlings late in August, reported to her husband the surprising news that "*The Book* seems to be much more *popular* than I ever expected—Archdeacon Singleton finds 'nothing Radical in it'!!"[19] It was soon selling remarkably well, "abundantly reviewed, praised and discussed."[20] When Carlyle returned home in the middle of September, he discovered his wife in bubbling good spirits, though her health was still worrisome. She waited for him behind the door, eager to proclaim the fact, whatever his grumpy reservations, that he was famous as far as she was concerned. Her fear that her saturnine husband might cart her off to some gloomy exile innumerable miles from London now seemed preposterous. The logic of success was on her side, and no matter how great the tension and unhappiness caused by his complaints, it seemed likely that the couple would be permanent residents of the only place she wanted to live in. Under these circumstances, Jane could better appreciate how well matched they were. Even her dependency was more acceptable if it was fulfilled by his success and if she could have her way in the matters most important to her, for, as she told her mother-in-law, "I have only him . . . to love me and take care of me. . . . Not but what numbers of people love me after their fashion far better than I deserve; but then *his* fashion is so different from all these and seems alone to suit the sort of crotchety creature that I am."[21] She needed his love. But, having married him for his genius, the highest confirmation of her choice came not from her own feelings but from the world's recognition that she was right.

2.

As the winter came on, certain things had been clarified, though not all of them resolved. The money problem was still serious. Though Carlyle had no desire to write for the periodicals, he accepted Mill's offer to do a review-article on Sir Walter Scott for the *London and Westminster Review.* With unhappy determination, he volunteered to write a steady stream of such articles throughout the year for approximately £200. But the *Review* had begun to have serious financing problems and, probably aghast at the notion of that much Carlyle, Mill made transparent excuses. Carlyle did what he thought "a long, occasionally rather stupid Article" on Scott, which he finished early in December 1837.[22] Though he had mixed feelings about London, his summer stay in Annandale had reinforced his conviction that he could not live there or anywhere in the country for very long. Was it his fate to continue to live unhappily in London, "the only vestige of neighbourhood . . . I ever had among my fellow men in this world?" By the end of 1849, he was almost resigned to it, and drew upon one of his recurrent images to describe his necessary ordeal: "Since my life seems cast here one has to do like the fabulous salamander: learn to live in fire!"[23]

Though he had preferred not to suffer the nervous torment of lecturing again, by late September 1837 he had resolved to do so.[24] It was the only secure source of money he had. Emerson soon made arrangements for the publication of *The French Revolution* in America. By December, Fraser, encouraged by the recent success, not only had agreed to publish his "scattered reviews and articles," in Carlyle's view "a pregnant sign," but had actually consented to publish an English edition of *Sartor,* which had sold so well in America. Still, the proceeds to Carlyle from all this publishing activity were at worst risky, at best a year or so in the future. As the winter deepened, he confessed to himself that he would have to "look mainly in the *lecturing side* of things for some time," which he hoped to "get thro' . . . with less pain and more profit."[25] Although his friends encouraged him to lecture on the topic he was most closely identified with, revolution, he put that prospect aside for the time being. He decided to lecture on literature in general, a vast portmanteau subject that would allow him to sweep across Western literature from the Greeks to the present, an expert "about all things in the world."[26]

For a change, in this freezing winter Jane's health was "wonderfully well."[27] While he pondered the details of his lectures, they tried to keep snug in their upstairs front room by "shutting off folding-doors" and "by the aid of paper-stuffing." "From the first night" of the frost late in January "everything has been frozen in every room here when there are not fires. One's towel is frozen in the morning; the water-jug is an ice-jug; to get your hands washed is a problem." He never took off his cloak and, when he looked in the mirror, he saw "a shaggy almost dangerous-looking man."[28] But, for the first time, this Scotch "Doubting Thomas" was invited into the community of government and aristocracy. The worldly audience interested him. Though he feared being misloved and misled, he also hoped that he might help others into the paths of honesty and righteousness. At Jane's urging he accepted an invitation to a dinner party at the home of the chancellor of the Exchequer, whose daughter, Miss Spring Rice, admired his new book. " 'It will help your lectures,' " she said. He could not help thinking, as the well-dressed and brightly-wealthy evening passed, that "here is the man that disposes annually of the whole revenue of England; and here is another man who has hardly enough of cash to buy potatoes and onions for himself."[29] Having dined at the Spring Rices, he was soon also on intimate terms with John Marshall, a wealthy Leeds manufacturer connected to them by marriage who kept a stately house in London for his family and for entertaining his friends. Carlyle expressed reservations about his ability to buy a horse that would provide him with the exercise he thought necessary for his health, and soon thereafter a four-legged gift from his wealthy friend appeared at his door. Probably neither of them noticed the irony of his naming it "Citoyenne," and kept it for only a short time. Altogether, it seemed a "restless dreaming winter," with "loud knocks at 'the wooden guardian of one's privacy.' "[30] But Carlyle answered the knocks whatever his temperamental and philosophical reservations.

On April 30, 1838, Carlyle gave the first of twelve lectures on European literature. To his wife he "looked a surprisingly beautiful man" on the platform.[31] He was back again at his "old trade of basketmaking, or lecturing . . . a tall, robust-looking man" entertaining "a well-dressed London crowd."[32] Convinced that sincerity was the highest value, he had no difficulty in demonstrating to his audiences that his own sincerity was no pose. His "low nervous voice, with a broad Scotch accent," flowed with rugged melodiousness across the high points of emphasis.[33] Stumbling and searching for the better phrase in the low points, carefully prepared, vividly graphic, seemingly spontaneous in his choice of language, he created the impression of a totally idiosyncratic speaker whose absorption in his own flow of ideas and words allowed his audience the privilege of being part of the thinking process of an extraordinary mind. Though there was an initial falling off in attendance, especially by his "fashionable friends," the audience soon lived up to expectations.[34] To some he was a Romantic figure, almost a primitive genius, "simple as a child, and his happy thought dances on his lips and in his eyes, and takes word and goes away, and he bids it Godspeed, whatever it be."[35] To others, he seemed too rugged, severe, forbidding. Those who found his literary style unattractive, found his lectures equally so. What seemed verbal genius to some seemed no more than "picturesque" to others. Leigh Hunt, covering the lectures for the *Examiner,* admitted that his fear that the speaker would not attain in public extemporary speech "the fluency as well as depth for which he ranks among celebrated talkers in private" was unwarranted.[36] With their occasional reservations and disagreements on minor points, Hunt's reports seemed to Carlyle unnecessarily carping, perhaps an expression of jealousy or resentment. But such extensive coverage in the *Examiner* and elsewhere affirmed what was undeniable: the lectures were widely recognized as a public happening, an attraction of the first order, whatever Carlyle's own reservations and anxieties about them.

Just before the lecture began, Jane had fallen ill again with influenza, the burden of her husband's strain evidently having been too much for her.[37] As soon as the lectures were over, Carlyle, who felt that he had already lived not four but twenty years in London, insisted on a long vacation in Scotland.[38] With profits of over £200 from the lectures, he could readily afford the trip, and he had no particular writing project in mind. It thus seemed a good time to leave for the familiar green hills and the people who were dearest to him. Also, he had been invited by Elizabeth Fergus, a middle-aged spinster who had enjoyed the Carlyle's hospitality at Cheyne Row, to visit at her family home in Kirkcaldy. Jane, however, made it clear that she would not go. Her health was against it. She had no desire to exhaust herself emotionally and physically as a tagalong while her husband visited his family and enjoyed the solitude that she found repellent. A visit to her mother at Templand held no attractions for her. As Carlyle sailed north at the end of August, he retasted the bitter words that had been spoken between them at parting. His "sharp tempered wife" apparently had made clear her dissatisfactions. Happy to have him gone, she felt physically better as soon as he left. Shortly, as was usually the case when they were apart, their letters became softer, more chastened, more loving.

Despite evident signs of success, the new literary star still had minor financial problems. *Sartor* had been published in England at last, an American edition of his *Critical and Miscellaneous Essays* and both an American and English edition of *The French Revolution* were out by the end of the year, but still the only money he received was from Emerson. Much as he disliked the public exhibition of his tormented nerves, the reward and the need were large enough to impel him to lecture again both in the spring of 1839 and the spring of 1840. In a last effort Emerson urged him to make a lecture tour in America, a message that was repeated in the spring of 1839 by Charles Buller, who had just returned from important service with the Durham Commission in Canada. Buller claimed that in America Carlyle was "the most esteemed etc, and ought to go over and Lecture in all great towns of the union, and make etc. etc.!"[39] But such an imperative did not seem urgent to Carlyle. Finding himself with a little time on his hands, he attended to some minor matters, "as idle as man could well be."[40] He thought of using some of his American money to buy a horse, which he would call "Yankee," to speed him "over the world for two hours daily." The "whirl" of violent exercise would be the appropriate setting for thoughts about his upcoming lectures on revolutions in modern Europe.[41]

By May, when he lectured again (six rather than the twelve of the previous year), Fraser had brought out the first English edition of the *Critical and Miscellaneous Essays,* a new edition of his translation of *Wilhelm Meister's Apprenticeship,* and a second edition of *The French Revolution,* which was matched by a second American edition. Carlyle now had no reason to accept Emerson's invitation to "Come, & make a home with me."[42] The new lectures created a "clear gain of £200," though he was less happy with them than the lectures of the previous years. Ironically, his lecture on the subject he knew most about, the French Revolution, pleased him least. After a frenetic gallop in "a kind of rage" to Harrow and back just before his final lecture, he finished the series with what he thought a "success."

On the day before the last lecture, Jane painfully joked that she assumed he would "hang himself *after.*"[43] She was disgusted with his nervous irritability. Of course, he had other plans. "The country hereabouts, so long as there falls enough rain, is among the beautifullest I ever saw, an ocean of wavy greenness," though without the music of "the clear-gushing streams . . . in the North." But "to me no country is or can be equal to my own, for tarrying in."[44] Shortly thereafter, he prevailed on Jane to travel to Scotland with him for the summer of 1839. She "nearly gave up the ghost" on the sail north and had a

Thomas Carlyle. Drawing by Samuel Laurence, n.d. Courtesy of the Carlyle House, The National Trust for Places of Historic Interest or Natural Beauty, London.

miserably irritable time at Templand with her mother, whom she called "the worst-natured of women."[45] Though they were in Scotland at the same time, they were hardly together. At Scotsbrig, he thought about his future as lecturer and writer. Though he was to do it once more, he was now certain of what he had sensed almost from the beginning, that "lecturing is a thing" he should "never grow to like."[46]

3.

In the first years of Victoria's reign the London literary and aristocratic world was in its golden brightness. Secure in its sense of privilege, the aristocracy rarely hesitated to make alliances with the newly wealthy. But both birth and wealth were attracted to that most unstructured and nonhierarchical of human forces, talent, the personal energy and magnetism of those individuals who had demonstrated, independent of any societal factors, what could neither be inherited nor bought. The narrow exclusivity of privilege welcomed the man of talent, who was in demand for dinner parties, hunting parties, and ongoing salons, and who found himself invited to participate in the glitter and fashion of bright ballrooms and used to help populate the uncountable rooms and long dining halls of cavernous country houses.

With his recent success as a writer and lecturer, Carlyle suddenly found himself eagerly pursued by the well-born, the wealthy, and the talented. By late 1838, the word had gone round that his was company worth having, though he himself met such popularity with the constant, self-deprecating reminder that worldly success encouraged pride. Edward Irving's fate was often on his mind. In addition, he believed that dinner parties disturbed his digestion and sleep. Whatever the immediate pleasures of company, ultimately such activities were idle entertainments for the frivolous, inconsistent with the earnest engagement with work which alone justified a man's life. The son of a family deeply proud of its special grace from God, whatever its outward expressions of humility, he did not think to pit the pride of religious election against the pride of birth or wealth. One was from God, the other from the World.

At the same time, however, he had a strong need for other people, both as a forum for the projection of his own personality and for the friendships that he valued so highly. His disparagement of the world of "getting and spending" sometimes made him feel that he could sample that world without being infected by it; at other times, he felt that it would be unfair to himself and others to remain separate from noble souls among the rich and well-born simply because they were rich and well born. In fact, he found most attractive those who affected no special pride in their possessions. Like the elite of his parents' spiritual community, they accepted the grace of election as natural aristocrats. He felt the honor of being sought after, the son of Annandale peasants in the glittering halls of the powerful. He also felt that he might influence the wealthy, the talented, and the powerful to follow wiser policies and more spiritual voices. And, whatever his hesitation before, whatever his suffering afterward, he enjoyed being in company, for he was eager to meet people with whom he could feel sympathetic. In addition, he could not give up the vision of special friendship, with its emphasis on a community of saints, which had been the heritage of his childhood.

One day in April 1839 an extraordinary apparition dazzled Cheyne Row—Count D'Orsay, dandy, amateur painter, and consort of the notorious Lady Blessington. He arrived in a glass and golden coach that seemed as if it had come right out of the coronation procession. D'Orsay flattered Jane, amused Thomas, and revealed himself to be, beneath the tailored brocades and elaborate color coordination of his appearance, a man of some good judgment of people. His minor talent as a painter soon produced a sketch of Carlyle, who accepted an invitation from the debonair count and the aging Lady Blessington in order to meet Walter Savage Landor, whom he admired and immediately liked. Through D'Orsay, he made an appearance at Holland House, sufficiently curious about the great lord and lady to keep his observant eyes on them and their guests throughout an evening at which "Lords and Ladies" were "as thick as blackberries!"[47]

D'Orsay, understandably, soon faded out of Carlyle's life, but at about the same time he was introduced to another, very different aristocrat. Bingham Baring's nobility was the result of his father's recent rise from relative anonymity through trade and banking to one of the major fortunes of the period. Baring, who would inherit the title of Lord Ashburton, dressed somberly, spoke softly, and communicated his presence by obvious competence and gentle reticence. His wife, Harriet Montagu, was a lively, aggressive, and sometimes witty woman whose aristocratic family had been at the center of English power for centuries. A small portion of the vast Baring and Montagu wealth went into the future Lady Ashburton's lavish entertaining at her various homes—a summer farm at Croydon (a short ride from London), an elaborately impressive mansion called Bath House in Piccadilly, and two magnificent country homes of which she was soon to be mistress, one on the seashore at Gosport near Portsmouth, the other a spacious, neoclassical enormity called "The Grange" at Alresford near Winchester in Hampshire. She was a hostess on the grand scale who delighted in collecting an appreciative salon, had a taste for literary celebrities, and felt certain that she was the ornament around which bright

Harriet Baring, Lady Ashburton. Drawing. Courtesy of the Carlyle House, The National Trust for Places of Historic Interest or Natural Beauty, London.

lights would shine even brighter. Toward the end of the winter of 1839, while pondering the subject of his lectures, Carlyle made his first appearance at Bath House at a dinner. Some of the aristocratic guests had attended his lectures on world literature. "The Lady of the House, one Lady Harriet Baring, I had to sit and talk with specially for a long long while," he wrote to his mother. She is "one of the cleverest creatures I have met with, full of mirth and spirit,—not very beautiful to look upon."[48]

Jane herself, who in the Victorian custom was often not included in her husband's invitations, actually "got up" a "*soirée*" with "between 20 and 30 entirely brilliant bits of personages" which "went off in the most successful manner."[49] Soon after that evening, bright spring weather provided an appropriate prelude to Carlyle's fashionably attended 1839 lectures. With his keen eye for the swirling richness and variety of the social scene, he was beginning to be a participant as well as an observer. "This time of year is precisely the heyday of London," he wrote to Jack. "Perhaps 100,000 additional people crowd into it, in May and June, from all parts of England and the world. The religious people hold meetings incessantly; the fashionable people dine and dance . . . one enormous beehive of human creatures, all buzzing their loudest in the burning weather," until by "the end of July . . . nearly dead with waste and weariness," they are "glad to fly into the country and hide themselves."[50]

Whether or not Richard Monckton Milnes was at Jane's *soirée,* the relationship between Carlyle and this wealthy and charming young literary critic, poet, and Tory politician presented the immediate possibility of real friendship. They met early in 1839. Quick to appreciate Carlyle's virtues, Milnes soon invited him to dinner and thereafter to his favorite form of entertaining, breakfasts at which the well-known were lured by gracious hospitality and famous names. Introduced by Carlyle to Emerson's essays, Milnes responded appreciatively, and Carlyle thanked him "for liking that man."[51] The next June, he breakfasted at Milnes's for the express purpose of talking to Daniel Webster, Emerson's "brave senator . . . a terrible, beetle-browed, mastiff-mouthed, yellow-skinned, broad-bottomed, grim-taciturn individual; with a pair of dull-cruel-looking black eyes, and as much Parliamentary intellect and silent-rage in him . . . as I have ever seen in any man."[52]

Later to become Lord Houghton, "Dicky" Milnes provided for Carlyle at this time his most cherished example of the propinquity of wealth, talent, and the good heart. He became a lifelong friend, his estate at Fryston in Yorkshire an occasional refuge for the restless and often tired writer. Despite Carlyle's bitter contempt for the useless Tories, who perpetuated the absurd and unjust Corn Laws, he had

Monckton Milnes. Drawing by Alfred D'Orsay, 1839. Reprinted from T. W. Reid, *The Life, Letters and Friendships of Richard Monckton Milnes* (New York, 1891).

enough loyalty and good humor to tease his friend on his prospects in the general election of 1841: "May *you* be 'returned' in your Burgh,—and hardly any other Tory at all in any Burgh whatsoever!"[53] Milnes's arms were always open and the two friends never seem to have quarreled. In a moment of gloom in the summer of 1841, unhappy with

London and with Scotland, Carlyle turned to Milnes with a half-serious question: "Why does not a pious man like you think of founding some kind of *modern* priests' cell . . . whither many a half-distracted Poet (modern Priest, if we are ever again to have Priests) might run."[54]

The distractions of the modern world, Carlyle felt, were having a particularly pernicious effect on poets, and he frequently told young poets that in this "iron age" prose was a more suitable vehicle for their feelings and ideas. Sterling, an insistent but uninspired poet, heard the lecture numbers of times without being in the least discouraged. Jane had nice things to say about his poems; so too did her husband, who kept his true feelings from Sterling in the interest of friendship. When "a huge horrible manuscript Poem" from Sterling arrived at Cheyne Row in November 1840, Carlyle knew he would "never read it; that is certain," but pretended to have done so, keeping his comments as general as possible. Having written a small number of poems himself, Carlyle had concluded, partly by making a virtue of necessity, that the highest poetry is the prose epic of reality: rhyme, meter, and the arbitrary arrangements of poetic line could only interfere with the creation of a literature that would respond to the needs of the contemporary world.[55] This attitude did not, however, detract from his responsiveness to the great poetry of the past and to the two best poets among his younger contemporaries.

When he met Robert Browning at a party at Leigh Hunt's in early April 1836, he found him "a modest youth, with a good strong face and a head of dark hair," dressed in "a turn-down shirt collar with a ribbon for neck-tie, and a green coat."[56] Noticing the poet's green coat in particular, Carlyle got the mistaken impression that Browning was a frivolous sporting man. Browning, however, pursued the older man's company during the next years, impressed by Carlyle's personality and his writings, especially *Sartor.* Noticing Browning in his lecture audience in 1840, Carlyle stopped him on the way out, to the surprise of the poet who doubted that the famous man remembered him. " 'O yes, I recollect you very well,' " Carlyle said, " 'Will you come and see me? I live down in Chelsea.' "[57]

Eagerly accepting the invitation, Browning became a regular visitor until his flight to Italy in 1845 changed his life radically. Carlyle, on his rides into the countryside, sometimes found it convenient to visit the young poet at his parents' home in Surrey. Whatever his reservations about Browning the poet, who often seemed obscure, rugged, and idiosyncratic, and Browning the man, who "dwells in an element of Charles-Lamb-ism, British-Museum Classicality and other Cockney encumbrance," Carlyle recognized that his new friend had great strength of personality.[58] Perhaps he also realized that some of the qualities of

Browning's poetry were similar to those of his own prose. Though he advised Browning also to give up poetry for prose, Carlyle was confident that the young man would eventually triumph over limitations and encumbrances. Despite a moment or two of tension, particularly when Browning learned of disparaging remarks that Carlyle had made about his wife, of whom the older man never thought much, Browning's love and respect for the man he came to look upon as an older brother or a father to them all never flagged. To Browning, he was a "beloved friend" whose opinions he did not always agree with but whom he honored in his heart.[59] After Carlyle's death, Browning told a mutual friend, "I feel towards him as John Forster did to Landor: . . . 'If he were standing here before me—I'd hug the old man!' "[60]

Tennyson, whom Carlyle met in 1839, had been an admired member of "The Apostles," a group of talented students at Cambridge, and was now patiently, sometimes indolently, enduring an engagement that was to last almost twenty years. But family and personal nightmares brought on by his father's alcoholism and his brother's madness did not prevent him from functioning effectively, though erratically, as a young man determined to devote his life to poetry. From his earliest days, the future poet laureate was an acknowledged and admired part of an important branch of the Victorian family, some members of which Carlyle had already become connected with before he first met the tall, shaggy, "dusty-dark" headed poet. At Cambridge, John Sterling, Charles Buller, and Richard Milnes, three of Carlyle's closest London companions, had been members of "The Apostles" and fervent admirers of the young poet. Even Thackeray, through Buller, had occasionally clasped hands in the same circle. When Carlyle and Tennyson were introduced, probably by Sterling, the two men began a friendship that was to last the rest of Carlyle's life, though it was at its most intense and companionable during the 1840s. Carlyle was immensely enthusiastic about his new friend, "a true human soul . . . to whom your own soul can say, Brother," an alter ego who is "carrying a bit of Chaos about him . . . which he is manufacturing into Cosmos!"[61]

During 1840 Tennyson was a frequent visitor at Cheyne Row. Like his host, he was a habitual smoker, and their pipes constantly sent mingled wreaths of smoke into whatever air they shared. The older man immediately admired Tennyson's humanity, warmth, musical voice, quiet patience, and distinctive looks. With the complexion of a gypsy and the soul of a poet, Tennyson seemed in touch with the mysteries of life and "eloquent" even in his "very silence."[62] The poems that Tennyson published in 1842, particularly "Dora," "The Vision of Sin," and "Ulysses," corroborated Carlyle's intuition about the poet's genius. He did not tire of recommending "Ulysses" to his friends and acquaintances, but his enthusiasm for the major poems of later years was minimal. *In Memoriam* seemed to him inexpressibly dull, in part because of the substantial disagreement between the two men, frequently expressed in hot arguments during the 1840s, on the question of personal immortality. By this time, Carlyle was willing to argue in private that he thought it a senseless doctrine, but Tennyson clung to it with emotional desperation, capable of convincing himself that without such a belief life had neither meaning nor hope. Like Jane, Carlyle found *Maud* unbearable. *Idylls of the King,* "the inward perfection of vacancy," he read "with considerable impatience at being treated so very like infants, tho the lollipops were so superlative." In his judgment, Tennyson had declined from the strength of his early poems into "mere aestheticisms."[63]

But his warm feeling for the poet sustained a lifetime of friendship, correspondence, and visits. Whatever their judgments of one another's works and temperaments, the bond remained indissoluble. Carlyle thought Tennyson lazy; Tennyson occasionally found Carlyle loud, overbearing, and irrational. He could not have been pleased by the older man's occasional urging that he put aside poetry for prose, though apparently, perhaps because he responded to the bardic element in Tennyson's verse, the advice was not proferred as frequently and as strongly as it was to Browning. When Tennyson was in desperate need of money, Carlyle helped him to obtain a government pension. He returned the poet's fondness for Jane with strong affection for Tennyson's wife when the younger man finally married in 1850. The poet's son claimed that Carlyle "took a fancy to her partly because, in answer to one of his wild grumbles, she said, 'That is not sane, Mr. Carlyle.' "[64] When they first met, Carlyle had seen in Tennyson some of the same passion, suffering, and hope that he still experienced himself. He saw him as a fellow voyager through the chaos of modern confusion toward some kind of acceptance and peace, the voyage that Goethe had been the first to complete successfully. From the beginning of the relationship, he felt that he and his new friend, like the poet's Ulysses, were traveling together on some cultural and personal journey "beyond the sunset, and the baths / Of all the western stars."

Unlike Carlyle's immediate affection for Tennyson, the embrace between Carlyle and John Forster was initially a formal one, but between 1837 and 1841 they gradually developed a close friendship, and in the next decades the relationship took on a special intensity. Even more than Carlyle, Forster expressed himself loudly in company, as if he imagined himself addressing a vast audience in a cavernous hall no matter how small the gathering and intimate the group. Nicknamed *'Fuzbuz,"* he seemed "a most noisy man, but really rather a good

John Forster. Photograph, n.d. Courtesy of the Rare Book and Manuscript Library, Columbia University.

fellow."[65] Eager to make his living as the traditional man of letters, as reviewer, biographer, and historian, the overbearing Forster had an extraordinary amount of energy to expend on advancing the interests of his friends. With a clever head for business, he soon made himself immensely helpful to Carlyle and indispensable to Dickens.

The difference in temperament between Carlyle and Dickens, however, was even more important than the difference in age. Both in his writings and in his life, Dickens' public side was a necessary expression of his imagination: the swirls of comic sociability and the sheer emotional satisfaction of making people laugh and cry which Carlyle thought self-indulgent were essential to Dickens. Dickens admired Carlyle immensely; Carlyle's explicitly stated views on social matters seemed an embodiment of his own strong feelings on such issues. With his reading of *The French Revolution, Chartism,* and the books that followed, Dickens found Carlyle one important step ahead of him in dramatizing revolution, class conflict, urban degradation, and the battle between spiritual needs and material temptations in a materialistic society. After *Pickwick* and *Nickleby,* Dickens' emotions gradually caught up with Carlyle's perceptions. By the 1850s he could proclaim that *Hard Times,* which he dedicated to Carlyle, "contains nothing in which you do not think with me, for no man knows your books better than I."[66]

Carlyle could not say the same. In 1837 he "sent for the Pickwick on the faith of" a positive review by Buller in the most recent *London and Westminster Review,* inclined in advance to agree with "an intelligent . . . youth in Dumfries" that such light entertainment did not deserve to be reviewed in a sober journal.[67] His suspicions were confirmed: "Thinner wash, with perceptible vestige of a flavour in it here and there, was never offered to the human palate." But "the human constitution has many wants. *Resquiescat* Pickwick!"[68] *Pickwick* seemed pure entertainment, without moral or message, to be tolerated and occasionally praised but not to be confused with higher aims and achievements that touched on the crucial questions of Man, Society, and God. Aware that the matter had its human side, he tried to understand and be tolerant of Pickwickmania. He was incapable of keeping a straight face or suppressing the story when an archdeacon wrote to him of "a solemn clergyman who had been administering ghostly consolation to a sick person; having finished, satisfactorily as he thought, and got out of the room, he heard the sick person ejaculate: 'Well, thank God, *Pickwick* will be out in ten days any way!' "[69]

When they first met in March 1840, Carlyle thought Dickens "a fine little fellow," with "clear blue, intelligent eyes, eyebrows that he arches amazingly, large protrusive rather loose mouth, a face of most extreme *mobility,* which he shuttles about . . . while speaking. . . . A small compact figure . . . and dressed à la D'Orsay rather than well." He sensed that beneath the dandyish exterior was "a quiet, shrewd-looking, little fellow, who seems to guess pretty well what he is and what others are."[70] Dickens' intelligence and talent were beyond question, his public cheerfulness and high spirits admirable. But Carlyle felt little incentive to read novels at all, and the later, serious, if not dark Dickens had no chance to impress a man who had formed his opinion on *Pickwick Papers* and *Nicholas Nickleby,* which he "never read, except pieces of it in newspapers."[71] Reports on the novels naturally reached him from his wife and other avid Dickens readers over the next decades, but he was rarely in the mood to give Dickens the novelist another chance. His slighting words for the novels decreased, however, mainly because his once ambivalent feelings about the man became unequivocably positive as the years went by.

For Dickens wore well. Carlyle's ambivalence resolved itself into solid admiration for the younger man's energy and wit, and particularly for his cheerful optimism. Whatever his own gloom, Carlyle believed that this earth is a place of hope and that it demands visions of hope. He felt increasing respect for Dickens, in contrast to Thackeray, whose intellect he admired but whose cynicism repelled him. Thackeray, of course, in his charming but realistic way wanted something from the Carlyles, particularly during his own years of struggle. In a minuscule comic handwriting he did not hesitate to ask Jane (and through her Thomas) for help in getting favorable reviews for his new book in early 1841. Not that Carlyle did not sympathize with the "poor man . . . just come in from Paris; where his poor wife is left . . . *insane,*" and the husband "not well off for cash."[72] But with a natural tendency to value people the more as the years went by, as if the very length of the friendship hallowed it in a way that diminished earlier qualifications, Carlyle increasingly cherished Dickens. He was to survive the younger man by eleven years. When Dickens died in June 1870, Carlyle consoled himself and Forster: "How strange, how sad, and full of mystery and solemnity to think of our bright, high-gifted, ever-friendly Dickens, lying there in his final rest!" While visiting his family in Scotland, among the graves of his past, he gave Dickens a special place in his haunted imagination. "Poor loved Dickens. . . . The figure of him . . . often visits me, among the Shadows of my other Loved Ones that are gone."[73]

For a man who tended to think of himself as alone and friendless, Carlyle had managed by the beginning of the 1840s to create a number of lifelong friendships, the need for which and the nature of which do much to define the Victorian experience. Whether together or apart, in London or separated by the vagaries of circumstance, the record of these long friendships is deeply impressive and often moving. Milnes, Sterling, Thackeray, Browning, Tennyson, Forster, Dickens, soon Edward FitzGerald, and later John Ruskin—together they wove a rich texture of experience, talent, achievement, and mutual affection which created a family connectiveness of the sort that Carlyle thought essential for human relations. For Carlyle, a personal need and a cultural structure became happy mirror images. But it was only as time and death removed his loved ones and tarnished the golden era of high Victorian literary culture that the aging writer became aware of what he had lost—more aware of what he had possessed than he had ever been in the act of possessing it. Even in friendships, he loved more within himself, as an act of Protestant introspection, than in communion with others. The past of what had been often stirred his emotions more than the present of what is. He lived most fully in elegiac moments.

4.

In the middle of September 1839, the Carlyles dashed home from Scotland "through the confused darkness" of their first railroad journey, hurtled by "the huge Steam mystery."[74] During the next few months Carlyle kept himself energetically at work, concentrating on an essay that he had been contemplating a long time, an "Article on the Working people" that had "been delayed two years too long."[75] Encouraged by Mill to make it suitably optimistic, he assumed that the *London and Westminster Review* would publish it only if it claimed that the conditions of the working class had been improving. This was not a position he could defend. He offered it to Mill for the last number of the *Review,* though he was concerned that the article would loose impact by association with the swan song of the soon-to-be defunct Radical journal. To his surprise, the editor of the Tory *Quarterly Review,* John Lockhart, the son-in-law and biographer of Scott, expressed sufficient interest in publishing it to meet with him in the late fall. But, since both men were uneasy with the prospect of Carlyle appearing in such a conservative journal, the negotiations soon collapsed. Finally, at the beginning of December 1839, he arranged to have Fraser publish it as a separate pamphlet and told the disappointed Mill of his decision.

Two other projects absorbed his energy during the rest of the winter and through the spring: his efforts to organize a committee to create the London Library and the preparation of what he vowed would be his last lecture series. There was an element of idealistic selflessness in his work for the library, though years of frustration in obtaining books had provoked his interest and nurtured his determination. By late

1839 he had a new project in mind, whose scope was so broad and also so specialized that he would undoubtedly need access to a large collection of books. Though he told almost no one until he felt certain that he would carry it through, the project was a biography of Oliver Cromwell. He asked Frederick Denison Maurice to look into the possibility of a small private room at the British Museum where he might read without noise and discomfort. Maurice suggested that he might be able to borrow books from the Cambridge University Library. But "for immediate purpose . . . there is no hope except in the Museum," where, apparently, such arrangements had been made in unusual cases.[76] But the new Keeper of Printed Books, Antonio Panizzi, flatly refused, eager to assert his authority and suspicious that any advantage given to Carlyle would not be sufficiently appreciated. Like Giuseppe Mazzini, whom Carlyle had recently met, Panizzi was an Italian republican exile with grand ambitions. The librarian and the library-user gradually generated small antagonisms toward each other which culminated in Carlyle's public criticism of the Museum and its keeper during Parliamentary hearings on the future of the Museum in 1849. Panizzi was one more example absorbed into Carlyle's archetype of the anal librarian who stands like a jackal at the gates of the library to preserve and protect books by keeping readers away. The main advantage of the London Library would be that its books could be borrowed.

Soon the "scheme of London Library" was embodied in a prospectus, copies of which were circulated to elicit support from the wealthy and the well-known. Four hundred of the necessary five hundred subscribers were committed by the time a group of the library's supporters gathered at the Freemason's Tavern toward the end of June 1840 to hear Carlyle and other speakers. He gave a brief, well-received speech, arguing that the first requisite of a civilized society was to make books freely available to qualified readers. He soon allowed his name to be entered as secretary of the committee for the new library, and while the young Scotsman W. D. Christie did the actual secretarial work, Carlyle acted the inspiring cheerleader: "We *must begin advertising;* we must begin working the great bellows-machinery of the Newspaper Press. To it! I say to Forster and you; to it, like lions!" Prodigal with advice to "leave no stone unturned" and to "fire away," for "all *depends* upon the *gunners,*" he thought at the end of December 1840 that the library would probably open by the next winter. By the beginning of the new year he looked forward "before many months . . . to be handsomely out of the thing altogether."[77]

The lectures in the spring of 1840 were a public success but a mixed blessing. Though he intended to "speak" the lectures, he wrote out in advance a fairly full text, with the expectation that he would publish it in book form. Working through the winter and spring, he had sensed that "On Heroes and the Heroic" would synthesize ideas and feelings he had been developing for a long time. With the prospect of a full-scale biography of Cromwell in mind, or at least a treatment of Puritanism and the age of the Civil War, he thought the section of the lectures devoted to Cromwell might indeed provide an occasion to articulate the central ideas of the new book. Would it not be necessary for a sustained study of Cromwell to be the product of a larger theory about the relationship between great men and the historical culture from which they are inseparable? Drawing his heroic figures from disparate cultures, he would have the opportunity to delineate the underlying forces of personality and nature, whose basis was the unconscious and the mysterious. The first lecture would be on Odin, the second on Mahomet, an attempt to tell parochial English Christendom that divine inspiration and individual genius transcended sectarian limitations. The lectures on religious heroes like Knox and Luther would demonstrate that the reforming spirit of Protestantism touched the spiritual core of those unconscious powers within modern man which needed only to be spoken to in a bold voice to be awakened. The lectures on the poets and writers—Dante, Shakespeare, Johnson, Rousseau, and Burns—would claim what Carlyle felt deeply embodied in his own mission: in the modern world the artist is the new priest, the vehicle of the divine force of the universe.

Fascinated all his life by the relationship between spiritual and secular power, Carlyle believed, as he mulled over the lectures, that figures such as Napoleon and certainly Cromwell had succeeded as leaders of men to the extent that they had incorporated in conscious and unconscious form the central spiritual truths that any keen eye could see in the words and deeds of all great men. Might did not make right in any simple sense; political and military power might be used for good or for evil. To the extent that such leaders had an element of God within them, their power would be in the service of right. But whatever had been built on wickedness, no matter how permanent it might appear, was, in Carlyle's eyes, neither lasting nor right. "No man who is not in the *right,* were he even a Napoleon I at the head of armed Europe, has any real *might* whatever, but will at last be found *mightless,* and to have *done,* or settled as a fixity, nothing at all, except precisely so far as he was *not* in the wrong. Abolition and erosion awaits all 'doings' of his, except just what part of them *was right.*"[78] If there was a providential God, then why doubt that in the long run all visible and invisible things on this earth would finally manifest the goodness and the justice of that divine power? Stripped of sectarian and theological matters, except in tone, the premise of Carlyle's religion (which some of his contemporaries would not call religion at all) was that there is an element of divinity within each man. In some, the conflict between the divine and the antidivine force plays itself out in personal anguish and public disaster; in others, the divine force eventually triumphs and shows itself in great works. For the vast majority of mankind, without the energy and the character of greatness, the supreme victory is its recognition of the divinity within God-inspired fellow human beings like Jesus, Shakespeare, and Cromwell.

The first lecture, delivered to an audience "about a third more numerous this year," was a modest success.[79] Free tickets had gone to John and Edward Sterling, Cavaignac, Forster, Mazzini, Thackeray, Hunt, and the Pepolis (the middle-aged Elizabeth Fergus had just become the Countess Pepoli), who, among others, found the second lecture, an invocation of the great Islamic leader Mahomet, powerful but bewildering. His words "vomited . . . forth on them," he boasted to his mother, "like wild Annandale grapeshot."[80] Though his nerves felt "shivered," he thought it "the *best*" lecture he had "ever delivered."[81] But since he had hoped that he could publish the lecture transcripts with only minor revisions, he was disappointed when the "transcript" produced by the reporter whom Fraser had engaged seemed "nothing for printing . . . like soda-water with the gas out of it."[82] In the days between the lectures, which he gave every Tuesday and Friday from May 5 to May 22, he galloped wildly out to Highgate and Hampstead in the hope of killing his nervous "pain and anxiety." Jane felt ill; "the Lecturing agrees with her almost rather worse than it does with me." If he were ever to lecture in America, he would certainly leave her at home. Why have "two persons made miserable by it instead of one!"[83] But, as he well knew, he would never lecture again, either in England or in America.

Regretting that he had not decided to "write the thing as a Book" from the beginning, he soon discovered that he had to write it almost as if it were being done from scratch.[84] By the middle of June he began "somewhat in the style of *speech*." In the hot weather he stayed indoors all day, venturing out only at night, taking rides into the countryside "away from the Monster."[85] By the middle of July he had finished writing the third lecture. His stomach was queasy with "violent extremes of indigestion." In his nervous state, the lectures seemed to be "pure trash." He begged Emerson to forgive his long silence. "I have been lecturing, I have been sick; I have been beaten about in all ways."[86]

Since it now seemed unlikely that he could finish the task in time to vacation in Scotland, he paused between the fourth and fifth lectures and took a riding excursion out to Herstmonceaux in Sussex to see

Julius Hare, Sterling's old mentor, who had urged him to visit. At first he had hoped that Sterling would ride in from Clifton to meet him at Stonehenge. When that was not possible, he arranged that he and Cavaignac would ride to Herstmonceaux, after which he would return Citoyenne to John Marshall. He had gotten it into his head that he could not afford to keep the horse, though at the same time he believed that his health depended on such exercise. But when he postponed the scheduled start of the ride in order to finish some work, the new date at the last moment turned out to be impossible for Cavaignac. Carlyle thus rode off by himself during the first week of August on "a rural ride *into England,*" a round trip of about one hundred miles. "Nothing so remarkable" had been seen "since Quixote took the road."[87] The notion of learning more about England in this direct physical sense appealed to him.

At the end of August he had finished the fifth and begun writing out the sixth lecture—"The writing goes like fire well *kindled,*" he told Jane—and by the end of the summer the task was done.[88] He felt exhausted and it was clear that he would not go to Scotland. He contritely apologized to his mother, guilty that he was not fulfilling his longstanding promise. But he was meditating "*a new book . . . sitting quiet.* . . . My Book is to be about—But indeed I had better not yet tell anybody."[89] He promised her that he would spend the entire next summer nearby in Scotland. But he felt sorry for himself, so much so that he made what was to him an immensely painful comparison: "I travel no whither," he told Milnes, "but sit still here, and wait till my friends return to me. . . . It is like the life of Samuel Coleridge."[90] He was forced to sit on a special jury for two days, in spite of his irrepressible complaining, as if his immersion in what already seemed insufferably dull books on Cromwell and the Civil War were still too precious to be interrupted by anything. His new project seemed to him clearly a much less interesting subject than the French Revolution, and at times seemed to "*retro*gress."[91] Through the intervention of Cambridge friends, however, he found that he had no want of books in general. When "a huge hamper of Cromwell Books" arrived, it was "frightful to look upon."[92]

In principle, the subject seemed important enough, but the preparation was painfully tedious. Through the winter of 1840–1841 his "whole work" was "reading."[93] The weather was the "roughest . . . wettest . . . in any winter here," he complained to his brother Alexander, almost like Craigenputtoch.[94] He could remember no winter as bad "since 1819–20. . . . First it blew, as the American said, then it *snew,* then it *friz,* then it *thaw,* and then it *friz* again!"[95] He felt exhausted, bored, restless—eager to be somewhere else but having on his list of possibilities no place that was superior to where he was. He seemed to hardly get on with his project, no matter how many books he read, as if he were preparing himself "for some Coroner's verdict of *Died by the effect of stupid reading!*"[96]

After the hard winter, the first signs of spring brought out his restlessness. Though he had declined Fraser's initial offer of £75 for the publication of the lectures on heroes, he accepted £150 for the new edition of one thousand copies of *Sartor,* and both were in print by March 1841. Carlyle now wanted to get "out of London . . . to witness one other Summer before I die."[97] An attack of "ugly *Influenza,*" which he found it hard to shake off, sapped some of his strength.[98] Jack, who had the "best wages" for "*imaginary* employment," urged his brother to join him for a week on the Isle of Wight, where he attended his latest employer, a wealthy Irishman.[99] Convinced that "not since" he "came to London" had he "felt so thoroughly out of order," he asked Alick to keep his eye open for a summer place for him in Annandale.[100] He wanted to keep his promise to his mother to spend the entire next summer there. But the unresolved burden of the Cromwell project weighed heavily on him. With his fame and economic security established, he now felt the anxiety of a writer whose freedom to write whatever he wanted was as much burden as opportunity.

So eager was he to get back to his roots that he took advantage of Milnes's invitation to visit Fryston and made the journey to Yorkshire the excuse for both a spring *and* a summer visit to Annandale. Jane, who had been "sore confined and stagnated by a continuous cold," looked haggard and exhausted when her husband left Cheyne Row early in April 1841.[101] She resented, among other things, the competition of Scotsbrig. On his way north, "the last look on [her] face. . . . haunted [him] all the way. . . . Would I could make thee happy!" It was clear that he could not. Their nerves and tempers clashed. His habitual weapon against her was his ceaseless complaining about London. He claimed that he must find some relief from its miseries or die, and that meant long summers in Annandale, a summer home of their own closer to London to which he could flee regularly, or even permanent residence someplace else, the last an unspecified but always threatening possibility. At Fryston, where the entire Milnes family received him into their accustomed luxury as their son's honored guest, distance soothed the pain. His conscience, however, reproached him. Apart, he and Jane both put things into perspective; correspondence was a cooler medium of communication than direct confrontation. He begged her, "think not hardly of me, dear Jeannie."[102]

The strain on the marriage was considerable, however. "O my wife," he soon wrote, "Pity me, do not cease to love me!"[103] "All would be well," he believed, "if I *could* but *sleep.*"[104] Jane had collapsed onto her couch, "worn out by what the cockneys call 'mental worry.' " But, she wrote to Sterling, it was her husband's "jury-trials, his influenza, etc.," that composed the "all things" that have "been against me. . . . Day after day has found me stretched out on my sofa with a circulating library book in my hand. . . . I shall have to return to my post again presently. One has to die at one's post, has one not? The wonderful thing for me is always the prodigiously long while one takes to die."[105] So depressed was she that she complained to her physician brother-in-law that she wanted "no paradise but rest."[106] She could have that only when separated from her husband.[107] She raised the possibility in her own mind of a permanent separation either in life or in death. In many ways, the latter seemed the more practical alternative, if one did not have to wait so long to realize it.

Leaving Fryston, after a stop nearby at Headingly near Leeds where he stayed briefly with a combination of the Marshalls and the Spring Rices, Carlyle continued on to Scotsbrig via Liverpool and the Annan steamer. On the way to the railroad with Milnes, he received a letter from Emerson, soon to be followed by a draft for £100 and the flattering but unprofitable news that the authorized American edition of *Heroes* had been "driven from the market" by "New York Pirates" and "New York Newspapers" which "print the book in chapters. . . . You circulate for six cents per newspaper at the corners of all streets in N.Y. & Boston: gaining in fame what you lose in coin."[108]

But the silent Annandale moors suggested the grounds of revitalization. Too often the struggles of recent years had dimmed the vision of spiritual independence which he had fought through to during his life's deepest crises, the moments of sustaining transcendence which had crystallized during his "sabbatical" year at Hoddam Hill and the vision of liberation from material encumbrances which had sustained his moments of joy during the six years in the silent wasteland of Craigenputtoch. He now needed to reaffirm his vision of the supernatural in the natural, and Annandale was the best place for that. No matter how ghost-like the territory of the past might seem, it had a sustaining capability to revitalize him, particularly as long as his mother was alive. Only by kissing the ghosts on their shadowy lips could he feel the pressure of his own reality.

Through the rest of the year he struggled unsuccessfully with his intent to do something important with his Cromwell project and to keep his nerves from getting the best of his body. Jane could not say of him what she acidly said of Jack after he had visited a phrenologist to have "his character given," that he is "capable of *anything* but not capable of turning his capability to account!"[109] Against her wishes, he insisted on their spending a long summer at a beach house at Newby on the Solway near Annan. She accepted her isolation with grace, however, mainly because her husband for the first time admitted openly that he did not think he would ever leave London except for annual summer excursions.[110] On the way to Scotland, he had stopped at Newcastle-on-Tyne to visit Harriet Martineau, as both Carlyles did on their way back at the end of the summer. He found her tediously talkative, especially on the second visit. Suffering from an unexplained but supposedly serious illness, which a "celebrated London Doctor" pronounced "*hopeless,*" she had become a semi-invalid, confined to her couch, under the impression that she had an incurable cancer of the womb. The Carlyles suspected that "this celebrated London Doctor knows almost nothing about it!"[111] On his way to Newby in July he actually seemed to Harriet "happy . . . gleesome . . . his whole face was released,—his laugh was loosened,—his soul was merry that day. We all rejoiced in it."[112] At Newby, he bathed frequently; his mother visited for weeks.

Rather than return directly to London, he made a Cumberland excursion in the company of James Spedding, a friend of his Cambridge friends, who lived among the lovely lakes and mountains. They drove around Derwentwater, "the beautifullest view I ever in my life looked on."[113] He preferred Newby, however, for its ugliness, which was "very strange, very sad."[114] But it was an honest and homely place, conducive to his long "vagabond" night walks and his desire for solitude.[115] When Jane came "all in tears" to report that an American steamer had shipwrecked in sight of their cottage, he watched the rescue operation with the tragic sense that such realities were the essence of life; it was better to confront than to evade them. In October, James Fraser suddenly died, no more than thirty-five years old. Francis Jeffrey was seriously ill. "The only use of living is to do some good work," he wrote his mother.[116] But his new work was not going well, "confused puddling."[117] By December 1844, as he sat "at the bottom of" his "inkwell, in this horrible black Babylon,"[118] he was sustained, as he had been since the previous spring, by one of those crucial moments of vision that had come to him on the Annandale moors. "The moors are silent as death," he had written to Milnes. "So much has altered. . . . I study to live silent . . . like a ghost,—which indeed I am, and you are. Yet outside . . . larks are singing. . . . We are *alive*. . . . All the jargon *you* can utter, is it not like a kind of personal insult in the presence of that entirely unutterable Fact!"[119]

[11]

Revolutions (1) 1841–1843

Having broken the closed circle of his parents' world, Carlyle felt with new force the fright and the challenge of his own precarious position and the broad threat to traditional European culture. In the revolutionary decade of the 1840s, the Victorian Carlyle emerges definitively, an explosive paradox: the visionary radical, tortured by personal and public misery, and the visionary conservative, furious at what seemed "solutions" that could only make matters worse. No matter how hard he "studied to remain silent," he often found that an inner urgency forced him to speak out in ever more controversial public statements, culminating in *Latter-Day Pamphlets,* the shriek of satiric and Swiftian despair published in 1850. During the controversy in the spring of 1844 about the "proposal to restrict the hours of factory laborers to twelve with *two* allowed for meals," against which "numbers of people were loud and bitter," he told Lord Elliot that "the government were absolutely bound either to try whether they could do some good to the people, or to draw them out in line and openly shoot them. . . . That would be a mercy in comparison! He seemed much astounded."[1] The *reductio ad absurdum* exaggerations of his passionate anger sometimes seemed all too literal to his readers. But, though he ended the decade in anger and frustration, he began it with uncertain hope.

He approached the new decade "through the confused darkness" on the newly opened Preston to London railroad line in September 1839, feeling like Faust flying on the cape of the devil.[2] The steamers on the lake at Greenock twenty years before, the fiery mass of dark mills at

Birmingham, now the railroad hurtling in the night—all were images of a new relationship between man, space, and time, a relationship forged in that iron furnace at Muirkirk into which the mysterious old woman had disappeared so many years before. The destination was "unknown." The steam engine could consume or it could create. But certainly it would intensify the fire, shorten the process. Since what would happen would now happen more quickly than anyone had ever imagined possible, the time in which to put the world back in joint seemed so much less. Whatever the threat of steam power, however, it could bring closer together friends and family who had heretofore been separated by formidable distances. Emerson still urged him to come to America. But, Carlyle reminded his friend, the marvelous steamers plied the waters in both directions, bringing London and New York closer than they had ever imagined possible. With a sincere but globe-swallowing egocentricity, he argued that all the distant children of England would now be able to make regular and swift pilgrimages to the mother of them all. He preferred to stay in London and wait to be visited.

Unlike the railroad, the penny-post seemed to Carlyle an unambiguous blessing, a technological advance that he could praise unstintingly.[3] During the Parliamentary debate in 1840, he reminded Richard Milnes that he would not have fulfilled his duty unless he voted "to abrogate the Corn Bill, and give an approving vote to the Penny Postage."[4] Cheap postage facilitated the expansion of one's circle of correspondents, knitting the members of the Victorian family more closely together. There was the danger, of course, that unsolicited and undesired letters would infringe on one's privacy. On rare occasions, strangers could be entertaining, prompted by the comic impulse to send him funny or satiric letters, such as the two from the spurious mayor of Bury St. Edmunds, Marmaduke Wright, who threatened to sue the author of *Past and Present,* who had "taken the liberty" of referring to Wright "as the *respectable* mayor of Bury. This is an insult to me which I will not stand."[5] Unfortunately, however, Carlyle soon began receiving letters from mad people, from beggars, and from a considerable number of serious and sometimes pathetic young men (and women) who pleaded for advice and even assistance. But, no matter how hard he tried to help and how deeply felt each new cry for assistance, the words he had to offer usually only repeated those he had offered before. Letters came and went to friends and family with extraordinary regularity, however, and, more than whatever book he might be working on, they became his most characteristic and self-defining form of literary expression. In letters he could say things to others and himself that he could say no place else.

At some level Carlyle feared that "progress" was a bargain with the devil, and he vaguely sensed that part of his own anxiety stemmed from his suspicion that, in rejecting his parents' religion and embracing a literary career, he had himself entered into some kind of Faustian agreement. But if he had, Carlyle could not believe that it was binding. The railroad embodied power. Power could be used for good as well as for evil ends. And his pen had the potential to influence others, perhaps even directly. Although he feared both the misuse of power and the dangers inherent in political commitment, he flirted a number of times in the next decade with the notion of direct involvement in government. Underlying his ambivalence was his pervasive and sensible fear that, whatever they did, whether speaking from the sidelines or actively engaged, he and his contemporaries would be the victims of power. Still, he began the decade with at least some hope that they might yet be able to beat the devil.

2.

When he returned to London on the "steam monster" in the late summer of 1839, he faced this quickly moving and rapidly contracting world with some hope and much apprehension. Changes on various levels had to be grappled with, for better or worse. But how does one change the governance and the distribution of wealth in society if one abhors violence and fears that revolution will leave society no better off than it was before, except for the additional corpses? Peaceful "reforms," such as those advocated by his Radical friends, hardly seemed to have much chance of passage, even if they were desirable. And he had grave doubts that they were. Though parliamentary reformers like Buller and Mill were not completely wrong, they seemed to Carlyle not to be right enough, and furthermore they were constantly engaged in partisan politics. Ideology and advantage often seemed more important to them than practical results. To Carlyle, one of the immediate answers to poverty and overpopulation was emigration, which he had dramatically urged in 1839 in *Chartism.* But the Radical party opposed emigration, for reasons that seemed to him narrow and ideological. For over six years he was to watch the badly led and often deceived workers of the Chartist movement search for effective political leadership. But their energy proved sufficient only to help persuade the government to repeal the Corn Laws, not to give positive shape to new policies for a new age. He believed that without effective leadership mass movements could do nothing more than clear away the old. "Black, atheistic, unsympathetic Radicalism" seemed to him a failure. But there was a new and "nobler" radicalism struggling to be born, which he might help to lead.

In the autumn of 1841 he proposed "a right Radical *Review*," with himself as editor, arguing that "your only Church and Pulpit, in these times, is a Periodical Book . . . to preach and prophecy in all ways that Labour is honourable, that Labour alone is Honourable."[6] For "a man willing to work, and unable to find work, is perhaps the saddest sight that Fortune's inequality exhibits under this sun."[7] And if labor were not available in Great Britain, because the government foolishly declined to create jobs, then it should be sought in the colonies or wherever, with the active support of the government. For a short time he actually hoped that, if Bingham Baring became responsible for the ministry, he might be offered the chance not only to influence emigration policy but also to further mass education, which he saw as another practical way of creating a more harmonious future for the society. "Were it not far better for you practical Reformers," he recommended, "if you went first of all with exclusive energy upon Education; got all the people to demand in an imperative manner, 'Educate us, we say educate us, or!' "[8]

But in his personal life he wanted as little government assistance and interference as possible. He did not see why he should even vote in such a corrupt society; to do so was only to lend support to a partisan and materialistic system. He angrily opposed what seemed unfair attempts to tax his royalties. As the day, so often fearfully anticipated in the Carlyle family, for Alick to depart from Liverpool for the New World came closer, he and Jack between them made sure that their brother was well provided for. But, for the country as a whole, laissez-faire seemed to Carlyle a disastrous policy; the present problems were so serious and widespread that only national plans funded by the government could provide effective solutions. At the same time, however, he increasingly doubted that the corrupt web of business, bureaucracy, aristocracy, and government would support practical solutions. He increasingly felt that he was looking down a deep, widening, and magnetic chasm into which everything was destined to fall.

His desire to have a forum of his own alternated with his desire to retreat into the work he knew and did best, which was solitary, impractical in the ordinary sense, and unlikely to have any immediate effect on the affairs of the nation. He had hoped that *Chartism* would help change society. Richard Milnes had remarked that if it had been written in the language of ordinary men it might have been incendiary. But Milnes was probably wrong and Carlyle was certainly incapable of writing in any but the brilliantly contrived prose that he had invented as the best expression of his own personality, his background, and his aspirations as an artist. Over the next decade, whatever glimmer of hope he had had that his writings could make him a public force for political reform slowly dimmed. It was extinguished with the hostile reception of *Latter-Day Pamphlets.* He himself had recognized that there had never been any possibility that he could actually work in some partisan way with an organized group like a political party. Unable to appreciate that only organized groups could exert sufficient pressure to influence the direction of the nation, Carlyle insisted that his own views should be above party. In his Romantic idealization of the "miracle" and the power of the individual, he looked to particular leaders and the concept of elite leadership rather than to the common denominator and the compromises of democracy.

Sometimes his intuition served him well. Early in December 1841, despite ridicule from all his "Radical friends," Carlyle maintained "that Peel will perhaps try to *abrogate* these insane corn-laws." He prophesied that Robert Peel and the conservatives may actually try to "*do* something,"[9] and his intuition proved correct. But he never bent his positions for party or friends. Even as he proposed a new Radical review, he insisted on making clear that he had "no faith at all in extension of the suffrage at present—yet I heartily honour you who do pursue it."[10] He believed that education must precede the extension of such privileges. Such an attitude could not, of course, attract supporters, and the new review never got off the ground.

On the whole, the disappointment was a relief. He had already started his study of Oliver Cromwell and the Puritan Revolution and, moreover, he had a strong sense of himself as a private citizen whose profession was the "black inkwell" rather than that of public wielder and shaker. He wanted sometimes to be a leader of men, to have the glory and the satisfaction of being a man of action rather than of thought. But he had already been defined and defined himself as a man who writes and thinks, who places the highest value on individual conscience and literary creativity rather than on mass movement and political rhetoric. Whatever the frustrations, he could not change himself.[11]

A new friend, with complicated problems of his own, saw the dilemma clearly. Giuseppe Mazzini had been introduced to the Carlyles in 1837 by John Taylor, Harriet Taylor's husband. Lonely, impoverished, and intensely proud, this idealistic clarion of Young Italy believed, like Carlyle, that moral and spiritual idealism were the necessary determinants of political and social change. But, unlike Carlyle, he thought of himself as an active and practical revolutionary who, despite his Romantic idealism, had no doubt about what he wanted to accomplish and the best means to do it. Actually more bold than sensible, more visionary than practical, Mazzini found himself constantly expending his energy to support himself and other exiles while advancing

Giuseppe Mazzini. Photograph, n.d. Courtesy of the Rare Book and Manuscript Library, Columbia University.

more than a few impractical schemes for the invasion of Italy. He imagined that a charismatic leader with a handful of loyal supporters would be able to awaken the suppressed soul and conscience of all Italians, who would then rise up and throw off the Austrian yoke.

Both Carlyles liked Mazzini for his innocence, his virtue, and his courage; Jane in particular found men like Cavaignac and Mazzini attractive and supportive. At first, the couple attempted to be helpful to Mazzini, who was often hungry, tired, and occasionally ill, and who had almost no one to assist him. Carlyle recommended him to an influential editor as "a man of true genius, an honorable, brave and gifted man."[12] Mazzini's initial response was hesitant, for he did not want the Carlyles or anyone else to patronize him. Though he occasionally accepted dinner invitations, he kept his distance, in part out of embarrassment at his poor English, which Jane found a delightful source of comic misstatements and mispronunciations. Having read *Chartism,* Mazzini believed that he and Carlyle felt equally strongly about authoritarian repression, though he soon discovered that they differed in emphasis: Carlyle directed his energy toward sympathetic and dramatic depiction of the plight of the poor, whereas Mazzini focused *his* on the condemnation of, and the call for rebellion against, repressive authority. For Mazzini, the enemy was military, political, tangible—a particular army and a particular repressive power, whatever its name at the moment, which attempted to stifle a people's aspirations toward republicanism and democracy. For Carlyle, the enemy was materialism, the spiritual deadness that blinded individuals to the demands of justice and charity.

The two men argued, on good terms, aware of the distance that separated them. Between 1839 and 1841, the intimacy increased. Mazzini was actually more troubled by Carlyle's ideas than Carlyle was by Mazzini's. When he had the opportunity early in 1840 to publish a review of *The French Revolution,* Mazzini's own high sense of mission prompted him to write frankly about his friend's dilemma. Why was it, he asked, that Carlyle's history of the Revolution had been received so favorably? Of the two kinds of popular historians, the materialist who attempts to give only the objective facts and the artist who attempts to dramatize the subjective element within great events, Carlyle was, of course, the epitome of the latter. Of the two, Mazzini preferred the artist; but neither of these kinds of historians provided effective guidelines for applying the lessons of the past to the needs of the present. Should not history be a guide for the future rather than merely a dramatization of the past? Mazzini looked to history for help for today and hope for tomorrow. He thought that, by serving art, valuable as that may be, Carlyle had abdicated his responsibility to answer the crucial questions of the revolutionary situation. For "ought he not to learn from history rather how to dry up, to prevent tears, than to weep?"[13] But why, Mazzini asked, did this poetic historian abdicate his responsibility to provide an active program for revolutionary activity that could apply to Austrian oppression as well as to Bourbon stupidity? He concluded that "Mr. Carlyle does not recognise in a people, and *a fortiori* not in humanity, a collective life. . . . He recognises, and is occupied with, individuals only. . . . Individuality being everything, the doctrine of *unconsciousness* follows. . . . God and the individual man—Mr. Carlyle sees no other object in the world."[14] The great historian must have all the powers of an artist but he also "must possess a conception of humanity, and Mr. Carlyle has none, and seeks none."[15]

Mazzini had made a telling observation with which Carlyle himself could hardly argue. In fact, he had already recognized, within the confines of his own rhetoric, that much of his ambivalent feeling about change, progress, and his own role as a leader of men resulted from his inability to believe in an abstraction called humanity. As with many artists, what was most real to him was the singular, the particular, the vivid fact—generalizations about abstract entities and broad masses seemed the refuge of politicians and the sentimentality of the deceived. It was the obligation of each individual, Carlyle believed, to impose upon his daily life the highest moral and spiritual standards. The collectivity called humanity moved forward only by individual movements. For Carlyle, his Italian friend's Romantic idealism was a sentimental luxury. For Mazzini, Carlyle was doing the wrong job; rather than discover "the causes of the revolution," he had brilliantly "illustrated" its scenes. What was needed was a "progressive" school of historians with a "philosophy of history." Perhaps Mazzini was partly correct when, in another essay on Carlyle published in early 1844, he claimed that his friend's "instincts drive him to action, his theory to contemplation."[16]

Mazzini was no less welcome at Cheyne Row because of his outspokenness. Jane, in fact, admired his courage the more, and even Carlyle readily granted that he was "beautiful, and merciful, and fierce."[17] But they were on opposite sides of the radical coin, one shining with partisan enthusiasm for a republican cause, the other convinced that revolution was a matter of the individual soul. The liberal programs and the liberated fashions of which Mazzini thought so highly seemed to Carlyle either wicked license or stupid sentimentality. It made no difference, other than as a matter of wonder, that such a good, sincere man—"the most *pious* living man I now know"—believed in them.[18] It simply demonstrated that personal virtues of the highest kind did not necessarily triumph over weakness of intellect. At the same time, Mazzini found "something very incomplete, very narrow, in this kind of contempt which Mr. Carlyle exhibits, whenever he meets in his path with anything that men have agreed to call political reform. The forms of government appear to him almost without meaning: such objects as the extension of suffrage, the guarantee of any kind of political right, are evidently in his eyes pitiful things, materialism more or less disguised. What he requires is, that men should grow better, that the number of just men should increase."[19]

More and more, Carlyle remained upstairs at work or was out on evenings when Mazzini called. After 1842, they rarely had their old spirited arguments, though, when they did, Jane sympathized with her Italian friend, to whom such issues were matters of life and death. To her husband, they were merely interesting or uninteresting arguments in a life dedicated to verbal jousts and the writing of books. But Mazzini momentarily expected to find himself on the shores of Italy, with sword in hand. Even Jane occasionally found some of the Romantic Italian's schemes ludicrous, among them his certainty that the invention of a stable balloon not only made his invasion of Italy imminent but that Jane, who experienced violent motion sickness on water, would now be able to accompany him through the calm stratosphere. The Carlyles were not alone among his English friends in fearing for his life and his sanity. "Surely between the highest virtue and the beginning of madness the line of separation is infinitesimally small!"[20]

Not surprisingly, Jane and Mazzini developed an increasing intimacy during the first half of the 1840s. Sensitive to her emotional needs, he treated her with warm admiration; she was a comforting presence who could provide him both with affection and consolation. Jane had a deep need, which her husband could not satisfy, for such compassionate companionship. The unhappy wife and the lonely exile engaged in the complicated rhetorical disguise of brother and sister, confiding in one another during long walks around London and quiet evenings by the Carlyle fireplace. Whether Jane expected more from Mazzini (or even allowed herself to believe that more was possible) is unclear. The relationship suddenly changed and its intensity declined in the summer of 1846, the moment when the Carlyle marriage faced its most threatening crisis. Jane asked her friend's advice about whether or not to leave her husband. He strongly advised her not to.

3.

At the beginning of the new decade another friendship began with the arrival of a touching letter from Geraldine Jewsbury, a woman who for Carlyle soon came to represent the danger of the new freedom in personal relations, just as Mazzini had come to represent the danger of republicanism. Geraldine—as both the Carlyles were soon to call her—cared little for national movements; Mazzini hardly cared at all about the personal problems of the unsatisfied heart and the special oppression of women in a male-dominated society. Though in principle he

Geraldine Jewsbury. Photograph, April 1855. Courtesy of the Rare Book and Manuscript Library, Columbia University.

believed in liberation for all the oppressed, Mazzini's notions about female duty and his definition of women had been created in the traditionalist atmosphere of a pious Italian home. He preferred that problems of religious crisis and emotional dissatisfaction be subordinated to the struggle for the needs of "humanity." Carlyle, of course, also preferred that they be subordinated—but to "work" of some practical and constructive kind. Mazzini and Geraldine never became friends, though they were to be Jane's two closest friends during the 1840s.

Geraldine's initial fascination was with Carlyle. She wrote to him in the spring of 1840, at the age of twenty-eight, asking advice about her religious doubts. Her father, an unsuccessful Manchester merchant, was soon to die; her mother had died young, leaving first her older daughter and then Geraldine to oversee a large family that was in the process of dispersing. The unmarried, aggressive, imaginative, and intelligent young woman shortly went to keep house in Manchester for her favorite brother. But she was anxious about her inability to believe in traditional Christian concepts and about what kind of future she could expect given her limited circumstances. She also had literary aspirations, having long dreamed of being a successful novelist, but no sense for the moment of how to go about fulfilling them. A deep admirer of Carlyle's books, she wrote to him, with customary apologies for intruding. She carefully emphasized not her interest in writing fiction but her need for guidance in coping with her own heterodox religious opinions.

Touched by her plea for help, Carlyle wrote a deeply pondered letter in which he gave the expected advice, some of it conventional, much of it his own particular vision of how best to confront fear, pain, and change: for "doubt is always a disease. . . . Like so many others, of a noble sort; better than many sorts of health! . . . All *expansion,* in all things . . . is it not a kind of disease? . . . The bird is sick in moulting-time; the Phoenix has to *burn* herself before she can become new and young again." An avid letter-writer, Geraldine took seriously Carlyle's suggestion that "if I at any time can help you in any way whatever, write to me frankly as to an elder brother." Jane felt no more uneasy than she ordinarily did about her husband's female admirers. She did not know, however, that her husband had urged his young friend to "pray understand . . . that it is always with me you correspond, not with her and me; that she is to know no more than I judge publishable, and expects or desires to know *nothing* if that please me. Write always as to me alone." The ostensible reason for such privacy was his desire to encourage Geraldine to feel free to write to him about her deepest concerns, imagining (quite incorrectly) that she would be embarrassed if anyone else knew about her religious doubts. More likely, he wanted, for the time being, to keep this young disciple all to himself. But he could not help but acknowledge that Jane "is as heterodox as yourself. . . . Some mutual esteem could not fail between you if you met."[21]

Carlyle's sympathy for his new friend increased considerably when he learned in August that her father had died. The news touched one of the deepest chords of his own concern. The deaths of his father and sister were always a strong memory; the anticipated death of his mother was a constant living presence, for the death of one's parents "comes on every one of us," no matter how much we prepare for it, "with a stern *originality,* as if it had never befallen till now. We ourselves, as you remark, seem far nearer to Death; there is now nothing between us and Death." But certainly, he reminded her and himself, the anticipation of death makes our lives much the more vital and meaningful to us. "It makes the meanest life divine. Dying we do become a kind of Gods."[22] He urged her to use literature as a resource in which she would find depicted the "struggle" that "all men in all ages . . . have had. . . . We are *not* alone then; we are an endless *army* of comrades!"[23]

Initially Geraldine appeared as attractive in person as in her letters, an "interesting young woman" with "clear delicate sense and courage" whose "small sylph figure" appeared at Cheyne Row for the first time at the beginning of March 1841. She had, in fact, been invited by Jane, who had broken through the privacy of Carlyle's relationship with his Manchester friend into a correspondence of her own. Within a few weeks, Geraldine was "a great friend of Jane's and mine" and still seemed "a good lovely young woman."[24] Probably somewhat surprised that Geraldine's emotionalism and her fascination with liberal attitudes about sex and life did not immediately disenchant her husband, Jane shortly discovered that her new friend dared to think and say things that even she, dissatisfied with the limitations imposed on women, found imprudent. "She is far too anatomical," for example, on "the passion of love."[25] With Carlyle busy most of the time in his study, the two women spent a great deal of time together. Jane was soon exhausted by the demands of Geraldine's emotional intensity, but this was not the only reason her spirits were low.

Constantly ill and dissatisfied, she felt that her husband considered his work more important than her welfare. His moods had become a constant trial for her strained nerves. When he left early in April 1841 on his trip to Fryston and Scotland, both husband and wife were unhappily aware of the corrosive effect of their bickering. Geraldine wrote from Manchester, trying to console her new friend. The young woman certainly realized that whereas Carlyle had been willing to offer her advice, he had no intention of offering her intimate friendship. But she thought that Jane might. She tried to help Jane by sharing her own belief in the superior sensitivity of women, for "a man does not, in a general way, understand our refinements in the matter of love." But, she counseled, since it was a wife's destiny to love her husband, she should "submit without vain struggling as to the conditions." For men act only according "to their nature, and are not altogether to be blamed." If her friend were suffering, for love "brings suffering as surely as life brings death," then she should remember that "it takes a great deal of misery to kill."[26] Geraldine had found then, that, whereas she and Carlyle could communicate about matters of the mind, she and Jane could confide about matters of the heart. Perhaps they could help one another to fulfill unfulfilled emotional needs. She urged Jane to visit. "I want to see you more than I can tell you. . . . There is not a day that I do not most sadly want you. . . . I cannot write half I want to say, and I dare not write even a quarter of what could be written."[27]

By June it had been decided that Jane was to join her husband for the summer in Scotland. On her way, she stopped at Manchester to visit her new friend. She was soon introduced to a number of people in Geraldine's Manchester-Liverpool circle, some of whom were admirers of Carlyle, and one of them, Elizabeth Paulet, became her good friend. Geraldine tried to comfort her with attention, entertainment, and emotional sympathy, almost overwhelming her in the process. Geraldine seemed not to want to share Jane with anyone else, and in the deepest ways, though on his own terms, neither did Carlyle. He wrote from Scotsbrig, urging her to come north quickly. As to Geraldine, though recognizing all her virtues, he wished that "she could once get it fairly into her head that neither woman nor man, nor any kind of creature in this universe, was born for the exclusive, or even for the chief, purpose of falling in love, or being fallen in love with. . . . It is *one* of the purposes most living creatures are produced for; but, except the zoophytes and coral insects of the Pacific Ocean, I am acquainted with no creature with whom it is the one or grand object."[28] Jane unhappily found herself between a woman who showed her love too readily and a man who repressed his love too easily.

4.

At the end of February 1842, Grace Welsh, living alone at Templand with a servant, had a stroke. Messages immediately went out to her brother in Liverpool, to her daughter in London. Though attended to at once by her friend and neighbor Dr. James Russell and his wife, Mary, she died within a day, having sunk rapidly into an incoherence out of which at the last moment she was heard to murmur, " 'I am dying. . . . Oh my poor Jeannie!' "[29] The news that her mother was seriously ill threw the already unhappy, lonely daughter into a panic. Her husband's heart fell for her sake and his own. Mothers were sacred creatures. The mystery of death was the most solemn and tremulous of the experiences of life. He could not know that on the same day that the foreboding message came from Templand, Emerson had written to him that "my son a perfect little boy of five years and three months had ended his earthly life. You can never sympathize with me. . . . Tell Jane Carlyle our sorrowing story with much love."[30] Desperately eager to reach Templand as soon as possible, Jane took the evening train to Liverpool, her guilty suffering evident in her face as the train left Euston Station. In the "wild, blustering, rainy night," her husband returned home, unable ever to forget "her beautiful eyes full of sorrowful affection, gloomy pain, and expectation, gazing steadily forward, as if questioning the huge darkness, while the train rolled away."[31]

When she arrived at her uncle's house in Liverpool, she immediately learned what her husband already knew. Another letter had arrived at Cheyne Row soon after her departure stating that on "February 26 . . . her mother had departed; that 'first stroke' mercifully the final one."[32] No railroad or penny post could travel fast enough to outpace death and confusion. Jane collapsed into bed with nervous exhaustion and severe headache, incapable of going forward or returning. John Welsh had left before she had arrived to see if he could be in time for his sister's funeral. Paralyzed by despair, Jane immediately gave up all hope of seeing her mother again. She did not really want to see a corpse. Her mother's death, let alone her mother's presence in death, seemed too formidable a representation of her own failure as a daughter. She had never forsaken the hope that some day she and her mother would be able to give one another the daily exchanges of love which each had so much wanted to give and receive.

Though he did not yet have word from her in her own hand, Carlyle felt the anguish of his wife's situation. His vivid imagination could not suppress the painful thought of what she must have felt when she arrived at Liverpool to learn that she was forever too late. Deeply tied to his own family, he could readily identify with the pain and the loneliness of what it was like, at whatever age, to be an orphan. Though Grace Welsh had for a long time opposed her daughter's marriage, the fact of death overwhelmed all Carlyle's reservations about her and whatever resentments he may have borne. The dead were sacred. How much more so a dead parent. "You need—more than almost any one that I know—a father's love or a mother's love—a heart, which you may hide yourself in and make your home of—a heart that might care for your least feeling," a friend was to write to Jane toward the end of the decade. But "you must go to God, if you would find such a heart—you are not in the way of finding it in this world—that is,—in any human being but you must find it, or remain a very wretched creature."[33] But the nonbelieving Jane, who found God most unhelpful and usually absent, could not fill the void created by the death of her mother. She never overcame the intense guilt that resulted from her conviction that through fault of her own she had not been a loving daughter and had missed the one dear relationship without which life cannot be fulfilled.

"O my poor little broken-hearted Wife," Carlyle wrote to her at noontime on March 1, "we shall never see her more with these eyes." To the visitors who came to Cheyne Row he gave the sad news and accepted their sympathy. He immediately sent letters to his family; he wrote to Geraldine. But did Jane want him to do anything? He could advise nothing, but he would do whatever she wanted. A few hours later he thought that perhaps he "ought . . . to *be there,* with or without thee . . . to testify my reverence for one who *will* be forever sad, dear and venerable to me."[34] It was almost immediately decided that he would attend the funeral. Perhaps he could arrive in time. He quickly bought a new suit and hat—he had nothing appropriate for such an occasion—and took the next train to Scotland.

At Liverpool he spent a few hours comforting Jane, who was inconsolable. She had not imagined that her mother's loss could so completely change the face of her existence. "So many fine schemes I had in my head for her future comfort!—too late." She felt as "helpless and desolate as a little child turned adrift in the world! . . . what are friends?—what is an husband even compared with one's mother?—of her love one is always so sure!—it is the only love that nothing—not even misconduct on our part can take away from us—."[35] For the moment she preferred to console herself with this illusion rather than admit the probability that none of her schemes would have been realized no matter how long her mother might have lived. Unable to cope with her practical responsibilities, she fell back into exhaustion and depression, grateful that her husband had agreed to preside over the melancholy end of her mother's affairs. He arrived at Templand at noon on Saturday, March 5, compassionately aching for "one of the sorest wounds a human heart can experience here below."[36] He was too late for the funeral. Grace Welsh had already been buried, accompanied to her family grave at Crawford, some twenty miles away, by local friends and by her brother John and nephew Walter. Her son-in-law was pleased to learn that his own brother Jamie had driven across from Scotsbrig to represent the Carlyle family at the funeral.[37]

While Jane painfully cherished her wounds at her uncle's house in Liverpool, her husband and her uncle did what they could to dispose of the practical problems created by Grace Welsh's death. Her daughter had been left everything. By the terms of her father's will and Jane's agreement at the time of her marriage, Craigenputtoch of course reverted to Jane's sole possession. Though she revered her father's memory, she still detested the place; the very name invoked the possibility that her husband would in his irritable moments propose its hated isolation as an alternative to London. But the market for farm property was slack; she could not immediately contemplate its sale; and the most reasonable solution for the time being was simply to continue letting it. The Carlyles unexpectedly found themselves with an additional £200 per annum, money for which they now had little need. And Carlyle vowed that his increased income would not affect his commitment to frugality: "*Servitude* was a blessing and a great *liberty*," for man would not take the trouble to create if he were not faced by necessity.[38]

Certain that she could not bear to see Templand again, Jane insisted that the lease be disposed of and that all her mother's personal property, except for a few token items, be sold. No one considered it appropriate to argue with her, though her husband had for a moment thought that Templand might serve them (or him) as a summer retreat. Within a little more than a week, Jane returned to London, accompanied by one of her favorite nieces, whose cheerful face and helping ways she and the family hoped would do her good. In her sorrow, she preferred her own home. Carlyle stayed at Templand for almost eight weeks. There was an auction of the household goods to be arranged and advertised. Also, he had to negotiate with the Duke of Buccleugh's agent the disposition of the lease; he preferred that the duke repurchase the remaining equity. In the meantime, he could visit with his family in Annandale or be visited and helped by them, all the while tasting the fresh bright silence and the sacred "mystery" of earth and springtime.

During the next week the "little dwelling" at Templand was gradually shut down. Toward the end of the second week of April the auction, or "roup," finally occurred. After three days the house was virtually empty. In the morning, with the "cold bitter Northwind" in his face, Carlyle traveled alone to the cemetery at Crawford. He had not yet seen the grave, and wanted to make a copy of the inscription on the stone. The stonemason had cut the letters "deep, correct and very well." But there were "one or two mistakes" of punctuation which he "could not bear to leave." He "went to the nearest farm-house . . . borrowed a chisel and hammer, and succeeded in making it all correct." With a writer's respect for preciseness of language and completeness of scene, he saw also that the only living things visible were "one ewe and her little blackfaced lamb. . . . The Clyde rolled by, its everlasting course."[39] He returned to Templand where the auctioneer was in charge, then to Scotsbrig to stay with his mother, accompanied by Alick and Jamie. He had to return to Templand once more, though he found it increasingly painful to do so, for the house was empty and under the rule of strangers. He knew it would have broken his wife's heart to see it that way.

But late in the month he was there again; the repurchase of the lease by the duke seemed finally arranged. The River Nith, which had been in flood the previous month, had partly subsided, and just a few miles downriver the Bridge at Auldgirth, which his father had helped build more than half a century before, spanned the calmer waters. "Poor Templand" was "solitary in the still sunshine!" He stayed at a familiar inn in Thornhill, a short distance away, while completing the sale of the lease. Within two days everything was "finished at Thornhill" and he prepared to turn "homewards again." But another memory, one even older than that of his marriage at Templand, stirred his emotions. Twenty-two years before, "on a day of April not unlike this I first passed thro' this village: I sat probably in this very room. . . . I had walked from Muirkirk. . . . Edward Irving had parted from me the night before." He had not yet met Jane and knew only her name.[40]

5.

At Chelsea a distraught wife and an impossible project awaited him. Jane found it difficult to deal with her guilt, except through tears and depression. In his letters her husband was gentle, understanding, sympathetic, but in their daily life he was preoccupied with his work: the frequency of their personal contact brought out more strongly the force of his stern stoicism, which was no comfort to her at all. Often it was an irritant. She felt weak and lonely, and she had no work to do. He agreed that it would be better if she had some "imperative employment to follow: a small portion of the day suffices for all her *obligatory* work; and the rest, when she cannot *seek* work for herself, is apt to be spent in sorrowful reflexions."[41] But the prospect of busy work, superfluous philanthropy or household chores, seemed demeaning to her. Of the two, she preferred the all-consuming mental and physical exhaustion of household projects. At home she could pretend that she was working in her proper sphere and fulfilling a personal duty. But for the moment not even the good cheer of her young cousin could bring her out of her depression. She wanted compassion rather than stoic philosophy. She wanted now the one person she could no longer have, or some substitute. She wrote to Mary Russell, who had become sacred to her through her connection with her mother, that she wanted to "throw" herself on her "neck, and cry . . . to rest like a sick child."[42]

Jane Carlyle. From a drawing by Samuel Laurence, c. 1840. Courtesy of the Carlyle House, The National Trust for Places of Historic Interest or Natural Beauty, London.

As spring advanced into summer, Carlyle became increasingly anxious about his book on Cromwell. Everything he had written he had burned. Though tempted to return all the books he had borrowed from Forster and others and to act on his confession that he had "never yet" been "in the right track to do that Book," his native stubbornness and his admiration for Cromwell kept him at it. But it did seem to him as if he were in a period of crisis. Thinking of Cromwell and of death while in the Templand solitude, he had confessed, "The time of my youth is past; that of my age is not yet fully come."[43] If he did not do the Cromwell book now, would he ever do another substantial book again?

On the way home from Scotland, he had stopped at Rugby, where Thomas Arnold, whom he admired as a historian but whose attempts to revive Christianity he thought unsuccessful, escorted him to Naseby Field, the site of one of Cromwell's important battles.[44] He and Arnold believed that they were standing on the very spot where the battle had raged at its height. But his collection of visual impressions and his extensive reading in primary and secondary documents only compounded his difficulty. The more he collected, the more confused his sense of control and literary structure became. The more he read, the more distant Cromwell seemed. "There is no use in writing of things past, unless they can be made in fact things present: not yesterday at all, but simply today and what it holds of fulfillment and of promises is *ours:* the dead ought to bury their dead, ought they not?"

His own opinion of Cromwell had risen into intense admiration. Whatever Cromwell's faults, he had made moral-spiritual leadership inseparable from practical results. In the contours of Cromwell's Puritanism Carlyle could clearly see the shape of his own parents' world, that closed circle of duty, asceticism, and religious vision, the very qualities his own society seemed most in want of. An effective life of Cromwell, Carlyle concluded, must dramatize to his fellow Victorians the need for the virtues that Cromwell had embodied. But the more he became aware of the complexities of Cromwell's life and culture, the more he began to doubt that he could bring them vividly to life for his contemporaries. The subject was hoary with age, and it had been further obscured by an accumulation of inaccurate "facts" and false interpretations. Would they not have to be combated first? Could one simply tell the true story and let the falsehoods and misimpressions disappear in the brightness of fact?

He doubted that it was possible. By temperament, by conviction, and by experience, Carlyle firmly believed that the old must be cleared away in order to let the new appear. But to do that in the case of Cromwell meant endless and detailed confrontation with false books, false facts, false interpretations. It seemed, indeed, that this was the direction in which he was going. He felt himself increasingly ground down by the eye-blearing tediousness of the task and unsatisfied with whatever he put down on paper. In addition, he had no confidence that anyone would want to read what he had to say. If the book were mainly a clearing away of the old, then readers would find it tedious and it would fall far short of his aim of using the past to illumine the present. If it were a biography, then it seemed probable that it would invoke opposition based on misunderstanding: the Victorians could not sympathize with Cromwell and his culture sufficiently to respond to the man as a human being. Moreover, how could he possibly transform this huge bulk of disparate material into a manageable literary structure? A strictly chronological biography would be antithetical to his amibition to make the past come alive as a document for the present. But a highly selective and subjective dramatization of the key events of Cromwell's life would come up against the negative preconceptions and general ignorance of his readers. By midsummer 1842 he gave more thought to abandoning "the task," for "what a talent have I for getting into the Impossible!"[45]

In the "warm blazing days" he stayed indoors until nighttime, then took "long solitary walks," brooding about his inability to write this book. Also, something else, connected but still distinct, was always on his mind. The economy of the country was becoming increasingly depressed, the visible images of the "hungry forties" appearing on the city streets and in the country lanes. During the winter, for the first time in his life he had seen fences being torn down and stolen for fuel by the poor. Passing through the industrial midlands on his way home from Scotland in May, he had noticed the preternatural clearness of the air in Manchester and Birmingham. So many of the mills were closed, the workers without employment.[46] He reminded Richard Milnes of traditional wisdom:

> Blessed is he that wisely doeth
> The poor man's case consider;
> For when the time of trouble is
> The Lord will him deliver.[47]

"We are *all* to blame," he believed, for "the distress of the country."[48] And the inevitable "trouble" that would result from allowing the continuance of such misery would be visited on everyone, not only on the politicians and the government.

There was some truth in his late August claim that "I cannot write *two Books at once!*" But the second book was an imaginative, moral, and political preoccupation rather than a focused plan to put something down on paper. He wrote that he could not "be in the seventeenth century and in the nineteenth at one and the same moment. . . . For my heart is sick and sore in behalf of my own poor generation; nay I feel withal as if the one hope of help for it consisted in the possibility of new Cromwells and new Puritans: thus do the two centuries stand related to me, the seventeenth *worthless* except precisely in so far as it can be made the *nineteenth;* and yet let anybody *try* that enterprise!"[49] His intention had been to contrast the leadership of Cromwell and the vigorous spiritual health of the Puritans with the leaderlessness and the corrupt materialism of his own time. The materials were there. But somehow he could find neither the clarity of mind nor the appropriate literary structure.

Perhaps the horrid reality of present conditions had to be dealt with first. Noticing (in a copy of the *Sanitary Report* sent to him by Edwin Chadwick) "the frightful difference of the duration of workman life in [urban] Manchester and in [rural] Rutland," he thought it "one of the most hideous facts . . . in the history of *Mammon-Worship* and *Laissez-Faire.*" If the government did not do something about it, there would certainly be an explosion. One could not expect the millowners and industrial barons to do anything about it themselves, except perhaps for James Marshall of Leeds, John Marshall's son, who "of all manufacturers" is "the most enlightened and humane, and anxious on these subjects."[50] "We must have industrial *barons* . . . the real aristocracy."[51] If only the industrialists would recognize and accept their responsibility to the workers and to the country. But it hardly seemed likely that they would. Matters could be expected to go from bad to worse.

Asked if he were " 'working very hard,' " Carlyle said that he "had to answer, 'Idling very hard.' "[52] Fortunately, his sense of humor was titillated by Bronson Alcott, another American visitor sent by Emerson. He was beginning to find the stream of eccentric Americans introduced by the idealistic Emerson somewhat objectionable, but Alcott's insistence that his vegetarianism or "potatoe-philosophy" would save the world so amused Carlyle that he finally could not resist telling Alcott that he was a "potatoe-Quixote" and his "gospel a mere imbecility." Browning, who was present at Alcott's third and last visit to Cheyne Row, thought him either "crazy or sound asleep," and also offended him with his laughter. Carlyle and Browning walked Alcott "up to town." They were not surprised to hear the eccentric American answer Carlyle's question, "When shall I see you again?" with a solemn "Never I guess!"[53] Alcott seemed hopelessly out of touch with reality. Though Carlyle recognized that this was not an exclusively American disease, he worried that Emerson might be infected with it also. But his immediate concern was with himself, his work, and his own country. He was depressed; his work was at a standstill; his country seemed on the verge of violent change.

At the beginning of August 1842 his "kind Palinurus," Stephen Spring Rice, invited Carlyle to accompany him and his brother on a quick semiofficial trip to Belgium. Here was a suitable excuse for running away from the "impossible."[54] Stephen's sister, who had married James Marshall, had been his admirer for years. Immensely wealthy and influential, the Spring Rices and the Marshalls enjoyed and respected Carlyle's companionship. Jane, who felt that the longer he took to write a book the more she suffered, thought it an unwarranted desertion. But it was hardly a matter about which she could make a fuss and it was to be for only three days. "I ought to go," he told Spring Rice. "Tomorrow, therefore, about noon, I will . . . meet you at the Custom-House. . . . You shall provide tobacco, cigars, and if possible, pipes; you shall undertake to bring me back on Tuesday; and in the meanwhile sail with me whither you will."[55]

The next morning, with the weather turning gray, he took the Chelsea steamer and joined Spring Rice and his brother Charles for a short railroad trip to the Margate steamer. After dinner and a brief walk around Margate, they set sail for Ostend in the coast-guard cutter *Vigilant,* purposely designed to be the fastest boat sailing the Channel and always at the complete disposal of the commissioner of customs. Carlyle admired the professionalism of the crew, but his "sleep, that night, was a sleep as of hospitals, of men in a state of asphyxia; a confused tumbling, a shifting from headache to headache,—which after three miserable hours [he] gave up altogether, and exchanged for a place on the deck, with early sunshine and the breath of the fresh sea. The ship had hung out all her canvas, an enormous expanse of cloth high and wide, and was dashing through the waters, in a heeling posture, with very great velocity,—a mad little wasp for sailing!"[56]

By midmorning, they were in sight of Belgium. The party went first to Ostend, which Carlyle thought "a circular dead-flat kind of place with straight clean streets." His head ached in the heat. Attracted by the restorative seawaters, he found himself the object of somewhat hysterical attention when, having misunderstood the attendant's instructions, he plunged naked into "one of the most delicious tepid sea-baths. . . . I found that men and women we were all bathing here in a heap, and that among my apparatus were not only two . . . towels, but a jacket and breeches of blue gingham, which I decidedly ought to have put on first!" He found the incident funny; fortunately, his headache was gone.

From Ostend they went by railroad to Bruges, where Carlyle particularly admired the churches, four of which they visited in as many hours. Though he detested Catholic ornamentation, which to his Protestant imagination seemed insincere and decadent, the "enormous" churches themselves impressed him with their beauty and solemnity. The buildings, as structures, pulsed with the religious commitment of their builders, though the current priesthood seemed the repellent embodiment of a religion whose "brains . . . have been out for three centuries." But "at bottom, one cannot *wish* these men kicked into the canals; for what would follow were they gone? Atheistic Benthamism, French editorial 'Rights of man' and *grande nation,* that is a far worse thing, a far *untruer* thing." In one of the churches a sculpture of "Mother-and-child" by Michelangelo deeply impressed him: also a painting of the Nativity "in a chapel of the same Church" gave him "real pleasure: a thing pictures and statues . . . seldom do." The ancient churches of Ghent contrasted dramatically with the modern monuments to "brutal heathenism . . . our Railway Terminuses, Pantechnicons, Show-bazars."[57]

Such a past was "altogether poetic, next door still to sacred," even though it was Catholic, not Protestant. The spiritual twists and the artistic turns of the Gothic imagination seemed "fantastic on the great scale." His observant eye, as imaginatively precise as that of his friend of the future, John Ruskin, saw "confused flutings, stalks and branches; high shafts suddenly swelling out in the middle into some annular bulge, and as suddenly contracting again, the annular bulge covered on its upper and even its under side with slate. . . . These buildings have a luxuriance as of plants growing in rich mould under the influence at once of heat and darkness." But the forms of Catholic worship were dead. "The noisy hoarse growling of the mass" seemed a desecration. He walked into a small "niche dizened round with curtains, laces, votive tablets. . . . Within this niche sat a dizened paltry doll, some three feet long, done with paint, ribbons and ruffles,—this was the Mother of God; on the lap of it lay a much smaller doll . . . —this was itself God."[58]

After a day in Ghent, they took the railroad back to Ostend in the evening. The Spring Rices had been good and undemanding company. Very early the next morning the *Vigilant* sailed on a windless sea. Carlyle had enjoyed occasional moments of peace, smoking by his hotel window above the town, standing quietly in the cavernous beauty of strange churches. He sat all the next day "in the shadow of the large sails, screened from the over-brightness of the brightest of days; well pleased to look at the clear green sea with the boat-keel lightly dragging through it, the great silent sky in pure and perfect hemisphere spread over it." Not even the *Vigilant*'s sail-speed could overcome Nature's unwillingness to provide wind. It was a moment out of a less threatening past, one that seemed to hold at a distance the threat of speed and accelerated time, the steam engine and the factory. That night the lights of Margate came into view. Suddenly the breeze came up, then rose briskly. Soon they "were swiftly rushing up the Thames-stream, overpassing its multitudes of ships; whose marching regiments . . . with their canvas all spread Londonward,—beautiful enough to see." The five-day excursion, two on water and three on land, was suddenly over. At the custom-house steps Carlyle said goodbye to his hosts. Going their separate ways, they were "swiftly re-absorbed into the great smoky simmering crater, and London's soot-volcano had again recovered" them.[59]

6.

Carlyle now found himself back in the fire. Jane departed the next day for Troston, the home of Reginald Buller, where the elder Bullers had gone on a prolonged country visit to escape the London heat. Charles Buller led an active political and social life; Arthur was in India; Reginald, the least accomplished and least talented of the children, rusticated year-round as a gentleman of religion, looking after the local souls at Troston with gracious Church of England indifference. For the first week, every night brought "forth some new variety of assassin to murder" Jane's "sleep!"[60] Her major concern was her husband's uncertainty about when he would arrive. He did not even feel that he had completely committed himself to come. Despite the tropical heat in London ("at midnight, it was still above 80°"), he was determined to get work done.[61]

Instead of starting on Cromwell, he decided first to write an account of his recent trip, which he did in four days in the middle of the month. Though Jane considered it an evasion of his real task (and did not see why he could not come to Troston immediately), she and the Bullers were delighted with it when it arrived in the mail a few days later. Jane thought it demonstrated his clarity of mind and keen powers of visual observation without any of the rhetorical and emotional complications of his sustained literary essays and books. Carlyle had a marvelous capacity for "instantaneous writing," and in his travel essay revealed the virtues so characteristic of his letters and diaries: vividness, immediacy, clarity, honesty, and descriptive brilliance. Clearly, writing "Notes Of A Three-Day's Tour To The Netherlands, " which he had no thought of publishing, was as much a holiday as the tour itself.

By August 20 he was "writing, writing," something else, "God knows at what precisely!"[62] It may have had something to do with Cromwell, but it may have been his first attempt to get down on paper his ideas about the "condition of England." He wrote to Emerson that he just could not be in two centuries at the same time.[63] The condition of England seemed desperate, the threat of anarchy and violence rising with the summer heat. At the middle of the month he noted the anniversary of Peterloo, the shock of which he had felt as a young man, and in Manchester a large Chartist rally reminded the entire nation of that shameful episode. He heard "a secret voice" whisper "now and then," that whatever happened, he "*must* be of it!"[64] In anticipation of the impending catastrophe, he invoked the name of the one contemporary politician who seemed to offer some possiblity of leadership, "O Peel, Peel!" But he also invoked his own name: "O Carlyle, Carlyle, for it is *thou* too, and all the world."[65] But whatever he was writing, it was clear toward the end of the month that it was coming to nothing. On August 29, he finally told Jane that he would be at Troston shortly, to take her home after a brief stay and perhaps to make a short excursion in the area around Ely and Cambridge, about thirty miles to the west, a region associated with Cromwell.

Though his mood improved, inspiration did not come easily. The green countryside cheered him. Jane actually seemed better. Despite his desire not to submit to Mrs. Buller's pressure to keep them longer, he found that he could not resist the combined urging of wife and friends. Even Charles Buller arrived late one night. The countryside was a delight and a challenge. Eager to please him, Mrs. Buller borrowed a barely satisfactory but still serviceable horse from a local farmer and put it at his disposal. To Jane, "his contentment with the place" verged "on the ecstatic."[66] Despite his frustration with his work, he felt comparatively relaxed, so much so that, early one morning at the end of the first week of September, he mounted his horse and rode off toward Cambridgeshire. He had spoken to Jane and the Bullers of the likelihood of this "pilgrimage" all the previous weeks. But "the Great Traveller" had been gently mocked by his wife and friends: he was well known as a man who advocated such journeys but rarely took them himself. True to form, as he rode off, he remarked that he felt " 'like a man setting out on some great commercial speculation by which he hoped to make his fortune; yet full of apprehensions and an invincible repugnance!!' "[67]

By late afternoon, he could see Ely Cathedral on its chalk elevation above the drained fens, hanging "venerable and majestic in the air." In "the yellow evening sunshine" he spent two hours exploring the cathedral, thinking of Cromwell's dramatic appearance there two hundred years before.[68] He visited what he had been told was "the very house" that Cromwell had lived in, and "smoked a pipe about nine o'clock under the stars" at the "Horseblock," which legend claimed Cromwell "had often mounted from." The next day he rode to St. Ives and Huntington; that night he relaxed "in a spacious apartment, blazing with gaslight," in the Hoop Inn at Cambridge, while a "magnificent thunderstorm" burst into heavy torrents of rain.[69] The next morning, pursued by a storm that overtook him late in the afternoon, he rode eastward to Troston, arriving in the evening, drenched but quite lively and proud of himself. He had "accomplished all he intended, and a vast deal more."[70]

But the culmination of all these intentions in a book still seemed as distant as ever. He wrote nothing in September. He did, however, make a new friend, Edward FitzGerald, whom the painter Samuel Laurence brought to tea.[71] FitzGerald, the wealthy heir of Irish estates, was a retiring, sensitive man with poetic talent and an innovative literary imagination. Fourteen years younger than Carlyle, he had become the close friend of Thackeray and Tennyson at Cambridge. Like Tennyson, FitzGerald made occasional, often unannounced visits to London from the eccentric but amiable solitude of his country retreat in Suffolk, to which he had retired in 1837. Carlyle and FitzGerald liked one another immediately. That FitzGerald's father actually owned the property on which the Battle of Naseby had been fought was a useful coincidence. While attempting to provide Carlyle with additional information about the battle, FitzGerald not only informed him that Thomas Arnold had been completely wrong about the site of the most intense fighting but said that he would prove it. Late in September he had deep trenches dug and graves exposed. The bones lay on the surface bright in "the full harvest moon." Carlyle vividly imagined "that warm 14th of June when the Battle was fought, and they fell pell-mell: and then the country people came and buried them so shallow that the stench was terrible, and the putrid matter oozed over the ground for several yards; so that the cattle were observed to eat those places very close for some years after."[72]

Carlyle was convinced by FitzGerald's evidence; but it brought him no closer to the actual writing of this book. FitzGerald suspected that, despite his new friend's passion for historical accuracy, he would "make a mad book." Even his talent for reconstructing historical events would not prevent him from spoiling it, FitzGerald wrote to his friend Bernard Barton, "by making a demigod of Cromwell, who certainly was so far from wise that he brought about the very thing he fought to prevent,—the restoration of an unrestricted monarchy."[73] But FitzGerald and most of Carlyle's friends had no idea that the author had not yet decided on the form the book would take. The writer felt "like a poor old spavined horse; cannot mark the ground at starting; but if you whip him on."[74] By late October he had "not yet got one word to stand upon paper in regard to Oliver." But the situation was worse even than that. He had lost all confidence in his ability ever to do the book as he had planned it: the subject was intractable, and his own confusion both emotional and literary. Ironically, he wished that he could write "rhyme"; perhaps some totally new form was necessary for this extraordinary subject. Completely demoralized, he felt as if he "were . . . without a language."[75] To some extent, it seemed as if his own sloth and sinfulness were responsible. "How easily might good books be made, if people were not themselves bad!"[76] For the moment, the very name

"Laborare est orare." Cartoon. Courtesy of the Rare Book and Manuscript Library, Columbia University.

Cromwell seemed hateful to him. That sunbeam seemed "*buried* under rubbish-mountains."[77]

But by November 1842 he had begun to write again, though much of it went into the fire at first. It was a book about the nineteenth century, however, not the seventeenth. By early December 1842 he was writing intensely, "all the forenoons till three or four o'clock—and often in the evenings also."[78] England's pursuit of "money, money, and one folly and another," took on dramatic form, a literary expression of his urgent call, "*Let us all repent, and amend.* Let each of us for himself do it:—that is the grand secret!"[79] By the end of December much of the book was done. It seemed comparatively easy to confess that "no Cromwell will ever come out of me in this world. I dare not even try Cromwell."[80]

Jane had herself already discovered the strange turn of events. When she glanced at his confusing "hieroglyphics" in his study and saw what seemed to her a biography of someone called Abbot Samson, she asked him "what on earth *has* all this to do with Cromwell—and learned that Cromwell was not begun—that probably half a dozen other volumes will be published before that. . . . He lets everybody go on questioning him of his Cromwell and answers so as to leave them in the persuasion he is very busy with that and nothing else."[81] But by the end of the month he was informing selected friends that he was writing a " 'Tract for the Times,' " though "*not* in the Pusey vein."[82] By late February 1843 part of the manuscript was already at the printer's, and only the final section remained to be written. He expected it to be out before the summer. He wrote to James Marshall, his model of a progressive industrialist, to announce the new book, which would advocate the replacement of the old aristocracy by "a *real* Aristocracy . . . the Captains of Industry, not the Captains of Idleness." He had decided on the title *Past and Present.* "It is partly historical, partly oratorical,—dreadfully difficult" to "keep from looking too bedlami*cal*! A 'Tract for the Times' full of the most portentious speculative-Radicalism ever uttered in . . . English, or even in *Carlylese* as they call it!"[83] The new book was passionate, "redhot, indignant," a curious confirmation for Carlyle of John Sterling's comment that his nature "was Political." It seemed to the author a product of the searing, furnace-like intensity in which he flourished as a writer, exploding dramatically like a volcano that consumed itself in the flames it produced.[84]

The Cromwell project had been like heavy earth, cutting off oxygen and light. But, rather than admit that *Past and Present* satisfied the political and emotional needs that heretofore had been invested in the prospect of writing a biography of Cromwell, he still wondered whether or not he should now return to his original intention. Before the middle of March 1843, *Past and Present* had been finished and sent to the printer to be published in one volume. He expected to be finished with the proof-sheets by May. In his own mind, however, he was still confused. Was this new book a "preliminary to *Oliver* or not; but it had gradually grown to be the preliminary of anything possible for me," he admitted to Emerson. "So there it is written; and I am a very sick, but withal a comparatively very free man."[85]

But, in fact, he was not free. He tacitly shared Jane's opinion that *Past and Present* was "a *great* book—calculated to waken up the Soul of England if it have any."[86] But he had already put in four years on Cromwell. Should he not still write the book he had intended on the Great Protector? During the summer and fall the question was always on his mind, whatever he was doing. He took a long vacation, visiting Wales for the first time, the guest of the stolid, dull, but affectionate and admiring Welsh lawyer, Charles Redwood. But while in Scotland early in September he visited Dunbar, the site of one of Cromwell's great battles, and continued to consult and collect books on Cromwell and the Puritans. By late October 1843 he confessed his dilemma to Emerson: "After four weary years of the most unreadable reading . . . I have come at last to the conclusion that I *must* write a Book on Cromwell; that there is no rest for me till I do it. This point fixed, another is not less fixed hitherto, that a Book on Cromwell is *impossible!* Literally so."[87] But he would try.

The compulsion to do so hardly seemed rational. But the depth of his stubborn *need* to do so—the complicated product of his sense of himself and of his unwillingness to leave something incomplete—was intensified by the very fact of his continual awareness that he could never write the book on Cromwell he had originally planned. Through November and part of December he either faced a blank sheet or wrote totally unsatisfactory sentences. Shortly after the middle of December 1843 he deliberately and solemnly gathered together everything he had written about Cromwell and "committed" it "at one fell swoop to the fire" in the same room in which Jane was "peacefully darning his stockings."[88] Once he had been the victim (and perhaps partly the beneficiary) of an accident whose flames had destroyed his manuscript. Now he had deliberately put his own work into the fire. With *The French Revolution* accident had not been able to defeat his ambition, and with "Cromwell" too arson was the beginning of a new plan rather than the end of the entire project. Since he could not do what he thought he had to do as a biography, he had decided to try "another tack." He would do an edition of Oliver's speeches and letters and let the Puritan leader's words speak for themselves. "If one had not the obstinacy of a mule (among other gifts), there would be no getting on in Literature,—or elsewhere."[89] Carlyle devoted the next three years, not without anxiety and complaint, to editing this edition. It proved the best strategy for dealing with disappointment and failure.

[12]

Revolutions (2) 1843–1849

When in December 1842 Carlyle asked Jane to give her opinion of the sections of *Past and Present* which he had just completed, she had already committed herself to another reading chore. Late in November she had "received . . . a bundle of manuscript from Geraldine." But now she left the parcel unopened; for "*decency's sake*" the manuscript by her husband had to take precedence over the one from her friend. By late December, however, she finally got to read *Zoe: the history of two lives,* and found that she did so "with a feeling little short of *terror*!" If her husband condemned George Sand, then what would he have to say about Geraldine? Some of her best passages seemed not only equal to Sand but to have their "indecency or want of reserve" heightened by appearing "so purely scientific and essential."[1] Jane squirmed with both disapproval and admiration while reading the sexual passages in the manuscript, finding that she was particularly sensitive to Geraldine's focus on the feminine psyche and the position of women in a male-dominated society. Her own instincts on both matters were prudent and repressed. Her self-consciousness about her situation and about that of her sex in general was sufficient to make her unhappy. But by training and temperament she always thought it best to restrict her comments to private letters or to bury them silently within herself. She often sounded like an echo of her husband, claiming that "the less *passion* in the world the more *virtue* and *good-digestion*!"[2] But it was one thing to write passionate personal letters, quite another to publish a novel whose heroine's sexuality would inevitably be associated with that of her creator.

By late 1841, Geraldine's letters to Jane were indeed intensely passionate. They were the letters of a woman at least partly conscious of her lesbian desires. "I love you, my darling, more than I can express. . . . You will laugh, but I feel towards you much more like a lover than a female friend!"[3] Unaware of Geraldine's amorous feelings and expressions, Carlyle astounded Jane by suggesting that Geraldine come to visit them at Cheyne Row "for a little while." Jane was almost suspicious; she certainly felt uneasy, for such an invitation from Carlyle was unprecedented. Perhaps it was an attempt to provide some companionship for his wife at a time when she was still extremely depressed and he very busy. But Jane, concerned that Geraldine might be interested in her husband, needed to reassure herself that her husband's consistent "indifference to *all* women *as women,*" probably including herself, *should* be sufficient protection against the "mischief" that a young woman like Geraldine might stir up by her very amorous nature.[4]

Unfortunately, Jane by this time had another reason to be apprehensive on the matter of female competition. Carlyle had met Lady Harriet Baring three years before. Bingham Baring's wealth and political prominence brought him to some of the same breakfasts and dinner parties that Carlyle's political and literary friends hosted and attended. It was inevitable that the sociable, aggressive Lady Harriet would soon invite Carlyle to be an active member of the circle that she was attracting to her father-in-law's mansion in Piccadilly and gathering for holidays in Hampshire at the Grange. She and her husband had a small villa of their own called Addiscombe just ten miles from London and had recently purchased Bay House, a newly built seashore home at Gosport.

When Carlyle returned from Belgium early in August 1842, he found an invitation from Lady Harriet to visit Addiscombe. Bingham Baring, whom he frequently saw in town, had alerted him to its arrival. Exhausted, and torn between Cromwell and Troston, he declined, but his hope that "perhaps this first is not the last Note you will ever write to my poor address" was soon fulfilled.[5] Such invitations soon came regularly and Carlyle began to appear occasionally at Bath House for personal conversations with the Barings or for parties. Jane was not invited. Sensitive to her husband's inclination to enjoy Lady Harriet's company, she hovered between slight jealousy and intense discomfort. She did not see any direct connection between her "husband's having received a seductive letter" from Lady Harriet and his unexpected suggestion that Geraldine be invited to visit. And she expected him to be above the ordinary temptations. But Lady Harriet's epistolary "love-making" to her husband was annoyingly effective. She "writes . . . that she is ill . . . and that 'there is nobody . . . she likes so well to speak with as him'. . . . When a handsome, clever, and reputedly *most haughty* woman appeals to the *charity* and *piety* of a simple man like Carlyle you may be sure she will not appeal in vain."[6]

Geraldine came at the beginning of February 1843 for a visit scheduled to last two to three weeks. She stayed almost twice as long. Carlyle remained upstairs at work most of the time. In the evenings, he frequently arranged to go out without Geraldine or Jane, especially to the Barings'. Whereas Jane repressed her feelings, Geraldine was outspokenly jealous of Lady Harriet, the presumption of which made Jane even more short-tempered with her friend. After three weeks, Jane was intensely weary and critical of her visitor, but Geraldine was determined to make the most of her London opportunity. She tried, mostly unavailingly, to get Carlyle to talk with her about intellectual matters. Eager to have Jane's friends like her, she attempted to ingratiate herself with Mazzini, Erasmus Darwin, and others. But they found her aggressiveness masculine and overweening. For a while she focused her feminine wiles on John Carlyle, an eligible bachelor, shocking his conservative Scots eyes (and Jane's as well) by coming down to Sunday dinner with a good deal of neck and bosom exposed. She also affronted his pocketbook by expecting him to pay for theater tickets and such things. Like a fashionable mesmerist, she had great faith in the power of her "gaze," and sat for hours, to Jane's irritation, staring at *her*. "To be sure," she also gazed at Carlyle and tried "all sorts of *seductions* on him . . . but the poor man proved absolutely *unseducible*. . . . Even when she [lay] . . . on the hearth rug at his feet . . . sleeping there."[7]

Geraldine's eagerness to please exhausted her hostess; her emotional extravagance seemed a combination of presumption and coercion. Finally, she was maneuvered out of the house, though she stayed in London a bit longer, returning to Manchester at the beginning of April. Jane was "sick to death of her. . . . *I* will never . . . be the means of bringing her again—she is 'a vile creature.' "[8] Unaware of (and perhaps uninterested in) the severity of Jane's judgment, Carlyle generally agreed that Geraldine had been a nuisance: the extent to which her attitudes had been influenced by George Sand's unorthodox views came as an unpleasant surprise. But, having kept his distance, his response was amiably critical and comparatively impersonal. Jane, though, regretted that she had confided intimately in Geraldine. She soon found herself being drawn back into that intimacy, however, unable to resist the flood of passionate letters that came from Manchester in the next months.[9] Jane soon realized that she had gotten used to and even enjoyed being so adored, especially at a time when her husband seemed increasingly absorbed in his work and in the thirty-seven-year-old Lady Harriet.[10]

During the next year Carlyle's relationship with Lady Harriet deepened. His friendship with Bingham Baring provided a normalizing background, for the quiet, proud husband was eager to support his wife's wit and social extravagances. Weekly visits to Bath House, usually in the evening after his work, increased Carlyle's appreciation of the virtues of his new friend, whom he urged to study German. Despite Jane's claim that she was "singularly inaccessible to jealousy," her resentment at "how marvellously that liason has gone on" was certainly an emotion that could hardly be distinguished from jealousy. She had no reason to fear that her husband would have an "affair" with Lady Harriet: her position, his sexual reticence, and his Puritan sense of duty meant that a physical relationship was out of the question. But that Lady Harriet seemed to have no interest in her and that her husband seemed to have an extraordinary interest in Lady Harriet left Jane doubly neglected. Her vanity was hurt; she felt rejected by both of them. Her initial response was sarcasm at "the flights of charming little notes" between her husband and the "Intellectual Circe." She alternated between aloof forbearance and sharp retorts.

Accepting an invitation to meet Lady Harriet at the Bullers', Jane finally saw her rival face to face in May 1843. The experience was curiously reassuring. Lady Harriet was both physically unattractive—"she is immensely *large*—might easily have been one of the *ugliest* women living"—and "almost beautiful." The "intelligence and cordiality of her expression," the openness of her manner, the absence of arrogance, her high spirits, and her delightful wit—"just the *wittiest* woman I have seen"—impressed Jane; rather than fearing she would lose some part of her husband to this woman, she now hoped she might find in her a new friend. And Lady Harriet, who had previously been unaware of Jane other than as Carlyle's wife at a home she had no intention of ever visiting, now seemed prepared to pay her "respects to Mrs. Carlyle. . . . A *reality*" whom her husband had "hitherto *quite suppressed.*"[11]

But Carlyle was soon on his way to Wales and Scotland, and Lady Harriet made no attempt to exchange intimacies with Jane. Love letters constantly came from the slim, boyish Geraldine, who was eager to caress Jane as best she could. Carlyle returned in late September 1843, determined to "set" his "workshop . . . in order, that I may begin working, or else go mad!"[12] Cromwell came before anything else, and Jane "hardly ever" saw "his face from breakfast to dinner." Headaches and tiredness frequently forced her to bed. "That red bed is such a horrid sojourn for me in the day time!—so associated with 'all things most *unpleasant* in life!' "[13] Though she had visitors, particularly Mazzini and Darwin, she felt worn out and deserted, especially when ill. "Send me to my bedroom for a day," she confessed to her Uncle John, "to that great red bed in which I have transacted so many headaches, so many influenzas," the bed in which she and her husband had spent their marriage night, "and I feel as if I were already half buried! Oh, so lonely!"[14]

Fortunately, Carlyle's decision to collect and edit the letters and speeches of Cromwell diminished the intensity of *his* self-torture for a while. But, as soon as he set to work, the problems of collecting and annotating a large number of documents renewed his sense of how miserable he was both when he was working and when he was not. Though the task was excruciatingly tedious, he did console himself with the thought that it was sensible to be usefully employed at this lesser task until he could return to the biography that he had originally planned. So he had little time for Jane, who was bored to death with his ceaseless talk about Cromwell anyway. His preoccupation was so intense that it seemed to her that they were doomed to live forever " 'in the valley of the shadow' of Cromwell now, as of Death."[15]

Not that he was insensitive to her constant illnesses. The loss of her mother was a bereavement with which he could identify. Her lack of some productive work seemed to him unfortunate. But they were both reserved people, except when angry, and they tended to talk together less than they had ever done before. Jane could accept that his "genius" demanded a certain amount of separateness, that his work required solitude. But the increasing distance between them now seemed to enforce separation even when there was no necessary reason to be apart. At the same time, however, they found certain of these separations refreshing, or at least ameliorating. When apart, they could not argue. When distant, their letters tended to be more tender than the words they spoke when together. But the weekly visits to Bath House and the occasional Sundays at Addiscombe, which were becoming more frequent, seemed to Jane an actual embrace of someone else. Did her husband prefer Lady Harriet's company to her own? She had never thought, when she had agreed to marry this man for the sake of his "genius" and the advantage of his company, that she would ever have to ask such a question.

Early in 1844, already exhausted in all ways, Jane came down with a case of her recurrent influenza, which was much worse than usual. Hammered constantly by headaches that beat her to a "pulp," she spent a good deal of time in bed; in the evenings her husband was either out, or working, or poor company. When she was on her feet, she welcomed visitors, though not all of them brought pleasure. Darwin's soft manner was always soothing. Mazzini's noble gentleness, bright idealism, and pathetic isolation tugged at her sympathy. If she loved him like a brother, he returned her affection with the constant attendance of a loving friend.

She was momentarily cheered by reading Geraldine's revised manuscript of *Zoe,* which "by the powers . . . is a wonderful book!"[16] Acting as agent, she persuaded Chapman and Hall, who smelled a popular success, to publish it on reasonable terms. But as much as she admired Geraldine's talent, she was irretrievably miserable at her inability to do anything constructive with her own. And increasingly she resented her husband's regular visits to Bath House, made when he seemed to have no time for her. By early spring, her temper was unusually edgy. "The air is full of madness at present," she wrote to Jeannie.[17] There were in fact two instances of literal madness among her friends, one of whom she directly tried to help. Carlyle found his own nerves short, as if he were confronting madness in his work, wondering whether he would make his work sane or it would make him mad.[18] Husband and wife could hardly say a word to one another without quarreling. It seemed to Jane "a stupidity rather than a heroism in me to stay till my life is crushed out in it, . . . the necessary efforts and endurances of my lot of *Man-of-Genius's wife.*"[19] In her anger, she threatened to leave him.[20]

Late in June 1844 she left to visit her uncle in Liverpool and to spend some time at Seaforth House with Geraldine and Elizabeth Paulet, a new friend who was gentle, gracious, and eminently sane, the well-controlled embodiment of middle-class and matronly calm. Without rejecting Geraldine, whose "Tiger-jealousy" was irrepressible and a "*revelation*" to Jane, she "swore everlasting friendship with Mrs. Paulet" and joked quite perceptively that Geraldine had no right to expect good treatment since she had the gall "for a whole evening" to be "making love before my very face to *another man*!"[21]

While Jane calmed her nerves at Seaforth and attempted to reconcile herself to being her husband's "necessary evil," Carlyle busied himself with Cromwell and took advantage of the Baring's generous hospitality at Addiscombe. He spent a day early in July in the "green and leafy country," and stayed overnight. Though he had been pressed to stay longer, when he awoke at 4:00 A.M. he restlessly determined to return to his desk that day. But he visited again the next week. The important people and the grand style of life seemed a pleasant relief, actually "entertaining." His usual criticism of idle aristocracy was suspended; the more he got to know Lady Harriet the more he bewailed that her high position did not allow her to use her talents in more constructive ways. "Real good breeding, as the people have it here, is one of the finest things now going in the world," he wrote to Jane. "The careful avoidance of all discussion, the swift hopping from topic to topic, does not agree with me; but the graceful style they do it with is beyond that of minuets!"[22] Lady Harriet even took her dinner earlier than her guests so that she could orchestrate the dinner conversation more readily.

But it was the hostess, rather than her company, who had motivated Carlyle to become a more social creature than he had ever been before. Jane did her best not to be jealous. But when Mazzini declined an invitation to dine at Bath House in late July, she exulted in having found at least "*one* man that can resist [Lady Harriet's] fascinations," though she recognized she was harming herself "by writing even this sort of babble."[23] To her chagrin, it turned out that Mazzini had declined only because he felt that he did not have suitable clothes to make the impression that might further the cause of Young Italy. He soon went to Bath House, properly dressed. Jane confessed, "I begin to have a real *admiration* for that woman—her *fascination* of Carlyle proves her to be the most masterly coquette of Modern Times!"[24]

But Harriet Baring was, in fact, not a coquette at all; there is no evidence that she ever purposely attempted to use her sex to attract Carlyle or anyone else. Lady Harriet had the advantage, unlike Jane, of being partly independent of her gender. She was the rare Victorian woman who found that, by education, temperament, and social position, she was capable of asserting herself among men. From earliest childhood she had successfully insisted that the world revolve around her. Her aristocratic birth supported her self-confidence, and her marriage reinforced it. Her husband, who provided her with immense wealth, had no greater delight than to see his wife shine. Also, the death in infancy of her only child had left her determined never to look back at the mother she might have been but only forward to the assertion of her personality in glittering halls and brilliant salons. Considering herself above both the possibility of slander and the temptation of sin, Harriet Baring felt free to associate with men in a way that most Victorian women found impossible. If those associations should produce unusual friendships, she did not see why she should not have the advantage of them. She felt the equal of any man or woman, absolutely certain not only that she could hold her own but that she would always lead the way in any company. Other women might resent her freedom (and the temporary loss of their husbands, if that were the case) but Lady Harriet apparently had not in general any concern about jealousies. She thought hardly, if at all, about other people's feelings and a great deal about the success of her social creations; and she encouraged unusual friendships without any regard to propriety.

Early in September 1844, Carlyle went for the first time to the Grange, a sumptuous Palladian mansion of 120 rooms whose baroque features had been partly transformed by architects of the Greek Reviv-

The Grange. Photograph. Courtesy of the Carlyle House, The National Trust for Places of Historic Interest or Natural Beauty, London.

al into an imitation of the Parthenon. Jane, who probably had not been invited, stayed at home, busying herself with papering and painting. Carlyle's invitation had come from Lord Ashburton, Bingham Baring's father, with whom he immediately got on well. But it was really Lady Harriet's invitation. She seemed to him, he quietly told his mother, "one of the Queens of the world, really a most clever woman."[25] To Jane it seemed that her husband had been "summoned" and obeyed. "*He never* by any chance refuses a wish of *hers*—the clever woman that she is!"[26]

During the winter, Carlyle tried to express his concern for his wife. But his small though appreciated presents at her birthday and on the New Year could not make a dent in Jane's resentment. She was very ill through much of the winter. In the bleak February of 1845, she wrote that Carlyle was "about as deep in the *Hell* of his Cromwell as he is likely to get." They were a "grim pair," she told Jeannie. "I do not think he has the smallest idea how ill I am."[27] His regular visits to Bath House continued, and Jane felt immensely lonely. Unknown to her, her husband was writing extraordinary notes to Lady Harriet. He was the dark man, the man of dross and dirt and confusion; she was radiant with light. "Sunday, yes my Beneficent, it shall be then: the dark man shall again see the daughter of the Sun, for a little while, and be illuminated, as if he were not dark! which he very justly reckons among the highest privileges he has at present. Poor creature! . . . Also be patient with the dark man, who is forever loyal to you."[28] Associating himself with winter, failure, sin, and the excremental dirt that had been one of his lifelong metaphors of anxiety, he found it both comforting and exciting to play his exaggerated darkness off against her imaginary brightness.

2.

Lady Harriet did not discourage him, but she answered his metaphorical lovemaking by indicating a willingness to tolerate it only in *his* letters; it was a private, one-sided affair. Her own letters were prosaic—messages rather than invocations. There was nothing that she needed to reveal to him other than her loyal friendship. She had a bracing and somewhat dry cheerfulness that probably, for Carlyle, contrasted refreshingly with the hysteria and unhappiness he often observed in Jane. But his expressions of devotion in his letters to Lady Harriet were completely acceptable; she did not feel in the least compromised, and was only minimally sympathetic as her friend gradually revealed that Jane was intensely jealous, imagining all sorts of things that were not so. She hardly granted Jane's right to be jealous in such a case. It seemed presumption. But, for Carlyle's sake, she made an effort to be friendly and to include Jane in some of her invitations. Early in May 1845 she actually came to Cheyne Row to take tea with the couple. Apparently she had decided that Carlyle's continued presence at her dining table merited concessions of that kind. Late in June, Jane allowed herself to be "taken to the opera . . . with Lady Harriet," her "*debut* in fashionable life." She was less grateful to Lady Harriet than astounded that her husband had not only gone "to ride in the Park at the fashionable hour" but that when he had returned he "dressed for the Opera!! Nobody knows what he can do till he tries! or rather till a Lady Harriet tries!"[29]

But the opera could do nothing for Jane's depression, exhaustion, and resentment. She feared for her own sanity. In June she broke down, to her husband's horror, in tears and hysteria, leading him to insist that she spend four days in the country at Addiscombe and get out of London for the summer. Addiscombe was like torture to Jane. The house was filled with "fine people," and she and Lady Harriet had no opportunity for private conversation, even if they had desired it. She hardly slept, and felt increasingly trapped by both her husband's insistence that he knew best and her own fear that disobedience would only make matters worse. Though he urged her to come to Scotland with him for the summer, she had a greater horror of revisiting the places associated with her mother than of resisting his suggestions. In the end they compromised; she would go to Liverpool again.

Arriving there in late July, Jane stayed on until mid-September. Ministered to by Elizabeth and Geraldine, she gradually relaxed into a lassitude that for the moment seemed worse than her previous anxiety. By late August her husband, who had stayed at Chelsea to work, had finally "*ended* Oliver," though it was not to be published until the autumn.[30] Always slow to get under way, he irritated Jane by not starting immediately northward to see her on his way to Annandale. They had been apart almost six weeks. Geraldine and Elizabeth competed for her company, but her husband seemed to get along well enough without her. She resented that he insisted on almost daily letters from her for she suspected, quite rightly, that between his work and Lady Harriet he was almost self-sufficient.

Early in September, Carlyle joined Jane at Liverpool, going on to Scotsbrig while she returned to Chelsea. He stayed there for almost two months, resting, reading, and enjoying the company of his mother. He felt so "dreadfully lazy" that if he could persuade Jane to continue writing to him from Chelsea "without needing a reply," he would "have little temptation to write."[31] On the day Jane returned home, he wrote to Lady Harriet, asking her to accept his "salutations from the *Shore of the Departed* whither I am now come. . . . Indeed I think you seem beautifuller to me here from Hades than you ever did before." Among his "contradictions and bewilderments" were "streaks of Heaven's own brightness . . . figures as of 'realized ideals' . . . . Figures beautiful exceedingly, of which I had better say no more at present, till I recollect myself better."[32]

At home, Jane felt happier than she had for months, enjoying Mazzini's company and delighted to attend an amateur but extremely "expensive" charitable theatrical put on by Forster and Dickens. Lady Harriet, prompted by Richard Milnes, sent her carriage for Jane, insisting that she visit Bath House for the first time, as if there were no reason why she could not have the company of the wife when it suited her as well as the adoration of the husband. Jane could not say no. Their first extended private conversation came off better than she had imagined it would. She could not dislike Lady Harriet personally, but she doubted that she could be the friend of a woman who seemed so unwomanly, so unable and unwilling to express "warm affection." She was soon to compare Lady Harriet, who was generous with gifts, to Geraldine, who was generous with emotions.[33] If only "she were as loving as she is charming."[34]

Initially she had hoped that they would "get on very well together," she wrote to her husband, "although I can see that the Lady has a genius for *ruling,* whilst I have a genius for—*not being ruled*!"[35] It turned out to be more a boast than a fact, for Jane soon found herself being manipulated by both her husband and his friend. Lady Harriet insisted that the Carlyles spend a long winter vacation at comparatively sunny and mild Bay House, "a large fantastical looking *New* Building on the shore of the sea. . . . It is warm enough and magnificent as money and taste can make it," with a view "of a beautiful narrow arm of the sea, looking over to the towns and hills of the Isle of Wight . . . with all the shipping of Portsmouth coursing to and fro" and "clear flinty" beach "for miles on either hand."[36] Feeling calm and in full possession of her senses, Jane resisted only the length of the proposed visit, and was sharply precise when her husband complained that Lady Harriet had told him that she had agreed to stay the whole winter. They finally consented to come for three weeks, but stayed for almost six. By the beginning of December Jane determined that if necessary she would go home by herself. She had erroneously assumed that her husband's "need to be ugly and stupid and disagreeable without restraint" would send them "back to London in a month or so."[37] It was not Lady Harriet's fault that all the men "go out of their sober senses beside her."[38]

Jane no longer had the luxury of blaming the other woman, and she felt further diminished by her own irrelevance: "Lady Harriet *does* all the wit herself."[39] The woman's capacity to have her way, whether by manipulation or by self-assertion, seemed to Jane both unacceptable and enviable. At a visit to the Grange over a year later, she was astounded that Lady Harriet did not in the least "fear to speak thro' " Carlyle. She thought nothing of chatting with her pet parrot while Carlyle was in the midst of talking to her. Such boldness took Jane's breath away. Lady Harriet could assert her personality in ways that made her the equal of men like Carlyle. In addition, since Lady Harriet seemed to Jane a totally useless person, one who did not help her "fellow creatures" in the least, she felt distressed and betrayed that her husband obviously cared for a woman of the very kind for which he had all his life expressed only contempt. It seemed a bad sign. She sensed that her relationship with her husband had been reversed in a perverse and insulting manner in his relationship with Lady Harriet, but she could not suspect the depth of his self-punishing servitude as he urged Lady Harriet to "employ me, do, order me this way or that, it is all I am good for at present. . . . See if I will not obey. . . . I must kiss your hand."[40]

From the Grange in December 1845, Carlyle wrote to his mother on his fiftieth birthday. It took his words and breath away to realize that he had already "lived half a hundred years."[41] Though he spoke against pursuing happiness and advocated stoic acceptance of limitations, he still felt a great deal of repressed anger, some directed against the state of the world and general folly, much really directed against himself. *Cromwell* hardly gave him any satisfaction. Though he permitted himself to hope that it might be the most influential of his books, he recognized that at some important level it had resulted from a failure for which he could not forgive himself. And it kept tormenting him: new letters turned up, necessitating an appendix when he thought he was finished with the project forever; soon there were to be even more new letters, some of them fake, and the demand for another edition. He could not say that he and Jane were happy; he keenly felt his shortcomings in their relationship; and though never a word was said about sexual incompatibility, his depression and self-disgust may have been related to the obvious fact, no matter how repressed, that at the age of fifty there would never be a second chance for so many of the things that he had not worked out successfully. With Lady Harriet, however, he could express some of the emotions that touched on these failures, and her hospitality and companionship relieved the dreariness that he felt so much of existence to be. He now visited at Bath House at least once a week; Lady Harriet was a bright glow in a dark middle age.

Sometimes, when Carlyle worked at night, Lady Harriet's carriage called for Jane and brought her to Piccadilly. Jane felt miserably sick, constantly depressed, and Lady Harriet showed hardly any emotion. But Jane felt she would only make matters at home worse by declining such invitations. Her husband, who often paced the house "like a chained tiger,"[42] seemed already mad in his own peculiar manner; and for years her own mind had been "dreadfully haunted" with the fear that she would go "*mad* some day." At the beginning of spring 1846 it seemed incredible to her that she and Lady Harriet were going to Addiscombe "for a month," mainly because her husband was convinced that it would do her "good."[43] But Lady Harriet rose to the occasion, and, somewhat nervously, Jane concluded that Lady Harriet actually liked her, for "if she does not like you, she would blow you up with gunpowder rather than be bored with your company; so that one clearly understands one's footing beside her."[44]

But she could not keep up the self-deception for long, even for the sake of her marriage or her sanity. She did not know what was said in the private communications between her husband and Lady Harriet, but she wished herself rid of the whole matter—her jealousy, her resentment, her pain, and the pervasive unhappiness that collapsed in on her with the threat of madness, the hope of self-extinction. "One escapes so much suffering by dying young!" It was abysmal to survive, she wrote to her cousin Jeannie, "one after another of all one loved—one after another of all one's beautiful illusions and even most reasonable hopes, surviving in short one's original self!"[45] When she looked in the mirror, she saw a middle-aged woman who looked old, frail, and desiccated; when she looked into her heart, she saw the probability of more unhappiness; when she looked into the past, she saw hopes unfulfilled and promises broken. Whatever her husband's actual relationship with Lady Harriet, the part of it that she could glimpse revealed that he preferred Lady Harriet to his wife, though he had sworn, on various levels, to prefer her to anyone else.

Late in June 1846 she told him how she felt and insisted that he could not have them both. He was astonished by the depth and bitterness of her anger. Aware of the occasional gossip about his attachment to Lady Harriet, Carlyle had not imagined that his wife of all people would give any credence to the thought of Lady Harriet as a rival for his affections. He did not feel guilty of the accusations she leveled at him. Jane, angry at both herself and him, left for Seaforth House early in July. Bitter remonstration had been followed by tight-lipped hostility. They had never parted before with such an emotional distance between them. "And all for literally—Nothing!" he wrote to her. "Composure, and reflexion, at a distance from all causes of irritation and freaks of diseased fancy, will shew us both more clearly what the God's Truth of the matter *is*."[46] If only she would not doubt him, they would overcome this problem together. But his solution did not necessarily require him to make a choice between rivals, the threat of which seemed to him a nasty trick of perverse fate. He wanted the advantage of both women, but, if such a choice were necessary, he assured Jane that she was "dearer" to him "than any earthly creature."[47] Why could she not believe that?

Within a week she was asking herself the same question. She had arrived at her "house of refuge," exhausted and already relenting. Her hosts thought she looked "shockingly" bad. Whatever her husband's relationship with Lady Harriet, Jane felt such hysteria unworthy of her; she was a burden to herself and a heavy weight to her husband. "For *you,* you must feel as if a millstone had been taken off your breast."[48] She thought it might be best to leave him permanently, though Mazzini responded to her request for advice by saying that she had a higher "duty" to remain. She was disappointed that he had not encouraged her in more personal and romantic terms to assert herself.

When Carlyle did not hear from his wife for the first week, he feared that she had resolved to increase the separation between them. But, when a letter soon arrived, it was clear to him that the matter could be worked out, despite her anxiety and bitterness. Her unfounded jealousy was more than ever an indication of her deep dependence on him. She watched the mail closely, eager to hear from him, especially since July 14 was her forty-fifth birthday. Her own sense of failure and rejection increased as her birthday approached without a letter or a present from her husband. Did he so hate her that he refused to write ever again? Was he so busy at Addiscombe with Lady Harriet that he had no time for her? When a letter that had been delayed in the mail arrived, she almost broke down with relief, furious at herself for not being able to believe what she still could not believe, "that, with all my faults and follies, I am 'dearer to you than any.' "[49] It infuriated him that he should be held responsible for the inefficiency of "that wretched puddle of a Seaforth Postmistress." Why should it even "matter whether I write to you or not?" Her hysteria was a sign that she was still sick. Rather than come to Seaforth, where he was expected within the next week or so, why, he asked Jane, could he not escape into a walking tour through England, into the green solitude and the open country?[50]

But the needs of his wife demanded that he come to Seaforth soon, his attachment to his mother having already determined that he would vacation in Scotland, where Jane still refused to go. He made haste to leave London very, very slowly. Soon after the middle of the month he went to Bath House and, shortly thereafter, he announced to Jane that he had declined all invitations to Addiscombe "for an indefinite, perhaps infinite, time to come!" There had been no need to discuss the details of Jane's illness with Lady Harriet. She had intuitively understood the problem and would accommodate Carlyle's purposes; whatever changes he should determine necessary in their relationship, she would cooperate completely. He assured Jane that if necessary the relationship would "cease altogether before long."[51] The next week he said good-bye to the Barings, reminding his wife that, as far as he and the Barings were concerned, any unwholesomeness that might be associated with the relationship existed not in fact but only in Jane's eyes. At the beginning of the fourth week of July, he finally left for Seaforth. Husband and wife had an understanding that he would see little or nothing of Lady Harriet, and write to her only when it was necessary to do so.

Almost immediately after leaving London, however, he surreptitiously wrote to Lady Harriet, meditating "on the various madnesses of human life, and of one's own among the number! . . . Last Wednesday . . . while you were at Landsdown House, all radiant to see and beautiful there, I, very ugly at Chelsea, amid my packages and lonesome wrecks, wrote you a note: but that also you never heard of; I put it straight way in the fire. . . . O daughter of Adam most beautiful; O son of Adam, in several respects, most unbeautiful!" Jane and he had talked of her: "Do not suppose that she does other, or ever did other, than respect and love you, tho' with some degree of terror. Baseless I do believe. . . . You are full of charity to me. . . . I, if I could ever reward you, oh, would I not. But it is a vain hope that."[52] Lady Harriet answered with a "little note," which he received at Scotsbrig early in August. He thought it "beautiful, in its words and in its silences. You are all good and beautiful, and I am bound to be forever grateful to you. *Bound;* and do not need much binding."[53] She even wrote to Jane, a polite, friendly letter, inviting her to join them at the middle of August at a hunting lodge they had rented near Moffat. Jane declined, though for her husband's and her sanity's sake she answered the letter politely; he constantly urged her to maintain the relationship with Lady Harriet.

But it was reasonably safe, Carlyle felt, for him to accept the invitation, since Jane had been invited and had declined to go. To Jane, this decision seemed a direct violation of their agreement. But what could she do, except resent it? At Manchester, Geraldine gave Jane "intelligent sympathy" and did not leave her alone for "a single vacant minute."[54] She felt morbidly depressed, but was aware that she could blame her husband only in part. While at Scotsbrig he anxiously looked for a letter from her, painfully aware that his mother now knew of the rift between husband and wife. During the early days of August, he thought that Jane was punishing him by not writing. But she denied that she had ever caused him "*intentional* pain," so far as she could remember.[55]

He joined the Barings at Beattock Inn at the middle of the month and spent four unhappy, rain-drenched, and claustrophobic days with them. In the bad weather everyone's temper, except Bingham Baring's, was short, and "fair weather" seemed the only "alternative" to "suicide."[56] Probably at Carlyle's suggestion, Lady Harriet was induced to write to Jane. With her usual cheery and insensitive briskness, she observed that "the only check to our felicity has been the missing you" and expressed her certainty that Jane's health could be improved if only she would take care of herself or allow her friends to look after her, say "in November" at Bay House. "You must spend that dreary month with us."[57] Jane was at a loss for a response; the note, like most of Lady Harriet's communications, did not seem to encourage an answer beyond the acceptance or refusal of the invitation. She eventually accepted, as over the next ten years she was to accept almost annual invitations to Addiscombe or the Grange or Bay House, particularly because her husband wanted to go and she no longer had the will or the strength to resist. She made the best of it, though the best was often painful.

3.

Carlyle felt deeply the turmoil of change in his private life and in public affairs. But the one center of stability that he clung to was his family. Whatever his opinions about social and political revolution and whatever his relations with his wife and friends, his emotional life focused on his work and on the irreplaceable family whose members were dearer to him than anyone else on earth. At the same time, he was acutely aware that nothing stayed the same. Driven each summer to return to Scotland, almost like a salmon going upstream, he felt Annandale increasingly inhabited by ghosts, the most prominent of which was his own former self. It occasionally sent strange quivers through him—as if he were no longer there as a bodily creature—to walk or ride in familiar places without being recognized, the person he had been not readily visible in the person he had become. Frequently he recognized the children, now adults who did not know him, of his childhood contemporaries. He was, indeed, shocked when he received a daguerreotype from Emerson, in whose features he saw an elderly man he did not recognize at all. To Emerson's reply, "What have we to do with old age," Carlyle thought it useless to give the direct answer which was constantly on his mind—"everything!"[58]

In the middle of October 1842 an oil portrait of his mother which he had commissioned to be painted in Dumfries came by Chelsea carrier. He was exhilarated. "My good old Mother exactly as she looks; with her air of embarrassed *blateness* [shyness], yet of energy, intelligence and true affection."[59] To Jane's distress, he urgently proposed that the portrait immediately be framed—he repeated the request three times the next morning—and installed in the most prominent place in the house, directly over the living-room mantlepiece. Not only were all her favorite mantlepiece ornaments to be scattered around the house but she was to have as a great looming presence in her living room the pervasive features of that dour matriarch. "I could never feel alone with that picture over me! I almost *screamed* at the notion."[60] But her husband could never feel anything but lonely without at least that picture. It soon hung "over the Mantle-piece" in his study, "on my right hand, while I write; she seems always to be looking down, wishing me good speed!"[61] He moved his writing table so that everytime he looked up he saw her "affectionate sorrowing face."[62] But at least, to Jane's relief, it was not in the living room.

At the same time, however, it pained him to look at the portrait. The

Margaret Carlyle. Painting by Maxwell of Dumfries, c. 1842. Courtesy of the Carlyle House, The National Trust for Places of Historic Interest or Natural Beauty, London.

image of Margaret Carlyle's face was a frequent reminder that she could not live very much longer. "That constantly advancing inevitability" had "terrified" him all his days.[63] He could not keep images of death in life out of his mind, as if impersonal eternity demanded always to be visible in time.[64] Sometimes such visions of preternaturalism were brilliant, alive with fire or almost sweet with peaceful sadness; other times images of death as decay and loss dominated his inner vision. He knew the death of his mother would alter the family structure irrevocably; the center of the family would disappear into a mystery that, at certain times, he could stoically revere but that, at other times, frightened him severely. The concept of death seemed organic, desirable; the actual loss of loved ones seemed terrifying.

By the beginning of 1843 what had been likely began to appear inevitable—the Carlyle family was about to lose the second eldest child not to death but to distance. Thomas was deeply fond of Alick, though much separated them. Since the days when Alick had farmed Craigenputtoch, he had not prospered, except in his marriage and children. With a population of farmers which far exceeded the amount of arable land available for rental (rarely could land be purchased) and fees that made profitable operation difficult, Scotland was a land where agricultural failure was commonplace. Jack was safe in medicine, Thomas in literature, Jamie at Scotsbrig, the daughters of the family in marriage. But Alick had the misfortune of having to find some economic refuge in the only work he knew in the worst of times for Scottish farmers. In desperation, he had opened an agricultural supply and general store in Ecclefechan. Carlyle was not surprised when it did not work out.

Canada, the alternative that had been on Alick's mind for years, now surfaced again. But Canada had many "drawbacks," and the family was not confident that Alick would succeed there any more than he had in Scotland. Though there would be an advantage in land, the man himself would stay the same. His elder brother was certain that Alick's failures had been due only in part to external economic and agricultural conditions; the weaknesses of the inner man had played an important role as well.[65] Alick was impatient and violent; he occasionally became drunk in public; and his anger often overcame his good sense. Carlyle believed that Canada was his brother's last best chance for self-improvement: "You are now called as it were to make a revolution, a radical reform; and that is no easy business!"[66] He assured his mother that he had "a real expectation that this will be the saving of our poor Alick."[67] The economic concern, though real, was for the moment secondary: the salvation of Alick's character and soul was more important. This then, Thomas argued, would be "a most blessed change; worthy of being purchased at very great cost of pain." He remembered his own departure from Scotland for England almost ten years before—the look on his brothers' faces as the steamer pulled away, the heartbreaking sadness, the stoic acceptance of necessity. "I felt that I was gone from you; but that I had been bound and compelled to go. . . . It is good for a man that he be cast, from time to time, forth from his old refuges."[68]

As preparations for departure continued through the spring of 1843, the family was in turmoil. In London, Thomas tried desperately to keep his mind on his work. Though he detested doing articles, he had agreed to write a review-essay on the former dictator of Paraguay, Dr. José Gasper Francia. His work on Cromwell seemed unfulfilling and he thought it might be useful to make some sense out of Francia as a modern Cromwell, a man who was unafraid to use force on behalf of right. Unfortunately, he had imposed upon himself a late June deadline and the writing of the article thus coincided with the final month of Alick's life in Great Britain. Such schedules were sacred and a refuge, and he stubbornly worked away at it, cursing both the commitment and the timing, more compulsive about his work than about his relationships.

But the work also provided him with an acceptable excuse to avoid the even greater pain of involving himself with Alick's preparations for departure. Thomas stayed in London, working. Jack and he each provided £150, with the promise that more would be available shortly, a gift if Alick could accept it, a loan if not. He wrote two letters to a contact in America in the expectation that his brother might settle among fellow Scots in upper New York State. But Jane, who brought them to the post office, had forgotten to put stamps on them. They could not be retrieved until the next day. Exhausted with work and anxiety, Carlyle awakened after an unusually long daytime nap to the realization that the letters probably would not make the next steamer to America, thereby delaying them by at least two weeks. Only when Bingham Baring offered to enclose any new letters Carlyle might write in a government pouch destined for the original steamer was the matter finally straightened out.

But his nerves were on edge, his head in a "whirl." His brother was going, he claimed, sooner than "expected." Feeling ambivalent and guilty, he wrote to Alick at Scotsbrig that if he should "wish it," he would act on his "daily" thought that he might "run up to Liverpool, and see you all before you went." But, at the same time, he complained about how busy he was. He would not initiate the trip himself; his brother would have to express a desire to have him come.[69] Unwilling to bear the pain of seeing his brother for the last time, Carlyle maneuvered himself into staying in London.[70] Late in June Alick brought his family to Liverpool and soon "bargained for a stateroom" on a liner owned, ironically, by the Ashburton Line. With Jamie standing on the dock on a Sabbath morning, disturbed, to Alick's horror, by the blasphemous cursing and the hectic activity of the sailors, the *George Stevens* slowly departed from Liverpool harbor. A large crowd of idle onlookers were "gazing heedlessly" at the casual spectacle. As the boat steamed away, and for a long time thereafter, Alick could recognize Jamie on shore by his bright Scotch plaid coat. He was never to see any of his family again.

Within the extended family of friends there were also changes, some of them even more final than Alick's departure for America. Public figures died, some of whom Carlyle knew, among them Thomas Campbell. Late in the year that Grace Welsh died, he noticed in the newspaper "with a painful shock . . . the death of poor Allan Cunningham."[71] They had not been particularly close in recent years. But, to the younger man, Cunningham had been like an infrequently seen but warmly regarded "elder Brother" whom he deeply admired as a human being.[72] Carlyle had met and spoken to him while walking three weeks before. The suddenness of his death came as a shock even to a man who worked hard at preparing himself for terminations of all kinds. He went immediately to visit the widow. Late in November 1848 Charles Buller suddenly died from the side effects of minor surgery, throwing the Carlyle, Buller, and Ashburton circle, where his liveliness had always been admired, into gloom. Carlyle had long given up his hope that his former student would make great contributions to solving the problems of society. But that the bright, good-humored, intelligent young man had suddenly ceased to exist shocked his friends into a protective numbness. Charles's father had died recently and Mrs. Buller, now an old woman and unable to recover from the loss, soon died as well. Even Lady Harriet was "sad as death."[73]

At the same time an entire family of friends was creating widows, widowers, and mad people at a tragic pace. For a few years the Sterlings had been like a family to the Carlyles, especially to Jane. In April 1843 the elder Mrs. Sterling died, leaving her compulsive, manipulative, and argumentative husband a thunderer without any real lightning. His mind slowly disintegrating into senility, he made frequent difficult visits to Cheyne Row, most of which Carlyle avoided. At the same time, his son Anthony's wife became deranged; among other things she was obsessed with the notion that her husband was madly in love with Jane. But the disaster that wrung Carlyle's heart was the slow but inevitable decline in John Sterling's health. Suffering irreversibly from consumption, Sterling spent much of his time abroad or in southwestern England. After trying Clifton and then Falmouth, he soon settled on the Isle of Wight, making a valiant attempt to continue useful literary work as his health deteriorated. In the middle of April 1843 his mother died and two days later, unexpectedly, his wife. "It is the old story," Carlyle wrote to him, "as old as the first existence of mankind in this Earth; and yet, to every one of us, it arrives with a strange originality, sharp and astonishing as if it had never happened before." He urged him to "grieve not, all grief is useless;—we are but a little way behind."[74]

This was advice that Sterling, with his faith in a personal God and his belief in the immortality of the individual soul, had less need of than Carlyle. And he had less time remaining to him in which to grieve. His health was a little better in late 1843, when he visited London, the last time the two friends were to be together. He seemed "the old unresting brilliantly radiating man." But such brilliance was unnatural, as it always seemed to Carlyle, too intense to last, too unresting to endure.[75] In the spring, Sterling was very sick again, consumptive and spitting blood. By June it seemed likely that he would not recover. Despite his own problems, Carlyle could not get his "much-loved Friend" out of his mind. "It all lies in *these three words!*"[76] Throughout the summer of 1844 the news from Ventnor was so unrelievedly bad that there could be no doubt that he was dying. Should he visit? What could he say to him? That "we are journeying towards the Grand Silence; what lies beyond it earthly man has never known, nor will know" could not have been a help to his friend. Jane was in tears. "There would be a kind of satisfaction for me," Carlyle wrote, "could I see you with these eyes yet again. But . . . perhaps I should be but a disturbance."[77] Again, he could not get himself to go to Ventnor, whatever Sterling's wishes (he had never asked him not to come), and confront the pain and the parting directly. A few deeply tender letters passed between them. Sterling made no demands. Early in September 1844 he wrote a brief poem (no better in quality than the weak pieces he had been writing for years) in praise of Carlyle, "More than the Sage the Man commend."[78] Carlyle was at this time visiting the Grange for the first time. He was not more than twenty miles from Ventnor. While he was at nearby Winchester on September 20, visiting with the Ashburtons the tombs of ancient kings, he received the news that his "brave" and "most intimate" friend had died late in the evening two days before.[79]

4.

Work and friendship were Carlyle's shield against middle-age fears. Neither proved totally satisfactory. By early 1845 he had basically completed *Cromwell* and between 1845 and 1849 he wrote very little for publication, even making almost no entries in his private journal. With sufficient income from royalties and the rent from Craigenputtoch, he felt liberated from the need to write for money or ever to lecture again. He managed to persuade himself that his edition of Cromwell was a fine accomplishment, though he knew while compiling it and thereafter that it was at best a poor substitute for the biography he had failed to write. But it was a critical and financial success in which he took some pride, particularly since he still hoped it would help lay the ground for a modern Cromwell who would lead England out of its miseries.

Though these miseries now preoccupied him more than any vision of literary form or artistic fulfillment, the creation of a book that would effectively embody his concern about his country and modern civilization seemed constantly out of reach during these years. It was a frustrating experience. No matter how much he tried, he could not settle into anything—a situation that added to his anxiety and anger. He constantly advocated silence but found himself obsessively talking, occasionally with wit and laughter, often with passion and explosive anger. Visitors to Cheyne Row sometimes found him overbearing, compulsively garrulous, an entertainment for the thick-skinned rather than a man with whom to exchange ideas. To some it was exciting, to others unbearable; as had been the case with Coleridge—and the irony here is striking—an increasing number of young people came to listen to his monologues, as if they were listening to a seer or a prophet.

To friends of his own age, he often managed to lower his voice, to pursue conversation rather than monologue, unless particularly angered. Richard Milnes took great delight in provoking him into abusive torrents, particularly about well-known people. But that was an acceptable and purposeful interaction, part of the deep friendship between the two men. Tennyson, Dickens, Forster, Thackeray, Browning, and FitzGerald loved and respected their friend at Cheyne Row in full awareness of his faults; his virtues far exceeded any reservations they had about him. Between 1842 and 1850, he saw Tennyson frequently; they argued about personal immortality and smoked long hours together. Carlyle admired Tennyson's poetry, and both men loved poetic emotion. "One . . . unforgettable day" Tennyson "staid with us till late; forgot his stick; we dismissed him with Macpherson's Farewell . . . on his way to the gallows. . . . The tune is as rough as hemp, but strong as a lion. . . . Alfred's dark face grew darker, and I saw his lip slightly quivering."

Dickens, who was constantly busy at his own writing and at social projects, became a friend without ever becoming an intimate. Both Carlyles enjoyed his satire of Americans in *Martin Chuzzlewit,* sections of which Jane read to Thomas. "The last *Chuzzlewit* on Yankeedoodledom is capital," he told Forster, and asked him to tell Dickens that he had said so.[80] Dickens responded appreciatively, emphasizing to Jane that "it is *impossible* . . . to caricature that people. I lay down my pen in despair sometimes when I read what I have done, and find how it halts behind my own recollection."[81] Carlyle declined Forster's invitation that he attend a banquet in Dickens' honor, but the lavish praise he offered was more than the occasion demanded: "I truly love Dickens; and discern in the inner man of him a tone of real music."[82] When the novelist left for a year in Italy in the summer of 1844, Carlyle implied that he would miss him and told Jane that he wished him "good luck. . . . There is something very good and gifted in him, and in his lot are tragic elements enough capable of unfolding themselves."[83] Having completed *The Chimes* by December, Dickens returned to London for a brief visit, because, among other reasons, he wanted the author of *Chartism* to be one of the first to hear him read it. Carlyle joined other friends of Dickens at John Forster's rooms late in 1844 to hear the first reading performance.

Unlike Dickens, Forster did become an intimate, visiting Cheyne Row constantly throughout the decade and often dining with the Carlyles. So too did Thackeray. Though Carlyle had reservations about his comic but satiric tongue, his man-about-town "gentleman's" code of values, and his cynical depiction of "reality" in his fiction, Thackeray was a frequent caller at Cheyne Row and became a member of Lady Ashburton's circle at Addiscombe and the Grange. His daughters called regularly on Jane. His determination to do his best for them elicited Carlyle's respect. Thackeray's relationship with Lady Harriet was more stormy, less repressed, than Carlyle's. After an argument, which kept them apart for months, he finally accepted one of her persistent invitations and sent back her card with a drawing of Lady Harriet pouring hot coals on his head as he knelt at her feet. Browning's visits with the Carlyles of course came to an abrupt end when the poet "suddenly *married,*—a Miss Barrett, *Poetess,* who lay lamed on a sofa for many years, but is now suddenly on her feet again." Carlyle wished them "heartily . . . as happy a pilgrimage as can be had."[84] The "pilgrimage" took them to Italy and reduced the friendship to correspondence for many years. FitzGerald also matched his feelings of friendship with frequent visits, though the whimsical, perceptive FitzGerald loved the man more than he admired his words.

There was, however, a steady stream of less well known admirers who made their way to Cheyne Row. Some became friends, providing Carlyle an audience for his talk and companionship in his exercise. Some were contemporaries, among them the generous and stolid Charles Redwood, a Welsh attorney who each year sent him a basket of game and fruit and prevailed upon him to take a summer holiday in Wales in 1843. He spent a lazy, dull, but restorative month at Cowbridge with Redwood before going on to Abgerwili to visit another new friend, Bishop Connop Thirlwall. Subsequently he joined Jack for a walking tour of northern Wales during which he "climbed" Mount

Snowdon in "bitter windy mist."[85] Though he found Redwood, Thirlwall, and similar friends dull, especially for long visits, they had the virtue of being honest, companionable, and serviceable men who could sometimes relieve his solitude. Other admirers were younger men, usually bright and ambitious; some, like Francis Espinasse, had literary ambitions, others, like W. E. Forster, were men of business and potential leaders of government. Another new friend, Charles Gavin Duffy, a partisan of young, rebellious Ireland, eager to assert its national and ethnic independence, was one of those attracted to Carlyle as a voice of revolution. Ironically, Carlyle rarely agreed with their revolutionary impulses or their specific programs. On his way to Scotland in 1846 he made a quick trip to Northern Ireland, accompanied by Duffy, a national hero in his own country. In 1847, for the first time in many years and as an act of reconciliation, he and Jane vacationed together in Yorkshire, visiting Matlock Bath, to which Jane was attracted by the restorative waters. They were escorted by W. E. Forster on a tour of the picturesque countryside around Derbyshire and Leeds and spent some contented time as Forster's guests at his home in Rawdon.

Late in July 1847 Emerson wrote to Carlyle, "In my old age I am coming to see you. . . . I mean in good earnest to sail for Liverpool . . . about the 1 October."[86] Though forwarded from London, the letter failed to catch up to Carlyle in Yorkshire, where he had been alternating between interest in the sights and a dreamy state of silent indifference, "as if for the time one had *got* into the country of the Lotos-Eaters."[87] He assured his friend "that a prophet's chamber is ready for you in Chelsea . . . on whatever day at whatever hour you arrive."[88] He immediately wrote to one of his young disciples and Emerson's admirers to meet the American at Liverpool and put him on the first express train to London.

Carlyle's relationship with Emerson was unique among his friendships. They had not seen one another since 1833. Yet Carlyle had retained a genuine affection for him during these years of separation, partly because of the glow of pleasure Emerson had brought by his unexpected visit to Craigenputtoch, partly because Emerson had worked so hard on his behalf to further his reputation and to sell his books in America. The "pleasing dream of going to England" had been in Emerson's mind for some time.[89] There were domestic and personal reasons for seeking the excitements of travel, and his brooding efforts to isolate the particular nature of what it was to be an American prompted him to revivify his sense of the special qualities of the English and England.

By the mid-1840s Emerson's essays had received wide circulation in England, with help from Carlyle, and his reputation as a representative Yankee of genius ensured him a generous welcome. If his English friends thought it desirable, he would "read lectures," particularly at the new workingmen's or mechanic's "Institutes" that had been founded in major industrial cities, such as those in Manchester and Liverpool. He could count on an enthusiastic welcome. Many of Carlyle's devotees were also Emerson's, among them Francis Espinasse and Alexander Ireland. They assured him of lectures and profits. Sterling, whose recent death had deprived Emerson of a much-anticipated meeting, had been one of his strongest admirers. Milnes was eager to meet him. Carlyle, however, effectively expressed to Harriet Baring his own reservations about Emerson the artist, who "writes very much into the vague, like a man soliloquizing in unpeopled vacancy . . . sometimes in a distressingly fantastic manner. . . . His little aphoristic enigmatic sentences do not cohere: the paragraph, the Essay generally, is not like a solid ingot of metal but like a well-tied bag of shot,—so many pounds of lead-drops held together by a tight piece of canvas!"[90] Emerson's writing could not meet the test of Carlyle's organic Romanticism: successful prose had to burn with the hot intensity of the author's creative passion. But Emerson's showed no sign of having gone through the furnace; out of the mysterious currents of his own life Emerson had struggled to create a surface of calm in both his prose and his personality. Despite his idealized longing for an ascetic serenity, Carlyle needed to feel the blood pounding in the heart, the pulse jumping with electric excitement: anger, outrage, and passion authenticated life; gentleness, compromise, and calm were admirable but inhuman. He found it easier to admire Emerson from a distance.

Upon arriving in England Emerson first spent a few weeks in Liverpool and Manchester, where he was warmly welcomed and entertained by Francis Espinasse, Alexander Ireland, Elizabeth Paulet, and even Geraldine. When he arrived in London in late October, the details of a lecture tour had been arranged. During his week at Cheyne Row, old affections were strengthened but prevailing differences of outlook and especially of temperament were dramatically vivid. Emerson found Carlyle's political bluntness and his advocacy of authoritarian leadership alienating, but, except for an occasional reservation, he hardly argued. His insistence on repressing tension and hostility confronted Carlyle with a calmness, a gentleness, a refusal to fight which he both admired and at the same time found unbearable. To Jane, Emerson seemed like a long, thin, devitalized "reed," a man without life or blood. Though the civilities were maintained, everyone was relieved when he left to begin his lecture tour. But Carlyle hoped to have him "here again before long."[91]

In the next months Emerson successfully lectured through much of central and northern England, gradually increasing his awareness of the English character. He visited Harriet Martineau at Ambleside and spent an afternoon with Wordsworth before continuing on to Scotland. He returned to London early in March 1848, but he did not stay with the Carlyles. At first he resided with his publisher, John Chapman; then he found rooms of his own. Carlyle took him to a lively dinner at the Barings', attended by "quantities of Lords, Townwits (Thackeray, etc.), beautiful ladies." Emerson "kept very quiet; mild modest eyes, lips sealed together like a pair of pincers, and nobody minded him much."[92] He dined in more modest company numbers of times at Cheyne Row, where his host noticed, with mixed feelings, how perfect "a 'gentleman' " Emerson was "and what is still more interesting, of the American type (a rare species . . .)."[93] For the first time, Emerson lectured in London, a series that Carlyle attended regularly even though he did not particularly enjoy the lectures.[94] James Anthony Froude, later Carlyle's disciple and biographer, was accompanied to the last of the lectures by his friend Arthur Clough, the young poet and close friend of Matthew Arnold. Clough pointed out Carlyle, and they "heard his loud, kindly, contemptuous laugh when the lecturer ended."[95]

Emerson and Carlyle had strikingly different lecture styles. Carlyle spoke extemporaneously, striving to create the effect of inspired talk. Emerson read in a monochromatic voice from texts that had been written out in advance. He avoided eye contact with the audience, and even kept voice contact to a bare minimum. To the surprise of his English supporters, he did not seem the least bit ruffled when members of his audience whispered among themselves or rose to leave while he was reading. Emerson calmly explained that he was quite used to that in America. He seemed much less interested in the English impression of him than in his own impression of England, which he was storing in his mind and notebooks for later use in his essays and in *English Traits*. To Carlyle, Emerson seemed blind, uncritical, "in a languid kind of way . . . content with everything." The subjects he was interested in no longer concerned Carlyle; his opinions seemed "moonshiney, unpractical"; his favorite people in England were "a washy set, 'friends of humanity,' etc."; and the best Carlyle could do was either restrain himself from disagreeing vehemently or occasionally relieve himself with sudden outbursts. In general, the two men kept a distance almost as great as the ocean that had separated them for over thirteen years.

Early in July they went together to Salisbury and Stonehenge, "a wild mournful . . . enigmatic and bewildering sight," Thomas wrote to Jane, "utterly solitary . . . studded with . . . 'barrows' . . . the tombs of extinct nations, and that huge mass of dark, meaningless, gigantic dislocated stones; of which no creatures will ever tell us the meaning, except that it is the extinct temple of an extinct people seemingly sunk very deep in *error*."[96] The two friends talked about the relationship between past and present, England and America; Carlyle hoped that the great strength of England and the English character would be revitalized and endure; Emerson felt that only in its American children would England have new life again. The next week Emerson sailed for America. Carlyle, trying to look squarely at change and necessity, thought the two aging men would never see one another again.[97] But no amount of stoicism could quite overcome his awareness of his faults as a host and the ambivalence with which he had treated his friend. At the end of the year, with the Atlantic separating them once again, he remorsefully pleaded, "Forgive me my ferocities; you do not quite know what I suffer."[98]

5.

For Carlyle, all public revolutions were questionable; what the individual could not do for himself it seemed doubtful that society, whatever its virtues, could do for him. During the 1840s his hope that society would become better through sudden changes diminished considerably, though he recognized that revolutions of various kinds were occurring in his private and public life and in that of his culture. The most demanding challenge was to confront and make the most of the inevitable changes. Some of the public changes—massive enough to be recognized as revolutions—he confronted with keen perceptiveness, others with blunt hostility. His intelligence almost never failed him, but sometimes his emotions overcame his insight and humanity.

What good, he wondered, is it to be humane to people when the outcome only prolongs and intensifies their misery? The "condition of England" did not seem to be getting any better. Without effective education and emigration policies, unemployment would leave the mass of the population demoralized and malnourished. The Corn Laws kept the price of wheat artificially high without in any way expanding the need for agricultural labor. Men like George Hudson, the "railroad King," pyramided huge paper wealth on a base of speculative greed. Those with capital considered their personal profits sacred. They put the nation's resources into creating the greatest railroad system in the world while much of the working class was impoverished. Ragged bands of beggars, most of them Irish, roamed the countryside; the pinched look of hunger, the glazed eye of misery, stared from random faces in the "chartered" London streets. In the countryside, the unemployed ate weeds and grass; in the city, they burned fences for fuel and stole food. In the industrial centers, huge outdoor meetings enthusiastically cheered the Chartist leaders; the energy of desperation channeled itself into the naive notion that Parliament would be sufficiently impressed by millions of signatures to enact legislation that would benefit the working class. Behind the semicoherent protests was the potential if not the actual threat of revolution; the "hungry Forties" were proving an unsettling challenge to the class structure that English leadership had assumed unalterable.

During his brief visit to Ireland in the summer of 1846, Carlyle concluded that the poverty and despair of Ireland presaged the condition that would develop in England unless steps were taken to prevent catastrophe. He believed that if England did not have the means to save Ireland, then it did not have the means to save itself, for underlying the plight of Ireland was English irresponsibility. But the solutions, he believed, were not mainly political; politicians could do no more than alleviate immediate misery through changes in government policy. For Carlyle, external disorder, which he deeply feared and deplored, was the result of inner corruption; the inability to act wisely stemmed from the loss of soul and vitality within individuals and within society. "The outer miseries of Ireland, and of all lands," he wrote in his journal in 1848, "are nothing but the inevitable body of that soul."[99]

Between his first trip to Ireland and his second in the summer of 1849, Carlyle spent much of his time brooding, worrying that it would soon be too late for England. He desperately wanted to influence his contemporaries to do what had to be done, but his frustration, both as a writer and as a citizen, was immense. There is no evidence that he himself ever voted; by the 1830s he angrily questioned the meaningfulness of the ballot box and frequently claimed that there was no deserving candidate. One night at tea he was "more savage" than Erasmus Darwin had ever seen him before. His "ferocity" was "like a child's . . . only unfortunately he has no Ma to carry him off cursing and swearing as some beloved angels sometimes do."[100]

Carlyle thought that radical improvement was unlikely. Democracy tended to institutionalize the power of the lowest common denominator. The policies of democracy might be ameliorative. But, having grown up in a tradition of spiritual and intellectual elitism, Carlyle did not see any wisdom in compromises that only made misery and the fallen state of man more bearable. Spiritual perfection should be the aim of human life. As a secular form of government, democracy rejected spiritual distinctions; indeed, it even seemed to have the potential to reject any spiritual values whatsoever. Inevitably the government of the lowest common denominator would be a government dedicated to materialism—to the "good life" as defined in material terms. In a time of crisis, with the social and economic stability of the country precarious, Carlyle thought it unlikely that the ballot box would produce leadership that could transcend material needs and narrow special interests. The history of Western culture provided no precedent in which the leadership produced by a popular election enabled a country to weather severe storms. Carlyle took exception when American historians such as George Bancroft claimed that "the American colonists founded their institutions on popular freedom, and 'set an example to the nations.' "[101] The ballot box had not created Washington's leadership, but only ratified it after the fact; and the example of America, with its endlessly fertile and unoccupied prairies, was of no use to the crowded, overpopulated European nations. From Moses to Washington, great men had risen to power because of their spiritual strength; their leadership was ratified through history's universal acknowledgment that they had provided enlightened guidance for their less capable contemporaries. What England needed now was another Cromwell—some man of goodness, vision, and spiritual dedication to provide national leadership.

But such a man was not in sight, with one possible exception. Carlyle's early opinion of Robert Peel had not been especially high. Unlike Wellington, whom Carlyle had caught glimpses of in Parliament, on the street, and even at the opera, Peel appeared to be a Tory without any particular inner strength or stubborn principle. Wellington, of course, seemed a venerable anachronism by the 1840s, a national hero without a contemporary role.[102] But at the end of 1841 the rumor that Peel might propose the abrogation of the Corn Laws lifted Carlyle's expectations. In 1842 he caught sight of Peel at the House of Commons, to which he had been persuaded to go to hear Charles Buller speak. In "the summer twilight" Peel seemed "an honest figure of a man . . . clever-looking . . . large substantial head, Roman nose, massive cheeks with a wrinkle, half smile, half sorrow on them."[103] But Peel did not seem so superior that he could avoid being lumped with his fellow politicians in the contrast between Cromwell and contemporary leaders which was so strong for Carlyle as he struggled with his book. For Cromwell was "an astonishing spectacle; unexampled;—altogether incredible to the poor . . . beggarly Peel-Russell & Company."[104]

But the strength that he had glimpsed in Peel's physical appearance surfaced dramatically when at the end of 1845 Peel "decided to abolish the Corn-laws: total and immediate!"[105] For Carlyle, it was matter for "rejoicing." The repeal bill was introduced into Parliament in January 1846. For almost six months the debate was heated. Determined opponents tried to speak over the shouts of public demonstrations, "the

Aristocracy struck almost with a kind of horror at sight of that terrible Millocracy, rising like a huge hideous Frankenstein up in Lancashire." Though Carlyle believed strongly in the necessity of repeal, the sight of the mob repelled him almost as much as the stupidity of the ruling class. "I will not fire guns when this small victory is gained; I will recommend a day of Fasting rather, that such a victory required such gaining."[106] By the end of April the victory was still in doubt. But within the next two months "Peel's Bill" attracted sufficient votes to make passage likely; the liberal Tories, among them Bingham Baring, who served under Peel, prepared for celebration. On June 19, when Carlyle sent a presentation copy of *Cromwell* to Peel, there was no doubt that the bill would pass, that Peel would be "victorious in spite of the world" and the world "a little better supplied with bread in years coming!"[107] Proclaiming that they were brothers in labor, Carlyle asked Peel to "let this poor labour of mine be a small testimony of that sort to" the minister's "great and valient labour."[108] Almost by return mail, Peel acknowledged the gift and offered tactful praise: "Whatever may have been the pressure of my public engagements, it has not been so overwhelming to prevent me from being familiar with your exertions in another Department of Labour as incessant and severe as that which I have undergone." The gift was deeply "gratifying" to him "as a token of [Carlyle's] personal esteem."[109] Three days later the repeal act passed Parliament. Was it not possible that Peel would provide the leadership that England so desperately needed?

Carlyle, however, had not the slightest desire that strong leadership be exerted at the expense of traditional civil liberties, at least insofar as civil liberties had been in practice the privilege of intellectuals and the upper classes. When, in the spring of 1844, it became publicly known that the government had interfered with one of an Englishman's most precious liberties, the sacredness of his private communications, it made no difference to Carlyle that Mazzini was not an Englishman. That it could happen *in* England was horrendous. The home secretary, he believed, had no right to open anyone's mail. It was "scandalous. . . . I think all men ought to denounce it and declare that they would not endure it."[110] For the working people, the priorities were perhaps not quite the same. Carlyle certainly knew that Peel, both by personality and by principle, hardly had the makings of a dictator, and that Carlyle thought him the hope of the country suggests that there was a wide gap between his occasional hysterical calls for authoritarian leadership and his practical sense of what was possible and best for England.

The most pressing problems, to Carlyle's mind, were poverty and unemployment. They were at the heart of the revolutionary situation. The symptoms had been produced by "old causes innumerable, deep-seated, wide-spread, engrained into the very blood of us . . . and which must be cast out, or social death itself, in the shape of 'red republic' and bottomless ruin and delirium, seems not to be far off!"[111] He had said much the same before, particularly in *Chartism* and *Past and Present,* but the events of recent years, and particularly the upheaval in France in 1848, had convinced him that one of the forms such disaster would take was an egalitarianism so complete that it would force an unnatural equality on all human situations. He could not know, of course, even when he used the phrase "red republic," that Friedrich Engels was in the process of distilling his experiences in Manchester into the pamphlet on the English working class that would be the first important document of modern communism. (Engels had read Carlyle carefully, deeply moved by *Past and Present.*)[112]

The solutions to the underlying problems which Carlyle had been advocating for years were necessarily abstract—they involved that vaguest of calls for change, spiritual reform. But the symptoms could be dealt with more directly. It seemed to Carlyle that it was the purpose of government to do everything necessary to relieve poverty and to prevent unemployment. All who wanted to work should be provided jobs. All who did not want to work should be persuaded through a process of education that it was necessary for them and for society that they too become laborers "in the vineyard of the Lord." The government that could not do this was "no Government otherwise." It seemed to Carlyle that under effective leadership "an actual Government (with one brave man in the heart of it)" could "begin *enlisting* mad perishing mobs of unemployed Paupers into 'Industrial regiments,' and under strict military drill . . . to find employment for them, in Colonies, in Bogs of Allen, in hundreds of square miles of waste improveable land . . . and on the whole to get sufficient work out of them for their own subsistence." Just as governments created armies of soldiers in times of national emergency, weren't they justified, in this different kind of emergency, in creating armies of workers? The military metaphor was perfectly acceptable to Carlyle and his contemporaries. Such an army would be transformed into "Christian soldiers" who would move on to "the bounds of the waste, / On, to the City of God," as Matthew Arnold was to write a few years later. Was it not possible that the "one brave man in the heart of it" could be Peel?[113]

In March 1847 Carlyle passed Peel while walking in Kensington Gardens. "He looked across very kindly at me, whom I believe he knows by face."[114] A year later Carlyle found himself seated next to Peel at dinner at Bath House. They talked much of the evening, enjoying the wide range and the common sense of the conversation. He admired Peel's ability to laugh and wrote to his mother, "I decidedly liked Peel; and could not but hope some real good might yet lie in him for the country. . . . Incomparably better furnished both with talent and disposition than any other we have at present."[115] In Ireland misery outpaced the possibility of remediation; in Europe, revolutionary explosions threatened chaos and its spread to England. Still, if Peel would come in, it might be "the *beginning* . . . of salvation . . . to England."[116] Throughout 1849 and 1850 Peel delayed attempting to take office, carefully assessing the prospects for effective government. The fragile Whig coalition governed at the sufferance of the bitter divisions within the Tory majority, for Lord Edward Stanley, soon to be the fourteenth earl of Derby, and Benjamin Disraeli were unremittingly hostile to Peel and his free-trade followers. On the last day of June 1850, Carlyle received the disturbing news that Sir Robert had been seriously hurt in a fall from his horse while riding on Constitution Hill. Contradictory rumors prevailed for the next few days, but the general atmosphere was gloomy. On the fourth day, Peel died. The country mourned the dead man more expressively than it had appreciated him when alive. Lady Harriet, who "all in tears" brought the news to Carlyle, went to Addiscombe to be alone with her close friends.[117] Carlyle felt that the "one statesman" who offered the country hope of "peaceable improvement" had been "suddenly snatched away."[118]

One of the subjects that he and Peel had spoken about at Bath House, the revolution that had just occurred in France, was now on everyone's mind. It seemed to Englishmen that whenever they looked across the Channel the French were again engaged in some violent adventure. In the summer of 1847 France was "in a shocking state of unprincipled depravity"; a new revolution threatened, but Carlyle's sympathies were clear.[119] Louis Philippe was a weaseling corrupt politician, not a royal bone in his body, whom the French were wise and right to dispose of. He went out "not like a King, but like a felon . . . supervised by the police."[120] But with what or whom would they replace him? The republic that had been established by February 1848 inspired a "joy-dance" in England of which Carlyle did not disapprove, mainly because he was so pleased by the expulsion of Louis Philippe, which seemed clear evidence that "the righteous Gods do 'live and reign.' " In March 1848 he published a brief article in the *Examiner* in which he lauded this third generation of French revolutionaries who were protesting, "with their heart's blood, against a universe of lies." He had not felt for a long time "such deep-seated pious satisfaction at a public event."[121] His general hostility to France and the French was less controlling than his firm conviction that it was essential to clear away the old in order to create the new. It was a "natural step." And the English, whose turn was next, could learn from the French. Not that he approved at all of the anarchy of the Second Republic. It was "No-Government" at a time when firm government was needed. But it was better than "False-Government." Though it might take generations to work out the problems, the end certainly would be better than the beginning.[122]

For the first time Carlyle subscribed to a daily newspaper, the *Times*, sharing the cost with Jack. He soon gave it up, however, "wearied out, reading night after night . . . of human violence and imbecile delirium from Paris and all other places."[123] Shaken by the thought of how many would die, he responded compassionately to the ironic news that General Louis Cavaignac, the younger brother of their republican friend, had assumed responsibility for putting down the street crowds. It seemed likely to him that General Cavaignac would die too. Soon Mazzini was off for Rome, where there was at last a reasonable opportunity for him to put his national hopes into practice. Carlyle's old depreciation of his friend was now muted by his admiration for Mazzini's evident courage and by the possibility that he might become a national hero who would "rouse the whole Italian nation." But it seemed unlikely that he could defeat both the French and the Austrians, and more likely that the Carlyles would never see him again.[124]

Revolution was inevitable; but Carlyle did not believe that revolution could solve the long-term problems. Without some change within the individual, the improvements in the conditions of society could not be sustained. And applying a bandage to the surface would not cure the deep wound. Though he did whatever he could to find and encourage the use of appropriate bandages, it seemed to him that all political and economic reforms, important as they might be in relieving misery, left the crucial wound of spiritual and moral depravity to fester. The world needed to rebel against materialism on every level—to seek spiritual gods rather than to worship the marketplace and the phallus, money and sex. He sketched briefly a number of topics to write about. But the absence of any vehicle to transform his opinions into literature aggravated his sense of failure and frustration. He grappled with the greatest personal revolution of all, the approach of what seemed to him useless old age. "What will become of me? I am growing old; I am grown old. My next book must be that of an old man, and I am not yet got into that dialect. Again and again I ask myself: Wilt thou never work more then? and the answer is a mere groan of misery, and also of cowardliness and laziness."[125]

He thought of writing a book that he would call "Democracy," exposing the delusion that wise leaders could be elected and the problems of the country solved by the ballot box. "Only the vote of the wise is called for, of advantage even to the voter himself."[126] But he felt too "sick, lazy, and dispirited" to begin it. He had long been meditating a project called "Exodus from Houndsditch," and perhaps a companion volume to be called "The Scavenger Age," both of which would dramatize his conviction that the contemporary age could best be defined as one that was sweeping out corrupt Christianity in preparation for the "New Church" that had not yet been born. But, though he recognized the importance of declaring that institutional Christianity was dead, even now he did not feel that he could tackle the problem head-on. He could not publicly renounce the Christian world into which he had been born, particularly as long as his mother was alive. William Gladstone, reading Froude's biography, recognized Carlyle's dilemma: "When he writes to his mother he assumes the phraseology of a Christian. . . . This is not hypocrisy but it is fiction; it is deception, beginning probably in self-deception. He could not bear to give pain to his mother he dearly and deeply loved."[127] After her death in 1853 his courage waned further, his sense of respect for the dead intervened; he thought such a public renunciation would be a useless gesture anyway. But, it occurred to him, it would not be useless to write, as an act of respect and affection, a life of his friend John Sterling. It would be possible to say a great deal about the current spiritual life of the nation while at the same time doing homage to a misunderstood "gifted soul." But in early 1848 all these projects seemed just out of reach, as the explosions from across the Channel sounded in his ears and the Chartist crowds threatened revolution in England.

Determined to write something, he began an essay, the purpose of which was to denounce the worship of the marketplace and the phallus. Though he would not mention Geraldine, he had her new novel in mind, believing that it had been influenced by immoral French models. When it arrived at Cheyne Row in manuscript in 1847, even Jane had been repelled by the extent of her expressiveness on sexual matters. He also had in mind a young friend, George Henry Lewes, who was making his living publishing such steamy fictions of the George Sand type as *Rose, Blanche and Violet* and *Ranthorpe;* in the margins of Jane's presentation copy of the latter, Carlyle had written severely critical remarks.[128] But the French disease was simply an advanced stage of a European-wide infection. "The New Sand religion is not yet developed in articles; creeds, and bodies of divinity." Even more than Mammon worship, "Phallus-worship" had become the center of post-enlightenment religion; the circulating library filled with sentimental and sensual fiction was its church, and George Sand, a "veritable new Virgin and *Mater Dolorosa,*" was its "melodious Anti-Virgin, Evangelist of Anarchy." In the reshuffling of central human values, the highest aspiration of human beings had become fulfillment in love. The "phallus" had become the "Symbol of the Divine." "Unhappy generation of the world, which has no marching standards but these two: a Phallus and a moneybag."[129]

He put the unfinished essay away. Perhaps its emphasis on sex seemed too explicit both as a public statement and as an allusion to his own sexual inhibitions. The very use of the word "phallus" would most likely provoke public criticism; his own confusions probably encouraged him to bury the essay in his unpublished papers as quickly as possible. What is remarkable is that he felt sufficiently liberated from personal demons to write the essay, and then, having written as much of it as he did, that he had not destroyed it, even though he had no intention of ever publishing it. Probably he never showed it to anyone, even to Jane. He did, however, have another writing project in mind, safer than an essay on "Phallus-worship" or a book on the obsolescence of Christianity: a series of "spiritual sketches" of Ireland, a country whose problems had increasingly preoccupied him throughout the decade. But in order to write that book he needed to know more about Ireland; it would be necessary, in fact, to visit again, but this time to make an extensive tour of the entire country. On the last day of June 1849 he waved good-bye to Jane from the Chelsea steamer, his white hat visible to her for a long while after he could not be seen; by that afternoon he was on a Dublin steamer heading toward the Irish Sea.

[13]

"Fierce Rage" 1849–1851

Carlyle had purposely chosen "a dingy, dirty-looking Dublin steamer" in which to make the voyage. He wanted time to think and the long, slow voyage would provide that. He anticipated that what he would see in Ireland would cause him great pain; the pleasures would be at most secondary. If he were ever again to write anything germane to the central problems of his society, he believed not only that he would have to deal with Ireland as a political, economic, and cultural problem for the English but also that he would have to confront his own complex responses to Ireland as they had developed during the past decade. To look closely at Ireland, he believed, was to look into the future, the destiny of Western culture. But, at the same time, such an experience compelled inner scrutiny, an examination of his personal frustrations, expectations, prejudices, and hopes. The subject had the potential for the same dramatic and resonating interplay between the public and the personal which he had found in the French Revolution and which had permitted him to write his seminal work on that topic. He had published *The French Revolution* at the age of forty-two. It was not a young man's book. But it was the work of a Romantic visionary who had seen both the beauty and the terror of the chaos. He was now fifty-four years of age; the wear and tear of the accumulated years of psychogenic "dyspepsia" and the self-punishing compulsions of "work" and "duty" showed more in his emotional tenseness than in his physical presence. He usually dressed in dark clothes, softened by the distinctiveness of his wide-brimmed hats. He "had a strong, well-knit frame, a dark, ruddy complexion, piercing blue eyes, close-drawn lips, and an air of silent composure and authority."[1] The distinctive feature of his long face, beneath the pale, extremely bright blue eyes, was his firm jaw and an overlip so thin that it accented the gravity of the lower part of his clean-shaven face.

Like many of the great writers of English literature, he instinctively overdramatized public and personal change, as if "yellow leaves, or few, or none" had been poetically grafted onto a tree that was still in its middle age. Part of this was convention, a purposeful attempt to heighten the intensity of the present moment. But, for Carlyle at fifty-four, there was now a certain reality to his confrontation with time and change. He had become an artist whose expressiveness was inseparable from constant involvement with and comment on a rapidly changing society. Because he increasingly found himself a voice that opposed these changes, his sense of his own subjective time, a separate personal calendar, stood out even more sharply. As the *Athlone* steamed southward down the eastern coast of England, he had time to appreciate that he was an outsider, a man who was leaving behind an England that represented a dying past and sailing toward an Ireland that represented a horrible future. So many of his complaints, so much of his tiredness and his sense of premature age, stemmed from his dissatisfaction with the present, as if only the past and the future might provide emotional reward. But the future, he believed, was likely to be revolution and apocalypse, bloodshed and chaos. And the past, as he grew older, seemed more and more a time and place of tombs.

As the ship passed Dover in the twilight of Saturday, June 20, 1849, Carlyle peered into the distance at the town in which he had spent some weeks with Irving, the Stracheys, and Kitty Kirkpatrick twenty-five years before, on the eve of his first trip to Paris. He "could recognize almost nothing of" his "old localities."[2] On a "beautiful sunny" Sunday morning the ship lay becalmed, "waiting for the turn of the tide," near Ventnor on the Isle of Wight, where John Sterling had died five years before. In a cluster of houses shining in the morning sun he tried vainly to make out the one that had been his friend's.[3] The next day, passing off the Cornish coast near the Buller family home, he thought of the recently dead "poor [Charles] Buller, poor old years of his and mine!"[4] It was as if the road to Ireland were marked with gravesites, among them an anticipation of his own, especially if he could not live again as a writer, dedicated to a subject worthy of his vision and talent.

Not that he was always gloomy. There were moments of laughter, humor, and very energetic activity, though much of the latter was the result of the frenetic restlessness that he believed a sign of inner illness when he perceived it in others. But his basic temperament was elegiac, so reconciled to loss that he found pleasure in embracing the harsh fact of the inevitable deaths of those whom he loved; the process of acceptance was so constant, so passionate, so self-involving and self-consuming that it dramatized how deeply he felt and feared these personal losses. His religious background had taught him stoic acceptance. But the promise of heavenly reward (of any kind of Christian heaven at all) which had been the emotional basis of such stoicism in the lives of people like his father and mother had little credibility for him. Those who died disappeared from his life, except as memories; and the memories more than anything else were painful reminders that they were no longer there. The prospect of personal reunion was only a hope. But the dead at least were surrounded by the sacredness of silence and peace and, as he grew older, that came to seem almost reward enough. Now, as the *Athlone* steamed slowly westward along the southern coast of England, he thought of the dead calmly, without anger or resentment, almost without fear. Such moments were cathartic in their sadness.

The anger that he so frequently felt could be stilled for the moment. He was angry at England for its blindness and stupidity; he was furious with himself for his inability for the time being, perhaps forever, to make some effective contribution to the reawakening of England and to the solution of corrosive social problems. Both the personal and the public future appeared fraught with dangers, as if he and his society had gotten themselves involved with "impossibilities." Between social madness on the one hand and personal anxiety on the other, there seemed little to be happy about. But the change was good for him. The voyage stimulated his keen visual and analytic responses, and the pleasure of observation imposed itself on the sadness of what he saw. Soon the variety of Irish faces among the passengers caught his attention. One passenger, drunk, disappeared forever into the sea on Saturday night. At Lands End, before the ship turned northward, "the evening light glared wild and sad." They passed "the light-house, at the distance perhaps of a mile," and he recorded that it was "the wildest, most impressive place I ever saw on the coasts of Britain."[5] On Tuesday, in gusty cold weather, Ireland came in sight.

Late that night, at the Imperial Hotel in Dublin, he and Charles Gavin Duffy sat down together to "scheme out a route" and a timetable.[6] Duffy and Carlyle had first met in the spring of 1845 when the young revolutionary, who strongly advocated an independent Ireland, came to Cheyne Row with two of his colleagues in national resurrection. They astonished Carlyle by proclaiming that they were "all sworn disciples" of his, young men who saw that beneath their superficial political differences with the older man was a fundamental agreement in spirit and principle. They were basically right. *Sartor Resartus* was to them an al-

Gavin Duffy. Photograph, 1865. Courtesy of the Rare Book and Manuscript Library, Columbia University.

most sacred book, whose stirring passages they read aloud to one another. The sympathy for the poor and oppressed and the absolute detestation of injustice which *Chartism* had directed toward the plight of the English working class seemed equally applicable to their suffering fellow countrymen. "England is guilty towards Ireland," Carlyle had written in *Chartism,* "and reaps at last, in full measure, the fruit of fifteen generations of wrong-doing."[7] In their enthusiasm, they thought they might be able to persuade Carlyle, who opposed repeal of the Union and thought an independent Ireland would not solve the problems of poverty and mismanagement, that the best penance England could pay would be its positive support of Irish national aspirations. The author of *The French Revolution* should be able to understand young Ireland's passionate hope to transform a revolutionary situation into a new nation.

Again they were right, to a point. Carlyle did admire their sincerity and their passion. Duffy seemed to him "a really interesting young man . . . full of zeal, of talent, and affection; almost *weeping* as he spoke of his poor country." He genuinely liked "poor Duffy very much."[8] It was refreshing to be in the company of young men who were willing to die for their national and spiritual aspirations. Duffy, indeed, had already been in jail, and he was soon to be imprisoned again by the British, though only for a short time. His magazine, the *Nation,* circulated freely throughout Britain and Carlyle, who was soon placed on the mailing list courtesy of the editor, read it regularly. After his second imprisonment, Duffy became an Irish national hero; the death of Daniel O'Connell, whose blustering oratory Carlyle hated, encouraged Duffy to pursue a parliamentary career and to distance himself from the extreme positions and programs of the Irish radicals. Eventually disillusioned with the raw politics of Irish-English relations and feeling bitterly betrayed by some of his own countrymen, Duffy emigrated to Australia in 1855 and began a new career as a distinguished public official. One of his minor accomplishments was to have a town named after the man he had come to in 1845, hoping to persuade him to support the repeal of the Union.

Carlyle could not be persuaded. As much as he admired Duffy, he strongly believed that repeal would be disastrous for both England and Ireland. Separated by only forty miles of briny water, wedded by centuries of mutual pain and shared responsibility, England and Ireland were one. To pretend differently, Carlyle thought, was to disregard the unalterable facts. Despite the differences in dialect, they were bound together by a common language. Despite the differences in religion, they were united by both history and destiny. The problems were formidable, the solutions difficult; but, for Carlyle, the best hope resided in a common fight, "a general insurrection *against the Devil* first of all";

separation would take vital energy away from this main battle and provide no solution at all.[9]

From 1845 to 1849 Carlyle gave much thought and energy to the Irish problem, partly because he was searching for a topic to write on, partly because he doubted that a book on any topic would actually effect a change for the better in public affairs. The great landowners were too busy spending money to attend effectively to the sources of that money, their estates and dependents in England and Ireland; and the industrial barons were too busy making money to take the time to show other people how to organize society in order to defeat poverty.

To his mind, little or nothing could be expected of literature or literary men, most of whom found it difficult enough simply to make an honest living in such a dishonest and materialistic society. His own good fortune had placed him above economic need, mainly because he continued to live modestly, most years spending far less than his annual income. His books continued to sell well to an awkward coalition of readers, among them young men who looked to him for spiritual leadership, entranced by his combination of poetic prose and exhortation into placing immense trust in the general values that he represented. If, as with Duffy, they differed on practical particulars, the consonance of the heart was more important than the differences of practical application. *Sartor Resartus* especially, and *Past and Present* as well, had found a vast audience among the young who were spiritually adrift and antimaterialistic. *Chartism* attracted the social and political radicals. *Cromwell* had temporarily become a national "classic." What the great writer would do next was a matter of some anticipation. Not even intimates, however, were fully aware of the depth of his ambivalence about what his next book would be.

To Duffy there seemed good reason to hope that the subject would be Ireland and that what Carlyle had to say would be a valuable contribution. Early in September 1846, after much hesitation, Carlyle had made a lightning trip to Ireland, crossing from Scotland to Belfast, where he had been joined by Duffy, who was eager to show him the miseries of a country in which the potatoes were rotten, the wheat stunted, and the paupers numerous. Carlyle's expectations were fulfilled by what he saw—rags, beggars, disease, filth, and starvation. From Belfast, he had gone to Dublin, where he "saw O'Connell haranguing his beggarly squad . . . perhaps the *most* disgusting sight to me on that side of the water."[10] Demagoguery that exploited other people's misfortunes seemed even more repellent than the misfortunes themselves. When O'Connell died the next year, Carlyle's bitter epitaph was that "the wretched blustering quack" had been "*lying* . . . for fifty years. Preaching to the Irish that they were just about to get repeal from the English."[11] But the reality of Irish misery depressed him deeply. After only a few days on Irish soil, he had crossed to Liverpool and returned to London.

He could not forget what he had seen. "I think often we are perhaps on the edge of great and terrible times. For all Reform Bills are a small matter to this of the Potatoe, if it continue dead!"[12] The reality of "fierce actual *Starvation*" in Ireland weighed heavily on his conscience.[13] That the Irish were "sitting *idle,* in the midst of famine," seemed a tragic absurdity to the son of a tenant farmer who was keenly aware that the landlords were more to blame than the peasants. Since the landlords would seize "all" the crop "for rent," it was understandable that the peasants declined to work *and* starve also.[14] With desperate common sense, responding from the deep side of what was already evident failure, he argued that it would be in everyone's long-range interest for the potato crop to fail decisively and forever. "For it is want of sense and honesty, not want of potatoes, that we suffer under: all the yearly potatoes of the British Empire are supposed to be worth some 20, or 25 or 30 millions; and all the yearly *harvest* . . . must be between 200 and 300 millions: a Nation . . . that reaped such a harvest . . . and has so many Manchesters and other big Workshops going . . . should not die for the loss of a few potatoes, if it *had* 'sense and honesty' in it."[15]

In Carlyle's view, "sense and honesty" demanded that the nation fulfill its responsibility to organize Irish labor and wealth so that Ireland could eventually feed itself; until that day arrived, the rest of the empire should provide the energy and resources necessary to relieve its misery. The solution was not repeal but the organization of labor and land into productive units with varied crops which would put the country's economy on a sound footing and encourage Irish small industry as well as agriculture: the "Devil" in this case was a combination of English stupidity and selfishness on the one hand and Irish superstition and sloth on the other. What the Irish could not do for themselves, however, it was the responsibility of England to do for them; and it was precisely England's irresponsibility, he concluded, that intensified the problem, encouraged a revolutionary situation, and created the desperate courage of the brave men of young Ireland. Since it was calculated that "from one to two millions of men . . . will perish" from starvation, how was it possible not to be sympathetic to the young revolutionaries?[16] That they were likely to "get themselves shot, or hanged for treason, by and by," was more an exposure of English baseness and stupidity than a condemnation of Duffy and his friends.[17] But, though the blame for their folly could be laid at England's door, Carlyle's anxiety about what might acually happen to his new friends increased his obsession with the problem. He believed that such a situation was a deadly disease that had to be cured to prevent its spread. And perhaps his own counsel could contribute to the cure.

In 1848 and early 1849 Carlyle seemed to be honing his pen to write at length on Ireland. He published a number of brief newspaper articles in the *Spectator* and the *Examiner,* mainly attacking the maladministration of Ireland by the English landowners and by Lord John Russell's government. He emphasized that England had to solve the problem of Ireland or sink itself. The longest of the articles, "On the Repeal of the Union," strongly argued his conviction that repeal would solve nothing and was not in the best interests of either Ireland or England. A few months before leaving for Ireland, he publicly expressed his hope that Peel's recent speech on the Irish problem was the harbinger of a new attitude and new leadership. But not long before he had written to his closest confidante, "How can I write on Ireland, or on any earthly thing, when day and night my poor head is in a welter of bewilderments . . . my Beautiful Lady. 'Beauty and the Beast'; the beast undeliverable?"[18] Might not his own deliverance be inextricably involved with his ability to write about the redemption of Ireland?

2.

The route that Duffy and Carlyle worked out committed them to a heavy schedule of travel for the rest of July and part of August 1849, a circular swing from Dublin through the South to Cork and Killarney, then northward and eastward along the western coast, eventually to Londonderry. From there Carlyle would sail for Glasgow in early August. To complete the circle he would rely on his memory of the trip made three years before from Belfast to Dublin. Duffy's judgment determined some of the route, and other stops were fixed on because Carlyle had had them particularly in mind. But he had also come with a rather full envelope of letters of introduction, many of them from FitzGerald and William Forster. FitzGerald's family was Irish; in fact, Carlyle's enthusiastic reception at the Imperial Hotel was due partly to its being owned by relatives of FitzGerald. Forster, whom the Carlyles had visited in Yorkshire, had led a Quaker commission of inquiry to Ireland two years before and helped to write a sensible, perceptive, and honest report on the Irish problem. Carlyle, in fact, had hoped that Forster would accompany him on the entire tour. But the ex-Quaker, who years later became the stern chief secretary for Ireland, had other obligations, though he made plans to meet Carlyle and Duffy later in the month.

The letters from FitzGerald and Forster directed Carlyle primarily toward the Anglo-Irish, and it was Duffy who provided the desired balance. The national hero could introduce him to Catholic Ireland as seen through the eyes of a sympathetic patriot. Of course, Carlyle's fame by itself opened many doors, though he often preferred not to step through. That he was visiting Ireland was common knowledge in London; the English authorities in Ireland were keenly aware of his presence. That he was being guided by Duffy was not to be taken lightly. Lord Clarendon, the British chief administrator who had been instrumental in indicting Duffy twice and in attempting to suppress the *Nation,* expressed his disapproval. By inviting Carlyle to visit at Phoenix Park, he made it clear where he thought the visitor should find his friends. Carlyle politely but emphatically made his position known. Whatever their disagreements, his heart was with Duffy.

A busy schedule of visits to well-known people in Dublin proved dull. The constant talk of "*England versus Ireland*" depressed him. But it did give him some insight into the pervasive Irish sense of alienation and victimization. As always, the tumult of travel set his nerves on edge. He was in "such a state of nerves" that he "couldn't *write*" his "name, except all in a tremulous, scratchy shiver."[19] He never doubted, though, that he had been right to come. This was a necessary experience. At University College Museum, he saw a "plaster cast" of one of his heroes and alter egos, Swift, with whose satiric tongue and acid vision he had been associated since his earliest college days. These days it might also be possible to find a correspondence between Swift's and his own obsessions about the condition of man and the state of the British Empire. He was visiting a city that Swift had lived in for many years. He was about to travel through a desperate and deprived country whose visible misery had inspired some of Swift's most devastating imagery in *Gulliver's Travels* and "A Modest Proposal."

After a week he was happy to leave Dublin "and environs" for Kildare and then Kilkenny. Dublin had seemed provincial, quiet. The city had no economic vigor; the streets were often empty of traffic. Compared to London, it was not a capital at all. The Irish leaders he met were spending their energies in sullen animosities rather than on the hard work of building an economy and a country. On Saturday, as he was riding through the muddy streets, a "car-boy, coming over one of the bridges, drives against the side of our car; seemed to me to see clearly for some instants that he *must* do such a thing, but to feel all the while that it would be so convenient to him *if* he didn't—a reckless humour, *ignoring* of the inevitable, which I saw often enough in Ireland."[20] Once outside of Dublin, however, the country seemed an unbalanced antiphony, huge hoards of impoverished beggars and occasional small model farms. As he entered, Kildare "looked worse and worse: one of the wretchedest wild villages . . . full of ragged beggars."[21] At Kilkenny the paupers and the workhouse were both wrenchingly painful to see. "The howl of a woman from the opposite flank of the valley, in wild rage of lamentation . . . like the *voice* of wretched Ireland at large."[22] At Waterford the dominant motif hardly changed. A few days later, in Cork, he heard the "loud song of the blind beggar on Lea Bridge; gave him a penny and stopped silently to listen: 'Oah Kehristins, may the Lard protec ye from the dangers av the night, and guide yer sowls, etc., etc.; and may ye never know what it is forever dark, and have no eyes—and for Kehroist's sake, lave a penny for the blind that can never see again!' "[23]

Catholicism, whose symbols were much in evidence, seemed one source of the country's miseries. It was not so much that the clergy had grown rich on the land and the labors of the people; indeed, this was usually not the case. But Carlyle saw much that confirmed his Protestant belief that Ireland's rejection of the Reformation had been a crucial factor in precipitating its modern misfortunes. To Carlyle, Catholicism was a religion of sloth and medieval corruption, and the Irish were a race of inferior Celts, whom the English visualized as both apishly bestial and mercurially irresponsible.[24] They were neither a Puritan nor a productive people; they lacked Protestant piety and seriousness, and the work ethic that Calvinism had used to build the modern commercial world was alien to them. If the Irish could only cast off old superstitions, Carlyle felt, they too could be redeemed. But, in the meantime, the problems were immediate and practical. Starving human beings of whatever religion or temperament had first to be fed and then to be taught how to feed themselves.

Carlyle's faith in education was considerable. The "facts" could make men free. "If the devil were passing through my country, and he applied to me for instruction in any truth or fact of this universe, I should wish to give it him. He is *less* a devil knowing that 3 and 3 are 6, than if he didn't know it. . . . If he knew *facts enough,* continuous light would dawn on him; he would (to his amazement) understand what this universe *is,* on what principles it conducts itself, and would *cease* to be a devil!"[25] These were not utilitarian but spiritual "facts." But it was necessary to start with the simple facts of arithmetic, common sense, and food production. When the young and the old were dying of starvation, these were the facts to teach first. By early July 1849 Carlyle had "already lost the heart to continue" his "old prayer . . . that potatoes might continue dead."[26] He was overwhelmed by the sight of naked starving children sent by their parents into the road to beg. The sight was more than horrible, for even "human *pity* does away into stony misery and disgust in the excess of such scenes."[27]

Arriving late in the month at Westport, in Mayo, he saw the largest concentration of the unemployed he could ever have imagined, almost half the population of sixty thousand, many of them begging, with the workhouse able to contain only three to four thousand. The workhouse itself seemed an "abomination." Instead of being organized into a productive work force, the men were forced into makeshift work whose uselessness demoralized them—for example, simply moving mounds of dirt from one location to another for no reason other than to comply with some sterile regulation. "Can it be a *charity,*" Carlyle asked, "to keep men alive on these terms?" His outrage burst into exaggerated rhetoric, the extreme terms of a man who believed he could express the full misery and pain of what he was seeing only by invoking such horrible crimes as bloodshed and murder. "In face of all the twaddle of the earth, shoot a man rather than train him (with heavy expense to his neighbors) to be a deceptive human *swine.*"[28] But at the same time he was clearly aware that the local and national landlords who took more from the land than they put back into it were the real causes of this misery.

Not everything in Ireland, however, was as grim as this; and there were moments both of personal and social pleasure. On the way to Cork, he and Duffy stopped at Youghal, "a dingy town" but one whose bay and harbor sweetly reminded him of a song called "Youghall Harbor" which Alick had often sung as a boy. At Cork a slightly drunk, squat, red-faced priest burst in with explosive welcome. The man who announced himself as Father O'Shea had been "one of the two souls in the world," besides Jane, "who approved of *Sartor* in Fraser's time."[29] Emerson had been the other of the voices from the distance which had meant so much at a time when the adverse reaction to the serial publication of *Sartor Resartus* had threatened to alienate the publisher and to sink a career that had hardly begun. Carlyle had thought Father O'Shea long dead but, to his delight, the priest now proved lively and hospitable. O'Shea insisted on arranging both an excursion and a dinner that, though the latter was "much too crowded," showed to advantage both the beauty of Cork in the twilight and the gentle spirit of this man who had touched his life so long ago.

Despite his lack of sleep, Carlyle managed to impress those he met, and especially those he liked, with his conversational good spirits, as if he were unquestionably enjoying the opportunities that travel created. In the coach on the way to Sligo, Duffy and Carlyle were joined by "a young bride and bridegroom on their honeymoon. . . . The bride was charming, and Carlyle courteously talked to her about sightseeing and the pleasures of traveling . . . like a man who never had a care. . . . He was as much disconcerted . . . as a beau of four-and-twenty" to learn later that the bride had taken advantage of his absence from the coach for a moment to ask Duffy, " 'Who is the twaddling old Scotchman who allows no one to utter a word but himself?' "[30] Duffy, however, never tired of hearing his mentor talk. He took advantage of the long hours they spent together to pump him with a wide variety of questions, particularly about famous literary people whom Carlyle knew. Years later, in *Conversations with Carlyle,* he reconstructed Carlyle's pungent remarks into brief essays and character sketches, capturing some of the flavor of his talk as they jolted over dusty roads and across picturesque mountains. Though Carlyle complained that his young Irish friend was not particularly well organized and found it barely forgivable that he slept so soundly, Duffy was as good a traveling companion as he could ever have had—a man who loved and admired Carlyle, a special kind of disciple and son. After a short separation, they reunited at Limerick, in the rain, at a confused railroad station: "and Duffy stands there, with sad loving smile, a glad sight to me after all."[31]

Visits with a variety of Anglo-Irish and Catholic Irish, from FitzGerald's uncle to Sir William and Lady Beacher (the latter had once been a "famous Irish actress"), proved to have less relevance and emotional impact than his constant search for men of action who were actually doing something constructive about Irish poverty. It was easy for Carlyle to bewail the absence of such men. But, conversely, he was prepared to appreciate even more those few instances in which he could find hope for the future.

The creation of a sound agricultural economy seemed to Carlyle the prime requisite for the salvation of Ireland. But the production of food to feed the population depended on the attitudes, skills, organization, and capital investment that the Irish themselves lacked: the soil needed to be made arable through draining, irrigation, and fertilization; labor needed to be organized, disciplined, and properly rewarded. The first step, Carlyle believed, had already been taken in the creation of model farms, which were usually owned and managed by practical but idealistic English and Scotch who brought with them the agricultural techniques of more successful countries. What was needed was not charity or "welfare" but work—real work, productive work; whereas "welfare" perpetuated and even increased economic and spiritual misery, work promised rebirth for the individual and the nation. But he did not see how the Irish could rise from misery and barbarism without leadership that transcended partisan politics and party interests.

Forster, "very blue in the face, but otherwise brisk and lively," joined him in Mayo late in July, only to dash off again on business.[32] When

Duffy returned to Dublin, Forster suddenly reappeared in Donegal, where Carlyle had made a new friend, Lord George Hill. Of all the men Carlyle met in Ireland, he probably admired Hill the most, "an exceedingly beautiful little man" whose "sad and grievous enterprise" is "to reclaim these savages" and "these desolate bogs. . . . A fine, nimble, gravely-smiling, most earnest truthful and courteous little man of fifty," with an "*elegant* club-nose, and intellectually protrusive mouth."[33] Carlyle liked him immediately, not only for himself but for his works. Much of his energy and fortune were being invested in the attempt to turn his large estate into a productive model farm: the bogs had been drained, hardy crops planted, enclosures constructed, schools opened. He had been at it for almost twenty years, with some success.

But the "dismal moors" were recalcitrant, and Lord George found himself struggling with the need to persuade as he attempted to educate the peasantry into more productive habits and commitments. To Carlyle, it seemed as if Prospero and Caliban had changed places: a noble man enslaving himself to slaves who were far beneath him in education, intelligence, and spiritual dedication. This was "the largest attempt at benevolence and beneficence on the *modern* system (the emancipation, all-for-liberty, abolition of capital-punishment, roast-goose-at-Christmas system)" he had ever seen, and he did not believe it could possibly prosper. Those who were by talent and training equipped to be leaders should lead; those who had neither the talent nor the training should follow. Otherwise, it seemed to Carlyle, hunger, brutality, misery, and materialism would inevitably result. What good were liberalism and democracy if they produced injustice and chaos, no matter how well intentioned and inherently noble some of its practitioners? Lord George was ignorant, not evil. The fault lay in the misconceptions and the misarrangements: the quality Carlyle thought of as "wisdom"—common sense and an appreciation of arithmetic and spiritual "facts"—was tragically missing.

After being shown over the estate on a long day early in August 1849, he "finally" went to bed "with pathetic feelings, gratitude, sorrow, *love* for this noble man, and *hope* as if *beyond* the grave!"[34] Ironically, the crops were excellent that year, even the potatoes. Despite "beggary" and "rags," Carlyle was convinced that Ireland "*will* surely improve." He could not resist being hopeful, no matter how deep his pessimism and his fear. He had often enough exchanged with his mother the conviction that "this earth is the place of hope." If one day he was in despair, the next he raised his eyes. Ireland was redeemable. For "seeds of great improvement are germinating visibly everywhere."[35] Late in the first week of August he sailed from Londonderry, "the prettiest-looking town" he had "seen in Ireland." Fortunately, he had no crystal ball in which to see the future misery of that striking city, "rising *red* and beautiful on [an] elevated hill."[36] In a little more than a day the overnight steamer brought industrial Glasgow into sight, like "pulses of some huge iron-furnace."[37] The contrast between failed agriculture and flourishing industry, between the horror of the primitive past and the ugliness of the industrial future, was striking. But at least in Scotland there was thrift, sobriety, industry, and order, "fenced fields, weeded crops, and human creatures with whole clothes on their backs."[38] The next day he was at Scotsbrig.

3.

As he arrived in Scotland late in the summer of 1849, Carlyle had none too secure a grip on a number of the strands of his life. He had gone to Ireland in order to prepare himself to write a book, but its shape and substance remained as ill defined as they had been before the visit. His nervous system was tense with his need to express his emotions—anger, outrage, fear, and a volatile mixture of tenuous hope and heavy gloom. But now, in the bosom of the family again, he tried to rest and revive himself, with some success. Fortunately, that summer found his mother reasonably well and active for a woman of seventy-eight. She read a great deal, and mother and son had long talks.

Jane was also in relatively good health during the spring and summer of 1849, good enough, in fact, to travel to Scotland for the first time since her mother's death. She visited William Forster at Rawdon, and then, while he "shot off for Ireland" to meet Carlyle, she went northward to confront the past and the dead.[39] Just to be in Scotland again was nerve-wracking. Her mother's grave at Crawford and the site of her death at Templand were too formidable to confront; they would have to be approached gradually. She decided to go first to Haddington to revisit scenes from her childhood. She went unannounced, determined to confront her memories alone before visiting her old friends, the Donaldsons, whose home at Sunnybank in Haddington quietly glowed with some of her sweetest remembrances. It was now the nearest thing she had to a home in Scotland. Her first evening in Haddington she sat alone for a while "amidst the silence of death" at the George Inn, where she had been shown to the best room. Almost thirty years before, Edward Irving and a young man whom she had just met for the first time had stayed the night there while visiting her in Haddington. The streets, the houses (her former home, where she had spent that part of her life in which her father had been alive) seemed the same, "but so silent, dead petrified!" And "the churchyard had become very full of graves."[40]

Attempting to remain anonymous, she arranged to be escorted to the church, as if she were a tourist. She looked at the family pew "in the dim twilight till I almost fancied I saw my beautiful mother in her old corner, and myself, a bright-looking girl in the other!" Her actions and the dimmed outlines of her youthful appearance provoked the elderly guide to recognize her. When she revealed her name the next day to another resident, "he looked pleased, and asked how many children I had had. 'None,' I told him. 'None?' in a tone of astonishment verging on horror. 'None at all? then what on earth had I been doing all this time?' 'Amusing myself,' I told him."[41] In Edinburgh, her "mother's old nurse," whom she had not seen for twenty year, said, " 'there's no a featur o' ye left but just the bit smile!' "[42]

During the rigors of his Irish journey Carlyle had had more than a few thoughts to spare for his wife in Scotland. Words of comfort and commiseration flowed quite readily from the distance. He knew what pain the return to Haddington had caused her; yet for the past few years he had been hoping that once she had gained the courage to confront the complex emotions represented by the country in which her mother had died and in which so much of herself had been left behind, she would indeed have taken a considerable step toward restoring her health. He understood that his wife felt orphaned. She needed the assurance that she was loved as a child is loved, unhesitatingly and without reservation, loved in the way he felt that his own mother loved him. And she needed to have her self-esteem restored.

But for her self-esteem he could do little. More often than not and without intending it he damaged and decreased her sense of self-worth simply by being himself—self-involved, irritable. He shut her out from his work; in company together, his urge to dominate the conversation often reduced her to his subordinate; and much more often than not he preferred to take his recreation either with male friends or by himself. He could not imagine anyone might conclude from this that he valued her less. Occasionally, he actually ministered to her need to feel loved. From Ireland, aware of her journey to Haddington, he assured her that his "heart" was "sore for" her. He wrote that she could feel certain that there was "one soul still alive who can never cease to love thee. Yes, after his own wild way,—stern as the way of death,—to love thee: that is a truth, and will remain one."[43]

But Carlyle's "own wild way" had curious twists. The warmth of his love was stronger at a distance. His actions rarely directed themselves toward her needs, especially when some need of his own intervened, as so often happened. When their separate travels finally converged in the middle of August, they managed to spend only a few days together. Carlyle insisted that he had to honor an invitation to join the Ashburtons for autumn hunting at their rented estate in the Highlands. Though urged to join them at Glen Truim, Jane refused. She preferred to make the rounds of Haddington, Edinburgh, and even Scotsbrig rather than be a dependent of her husband's dependency on Lady Harriet's company. Hurt and furious, she felt as if she had been slapped in the face again, as if the agreement they had made three years before had been unilaterally abrogated. They parted unhappily. Worst of all, he insisted that he did not deserve her anger.[44] At Glen Truim, he felt irritated by the small crowded house, the merciless rain, the cold, fireless, hunting-lodge ethic, the absurdity of hunting in general and particularly where there was no game, and the vast expenditure (about £1200) on inferior quarters. Jane shortly refused Lady Harriet's invitation that the Carlyles come to the Grange for a long visit in the autumn. Lady Harriet somewhat tartly answered that she too "should be very glad to live a little alone if it were possible also. The only drawback on my enjoyment here has been the number of people—with only two servants."[45] Jane would have been happier if the number of guests had been one less.

At Scotsbrig she felt constrained. There was a momentary flutter about her health, perhaps her heart, that Jack attended to but that seemed only an isolated episode. Intensely angry at her husband, she found it even harder than usual to be among the Carlyle clan, who seemed so obsessively intimate with one another. She could hardly complain to them about what was really bothering her. Even in her letters to the sister-in-law for whom she felt most affection, Jean Aitken, she had to confess that "I durst not let myself *talk* to you at Scotsbrig" and that she preferred that her letter be burned as soon as read. She still did not complain of her husband directly to her husband's family. For "there is a circulation of letters in families that frightens me from writing often—it is so difficult to write a circular to one."[46] Because she felt that she could not confide in all the Carlyles, she felt that she could not confide in any one of them. And she had no family of her own, except perhaps Mary Russell at Thornhill, to whom she could write from the heart.

Back in Chelsea late in September, she was glad that she had "been in Scotland once more."[47] But she felt exhausted; she needed morphine to relieve her pain and sleeplessness. By early October her husband was home also. He informed his family that Jane seemed much improved. But she protested bitterly that, whatever her health, "Mr. C's 'decidedly stronger' is never to be depended on or any account he gives of me—as so long as I can stand on my legs he never notices that any thing ails me, and I make a point of never *complaining* to him unless in case of absolute extremity."[48] The best end to her "useless existence" would be withdrawal from life, though her sense of guilt on this matter prevented her from being explicit about the quickest exit.[49]

What could he do about her unhappiness when he felt that he had more than enough of his own to confront? His mother suddenly became sick at the beginning of October 1849, though fortunately Jack was there to look after her. At the same time, his head ached with the memory of what he had seen in Ireland. The visit had been "painfully impressive and oppressive." "Under the sky at present" there seemed "no such detestable and profoundly damnable spectacle as . . . the West of Ireland."[50] So moving had the experience been that, for the moment, he did not want to talk about Ireland at all. His own "passage thro' it" had been "like a bit of the Flight of Satan Thro' Chaos."[51] And, like Lucifer, he felt the threat of both chaos and despair as he passed through middle age. Much of his capacity to feel, he thought, had been diminished by time and circumstance, by endless quarrels, baffled hopes, and persistent anxieties. His strong opinions, his forceful personality, and his introspective involvement with his work made the armor that hardened around him increasingly impervious. "I consider it good, however, that one do not get into the state of a beetle," he wrote to Jane, "that one try to keep one's shell open, or at least openable."

He meant to "persist" in trying.[52] No doubt he had been successful with Lady Harriet and his mother; but much less so with Jane and most others. For so much, and especially for his childhood and family, "all the old tremulous affection lies in me, but it is as if frozen . . . lain down in a kind of iron sleep."[53] When young, in moods of indolence and frustration, he had imagined that he was under a kind of enchantment whose spell he would soon break. But now he had no expectation that he could break the spell except through work. Only through work could he feel useful and whole again. But the greater his effort, whether successful or not, the less time, energy, and flexibility he would have for Jane, who desperately needed his attention. His own desperation, however, was stronger than his commitment to her needs. His work came first. And Lady Harriet, he felt, was necessary to that work.

Carlyle did not think his wife's humiliation or angry withdrawal too high a price to pay for Lady Harriet's company. Indeed, since it was not he who was asking that price, he thought he was not really responsible for the fact that Jane insisted on paying it and forced him to share the expense. If only she would recover that vague thing called her "health," he was certain that she would see his relationship with Lady Harriet in a different light. But, frequently ill with headaches, bodyaches, nausea, colds, sleeplessness, and exhaustion, Jane was probably in a particularly difficult menopause as well—childless, vocationally unfulfilled, and with a husband whose interests seemed to lie elsewhere. The prattle of literary wits like "old Rogers," who teasingly asked her at a party if her "husband" was "as much infatuated as ever with Lady Ashburton," did not allow her to forget that there was also a public dimension to her humiliation. Every time the door at Cheyne Row closed behind her husband on his way to Bath House, she felt it had shut painfully on her heart. Each time she went with him, the experience was miserable enough to make the next decision about whether to go or not torturously difficult. When she had the energy there were arguments, otherwise not, but despite the obstructions he still went to Bath House, so strong was his need. And he continued to write secretly to his "Queen" in intimate terms. "O heaven! God save the Queen—my own Queen" whom he could "always . . . see" with his "mind," in spite of "all the Devils!"[54]

Unfortunately, no one and nothing allowed him to make "cosmos" out of the "chaos" of his ideas and feelings about Ireland; the kind of book he valued and wanted to write seemed unrealizable. Neither Jane nor Lady Harriet could help. He had some fragments that he had written during the previous year, some of them early in the summer. But they did not deal with Ireland directly and, more troubling, they did not cohere into any wholeness of form and statement. Perhaps he could begin to get his thoughts in order and the material under better control if he were to write a chronological account of his tour of Ireland. He had no intention of publishing it. He desired to clear his "own mind, as some kind of 'preparation for action.' "[55] And the very act of writing itself was cathartic. Despite his exhaustion, he began to write his "Reminiscences of My Irish Journey in 1849" a few days after his return from Scotland and finished it just after the middle of August. Without showing it to anyone, he stored it away in the bureau drawer in which he had been collecting over the years small bundles, some of them carefully tied, of all sorts of disparate manuscripts, destined in his own mind for either posterity or, more likely, oblivion. He would do the same with his "Excursion (Futile Enough) To Paris," which he was to write the next year.

Regrettably, Carlyle's sense of his mission and his definition of himself as a writer did not permit him to give serious consideration to publishing travel accounts or personal journals; in his opinion, it was something that serious writers did not do. Thus, Carlyle did nothing to prevent Thackeray from learning of his disapproval when the novelist took free passage and perquisites as partial payment for his writing about his travel experiences to the Middle East, as if his pen were for hire. (By October 1850, it was no longer an issue between them; Thackeray, who was seriously ill, had had to stop for the time all work on *Pendennis.*) Carlyle, who always felt compelled to write accounts of his external experiences as well as his inner ruminations, had a sharp eye for the visually significant and a marvelous memory that could recall physical details and the emotional ambience of the people and places he had visited. But his background and his principles constrained him from the full expression of these talents.

However, his need to express himself on serious issues was not to be balked by his inability to discover an appropriate book-length form for his ideas and feelings. The "black mass of a 'Book' " that he had within him might be discharged in small, more manageable parts. He felt a fire burning within, but at the same time he felt himself immersed in "a *continent* of foul liquid" and mud.[56] He reached for some cleansing power, which he visualized as fire, some "divine rage," whose hot anger would burn away the confusion and the filth. Aware that such a flame might also burn away the author himself, he felt that such a sacrifice might well be justified by the benefits that would result from his endeavor. In order to begin writing he needed to convince himself that what he would write would make a difference—a conviction he could never maintain for very long. And in this instance the controversial nature of his subject demanded that he be prepared to consume himself in the effort.

By November 1849 Carlyle had finished an essay called "Occasional Discourse on the Nigger Question," which *Fraser's Magazine* published at the end of the month. He attempted to write a new essay deploring the results of laissez-faire policy, "Leave It Alone; Time Will Mend It," but the fragment went into the drawer with the other unpublished material. By the middle of December, he felt that he was in the writing vein again. His subject was "democracy," "work," "labor," "modern government"; his vision that of the interplay between unalterable "facts" and human manipulation. The main question was "whether it ought to be as a Book or as a Series of Pamphlets."[57] By the new year, he had not only decided but had already begun what he conceived of as his own "*Tracts for the Times,*" a series of pamphlets, probably twelve in all, to be published in monthly installments over the next year. Writing quickly, he had completed the first two before the middle of January 1850, the first a general introduction to his opinions about democracy called "The New Era," the second a practical example of the folly produced by an application of democracy to "Model Prisons."[58] The entire work was to be entitled *Latter-Day Pamphlets,* a title with curious overtones of both religion and journalism, fiery vision and strident propaganda; the vision was basically religious, but the voice was shrill and satiric.

Now that he had "decided at last to give vent" to himself, regardless of the consequences, his anger expressed itself with less restraint than ever before.[59] He appreciated the practical advantage of being pursued every month by the printer, the "devil" at the door bringing proof sheets and waiting to carry away corrected copy. Such a procedure demanded that he write quickly, and second thoughts were thus less likely and certainly more difficult to act upon. Unquestionably, he would have been more satisfied had he been able to create in his imagination and then transform into a book the major and perhaps final work he had for so long conceived of. "With painful intense distillation" this "might perhaps have been done,—perhaps should have been?—but in" his "heart there remained no longer patience enough for that feat on such a subject: so a Book of *Sermons* is what you get, some dozen or so." With "only one . . . to be done at a time, this is a much easier way of harnessing oneself."[60]

As the months went by, however, Carlyle became increasingly aware that serial publication also had disadvantages. Though he recognized at the outset that "these Pamphlets" were "sure to shock and enrage great quantities of people," he overestimated his own ability to withstand the vehemence of the criticism that surfaced month by month.[61] And the comparative formlessness of the conception left the project more vulnerable to criticism than would have been the case had it been structured by the devices of serial fiction or at least completed in advance of publication. Though he had decided that there would "probably" be twelve such pamphlets in addition to "An Occasional Discourse," he had no precise sense of what the later sections would contain and was primarily trying to endow his rather formless literary concept with at least a temporal symmetry. The broad subjects were clear; he knew his own mind about them. But the length to which he would extend or curtail his comments would not be dictated by any literary determination about wholeness and structure. If his energy declined, if he felt that he had said enough, he could just as well end after ten "sermons."

By the beginning of February 1850, when the first pamphlet appeared, he was ready to confess that it was "a questionable enterprise," but that he "could not help it," whatever the "loud astonishment" and "condemnation."[62] Writing itself was his "remedy for all misery," but "that unfortunately is itself a misery."[63] He rode up from the Grange, to which he had made a short visit without Jane, aware that Richard Milnes's and Lady Harriet's reactions, as they read his pamphlet on the train, were not enthusiastic. Erasmus Darwin was "rather alarmed, as one can't stand a great deal of such stuff." One segment of the literary world agreed with Anthony Trollope's private comment that he had long looked on Carlyle "as a man who was always in danger of going mad in literature and who has now done so."[64] However, Carlyle was determined not to be shaken by hostile response, or even by the most undermining kind of praise, barely sincere cool phrases from friends. But doing the work was "terrible . . . so lonely as I am, no man sharing my adventure."[65] Still, the public was buying the pamphlets; at least he was being read. Chapman, delighted by the " 'vigorous sale,' " urged him on.[66] The "last *Punch* was full of barking and bantering . . . which gratifies Chapman amazingly."[67] The public reaction was pungent, satiric, outraged. Various "sects" discovered that whatever aspect of Carlyle they had previously taken for the whole and used to absorb him into their own ranks could no longer be distorted or seen in sufficient isolation. The second pamphlet, "Model Prisons," was out at the beginning of March. After a great deal of difficulty in bringing the material under control, Carlyle divided what was to have been the third pamphlet into two parts, each dealing with "Downing Street" and the nature of political and moral leadership in the modern world. The first section was published at the beginning of April, the second in the middle of the same month. By that time he had already finished writing the fourth pamphlet, "Stump-Orator," and late in April he was struggling with the sixth, "Parliaments."

He still had it in his mind to do a "dozen," but his energy and commitment were waning.[68] The writing now was more painful than pleasurable. Despite his stubbornness and defiance, the hostile reaction unnerved him, though he fought hard against admitting it even to himself. Suddenly his health seemed uncertain, and within a short while he thought of himself as wretchedly ill.[69] By the end of May the disease had been located in the familiar physical centers of his lifelong psychogenetic despair, the "liver and stomach and whole inside machinery . . . which aggravates every other distress and confusion (and I have my private share of these too)" about which he would "hold" his "tongue." If only his "poor *clay case* were like other people's," then life would have been and would be so "*easy*."[70] He had already finished the seventh pamphlet. He could not help thinking how much easier it would be if he simply stopped at eight. "I think sometimes of making out the dozen; but ten seems likelier for the present; nay something (a cowardly something) whispers occasionally, 'If the thing grow *too* hot, you may finish with *eight*,' which is only one more."[71]

By June 1850 he confided to his mother that he had decided that the eighth, "Jesuitism," would "be the last. It will be a great relief to be out of that job."[72] The seventh was scheduled for the first of July, the eighth, which he was already writing, for the first of August. In early July the death of Robert Peel, the one man who Carlyle hoped might fulfill the model of leadership presented in *Latter-Day Pamphlets,* seemed to provide an ironic addendum to his decision to stop at eight.

Carlyle was not ashamed of his *Pamphlets.* They had been "beautifully abused, and extensively read."[73] But he had little hope that they would really make any practical difference. Now he wanted to rest. There was nothing wrong with his health, he assured his mother, that rest and

Thomas Carlyle. Sketch by Richard Doyle, c. 1855. Reprinted from *New Letters of Thomas Carlyle,* edited by A. Carlyle (London, 1904).

sleep would not cure. Indeed, "a sleep amid the wilderness of Craigenputtoch itself" seemed "almost inviting."[74] Late in July 1850 he left for Wales, via Bath, where he was to visit Walter Landor, and for Scotsbrig.

4.

To many of Carlyle's contemporaries the publication of *Latter-Day Pamphlets* represented a dividing point in his career, and to some extent it was, though more in appearance than in fact, more in reputation than in substance. What he dared to write in *Latter-Day Pamphlets* he had already said many times before, though in different ways and in more guarded tones and phrases. The sermon form and the serial procedure both heightened the intensity of the separate parts and extended the period during which the work was the focus of excited attention. For a short while the best known of his works, it consequently played an undeservedly pivotal role in shaping how his audience looked at him thereafter. Whatever its actual qualities, the exaggerated and distorted response to the book was unfortunate for Carlyle's future influence and stature as a writer. Part of the fault, of course, was the author's; *Latter-Day Pamphlets* has much sense in it and many merits; its crucial failure is not that of substance but of literary form.

In *Latter-Day Pamphlets,* Carlyle's anger overwhelmed his artistry. He was an impatient and often an angry man. But there were depths of tenderness as well, for "much of his fierceness is an inverted tenderness," as Mark Rutherford realized.[75] Certainly the decision to publish his views in serially published "sermons" was a mistake in judgment which undercut the possibility that his anger would be subordinated to form. But the deeper source of Carlyle's failure to make an artistic success of *Latter-Day Pamphlets* was the accumulated fatigue, anxiety, indecision, and anger that had brought him at the age of fifty-five to think that much of life was behind him, that satisfying human relationships were difficult if not impossible, and that neither his own frame of mind nor the condition of his culture permitted him the liberality of imagination and the concentration of intellect which great works of art demand.

What Carlyle had to say, even if he had found an appropriate form, would still have been disagreeable to many. But his criticism of modern democratic culture, even at its most extreme, always contained a degree of cogency. He himself tended to exaggerate the potential offensiveness of his criticism, probably because throughout his life he feared alienating from himself those whose values he rejected but whose affection, even love, he desired. He was not alone in calling attention to fundamental flaws in the procedures and values of the new society. But he was probably the only Victorian of national stature and prominent literary gifts—with the exception of his disciple John Ruskin—who stepped forward to deliver sharp criticism in a distinctive voice. Carlyle was not the only one who feared rule by the lowest common denominator. Nor was he alone in his condemnation of bureaucracy, political propaganda, false promises, laissez-faire, uninspired and self-serving leaders, and unlimited exploitation of the working people. Tyranny and repression, however, were no solution: Carlyle did not believe that leadership entailed the abrogation of civil liberties and the destruction of the state's respect for the integrity of the individual. Nor did his conclusion that the ballot box rarely if ever produced collective wisdom mean that those who governed should be independent of the will of the governed.

On the contrary, Carlyle was convinced that it was not possible to govern without the consent and the approval of the people, whose "opinions . . . are the unspoken sense of man's heart, and well deserve attending to. . . . It will be . . . indispensable, for the King or Governor to know what the mass of men think upon public questions. . . . To which end, Parliaments, Free Presses, and suchlike are excellent." Without in some way "knowing" what the people think, "[the leader] has not a possibility to govern at all."[76] As a student of revolutions, Carlyle could not imagine that any government could remain in power indefinitely without the consent of the majority of those it governed. Such a government would eventually collapse because it was unwise in its policies and unjust in its distribution of the wealth and the privileges of the community. But, to establish justice and wisdom in the nation, its leaders needed to be just and wise. The purpose of any nation was to put such leaders in power. The critical question was, how to do it?

Carlyle argued that people exhibit a natural tendency to recognize and give power to superior people—superior in intelligence, moral stature, and sometimes in education. The source of such superiority was neither high birth nor worldly power but the mysterious spiritual forces that Carlyle described in vague religious terms, sometimes drawing on his Calvinistic inheritance to talk of "God," other times on his nineteenth-century ethos to talk of "world-force" and "vital energy of the universe." The distinction inhered, so to speak, in the genes. And the complex interaction between what "God" contributed and what the environment contributed was so subtle, mysterious, and ultimately incomprehensible that it was a mark of wisdom to accept the beauty and the inexplicability of what could never be understood in rational terms.

For Carlyle, the wise man recognized that the universe was organized hierarchically, with a responsible world-force or God of justice at the apex, whose definition was moral and spiritual, not amoral and materialistic. Such a hierarchical view of cosmic organization implies that some human beings are higher in the scale than others. Though Carlyle believed in the sacredness of each individual, he emphasized differentness rather than equality. Whereas we are all equal before the divine force, we are all different in our talents and capacities. The evidence of common sense clearly reveals these differences, and these differences demand that different human beings fulfill different functions. To the extent that education could make human beings wiser—more capable of discovering and fulfilling their abilities and more accepting of their roles in society—he strongly advocated education. Too little of the nation's resources of both money and wisdom were being devoted to that crucial enterprise.

But Carlyle believed that the natural tendency to accept a vertical structure in God's and man's world and to find wise leaders was being balked by misconceptions, endless stupidity, and a conspiracy on the part of people who embodied a fatal combination of sentimentality and materialism. If the purpose of democracy—or rule by the people—was to provide for the nation wise and effective leadership, capable of creating policies to deal with the needs of the present, then clearly democracy was not succeeding. "Where there is a Pauper, there is a sin; to make one Pauper there go many sins. Pauperism is our Social Sin grown manifest."[77] Collective wisdom was a fragile thing; collective ignorance and collective error seemed dominant. Democracy, like all other political systems, had as its foremost aim the installation of effective leaders, chosen without regard to birth or wealth. In Carlyle's eyes, it was proving a dismal failure.

The adage that a nation often gets the rulers it deserves, men who embody the values of the culture that has created them, was often on Carlyle's mind. But he did believe in the honesty and the nobility of the British common man, and, in the months that he worked on *Latter-Day Pamphlets,* the possibility that Peel would soon return to power seemed to suggest that all was not lost. If a minister of real worth were in office, then the people he governed would have their value and their values authenticated by their choice. One strong-willed man of wisdom could, in the proper office, make all the difference: he could initiate the changes that would restore "honesty and sense" to government and to the nation. Peel was not the hero of *Latter-Day Pamphlets,* as has sometimes been suggested. But he was a potential hero of the nation, a man whose very existence demonstrated that the nation was probably governed by rulers who were worse than it deserved. But how much worse, Carlyle realized, only time would tell.

In addition, the delusion that wisdom in electoral matters and state decisions can be achieved through the ballot box seemed to Carlyle inseparable from the widespread conviction, particularly among the non-evangelical middle and upper classes, that morality is relative and a private matter. The shifting public standard relied on social acceptability rather than on the interaction between absolute principle and the individual moral conscience. Morality itself, for Carlyle, was a hierarchical concept. Human intellect and moral conscience can distinguish between the relative value of different acts and thoughts and establish a scale of preference in a formal arrangement that makes it absolutely clear which are superior. One of the characteristics of wise men is their ability to see more clearly than the rest of humanity the preferred modes of thought and conduct. But inherent within democracy, Carlyle believed, was the worship of the lowest common denominator, not the highest morality but the base middle ground, the compromise that ultimately made the wishes of the majority the standard by which thought and action are judged. If the majority wished to avoid all such judgments in its pursuit of material advantages, then wisdom was irrelevant and morality a completely relative matter. Material expediency itself became the standard. And if one rejected hierarchy and wisdom, then why should one not also reject sexual restrictions and moral scruples? For Carlyle, they could not be separated. He had no doubt that "Phallus-worship" and the new religion of sex and sentimentality contributed to social chaos and moral confusion. From George Sand to Geraldine Jewsbury, from France to England, the future in regard to women, marriage, sex, and social stability seemed to him potentially more pagan than Judeo-Christian. Even if Moses or Christ should return, the England of the future would provide no role for either of them.

It seemed clear to Carlyle that the defeat of Presbyterian values at the end of the seventeenth century and the general victory of Counter-Reformation attitudes—typified for him by the career of Ignatius Loyola and the creation of "Jesuitism"—had marked the beginning of Britain's gradual descent into materialism and all that followed. With biting sarcasm he called it the "Pig Philosophy," and listed its dominant tenets, among them that "the Universe, so far as sane conjecture can go, is an immeasurable Swine's-trough, consisting of solid and liquid," and that "moral evil is unattainability of Pig's-wash; moral good, attainability of ditto." Paradise is the "unlimited attainability of Pig's-wash; perfect fulfillment of one's wishes, so that the Pig's imagination could not outrun reality," for "it is the mission of universal Pighood, and the duty of all Pigs, at all times, to diminish the quantity of unattainable and increase that of attainable."[78] But the inevitable result of materialism, Carlyle insisted, was the unsatisfying pursuit of that which, if it could ever be realized, would prove abysmally unsatisfying. Whatever man's material and technological accomplishments, they would never answer, even for "pigs," the need for spiritual achievement and communal harmony. The final words of *Latter-Day Pamphlets* rise beyond the rhetoric of despair into both a warning and a hope:

> Mount into your railways; whirl from place to place, at the rate of fifty, or if you like of five hundred miles an hour: you cannot escape from that inexorable all-encircling ocean-moan of ennui. No: if you would mount to the stars, and do yacht-voyages under the belts of Jupiter, or stalk deer on

> the ring of Saturn, it would still begirdle you. You cannot escape from it, you can but change your place in it, without solacement except one moment's. That prophetic Sermon from the Deeps will continue with you, till you wisely interpret it and do it, or else till the Crack of Doom swallow it and you.[79]

5.

The practical proposals that Carlyle presents in *Latter-Day Pamphlets* are not the most important aspect of the book, but they are relevant and forceful. In order to strengthen the executive and liberate it from the vagaries of the ballot box, he proposed that ten appointive ministerial positions be created, each with a vote and a voice in Parliament. The prime minister, acting not as the leader of his party but as the queen's representative, that is, as the leader of the nation, would choose the ten wisest, most hard-working men in the country, regardless of their class, wealth, party affiliation, or previous profession. They would be put in charge of the most important ministries, particularly Foreign Affairs, the Home Office, and the Office of Education. The prime minister, himself an elected official, would take ultimate responsibility for the acts of these appointed ministers.

The minister of education would be given the power to reform the existing establishment completely. The level to which people would be educated would depend on talent, regardless of birth or wealth. The system would be universal, demanding a certain minimum level of education. And the educational procedure, though it would certainly stress factual information, the teaching of both "what" and "how" as knowledge and vocation, would also emphasize moral and spiritual values. Carlyle believed that the problems of "The Irish Giant called Despair," in all its various forms, were susceptible to the corrective of vocational training and universal "work." But the primary function of the educational system must be to perpetuate and reinforce the highest moral and spiritual standards of the community, to teach both the rejection of materialism and the embrace of wisdom. Once such a system was working effectively, then the problems of the economy, of foreign affairs, and of national leadership would be considerably less severe: the discipline of work would be enforced; the promotion of emigration would relieve the pressure of excess population at home and create a worldwide Anglo-Saxon hegemony; the true well-being of England would be seen to lie in amity with its world neighbors; and the community at large would both create and authenticate its own wise leaders.

Carlyle did not think such a scheme particularly utopian. Despite the widespread dominance of materialism and the "Pig Philosophy," he was reasonably confident that the English people had the capability to recognize and accept effective leaders. The instincts of man were inherently good, capable of responding to the noble and the divine. Years before he had said in "Characteristics" that self-consciousness was the modern disease, yet he believed that most human beings had preserved an instinctive un-selfconsciousness in regard to certain fundamental emotions. He had no doubt that such emotions and a belief in them were still widely shared and could help society attain the common consent that would produce communal health. No matter how corrupt the society, there remained within individual human beings responses that reflected an instinctive awareness of good and evil and the divine facts that governed the universe.[80] If these could be drawn on, then indeed the community at large could be transformed into a moral force for order and harmony. Though the community could not lead, it could instinctively recognize and respond to leadership.

To Carlyle, Peel had seemed the only possibility for such leadership. Carlyle had certainly misjudged the extent to which parliamentary convention and the intricacies of political maneuvering influenced Peel's performance; but his unexpected death left *Latter-Day Pamphlets* even further removed from the political realities of Britain at midcentury. Inherent in Carlyle's vision was the belief that without a leader to initiate the change the whole program was unrealizable. He had no doubt that there were at least ten wise men in the kingdom to fill the appointive positions. Indeed, there is good reason to believe that he himself hoped to be chosen to fill the position of minister of education, if his scheme were ever acted on. Throughout the 1840s the prospect of becoming a man of action, a public actor rather than a private thinker, had attracted him strongly. His Calvinistic heritage and his attitude toward work and the world had saddled him with ambivalent feelings about whether what he did as a writer was actually work. And since it was to him a painful profession, and not necessarily the best mode of fulfilling his spiritual mission, he could not resist imagining that he would be happier and a more useful member of society if he played some more active role, perhaps in government. Given his friendship with Bingham Baring and his relationship with Peel, the possibility of a new career in public service was more than wishful thinking. But after Peel's death, not even a wishful thought seemed possible.

[14]

"Imperfect Sleep"
1851–1857

The writing of *Latter-Day Pamphlets* had been Carlyle's most intense attempt to speak directly on public matters and perhaps to promote one final effort to involve himself directly in public affairs. However, the combination of Peel's death and the hostile reaction to the *Pamphlets* sent him hastily back to creative and scholarly solitude. Having shouted at the top of his voice to no avail, Carlyle collapsed into a renewed appreciation of silence. Charles Redwood, in his new cottage at Boverton, Cowbridge, South Wales, provided early in August 1850 "the most perfect hermitage," including a kind of tree house in which he could sit, smoke, and gaze at the sea in the distance.[1] From this vantage point, as so often when they were apart, Carlyle found that the noisy tension between Jane and himself became a more harmonious music. Recognizing that much of her pain was self-inflicted, Jane tried to accept that her loneliness was insurmountable, her dependence on her husband destructive but unalterable. "Half your loneliness," Geraldine remarked, "comes from having no outlet for your energies and no engrossing employment."[2] Her husband offered to take her away from London and housewifely chores. But she felt that it would hardly help to deprive her of her only vocation. "I shall try in time coming to be a better housewife at least; that career being always open to talent. . . . If I died, all my drawers would be found in the most perfect order."[3] Her bitterness could never be suppressed completely; his inability to help her could never be overcome. He was having difficulty enough helping himself.

Carlyle left his kind but "fussy" Welsh friend late in August and set out for what he hoped would be the even deeper silence of Scotsbrig. Jane absolutely declined to join him. He justified his constant complaints to her about the miseries of travel, particularly the overcrowded steamer from Liverpool to Annan, by asking, "To whom can we complain, if not to one another, after all?"[4] She agreed that they were both too sensitive but that their sensitivities suffered less when they were apart. He would be better off without her company, which, she had "no illusion . . . is generally worse than none; and you cannot suffer more from the fact," she confessed to him, "than I do from the consciousness of it. God knows how gladly I would be sweet-tempered and cheerful-hearted, and all that sort of thing for your single sake, if my temper were not soured and my heart saddened, beyond my own power to mend them."[5] He did find a Sabbath-like peace and some healing at Scotsbrig. The early September days were "of surpassing beauty . . . clear . . . [and] calm. . . . The hills are all spotted with pure light and pure shade; everything of the liveliest yellow and the liveliest green."[6] But he "could not lie down in silence for ever."[7]

After almost a month at his mother's house, he began his return trip to London, traveling by way of the Lake Country. He had accepted an invitation from James Marshall to visit at the wealthy industrialist's summer house at Ambleside. Late in September, Jane had gone to the Grange. She had been pressured by the forceful and capriciously solicitous Lady Harriet into agreeing to a long visit. For Jane, it was like being at a special kind of hotel. "The longer" she and the mistress of the house "know one another and the more we are intimate to outward appearance the less have we to say to one another *alone*."[8] When she went to the Grange, she did not expect her husband to return until the end of October, but the visit to Ambleside did not go well and he returned home early. Not even the Tennysons' company at Ambleside could compensate for his sleeplessness. Mrs. Tennyson delighted him; she seemed a woman of practical sense and temperate spirits; no doubt the wandering poet had been much improved by the responsibilities of marriage. But, restless and irritable, Carlyle insisted on leaving the next day. After a good night's sleep the second night, however, he thought he might remain, but his hosts did not renew their pressure to have him change his mind. He resented what seemed a breach of hospitality and, in his thoughts, accused the Marshalls of liking to "keep" a poet, as long as he was tame. He angrily boarded "an Express train, and after about 10 hours of screaming . . . chaotic raging dissonances . . . was shot out at Euston Square."[9] Jane, however, was deeply disconcerted to learn that he had arrived home while she was still at the Grange. It had never happened before. On some level it seemed a betrayal, however accidental, though characteristically she turned the blame on herself.

With the noise of London loud in his ears, he thought it best to join Jane in Hampshire. Some of the noise was criticism of *Latter-Day Pamphlets,* to Carlyle's mind the "screaming and squealing" of pigs, "the stupid blockheads of this generation."[10] But much of it was the cry of inner pain. He thought of his mother and urged that we "all learn to grow *old,* as we must; and know that age too has its beauty to the rim."[11] He associated his own "old age" with a noisy sickroom. Despite the long vacation, his "nerves" were "in a sad state of disorder."[12] He felt "*as* sick, according to all indexes of personal sensation, as when" he "had left. A hopeless thing this of ministering to an Incurable!"[13] As autumn came, he wanted to be let alone, for "nobody comes whose talk is half so good . . . as silence."[14] But even in the dead of winter the threat of noise could not be eliminated.

In London, Carlyle concluded, he was doomed to the "mere silent endurance of pain." But if he had "a house in the country" to which he could flee "for shelter and seclusion" would he not be considerably better within a year? Late in 1850, he had hesitatingly encouraged his sister Jean to provide him with details about an inexpensive house for rent in Dumfriesshire. For the next three years he struggled with the problem. Keenly aware of the "straps and tethers" that bound him to London, he either had to make London more bearable or leave it altogether. At moments of emotional crisis he thought flight the best solution. But, as soon as he felt better, the attractions of London again asserted themselves. "Abundant books, total *freedom* from the question of money-income, power to choose my society from the best of the Kingdom. . . . I feel as if it would be very rash to cut London, too. And so one wavers hither and thither; and is a fool."[15] The fact was that in London he could have what he cherished more than anything else, his independence. "If you lived in a country place, and did not fall in with the cants and the pietisms of the little sets there, they pointed the finger at you, and there was no living quietly."[16]

Perhaps it would be possible to remain in London and avoid the kind of noise represented by the Great Exhibition, with its extraordinary Crystal Palace. In the end, however, he found the crowds less pressing than his curiosity to see for himself the "noise, nonsense and confusion" of "this big Glass Soap-bubble."[17] With two press passes from John Forster, the Carlyles visited early in March 1851. Though he condemned the "monster of a gigantic-Birdcage . . . a Sanhedrin of windy fools from all countries of the Globe," he admired the practical ingenuity of its construction. When another piece of windiness presented itself in the form of Thackeray's entertaining but thin public lectures, he felt compelled to attend. At the last lecture, Harriet Martineau found herself sitting between Jane and Thomas. After a short time, he constantly looked at his watch, holding it across her and showing it to Jane every two minutes. "He filled up the intervals with shaking himself, & drumming his elbow into" her "side."[18] Though he admired Thackeray's "comic acting," he found the air stale; his only desire was to be away from the crowd and the noise.[19]

Through the fall and winter, he could not suppress the thought of fleeing into the countryside for good. But the impossibility of ever living in Scotland again seemed undeniable; his temperamental and philosophical abhorrence of nomadic movement was strong.[20] Despite his frequent advocacy of solitude, he rightly feared that wherever he lived in the country he would be dreadfully lonely. Jane, of course, had no intention of leaving London. But it was particularly galling and painful to have to refight a battle she thought she had won ten years before, especially with her complicated but bitter feelings about their marriage now close to the surface. Since it was clearly an impossible alternative, one that would create many more problems than it would solve, she thought her husband's constant comments and complaints about London another glaring instance of his selfish insensitivity to her needs. His obsessions on the matter of his health were, Jane believed, simply not controlled by good sense, let alone wisdom.

He was not unwise, however, to accept an invitation from Dr. James Manby Gully and spend the month of August 1851 at the village of Malvern in the rolling hills near Worcester. Eight years earlier the doctor had cofounded a now famous center for applying the "Water Cure" to chronic diseases, particularly those of the nervous system. Hydropathic cures had become popular during the 1840s. Tennyson, who spoke very highly of Dr. Gully, had been a patient at Malvern in 1847. Water-cure proponents "held that all chronic disease was caused by a faulty supply of blood to the viscera; either the blood was poor in quality or owing to defective circulation it was not carried off and the viscera became engorged with it. The application of cold water to the skin by various methods: compresses, or packing in sheets wrung out of cold water, or sitz baths or jets or douches was used to animate the circulation and get it working normally."[21] Constant moderate exercise, particularly walks in the lovely countryside around Malvern, was an essential part of the regimen. And all drugs and internal medications were absolutely forbidden, perhaps a significant factor in whatever patient improvement occurred, for this was an age when the whole pharmacopoeia, from castor oil to laudanum, was easily available and often abused. That the "Water Cure" deprived Carlyle, who regularly took cold showers anyway, of castor oil and "blue" pills certainly benefited his body more than did any discomfort produced by the constant exposure to cold water.

At Malvern, Dr. Gully and his wife, who seemed generous and pleasant people, made the Carlyles particularly comfortable. The doctor was anxious to impress the well known and influential with the virtues of his system. He insisted that the Carlyles, who readily accepted, stay as long as they liked as his guests. Carlyle plunged into the cure, "a strange half-ridiculous and by no means unpleasant operation."[22] Jane declined and found other ways to spend her time at what was basically an elegant country retreat for the well-to-do. Though he doubted that he would benefit in any important way from the regimen, Carlyle was not sorry that he had come and stayed for almost a month. So many people had urged this cure on him that at least he could now say that he had already tried it. "As poor Lord Melbourne liked, when a Poet *died,* for then, said he, 'you get all his books on your shelf and have finished with him,' so may *I,* with better reason, of the Malvern puddles."[23] In the fall he speculated that perhaps he had been helped a little. But the crucial problem of his mental health had been neither washed nor floated away by the Malvern waters.

By the summer of 1852, Jane's insistence that she would stay in London whatever her husband did and Carlyle's own fecklessness on the matter had finally combined to produce the decision that they would attempt to secure a long-term lease on their house in Chelsea, make whatever improvements were desirable, and make do with London. Fortunately, they had no problem in obtaining a financially advantageous lease. His occasional "wish" that he "could purchase it on reasonable terms" bowed to a very satisfactory compromise. While he was away, extensive renovations were done. Their first thought had been to create for Carlyle a soundproof study with a skylight, almost totally rebuilding the attic. But since the estimates seemed terribly high, they decided against it and concentrated on enlarging rooms to make them more suitable. Jane spent a long hot summer exercising her formidable skills as architect and contractor in charge of all renovation decisions. Such moments, occasionally repeated and often imitated in a small way over the years, provided her with a sense of purpose and vocational fulfillment greater than anything else she did in her adult life. This renovation went on from July 1852 to the next January. The time and the expense constantly expanded, but the hope was that the external noises of London would finally be muffled, thereby comforting Carlyle's obsessively sensitive inner ears.

For over a decade he had been complaining about street noises, from poultry to organ grinders to heavy traffic to the tearing up of Cheyne Row for a new sewer system. After his complaints, he usually felt relieved; he often slept. But Jane was anxious that new complaints were imminent, and this anxiety compounded her own insomnia and mental restlessness. In moments of hysteria, he shouted and screamed at the closest object on which he could vent his feelings. At other moments, as when an organ grinder played beneath his window, he found enough control to wonder why the universe had been constructed so that another person's need to earn his simple living conflicted with his own need to have silence for his work. "The question arises, whether to go out and, if not assassinate him, call the Police upon him, or to take myself away to the bath-tub and the other side of the house? Of course, I *ought* to choose the latter."[24] At one time some neighbors who shared a side wall with the Carlyles had the temerity to have a piano-playing daughter. A diplomatic compromise, engineered by Jane, brought some relief. At another time, Jane negotiated a legally binding arrangement with a neighbor who kept roosters and macaws.

But by early spring 1853 it seemed clear that the previous renovations were insufficient. In March there were "vagrant *musical* scamps" under his window, "with *clatter-bones,* guitars and Nigger songs."[25] The idea of building a soundproof attic study, which had been raised as early as October 1843 and dismissed regretfully in 1852 because of the cost, was now revived. That summer the upper stories of the house were turned over to an honest but unreliable contractor and his laborers, who provided the Carlyles with "a *last* desperate spasmodic effort of building,—a new top-story to the house."[26] In the middle of May 1854, Carlyle sat down at his desk there for the first time. His first thought was that "the room considered as a *soundless* apartment may be safely pronounced an evident *failure.*" Complete silence was unattainable. The skylight leaked. The wind blew furiously in the winter weather, creating whirlpools of noise. Still, it was quieter than any room he had ever had before. How satisfactory it was depended to some extent on his mood. The "garret" was as "luminous as day, almost too much light rather, and almost perfectly silent" when he got it "shut completely," which was difficult to do. It seemed impossible to eliminate the howling of the east wind.[27] And the greater the external silence, the more he listened for internal noise.

2.

Literary reputations are fragile gifts, quickly altered and often withdrawn. The publication of *Latter-Day Pamphlets* did not create new divisions in Carlyle's audience, but it did intensify the hostility of those who already had reasons for disparaging his work and provide a more explicit, public set of issues around which to focus criticism. Riding down to the Grange at the end of January 1850, Carlyle received the saddest reminder of one of his first and most perceptive critics. "A gentleman in the rail-carriage . . . read out from the *Times,* an announcement that *Lord Jeffrey* in Edinburgh was just *dead.* . . . Our poor little Jeffrey is no more!"[28] An embodiment of the Whig middle way in literature and politics, Jeffrey had been among the first to publish Carlyle, doing so despite his distaste for his friend's "Germanic" style. Jeffrey's private criticism of Carlyle's style had long since become a widespread public accusation. After 1837, the peculiarities of Carlyle's mind and style, often referred to as "Carlylese," provided a focus for both his admirers and his detractors, though in a number of instances, such as Jeffrey's, the recognition of vices did not preclude the appreciation of virtues. His detractors usually granted his "genius," generally conceding that his satiric inventions were powerful, his use of metaphoric language rich, and many of his targets deserving of condemnation. And his supporters often conceded, however hesitantly, that some pruning of his complex rhetoric and more concessions to traditional uses of language might indeed make his prose more effective, his ideas more accessible.

Some of Carlyle's most fervent admirers tried to rescue him—and themselves—from his more extreme statements, particularly on current affairs, by claiming him for poetry rather than for politics. Whatever the response to his ideas, his originality lay in his "medium," his language, as Elizabeth Barrett claimed in a perceptive essay published before she had met her subject. She agreed with Mazzini that "his great forte and chief practice is individualization." He is a "true poet" who recognizes

> the same human nature through every cycle of individual and social existence. He is a poet also, by his insight into the activity of moral causes. . . . He proceeds, like a poet, rather by analogy and subtle association than by uses of logic. His illustrations not only illustrate, but bear a part in the reasoning;—the images stand out, like grand and beautiful caryatides, to sustain the heights of the argument. . . . His language . . . somewhat too slow, broken up, and involved for eloquence, and too individual to be classical . . . is yet the language of a gifted painter and poet, the colour of whose soul eats itself into the words.[29]

In America, Henry David Thoreau, introduced to Carlyle's works by Emerson, presented an equally strong and perhaps even more eloquently expressed defense of Carlyle. The two writers had exchanged greetings indirectly as early as 1841, through the channel of their common friend at whose home Thoreau was visiting. Emerson wrote to Carlyle that he is a "reader & friend of yours."[30] While in Ireland in the late summer of 1849, Carlyle had carried *A Week on the Concord and*

Merrimack Rivers, which he read appreciatively while he rested in Scotland. Like Elizabeth Barrett, Thoreau turned to his own definition of art for his justification of Carlyle's stylistic originality. "If you would know where many of those obnoxious Carlyleisms and Germanisms came from," he explained, "read the best of Milton's prose, read those speeches of Cromwell . . . or go and listen once more to your mother's tongue. . . . For fluency and skill in the use of the English tongue, he is a master unrivaled." Indeed, "no man's thoughts are new, but the style of their expression is the never failing novelty which cheers and refreshes men." And to the accusation of exaggeration, Thoreau replied that "he who cannot exaggerate is not qualified to utter truth. . . . Moreover, you must speak loud to those who are hard of hearing, and so you acquire a habit of shouting to those who are not."[31]

Carlyle's own attitude toward America was skeptical. When in *Latter-Day Pamphlets* he referred, in a moment of rhetorical exaggeration, to America as a nation of eighteen million "bores"—a statement that reflected his increasingly wearisome experiences as a local tourist attraction for visiting Americans (especially Emersonians)—he naturally evoked a pained response from that country's defenders. But Carlyle's skepticism cloaked his deeper responses to that distant continent, the intensity of which resulted from his own sense of shared qualities and inseparable destinies. His first income as a writer of books had come from America; the strongest and earliest affirmation of his work as a writer had come from his American readers; that distant land had become both attractively and threateningly close with the constant invitations from Emerson and the possibility that his own choice was either to lecture in America or to starve in England; and, of course, in 1843 Alick had made the irreversible journey across the ocean. In a sense Carlyle actually owned property in Canada and the United States; his funds had partly paid for the purchase of Alick's Canadian farm and he had invested with Jack in State of Illinois bonds. Despite his reservations about American democracy and frontier culture, he placed great hope in its contribution to what he envisioned as an Anglo-Saxon hegemony: the aging mother of strong sons would find, he predicted, her future realized in the deeds and wealth of her children.

Many of Carlyle's American readers believed that the boldness of his prose reflected their own sense of themselves and their country as experimental and prophetic, exaggerated and ambitious. His style seemed to correspond with their own fascination with ruggedness, individuality, biblical prophecy, and journalistic extravaganza; it seemed to echo both their condemnation of the corruption of the old world and their grand expectation that America was the hope of the future. *Sartor*

Resartus and *The French Revolution* were particularly admired in America. Carlylese met somewhat less resistance in this more loosely structured and experimental society, and the apotheosis of Cromwell in particular appealed to an antimonarchical republic whose strongest religious identification was with Puritan dissent. American idealism responded to Carlyle's admiration of heroes; American realism found his attacks on "cant" refreshing.

America was also more tolerant than England of the "habit of shouting" because it was itself more given to doing so. Still, some of the divisions that characterized the English response to Carlyle also appeared in the American, particularly before 1850. Perhaps the severest condemnation came from one of America's most troubled but original literary minds. In an essay published in 1843, Edgar Allan Poe claimed that if Carlyle meant "to be understood" but took "all possible pains to prevent us from understanding . . . we can only say he is an ass—and this, to be brief, is our private opinion of Mr. Carlyle, which we now take the liberty of making public." In private notations, three years later, he confessed "not the slightest faith in Carlyle. In ten years—possibly in five—he will be remembered only as a butt for sarcasm," since the only "important service" he can be credited with is having pushed "rant and cant to the degree of excess" that must create a negative reaction to the absurdity of hero worship. Three years later, in another private notation, he humorously attacked Carlyle in a satiric exaggeration worthy of his subject: "The next work of Carlyle will be entitled *Bow-Wow,* and the title-page will have a motto from the opening chapter of the Koran: 'There is *no* error in this Book.' "[32]

Particularly in America, "An Occasional Discourse on the Nigger Question" (1849) and the *Pamphlets* assaulted such sensitive cultural issues that the old divisions were intensified and Carlyle's opinions became detached from the literary texts in which they had appeared. They became part of a debate in which the qualifications and nuances of Carlyle's prose and thought were irrelevant. The old detractors joined a broader group whose interest in Carlyle was considerably less intense than its interest in political and economic controversies concerning class struggle, the slave economy, emancipation doctrine, sectarian theology, and an assortment of nineteenth- and early twentieth-century ideologies, ranging from antebellum plantation Christianity to National Socialism.

When Carlyle had opposed abrogation of the Union with Ireland, Mill had temperately responded that to assume, as Carlyle did, that England had a "mission" to impose "good government" on the rest of the world was to deny the evidence of England's failure in all its previous attempts to do so, especially in Ireland.[33] But when Carlyle defended slavery as justifiable under certain special conditions, Mill responded with the outrage of someone who correctly anticipated the use to which Carlyle's opinions would be put. The Northern abolitionists were horrified. "It is a sad thing to find so much intellectual power as Carlyle really possesses so little under the control of the moral sentiments." The radical humanitarian of *Chartism* had betrayed "the poor and the wronged" and "had swapped his heart of flesh for a cobble stone."[34] But Southern defenders and apologists for slave labor and plantation culture were delighted. "Occasional Discourse" and the *Pamphlets,* frequently reprinted, became popular reading and the focus of a great deal of commentary in Southern journals: Southern intellectuals, educators, and editors gratefully accepted and exploited the gift of an unexpected but world-famous ally.

The apologists for slavery embraced Carlyle's advocacy of a hierarchical universe; the abolitionists found that the "genius" that New England had welcomed had become the voice of perverse doctrines that denied spiritual equality. Under strains so immense it took at least a Thoreau or an Emerson to resist the narrow view and the partial judgment. The subtleties of Carlyle's position on heroes, power, and slavery, let alone the literary and philosophical context he had established for his words and ideas, disappeared behind the emotional and intellectual reductionism of partisan slogans and ideological banners. The misuse of Carlyle to support visions of society and human relations which he would have abhorred abated at different moments over the next century, but the publication of *Latter-Day Pamphlets* made its author vulnerable in a way that he was perhaps shortsighted not to anticipate. But even if he had, it seems unlikely that he would have acted differently. He would instead have taken refuge in the sanctity of his obsessions and in his contempt for literary reputations, especially his own.

Such contempt, however, did not extend to the reputations of his friends. In the case of one friend, John Sterling, he had been assigned the special trust of coexecutor in 1844. Sterling had left instructions that his friend Julius Hare, an Anglican clergyman, and Carlyle were to sift through his unpublished literary materials and publish with appropriate introduction whatever they thought of permanent value. Numbed by his friend's death and deeply exhausted by the enervating work on *Cromwell,* Carlyle relinquished his own obligation to Hare. For the time being, the tears he shed for Sterling were real but unrealizable as work. The increasing rage that directed his energy toward the explosive public denunciations in *Latter-Day Pamphlets* made contemplative biography impossible. In addition, some of the issues that related to Sterling's life were personally painful; to deal with them effectively demanded a self-confrontation for which he did not feel ready. But the writing and publication of *Latter-Day Pamphlets* had a cleansing effect; his anger had been softened and he now felt calmer.[35] Moreover, his conscience in regard to the bequest from Sterling had been additionally unsettled by Hare's biographical introduction to the edition of Sterling's selected works published in 1848, a portrait of Sterling in which the dominant emphasis was on his Anglicanism.

By December 1850 Carlyle was thinking "of trying some book again."[36] At the end of the year, in the "opaque" London fog, he had made no progress. With nothing to do, he cleared his desk until there was nothing more to clear. He continued (without ever admitting that he enjoyed) the routine of social relationships, which mainly involved receiving guests at Cheyne Row, the regular friends and companions of the past decade. There were occasional new faces, among them two young men of great talent and energy, Charles Kingsley and John Ruskin. The relationship with Kingsley, whose novel *Alton Locke* he had read and admired, especially for its flattering portrait of himself, was never to become a close one; the relationship with Ruskin, whose genius and loyalty he was soon to recognize and encourage, developed into an intimate friendship that lasted until Ruskin's illnesses and Caryle's death.

Jane had little more than her pet dog Nero to divert her while her unhappy husband stared unrelievedly at a blank sheet and an uncertain future. The illusion that he could write extensively and effectively on Ireland or democracy or any other current social issue had been shattered. In fact, any long project was at the moment beyond him. What awakened his suppressed expectation that he would one day set the record straight about John Sterling is unclear. Probably Sterling's older brother Anthony urged him to restore both accuracy and the family honor. Late in January 1851 he was at the Grange, without Jane, where he took the occasion, in the company of two distinguished Anglicans, to express strong criticism of the church. The civilized response to his "dreadful onslaught" served only to emphasize the hollowness of modern religious commitment. By the end of the month he had decided that he must discharge his debt to Sterling. His emotions immediately interacted with his powerful memory. The debt seemed sacred. He could recharge the present and himself with the power of the past. And here was a manageable project, work that would give him a sense of worth and purpose.

After gathering and reading all the available documents, mainly letters, he spent February and most of March 1851 writing, with hardly a complaint. In comparison to the time and anguish he had expended on *Cromwell* and *Latter-Day Pamphlets,* this seemed a small, sweet task. He did not necessarily intend it for publication, he claimed: as with his travel writing, there was a personal element in such a volume which he tended to see more as private ritual than public performance. But he could hardly expect to set straight the record of Sterling's life if he put the manuscript away in a drawer. At the end of March, Jane read it. Her own friendship with Sterling had been particularly close, her relationship with the entire Sterling family especially intense. She "warmly" voted for "immediate printing."[37] The proof sheets were done in the late spring and early summer, completed just before the Carlyles left for the "Water Cure" at Malvern and an extended summer holiday. But, because of the general diversion created by the Crystal Palace, it had been decided not to publish the book until autumn. On the same day that the Great Exhibition closed, Carlyle's biography of his friend appeared.

3.

The contrast with *Latter-Day Pamphlets* escaped few readers. Though it was not entirely free of controversy, the response to *The Life of John Sterling* was comparatively muted and quite favorable. It was as if there were two Carlyles: on the one hand, the angry, uncontrollable prophet; on the other, the gentle, contained, and incisive artist, concerned more with vivid depiction than with strong-voiced persuasion. When he dealt with social issues, he sometimes shrieked incoherently; when he wrote about people, though he was occasionally ungenerous, as with Coleridge, his clear-eyed artistry and his deep sympathy with the condition of the individual human being usually triumphed. And his deep affection for Sterling cast a beneficent warmth on the book as a whole. He wrote that it was "a light portrait, the truest I could easily sketch, of an unimportant but very beautiful, pathetic and rather significant, human life in our century."[38]

Such qualities were immediately appreciated by many of Carlyle's Victorian readers. Writing anonymously in the *Westminster Review,* Mary Ann Evans (who was not to make her appearance as George Eliot for another five years) saw the significance of Carlyle's comment that "artist, not saint, was the real bent of [Sterling's] being." Carlyle may very well have seen himself in the mirror of his friend's life; the book is as much autobiographical as biographical. Two of Carlyle's strongest impulses, despite his many failures to act on them, were his delight in human beings in all their various shades and his compulsion to create in rich language some projection of the interaction between the reality of "character" and his own emotions. "This *Life of Sterling,*" Miss Evans wrote, "is a touching monument of the capability human nature possesses of the highest love, the love of the good and beautiful in char-

Thomas Carlyle. Photograph, July 28, 1854. Courtesy of the Rare Book and Manuscript Library, Columbia University.

acter, which is, after all, the essence of piety. The style of the work, too, is for the most part at once pure and rich; there are passages of deep pathos which come upon the reader like a strain of solemn music, and others which show that aptness of epithet, that masterly power of close delineation, in which, perhaps, no writer has excelled Carlyle."[39]

The most intense criticism, some of it quite outraged, came from those who felt that Carlyle had finally and fully revealed the extent of his hostility to Christianity. Hare had concentrated on Sterling's religious commitments and values; Carlyle thought a corrective was necessary, for in his eyes Sterling's Christianity had been much less orthodox and his faith much less certain than Hare had claimed. Sterling's eight-month ministry had just ended when Carlyle and Sterling met in the spring of 1835. The young man had decided that he was a poet, not a divine. Though the decision was grounded in his character, it had a doctrinal level as well. Sterling soon discovered that he stood somewhere halfway between the liberal orthodoxy of Coleridge—and of many of his Coleridgean friends like Maurice and Kingsley—and the ethical existentialism of Carlyle, who urged him to turn away from the fables of Christianity and the deadness of its churches. It seemed to Carlyle a gross distortion for Hare to depict Sterling as Christian and unwaveringly Anglican.

By focusing his biographical sketch on the religious dimension of Sterling's life, Hare had, in Carlyle's view, completely neglected Sterling the artist. For Sterling's character was neither devotional nor ascetic, and he had little sense of religious mystery and wonder. "He had endless admiration, but intrinsically rather a deficiency of reverence."[40] Over and over again, Sterling had attempted to define himself as a poet. That Carlyle had great respect for Sterling's effort but little respect for the poems themselves made the biographer's attempt to readjust the emphasis especially difficult. The biographer risked depriving his readers and Sterling's friends of both Sterling's religious aura and his artistic achievement.

In his biography of Sterling, Carlyle presents a memorably vivid but intensely hostile pen portrait of Coleridge, based partly on his visit to Highgate with Irving in 1824. Carlyle detested Coleridge's mind and manners, and felt that the poet represented an ignoble model of manliness in contrast to Carlyle's father and to Goethe. But the hostile portrait was not entirely personal: it proceeded partly from his need as an artist to make clear the grounds for Sterling's rejection of Coleridge's influence and partly from his need to put his own rejection of Coleridge in a favorable light. In order to elucidate the relationship between Sterling and Coleridge, Carlyle had, of course, to reveal his own long-held but only indirectly expressed views on the church and Christianity. To some it came as a shock; to others it was also an affront. It was clear that despite the Christian resonances of Carlyle's prose there was no Christian substance, if substance was to be defined theologically. In the eyes of many Christians, such a position was hardly to be distinguished from atheism.

The real achievement of *The Life of Sterling,* however, lay in its artistry, not its apologetics. The book granted that Sterling was neither a model of religion nor a successful artist, two concessions that necessarily provoked resentment. For Carlyle, Sterling's early death explained the failure of his ambitions. Carlyle's view of Sterling was basically tragic: his unfulfilled promise and early death were neither accidental nor unique but symbolic, representative of the condition of modern man, particularly of the corrupt condition of modern culture and the delusions and evasions it demands. That Sterling had been implicated in the revisionary attempt by Coleridge to strengthen conservative Anglicanism (of which Hare's biographical sketch was an extension) reveals that even the noblest and most sincere of modern men could not fully escape the dead hand of the past, though Carlyle believed that his friend had eventually been perceptive enough to liberate himself from that particular influence.

At the same time, however, Carlyle thought that Sterling erred in his claim that poetry or literature as "Art" could sustain the spiritual vision that religion no longer embodied effectively. "It is expected in this Nineteenth Century that a man of culture shall understand and worship Art: among the windy gospels addressed to our poor Century there are few louder. . . . And if the Century expects that every man shall do his duty, surely Sterling was not the man to balk it!"[41] In a culture in which the old certainties had been destroyed, the variety of potential replacements encouraged uncertainty and bewilderment. Thus, Sterling had been born into a confusion that he himself inevitably came to embody. Carlyle, drawing in part on his own experience, deeply appreciated the extent to which man is culturally determined. Different as he and Sterling were in personality, they shared many of the same external givens; and Sterling's struggle with his Christian identification and his attempt to define himself as an artist had much in common with Carlyle's own dilemmas.

But whereas Carlyle envisioned himself as asocial, idiosyncratic, and alienated from the community, Sterling had all his life seemed a golden child of the culture into which he had been born. Everything came easily to him: eonomic security, university honors, warm friendships, and the widely and readily granted view that his would be a brilliant literary future. In his own struggles, Carlyle believed that he had been toughened, that he had developed the will to face unalterable "facts" head-on and to forge on the anvil of life a defiant art consonant with those "facts." But Sterling, like Edward Irving—who was much on Carlyle's mind as he finished this biography—had had an "almost childlike faculty of self-deception." He "usually substituted for the primary determining motive . . . some ultimate ostensible one, and gave that out to himself and others as the ruling impulse for important changes in life."[42] Though Carlyle recognized that he too had not escaped the need to rationalize, the difference in degree was important. Because of the particular nature of Sterling's gifts and his social position, he had more readily and more frequently succumbed to destructive tendencies within the society and evasive tendencies within himself. He had not been able to defeat a whole host of restless fantasies. Carlyle had fought many of these same fantasies to a standstill, but they had possessed and then destroyed Sterling. In Carlyle's eyes, the consumption that killed him was not the real cause of his death. "In this as in other cases known to me, ill-health was not the primary cause but rather the ultimate one, the summing-up of innumerable far deeper conscious and unconscious causes,—the cause which *could* boldly show itself on the surface, and give the casting vote."[43] As in his own case, the inexplicable interchange between flaws of character and the society that had malnourished him threatened tragedy. Carlyle realized that he himself had fortunately survived, though at great cost, probably by destructive because overly strenuous exertion of the will. Sterling's was "the tragic story of a high endowment with an insufficient will."[44] All his virtues—sweetness of temperament, brilliant wit, nobility of character, and love of life—had not been able to save him.[45]

4.

From Malvern at the end of August 1851 Carlyle went to Scotsbrig; his wife went to Manchester, where the faithful Geraldine provided emotional comfort. Jane had grown accustomed to her friend's aggressive excesses. Geraldine fantasied an intimate life with Jane in "a cottage in the country. . . . You should keep the house absolutely—keep the accounts, keep the money—and I would write; and you should make me work."[46] Ironically, Geraldine's vision offered Jane a mere exchange of spouses rather than a liberating restructuring of her role. Despite the force of her erotic imagination, however, Geraldine recognized that the problem transcended individual peculiarities. Jane, who had no hope for her own marriage, could probably muster only a little enthusiasm for her friend's evocation of "better days, when women will have a genuine, normal life of their own to lead. There, perhaps, will not be so many marriages."[47]

Jane Carlyle and her dog Nero. Photograph, July 31, 1854. Courtesy of the Rare Book and Manuscript Library, Columbia University.

Jane had by now become quite cynical about marriages. Her husband's involvement with Lady Ashburton continued, whatever her own demands: she had been effectively outmaneuvered by stronger personalities, and her visits to the Grange, which she recognized were not unmixed evils, symbolized her defeat. Almost thirty years before she had warned her suitor that in a Romantic friendship one person gives pain and the other receives it; but at that time she had expected that she would always control the emotional flow of their relationship. When she left Malvern, she bitterly acknowledged that their vacation had to be "cut short to suit the movements of another Lady—Lady Ashburton—who wrote that *she* is to be in Paris on the 10th—instead of at the end of September when Mr. C. engaged to spend a fortnight with *them* in Paris."[48] The invitation had been in the air for a long time. Jane found in Geraldine's advice confirmation of her own feelings: "As to Paris and Mr. Carlyle, you would have no comfort in that arrangement—going in that company, you would be worried and tantalised to death."[49] Jane, who had never been out of Britain, declined the invitation. But her husband, who had been to Paris before and had no personal wish to return, could not resist Lady Harriet's urging, for, as he rationalized, "it seemed stingy and cowardly not to take advantage of so handsome an offer."[50]

The trip was doomed from the beginning. Every aspect of his life except one demanded that he stay at home to deal with his problems. But that one need had the propelling force of a fantasy that idealized love and servitude, beauty and the beast; in the service of this "Principessa" all "shall be as you desire: how else?" For "in all things you are beautiful and good."[51] Despite the contradictions and confusions, he had determined to maintain this relationship, as if his fulminations against courtly love and George Sand somehow did not apply to himself: allegations, from Jane or anyone else, that there existed anything improper in his attachment to Lady Harriet were to be resisted with all the rhetorical force and moral passion of a man who had convinced himself that his intentions and feelings were completely pure. He was, in fact, joining *the Ashburtons,* who were returning to England from a summer on the Continent, and Jane *had been* invited.

Fortunately, he had good luck in the arrangements for the journey itself. At the beginning of the third week of September 1851, he learned that the Brownings, who had spent the summer in London, were about to leave for Paris. The advantage of experienced traveling companions, who were happy to have his company, seemed more than sufficient to motivate him to postpone his departure for a day. To Jane, Browning seemed always a "ball of fluff" whose company she would gladly avoid. But Carlyle liked him very much. His affection and respect for Browning actually increased during the next years, especially with Browning's publication of his preface to an edition of Shelley's poetry and a volume of his own poems, *Men and Women,* which Carlyle thought superb. Whereas Elizabeth's poetry seemed to him flat, sentimental, and conventional, the unusual rhythms and striking perceptions of her husband's dramatic monologues soon persuaded Carlyle to desist from advising him to give up poetry for prose. The Brownings' intention to spend the winter in Paris, rather than return to Italy immediately, seemed to Carlyle a positive sign, for it would bring the poet closer to repatriation with the land of his language and the home of his friends.

The energetic Browning took charge, guiding his revered friend, his own delicate wife, and his precious son through the practical obstacles of the trip. Carlyle indulged his sense of technical ineptness with controlled passivity, while Browning shepherded the luggage, arranged the hotel at Dieppe, and negotiated with customs. The poet did not seem to mind. At Dieppe, Carlyle "woke dreaming, confused things about [his] mother."[52] But he managed to be good enough company to entertain Elizabeth with his talk. She perceptively commented that "all the bitterness is love with the point reversed."[53] At the tumultuous Paris station, "the brave Browning fought" for them, leaving Carlyle "to sit beside the women."[54] Some additional confusion and delay got him to the Hotel Meurice, where the Ashburtons had taken a large suite. He was an hour late and the Ashburtons were out. They returned in time for them to dine together and then go to the theater, where Carlyle found the box drafty, the "play wretched." The noise of the hotel and the street kept him awake most of the night.

Paris itself seemed morally as vacuous as when he had been there in 1824. A worshiper of hollow show and ornamental illusions, the city had no soul. It was also in a "dingy, dirty, unswept condition . . . a sordid, ragged kind of object," heavily patrolled by armed soldiers, and showing the wear and tear of the past three years of revolution and public misery. Carlyle was ambivalent about Louis Napoleon's tactful maneuvering toward complete power. On the one hand, having met him in London and watched his career, he thought him a hollow simulacrum of the great leader whose name he bore; on the other, any consolidation of order seemed better than the continuation of national chaos.[55] When the bright October sun shone, however, Paris did look "brisk and beautiful."[56] Unfortunately, he had really nothing to do. Ordinary sightseeing did not appeal to him. The one man he wanted to see, Louis Cavaignac, was out of town. Adolphe Thiers, the historian, he could not help meeting again; his company was tolerable, but nothing more. Carlyle later described him as

> a noticeable subject . . . with the light eupeptic practical Gascon spirit very strong in him, has a most musical, plaintively-singing, and yet essentially gay and jaunty *treble* voice; talks unweariedly, and in a very neat and clear and carelessly frank and ingenious way . . . close-cropped, bullet-head, of fair weight, almost quite white; laughing little hazel eyes, jolly hooked nose and most definite mouth; short, short (five feet three or two at most), swells slightly in the middle—soft, *sausage-like* on the whole—and ends neatly in fat little feet and hands.[57]

Everyone else he met, including Prosper Mérimée, he "did not *much* care for. . . . A sad incredulous shallow grimacing set."[58] Lady Ashburton, who felt increasingly ill, was not very companionable, and Carlyle spent more time with her husband and with the Brownings than with "the one glow of radiancy that still" looked "of heaven" to him, "on a ground which is black and waste."[59]

Carlyle returned from Paris on October 2, 1851, "through muddy rains"; after sleeping on the train, he felt like Jonah finally expelled from the whale's belly. For a week it seemed to him that he did nothing but sleep, though he did manage to dash down and throw into a drawer his impressions of his Paris trip.[60] Such compensation for his previous sleeplessness was also an intuitive preparation for some new task, the subject of which he had not yet determined. From Paris, Browning, to whom he felt grateful and affectionate, urged new voyages, particularly to reunite with them in Paris during the winter. But, by the end of October, he eagerly anticipated the isolation that winter would bring, rushing the season by comparing the occupants of Cheyne Row to "Greenland ships *frozen in*. . . . Weather, dark, dusty, smoky, windless and sunless . . . an evil it were useless to rebel against."[61] He preferred to read in solitude, particularly about William the Conqueror and the Normans who he had years before thought a possible subject of a book. If he were to travel, Normandy would be the more likely destination than Paris. As the winter darkened, his mind turned more toward the brightness of Lady Harriet. He had seen her soon after her return to England in October. Though she had brought a present for Jane, she had also brought sufficient indifference to avoid going at all out of her way to see her. Jane, who had "long given up the generous attempt at loving her," felt bitterly resentful "to see *him* always starting up to defend everything she does."[62] It seemed that Lady Harriet could do no wrong. He constantly thought about her, "indeed *always;* but . . . on terms," he claimed, "which neither God nor man, if they could be well seen into, need find much to punish!" As long as he lived, he assured her, you "shall more or less belong to me."[63]

Jane felt coerced into accepting an invitation for a long winter visit at the Grange; otherwise, she felt certain, Lady Ashburton would quarrel with her, and then she would have to confront her husband's anger. She stayed for a full month, through December 1851 and into the new year; her husband, busy reading at Chelsea, joined her for the last two weeks of a holiday that turned out to be pleasanter than many of their visits. There were interesting guests, among them Thackeray and his daughters, and particularly Thomas Babington Macaulay, whom Carlyle had seen during his visit to London in 1832 and whose career he had followed with condescending interest. Macaulay talked marvelously, "a real acquisition while he lasted." He had a "truly wonderful historical *memory.*" But he seemed to Carlyle "constantly definable as the sublime of commonplace . . . not . . . the least tincture of greatness or originality or any kind of superior merit except neatness of expression."[64]

On Christmas night "secretly . . . a 'brass band' . . . stationed themselves, in the dark, under a huge greek portico . . . and suddenly the black night burst into *Auld Lang Syne,* and other soft-breathing . . . articulate melody which lasted for an hour, and was really touching to the feelings."[65] Inexpensive presents for a horde of servants and their children marked the festivities of Boxing Day night in the huge ballroom. During the formal presentation of gifts by the Christmas tree, Lady Ashburton put into the delighted Carlyle's hands a map-of-the-world puzzle, with the announcement that it was appropriate to his ambitions. Jane thought the money spent on gifts embarrassingly small. But, to her husband, who returned to his reading at Cheyne Row with a sense of the general futility and folly of the "rulers of the world" who "hunt foxes" and "make bursts of parliamentary eloquence," Lady Harriet herself was the primary blessing: "You are indisputably an astonishing woman; and have a gift like no other alive!"[66]

His major concern, however, was finding some work that would sustain him through the remaining years of his writing career. He had just celebrated his fifty-sixth birthday; despite his lifelong complaints about his health, he had no reason to believe that, having survived into middle age, he would be abruptly relieved of the burden of at least another decade of consciousness. Without some absorbing work, life seemed clearly insupportable. He wanted to do one last major book before ending his career. First, he mulled over and dismissed the suitability of William the Conqueror and the Norman episode in English history. The main objection was the difficulty of finding the appropriate source material, given the antiquity of the topic and the chaotic state of library resources and services in England. Other subjects that came to mind, including the episode of the Cid in Spanish history and its European significance, soon faded. The clear direction of his intention was to write a substantial work on some major figure in British or European history which, to some extent, would fulfill the intent of his never-realized biography of Cromwell.

Whatever historical figure he decided upon, the library problem loomed forebodingly. Even under the best of circumstances he had little patience for detailed research, especially if it had to be carried on in the uncomfortable public atmosphere of a library reading room. Even as a comparatively young man working on *The French Revolution,* he had suffered from the bane of "museum headache." Access to books had seemed to him among the most important services that a government could provide for its citizens. But his experiences at the British Museum, especially while working on *Cromwell,* were marked by both objective criticism and personal anger, though which came first is not easy to ascertain. Apparently Antonio Panizzi, the Keeper of Printed Books whose combination of genuine talent and political shrewdness had made him a crucial power at the library, deeply resented a critical reference that Carlyle had made in his 1837 essay "Parliamentary History of the French Revolution," in which "the respectable sub-librarian" had been directly blamed for the slow progress in compiling a subject catalogue.[67] Panizzi's was not a forgiving temperament and Carlyle stayed away from the Museum as much as he could.

His general complaints about the inadequacy of Museum services and the shortcomings of its physical facilities had considerable validity, however. Early in 1849, Parliament established a select Royal Commission, with Richard Milnes as one of the commissioners, in response to the widely discussed need to improve the Museum. Invited to testify at the commission's hearings, Carlyle spent "rather an agitated three hours" on the witness stand. He had "many *faults* to find" and "in strenuous Carlyle phraseology" gave them "a good mouthful of" his "mind." Rather eloquently, he emphasized the two major insufficiencies that he believed needed remedying: the absence of a printed subject catalogue and the inadequacy and improper arrangement of the physical space. "I have gone into that room when it has been quite crowded, and there has been no seat vacant, and I have been obliged to sit on the step of a ladder: and there are such a bustle and confusion that . . . I never do enter the room without getting a headache . . . and therefore I avoid the room till the last extremity. I may add, that I am rather a thin-skinned sort of student."

Questioned closely about his preference for a printed catalogue, Carlyle presented an argument that anticipated modern attitudes. He was "decidedly of opinion that any catalogue whatever . . . printed with ordinary correctness, is preferable to no catalogue." Without a catalogue, "for all practical purposes this Collection of ours might as well have been locked up in water-tight chests and sunk on the Dogger-bank, as put into the British Museum."[68] Under light prodding, he indirectly identified Panizzi, who was, of course, sitting in the chamber, as "the librarian with whom" he was "not acquainted" but with whom an acquaintance might have procured him a private reading area, had he been willing to adopt the proper tone in asking for special favors. Of course, he was never polite in his private references to this "fat pedant." In a self-satisfied mood, he boasted to his mother that "the accused official parties sat by; especially one big blustering half-quack (not entirely a bad fellow either) whom I have long had my eye on: he could make next to no defense, tho' he tried hard; I am really almost sorry for him now, poor blockhead."[69]

But Carlyle's emphasis on the library problem was primarily a feint. Whatever subject he chose to write on, he could easily afford to purchase a large number of books and to use as secretary any one of the many young men who offered their services. His preoccupation with practical difficulties thus served to disguise his deeply felt personal hesitancy. Without work, he would be miserable; with some time-consuming writing project his misery might take other, less self-destructive forms. He was always happier complaining about work than complaining about idleness, and the more difficult and definitive—the more life-absorbing—the project, the greater the chance that it would relieve him (to the limited degree that he believed relief possible) of what he felt to be impossible burdens.

He had had built, insofar as conditions permitted, the best isolation chamber in London in his attic study, ironically encouraged by Jane in further separating himself from her and imprisoning himself in "one sublime garret-room . . . impervious to sound, to—in short, to everything but self and work!"[70] Finally, in the late spring of 1854 he sat down for the first time at his desk in his garret-study to begin sustained work on the subject that he had decided on; it was to be the last book of his life, and by the very choice of subject he had determined that its making would inevitably absorb his life. It took him almost thirteen years to complete, a period that Jane painfully referred to in her lighter moods as "the Thirteen Years' War."

5.

Carlyle began serious reading on the subject of Frederick the Great in the late fall of 1851. He had considered the subject as a possible topic for a book as early as 1830, when he had proposed to an Edinburgh publisher that he write a single-volume biography of the "brave Fritz."[71] From a history of Frederick that Edward Irving had lent him

Thomas Carlyle. Photograph, May 25, 1855. Courtesy of the Rare Book and Manuscript Library, Columbia University.

in the spring of 1819 he probably had derived a maxim that he was fond of quoting: "If all efforts will not gain the object, [we] say with Frederick the Great: *Another time we will do better.*"[72] In 1851 Carlyle could write on any subject he chose with the certainty that he would have an eager publisher. But after his failure to write a biography of Cromwell, the critical problem was finding suitable subjects; his refusal to move in the direction of more personal or more fictional forms of expression left him anchored to either public affairs or factual history. And the response to *Latter-Day Pamphlets* of course discouraged him from further pursuit of his ambition to unite personal observation of public conditions with political philosophy.

By 1847 a book on Frederick had begun to seem a potential answer to his problem. He was perceptive enough, however, to realize immediately that the subject offered almost insurmountable difficulties, and it was not at all clear that this was the "better" time. In 1830, with the impetuosity of comparatively inexperienced youth, he probably could have written an effective single-volume biography, similar in scope to his biography of Schiller, and consequently have relieved himself of the desire to return to the same subject toward the end of his career. By 1851, however, the need for some all-absorbing subject had become compulsive; even his mature appreciation of the difficulties of writing on Frederick could not dissuade him. Indeed, had Frederick not been available, he would have sought out an equally intractable and life-consuming topic.

For Carlyle, Germany itself had always been an idealized country, a land brightened by its literary luminaries. His initial consciousness as a writer had been formed in large part by his interaction with the German language and its literature. Though it was a vast distance from Goethe's literary meditations to Frederick's battlefields, it was not necessarily any greater or any less continuous than the movement from *Sartor Resartus* to *Latter-Day Pamphlets.* For Carlyle, German culture was embodied in the piety of Luther, the sacred necessity of the Reformation, and the creation, by Goethe in particular, of Romantic Idealism, a literary antidote to both eighteenth-century rationalism and modern materialism. He believed that the Anglo-Saxon hegemony would be based, like Britain itself, on Teutonic virtues—virtues of the kind that were best repesented by his own father and that were deeply rooted in the racial inheritance of northern Europeans: piety, courage, reverence for work and legitimate authority, and the intuitive intelligence that recognized and attempted to realize in daily life the consonance between man's needs and the facts of Nature and the universe.

Carlyle's youthful idealizations about German culture survived into maturity, mainly because he wisely declined to put them to the test of reality. The journey to Germany that he had fantasied in the first years of his marriage had never materialized; he intuitively sensed that he had more need of the ideal than of the real. Moreover, by the time he had become an established writer, he had decided to put some distance between himself and Germany, with which he was almost exclusively identified by the public. Soon Germany had become "almost a necropolis, . . . with only the tombs of my loved ones for me there." And in the late 1840s, despite his restlessness, not even his formerly close attachment to and general curiosity about all things German could overcome his distaste for long trips. However, a substantial recent book on Frederick by J. D. E. Preuss, which Carlyle read during the summer of 1845, reawakened his long-standing interest in the Prussian king and again excited his imagination with the thought of a trip to Germany.[73]

But he did not go. His preoccupation with Ireland drew him westward. Germany and Frederick, however, remained on his mind. The direct correspondence that he had opened with Germany through Goethe now continued in his correspondence with Varnhagen von Ense, whose *Memoirs* he had reviewed in 1838. Varnhagen frequently sent him German books unavailable in London—Preuss's biography of Frederick was probably among them—and Carlyle returned the favor with gifts of English authors and autographs, for which von Ense had a collector's passion. By 1847 Carlyle's letters to Varnhagen frequently mentioned his special interest in Frederick; indeed, he told Varnhagen that "if" he "were a Prussian, or even German," he "would decidedly try" to write a book about the king.[74] By the late autumn of 1851, the urge to embark on such a project was already affecting his good judgment, though he tried to emphasize the important obstacles.[75] In late November 1851 he was rereading Preuss with "some considerable private love for Frederick."[76] He felt that he was "decidedly" growing "in love for" his "Hero."[77]

However, when he encountered a large number of what seemed insufferably "dull and dreadful Books" of repellent pedantry on his subject, he began to sour on the project.[78] Though he had assured von Ense and himself that he meant only to study Frederick, his pressing need to be busy writing *something* inevitably meant that his disclaimers were only reservations that he was in the process of overcoming. "The subject" had not "the least" grown "lovelier" to him; "nor will, I think," though it had the advantage of keeping him "*silent,* and busy in thought."[79] He kept on with the reading, of course, as if boredom were the price he must pay for some degree of inner peace, for the satisfaction of being at work on something. Perhaps, he speculated, his difficulty in "making almost any true progress towards understanding" Frederick "or his affairs" resulted from his inability to get the "right Books" in England. Restless, he imagined that a trip to Germany would overcome the problem. In the spring of 1852, he and Jane spoke about "lifting anchor, and going over . . . for six months."

Jane's reaction could hardly have been enthusiastic. Certainly supervising renovations at Cheyne Row could give her a great deal more satisfaction than trailing across Germany in the luggage of a bilious husband. And Carlyle himself still had reservations not only about the voyage but about the subject. "The *worst* is," he confessed to his sister, that "I do not care rightly about the subject; do not kindle readily now about it or any other subject . . . the chief fruit . . . of rapidly advancing years."[80] During the late summer of 1852 he tried to rest at Scotsbrig, torn between lassitude and despair.[81] At Chelsea, the extensive renovations sent gasps both of dust and determination from Jane, who gradually broke the news to her husband that he "ought to go to Germany" without her.[82] Carlyle still had his doubts. He felt that leaving his aging mother would be painful, especially at a time when her death could come at any moment. If he did go, however, the trip would not be a long one; and he could, as his mother's surrogate and messenger, visit and describe to her those places in Germany closely associated with their shared and deeply revered hero, Martin Luther. But, since he had not fully admitted to himself that he had decided *actually* to write a biography of Frederick, he could not yet accept the practical necessity of subjecting himself to the anticipated miseries of such a voyage. "Of pleasure" he "could expect absolutely none; of pain and disgraceful wretchedness very much."

On the positive side was the fact that he would at least have assiduous and devoted help in practical matters. Four years before, he had been introduced by Emerson to a successful Nottingham manufacturer of German-Jewish birth, Joseph Neuberg, whom Carlyle described as a "rather heavy brother-man of the seed of Abraham." Having retired early, Neuberg made himself increasingly available to help Carlyle in any way he could. Though he had lectured on Carlyle at the Mechanic's Institute in Manchester, Neuberg's talents were more supportive than original. Soon he began translating *Past and Present* and *Heroes and Hero-Worship* into German. Both the Carlyles immediately liked him; he was undemanding, flattering, and genuinely helpful. Between 1849 and 1851, the gentle Neuberg spent long hours doing research for Carlyle at the British Museum, sorting packets of his master's notes as a "volunteer secretary" at Cheyne Row, and serving as a companion on long walks both in town and between Neuberg's Hampstead lodgings and London. He now readily offered himself as an experienced and efficient escort on this German tour. By the middle of August 1852, Carlyle felt it necessary to let Neuberg, who was staying with his sister at Bonn, know whether or not he was coming. Though he allowed himself to hope that Jane would eventually join him for part of the tour, he finally realized that the decisive factors were self-definition and pride.[83]

Disgusted with his own lassitude, Carlyle thought a voyage, though painful, might be energizing. He was still somewhat ambivalent about Frederick, but if he did not go he could not write about him; and he had no other subject at hand. If he did not make this effort, his premature sense of old age would be intensified. And he was encouraged by the possibility that Lord Ashburton would join him at Berlin. By the end of August, he had made up his mind. The most practical route would be to go directly from Edinburgh to Holland, and then steam up the Rhine. After packing, he walked in the twilight to the top of a nearby hill with a broad view of Scotsbrig and his Annandale home; with a "strange earnest light" shining and in "solitude" and "silence," he reread all Jane's recent letters, sadly reminding himself how miserable she was and the extent to which he was responsible.[84] Two days later, at midnight on August 29, 1852, he left Leith on a heavily laden steamer, beginning "one of the most uncomfortable pitching, tumbling, tedious and dreary voyages" he had "ever made."[85] He did not feel in the least self-conscious about complaining.

Fortunately, despite his litany of regrets, the trip was a success, though he sometimes denied even that. It did not, of course, result in substantial progress in the writing of Frederick; that could be determined only by what he did in his study. The amount of actual research, in our modern sense of that term, was negligible. But Carlyle was in an early stage of his work on the subject: what he needed was to acquaint himself with what was available, to gain impressions, and to strengthen his commitment to the project. He did some reading in public libraries and private collections, particularly in Bonn, Weimar, and Berlin; but it soon became clear that since on the whole German collections of material on Frederick were chaotic and neglected, he would do best to purchase whatever books he could for later study in the solitude of Cheyne Row. Certain that he could not write a successful biography without obtaining some accurate drawings or portraits of Frederick, he felt fortunate to discover in Berlin what he was looking for. Neuberg provided the much-appreciated services of a diligent courier as the two men looped from Rotterdam to Dusseldorf, southward and eastward across Germany to Dresden, where they turned northward to Berlin. The sites of some of Frederick's major battlefields were on the itinerary, of course. But even Berlin, the best of German cities, so many of which, like Potsdam, were "dreadfully ugly," did not impress Carlyle: the city had "a rawboned awkward bare appearance," like "Manchester *without* the industry, or any *smoke* save that of bad tobacco, which penetrates all corners and sanctuaries."[86] To his disappointment, Lord Ashburton could not meet him in Berlin, though the British ambassador received him cordially.

On the whole, he felt kindly welcomed wherever he went. In Weimar, the ruling family extended its hospitality to a celebrity intimately connected with the great literary past of its city. In Berlin, he met

Preuss and Ludwig Tieck, whose Romantic prose-poems he had translated thirty years before. Traveling up the Rhine by steamer, he marveled at the beauty and grandeur of the river. It was "the most magnificent image of silent power" he had ever "seen . . . one's first idea of a world-river."[87] Unlike the Thames, the Rhine created a pathway between countries and a channel into the heart of Germany; he felt as if he were being carried along by Nature itself.[88] But "the *sublime* portions of the Rhine country" and the dramatic "mountain watering" heights of Bohemia impressed him more than did modern German culture.[89] His youthful and previously untested vision of Germany as a center of literary culture and artistic sensitivity crumbled immediately before the bourgeois stolidity of this "honest-hearted hardy population" who, "one becomes convinced, are not wise."[90] To be wise one had to have imagination; he felt that the tediousness of the books he read on Frederick embodied the widespread "prosy inconclusiveness" of the German people—"talk and thought that leads nowhither."[91] He did not dislike them in the least; indeed, he admired some of their virtues. But, in no more than ten days, he had determined conclusively that all Germans were vapid and dull, without sparkle or intellectual vision. Most of all, he was angered by the neglect of Frederick among his own people. The country that in his youthful fantasy had seemed bright with hope now seemed gray with dullness, as if the journey up the Rhine were a journey into tedious confusion.

At some level he worried that his projected multivolume exploration of Frederick and the eighteenth century would also be a journey into confusion. Eighteenth-century Germany and the Enlightenment in general, except for the literary heroes who wrote at the end of the epoch, were not congenial to him. The genius of Johnson and Voltaire had won only a partial victory over what Carlyle saw as the mind- and soul-damaging corruptions of rationalistic materialism. How could he possibly create an effective dramatization of Frederick's life when the century in which he had flourished had so severely stunted his potential and restricted the literary and spiritual atmosphere in which he lived? And it was not only Frederick who appeared forgotten in Germany; even the Germany of Goethe and Schiller seemed to have disappeared. It was actually *that* Germany which he was most interested in. In fact, his experiences in Germany on this first trip had nothing to do with Frederick directly but focused instead on the two people who had long been the dominant models for his life, Goethe and Luther, the representatives of German Idealism and the German Reformation.

At Weimar, Goethe's house was opened for him as a special "*favour*." The house and its rooms seemed so much smaller than he had imagined them to be from the etching that had been printed in his translation of *Wilhelm Meister,* smaller in fact than his own home at Cheyne Row. The father who had once seemed so imposing seemed quite mortal now. Looking over the books on the bookshelves, he was moved to discover a copy of the last book that he had ever sent to the Sage of Weimar, Taylor's *Survey of German Poetry*. Inside, "still sticking in, after twenty years," he found "a crumb of paper torn" from his own essay on Samuel Johnson. It was touching and unnerving.[92] In Frankfurt, he had another experience that resonated with the complex emotions of his discipleship and the changes that time had imposed. While shaving early one morning in his hotel, he glimpsed, out of the corner of his eye, a completely familiar face in the town square. It was the face of Goethe, in *stone,* in the middle of the Platz among the trees. He "had so longed to see that face alive; and here it was given to" him "at last . . . in stone, an emblem of so much that happens. . . . Goethe's face . . . now when I saw it, as I had often longed to do . . . could not see *me* at all."[93]

He journeyed to the Wartburg Castle to visit the monastic room in which Luther had lived; to him it was "a kind of holy place" in which an "authentically . . . great man" had confronted the voices of anguish and triumphed over them. As he looked out the cell window, into the deep chasm and across to the heavily wooded hills, he thought about his mother, her veneration for piety and her imminent death. Examining the relics in this "venerable" room, he "kissed the old oak table" that Luther had used as a desk and reverently touched the spot on the plaster wall against which Luther had thrown his inkstand in defiance of the voice of the devil.[94] He too had used ink as the means of expressing his defiance. Luther had left father and mother (and offended their values) to make his profession of faith. The words that Luther spoke and wrote reminded Carlyle of his own relationship with his parents and the mission that he had chosen for himself. "Here once lived," he thought, "one of God's soldiers," the creator of the Reformation and thus the man most responsible for the culture that his parents embodied and the Puritan vision that he himself most revered.

Like Luther, over and over again, despite his suffering, Carlyle had exclaimed, "Lord, here stand I; I can do no other!" Such defiance was one of the key sources of his own Protestant self-consciousness. Luther was his mother's favorite "saint" and his own alter ego. No matter how much he departed from the theological structures of his parents' world, he knew that the closer he could come to embodying Luther and Luther's vision of the inner life the more certain it was that he would eventually be reconciled with his mother and father. At Erfurt, looking at Lucas Cranach's famous portraits of Luther's parents and of Luther, he saw the idealized features and moral characteristics of his own parents and of himself, though the transference had been so lifelong and complete that he seemed unaware of the nuances of his special vision: "the Father with a depth of thrift, contention and worldly wisdom in his old judicious peasant countenance, the mother particularly pious, kind, true . . . a noble old peasant woman. . . . Luther . . . a bold effective-looking rustic man . . . with a depth of peaceable self-consciousness and healthy defiance."[95] The description was written expressly for his mother, who read her son's tender words with tears, sensing that her family had been absorbed into the most sacred archetype of Christian piety.

6.

By the spring of 1853 the event that Carlyle had all his life feared more than any other seemed imminent. The year had been an anxious one for the Carlyle family: there was no doubt that the best that could be done was to make Margaret Carlyle as comfortable as possible, in the hope that she could survive another winter. At home at Chelsea, struggling with his attempt to begin writing, Carlyle had his mother constantly on his mind. But he did not want to go to Scotland that summer, partly because he feared seeing his mother's frailty, partly because he felt desperate to get on with his work. Though he wrote consoling and confessional letters to his mother, he apparently had determined that he would not visit her until he had no choice: even at a distance of almost four hundred miles his voice was tremulous, his tears barely suppressed. The gift of a ham from Scotsbrig moved him to affirm that it was "one of a thousand such things with which my poor life, ever since it began, has been made rich by you. Whatever other things have gone wrong with me, the love of my true Mother never went wrong; but followed me ever inseparable, in good and evil fortune. . . . And, alas, what can I do in return for you, dear Mother? Nothing, Nothing!"[96] His helplessness tortured him. Long years of mental preparation to confront stoically the "King of Terrors" did not relieve him of the pain he felt anticipating her imminent death. After this time, he thought, he would only weep once more, when Jane died.

Over the winter, Jane's health had "greatly failed," though "she has a wonderful spirit in her still."[97] Desperate for a holiday away from her gloomy husband and before work began on the "sound-proof" room, she accepted John Carlyle's invitation to visit his new home in Moffat. To everyone's surprise, the stolid bachelor had finally married in the autumn of 1852. His wife was "a tall Ladylike" well-to-do young widow with three sons, Mrs. Phoebe Elizabeth Fowler Watts. "Not beautiful but handsome enough and healthfully agreeable," Carlyle reported to

Alick, she seemed to have good sense, "cheerful temper and honest heart."[98] Carlyle hoped that Jane would like her new sister-in-law. He thought her "very comely" and a "great improvement" for Jack.[99] But the visit the next summer was not particularly successful. "Phoebe's manner is so different from mine, so formal and cold," Jane told her husband.[100] Astounded by the suggestion that her sister-in-law might find her "formidable" and "sarcastic," Jane claimed that she was "perfectly unconscious of dealing in that sort of thing at all."[101]

From Moffat, Jack kept his eye on Scotsbrig and made the short trip frequently to administer medicine and advice. Though always far from comfortable among her husband's family, Jane went in mid-July to spend her birthday at Scotsbrig, where Margaret Carlyle had taken a sudden turn for the worse. For the moment it seemed "to be the beginning of the end . . . but . . . she rallied as by miracle . . . said you had been as good a son to her as ever woman had." It was clear that "no doctor can do anything against old age."[102] Carlyle was grateful for his wife's comfort; she returned at the end of July to face his irritability. If she went away again, she feared that she would find her husband "in the Prison" on her return "for having killed an Irish bricklayer because he had fallen thro' the ceiling. . . . It takes all my strength of mind to keep things from murder and utter insanity."[103] The Ashburtons, who were away, gave the Carlyles "liberty of their beautiful little place at Addiscombe," where he spent three weeks by himself in September.[104] He recollected there that just a year ago, in similarly bright weather, he had been in the presence of Luther's spirit at the Wartburg.[105]

When Jack reported in November 1853 that "she is evidently parting from us," Thomas had to confront the obvious and unavoidable fact that his mother was dying. Her children did all they could to make her comfortable; she stayed in bed in her room, where there was a fire night and day. Jack's presence made it easier for Thomas to accept the fact of his own absence. What could he do except add to the gloom and increase his own pain? At least Jack could provide expert medical attendance. Fortunately, Margaret Carlyle seemed piously resigned and uncomplaining; she had her wits about her still. Early in December, from the Grange, where he and Jane had gone for a visit during which it had been agreed he would carry on his work just as if at home, he wrote what was to be his last letter to her:

> Dear old Mother, weak and sick and dear to me while I live in God's creation, what a day this has been, in my solitary thought. . . . A dim silent Sabbath day, the sky foggy dark, with damp, and unusual stillness. . . . And it is this day gone fifty-eight years that I was born! And my poor Mother—Well we are all in God's hands. Surely God is good; surely we

> ought to trust in Him,—or what trust is there for the sons of man. Oh my dear Mother, let it ever be a comfort to you, however weak you are, that you did your part honourably and well while in strength, and were a noble Mother, to me and to us all. I am now myself grown old; and have had various things to do and suffer for so many years, but there is nothing I have ever had to be so *much* thankful for as for the mother I had. . . . For if there has been any good in the things I have uttered in this world's hearing, it was *your* voice essentially that was speaking thro' me: essentially, what you and my brave father meant and taught me to mean, this was the purport of all I spoke and wrote. And [if] in the few years that remain for me, I am to get any more written for the world, the essence of it, so far as it is worthy and good, will still be yours.[106]

Jane, in her usual bad health, felt extremely weak, nervous, and sleepless. Amid the crowds of "Bishops, Foxhunters, Lords and Commons, not to speak of Ladies great and little," they both felt lonely, though emotionally apart in their loneliness. The winter days seemed short, "shut out by . . . monstrous Ionic pillars and Greek architecture . . . under these grey frozen skies." Each morning the first thing he heard was the "hoarse melody" of "an immense assemblage of rooks" that roosted "around the Grange, . . . remembrances of poor old Ecclefechan."[107] He expected to hear from Scotsbrig at any moment. Jane, who thought herself better off at Cheyne Row than at the Grange, returned on Monday, December 19, to see if she could compensate for the inadequacies of the soundproof room by silencing her neighbor's parrots. A message from Scotland carried foreboding implications, but it was not clear whether the end was hours or days or weeks away. Vividly reliving the pain of her failure to arrive in time to see her own mother before she died, Jane urged her husband to leave immediately for Scotland. There was no time for rest. Otherwise, she was certain, he would be too late; there would never be another chance to be on time.

He left the Grange on Wednesday and London on Thursday. The overnight express brought him to Kirtlebridge Station early the next morning. His anxiety about whether he would find her alive propelled him to Scotsbrig in silence. He dared not question anyone until halfway up the staircase to his mother's room. She joyfully recognized him. Throughout the day she was restless; in her extreme weakness it seemed sometimes difficult for her children, gathered around her bed, to tell whether she was asleep or awake. Though her mind was mostly clear, she occasionally failed to recognize her eldest son. But each time she called him back, apologizing for her lapse. Jean kept a tireless nurse's vigil. That night Margaret Carlyle prayed for each member of her family, " 'going round by America too now.' " There was no chance of Alick returning from that distance even for the death of his mother. About midnight on Saturday Jack gave her laudanum. While his mother rested, Carlyle, who had sent Lady Harriet a note from London just as he was leaving, wrote to tell her that, "Thank God," he had found her still alive and able to recognize him. But she was "struggling and sinking."[108] The laudanum relaxed her. "A little after midnight, John said to her, 'Here's Tom come to bid you goodnight.' She looked kindly at me, as she had done even in the worst pain. . . . I kissed her cold lips; and she took leave of me in these words, 'I'm muckle obliged t'ye,' audibly whispered . . . which except a 'yes' and a 'no' in answer to questions from John about one and about four o'clock, were the last she spoke in this world."[109]

She soon fell into "deep and deeper *sleep* for near 16 hours," until she slipped gently into death, "almost as" into "a dream."[110] It was the late afternoon of Christmas Day 1853. An hour later he wrote to his "dear friend" at the Grange that "all is over here." The body was laid out in the bedroom. He went to sleep that night in the next room, "*her* Corpse and I the only tenants upstairs." He walked a few times quickly into the "white-sheeted Place" and tried to calm himself and his memories. "All manner of late and early things" were "walking in funeral procession thro' " his "heart." But he felt more composed than he had for a long time. His presence as she had wrestled "with the King of Terrors" had at least relieved him of the painful "remorse" he would have felt if he had not been there. For that, he was grateful to Jane.[111]

The next morning the sky was "bright like diamonds." The funeral procession walked through "iron frost, with a powdering of snow," and laid Margaret Carlyle to rest in Ecclefechan churchyard next to her husband and her daughter. At Scotsbrig, Jamie faced the continuation of his life in the house in which his mother had lived and died. Toward the end of the week, Jack presided over the dispersal among her children of "the mournful lot of remnants *she* has done with."[112] It was a painful moment. Carlyle remained through the weekend, after the others had gone, and wandered through the empty upstairs apartment, his mother's room "all full of litter."[113] He felt as if a "new epoch" had begun for him; but it was "the final one."[114] With his mother's death, his own seemed much closer. He came home on the second day of 1854, "extremely cold and miserable," and returned to his attic study.[115] He hoped "yet to do some work, in the years that may remain; no other consolation is conceivable. . . . One gets very dim," he told his "bright Queen," and "has need that the sacred fountains be again opened in one's stony heart."[116]

But his work on Frederick was hardly any consolation at all. He could not overcome its inauspicious origins, the sour feeling that had attached itself to the project almost from the beginning. When it became known that he was working on the subject, he squirmed under the expectation, expressed by Emerson and Geraldine, that he would write an extraordinary book. Until he returned from Germany, he emphatically denied that he was "*writing* on Frederick the Great; nor at all practically contemplating to do so."[117] But in the autumn of 1852 he confessed that he would either have to conquer "the chaotic heap of facts" or "they will abolish me." However, he found the material intractable: he had no conviction that he saw fully and perceptively into Frederick and, as in the case of Cromwell, he sensed the need for some effective organizing principle. After the return from Germany, he felt "utterly *demoralized*."[118] How, he asked himself, could he ever write anything on that man, despite the time and energy he had already put in, "so little lovely is the man to me; so dim, vague, faint and contemptible is the account I get of his life-element" and "too often" of him?[119] Like Cromwell, Frederick seemed buried in unreadable books, Prussian "dust mounds."

The best thing seemed to be to give him up. Carlyle tried to do so at the end of 1852. But, since he had no alternative project, to relinquish the task would be to admit that his life had lost its use and value. Though he went back to reading and making notes about Frederick throughout 1853, he did so with a dismal sense that he lacked the enthusiasm necessary to carry out the project. He was being driven by pain, not joy, but he simply could not "yet afford to be *beaten*. . . . If I can work no more, what is the good of *me* further?"[120] When he returned from Scotsbrig at the beginning of 1854, his desk was both his refuge from pain and his solace from suffering, "the perpetual misery" which had kept him company "for thirty-five years or so."[121] But the effort was distinctive in that he clearly expected it to be his final struggle with work: the scope of the project was such that if he survived to complete it he would have neither the time nor the energy to undertake anything more.

Through much of 1854 Carlyle felt that "enormous rubbish-mountains" surrounded him in his study.[122] The valuable material at the British Museum was "as good as invisible" to him;[123] documents at the State Papers Office were more accessible. Fortunately, the assiduous and faithful Neuberg provided research assistance. If necessary, Carlyle could readily afford to (and did) employ clerks to copy out passages relevant to his work. Near the end of the year, he confessed to his brother that his "work" went on "ill. . . . I really need to get sufficiently wretched over it; then I shall rise in despair, and *can* do it."[124] Staying more and more at home, he was even less of a companion to Jane, even more of a recluse in his study, determined that he would get this book done. Some of the material was actually taking shape on paper, though his satisfaction was undercut by the increasing consciousness that the bitterness of the process might somehow taint the value of the product. Recognizing that he would not have chosen to write this book if he had any alternative, he could not retreat from his commitment to complete what he had begun, no matter how close to a living death the process of creating the book might seem. Already his mind turned to fantasies of liberation: to Emerson and to Alick he speculated on the pleasures of coming to America to see them when once he were done. By March 1855 the bitter cold of the "severest winter" he had "ever experienced" did not seem quite as piercing as his own sense of depression and desolation as he struggled over "the ugliest mass of dreary work . . . in real horror" at the "darkness and meanness of intellect and mind" of the German books he had to read.[125]

When the warm weather came, he still did not change his mind about his subject.[126] He "quietly" admitted to Jack that his book "never can have much value," a claim his brother, who still idealized the family's famous writer, reluctantly came to agree with.[127] By the early spring of 1856, though he was "very unhappy; buried in endless . . . Prussian Pedantry, Prussian Stupidity and Infidelity; seeking a poor prize after all," he had made sufficient progress to see a glimmer of deliverance, for which "we must have faith."[128] Even though "the Book will . . . never be worth two-pence . . . it is only when I fall altogether idle, that I get altogether miserable."[129] At least he was at work and making progress; some pleasure had begun to infiltrate the pain. Two volumes would be ready for printing by autumn, about half the book, perhaps a little more. He anticipated taking a rest before returning to the "other two (or one), which ends it!"[130]

During the summer of 1856 he kept at it, "feeling obliged to do the Bad Book or go to Bedlam."[131] But it was going much more slowly than he had hoped, he confessed to his sister, "slower than *snails*."[132] Brief lightning strokes of genius could not sustain him through the long haul of tedious reading and insufferable detail. "The truth is I am wrestling fixedly to do a piece of work set to me for which . . . I am not equal," he told Lady Harriet. "I rather despise it too."[133] If he survived this, he had no intention of writing anything else again. If he still needed to work, could he not find some other employment, perhaps in government and education?[134] By the end of 1857 the first two volumes had still not appeared; and, worst of all, he recognized not only that his own inefficiency was slowing the process but that the scope of the project inherent in the first two volumes demanded more than the one or two additional volumes he had planned. There was nothing to do but go on with it. "I wiggle and waggle still along, and will not be beaten if I can help it. The book seems worth nothing to me, or less than nothing; that is the heaviest item of the problem."[135] Finally, in June 1858 volumes one and two were completed; they were published in the autumn, while their author glumly faced what he

"Carlyle writing 'finis' to 'Friedrich.' " Cartoon. Courtesy of the Rare Book and Manuscript Library, Columbia University.

realized were at least two or three years more work. To his surprise, Jane thought the first two volumes "a magnificent book. . . . The best of all your books . . . forcible and vivid, and sparkling."[136]

The recent deaths of friends and relations, however, heightened his sense of old age and of the worthlessness of what he was doing. The long-anticipated death of Margaret Carlyle was followed by an unexpected family tragedy. Like her husband, Carlyle's sister-in-law Phoebe enjoyed bustle and travel. Early in the winter of 1853 the newlyweds spent two weeks in Chelsea, near the Carlyles. The famous author, who saw his sister-in-law often, "was well contented with" her, though they "did not get to any intimacy."[137] Jane had found her company uncongenial, but differences of temperament rather than any failure of intention determined her response, and her ill health certainly made it less likely that she would make any special effort to get to know Phoebe better. Jack seemed unusually happy; the marriage appeared to be a success.

Early in the spring of 1854 Phoebe became pregnant; she was about thirty-nine, her husband fifty-three. Delighted by their good fortune, the couple left Moffat in June and took lodgings in Chelsea; they began immediately to visit frequently at Cheyne Row and to take rapid excursions not only to see London but to search for a house in the country. To Carlyle, "they did not seem in any haste to fix upon a house,—tho', as she was five or six months gone with child, we always silently thought it altogether desirable they should be *fixed.*" Phoebe, who had apparently always had easy pregnancies, saw no reason to confine herself unnecessarily soon. In the middle of August, on their way back from a house-hunting excursion, the fright of a minor railway accident seemed to have unsettled the expectant mother. After a few days of seemingly normal activity, Phoebe was suddenly seized with "hysteria fits," which lasted for two days. Soon the baby, in its eighth month, was born dead. The doctors expected Phoebe to recover; though she was exhausted, she seemed cheerful and her mind was clear. But a week later she unexpectedly died, "without pain . . . sheer weakness dragging her down."[138] The "railway accident" was blamed.[139] But Jane, sharply censorious, thought it "a *waste* of a woman and child" which could have been prevented "if she had staid at home and taken the ordinary care of herself that her situation required." She claimed that "even before the accident" it had "seemed to us often . . . a sheer tempting of Providence."[140] (If Jane herself had miscarried, after traveling to London in 1831, it seems likely that the memory of her own misfortune and the potential allegation of a similar recklessness would have discouraged her from such criticism.) Her husband held his tongue, except for his deep regret that his brother had had his happiness so cruelly snatched away from him. It was "perhaps the very saddest [scene]" he "ever was concerned with."[141] Jack's stolidity and stoicism came to his rescue. What could he do but accept what God had ordained? He went back to Scotland to attend to practical matters, since he now had three stepsons, and to wonder what he would do and where he would settle. Early in September 1854, pensive and sad, Carlyle "walked out to the Brompton Cemetery," where they had buried Phoebe the previous week, to pay his last respects to the dead. "All" was "still and smooth . . . hushed up into eternal rest." He "sat down on the stone nearby, for a little while, and thought painfully of many things." At home, "Jane . . . burst into a passion of tears, thinking of all that sad avalanche of death."[142]

The middle years of the decade saw only a slight decrease in his passionate friendship for Lady Harriet. Whenever opportunities arose to visit at Bath House or at the Ashburton country homes, he usually took them, unless Jane's attitude made it absolutely impossible. But there had been some subtle but important changes, particularly after 1854. His desperate need to complete his huge writing project demanded that he isolate himself more and more, staying at his desk in London as much as possible. At the same time, Lady Harriet's health had become increasingly uncertain; the cause was unclear, but consumption was suspected. The remedy was rest, fresh country air, and frequent trips to the south of France, especially to avoid the influenza and bronchial ailments that flourished in the damp English winters. Though the quality of Ashburton entertaining did not decline, the frequency of their London parties and even their extravaganzas at the Grange did. Between her increased absences and his obsessive work, she and Carlyle saw one another less.[143]

But Carlyle's emotional attachment to her, instead of declining, merely shifted its emphasis in order to adjust to the new conditions. It had always been necessary for him to express much of his intense feeling for her through indirection or displacement. Thus, he wrote that he had seen her "one night . . . in a Dream: strange nightmare figures, gathered out of various countries and various centuries . . . with something of grotesque, of the nightmare, in all of them, male and female, except your own self, who were brightly beautiful, good and spirit-like, as you have always seemed to me."[144] The dream appeared to him the best thing he had created in years. Many of his dreams had been nightmares for a long time, "waste scenes of solitary desolation, gathered from Craigenputtock," but intensified. For

> nearly all my dreams in this world have come from bodily conditions of the nerves . . . and ninety-nine out of every hundred have been ugly and painful, very stupid too, and weak, and, on the whole, by no means worth having, could one have avoided them. . . . I find nothing sublime in the act of dreaming, nor even anything very strange. Shut your eyes at any time, there will be a phantasmagory of thoughts and images begin parading in unbroken series through your head. To sleep is but to shut your eyes and outer senses a little better. I have an impression that one always *dreams,* but that only in cases where the nerves are disturbed by bad health . . . do they start into such relief—call it agony and antagony—as to force themselves on our waking consciousness.[145]

But his dreams about Lady Harriet had never been nightmares. He would do whatever he could, "encounter" even bores and worse, to see her directly; and, when he could not, he would resort to dreams and fantasies.[146] Throughout, Lady Harriet remained the imperturbable object of his needs. Her need for him was less than his dependency on her; and, in order to continue some of the satisfactions of a relationship he had come to rely on, he became even more the pursuer. Though eager to please her, he was sometimes cross, irritable, and even sarcastic. At the end of 1855, having arranged that he and Jane were to stay at the Grange for a month, he promised to be, he assured Lady Harriet, "a good boy; it is only by weakness of the flesh, not want of a willing spirit, that I shall fail of being exemplary."[147] To be successful, he would have to quell his complaints, his irritability, his impatience. After the visit, he begged her to "forgive all my sins. . . . They are many and great," but, he assured her, they were not directed against her. "I am a sinful son of Adam, and you—have no malice against me, have you? . . . Oh my Lady, my Lady, what could I write that were not a mockery of what one probably feels! . . . I kiss the hem of your garment."[148]

In the summer of 1856, despite Jane's deep resentment, he accepted Lady Harriet's invitation to vacation with them in the Highlands. The Carlyles journeyed to Scotland in a private railway carriage hired to carry the tired noblewoman and her entourage northward: she hardly came out of her private compartment throughout the journey, though Carlyle flattered her with his thanks for her "tearing me up from Chelsea, and whirling me off, with burning axle, in a whirlwind of dust, into these dumb regions: how beautiful you did it, too; I never saw better behaviour under baddish usage: but you do belong to the clouds . . . though some others of us do not."[149] Some mechanical problems with the train had increased the passengers' discomfort in the hot weather, and Jane found ways to express her hostility. In Scotland, the Carlyles made their usual visits, sometimes separately, to Scotsbrig, Haddington, Edinburgh, and Thornhill. Jane refused to join the Ashburtons in the Highlands. But Carlyle assured Lady Harriet that if "I were an insect I would rather bite you than almost any creature. . . . And will I come to the Highlands, I myself? Bright Lady . . . if it stood with me, the answer were not difficult. But it stands with so many persons, and with so many things and laws, I dare not yet answer at all."[150]

But it really *did* stand with him, if he were willing to face the consequences of fulfilling his needs. Despite Jane's feelings, he went to Loch Luichart for ten days with the Ashburtons. There he complained of everything, with some justification, even of Lady Harriet's company. She was irritable and kept to herself much of the time. He walked, and slept, and read. Back at Chelsea, he idealized the experience. "All was so beautiful. . . . I reminded myself of a banished soul (Satan without the devilry) taking a walk through Paradise. . . . The Paradise still in many respects belongs to us all; and all of us too . . . get our share of Purgatory, each according to his softness of nerves." He often looked at the portrait of Lady Ashburton hung over the mantlepiece, downstairs, opposite his own. One day, a stranger, a guest of Jane's, remarked, " '*There* is a beautiful woman: who is that?' " She then asked Jane if the man in the opposite portrait was Lady Ashburton's husband. " 'Rather hers than mine!' added this good judge of mankind and womankind," Carlyle, who had heard the story from Jane, reported to Lady Ashburton.[151]

When Lady Ashburton went to spend the winter at Nice for her health, Carlyle was dimly aware that she was not well. He had not seen her since October 1856; the rumor about her ill health had gathered intensity during the winter. By February 1857 he felt anxious, suspecting that her traveling did her health "mischief." His own mood was better than it had been for quite some time, particularly because with the coming of the bright spring weather he could also envision the completion of the first stage of Frederick. Yet he felt more aware of change than of anything else. "The Spring is beautiful again; but the eyes that once saw it with me, where are they? One's own eyes get old, even they are not the same!"[152] He was disquieted by the news that Lady Harriet was reacting badly to the medicines that were being prescribed for her, particularly mercury, whose disastrous side effects he knew from personal experience. He urged her to come home as soon as possible, to be "among your friends again."[153] Apparently, she was depressed. The doctors diagnosed dropsy; the swelling of tissues from excess fluid was obvious. More likely than not, there was the beginning of serious but undetected heart damage sometime in the early spring of 1857. Still, the doctors thought her well enough to travel. From Nice, she went to Paris. There, on May 4, while dressing for the evening, she collapsed; she soon died in her doctor's arms. The next evening Richard Milnes brought the news to Cheyne Row. It was an inexpressible shock to Carlyle; moreover, despite his expressive powers, he was not free to express his deepest feelings about Lady Harriet to anyone. Jane coldly watched the tumult of telegrams, meetings, condolences, and finally the funeral. Lady Harriet was buried at the Grange "with a kind of royal state; and all the men, who used to compose a sort of *Court* for her, were there, *in tears!*"[154] Carlyle took his mournful place in the funeral procession and said good-bye to his Queen.

[15]

A Victorian Sage
1857–1865

During the 1850s the intensity of Carlyle's "angry" public "dialogue with the world" gradually diminished.[1] He still made bitter, taunting observations, which were sometimes tellingly accurate, but he recognized clearly that the part of his career which had been based on the expectation that he could influence public life had come to an end. His "angry dialogue," however, had been deeply internalized, based on a vision of the world as an extension of the self rather than the self as an extension of the world. He had no doubt that human beings carried their own inherent miseries with them wherever they went. He could not imagine heaven or paradise other than as cessation of pain, the end of life. With the deaths of his mother and Lady Harriet, he had only two other crucial deaths to face; his own, he suspected, would be the easier of the two, provided that he could finish his "impossible" book before the end. At the age of sixty-two, he was curiously ambivalent about old age. He did not value his own life except in terms of the work that he found not only increasingly painful but possibly useless. As critical as ever of the materialism and corruption of contemporary society, he discovered that he was more and more admired by a public that found his image attractive but his message irrelevant. Not even the derisive hostility provoked by *Latter-Day Pamphlets* could do more than slightly slow that public's insistence that Carlyle help fulfill its demand for patriarchal totems.

Carlyle himself had unwittingly cooperated with the creation of comforting stereotypes by growing a beard in 1854. The previous year Lord Ashburton had elicited the promise that if put to the test Carlyle

Thomas Carlyle. Photograph, July 15, 1857. Courtesy of the Rare Book and Manuscript Library, Columbia University.

would match him and also grow a beard. It seemed to the writer a promise that he would not have to fulfill. To his surprise, Lord Ashburton returned to town in September 1854 with a long, white, silken beard. The shocked Carlyle bemusedly admitted that now he might have to pay off on his "careless" promise.[2] Throughout his life a clean-shaven face had been the fashion for poets as well as politicians; indeed, for over two hundred years clean-shaven cheeks and chin had been an essential affirmation of secular civilization. Keats, Shelley, Byron, even the longer-lived Coleridge and the very durable Wordsworth, had kept their faces smooth; their image was that of the youthful son. But suddenly, with the return of bearded soldiers from the Crimea, the beard had become fashionable. The characteristic Victorian seriousness had found its appropriate visual representation. Even Leigh Hunt, the most unserious survivor of Romantic spontaneity, "produced a copious beard, white or nearly so; he complained that there were two drawbacks, 1) the little boys laughed at him; 2) the beard abolished an uncommonly sweet smile he was understood to have." Carlyle observed that at least the "latter evil" would "not apply" to him.[3]

To his surprise, Lord Ashburton kept the beard. Carlyle granted that he also was an "enemy" of shaving in principle; it was a daily waste of time. But early in October 1854 Lord Ashburton appeared at Cheyne Row and, with Jane's collaboration, removed all Carlyle's razors. The stubble itched; the beard seemed to grow slowly, "the horror of surrounding parishes!" He did not think "it" would "ever do; for it grows daily more ugly."[4] But his resistance soon diminished. Apparently the transformation seemed suitable; in fact, it had been psychologically and culturally long in preparation. As soon as it was full-grown, mostly gray to match his slightly grizzled hair, it seemed not only natural and right but helped impose on the earlier Carlyle a definition so Victorian that it seemed as if that were the only Carlyle there had ever been. By the time the first two volumes of *Frederick the Great* were published, that shaggy, bearded, dour, but immensely handsome face was in great demand. Commercial photographers urgently requested the privilege of photographic sessions; photographs of the "new" Carlyle, and even occasionally of Jane in her capacity as wife of the "man of genius," became commonly available in booksellers' shops. Some of the photographs he liked; but most of them seemed unsatisfactory.

The photographs, of course, represented the society's idea of the man rather than the man himself. Looking at the bearded, unsmiling face, Victorian observers generally concluded that he was a wise, sad, and even gentle man with deep resources of spirit through whose special powers of insight truths that transcended the passing moment had been revealed. They were not altogether wrong. But they were far from completely right. Though he sometimes enjoyed the role of "sage," more often than not he found its mantle too heavy, inappropriate to his own sense of himself. He was frequently unhappy, and his self-consciousness about his inner anger served as a constant ironic comment on his elevation into a partriarchal figure dispensing wisdom to his society.

The sudden popularity of photography helped to fix this image of Carlyle in the public mind. Erasmus Darwin was an amateur photographer; so too were John Carlyle and Geraldine Jewsbury. Jane Carlyle decorated her bedroom with photographs of all the places she had lived in and all the people she had known who were dear to her. "Blessed be the inventor of photography!" she exclaimed. "I set him above even the inventor of chloroform. . . . I have a photograph of . . . every place I ever lived at as a home—photographs of old lovers! old friends, old servants, old dogs!"[5]

On one occasion, the camera was sent to see Carlyle as an embodiment of "work." Throughout his life he did not work any harder or longer than most working people. But his preoccupation with work as a concept had both its public and private dimensions. Over and over again he insisted to his reading audience that honorable work was a spiritual and economic necessity. Neither the individual nor the nation could be saved unless deeply involved in fruitful activity. The answer to painful self-consciousness was the sweet satisfaction of the subordination of ego which work demanded: the answer to poverty was productive labor. For Carlyle himself work was a driving necessity; but it was not a successful answer to dislocation and nervous anxiety, and it was an expression and an expansion, not a subordination, of ego. The reward, then, had to be partly the sense of a process honorably engaged in and partly a product well created. Work was not for the purpose of making one happy or wealthy in the ordinary sense. It was a spiritual test, an existential necessity. It allowed one to be useful; and since "use" was critical, work encouraged a life of dignity and self-regard. But why, then, was work always so painful to him? Was it because he could not fulfill his own standards? Was it because he had never overcome his suspicion that the work he did was not sufficiently useful, not sufficiently relevant to the needs of the society?

He could not answer such questions definitively, of course. And his own public comments on the nature and importance of "work" over a forty-year period are so rich and varied that they resist simple summary. But in May 1859 Ford Madox Brown sent his photographer to help him in a project designed to satisfy a public that demanded stereotypes and slogans. Brown had conceived of doing a painting called *Work* to represent the Carlylean doctrine of work as a spiritual and economic necessity. He sent a letter to the writer, who was bitterly working at a book that he hated, reminding him of his earlier promise to pose for photographs that would help the artist include in his painting a portrait of the man who most fully represented the "doctrine of

Thomas Carlyle. Photograph by Julia Margaret Cameron, 1867. The Metropolitan Museum of Art, The Alfred Stieglitz Collection, 1949.

work." Although Carlyle reluctantly agreed to fulfill his promise, he honestly responded, for reasons that Brown could not possibly grasp, "I think it a pity you had not put (or should not still put) some other man than me into your Great Picture."[6] The results were almost ludicrous; Brown painted an unconvincingly grimacing Carlyle leaning against a fence, watching work-in-progress on an underground tunnel on Heath Street in Hampstead.

Over seven years later, a brilliant amateur photographer and friend of Tennyson's, Julia Margaret Cameron, caught Carlyle in a very sensitive lens focused to produce an image of the literary artist as inspired seer. Cameron's photograph superimposes on the evidence of lifelong suffering the calm of wisdom; pain still flickers in the face, but the prophetic vision of old age redeems the pain and suggests the common bonds of humanity. Anger has given away almost but not completely to resignation and sadness. Cameron's photograph was taken after Jane's death, but probably Jane would have liked it; it was taken by an artist with a deep sense of human complexity rather than by an ordinary hero-worshiper or a commercial photographer feeding the public's needs. Jane herself had remarked with some exasperation that everyone seemed to get Carlyle wrong because they assumed that there was only one Carlyle. Continuously experiencing the full range of his moods, she could fully appreciate the complex reality of his temperament and had little reason to accept the stereotypical images of her husband that the society increasingly formalized. She had learned over a period of forty years that there were many Carlyles: the recluse, the friend, the monologuist, the complainer, the mourner, the neurotic, the charitable, the compassionate, the loyal, the loving, the dutiful son, the neglectful husband, the volatile arguer, the self-obsessed artist, the bitter satirist, the brilliant talker. . . .

But he was certainly not in her eyes the Victorian sage who had discovered the hidden truths of the universe. To the extent that he had an important message, it was not particularly new or original, though its mode of presentation was; and, to some considerable extent, Jane, who lived with the daily reality of that mode, realized that she both benefited and suffered from the distinctiveness of a personality rather than the brilliance of a doctrine. She lived with an artist, not a philosopher. Despite the growing tendency to elevate her husband into sainthood, she could hardly think of him as a particularly wise man. The greater the reputation of the "Sage of Chelsea," the greater the gap between the simple photographic image and the complicated reality. Jane saw him through the distortions of her disappointments; but her sense of him, allowing for the distortions, was more accurate than that of his public admirers. In response to the comment that the wives of great men tend to embarrass their husbands with their unrealistically exaggerated admiration, the elderly Carlyle playfully said that "in that respect" he had been "most mercifully spared."[7]

2.

During the 1850s, however, he gradually came to think of his new writing commitment as an inescapable misfortune. Yet the book that caused him most pain also provided him, as the culmination of a forty-year-long career as a writer, with an extraordinary public reward. From the very beginning of his work on Frederick, he had recognized that compulsion had triumphed over reason. With the death of his mother, his tentative commitment to pursue the project to the boundaries of common sense and just a little beyond became an irreversible emotional necessity. This was "not the work" he "would have chosen, had much choice been given" him. But "work, real work" is "the *only* remedy of grief."[8]

At some level his compulsion to finish this biography was also the result of an unspoken promise to his mother. He had become more conscious of the link between his mother's reverence for Luther and his own German studies during his visit to Germany in the summer of 1852. Though the eighteenth-century world of Frederick II had none of the religious intensity of Luther's century, the subject was clearly an extension of his earlier attempts to contrast the corruption of modern Europe with Reformation spirituality. The topic was perfectly consistent with his lifelong interest in the Reformation, the eighteenth century, German culture, German-English relationships, and modern "Heroes." Seen in such a light, it was a subject of which his mother would have approved.

For Carlyle, such work exemplified the values that his mother embodied. Whereas she had found relief from painful grief in contemplating God and eternity, her son found it in work and history. Early in 1855 he had seven photographic copies made of the portrait of his mother that hung in his bedroom. He sent them to various members of the family, including those who were across the sea.[9] He was grateful for the passage of time which decreased the pain, but her loss was always a potential motivating force in which he wept again "at grievances foregone."

Though he grieved mainly at his desk in his soundproof study, he had no sooner gotten done the first "small bit" of his book and sent it off to the printer in June 1856 than he took what he thought a well-deserved holiday in Scotland. It took the printer almost two years, however, to "chase" him to the completion and publication of the first two volumes.[10] He consoled himself with the fantasy of the country life that he would enjoy once this final work were completed. What need would he ever have of London again? To Alick he suggested that he would then visit America. Having parted as young men, the brothers would clasp hands on the way to the grave.

Jane found his fantasies irritating. They fueled his ability to go on working in *his* usual way. In the meantime, she was frequently ill in *her* usual way, and as her sixtieth birthday approached it was clear that the years of sickness and neglect had made her old and weak. She had "a very sickly winter" preceding Lady Harriet's death; her despair about her health was widely noticed.[11] Yet no doctor seemed able to help her. Her husband thought that somewhere "there ought to be one."[12] Though there seemed "nothing *specifically wrong* with her," by the early summer of 1857 she was on the verge of collapse. Scotland seemed the only available medicine.[13] While she spent two months visiting friends in Haddington and Edinburgh, Carlyle stayed in London, completing the proofs of the first two volumes and supervising through the press the volumes of a complete edition of his works being brought out by Chapman and Hall. He made efforts to begin the next part of *Frederick.* He now hoped to be done by 1860 or at the latest 1861. He imagined that two additional volumes would suffice.

Jane's own enthusiasm at the end of the next summer for the first two volumes of *Frederick* derived from her desire to be supportive and to protect her lifelong interest in her husband's genius.[14] This was the one area in which she would not suffer any doubts. But she had frequent doubts about herself, and at times even feared for her sanity. It was not, she claimed, her husband's fault that she was ill, weak, and useless. Short of death, however, the best she could do would be to suffer quietly and use whatever energy she had to praise her husband's work and protect him from interruptions.[15] So, though she felt frequently ill, for three months during the spring of 1857 she had the nerve-wracking job of making certain that Robert Tait, whom it had been agreed would be allowed to paint the Carlyles at home in their living room, did not create too much of a disturbance. He came twice a week. Toward the end, he seemed to be there "like a nightmare *every day!!*"[16]

When Jane went to see the painting on exhibition, she was charmed by her maid's astonished exclamation that she should hurry into the next room because her master and mistress and even Nero were hanging on the wall.[17] But she did not like the painting. "The dog is the only member of the family who has reason to be pleased with his likeness,"[18] she told Mary Russell. A new friend of the Carlyles, who was an acknowledged expert on "modern painting," criticized Tait's technical competence in creating the angular perspective and in his color selection, among other things. But John Ruskin still liked "this little composition very much," though he thought "it isn't quite right" and could not "suggest what would put it right." He soon came up with the claim that three inches off the top would mend matters.[19] But as a Victorian

A Chelsea Interior. Painting by Robert Tait, c. 1857. Lent by the Marquess of Northampton. By permission of The National Trust Photographic Library, London.

image, Tait's *A Chelsea Interior* transcends all its limitations. Carlyle leans gracefully against the mantlepiece, his pipe in his hand. He seems to have "world enough and time" in this extended moment of thought and relaxation. Jane sits comfortably on a chair in a corner, as if contentedly patient, approving of the details of their life. The room, well decorated and comfortable, is uncluttered. Though there are no children, the husband and wife seem a family. Carlyle wears the dressing gown that his mother had made him. There are no lines of illness or anxiety on Jane's face. And Carlyle's bearded face has enough youthful energy in it to assure the world that this writer still has the strength to add to his collected works.

Separate volumes of the 1857–58 edition of the *Collected Works*, coming out a volume a month, often got into the hands of reviewers at the same time as the first two volumes of *Frederick*. Readers could not help but be impressed simply by the scope of the whole enterprise. And at the same time to have in hand volumes of the newly printed *Works* inevitably demanded that readers be impressed, whether they admired Carlyle as a writer or not, with the extraordinary size and range of his achievement during almost forty years. No matter how cool a particular reader might be to the prose and the message of the early essays, and of *Sartor, The French Revolution, Chartism, Cromwell, Heroes and Hero-Worship, Past and Present,* and *Latter-Day Pamphlets,* the impact of the particular volumes and of the total career on English Victorian culture could not be denied. It was hardly possible now to deal with any new book by Carlyle without in some way taking into account his cumulative achievement and his reputation. He had reached that point at which a writer is no longer simply a creator of books but the embodiment of a cultural myth. For "a critic may, if he choose, assault" the highest mountains,

> but he had better leave Mr. Carlyle alone. For the veteran has grown grey, and hard, and victorious; and it is now impracticable to move him either to the right hand or to the left. The author of the *French Revolution* must be looked on and accepted . . . as *un fait accompli.* He stands there quite by himself, courting no sympathy, fearing no hostility,—a brawny, iron-bound, colossal Titan, against whom the surf of the sea, and the rain and lightning of heaven, beat in vain; yet not without hidden springs of love and laughter, and the sense of an antique pain which disquiets the heart of the onlooker.[20]

Not every critic, of course, let him alone. Christian critics frequently regretted his lack of belief in a personal god. The more severe of them found that though he had sought a religious antidote to the prevalent "scepticism of the day," his failure had infected his moral will as well as his religious beliefs. "He has little Faith, Hope, or Charity."[21] Those who found his temperament wilful and his anecdotal approach to history unscientific sometimes pricked him where he was most vulnerable:

> His method of treating history may be called the phantasmagoric, anecdotic, and comic. It has been said that the end of Mr. Carlyle's teaching is to show us God in history. What Mr. Carlyle does attempt to do is to show us the demonic in history . . . and his heroes, like Byron's Conrads, Alps, Giaours, and Manfreds, and all cut out of one block, all men of ungovernable temperament, all consuming noble efforts after their own wilful fashion, and scourging anarchy—everywhere except within their own hearts and minds. . . . Much as Mr. Carlyle raves against the age, he partakes of its literary vices in no small measure.[22]

Most of the favorable reviews purposely said little about Carlyle's politics or his theories of history. Many supporters and detractors alike granted that since nothing new could be said it was just as well to say hardly anything at all. Some appreciative criticism took the position that Carlyle was now a national treasure. The function of the civilized reviewer was mainly to excerpt a few of the "chief passages and a few famous acts out of this grand and dramatic history . . . for the delight and instruction of our readers."[23] His style was to be enjoyed, not complained of. But the more vehement critics found *Frederick* tedious and empty, both boring and frustrating, as if Carlyle, "with vast activity and perseverance," had built "up a Man of Snow."[24] To those who had not yet given up on Christianity, what is now seen as Carlyle's greatest strength was then judged his most serious weakness: his inability to resolve religious problems, to do much more than dramatize the conflict. "It is lamentable to think how trivial has been the result of all those agonized spasms—all the groans of this giant in torment."[25]

But even hostile critics granted that "he has become, while yet alive and at work among us, something of a classic."[26] In an anonymous review published in 1855, George Eliot had claimed that "it is not as a theorist, but as a great and beautiful human nature, that Carlyle influences us"; the next year, James Martineau, Harriet's influential brother, joined him to Coleridge and John Henry Newman as one of the three major influences on the religious spirit of the age.[27] George Henry Lewes, drawing on his personal knowledge of his revered friend, emphasized the power of "genius" to transcend its limitations, though "our eyes ache a little in gazing at this constant glowing . . . white heat." In *Frederick,* he saw "picturesqueness and . . . humour," the concrete visual evocations of the true artist, so powerful that "there is what we may call a tyranny of the picturesque in him. He makes some physical detail so vivid that it predominates over the whole." But criticism is "superfluous," for "Mr. Carlyle is not the kind of writer whose faults are to be amended, and his efforts directed . . . and he is now arrived at a time of life and has reached a position in literature, when all such 'criticism' is an impertinence."[28]

Months before the publication of *Frederick,* a longtime acquaintance of Carlyle's, James Fitzjames Stephen, with much of the new *Collected Works* in his hands, dismissed the question of politics and theology: "Regarded as works of art, we should put the best of Mr. Carlyle's writings at the very head of contemporary literature." And, "if he is the most indignant and least cheerful of living writers, he is also one of the wittiest and the most humane." With keen critical perception, Stephen claimed "a mixture of poverty and audacity in these books which is perfectly bewildering." For Carlyle is "one of the greatest wits and poets, but the most unreliable moralist and politician, of our age and nation."[29] Stephen's calm conclusion that "no one but a man of real and great genius could have done this" aptly crystallizes that remarkable process whereby at some late point in his career a great writer's reputation transcends the limitations of his individual works. A historian himself, and for a long time "Under-Secretary for the Colonies," Stephen's praise in *The Saturday Review* gave Carlyle the imprimatur of the establishment. Clearly, by late 1858, the writer who for years could not find a publisher for *Sartor Resartus* and who just eight years before had shocked the public with what were felt to be the mad barbarities of *Latter-Day Pamphlets* had been elevated to the Parnassus where "classics" reside.

3.

Unfortunately, the two volumes published in 1858 barely brought the young Frederick into the world. The Victorian reading public could have no doubt that it was being presented with a work on the monumental scale. And, on the whole, there was sufficient reason to believe that Carlyle the artist had his material under effective control, though the writer himself had growing doubts. Since his failure with his original plan for *Cromwell,* he had become increasingly aware that "writing is an art."[30] Intelligent commentators had more and more stressed the poetry of Carlyle's prose and his epic ambitions. The writer himself continued to think that even Browning would be better off if he turned to *his* form of poetry. When Tennyson, attempting to read *Frederick,* came across the sentence, "*They* did not strive to build the lofty rhyme," the poet laureate threw the book aside. Among other things, it seemed to him insufferably long.[31]

For a project of such extraordinary length, Carlyle needed help. Three different admirers did their best to lend a hand—Alexander Gilchrist, Henry Larkin, and Joseph Neuberg. The first two suffered the mixed rewards of being, for a short while, close neighbors in Chelsea. Earning a bare income as a writer on painting, the intelligent and observant Gilchrist supported his family more with literary ambition than with income. Soon after his move to Chelsea in 1855 he became a welcome visitor at the house of his illustrious neighbor. Carlyle, who thought well of Gilchrist's *Life of William Etty,* helped the young man search for a publisher for a biography that he had begun writing of the then comparatively unknown William Blake. Gilchrist gave Carlyle some pamphlets on Frederick which particularly described the costumes of the period. Eager to assist, Gilchrist soon found himself sharing with Joseph Neuberg, who had recently returned from Germany, some of the tasks of seeing through the press the new *Collected Works.* But Gilchrist's time was limited, his devotion noncompulsive; and Neuberg, though ten years younger than Carlyle, no longer had the stamina to take on the heavy burden of proofreading, dealing with the printer, and writing the indexes and chapter summaries. By the summer of 1856 a new "loyal friend" had been commandeered "to do the correcting" of this "cheap but handsome" edition, the first of whose sixteen volumes was scheduled to appear in November.[32]

Henry Larkin, a devoted worshiper of Carlyle but also a committed Christian, worked evenings for Carlyle after working all day as a cashier on the Chelsea steamers.[33] Larkin had literary and religious ambitions, among them the reconciliation at some level of the worship of Carlyle with the worship of Christ. Carlyle soon had "no doubt" that Larkin "could do acceptable service"; and by the beginning of January 1857 he complimented his new assistant whose work was "faithful, solid, and judicious . . . just what was wanted."[34] Soon Larkin was trusted with the indexes, summaries, and proofreading, though his "very elaborate, clever, and indeed poetical" summary of *Sartor* was too extravagant for its purpose and was withdrawn on Carlyle's insistence. But Carlyle recognized the young man's motive and sympathized with his need. He suggested that Charles Robson, the excellent printer who had handled his typesetting for thirty years, "throw off a few copies of this Proof which I now have, and we will keep *in memoriam.* And be patient with me, and with your fate," which now included not only the summaries (and, at the end, the cumulative index) for *Frederick,* but also, since he was discovered to be a good draftsman, the political and military maps, which he hated doing.[35]

By 1862, when he married and moved to Chelsea, Larkin found that he was doing personal errands for both Carlyles; he was a willing but increasingly sober general secretary, handyman, and copy editor. His moments of greatest satisfaction were those in which, in his effort to mediate between Carlyle's difficult handwriting and the baffled printer, he felt that he had not only interpreted Carlyle's words but in fact intuited Carlyle's meaning before reading the text fully, almost as if he had written it himself or at least succeeded in intermingling his own personality with that of his master. Though Larkin was paid small sums on an irregular basis, his work was a labor of love. Gilchrist's minor contribution ended in December 1861 when at thirty-three years old he died of scarlet fever caught from one of his children.[36] But Larkin plodded on, increasingly aware that Carlyle not only despised Christianity in its current forms but could not resist dealing roughly with him and others in moments of anger. He witnessed occasional scenes of uncontrolled rage and bitter sarcasm, gradually losing his enthusiasm if not his commitment. The son found that he could never really please the father enough.

Toward the end of the work on the index, Carlyle was ill-temperedly impatient about the return of some books that Larkin had borrowed for his work on the *Frederick* maps. When "the last stroke was faithfully completed," Larkin "gave vent" to his "pent-up feelings." Unable to do it face to face, he told Carlyle in a letter what the older man should very well have known, that much of the work he had done had been "utterly irksome and abhorrent" to him and that he had done it "out of personal loyalty." The next day, at Cheyne Row, Carlyle attempted to receive Larkin as if nothing had happened. But he seemed "greatly hurt." His conscience paining him, Larkin even imagined that Jane received him "with wide-open eyes of astonishment; which might have meant '*Et tu, Brute!*' " Whatever the attempt by Carlyle to make Larkin feel guilty, Larkin still had enough sense of self to imagine that perhaps Jane "in the hidden depths of her own heart" admired him for speaking out.[37] When *Frederick* was finally done, he received a letter of thanks and another check. He had already moved from Chelsea to Camden Town. Thereafter, the two men kept in touch, but infrequently and at a distance. Unfortunately, nowhere in the *Collected Works* or in *Frederick the Great* did Carlyle directly acknowledge Larkin's assistance.

Neuberg and Carlyle never argued; their working relationship benefited from Neuberg's stolid, unflappable temperament; and Neuberg was too old and disciplined to demand from Carlyle things that he could not give. Neuberg was away much of the time in Germany, where he studied and translated into German a number of Carlyle's best-known works. By the spring of 1858 it seemed that Neuberg might be of help again in the way that he had been in 1852. For months, Carlyle had been unsuccessfully attempting to wiggle away from a serpentine nightmare: in order to finish *Frederick* he would have to visit Germany again. Frederick's great battles could be dramatized vividly only by someone who had been to every site and absorbed the concrete details that would allow him to recreate the historical reality. During his 1852 visit Carlyle had gone to only a few of the battlefields, mainly because of his impatience but also because he was not yet committed to writing the biography.

By June 1858 a return visit had come to seem an unpleasant necessity.[38] He did not want to go to Germany. But "duty" said that he "*ought* . . . to go."[39] It was agreed in August that Neuberg would provide the same companionship and courier service he had provided six years before. He was told to make the tour arrangements immediately and to meet his friend in Hamburg within the week. Carlyle left Ecclefechan by train for Edinburgh on the "clear, bright morning" of Saturday, August 21.[40] In Edinburgh he spent a "dreary" afternoon "wandering" about the Calton Hill and talking to a "new companion," Frederick Joseph Foxton, whom he had first met about 1851 and who had offered to accompany him to Germany. A former Anglican priest, Foxton turned out to be neither particularly companionable nor helpful: Carlyle found him dull, blustering, and vigorously incompetent. The two men departed by a Leith steamer into a rising storm that plunged all the passengers into the "choking cesspools" below deck. But the next day was "bright and sunny, without wind." By late Tuesday they were in sight of Hamburg, "grey ancient still busy city; no smoke on it, many grey towers and steeples."[41] A stranger, "a bright young gentleman, with fine black eyes . . . hair, and long hook-nose, evidently of Abrahamic lineage, forced his way up" as soon as the ship had docked, "and addressed" Carlyle "in perfectly good English" with a message from Neuberg.

The young Jew, a member of a successful Hamburg merchant family, impressed Carlyle with his intelligence as he did the honor of showing the English visitor his native city. At the office of the family business, his "old Father," a "good old Jew," reminded Carlyle "of *Nathan the Wise,* so good was he."[42] Carlyle was impressed with the apparent stability and cultural integrity of the comparatively large Jewish population of Hamburg. But he had not come to see Hamburg or to rethink his prejudices about Jews, and he found the city uncomfortable in the late summer heat. Fortunately, he had accepted an invitation, extended as a result of Lord Ashburton's efforts, to visit a distinguished Prussian family, the von Usedoms, on the Island of Rügen, in the Baltic, before going to Berlin. Soon he was on the road to Rügen, first by rail and then by carriage, across what seemed to him the ugly flatness of Schleswig-Holstein. At Rostock he was surprised but delighted to be met by Madam Olympia I. von Usedom who had come to escort him the rest of the way. The next day he was on what seemed to him the "German 'Isle of Wight,' " where he stayed for over a week, bathing in the Baltic waters, recovering from a nasty cold, and exploring the rustic sights. Baron Karl Georg von Usedom soon joined them, eager to please his distinguished guest. Carlyle, who enjoyed Usedom's company, was delighted when his new friend agreed not only to help arrange his travel schedule with official government cooperation but actually to accompany him to Berlin, where Carlyle was to rejoin Neuberg and Foxton. They left on September 3, 1858, and were in Berlin late in the day, eager to rest from the journey and to escape the noise of the city in the same British Hotel in which he had stayed in 1852.[43]

On his one day in Berlin he visited Varnhagen von Ense, whom he was "glad to see . . . so alert." Varnhagen noticed that, despite his guest's complaints, Carlyle seemed "to be more healthy and livelier than when he was here before, and also more resolute." The next week Carlyle began seventeen days of rapid travel that took him to the battlefields of Zorndorf, Liegnitz, Leuten, Mollwitz, Hohenfriedberg, Sohr, Chotusitz, Kolin, Prague, Hochkirch, Torgau, and Rossbach. Determined to have the facts precisely right and to see the physical qualities of the landscape through Frederick's eyes, Carlyle now concentrated his energy on those hours in which he walked the battlefields, measuring with his legs and his eyes the exact features of the terrain. The weather was mostly good, though occasionally too warm. The landscape constantly changed: brackish river country, rolling plains, low hills, austere mountains, ancient cities. Neuberg and Foxton undertook all the practical arrangements, Neuberg never faltering in his patient competence. As usual, Carlyle had difficulty in sleeping on strange beds. "On seeing a German bed for the first time," he had said, " 'Do the Germans mean one to *sit* in one's bed?' " And the absence of bed curtains, which he had become used to, disturbed him.[44]

He awakened on a bright morning in Prague, after having driven through lovely countryside that reminded him of a "drive" that he and Jane had once taken "from Buxton to Derbyshire across the hills to Sheffield." The sight on the Moldau Bridge of hundreds "of sacred Statues crowded on the parapet" disturbed him, a striking reminder of the failure of the Reformation to cleanse much of Central Europe of its idolatry. In contrast to the Germans, the Bohemians, by which he meant not only the Czechs but all the Slavs, were "liars, thieves, slatterns, a kind of miserable subter-Irish people—Irish with the addition of ill-nature." But Prague itself he found beautiful. By the middle of the month even Neuberg was exhausted "and Foxton [was] good for absolutely nothing."[45] But Carlyle was comforted by the satisfaction of doing what he had intended to do; as the others wilted, he grew stronger. On September 15 he was in Dresden, "sitting on the Elbe bridge in the sunshine," reading a letter from Jane. The news was good; Jane felt better. He respected her right to control her own schedule: however long she wanted to remain with a friend at Lamm Hall in Scotland, where she had gone after leaving Bay House at the end of August, or with the Russells at Thornhill, suited him.[46]

At Leipzig, with only one more battlefield to visit, he and Neuberg were reunited with Foxton, from whom they had temporarily separated a few days earlier. To Carlyle's delight, Thomas Wilson, who with his sister Jane had helped arrange his first lecture series, was "blithely waiting" with Foxton, "friendly human faces."[47] Twenty years before, the Wilsons, Harriet Martineau, and Henry Taylor, among others, had come to the rescue of the impoverished writer, at a time when, despite his completion of *The French Revolution,* his future still looked desperate. Wilson was now living in Weimar. After inspecting the battleground at Rossbach, the four men hastened to Weimar, where they arrived before breakfast on September 19 "in the grey fresh Sunday morning. Gilt Statue in one of the public spaces, countryman looking at it could not tell me who, which was new to me; 'Goethe!' answered a second of the civic or gent species, who came up. 'Not the least like him!' said I."[48]

Entertained by Wilson and also by James Marshall, another old friend who was serving as secretary to the Grand Duchess of Weimar (partly on Carlyle's recommendation), Carlyle declined an invitation to join the Grand Duchess at Eisenach. He was eager to have the journey over with now that he had accomplished what he had set out to do.[49] A fifteen-hour railroad ride brought the three men to Dusseldorf. It was "the hardest day" of the entire trip, but they were on their way home. At Aachen, where he slept well in a clean hotel that to his delight actually had curtains on the beds, he visited the cathedral where Charlemagne is buried. As he stood for a moment on the lid of Charlemagne's tomb, the rising tones of the mass seemed to him a desecration of the holy spirit of man. Soon they were at Ostend, and then across the Channel. He had last been to Dover almost thirty-four years before, as a guest of the Stracheys and Irvings. The city seemed to have grown immensely. He walked through its streets with "company from the Land of Shadows." Where had they all gone? The noon train got him to London late in the afternoon, September 22, 1858. Foxton had left for Reading. Carlyle said good-bye to Neuberg at London Bridge and went home to Cheyne Row.[50]

4.

It did not disturb him that Jane was still in Scotland. At Thornhill, the Russells nursed her through relapse after relapse. Fortunately, the harsh cough that had plagued her all the previous winter and spring had almost disappeared. Mary Russell reminded her of her mother, Dr. James Russell of her father, "a *real* live Doctor!"[51] But her body constantly both anticipated and followed the pain of her emotions and the rawness of her nervous system. Lack of sleep frequently exacerbated physical exhaustion and emotional depression. In the tender hands of the Russells and close to places intimately associated with her mother, she felt more cared for than anywhere else in the world. Scotland now seemed a place of refreshment; the return journey was to be dreaded. In fact, ironically, she began to think of London as "a perfectly poisonous place" for her.[52] But she tried to prepare herself mentally to return "to that horrid Cheyne Row," where she was "always ill, and generally miserable."[53] Neither home nor marriage seemed attractive places. Still, despite her bitterness, it was her only home. And if she were not needed there, then of what use was she in this world?

That her husband had arrived home from his "long wanderings" in her absence made her feel morose and guilty.[54] She decided to return immediately, though she had just suffered a new "attack of Inflammation. . . . The idea of Mr. Carlyle going about at home, *seeking things* like a madman, and never finding them," and depending on the incompetent servants for everything, made her feel both derelict in her duty and frightened that he might actually get along quite well without her. She urged the still faithful Henry Larkin to "be a Mother to him, poor Babe of Genius, till I come."[55] She arrived home before the end of September after having played a trick on Larkin, whom she had asked to meet her at the station without her husband and then purposely evaded in order to arrive at home alone.

Though her husband was happy to see her, within a short time he was "as busy and private as before."[56] As was his habit, immediately on returning home he had begun to write out an account of his journey, partly based on journal notes that he had made while traveling, partly based on his memory. Like the rest of his travel writing, it found its place in the darkness of a drawer and remained unpublished in his lifetime; and, as in most of his efforts in the genre, the writing sparkles and the observations are vividly drawn, though perhaps the more businesslike nature of this trip provided fewer opportunities for exposition than some of his earlier journeys. With typical self-dramatization, he noted at the end of the manuscript that he had finished it on "10 October, 1858 (fast as my pen would go, and my many hurries would admit),—possibly enough never to be *read over* by me at all."[57] The completion of *Frederick* had the highest priority, and he was soon urgently at work again. It seemed to Carlyle that there were two more volumes to be done, about "two years of hard work," though he imagined that they would be less difficult to do than the two he had already completed.[58] Even his evenings were given over mostly to reading his way through dull volumes, while Jane sat bored and depressed in the long silences.

The winter was a brutal one. Miserably ill, Jane spent much of her time in bed, under the care of a local doctor whom the Carlyles respected. She often read through the night "to stave off insane thoughts!"[59] "Tormented somewhere in the region of the *heart,*" she was as ill as her husband had ever seen her.[60] Apparently there were recurring chest pains. Occasionally she took the air in "a second-hand brougham, with one horse," the hire of which Carlyle insisted on, but which Jane referred to it as "an expensive luxury" that her husband forced on her now that she was " 'old and frail.' "[61]

Almost every late afternoon he mounted his horse to ride for a few hours into "the dusk, like a distracted ghost."[62] Sometimes he noticed how ill Jane was, other times not. In January 1859 she seemed "very weakly."[63] By the end of the month, he generalized that she has been "very much better this winter than the two last."[64] But since his attention to her was so sporadic, his own obsessions so compulsive, his perception of her condition was usually distorted. And at times the facts hardly filtered through his own moods and preoccupations with anything like accuracy. In April Jane had a "bad cold" and the sudden warm weather renewed the cold that he had "always obscurely had" since bathing at Rügen the previous summer.[65] Scotland seemed necessary for both of them. His attempt to rent Cressfield House, near Ecclefechan, which his father had helped build, fell through. But at the end of June Carlyle sailed with their maid, a horse, and their luggage to Edinburgh and then across to Fife, where they had rented the second floor of a charming farmhouse called Humbie, within a short distance of the Firth and about ten miles from Kirkcaldy. Jane followed by train a few days later.

The view from Humbie was extraordinarily beautiful; Edinburgh was visible in the distance. Carlyle commented blissfully on the advantages of "seas, mountains, cities, woods, fruitful cornfields, . . . solitude, silence and a horse."[66] He bathed regularly in the sea, Jane's dog Nero often dancing in the small waves beside him. Since Jane could not sit a horse with any security, a donkey was obtained, which she rode with perfect safety and some delight. But, obsessed with the notion of recovering his health, which really meant his spirits, Carlyle tried to coerce his body into vigor and his psyche into joy by dashing around on foot and on horseback as if he were " 'more like a man of sixteen than of sixty-four.' "[67] It did not work. To Jane, he seemed "bilious." The benefit to her own health was undermined by the tension generated by her husband's moods. After five weeks, they moved from the "rough farmhouse" to a more comfortable "Country House," a few miles inland and closer to Kirkcaldy.

The move was unfortunate. From the beginning Jane had felt that it was "more like being keeper in a madhouse than being 'in the country' for 'quiet and change.' "[68] She vowed that she would never do it again and, in fact, this was the last time they were ever to vacation together. When, late in August, she received a letter from a young female friend, with whom she had established a surrogate mother-daughter relationship, she reacted with unhappy, self-pitying tears to the news that her friend was to marry.[69] Carlyle wandered the Fife countryside, increasingly restless. At Kirkcaldy he visited the place where he had lodged and where Alick had stayed with him for a short time when he had first met Edward Irving and become a schoolmaster. Fife too seemed inhabited by the ghosts of departed friends and loved ones. Superimposed on the landscape was his memory of what he himself had once been. At Ecclefechan, he went with his brother Jamie to the churchyard cemetery. A new grave had recently been filled. Jamie's wife, Isabella, ill for years, had died in June. They stood silently by familiar graves.[70]

While in Scotland, the problem of *Frederick* was never far from Carlyle's mind. No matter how hard he tried, he could not "get that terrible problem shaken out of [his] head altogether."[71] The necessity of returning to his desk at Cheyne Row filled him "with terror." But by early October 1859 he was not only back at his "heart-breaking Prussian concern" but determined not to push himself to get done more than his nerves would permit, as he had done the previous winter. The vacation had left him only a little less tired than he had been before. He asked himself which was worse—to exhaust himself rapidly by making intensive efforts to finish soon or to pace himself in a way that would keep him going for three or four years more, "pulling at a dead lift."[72]

By November it was clear to him that he would have both to work intensely hard *and* to accept that even then he would still not finish for three or four years. In the darkest days of the year, he kept working and riding. His marvelous horse, whom he had named Fritz, was his most frequent living companion. By the end of the month, he had enough material to get the printer started.[73] There was room for hope. "Please Heaven we shall get this tolerable slave-chain *filed thro'* at last."[74] By the spring of 1860 Jane had reason to complain that her husband was "working himself to death." Probably she would not be able to go by herself to Scotland for the summer, since she would not dare to leave him. If she stayed she could at least "put all sorts of hindrances in the way of his absolutely killing himself."[75] By the beginning of the summer, he was sleeping badly. A vacation seemed an absolute necessity.

With Jack, he sailed early in August 1860 toward Thurso at the northeastern tip of Scotland, having accepted an invitation from Sir George Sinclair to have the run of Thurso Castle. He would not be disturbed, but could work or play as he chose. Jane, of course, declined to go. To her it seemed worse than suicide to make a sea voyage of almost eight hundred miles to a desolate place where she knew no one in order to spend weeks or months while her husband fulfilled a schedule arranged completely to his own satisfaction. She had tried a week in Brighton in June; her husband had tried it for three days; noise and restlessness had defeated them. For weeks Carlyle had been awaking before dawn and staring at the ghastly possibility that he might never finish this book, "the first real assault of fear."[76] Though he faced that down, comparing it to Luther's being tempted by the devil, his sleep returned only with movement: the first night on the steamer to Aberdeen he slept for six or seven hours. Jack's prescription of "a long sail" had been successful. Jane, "on the verge of complete break-down into serious illness" when he left, was delighted to see him go.[77]

At Thurso he found Sir George awaiting him with deferential hospitality, so happy was the benign elderly man to host his great writer friend. Jack went south, to the Trossachs, reminding his elder brother of a walking tour he had made "with good Edward Irving and others, many long years ago. . . . Indeed all was new to me, and joyously impressive, at that time."[78] Though new, Thurso was not "joyously impressive" but stolidly comfortable, the "country equal to Craigenputtock for picturesque effects, plus the sea, which is always one's friend."[79] Each day, after bathing, he breakfasted privately, avoiding household prayers, and worked until two. In the afternoon, whatever the weather, he walked on the beach or drove around the Thurso countryside. He slept soundly.

At Cheyne Row, Jane supervised some repairs and slept badly, undecided abut how long to remain in London but thankful to have her husband off her hands. She resisted his pressure to join him at Thurso. The hospitable Sinclair pressed on Carlyle secondary invitations to anyone he desired, suggesting, in addition to Jane, Milnes, Ruskin, and Jack. Though he felt disturbed by Jane's continuing illness, Carlyle was not eager to have his working solitude disturbed. It was generally understood that he would stay as long as he liked and then continue his summer someplace else, perhaps in southern Scotland. But he refused to be firm about his plans. Jane complained that his letters were disturbingly impersonal, mostly about landscape rather than "about feelings," as if he were writing not to her but for the future readers of his biography—a charge that he denied.[80] By the end of the third week of August the tone of their letters was less tense. The exhausted Jane went to visit old friends, the Stanleys, at Alderley Park in Cheshire, escorted to the train at Euston Station by Henry Larkin and Geraldine. She intended, after resting, to go on to Scotland, eventually to spend some time with the Russells at Thornhill where she assumed her husband would join her.

A letter from Carlyle, forwarded from London, arrived on the morning of August 25, 1860, informing her that he intended to sail south shortly. The letter had been close to a week in transit. Jane assumed that just as he had sailed from London to Thurso, so he now was about to and might in fact already have completed a sail from Thurso to London, since his vagueness about a departure date might indeed mean that he was on his way to London or had already returned there. She was shocked and furious. Did this mean that he expected her to return to London immediately? And how could she act in any way independent of his expectations without making matters worse for herself? Tormented by indecision, she hesitated. Was he impatiently waiting for her at home in Chelsea or was he at his sister's home in Scotland? If he were in Chelsea, he would surely blame her for the mess left by the painters and plasterers. Her anxiety would not permit her to remain at Alderley. She "turned south" to Chelsea "with real mortification."[81]

Carlyle, of course, was still at Thurso, where he had just received a letter from Alderley telling him about his wife's dilemma. He had "seldom . . . been so vexed. . . . If you have actually gone back to Chelsea, and are sitting there this night instead of at The Gill, and all on a basis of mere mistake and delusion, I know not how I shall ever endure it." In fact, he had postponed his departure date until September 7; it had been his intention all along to sail south to Aberdeen and Edinburgh, and then visit his family in Annandale. He had no intention of being in Chelsea for at least three weeks. "*Are* you at The Gill; or [are] you at Chelsea (Heaven forbid!)"[82] Depressed, mortified, and furious, what could Jane answer? To some considerable extent she was responsible for a situation in which her husband's pressure and her exhaustion had undermined her good judgment. It would have been sounder to have remained at Alderley and to let the mail, which had created the confusion, clarify it. She consoled herself that the "error was quite natural, almost inevitable. But that doesn't make it the less mortifying for myself and others."[83] And her husband's self-justifying anger did nothing but increase her misery. He insisted on her complete culpability. Despite his urging, she refused now to leave Chelsea. No one could persuade her to do it. She did not even want to write to him.

By the end of the first week of September, 1860, Carlyle was on his way south.[84] But still not to London. He had decided to go on with the rest of his trip. The voyage "by sea and land" to Linlathen, where he visited Thomas Erskine, was "pleasant" but exhausting. He did not confide to his host, with whom he "had plenty of pious discourse for . . . two days," that he was emotionally weary of marital mistakes and confusions.[85] He visited the Gill and Scotsbrig. Jane soon gave up her resistance to writing. She was in bed with influenza. He wanted her to know how deeply and permanently he loved her. She responded that "passionate loves, not applied to practical uses, are good for so little in this matter-of-fact world."[86] At the Gill, he said good-bye to Jamie and Jack; both his brothers, of course, no longer had wives.[87] By the beginning of the last week of September he was back in London, where his anxiety about completing *Frederick* occasionally awakened him at night. Frederick the man hardly seemed worth this labor.[88] He returned to his two obsessions, writing and riding. He kept feeding manuscript to the printer, but the "rate is very slow." "It is a dreadful time for him—and me!" Jane told Richard Milnes.[89] He vowed that he would not return to Scotland again, even for the sake of his health, until he had finished. There were many things he would do, he promised himself, and Jane, and others, "some day when this horrible load, which has crushed me down in the bowels of Chaos these many years, is at length off my shoulders, and I am again alive among the living."[90] But not until then.

5.

Fortunately, Carlyle did not have to leave London to enjoy the company of both old and new friends—to the extent that his monomaniacal concentration on *Frederick* permitted such diversions. Even during the most trying years, those between 1859 and 1864, his daily work schedule often ended at about three in the afternoon and did not resume in the evenings; and even after his decision not to return to Scotland until he had finished, the lifelong pattern of taking short holiday breaks after completing chapters or major sections asserted itself. Large social gatherings were another matter, however. He regularly declined such invitations; so too did Jane, who could count on feeling ill and going alone if she accepted.

But in the late afternoon, when he rode Fritz, he needed companionship more than at any other time of the day. The loneliness of a writer's life extended from his work-desk to his recreation. The hours were not appropriate for those with ordinary work schedules and, as the years went by, old friends of leisure and youth became less available, lost to new obligations and the more insular routines of middle age. For her own protection and her husband's health, Jane touchingly appealed to Richard Milnes, whom she had just seen riding "a pony. . . . I saw you on it the other day . . . and I thought to myself; 'I wish to Heaven he would come to ride with Mr. C'. . . . *Riding with him* is the only 'delicate attention' to which [he] remains sensible,—the only human intercourse to which he lends himself!"[91]

Many of the friends of his first London decade still provided good cheer, though correspondence sometimes substituted for direct contact. Browning's voluntary exile deprived Carlyle of the "night to night" presence of a friend; such a loss was one of the "sorrows and lasting regrets" that could hardly be justified even by the occasional research chores that Browning did for the much-admired older man.[92] When in late 1855 Carlyle caught "a glimpse" of Browning's new book of poems,

Men and Women, he was delighted to have the opportunity to praise unhesitatingly some of the poems, particularly "How It Strikes A Contemporary." Over the years Carlyle's advice that Browning give up poetry for prose not only had failed to discourage his continuation as a poet but perhaps had actually increased his determination to prove himself. In only partly disguised ways, the younger man imposed the Carlylean presence on some of his poems, even to the extent of representing Carlyle's voice and values directly.

At the Grange at Christmas 1855 Lady Ashburton had read a selection of poems from *Men and Women* with the "*strong*" voice and fine intellect that Carlyle believed made her a superb reader. The audience listened with "rapt attention."[93] For the first time Carlyle tactfully and sensibly withdrew his reservations about poetry as Browning's proper medium. By the spring, he did not hesitate to admit that "*verse*" had "grown to be" Browning's "dialect," which came to him "more naturally than prose."[94] Browning, of course, was delighted with the totality of the concession; it was a vindication to be cherished. But Browning's capacity to be a friend to Carlyle was limited not only by distance. He could hardly mistake Jane's hostile attitude. When he had visited in the summer of 1856, his exaggerated courtly gestures, such as fervently kissing her hand, only increased her contempt for such "a 'fluff of feathers.' " She believed him to be insincere.[95] The publication in late 1856 of Elizabeth's poem *Aurora Leigh,* extolling Italian nationalism and liberal aspirations in rather tepid verse, emphasized an aspect of the Brownings which neither of the Carlyles admired. Carlyle could not disguise either from Elizabeth or, more important, from her husband, his contempt for Elizabeth's stupidity on such issues. Browning was "abstruse; but worth knowing," whereas Elizabeth, among her other faults, had taken a man "worth knowing" away from London, his natural home.[96] From the distance, both Brownings disapproved of the first two volumes of *Frederick.* Elizabeth, who in 1841 had extravagantly praised Carlyle as a great artist, exclaimed to a friend that "never was there a more immoral book in the brutal sense."[97]

Elizabeth's death in Italy in the early summer of 1861 did not completely restore Carlyle's friend to him. Aware of Carlyle's reservations about his wife, Browning became even more sensitive about her worth after her death. (Edward FitzGerald's harsh, and he thought private, comment "Mrs. Browning's death is rather a relief to me. . . . No more *Aurora Leighs,* thank God!" far exceeded anything Carlyle had said about her before her death or anything he said about her now.) Carlyle did sympathize with Browning's loss. "But I believe it may ultimately prove a great gain to him, if he come to England, and look after his own tasks, while it is yet time!"[98] Elizabeth was to be blamed for having kept "a soul like" Robert Browning's "weltering, in a *hobbled* condition, amid such a mass of thorns and hopeless cobwebs." Her death could be the beginning of "a *new epoch* for *him,* in regard to his own work in this world," if he would only return to England.[99] Browning did not need Carlyle's advice to reach the conclusion that his hope for a productive future demanded that he separate himself as much as possible from the ghosts of the past and the scenes of his married life. London became his home again.

But now Carlyle was not so much inaccessible as less attractive to Browning. The prospect of cultivating intimate friendship with one of his wife's antagonists had to be additionally unsettling to a man who already felt guilty about his disloyalty to her memory. In fact, for the next years, Browning had no special need for intimacy at all; he instinctively sought more public forms of companionship than Carlyle could ever tolerate. Though busy at *Frederick,* Carlyle did find time to ride out to Oxfordshire with Browning to attend the funeral of a mutual friend; and there were other social occasions for the two men, including an occasional meeting at a party or dinner of the kind Browning so frequently attended, much to Carlyle's disapproval. Browning's public good spirits seemed remarkable to Carlyle: "It's a very strange and curious spectacle to behold a man in these days so confidently cheerful."[100] Through a tacit understanding, the men agreed to maintain their friendship at an emotional distance; ironically, the gap between them was almost as formidable as the miles that had separated them before.

By 1858 another once vital friendship—that with Mill—had died, and although Carlyle partly understood the reasons, the disappointment still pained him. Mill was inseparably connected with what seemed in retrospect the most triumphantly creative period of his life, the years immediately prior to and just after his move to London. The destruction of the manuscript of the first volume of *The French Revolution* had not terminated the friendship. Instead, it died slowly (and for Carlyle sadly) over the next decade. Having declined intimacy with Harriet Taylor, the Carlyles were denied intimacy with Mill.[101] Mill did lend his old friend books while Carlyle worked on *Cromwell* during the early 1840s, but such impersonal objects epitomized the quality of a relationship that had in effect ended by the time John Taylor died in 1849. "How Mill has gone to a perfect scarecrow, when I saw him last," Carlyle remarked on learning of the marriage of the bachelor and the widow in April 1851. "The widow has been *hidden* (none knows where) ever since Taylor died. It is a sad, half miserable half laughable affair."[102] But he felt cordial enough to ask some impersonal information of Mill the next year and to assure Mill that he respected his "solitude."[103]

As the years went by, however, the solitude turned into almost total silence, though Mill's sharp disagreement with both the tone and substance of much of what Carlyle said in public during the early 1850s provoked published dissent. Mill made criticism of his wife and his marriage even more difficult by moving to France, where Harriet died in November 1858. One morning Larkin came into Carlyle's study, assuming that he was at work on *Frederick,* and was frightened by "a torrent of anathema" directed at Mill's recently published *On Liberty*—as if Larkin had been the author himself. Though he shortly apologized to Larkin, Carlyle could not rid himself of the notion that Mill's position was all the more destructive because of the clarity with which it was expressed.[104] When a young disciple asked for an introduction to Mill, Jane spoke for both her husband and herself: "We did once know him intimately, and he cut our acquaintance! For years and years we have stood apart like rocks. . . . So that it would no more suit *us* to send any one to *him* than it would suit *you* to be sent by us!"[105] The Carlyles had, for good reason, no expectation of ever seeing or hearing from Mill again.

With Richard Milnes, almost as old a London friend as Mill, the exchange of affection never ceased, though marriage and then the death of Lady Harriet decreased Milnes's carefree availability. With both Milnes and others recognizing the uselessness of his political career, he was offered and accepted elevation to the peerage and became the first Baron Houghton. He continued to write poems, which Carlyle did not care for, and to write criticism, whose championing first of Keats and then of Swinburne seemed to the "Sage of Chelsea" one more example of his friend's lack of seriousness. During holidays, Milnes was at Fryston or abroad; during the season, he was in London, but, by the mid-1850s, political, literary, and social activities made him a very infrequent visitor at Cheyne Row. Carlyle appealed to his conscience: "It will much beseem you to come and see whether I am dead or alive."[106] They walked together in Lady Harriet's funeral procession in May 1857. When Douglas Jerrold, whom Carlyle had known since the earily 1840s, died the next month, Carlyle thought of asking Milnes to ride out with him to the funeral, for he felt "outwardly and inwardly, much fitter for funerals than for dinners at this time!"[107] His own mobility limited by his absorption in *Frederick,* he reminded his old friend in mid-1860 that even his letters were becoming infrequent. "Are not you a shocking fellow, never to ask once this year whether I was alive or dead."[108]

But invitations from Milnes never ceased—to share elaborate dinners in London with other guests and to visit Fryston again, to which Carlyle had been just once, twenty years before. Late in 1861, mindful of her health but even more of her husband's intractability, Jane responded that she "should like" to accept Milnes's invitation "if the wind would change, and if Mr. C. would change. But—blessed are they who do not hope; for they shall not be disappointed." After "six hours consideration Mr. C." finally decided that "he 'will give himself the pleasure of dining with you'. . . . I am to write and say 'yes'—I hardly know how to form the letters of that almost forgotten word."[109] Milnes was initially successful in luring Carlyle to other dinner parties, but gradually, between Jane's declining health and his work on *Frederick,* invitations to the Carlyles began to seem a waste of paper. Carlyle's affection for Milnes was deep, however, and he hoped that his "dear old friend" would "be happy and merry . . . for many years to come! I still hope to see Fryston again."[110]

Carlyle was *never* to visit Farringford, the Tennyson's home on the Isle of Wight, though the relationship remained a cordial one and invitations were forthcoming. The once peripatetic poet became almost as immovable as his London friend during the 1850s and into the 1860s. They did occasionally meet in London and, before Lady Harriet's death, at the Grange, where Tennyson was thought a valuable addition to the literary salon. At the Grange, at the beginning of January 1856, Jane had been compelled to sit through the author's dramatic reading of *Maud,* which she had heard him read three times before. Tennyson looked "flourishing," with a new, wide-brimmed hat; his conversation, like his constant wreaths of pipe smoke, was as rich as ever. Carlyle, who refused to listen to his friend read the detested poem, "took a walk instead."[111] Though he delighted in Tennyson's private company, Carlyle thought him vain in his public role. Eager to visit Farringford, if her health would permit (eager to visit anyplace if only her husband would come), Jane reluctantly turned down numbers of invitations as her husband became increasingly obsessed with *Frederick.* She had become so pessimistic and habituated to self-denial that she sometimes responded to such invitations even before she had consulted with him. "And if by possibility—or rather by *im*possibility, I have put wrong words in his mouth, I shall be only to [sic] happy (I who am not writing Frederick) to unsay them, dear Mrs. Tennyson."[112]

Two of his old friends made an effective contrast: FitzGerald remained a relatively unknown country recluse, Dickens had become a world-famous celebrity. With FitzGerald, Carlyle had moments of warm and relaxed intimacy; but FitzGerald's avoidance of self-assertion in his private life and in his semi-anonymous literary career kept them at a distance from one another. And FitzGerald's admiration for Carlyle, especially after the publication of *Cromwell* and *Latter-Day Pamphlets,* was consistently punctured by his mordant, deeply skeptical assessment of his friend's political and cultural views. Still, mostly in letters and in occasional meetings, the warmth of their personal affection had a loving resonance. Dickens, in contrast, was effusive with his praise and almost worshipful of the master's energy and ideas, eager to identify himself with the imaginative power and implications of Carlyle's historical vision. But, even while Dickens lived in London, the two men were never really intimate; the more Carlyle committed himself to *Frederick,* the less he saw of Dickens; and, since Dickens had never been a member of Lady Ashburton's circle, the one compelling social scene that Carlyle had felt drawn to had not included Dickens.

About Dickens' fiction, Carlyle always felt ambivalent. He tried to keep up with the serial issues of *David Copperfield* but quickly fell behind, judging it the "innocent wateriest of twaddle with a suspicion of geniality,—very fit for the purpose in view."[113] Even Jane thought it "arrant nonsense."[114] And a few years later the second number of *Bleak House* seemed representative of this "new dud of a Book."[115] But Carlyle's heart responded to Dickens' sincerity, personal charm, and cheerful talent. When the Dickenses' infant daughter Dora died, he genuinely felt "heartily sorry for them."[116] And when the novelist and his wife separated in the spring of 1858 Carlyle refused to join in the common chorus of disapproval. It was "no crime or misdeameanour." They were simply "*unhappy* together."[117] And the next year Carlyle was delighted (and asked John Forster to pass along his response) that he could exclaim "Wonderful!" to *A Tale of Two Cities.*[118] Of course, in his preface to the novel Dickens had not only acknowledged Carlyle's influence but had claimed that though it was his hope "to add something to the popular and picturesque means of understanding that terrible time . . . no one can hope to add anything to the philosophy of Mr. CARLYLE's wonderful book."

With gift tickets from the author, Carlyle went to hear Dickens read in the spring of 1863. He reportedly said, "Charlie, you carry a whole company of actors under your own hat" and "there was no need of any orchestra."[119] He told his sister that Dickens was a brilliant actor, "a whole tragic, comic, heroic *theatre* visible, performing under one *hat,* and keeping us laughing—in a sorry way, some of us thought—the whole night."[120] These "mutual friends" maintained their warm feeling for one another over the years; but their moments together were accidental social ones. And when Dickens moved to Gad's Hill in Kent in 1856, such accidental occasions decreased.

"Poor dear Fuz," however, for whom Carlyle's affection never slackened, was often available, eager to do his friend whatever service he could.[121] During the 1850s Carlyle consulted Forster frequently, mostly on matters of business, but in all things it was Carlyle's confidence in

Forster as a friend and as a human being that sustained his respect. Carlyle found the walk from Cheyne Row to Forster's home at Palace Gate convenient and rewarding. Even in times of concentrated work and emotional reclusion, he found time to answer Forster's notes, sometimes even to knock at his door without warning late in the evening. While anticipating his own mother's death in the fall of 1853, Carlyle was considerably shaken by the news of Forster's unexpectedly serious illness.[122] Forster's weak heart threatened his life again in 1859. From Humbie, Carlyle expressed his guilty anxiety and his thanks that the episode had subsided. Deep in *Frederick,* he had neglected his friend. "I had intended, every day, for about a week before leaving Town, to call . . . and there is a mad feeling in me . . . as if that omission had been the guilty cause of what followed!"[123] When Jane was seriously ill in 1864, both Forsters offered help and hospitality; and Carlyle dined quietly at the Forsters' on Christmas Day 1864.[124] Forster was never too busy at his official work as commissioner of lunacy and at his literary projects to be available for assorted friendly duties. Unfortunately, there was little anyone could do; and between Forster's health and Carlyle's work their opportunities to be together decreased over the years.

While riding in Hyde Park a few days before Christmas 1863, his mind much on the anguishing problem of finishing *Frederick,* Carlyle met Thackeray out driving with his two daughters. He doffed his hat to them. The day before Christmas, Thackeray suddenly died. That the two men had been kept apart by differences of personality did not prevent Carlyle from warmly eulogizing the novelist who "had many fine qualities, no guile or malice against any mortal; a big mass of a soul, but not strong in proportion; a beautiful vein of genius lay struggling about in him. Nobody in our day wrote . . . with such perfection of style. . . . adieu! adieu!"[125] During the early London years, Thackeray had been a regular visitor at Cheyne Row. His prominent review of *The French Revolution* had provided helpful publicity for its author. The Carlyles had encouraged his talent and his career, particularly sympathetic to the personal misfortune that had in effect deprived the novelist of a wife and his daughters of a mother. Thackeray's humor appealed to Jane, especially his satiric wit, which had some of the bite of her own. And both Carlyles admired Thackeray's sheer intelligence as a writer.

But Thackeray's lectures in the 1850s and his social life kept him away from Cheyne Row on the whole; the Carlyles attended his lectures, wished him well in America, and, of course, sometimes met him at the Grange. When he came to Cheyne Row, he was welcomed but not embraced. Though Carlyle granted that "he is a friendly man," he could not work up any personal enthusiasm for him, perhaps because to his mind Thackeray's worldly pessimism had suppressed any element of the spiritual. And the veneer of witty cynicism could not obscure either from Carlyle or from Thackeray some tragic and destructive weakness in the novelist's character. "I rather dread explosions in his history. A *big,* fierce, weeping, hungry man; not a strong one."[126] Carlyle caught a glimpse of the novelist immediately before his departure for America in 1855, a venture that seemed to Carlyle to exemplify Thackeray's unfortunate lot and the fallen state of the writer in modern society, "with all loadstars [*sic*] gone out, locker emptyish, and the sea running high."[127] But Thackeray, who became "the Cortez and Columbus of that element," was "a very kind obliging soul too," whose success after the publication of *Vanity Fair* in 1848 never interfered with his generosity to his friends and his amiable but strained attempts to elicit love from those he admired.[128] The Thackeray daughters remained welcome visitors at Cheyne Row, and when their father came there was praise for his talent, "one of the best Novelists of the day."[129] Though his death in 1863 was not an intense personal loss to Carlyle, it nevertheless struck him forcefully. He was the first of Carlyle's early London friends to die. And he was sixteen years younger than the "Sage of Chelsea."

One of Carlyle's most eager friends throughout the 1840s, George Henry Lewes, who was twenty-eight years younger than Carlyle, also had less time and energy for the Carlyles by the 1850s. As a young man of eighteen whose ambition was greater than his talent (though his talent was estimable), he had met Carlyle soon after the burning of the manuscript of the first volume of *The French Revolution.* Carlyle introduced him to his neighbor Thornton Hunt, Leigh Hunt's son, and to the excitement of German language and culture.[130] Both had serious consequences. With an introduction from Carlyle to Varnhagen von Ense, Lewes went to Germany in 1838 where he learned the language; back in London, he attended Carlyle's lectures, imitated Carlyle's prose, attempted to earn his living as a journalist and as an author of semipopular George Sand-like novels, and soon married. With Thornton Hunt as his collaborator, he shared the editorial duties of a new journal, *The Leader,* whose radical spunk Carlyle admired, though he frequently disagreed with its positions. A regular visitor at Cheyne Row throughout the forties and into the fifties, Lewes was often a source of comedy and high spirits.[131] Considered physically ugly and nicknamed by the Carlyles "the ape," he was nevertheless warmly appreciated for his good cheer, his energetic willingness to tackle almost any literary task, no matter how formidable, and especially for his openly expressed veneration for Carlyle. Carlyle took Lewes' serious side seriously. He responded to Lewes' request for spiritual guidance that he "should very like to have a *credo*" but "better to be a good Christian and leave your Thirty-nine Articles very much to shift for themselves."[132] But both Carlyles found Lewes' novels, *Rose, Blanche and Violet* and *Ranthorpe,* "silly"; and Carlyle, who himself termed them "dreadful," made disapproving marginal notes, especially critical of the sexual lushness of many of the descriptions in *Ranthorpe.*[133] Nevertheless, he tactfully refused to allow the persistent Lewes to draw him out on his response to the novels.[134] To Jane, Lewes was still "the most amusing little fellow in the whole world—if you only look over his unparalleled *impudence,*" the "best mimic . . . and full of famous stories."[135]

Thornton Hunt's relationship with Lewes' wife soon became noticeable, and by early 1849 the Leweses' marriage had collapsed. Jane had prophetically observed that the Leweses were too warmly effusive with one another for the relationship to last. The Carlyles thought that Lewes was well within his rights to separate from his wife. With characteristic generosity, Lewes maintained the support and the legitimacy even of those children who were Hunt's. Hunt and Lewes struggled on with *The Leader,* which became increasingly socialistic, to Carlyle's dismay. But after some months Lewes resigned his position and determined, prompted by his long-standing interest in the "Sage of Weimar," to go to to Germany again and write Goethe's biography.[136] He took with him a note of introduction from Carlyle to James Marshall, which described him as "ingenious, brilliant, entertaining, highly gifted and accomplished." When he left for Weimar in the summer of 1854, he was accompanied by Mary Ann Evans.[137]

Though Carlyle could not condone the relationship, he also could not condemn it, unless, of course, "the strong woman of the *Westminster Review*" had been responsible for the breakdown of Lewes' marriage and his decision to leave his wife.[138] Deeply fond of Lewes, he shortly wrote asking him to deny or confirm the rumors that depicted him as an irresponsible libertine and Miss Evans as a marriage breaker. Lewes immediately responded with what to some extent Carlyle already knew, that his marriage had been fatally corrupted by his wife's behavior long before he had met Miss Evans and that the new relationship had begun only after he had abandoned all hope for the former. Carlyle had never met Miss Evans, though he was aware of her professional activities at the *Westminster Review* and as a translator. He did not know that she had paced up and down Cheyne Row almost exactly four years before while Chapman solicited Carlyle to contribute and to urge his friends to contribute to the *Review,* the name of whose "able Editor" he declined to reveal because she was a woman.[139] But Lewes' solemn denial of the scandal was convincing; and Carlyle thereafter honored his request that he should, "on all occastions, clear the lady from such unworthy aspersions and not allow her to be placed in so totally false a position."[140]

But, for Carlyle, there was a finer, subtler difficulty to take into account. In his mind, there was no doubt that Lewes had contributed indirectly to the loosened sexual atmosphere, even if only of a broad cultural sort, that had made his wife's infidelity possible. The author of *Rose, Blanche and Violet* and of *Ranthorpe* was not untainted by "George-Sand Philosophies" and "the Cesspool" of modern sexual licentiousness.[141] In principle, for Carlyle, "*continence*" was one of the highest duties; "a lewd being has fatally lost the *aroma* of his existence; and become" dead "in regard to the higher functions of intelligence and morality."[142] In fact, however, Lewes was still a valued friend, and when his *Life and Works of Goethe* was published in late 1855 Carlyle praised it highly to the author.

Though Lewes was welcome at Cheyne Row, Mary Ann Evans was not; and George Eliot, though welcome between the covers of a book, was no more considered an appropriate visitor as a celebrity than she had been as an unknown. It was not a personal matter. And Carlyle's sense of propriety overrode Jane's more latitudinarian curiosity. When the pseudonymous *Scenes of Clerical Life* arrived at Cheyne Row in January 1858, as a gift from the "author," Jane responded that she had found it a totally "*human* book—written out of the heart" and that on her urging her husband "had engaged to read" it. She felt the author to be a "sympathetic helpful friend." When *Adam Bede* arrived the next year, Jane found it "as good as *going into the country for one's health* . . . a beautiful most *human* Book!"[143] There is reason to believe that even Carlyle read it, the gender of its mysterious author in his opinion female, in Jane's male. Of one thing Jane was certain: the author was a great writer and certainly not "a clergyman."

Unfortunately, friendship with Mary Ann Evans was out of the question. Lewes "was not to be applauded, but it could scarcely be said that he had gone from bad to worse."[144] However, the bad was not to be cultivated; it might drive out the good. It made no difference that Miss Evans had been a deep admirer of Carlyle's early work, though she privately criticized *Latter-Day Pamphlets* and deplored *Frederick,* and that she spoke and wrote in praise of Carlyle the artist whose genius and personal attractiveness could be separated from his message. Only a completely casual if not accidental relationship outside the house was permissible. Carlyle apparently met her at least once while she and Lewes were living at Richmond soon after their return from Germany.[145] And one evening in the summer of 1861 Jane, to her complete surprise, found herself sitting "between Lewes and Miss Evans" at a performance of *Hamlet;* John Chapman had arranged the meeting. The tainted Miss Evans, whom Jane had been prevented from pursuing as a friend, looked to her like "Propriety personified!"[146] Lewes himself, perforce, came less frequently to Cheyne Row; and by the 1860s, though he was no less an admirer, his relationship with George Eliot and his increasing commitment to his work as a popular scientist deprived the "Sage of Chelsea" of his companionship.

6.

But many of his less famous younger contemporaries came to fill the void in companionship that the barriers of fame and time had created. Disciples, no matter how distinguished, remain subordinate and available to the master in a way that those whose talent and achievement equal his can never be. Browning, Dickens, Tennyson, and Thackeray followed a rather stringent imperative of their own that sent them on their separate ways. So too, though in a lesser way, did Lewes. There were others, however, whose private lives and careers had time for Carlyle's needs and frequent visits to Cheyne Row. Larkin, of course, gave himself up to Carlyle's demands; so too did Neuberg and, for a short time, Gilchrist. And Jack was sometimes in lodgings in London during these years. The distance from Manchester to London kept two young disciples, Thomas Ballantyne and Francis Espinasse, from providing daily companionship. For Geraldine, who had moved from Manchester to London in 1851, it was only a short walk to the Carlyles'. She met unfailing politeness and sometimes affection from Carlyle, but her intimacy was with Jane. Henry Taylor was still in sight but mostly out of mind. Emerson was sometimes in mind but, as always, far away; even their exchanges had become less frequent, though Emerson had high praise for the first two volumes of *Frederick.* A frequent and appreciated visitor during the 1850s, James Stephen, who as an official in the Colonial Office provided Carlyle indirect access to government attitudes, died in September 1859. His eldest and "inseparable son," James Fitzjames Stephen, had frequently accompanied him to Cheyne Row; years later he was to be a valuable help to Carlyle in his old age.

But the new young men who came as disciples and sustained the relationship long enough to make a difference to Carlyle's life were William Allingham, James Anthony Froude, and John Ruskin. When Allingham first came to Cheyne Row in the early 1850s, the ambitious young Irish poet had recently published his first volume; without private means, he earned his living as a clerk "in the Custom house service," a necessity despite his increasing success in publishing his poems in journals like Dickens' *Household Words.* Eager to rise in the literary world and deeply sincere in his admiration for Carlyle, he came as often as he could to Cheyne Row. In April 1854 he asked Carlyle to intercede for him with Carlyle's old friend, Stephen Spring Rice, the commissioner of customs. A few months before, ill, depressed, and under the influence of opium, Allingham had resigned his position at the Custom House and come to London again in the vain hope that he could make his living as a writer. "This poor Allingham" seemed to Carlyle "a young man of superior worth and faculty, a perfectly honest, ingenious and even genial young man" who deserved to be saved from his own folly. There was "something really good in . . . the foolish little Poet."[147] Spring Rice readily obliged his friend, and Allingham was returned to his former post and security for the time being.

Work, however, kept Allingham away from London, except for visits. Despite his limitations as a poet, his agreeable personality and general intelligence made him a welcome caller at Cheyne Row and an accepted though peripheral member of English literary society. His wife Helen, a talented watercolorist, added to Allingham's attractiveness. In the next few decades, he became an intimate of Coventry Patmore, William Morris, Edward Burne-Jones, and especially Dante Gabriel Rossetti, and a peripheral friend of Tennyson, Ruskin, and George Eliot, among others. As suits a man whose own inner drive demands that he make himself part of the community of writers even though his own talent is far beneath and different from that of his mentors, Allingham began in the 1850s to keep a substantial literary diary. The central figure was, of course, Carlyle, whom "he saw many times" during his London visits until his retirement from government service in 1870 gave him the opportunity to see Carlyle frequently. To Carlyle he seemed "a thoroughly transparent creature, simple-hearted, talky and ingenious." When Carlyle was told that Allingham had remarked to several people that he hoped to be his Boswell, "he replied, 'Well, let him try it. He's very accurate.' "[148]

James Anthony Froude, Carlyle's future biographer, first saw the "Sage of Chelsea" in the early summer of 1848. The thirty-year-old Froude sat behind him at Emerson's last London lecture. ("You pronounce his name *Frood* [in spite of the spelling]," Carlyle was to indicate years later.)[149] Without seeing his face, Froude "heard his loud, kindly, contemptuous laugh."[150] Froude was then a fellow of Exeter College, Oxford, but his position there was becoming untenable. In 1847 he had published under a pseudonym a volume of religious stories which anticipated the public expression of his disillusionment with Anglican Christianity in his autobiographical novel *Nemesis of Faith.* Honest doubt infuriated all parties, and by the end of February 1849 Froude had been forced by condemnation and censorship to resign from Oxford.

James Anthony Froude. Photograph, n.d. Courtesy of the Rare Book and Manuscript Library, Columbia University.

The controversy surrounding *The Nemesis of Faith* shortly brought the novel into Carlyle's hands. The "Book is not,—except for wretched people, strangling in white neck-cloth, and Semitic thrums,—worth its paper and ink," he wrote to Forster.[151]

Having been through a painful religious crisis of his own, and having resolved it on the far side of Christianity, Carlyle found only Froude's insistence on public self-exposure repulsive. His own strategy had been one of concealment and evasion. "What on earth is the use of a wretched mortal's vomiting up all his interior crudities, dubitations, and spiritual, agonising bellyaches, into the view of the public?"[152] But, despite his distaste for Froude's public agonizing, Carlyle might readily have guessed not only that the young writer was an admirer of his who had read during the past decade all that he had written but also that he believed that Carlyle himself, particularly in *Sartor,* had provided the model for public expression of religious doubt. He did not decline to meet the young man when Clough, whom Carlyle already knew and liked, arranged to have James Spedding bring Froude to Cheyne Row in June 1849. The meeting was a success. Carlyle was not critical of Froude's opinions but only of his having published them. Jane served tea in the dining room. Froude "had never seen a more interesting-looking woman." And at "fifty-four years old," Carlyle was "tall . . . thin. . . . His body was angular, his face beardless . . . the hair grizzled and thick and bushy. His eyes, which grew lighter with age, were then of a deep violet, with fire burning at the bottom of them, which flashed out at the least excitement."[153]

During the next decade Froude visited at Cheyne Row frequently, prompted by deep affection for both the Carlyles. In his new career as a historian, he identified himself especially closely with Carlyle. For a while, he sought "intellectual solitude" in Wales, for, as Geraldine remarked, his scorching in the heat of religious controversy had made him "rather like 'a lost sheep' " who needed to find his stability and inner peace again.[154] Fortunately, his heterodox opinions did not close the pages of the *Westminster Review* and *Fraser's Magazine* to him. By late 1853 he had decided to "write a History of Queen Elizabeth, and stand by his heterodoxies."[155] In 1856 he published, to sharp controversy among historians, the first two volumes of what later was to be titled the *History of England from the Fall of Wolsey to the Defeat of the Spanish Armada,* the final volume of which appeared in 1870. Throughout, he eagerly sought Carlyle's advice; the older man gave "heretic Froude" detailed help whenever he could, delighted to have the opportunity to assist in the development of a historian whose principles followed his own. Though his own *Cromwell* provided the model, he still thought "the earliest volumes of" Froude's history " 'meritorious, but too much raw material.' "[156]

Froude had much in common with the Carlyle of thirty years before; and Carlyle could see in him some of the conflicts, ambitions, and commitments that he had himself experienced as a young man.

Froude, whose father had died when he was an infant, found Carlyle an affectionate but at the same time rewardingly stern taskmaster. The major impediments to the development of the relationship gradually disappeared: in 1860 Froude moved to London and soon became editor of *Fraser's Magazine;* in early 1865 Carlyle finished *Frederick,* never to be so busy again; and in early 1866 Carlyle became a lonely widower. Froude later claimed that from the time he moved to London, "for twenty years," except during holidays, he "never ceased to see" Carlyle "twice or three times a week, and to have two or three hours of conversation with him."[157] Outside of his relationships with his family and his wife, it was the most sustained direct relationship Carlyle ever had. "I am glad to hear of you again," Carlyle wrote to him in October 1860, "especially after so long a silence. . . . Come then, and without fail."[158]

Early in July 1850 an avid and admiring reader of Carlyle came to visit briefly at Cheyne Row. Perhaps the thirty-one-year-old John Ruskin had met Carlyle previously; certainly the young man had been a careful reader of *Sartor, The French Revolution,* and particularly *Heroes and Hero-Worship* and *Past and Present,* the latter two at their times of publication. The recently married Ruskin, who with his wife visited Cheyne Row again late in the year, understandably struck Carlyle as "a small but rather dainty dilettante soul, of the Scotch-Cockney breed."[159] From his childhood, Ruskin had been encouraged by his dour Calvinistic Scotch mother and his successful, cultured, Scotch-merchant father to pursue learning and the arts. They were determined that their son's genius should have every support and encouragement that their discipline and wealth could provide. Private tutors and travel overshadowed his formal education, partly because the parents had an evangelical suspicion of English schools, partly because the particular brilliance of the young boy readily demanded expression outside institutional channels.

Ruskin had already begun to move from a focus on such traditional forms of expression as poetry and drawing to his passionate concern for color, architecture, landscape, and painting. He was fascinated by the interaction between language and visual experience. With an intense energy that seemed as much an expression of the nervous system as of the imagination, he wrote and published in 1843 the first volume of his *Modern Painters,* championing the controversial English painter J. M. W. Turner, whose appreciation of light and color Ruskin took as the symbol of his own commitment to the truths of the imagination. Certainly Carlyle did read "snatches" of *Modern Painters;* if he did not glance at *The Seven Lamps of Architecture,* which Ruskin had published in 1849, he was nevertheless aware of its existence. Early in 1851, Carlyle was reading *The Stones of Venice,* "a strange, unexpected, and . . . most true . . . *Sermon* in Stones," which the author had given him as a gift, as he was to give him a copy of everything else he wrote while they were both alive.[160] In the meantime, a personal relationship had been devel-

John Ruskin. Photograph, n.d. Courtesy of the Rare Book and Manuscript Library, Columbia University.

oping. There were exchanges of visits. Early in 1851 Carlyle rode over to the Ruskin family home at Denmark Hill, where he visited for hours, talking "in a most marvellous manner." Ruskin's eager father thought "it was a great catch to get him . . . to stay to dinner."[161]

Like Carlyle's, Ruskin's loyalty to his parents and his early training dominated his life in crucial ways. He wanted more than anything to please them; and the most difficult crises of his life developed when he became conscious that either in his career or in his beliefs he somehow fell short of his parents' expectations. As with Carlyle, the attachment to his parents overshadowed all the other relationships of Ruskin's life, one of which, early in the 1850s, was in the process of foundering. Among other things, the strain that led to the separation between Ruskin and his wife by the spring of 1854 kept him either abroad or away from London much of the time during those years; and the separation itself provoked widespread comment. "I know nothing about it," Jane said, "except that I have always pitied Mrs. Ruskin, while people generally blame her. . . . She was too young and pretty to be so left to her own devices as she was by her Husband, who seemed to wish nothing more of her but the credit of having a pretty, well-dressed Wife."[162]

By early 1855 it had been three years since the Carlyles had last seen Ruskin. But the two men had been much on one another's minds; and with Ruskin's return to London regular visits began, to the extent that health and work permitted. Carlyle soon introduced Ruskin to the Ashburtons. At one large party at Bath House, Jane, who resented "horribly ill bred people" staring at Ruskin, took his arm at the entrance door with "a *certain* force of mind" and had them announced as " 'Mrs. Carlyle and Mr. Ruskin!' "[163] Gifts of eggs, brandy, and cigars came frequently from Denmark Hill, prompted as much by John Ruskin's generosity as by his concern for his son's relationship with his distinguished friend. Ruskin's fondness for Jane increased; his concern for her health extended to concern for her feelings. When her dog Nero was ill in December 1859, he reminded her that "Nero . . . will love you just as much, even when he is blind."[164]

Despite Ruskin's association with aesthetic matters and Carlyle's initial criticism of him as a "dilettante," Ruskin had for almost a decade been moving in Carlyle's direction, increasingly advocating the need to speak out vigorously on crucial issues of social justice. It was heady praise to have Carlyle tell him that he was "the most eloquent Preacher" he had "heard these 20 years," one whose "beautiful enthusiasm" had only the minor fault of expecting the triumph of truth much before that victory would come.[165] By the autumn of 1860, Ruskin's long determination to speak out on contemporary social and spiritual issues had shaped, much to Carlyle's delight, the first essay of *Unto This Last.* Carlyle read it "with exhilaration, exultation, often with laughter, with 'Bravissimo!' " In his estimate, if Ruskin devoted himself to that kind of work for the "next 7 years," there was reason to have hope that England's future would be better than its past.[166]

But Carlyle's own disappointments colored his optimism with caution. When he joined a "most brilliant audience" in April 1861 at the Royal Institution to hear Ruskin's lecture on "Tree Twigs," he attributed the general "failure" of the lecture to "over-opulence," by which he seems to have meant Ruskin's tendency to be more emotionally and descriptively expressive than the context would bear.[167] By the early 1860s, severe anxieties disturbed Ruskin, some of which he communicated to his friend. "The heaviest depression is upon me I have ever gone through; the great questions about Nature and God and man have come on me in forms so strange and frightful."[168] His doubts about the reality of God in traditional forms shook the security of his relationship with his parents; his guilt increased his anguish. The notion that nature might harbor irredeemable destructive powers frightened him. His sense of his own mental fragility was keen; when he began to see hideous shapes superimposing themselves on the contours of Nature and invading his dreams and daydreams he turned with desperate energy to social problems and to friendship. Froude began to provide some companionship and, particularly on Carlyle's urging, published the first four installments of Ruskin's *Munera Pulveris* in *Fraser's Magazine* in 1862.[169] But the pressure of hostile public reaction forced Froude to discontinue the essays after the fourth installment, just as Thackeray had been forced two years before to discontinue publishing in the *Cornhill Magazine* the essays that eventually appeared under the title *Unto This Last.*

Prone to self-destructive idealizations, Ruskin became obsessed during the next few years with a young Irish girl, Rose LaTouche, who had been one of his art pupils. When he went to Ireland in the summer of 1861, he did not hide his motive from Carlyle. His longing for Rose caused him great pain, some of which he attempted to discharge and evade by frequent trips to Switzerland and Italy. From the Continent, he promised the Carlyles that he would be home for New Year's Day 1862. "But it was very cool of Mr. Carlyle to say I was leading a life 'with a trace of sadness' in it. I'm entirely miserable—that's all. . . . I love you both."[170] Carlyle returned the love with the highest praise for *Unto This Last* and *Munera Pulveris,* praise that was extended not only to Ruskin but also to venerated friends like Thomas Erskine and Lord Ashburton. "It's all as true as gospel," he told the author.[171] For much of 1862 and 1863 Ruskin was in Italy, but he saw the Carlyles on brief visits to London. By the spring of 1863, he seemed to be settling in at Denmark Hill, at least for a while, only to be threatened by a new catastrophe early in 1864. John Ruskin senior became ill, "suffering very grievously."[172] Jane, who was desperately sick herself, could be of no help, and Ruskin, who stayed at Denmark Hill, in turn felt guilty that he could not help his friends. His cherished father died early in March. Perhaps anticipating a guilt that Carlyle did not feel, he assured his mentor that "you had enough sorrow of your own, and could by no means help us in ours."[173]

Devastated by his father's death, Ruskin felt depressed and guilty. He resolved to devote his life to attending to his mother. Carlyle, who visited mother and son at Denmark Hill in August 1864, found them a pathetic couple. Ruskin seemed constrained, "insincere." Carlyle himself was nervous, exhausted, worried about Jane's health and desperately trying to finish *Frederick.* Some months later, with the end of *Frederick* finally in sight, Ruskin seemed to Carlyle more friendly and open. A gift of cigars from his friend cheered him. He went out to Denmark Hill to have Ruskin show him his "superb mineralogical collection."[174] Ruskin, whose spirits had risen temporarily, contributed eagerly and sensitively to a renewal of the friendship. The publication of Ruskin's *Sesame and Lillies* provoked from Anthony Trollope, whose fiction Carlyle judged frivolous and inferior without reading it, a hostile review that Carlyle condemned. Eager to protect Ruskin's feelings, he called Trollope a "nasty gritty creature, with no eye for 'the Beautiful.' "[175] With more and more paternal concern, he administered to his disciple, whose youth was fast becoming absorbed in suffering, whatever consolation and affection he could. Now without a father of his own, Ruskin increasingly sought Carlyle's blessing.

7.

During the later years of Carlyle's work on *Frederick,* Jane went through the most serious crisis of her life. The death of Lady Ashburton in 1857 relieved her of one emotional burden. But, unfortunately, the habit of suffering had become entrenched; and there were causes for pain which, though they may once have been associated with her husband's commitment to Harriet Baring, now had an independent life of their own. Her husband's devotion to his work outlasted his devotion to Lady Ashburton. And Jane's own disappointments in life were too complex and pervasive to be limited to that one focus. She did not shed any tears at the death of Lady Harriet; but she had other reasons to weep.

Lord Ashburton responded to his wife's death with "the silent firm fortitude" that Carlyle had learned to expect from him.[176] Over the years, the men had developed a deep mutual respect and affection. To Carlyle, Bingham Baring seemed the ideal representative of the "English country gentleman." One night, at a formal dinner at the Grange, a servant had brought a note to the master of the house indicating that there was "a fire somewhere in the neighborhood." Carlyle admired the tactful quietness with which Lord Ashburton excused himself, drew on his boots, and galloped off into the "wild squally night."[177] What

Bingham Baring, the second Lord Ashburton. From a painting by Sir Edwin Landseer, n.d. Reprinted from *New Letters and Memorials of Jane Welsh Carlyle,* edited by A. Carlyle (London, 1903).

Lord Ashburton thought of his wife's relationship with Carlyle remains a matter of speculation. But, more likely than not, his Olympian calmness and innate sense of security left him completely unruffled by what probably seemed to him his wife's natural aristocratic function. What Jane resented, Lord Ashburton accepted; and, in addition, his own friendship with the Carlyles eschewed any possibility of scandal in such exchanges of affection.

Both Carlyles assured Lord Ashburton immediately after Harriet's death that he was now even more precious to them. Despite his obsession with *Frederick,* Carlyle could not lightly decline invitations to Addiscombe and the Grange, especially during the next half year. For Lord Ashburton, loyalty to his wife's memory did not demand solitude or the long perpetuation of widower's grief. Of the three survivors, perhaps Carlyle lived most constantly with her memory, inclined to keep alive the past as long as he could. The Carlyles even accepted an invitation to spend some weeks near Windsor Forest in the summer of 1861 with Harriet's aged mother, Lady Sandwich, who was "a brave, airy, affectionate, and bright kind of creature."[178] While visiting the Grange the next winter, Carlyle wrote to her that he had made one of his "Pilgrimages" to her daughter's grave at the Church of Northington. "I walked silently round that building; visited the inside, and read a little tablet, '4 May 1857,' which will be memorable to me all the days of my life. . . . There is no forgetting possible in certain cases; and if I mention this one to *you,* it is sacred and silent from all other mortals."[179]

He certainly did not talk about it with Jane; and there was soon reason not to talk about it with Lord Ashburton. In the autumn after his wife's death, Bingham Baring found himself attracted to a Scotch heiress, Miss Louisa Caroline Stewart Mackenzie, whom Carlyle had already met "once or twice" and who had been for a short time one of Ruskin's drawing students. She was "a bright vivacious damsel, struggling fitfully about, like a sweet-briar, and with hooks under her flowers, too . . . for they say she is much of a coquette."[180] In early May 1858 Carlyle, at Addiscombe, remarked that "it was yesterday gone a year that the presiding Genius of it was called suddenly away; and left a blank that will never be filled up to those that staid behind!"[181] In October 1858, soon after his return from Germany, he received from Lord Ashburton the news that he and the thirty-one-year-old Louisa intended to marry the next month. "Life belongs to the living," Carlyle responded, "and he that lives must be prepared for changes. . . . I have had the honor to see that amiable lady more than once. . . . May a blessing be on this new epoch of your life."[182]

Soon after her return from her honeymoon in Egypt, Louisa Ashburton called on the Carlyles to assure them that she valued her husband's friends. The second Lady Ashburton seemed generous, impetuous, and emotionally expressive, to the delight of Jane who soon realized that she had been unexpectedly blessed with a sympathetic friend. When she visited the Grange early in 1860, "the new Lady . . . was kindness's self!

Louisa Lady Ashburton and daughter Mary. From a painting by Sir Edwin Landseer. Reprinted from Iris Origo, *A Measure of Love* (London, 1957). By permission of Jonathan Cape Limited and Pantheon Books and courtesy of the Marquess of Northampton.

A really amiable, loveable woman . . . much more intent on making her visitors at their ease and happy, than on shewing off *herself*, and attracting admiration."[183] It was delightful to be invited for her own and not her husband's sake. When Louisa gave birth to a daughter, Jane's usually repressed maternal instincts exploded into sentimental effusions.

For not only did Jane feel unloved but a series of neglects and deaths had left her without a sufficient number of people to love. Over the years she had occasionally lavished motherly attention on youthful friends and relations; but such objects of love inevitably escaped her embrace, sometimes involuntarily, as in the case of her cousin Babbie Welsh and the Sterling's daughter Kate. When her dog Nero died in 1860, she buried him in the garden at Cheyne Row and grieved "as if he had been my little human child."[184] "Beautiful Kate Sterling . . . was buried" in December 1860.[185] The birth of a child to the Ashburtons amid such general deprivation provided a sentimental and obsessive long moment of release for Jane. "O yes, I saw her . . . lying like a pearl in an oyster-shell in her pink and white basket. . . . The first human child that has ever . . . awakened what is called the *maternal instinct* in me . . . whose lines have always been cast in babyless places!"[186] But the object of her maternal instincts was not really the child but the mother, who was old enough to be Jane's daughter; and, though her love for the child was sincere, it was mainly a vehicle through which she could express her passion for Louisa.[187]

In the spring of 1861 a sudden crisis in the sixty-two-year-old Lord Ashburton's health weakened him considerably and anticipated another decisive change.[188] In 1862 the Ashburtons put the Grange at the Carlyles' disposal, joining their guests there in October. A photographer, who had been employed to take "views" of the place, took group portraits of the hosts and their company, who had gotten into the practice of exchanging photographs. A short while before, Carlyle had sent Louisa "one of the ugliest Photographic Pictures of the human countenance you ever saw: an old grim fellow (much older than I thought he was) in wool-white hair; features full of gloom, hard as granite, and looking out quite relentless upon life."[189] All these attempts to capture and make permanent the passing moment bespoke a general awareness that all moments were slipping away. In one of the photographs, Carlyle and Lord Ashburton were "sitting on one bench." Louisa described them as " 'two criminals in the same dock, hearing sentence of Death pronounced on them!' "[190]

A few weeks later, in Paris, Lord Ashburton suffered a relapse of his inflammation of the lungs. For six weeks he hovered "between life and death." The mail from Paris brought uniformly dismal prognostications. Eager to have her friend beside her, Lady Louisa queried Jane

Thomas Carlyle, Louisa Ashburton, and Jane Carlyle. Photograph, 1865. Courtesy of the Rare Book and Manuscript Library, Columbia University.

about her willingness to come to Paris. Despite the fact that she had never crossed the Channel before and was herself in precarious health, Jane felt conscience-bound to write, offering "to come immediately."[191] But Lady Ashburton had the good sense to decline to put Jane to that ordeal and took her expression of willingness as sufficient support. Jane felt relieved. Her own health and her husband's demands were by themselves almost overwhelming burdens.[192]

The thought of the impending death of one of his dearest friends filled Carlyle with a sense of the helplessness and hopelessness of all things except his work. "Our sadness of soul is very great," he wrote to Lady Ashburton. "If your loved partner is still with you, and can hear my message, let it be to him: 'God go with you, guileless, brave, and valiant man, who have accompanied me in my Pilgrimage so far, and been friendly to me like a Brother; whom I shall soon follow. Farewell!' "[193] In Jane's estimation, he was "the only intimate friend" that her husband had "left in the world."[194] It was like losing a member of the family. But on Christmas Day 1862 the well-known London doctor Richard Quain, who had just returned from Paris where he had been attending Lord Ashburton, brought the unexpected news that the patient was for the moment out of danger.

Throughout the winter the reports continued favorable. In the summer, the Ashburtons finally came home. There was an exchange of presents and a visit at the Grange. But it was clear that the patient had not fully recovered and could never be expected to do so. Very early in the spring of 1864 Lord Ashburton died. Too ill herself to attend the funeral, Jane "day after day" realized that she had "lost *forever* his beloved companionship and sweet society" and responded compassionately to Louisa's desolation.[195] She had no belief that the living and the dead would ever meet again. Neither did her husband. He went down to the Grange to say good-bye to "twenty years of friendly acts and offices on his part, all done in the same gentle, quiet and fine way."[196] The funeral exhausted him; Lady Ashburton, to his surprise, kissed him gently; in the taxicab back from the railroad station he lost his "*dear old black velvet cap.*"[197] It seemed appropriate; valued things were fast disappearing.

8.

One valued friend from the past unexpectedly turned up at a fortunate time and helped in a small but important way with what was to be the greatest loss of all. While Jane was in Scotland in the summer of 1862, the servant announced to Carlyle that someone named "*Bessy,*" who claimed to know him, wished to see him. To his surprise, it turned out to be Bessy Barnet, John Badams' mistress and quasi-servant who had been the Carlyles' first servant in London almost thirty years before. She was about to marry a widower, a doctor in whose home she had been employed. Jane, who had thought her long dead, could not "get that Bessy Barnet *rediviva* out of" her head, as if someone had actually been brought back from oblivion.[198]

At Holm Hill, the Russells' new home near Thornhill, Jane was attempting to recuperate from a painful minor accident she had had early in the summer. Trying to step up onto a curbstone, she had not lifted her foot high enough, and, banging it hard against the side of the stone, had fallen flat in the street. Her ankle had swollen painfully. Though morphine gave her some relief, she was sleepless much of the time. Gradually she made progress, however, and early in 1863 she was well enough to spend the night at the suburban home of a new friend, Margaret Oliphant, who had just published, with praise from the Carlyles, her *Life of Edward Irving.*[199] The Carlyles felt that the memory of their friend had been treated respectfully and fairly; for Jane, there was the reminder of what might have been, for Thomas deep regret for what he had been deprived of by madness and early death.

From Jane's point of view, the madness of *Frederick* went on relentlessly. Fritz collapsed, the rapidly aging horse having galloped thousands of miles with his compulsive burden. But Carlyle went on, first on foot and then on horseback again—the new animal, named Noggs with a bow toward Dickens' *Nicholas Nickleby,* a gift from Lady Ashburton. By the spring, Carlyle's right hand began to shake slightly. However, the slight deterioration in his handwriting hardly interfered with his work.

In June 1863 a "very tall . . . pale beautiful" Bessy Barnet appeared as Bessy Blakiston, now married to a "rather loud-voiced restless, but really good kind of man," who was in medical practice at St. Leonards, a few hours south of London.[200] Urged by Bessy to visit them soon, Jane ascribed Bessy's statement that she looked just like Dr. Blakiston's former wife when she was dying of cancer to an "imagination morbid almost to insanity!"[201] But Bessy had not seen Jane for almost thirty years: the changes were more than normally startling. And Jane's left arm had recently become painful and stiff, vaguely diagnosed as "neuralgia" but possibly a psychosomatic nervous disorder, possibly a heart and circulation problem. She went to St. Leonards for a week and had a delightful time. But, when she returned to Chelsea, she soon felt "as sick as a dog" again.[202] Three weeks at the Grange beginning at the end of August did her no good. The left arm hurt constantly. Dr. Quain called it "neuralgia" brought on "by extreme weakness." Frequent doses of quinine and castor oil did not help. She found her vaguely defined status of semi-invalid unbearable, and she was just as miserable in bed as out.

In late September 1863, on her way home at night from a visit to a young cousin who was living in London, Jane stepped off the pavement into the street in order to be in position to mount an omnibus that could not come close to the curb because of an excavation. Suddenly a "furious" taxi hurtled through the space between Jane and the "slippery" curbstone. Uncertain which way to go to save herself, she "spasmodically" moved both ways until she abruptly lost her balance and fell heavily, unable to protect her body with her lame left arm from the full force of the fall. She "was powerless to move or stand." Apparently, she had torn some sinews in her thigh.[203] She lay "on the flags, full length," her left arm under her. The pain was "unspeakable."[204] Having returned from his evening ride, her husband waited at home, expecting her momentarily, eager to hear news of her visit. The sound of the carriage wheels announced her return. But when the carriage lingered at the door without Jane appearing in the house, he "rushed down."

Larkin, whom she had sent for, was leaning into the cab. She was "in agony." The two men carried her into the house and up to bed. The doctor's assurance that there was no "breakage or dislocation, wholly a strain of the muscles, or sinews," did not lessen the sudden sense of disaster in the Cheyne Row household.[205]

The pain did not diminish. Various drugs, particularly morphine, which Carlyle suspected did more harm than good, kept her numb but awake much of the time. Whenever the physical anguish temporarily diminished, mental anguish increased and absorbed all her tolerance for pain. Among other things, she felt guiltily certain that her husband's work was being disturbed. She strained her nerves to be as quiet as possible. Though she could not "read, or rise to mend her fire," she would "not have anybody sit with her, absolutely *not*."[206] After some weeks she felt able to take a few steps from bed. Late in October, she came haltingly down to the drawing room, to her husband's nervous delight. But, in the middle of November, she had a relapse. "No sleep, no food, nothing but torture and agitation." Carlyle told Louisa Ashburton that he did "not recollect ever to have seen the poor soul so beaten before."[207] In December her cousin Maggie Welsh came to stay with her, proving efficient and compassionate; during the night shift a special nurse watched the patient. Unfortunately, Dr. Quain, Dr. Barnes, and Dr. Blakiston could do little or nothing for her: the side effects of the medicine they used to relieve her pain destroyed her appetite and her sleep, but without the medicine the pain was unbearable. Despite her husband's skepticism, even mesmerism was tried, "first a man, then a *quack* woman . . . who at least did no ill, *except* entirely disappoint."[208]

Carlyle watched in anguish, though he kept on with his work, partly because he believed that his book itself was "the prime source of all her sorrows" and that if he could only finish it there would be a chance for a "new life" for both of them. In bed, Jane thought of suicide. Her husband felt helpless, watching her "continuous agony . . . no sleep . . . weakness . . . utter restlessness, depression and misery."[209] When they stopped all drugs for a short while, it seemed to help. The new year was frigid and frightening. One wintry morning, as he walked out of the house for air, the "thought" suddenly "struck" him, "cold and sharp, 'She will die, and leave thee here!' "[210] The anxiety clung to him for twenty-four hours; it returned twice more. But he fought it off. He would not accept that she would die; *that* he would not admit, though "in all points except" that one he "was as if stupefied more or less, and flying on like those migrative swallows . . . after [his] strength was done and coma or dream had supervened, till the Mediterranean Sea was crossed!"[211]

It was crossed safely in the next half year, though the effort had made any future safe passage unlikely. Soon there were "some faint symptoms of improvement."[212] By the time volume four of *Frederick* appeared late in January 1864, her will to survive had strengthened sufficiently for her to ask Maggie to tell the Ashburtons that "she 'would like to live a little longer to thank' " them " 'for all' " their " 'great kindness and thought for her.' "[213] Now that she was well enough to think that she might not die, her desire to control the circumstances under which she would struggle for life asserted itself. One day late in February she "astonished" Larkin by telling him that "if she must die, she might just as well die elsewhere as remain where she was, with nothing but the dreariest associations about her." She might as well die in a less unpleasant place, since she now had the strength to move.[214] With the consent of her doctors, she determined to return to the Blakistons' at St. Leonards. Early in March, Larkin carried her downstairs in his arms "as easily as if she had been a child of twelve years old . . . appalled at the shadow to which she had become reduced."[215] She had warned her husband to stay out of the way, at least until she was downstairs; his impatience and nervous irritability in the presence of her suffering made her even more miserable. At the door, Carlyle joined Larkin and helped slide her feetfirst into a "hideous receptacle" that seemed "more like 'a hearse' . . . than a carriage." Jane stifled a "shriek." At the railroad station, the whole apparatus was lifted into a special area of the train and, accompanied by her husband, she "got the journey done."[216] Carlyle returned to Chelsea that same day. They had agreed that her recovery and his work could best be speeded by a temporary separation.

But not even the ministering gentleness of the Blakistons could soothe Jane's nerves sufficiently to make her feel well again. Improvement came, but very slowly. Unquestionably, Jane felt more than weak and physically ill: she felt deeply wounded as a person, subject to unexplainable stabbing pains from within that focused on "the most nervous part" of her, as if her lifelong sense of guilt in regard to her parents and her own aborted career as a writer and as a woman now found the most physically symbolic residence. "The malady is in my womb. . . . It is the consequence of that unlucky fall; no disease there, the doctors say, but some nervous derangement."[217] Dr. Quain, whom she had allowed to examine her internally, agreed with Dr. Blakiston. The pain had no identifiable physical source. Some days she felt well enough to go out for a carriage ride; others she lay in bed, sleepless and suffering. At the end of March 1864, as they had agreed, her husband came to St. Leonards, accompanied by the loyal and kind John Forster and his wife. Carlyle stayed at the Blakistons'; the Forsters, who stayed at a

Jane Carlyle. Photograph, n.d. Courtesy of the Rare Book and Manuscript Library, Columbia University. After Jane's death, Carlyle wrote on this photograph, "the worst."

hotel, did not see Jane, who could not bear to have any visitor other than her husband. Even he did not stay long. "Poor Jane," Carlyle reported to Louisa, "in her own sad mind is hardly at all better."[218]

The "burning, throbbing, maddening sensation" in her womb continued. She had frequent nightmares, and occasional opium visions. The past was constantly on her mind, particularly her school days at Haddington and all the dear people and places she had lost: the person whose loss she most regretted was the child of promise and bright hope that she had once been. She "had the beautiful dream of being able to run again."[219] She also dreamed of escaping into death. "Oh, my husband! I am suffering torments! each day I suffer more horribly. Oh, I would like you beside *me!* I am terribly alone. But I don't want to interrupt your work."[220] Perhaps, she thought, their "life together" was "indeed past and gone. . . . Shall I ever make fun for you again? . . . I want so much to *live,*—to be to you more than I have ever been; but I fear, I fear!"[221] At the end of April she moved from the Blakistons' into a nearby "small furnished house" that they had rented to have more privacy and to permit him to stay with her. Maggie Welsh continued at St. Leonards as companion and nurse. After one of Carlyle's brief visits, Maggie had felt it likely that the hysterically sensitive noise-hater would be "the better" for "the complete quiet at home."[222] But he shortly moved himself and all his necessary writing materials from Chelsea to 5 Warrior Square, St. Leonards.

Despite the crisis, he had been making steady progress in his work. To his regret, however, a sixth—and absolutely last—volume of *Frederick* was necessary. During the increasingly warm weather, he worked at proofs for volume five and the preparations for volume six, with the help of Larkin, who mediated between author and printer, attending to innumerable mechanical details. During the months in London without Jane he had pressed on with the conviction that the best contribution he could make to her recovery would be to finish as soon as possible and thus relieve her of her guilty conviction that she was interfering with his progress. During May and June he worked at St. Leonards. To counter depression and boredom, he took long rides in the countryside, imposing on the summer landscape the dark tones of his misery. Jane simply did not seem enough better, though it was clear that she was "really improving." He agreed with Maggie Welsh that "she must be gaining strength. If it were not for the terrible depression from which she suffers and the almost constant nervous pain." Maggie had the perception to recognize that Jane's hopelessness "about herself . . . may be really part of her ailment."[223] At the beginning of July 1864, Jane suddenly decided that she could not stay any longer at St. Leonards. The weather was too hot; she could not sleep. Did she have the strength, her husband worried, to go anyplace at all, especially to make a long journey? She had no choice, she felt. There was only one place she wanted to be—Scotland.

With the emotional decisiveness of desperation, she immediately acted on her decision. Carlyle was left at St. Leonards to dispose of the rented house. At her husband's insistence, Jack accompanied her, first to London, where she stayed overnight with the Forsters, and then by night train to Scotland. The Forsters unavailingly urged her to stay longer with them. They all feared that the long journey would destroy her. But, as the train sped northward, she felt some of her strength returning. She even had the energy to argue with Jack, who seemed too irritable, querulous, insensitive, and better-than-thou. "Fancy him telling me in my agony," she complained to her husband, "that if I had ever done anything in my life this would not have been; that no poor woman with work to mind had ever such an ailment as this of mine since the world began."[224] Working diligently in the heat of Chelsea, Carlyle agreed that "it was *cruelly* absurd of him to say that," especially in the light of Jack's own difficulties as a worker. But he assured her that Jack "really does desire to help."[225]

Fortunately, the Russells proved more sensitive and supportive. Close to such familiar sights and in such loving hands, Jane felt that she had a better chance to recover and live again. She desired to get well more for her husband's sake than for her own. But recovery came only partially and slowly. "The accounts" that her husband received in London were "mostly . . . bad."[226] During much of the first month at Holm Hill she hardly improved, "almost continually in very great suffering." To her husband, "the root of all the mischief" was her lack of sleep "for many years back."[227] She had a nightmare about Lord Ashburton that Carlyle reported to the widow. "She had met *Him* in her dream: 'his face was all transfigured, grown pellucid; he said to her, yours will be so too, when *you get out of your sickness!*' (which I could see she interpreted in a sad sense for herself). I have had him in my dreams too: what a 'dreaming' one has, not by night only; and how one's Life altogether is like a dream!"[228] But the nightmare of Jane's crisis was at this very moment dispersing. Toward the end of August she was unquestionably improving. She slept more; she ate regularly and started actually to regain weight. For the first time she began to believe "seriously" that she might recover. Late in the month "something occurred . . . which produced an extraordinary sensation! . . . My Dear, *I laughed!!!*"[229]

Frightened of the consequences of returning to Cheyne Row, Jane soon realized that, whatever the state of her health, the only thing worse than returning would be staying away. She feared, naturally, that her husband's "frightfully slow" progress with his book would be impeded by her return and that the atmosphere of Cheyne Row would so exacerbate her constant anxiety that she would become ill and "half-insane" again. However, to stay away would destroy a relationship that she could not live without. Her husband urged her to return to his "side again for weal and woe. We have had a great deal of hard travelling together; we will not break down yet, please God!"[230] By the middle of September it had been settled that Carlyle's "poor wife" was "coming home" to him "before long."[231] Jack, who had apologized for his insensitive remarks, travelled with her from Scotland to London on the last day of the month. At Cheyne Row, Carlyle rushed "out into the street to meet" her "in his dressinggown, and in violent agitation." Since he had been led to believe that she would arrive an hour and a half earlier, "he had been momentarily expecting a telegram to say" that she "had died on the road."[232] Tearful friends came to visit, as if she had risen from the grave, "rejoicing over" her "as if" she "were a Queen bee."[233] Many of them had expected never to see her again.

No doubt she was better, "an improved woman," for whom her husband bought "a nice little Brougham" and Lady Ashburton a "beautiful grey horse" so that she might take carriage exercise.[234] At night she usually took a little whiskey to calm herself; and she still took "pills at great rate," desperately eager to keep the dull irritation in her womb from becoming a tormenting throb. Fortunately, for the first time in years, she had a satisfactory servant, and early in the new year Jane asked her to help her atone for a wound she had inflicted on her mother when Grace Welsh had first visited Cheyne Row. When she died, would the servant take out of their hiding place two candles she had berated her mother for being so extravagant as to buy for her and burn them beside her corpse as an act of repentance? Clearly, she did not expect the occasion of repentance to be long delayed.[235] And her friends, despite her not being in any imminent danger, could not fail to observe that at the age of sixty-three she looked devastated, an emaciated, feeble old woman whose gradual liberation from "physical suffering" over the next months did not ease her torment for so much that she had lost and so much that she had never had.

Thus, in the last dark days of 1864, Carlyle realized that what seemed the worst year of his life had at least been merciful enough to return his wife to him alive and to bring him within moments of finishing the book that had made them both miserable for so long. Exhaustion, depression, "gloomy but quiet *collapse*" overwhelmed him.[236] During the summer he had wryly joked to Froude that he had "mainly consorted" with his "Horse" for the last eight years.[237] Indeed, Fritz had been a more amiable companion than *Frederick.* Despite all his efforts to like the Prussian king, he had been able to muster no more than respect; and his struggle to create order, both as a historian and as an artist, had been undermined from the beginning by serious doubts as to whether order itself existed and whether efforts such as his had any value. Nevertheless, *Frederick* pulsed with a vital energy that few of his contemporaries and few modern readers have had the perception or the patience to experience. But it was a book written in pain. At the edge of his own strength and certain that his own death was imminent, he could not help but accentuate the autobiographical impulse of all his writing and track himself toward the grave as he described Frederick's old age.[238]

Early in 1865, after thirteen years of work on *Frederick,* Carlyle mailed the last section of the manuscript to the printer. There was some additional proofreading to be done; and Larkin, of course, could not have the final comprehensive index completed until February. Fortunately, by the middle of that month it was completely done and out of the author's hands forever. His right hand could now no longer hold a pen steadily. If he tried to write for more than a short time, it had "taken to *shaking* at [an] unpleasant rate."[239] But he did not plan to write anything more. With a sense of relief and disgust, he left his attic study, never to use it again, and soon had it turned into "a bedroom for the servants."[240]

[16]

"My One Strong City" 1865–1870

" 'Your birthday, Carlyle!' " The irresistible Forster insisted on a party at Palace Gate. That the seventy-year-old celebrant remarked that it "went well enough" was a clear sign that he was more willing to be feted than his usual reservations would indicate. The company was intimate, mainly Forster, Browning, and the two Carlyles. The days surrounding his attainment of the biblical three-score and ten in early December 1865 brought an amiable balance of old and new friends to Cheyne Row. Tennyson came with "a dilapidated kind of look, but in talk . . . cheerful," accompanied by his London host, the sculptor Thomas Woolner, who had done a bust of Carlyle the previous spring. They met Froude and James Fitzjames Stephen at the door of 5 Cheyne Row. Carlyle soon maneuvered the unwieldy group out for a walk in Hyde Park, the five men talking animatedly as they trudged through the "muddy and clammy" turf.[1]

The aging Neuberg, hard at work translating *Frederick* into German, visited that night. From Denmark Hill, Ruskin kept constantly in touch. Despite the grim weather, Carlyle's pleas for companionship were answered directly by the author as well as by a copy of his recently published *Ethics of the Dust,* which Carlyle thought "a most shining Performance."[2] A young scientist and writer, John Tyndall, expressed his admiration for the older man during cheerful and chatty visits. And in Edinburgh a larger public audience was being arranged for the "Sage of Chelsea," who had already discovered that wearisome old age and public indifference to the substance of his writings were the price to be paid for national fame.

With the completion of *Frederick* at the beginning of 1865, he had sunk into bemused lassitude, mingling relief with depression. At first he hardly resented the increased shaking of his right hand, taking some comfort from the assumption that he would never have energy again and that whatever work he "had to do in this Planet" had been done. With no desire to write anything more, he could for the time being accept this new infirmity as the external symbol of "a gloomy but quiet *collapse*"; its only practical effect would be to diminish his letter writing.[3]

Jane had been in better than normal health through the winter. There had been no return of the "hysterical mania," the aching in the womb. At the end of the first week in March 1865 they had gone for a month to Seaforth, Lady Ashburton's home in Devonshire, where the "invalid" was lovingly cared for and the "idle" writer walked and rode by the seashore. The house was "within a hundred yards of a high cliff overhanging the sea." But her husband's characteristic all-purpose skepticism scotched Jane's enthusiasm for the purchase of "a Devonshire Craigenputtock." It would be, he objected, impossibly lonely there. When she proposed to resolve that by inviting all their friends, he made it clear that in his judgment that would be worse than "solitude."[4] Back in London her right arm unexpectedly "took ill." Dr. Barnes and Dr. Quain could do nothing. It felt "as if a dog had got it in its teeth, and were gnawing at it, and shaking at it furiously."[5] Dr. Quain somberly advised her to try to learn to write with her left.

For Carlyle, it was a time of transition; for Jane, a moment of reminder that there would never indeed be any real change for her. She had hoped to soften the disappointments accumulated during the years her husband had worked on *Frederick* by having more of his company now that he had finished. Certainly she permitted herself the fantasy that there would be renewed tenderness between them. And though there was some, it was far less than she had hoped, particularly because they had grown into the habit of not confiding their feelings to one another. While in Devonshire, bored by his "entirely idle existence under the chalk cliffs," Carlyle had even decided that some solitary travel might do him good, particularly a long summer in Scotland. Jane was "to be left alone at Chelsea."[6] The general excuse was, as usual, that Carlyle's sister at Dumfries had room for only one, and that Jane's health was not up to the exertions that the railroad journey would demand. In fact, he preferred to take the atmosphere provided by the "remnants" of his Annandale family without her; she preferred, as the pain in her right arm suddenly became all-absorbing in May, to be apart from a husband who could be of no help to her at all. Still, she "cried a very little" at being left by herself when her husband departed at the end of the third week of May for "Scotland and silence far away."[7]

Scotland calmed him. Used to being idle there, Carlyle did not have to confront, as he did in Chelsea, the likelihood that idleness would be permanent. It was a vacation time, more morbid and less restless than his usual vacations, primarily because he had finally let go "after the long deadly tug of pulling (12 years long!) at that last Book."[8] And, on the whole, he felt intact, though "worn out" and "very old." Though he imagined, almost hoped, that he would not live much longer, he certainly knew that physically he was in quite sound health.

As he rested, he became more capable, as he always did from a distance, of hearing Jane's voice of suffering. But it was not until she also came to Scotland at the middle of June that he was shaken by her condition. Dr. Quain thought that Scotland might again minister to her pain and sleeplessness. At the edge of her endurance, she had more to gain by the change than to lose by the journey. She left London, without her husband's knowledge, and passed by in the night within a quarter mile of where he was sleeping. Just before crossing the border, she wrote to explain that she did not want to create the dilemma for him of whether or not to meet her at the station.

From Holm Hill, she put a brave face on her debility and their separation. "Don't be bothering, making plans embracing me. The chief good of a holiday for a man is just that he should have shaken off home cares—the foremost of these a wife. . . . For the present summer, you have nothing to do with me, but write me nice daily letters, and pay my bills."[9] With his brother Jamie he awaited her visit the next day at the Gill in Annan; Jack, who had gone to the station with a gig to meet her, returned alone. Exhausted and ill, Jane had been forced to get off the train at Dumfries. Urged by her message to meet her at the station there, Carlyle soon joined her on the platform where they spent three hours in the late afternoon of a warm summer day. "She was so pleasant, beautifully cheerful, and quiet." He felt quite comforted by the warmth of the moment, as if there might be many more. Jane recognized an old local acquaintance, "remembered kindly after forty years," and spoke graciously to him for a moment, "the great, red, sinking sun flooding everything: day's last radiance, night's first silence." He "sat by her in the railway carriage (empty otherwise) till the train gave its third signal, and she vanished from [his] eyes."[10]

Family and solitude, constant reminders of love and death, soothed the tired writer through the summer. At the homes of his sisters he found that their undemanding affection brought relative peace. He reserved his curses for the inescapable railroad whistles that regularly pierced the air in Dumfries. "Whirlwind" nighttime gallops on the Solway Sands near Annan helped exorcise exhaustion. He slept better. Each morning at Scotsbrig "the shining *transparency* . . . the definite *purity* of all things in earth and air" delighted him. A visit to Craigenputtoch provided a sharp reminder of the days that were gone. The completely familiar Annandale and Dumfriesshire landscape was possessed by either completely unfamiliar people or a few worn, familiar faces, like that of his brother Jamie who had "grown very sad and saturnine" since the death of his wife.[11] Visiting Jane, who stayed first at Holm Hill, and then for two weeks with a friend at Nith Bank, he was worried by her exhaustion, depression, and lameness. On her birthday, Ruskin delighted her with a long letter, a copy of *Sesame and Lillies,* and the hollow assurance that he had "found a doctor . . . who will make you well if anybody will."[12]

At Nith Bank on Jane's sixty-fourth birthday the Carlyles discussed plans for the rest of the summer. Jane had decided to accept the invitation to visit at Folkstone a close friend of the last few years, Miss Bromley Davenport, a friend of Lord Ashburton's whom she had met through Louisa. Late in July Carlyle boarded her London-bound train at Dumfries and accompanied her for an hour as far as Annan. He felt "miserable," she seemed "agitated." He had no thought that "it would be her last railway journey."[13] Surprisingly, after a week or so in London her arm felt better; at Folkstone, in the second half of August, she actually experienced what seemed to her the miracle of sleeping "wonderfully."[14] In the meantime, Carlyle tried to shake himself into mental and emotional alertness. He wrote to Jane that he felt "as if there were still as much love in me—all gone to potential tears—as there was in my earliest days."[15] And the tears were even the more painful because he kept them mainly to himself. What he wanted to do and what he could do, both had changed. He offered his horse, Noggs, whom he had not cared for nearly as much as Fritz, to Neuberg, having decided that in his old age he could no longer ride. He had much of Jack's company, which he appreciated more than he enjoyed. Restless, he spent some time in Edinburgh. He decided against sailing to Thurso; instead, he made a number of closer visits, particularly to Linlathen to see Thomas Erskine, whose "paternal" assurance to Jane "that God is indeed a Father" poignantly reminded both Carlyles how distant they were from traditional religious comforts in sickness and old age.

When Carlyle abruptly returned to London at the end of August, Jane refused to panic. She could no longer persuade herself that her husband really needed her; and she was now beyond fantasying that the responsibilities of her home were more important than her health. Unfortunately, even this minimal liberation from such anxieties came only a short time before her death; that Jane herself sensed its nearness may have helped her to exercise personal choice for almost the first time in such a matter. While she stayed a little longer at Folkstone, Carlyle continued to try to learn to be "idle," reading in the shade of his awning in the garden at Cheyne Row and receiving his usual visitors. The effort to pass time without working sometimes itself seemed to him hard work. Not only was he finding it difficult to be idle graciously but to be idle at all, "with little prospect but that of continuing so for the remainder" of his "appointed days."[16] He could not yet convince himself that he had earned an honorably useless old age, as he had often told his mother she had done. To be idle was to be "unworthy." As he had done all his life, he set a standard for himself slightly beyond his grasp; and, often with vivid exaggeration, dramatized the distance between the ideal and the actuality. His complex emotions were most at home in that space purposely created for self-criticism.

2.

In November 1865 Carlyle began to be preoccupied with the latest and most newsworthy indication of his high status as a culture hero. After serving two terms, Gladstone had retired from the newly created and largely honorific position of rector of the University of Edinburgh. A new rector was to be elected by the students of the University.[17] Two names were proposed, Carlyle and Disraeli. Despite his reservations about such public honors, Carlyle did not decline his nomination, partly because of vanity, partly because of his desire to be a prophet even in his own land, and partly because of his disapproval of Gladstone and Disraeli. The students, some of whom had cut their teeth on *Sartor* and grown into hero worship on *Cromwell* or *Frederick,* deserved in his judgment something better than another politician.[18]

To his surprise, he was elected to the office before the middle of November by a vote of better than two to one.[19] It seemed a moment of triumph, and Jane especially took it that way. It was also a time of slowly growing worry. The principal duty of the rector was to give an inaugural address. He had not spoken in any formal way in public since he had given his last lecture in 1840; and in anticipation of this address both he and Jane began to relive some of the emotional anxieties that had made life a nightmare for them at that time. Despite misgivings, however, there was no turning back. At first he thought it best to get it over with as soon as possible, perhaps "before the Christmas Holidays." He soon changed his mind and suggested instead "either the first week of April or the last week of March."[20] By the time of his birthday party at Forster's, April 2, 1866, had been decided on.

He insisted Jane would have to decide herself whether she would accompany him to Edinburgh. "If the weather happened to be remarkably mild, and if" she "happened to be remarkably well," she "should like to go with him."[21] But she soon decided against making the trip, even as far as Yorkshire, where her husband had agreed, on Milnes's invitation, to "stop a day or two at good old Fryston."[22] "I am not afraid of the journey," she told Milnes,

> or of bodily fatigue, generally. For you see I am what is pleasantly called 'A Living Miracle!' Meaning a woman who, according to Nature, should have been dead and buried away two years ago, and is still here, going about in society live and well! . . . What *I am* afraid of . . . is the agitation that was getting hold of me about *his* agitation. I had visions of his breaking down in his 'address'! of his lying ill . . . and I unable to do anything . . . *but* just to take the terrible *pain in my back* which assails me under all violent emotion.[23]

By the middle of March both Carlyles were on edge, eager to have the "accursed adventure" over with. Dinner invitations had to be declined. Her husband seemed to Jane "in no humour" for "doing anything but committing suicide!" She was sure that "many a man, with a good thick skin, has gone to be hanged more comfortable in his mind, than Mr. C goes to make that tiresome *address.*"[24]

Accompanied by John Tyndall, Carlyle left for Fryston early in the morning of the last Thursday in March 1866. Jane provided a small flask of the brown Scotch brandy that he was used to. On the journey, Tyndall, who was to receive an honorary LL.D. at the same ceremony, provided companionship and distraction. The younger man was deeply attracted to Carlyle. As a youth he had read avidly and annotated *Past and Present.* As a mature scientist he had discovered that he had a gift for popularization, and resolved to demonstrate that the physical basis of modern science affirmed the mystery and the beauty of life. On the highest level, science and religion should be reconcilable. His revered mentor in the former was Faraday, his senior colleague at the Royal Institution, in the latter Carlyle, whom he had met at a luncheon at Bath House in the days when Harriet Baring had gathered around her distinguished men in all fields. Later they had also been fellow guests at the Grange. Actually, Carlyle believed that his own early background in science was a bond between them; and Tyndall refrained from pressing too hard when their disagreements on scientific matters revealed Carlyle's ignorance. Carlyle visited Tyndall's laboratory a number of times. On one occasion he was delighted to conclude that the scientist's experiments on the germ origin of disease, which disproved spontaneous generation, provided scientific support for his own belief that life could

John Tyndall. Photograph, n.d. Courtesy of the Rare Book and Manuscript Library, Columbia University.

arise only from life.[25] During the difficult *Frederick* years, Tyndall had done what he could to provide Carlyle with companionship; the now prominent scientist had a strong sense that when great men grow old they should have young shoulders to lean on.

At Fryston, the hospitable Lord Houghton did his best to make his guests comfortable. In the twenty-five years since Carlyle had last been there, much had changed, including the imposition of the dreaded railways and their shrieking whistles on what had once been a quiet rural landscape. "In the morning," claiming that "he had not slept a wink," Carlyle was "wild with his sufferings." He insisted on leaving for Edinburgh immediately. Tyndall did not oppose him, but Milnes's disappointment and his own conscience soon stirred his guilt. Tyndall suggested exercise, "a pair of horses" and a "gallop over the country for five or six hours." Though he had given up riding, Carlyle consented, and soon found himself mounted on a strong horse, "disposed to bolt," on which he galloped for over five hours, accompanied by Tyndall, whose fear that the old man would be killed or would kill himself gradually subsided when "the horse was at length clearly mastered by its rider." Encouraged to have a simple dinner and restrained from engaging in animated discussion afterward, Carlyle went to bed early, certain that he would not sleep at all. He slept perfectly soundly. It was 9:00 A.M. before Tyndall finally heard movement in the bedroom. Later in the day they took the railroad to Edinburgh, accompanied by Thomas Huxley, who had joined them at Fryston. A good friend of Tyndall's, Huxley was also to be honored with an LL.D., after which the two athletic scientists planned to hike in the Highlands. Carlyle and Huxley were cordial but not friendly, Carlyle certain that Huxley's view of the physical basis of life diminished rather than elevated man. But Darwin's "bulldog" and the "Sage of Chelsea" had no difficulty traveling peacefully together.[26]

At Edinburgh, Carlyle went immediately to Thomas Erskine's home. Despite invitations from David Laing, whom he had known for decades and who had helped him with books on Cromwell, and from David Masson, a young admirer and respected literary scholar, he preferred to stay with Erskine for reasons that had nothing to do with personal feelings. As Jane remarked, "The man he will go to . . . will not be the man he likes best, but the man who lives furthest away from—'*railway whistles.*' "[27] Treated to the highest, most isolated room in the house, he was prevented from sleeping by nervousness rather than noise. He blamed the state of his nerves on Milnes and the visit to Fryston. During the day on Easter Sunday he refused to see anyone, even Tyndall, insisting on "absolute seclusion." Except for a solitary walk, he kept silent, preoccupied with his nervousness, repeatedly rereading the notes he had prepared for his talk.[28] Unlike Gladstone, he refused to write out his speech in advance. He planned to talk, not orate.

That evening, while Carlyle, accompanied by Jack, visited David Masson, Tyndall dined lavishly at the home of his hosts in Edinburgh, among whose guests was the eighty-four-year-old Sir David Brewster, the principal of the University. Forty years before, as a scrappy and ambitious editor and journalist, Brewster had provided the young Carlyle with the opportunity to earn money writing brief entries for anonymous publication in the *Edinburgh Encyclopaedia.* There had been other literary business between them, though Carlyle had found Brewster's mind conventional, his manner unattractive. Brewster was now certain that Carlyle's oration would be "a *fiasco.* 'Why' " he " 'has not written a word of his Address; and no Rector of this University ever appeared before his audience without this needful preparation.' "[29] Carlyle, however, had no intention of betraying his lifelong commitment to spontaneity and sincerity as the driving forces of literary expressiveness.

Carlyle's admirers in Edinburgh, unaware that the principal feared a "*fiasco,*" crowded the Music Hall on George Street early the next afternoon. Edinburgh's social, literary, and academic elite, supported by a large number of students, dominated the audience of two thousand. In the anteroom Tyndall asked Carlyle how he felt. He shook his head, refusing to say anything. Soon he entered the crowded auditorium, robed unwillingly in the rector's pompous gold and purple. Huxley, Tyndall, and Erskine accompanied him in the "more somber" gowns of their doctoral status. The elaborate procession of university and city dignitaries who had gathered to honor him moved colorfully through the audience. It mounted the platform to resounding applause. "Carlyle took his place in the Rector's chair, and the ceremony of conferring degrees began." Huxley, "dark, heavy-browed, alert and resolute," accepted his. Tyndall, "young, lithe of limb, and nonchalant in manner . . . sat as if he had no concern in what was going on, and then rose with an easy smile, partly of modesty, but in great measure of indifference."[30] In looking at the eager faces of the students, Tyndall had forgotten for a moment about the degrees, as the dull, flowery encomiums introducing each one of the honored guests droned on. The audience greeted the final cliché with resounding cheers. A "fine tall young fellow rose" and introduced "the foremost of living Scotchmen. . . . More than fifty years ago he was a student in our class-rooms, and now we rejoice that it has been our good fortune to bring him back to you, and to give him the highest of all the honours we have to bestow."[31]

Slightly flushed, Carlyle rose and shook off his feudal robe. "In his carefully-brushed brown morning-coat" he "came forward to the table," grasping its leaf with nervous fingers. The students greeted him with sustained applause, as if everything that had come before had been a mere preliminary. Bowing his head slightly in acknowledgment, Carlyle raised his voice into a conversational tone whose first words were lost in the continuing noise. It took a few minutes for the audience to realize that he was already speaking, impulsively disregarding his notes. The spreading silence revealed a hesitant voice that gradually found rhythm and firmness in its conviction that "what comes direct from the heart" has value beyond oratory. He spoke to the students, as if the celebrities were accidental onlookers, pitching his tone to the dignity and the emotion of those who had been responsible for his invitation. "Your enthusiasm towards me, I must admit," he told them, "is in itself very beautiful, however undeserved it may be in regard to the object of it. It is a feeling honourable to all men, and one well known to myself when I was of an age like yours . . . this noble desire to honour those whom you think worthy of honour. . . . It is now fifty-six years, gone last November, since I first entered your City, a boy of not quite fourteen; to 'attend the classes' here, and gain knowledge of all kinds."[32]

Striking the delicate balance between a father and a friend, he spoke to "young Scotland" for over an hour. He himself, through a lifetime of influence, had helped create this audience; and with the unconscious, intuitive appositeness and the keen intelligence of an imaginative artist he suddenly found that both his years of unwitting preparation and the accident of the occasion had brought him to a moment of perfect expressiveness. He "ought," he acknowledged, "according to custom, to have written" his speech "down on paper, and had it read out."

> That would have been much handier for me at the present moment;—but on attempting the thing, I found I was not used to write speeches, and that I didn't get on very well. So I flung that aside; and could only resolve to trust, in all superficial respects. to the suggestion of the moment, as you now see. You will therefore have to accept what is readiest; what comes direct from the heart; and you must just take that in compensation for any good order or arrangement there might have been in it. I will endeavour to say nothing that is not true, so far as I can manage; and that is pretty much all I can engage for [A laugh].

He deprecated "fine speech. . . . For, if a 'good speaker,' never so eloquent, does not see into the fact, and is not speaking the truth of that, but the untruth and the mistake of that,—is there a more horrid kind of object in creation? [Loud cheers]."[33] Intuitively aware that a combination of sincerity and common sense often creates truth in oratory, Carlyle reminded the students that the ultimate virtue of speakers is silence. But, having accepted the responsibility for speech, he spoke with unaggressive and charming sincerity of the key values and concerns of his own life: duty, work, art, heroes, history, reverence, religion, and the lifelong process of learning, particularly from the larger university of books and life.

The difficulties of the struggle with the anarchy and corruption of modern life, he told the students, should not be complained of. "For that is the thing a man is born to, in all epochs. He is born to expend every particle of strength that God Almighty has given him, in doing the work he finds he is fit for; to stand up to it to the last breath of life, and do his best." For that task, he emphasized, health was essential, a sound mind in a sound body, though the conditions of modern life made such an ideal unattainable. "If, for instance, you are going to write a book,—you cannot manage it (at least, I never could) without getting decidedly made ill by it: and really one nevertheless must; if it is your business, you are obliged to follow out what you are at, and to do it, if even at the expense of health. Only remember, at all times, to get back as fast as possible out of it into health." And it was certainly not healthy to believe that "people are hostile to you or have you at ill-will, in the world. In general, you will rarely find anybody designedly doing you ill. . . . Only, that the world is travelling in a different way from you, and, rushing on in its own path, heedlessly treads on you."[34]

Having already invoked as a model of education *Wilhelm Meister* and its emphasis on reverence as "the soul of all religion," Carlyle concluded with his favorite poem by Goethe, which he had been reciting to himself for many years. Without the limitations of specifically Christian doctrine, it combined the fervor of a hymn with the lilt of a marching song. The religion of the heart embraced modern man's needs, not his theology. For

The Future hides in it
Gladness and sorrow. . . .

And solemn before us,
Veiled, the dark Portal;
Goal of all mortal:—
Stars silent rest o'er us,
Graves under us silent!

. . . . .

But heard are the Voices,
Heard are the Sages,
The Worlds and the Ages:
'Choose well; your choice is
Brief, and yet endless.

Here eyes do regard you,
In Eternity's stillness;
Here is all fulness,
Ye brave, to reward you;
Work, and despair not.'[35]

Tumultuous applause, a "roar of acclamation," burst from the enthusiastic students. "For an hour and a half he [had] held them spellbound."[36] Everyone was on his feet, arms waving, caps flying, students surging forward to touch him as he apparently had touched their hearts. In some eyes tears glistened. Surrounded by Tyndall, Huxley, and others, he knew beyond the shadow of a doubt that it had been an immense success. He tried to get down from the platform, to make his way with his escort to the exit. But they were prevented by hundreds of students. "The tumult was *prodigious:* never in the world" had he been "in such a scene." Finally, in the press of the crowd, he made his way to the door, buffeted by "a tempest of enthusiastic excitation" which followed him into the street with "vivats and vociferations."[37] For a moment, exhaustion threatened to overwhelm his own exhilaration. But the fresh air braced him. With Erskine on one arm, Jack on the other, he tried to walk back to the home of his host. But crowds of young people, milling in the street, joined by others pouring out of the Music Hall, pursued him with their admiration and even made gestures toward raising him on their shoulders and carrying him in triumph. Barely managing to evade that honor, he climbed into a carriage and escaped.

In the meantime, Tyndall had gone to the nearest telegraph office and wired to Jane, who had gotten it into her mind that when her husband "stood up to speak he would probably drop down dead!" that it had been "a perfect triumph."[38] When the telegram arrived early that evening she was dressing to go to John Forster's fifty-fourth birthday party. Faint with happiness, she and Maggie and the servants treated themselves to brandy, cheers, applause, and dancing until she went off "flourishing the telegram in her hand" to show it to Forster, Dickens, Wilkie Collins, and others.[39] She was the delight of the evening. Whatever the problems of her marriage, Jane had no difficulty sharing her husband's public triumph with friends. This celebration of her husband's genius confirmed that in choosing a husband all those years ago she had not chosen mistakenly. Throughout the evening her spirits were high, her husband's reputation probably more advantageous than his company. She suggested to Dickens "the subject for a novel, from what she had herself observed at the outside of a house in her street; of which the various incidents were drawn from the condition of its blinds and curtains, the costumes visible at its windows, the cabs at its doors, its visitors admitted or rejected." Delighted, Dickens made much of it; and they agreed to carry on the plot for "in a few days exciting incidents were expected."[40] The next day she received news from Moncure Conway, an American introduced by Emerson who had been a frequent visitor at Cheyne Row during recent years, which confirmed her joy, for "by far the most agreeable part of the flare-up of success . . . has been the enthusiasm of personal affection and sympathy on the part of his friends. I haven't been so fond of everybody; and so pleased with the world, since I was a girl."[41] She was keenly aware how long ago that had been.

Carlyle, of course, could not escape his post-address obligations. In his happy mood, however, he was more tolerant of such demands than he had ever imagined he could be. Concerned not to tax his guest, Erskine only at the last moment arranged a small dinner that night, followed by a larger one the next.[42] In the following days Carlyle perforce dined elaborately at David Masson's, where the guests jovially parodied in song "Stuart Mill on Mind and Matter," Carlyle, "with voice-accompaniment, swaying his knife to and fro, like the bâton of a 'conductor,' " and at a formal "banquet" attended by a large number of Edinburgh notables and distinguished visitors. Jack, now a minor Edinburgh celebrity himself, enjoyed the celebrations of his brother's fame and kept him constant company. One afternoon, on Jane's behalf, Carlyle briefly visited Betty Braid, Jane's old childhood nurse, and Jane's aunts; and a few hours were given to fulfilling the rector's obligation to preside over a meeting of the University Senate.[43] One evening, relaxing with his pipe in the room at the top of Erskine's house which had been designated his smoking room, Carlyle spoke reflectively to Conway about his parents and his youth. For a short time, the excitement of the moment had suppressed the past and denied the future; but he could not live in the present for very long. For some days, he had had not "one moment" to himself, "like a man killed with kindness."[44]

And he still had another obligation. His Inaugural Address, which had been published in *The Scotsman,* based on a verbatim transcript that Moncure Conway had made, had been immediately reprinted "in full in half the newspapers in the island" to "universal acclamation."[45] But it was not in a form that he considered satisfactory. Though Conway's transcript was reasonably accurate, Carlyle wanted the opportunity, as he had done with *Heroes and Hero-Worship,* to create a final version that would be the product not only of extemporaneous speech but also of the literary craftsman's belief in revision. Toward the end of the first week of April, he worked on the text in his room at Erskine's. Rather than return to London immediately, he had decided to go to Scotsbrig, where he could finish revising the address and rest for a week or so. Instinctively, he turned to his parents' home, though they were long gone, and to the place that was the source of his strength.

At Scotsbrig he worked through the weekend at revising the address and finished the correcting by Tuesday. He planned to have Chapman and Hall run off a limited number of copies to give to special friends. "I wish you had been coming straight back," Jane wrote as soon as she learned that he had preferred to remain among old family scenes rather than to return to her immediately. She was even more vexed when he "sprained" his ankle Tuesday night on "rough ground" in the darkness.[46] Immediately swollen, the ankle could not take a shoe; even if it had, he could not walk for the pain. But he was not particularly upset about the matter; he had family assistance and visitors: all his wants were cared for, and if he had a permanent "*Oberon* to attend" him, he "should be tempted to linger a good while perhaps!"[47] For amusement and exercise, he rode quietly on a pony provided by Jamie. Despite the permanent shaking of his right hand and the temporary inconvenience of his swollen ankle, he did not hesitate to concede that he had "seldom . . . been better in the last 6 months; so blessed is the country stillness . . . the purity of sky and earth."[48] Jane forwarded to Scotsbrig a pictorial representation of her husband's fame, a friendly caricature in *Punch* that "gave everybody a hearty bit of entertainment."[49]

Fortunately, the swelling decreased; but putting pressure on it still caused pain even by the middle of April. He wanted to "lift Anchor very soon"; but he would still have to wait at least a few days. By Tuesday, April 17, he cautioned Jane that Monday the 23d "may *possibly* be the day" for his return to London.[50] Jane was delighted, "my Friend coming home to me, day after to-morrow!"[51] Not having heard from her for a few days, he felt anxious on Thursday, and wrote to her the next day that "about 1 a.m. soon after going to bed, my first operation was a kind of dream, or actual introduction to the sight of you in bitterly bad circumstances; and I started broad awake with the thought, 'Ah, this was her silence, then, poor soul!' Send better news; and don't reduce me to dream."[52] His letter was not put into the mail until Friday night, too late to arrive at Cheyne Row until late in the day Saturday. On Saturday morning, Jane, who had finished her preparations for a small tea party that she was to host that night, wrote him a letter and mailed it when she went out to have lunch with the Forsters. Afterward, she planned to take her usual midafternoon carriage ride in Hyde Park.

At the Hill, in Dumfries, Carlyle spent most of Saturday idle. He gave his ankle a little exercise. At about 3:00 P.M. he was walking in the nearby fields, "among the silent green meadows."[53] Late that same afternoon, Jack in Edinburgh received a telegram from Forster, which he forwarded "at once" to his brother. Hours later he received a second telegram. By about ten that night they were both in Thomas' hands; taken together they told him the "saddest of messages," the shattering news that Jane was dead.[54]

3.

The shock left Carlyle too numb to deal with the immediate practical problems. Fortunately, he had assistance. Jean and Jamie were on hand, Jack in Edinburgh. In London John Forster and Geraldine would attend to the lachrymose details until his arrival. Actually, his London friends hoped that he would "stay in Scotland to receive her."[55] Early in the afternoon, the letter that Jane had mailed the previous day arrived at the Gill, "written in the most perfect spirits."[56] His sister Jean read it with him. Since he had a promise to fulfill, he wrote briefly to William Dods, a Haddington banker who had been one of Jane's schoolfellows and was one of her few remaining links to her childhood. "These two years," he explained, "she repeatedly made me promise, that I should write at once to you,—who would immediately, for her sake, undertake all the [funeral] arrangements."[57] She had received her husband's promise that she would be buried next to her father in Haddington Abbey Church. Implicit in the request was the assumption that he could not be buried there; but her desire to be buried next to the father she had lost so long ago, before she had even met the man who was to be her husband, readily outweighed any concern to be united in death with the husband she had spent forty years with in life.

Shortly after reading Jane's last letter, Carlyle wrote to Forster that he planned to "set out" in the morning "for what can never more be a home to me. . . . The stroke that has fallen on me is immense; my heart as if broken": and he confided that he had actually made the promise that she was "to lie beside her father" thirty-nine years before.[58] Early on Monday morning, joined by Jack at Dumfries, he traveled southward to London too numb to face any future but the week of nightmarish pain that confronted him. He doubted that he could manage even that successfully, except as a ritual in which he would take satisfaction in believing that the part of himself that he would be burying would soon be followed by the part of him that remained behind.

At Cheyne Row, Jane's body lay upstairs in the bedroom. John

Forster and Geraldine sent telegrams and letters to those people who in their judgment warranted personal notification. Geraldine wrote to some of Jane's friends with her usual dramatic intensity: "Nobody will ever see her again. *Mrs. Carlyle is dead.*"[59] On Sunday she wrote to Betty Braid, "I *have seen her*—and it has quieted me. . . . I shall have all my life long to be sorry but now I am comforted to have seen her so calm and placid and out of all pain and sorrow."[60] Tyndall, who sped back to London as soon as he read the newspaper announcement of the "sudden death of Mrs. Carlyle," found a note from Geraldine, urging him to come immediately. Carlyle had arrived. On the table at Cheyne Row lay the unopened letter that had been mailed from Dumfries Friday night. " 'For Heaven's sake . . . come and see the old man! he is utterly heart-broken.' "

Tyndall found him in the garden. They went "upstairs together." The widower's reserve collapsed into a long, rambling, tear-filled monologue of grief: "He referred to the early days of his wife and himself—to their struggles against poverty and obstruction; to her valiant encouragement in hours of depression; to their life on the moors, in Edinburgh, and in London—how lovingly and loyally she had made of herself a soft cushion to protect him from the rude collisions of the world." But now, in the next room, Jane looked "as tho' she were asleep."[61] Her husband "saw her dead face twice: beautiful as Eternity, soft as an angel's or as a babe's."[62] With her usual efficiency, Maggie Welsh, who had returned to Cheyne Row late Saturday night, kept the household functioning. She also expressed what many of those who had loved Jane most were feeling: "She did so dread another long illness . . . that one feels as if for herself her sudden, and truly *apparently* painless death had been granted her mercy."[63]

While the funeral arrangements were being made, Carlyle sought any details about the circumstances of her death which could supplement the fragmentary information contained in the telegrams. Her health, if anything, had been slightly more stable for the past few months, though "always when she was alarmed or agitated" she "had a great sudden pain in her *Back* which took her breath for the moment. . . . She used to say her mother had it and that some day it would kill her."[64] To Maggie Welsh, who stayed with her until just after the installation, Jane's spirits and health seemed better during this spring than at any time in years. About three in the afternoon the previous Saturday, after lunching with the Forsters, she had gone for her regular afternoon ride, the main route of which passed through Hyde Park. In the carriage she had with her "a small terrier, left to her care by a friend." Near Victoria Gate she put the dog out to run for exercise, but at Stanhope Place, approaching Marble Arch, another carriage "upset the dog, which lay on its back screaming for a while."[65] Jane got out and rescued the dog, which was not seriously injured. At her signal, her driver drove on. When he received no orders of any kind from within the closed coach, he took the carriage for another circle of the park, passing the spot where the dog had been injured; but when he passed the Duke of Wellington's house and the gate opposite St. George's Hospital, he declined to go on without instructions. When he looked into the coach twice at intervals of a few minutes and received no response, his apprehension became alarm. Jane's hands remained in the same position, her body "in the same posture." Frightened, he asked a lady to look in. Jane "was leaning back in one corner of the carriage, rugs spread over her knees; her eyes were closed, and her upper lip slightly, slightly opened."[66] She seemed dead. Another stranger, a man, agreed. A few minutes later, at St. George's, medical authority confirmed the obvious.

Forster, exercising his influence as a government official, prevented an autopsy, which would otherwise have been performed as a matter of law and routine; Carlyle was deeply grateful for this escape from "defilement." With Dr. Quain's cooperation, the death certificate was signed, the cause certified to be "disease of the spine which . . . stopped the action of the heart" under emotional stress.[67] Forster arranged to have the body released from the hospital. That night it was delivered to Cheyne Row, where Geraldine and Mrs. Warren, to whom Jane had confided the story of her mother's gift of candles, waited to receive it. "For two whole nights" the candles flickered on either side of her body until they burned to extinction.

On Tuesday morning, the widower sent a telegram to William Dods at Haddington requesting that the funeral be held on Thursday, April 27. Jack provided the necessary details, which he and Forster had worked out. He held the pen for his brother, "who is not himself able to write at present."[68] But, though he could not write, he was capable of attending to the tokens of grief and continuity that absorbed him. In her last letter Jane had written that she had seen "in an old furniture-shop window at Richmond a copy of the Frederick picture that was lent you. . . . Would you like to have it?"[69] Such last words were a sacred testament and testimony of her love. He sent for the picture immediately. As soon as it arrived, he had it hung, as if he were carrying out her wish as well as his own. The details of her deathday were not sufficiently vivid in his feelings until he had compelled her carriage driver to accompany him around the same route in the park, "making him show every point in the drive . . . ending at the hospital, where he gazed on the couch where she was laid."[70] The placidity of her face in death and the suddenness of the moment of expiration convinced him that she had died painlessly; he even was able to believe that "*she* died happy," relatively free of the suffering of the previous years.[71]

The next morning on the express train northward from King's Cross, Forster and Jack respected his silence. He struggled toward the consolations of dignity, silence, and order, though he felt a strong tug toward immoderate grief which he fought to contain, aided by a certain numbness, the remnant of the moment of heart-stopping shock when he had first heard the news. They brought Jane with them in an oak coffin, enclosing "a leaden coffin within . . . two feet wide by six feet four inches long." Her husband "looked out upon the Spring fields, the everlasting Skies, in silence."[72] She was coming back to Scotland in the springtime.

By special permission of the railroad authorities, the express made an unscheduled stop close to Haddington; at the station a hearse and carriage took the corpse and its mourners to the town that Jane had grown up in. Jack and Forster stayed the night at a hotel, Carlyle at Dods's home. He "could on no account bear that the funeral," which he wanted "as quiet as possible, . . . should proceed from a railway station."[73] He could not, however, escape the hospitality of old Haddington friends, which "almost drove" him "openly wild." Though he wanted to walk out that night alone, companionship was forced on him. "In the moonlit silent streets . . . I looked up at the windows of the old Room, where I had first seen her . . . on a Summer evening after Sunset,—five and forty years ago. Edward Irving had brought me out walking, to Haddington; *she* . . . the beautifullest young creature I had ever beheld; sparkling with grace and talent, though sunk in sorrow . . . and speaking little."[74]

After a sleepless night, "sunk in sorrow" and not speaking at all, he went to the Abbey Kirk at noontime. The day was beautiful. He wandered mournfully in the churchyard. From Dods's house, the pallbearers bore the coffin, its weight on the shoulders of Jack, John Forster, Edward Twistleton (who had quietly befriended the Carlyles for years and had come up silently from London on the same train), and an assorted group of the survivors of Jane's Haddington life, including her old schoolfellow Dods and the aged Dr. Thomas Howden, who had been her father's partner. The warmth with which Jane was remembered in Haddington brought out a small dignified crowd that kept silently in the background. About twelve men gathered around the grave that had been opened in the chancel next to John Welsh's. "In accordance with the Scottish practice," no funeral service was read. After she had been lowered into the grave, her husband "threw a handful of earth on the coffin."[75]

4.

Escorted home to Cheyne Row by Jack and by John Forster, he sat in the house empty of the one person whose life was so closely associated with it and expressed to Louisa Ashburton the suddenness of his loss in idealized terms: "She passed away as in a blaze of splendour . . . swift . . . almost as lightning from the Skies." He was far from completely wrong in thinking that "her life from the time we met was and continued all mine; and she had fought and toiled for me, valiantly at all moments up to the last, how loyally, lovingly, and bravely, and through what sore paths and difficulties, is now known only to God and one living mortal."[76] His knowledge that he had not rewarded her commitment in ways that would satisfy her needs was a heavier weight to bear now that she was dead and beyond compensation than it had been when she was alive. In a house filled with the memory of her presence, he planted in his own mind the thought that perhaps he might fulfill his obligations by sharing her virtues and triumphs with others.

But his hand shook. He was uncertain what vehicle was appropriate to such communication, and he really did not want to talk to anyone. Most visitors were turned away by the guardians of the door, Maggie Welsh, who stayed to look after things for the time being, and Jack, who thought that now that his brother had joined him in wifelessness they might give serious thought to living together. "Except Froude," he "admitted nobody."[77] And he found it hard, if not impossible, to answer letters, at least for the first week or two, though he did write to Louisa Ashburton and to Betty Braid, "aware that, except my own heart, there is no heart living more sad than yours."[78] Letters of condolence came from friends near and far. "I have not written to you" immediately, Dickens explained, "for a reason that I instinctively felt you would understand. Even now I touch your hand in the spirit. . . . My thoughts have been much with you. . . . To your great heart and mind little can come out of mine but sympathy—That has been with you from the first, and ever will be while I live."[79] By the time a letter from Emerson came late in May, however, Carlyle had gotten better hold of himself. He himself answered a letter of consolation written by Lady Stanley for Queen Victoria. And soon the door at Cheyne Row was less tightly closed, both to his own friends and especially to those whom he and Jane had shared, as if they were now more dear to him for her memory's sake. But, in Geraldine's eyes, he had "become a very old man all at once—broken and frail and very worn."[80]

That was an exaggeration, as Emerson well knew. His American friend touched a shared elegiac chord when he reminded Carlyle that it was "thirty three years in July . . . since" he had first seen Jane. But, he continued, "as I have not witnessed any decline, I can hardly believe in any, & still recall vividly the youthful wife & her blithe account of her letters & homages from Goethe, & the details she gave of her intended visit to Weimar, & its disappointment." The generous Emerson, that "thin reed," deeply familiar with loss, graciously eulogized Jane, whose "goodness to me & to my friends was ever perfect. . . . She was the rest that rewarded labor." But, unlike Geraldine, Emerson saw the reality and the problem that Carlyle now had to face: Jane's death would not kill him. In fact, he saw a virtue where Carlyle saw a liability—for "it is good that you are strong, & built for endurance." He urged his friend to do what artists who endure do best, to write "the book I wish & wait for,—the sincerest confessions of your best hours."[81]

But the idea of writing his autobiography repelled Carlyle; what he wanted to remember concerned others, what he wanted to forget concerned himself. And, though he frequently thought of the past, the possibility of embodying it in prose did not demand that the prose be made public, as Emerson's urging implied. Whatever his shaking right hand was capable of, he immediately rejected the notion of creating a biography of the self in the usual sense. He needed to work, "to repair" and "rebuild" his life "into something of order for the few years or days" that remained.[82] But he could not accept Emerson's challenge; and he had for the moment no other alternatives. Soon Ruskin urged that "a magnificent *closing* work for you to do would be to set your finger on the turning points . . . in European history . . . your own *final* impression of the courses and causes of things." He offered to come to Cheyne Row every day to write it out as Carlyle spoke it.[83] But to imagine that he could be an active historian again seemed to Carlyle absurd, though he certainly agreed with Geraldine that "work" was "the only real refuge" he could find from his "lonely sorrow."

To some of the friends who came in May and June he seemed hospitable, conversational, calm. To Geraldine, who saw him frequently, he noticeably shrank "from speaking of his great sorrow;—it is always there,—but a surface is beginning to form over it. He will never be comforted—but he lives on, and has taken up his life, and he is like one of the old Bible prophets in his mode of speaking."[84] Dressed in his "fresh mourning," Carlyle seemed to Duffy, who visited in May, "composed, and at times even cheerful."[85] Usually with Froude, who came frequently and was always admitted, he walked every day, making certain that he took exercise. He readily admitted the *possibility* of usefulness. "If by slow degrees I *can* rally to some useful work for the poor remainder of my days, it shall be well and fit; if otherwise, I already seem to see I shall soon follow wither she has gone."[86] Within a short time, the possibility came to seem a hypothetical intention of providence, for in a world ultimately controlled by a master spirit might not even this pain be a purposeful correction to be put to good use, "some other little *work* to do, under changed conditions, before I died?"[87] But what that work might be he did not know.

Neither did anyone else. The only external demand for work came from friends, some of whom, like Ruskin, imagined an additional contribution to historical studies, whereas others, like Emerson, thought an autobiography would provide a moving and influential personal model. During the summer, he urged on Froude and Ruskin that the three of them establish a new periodical, the purpose of which would be to create a public focus for the social, political, and cultural urgency of the message that he had initiated during the last four decades and that Ruskin and Froude were now championing. But it was less a gesture of involvement than of support for his disciples and companions. For good reason, Ruskin did not "*bite* very ardently." Froude, currently editing *Fraser's,* must have been relieved; and Carlyle shortly admitted that his own heart was in it more as an idea than as an actual work commitment.[88] But those among his intimates who urged projects upon him did so mainly because they thought his personal survival, let alone his happiness, depended on his feeling productive; the rest of the world, indifferent to his personal needs, had no expectation and little desire to hear from Carlyle again. The Rectorial Address had seemed an appropriate farewell; indeed, the circle of his public career seemed complete.

In late May 1866 Geraldine gave him a short biographical sketch of Jane which she had written at the request of Lady Lothian, one of Jane's friends. Naturally, Carlyle found the sketch faulty in important ways; so many of the details were inaccurate, though the "recognition of the *character* is generally true and faithful." The passion for accuracy in historical fact that had helped keep him at *Frederick* conditioned his gentle but critical response to Geraldine, who returned the sketch to him for his disposal without showing it to anyone, though as a matter of fairness he had given permission for Lady Lothian to see it. It was his intention to burn the manuscript, just as he had burned the letter from Geraldine which accompanied it. But he did not; he always found it difficult to destroy any manuscript that dealt with something or someone central to his emotional life, as if it were a kind of criminal suicide to destroy such extensions of the self. In addition, he was deeply moved by this account of Jane's early life, whatever its faults. The subject, distorted in its details, rose before him almost as if she were still alive; and precisely because of its insufficiency as a portrait Geraldine's account demanded correction and elaboration.

Carlyle soon began, in a little notebook of Jane's into which he inserted Geraldine's sketch, to evaluate and supplement her account of Jane's childhood. By the end of the month, having written a few pages of detailed response to specific points, he began to write another essay entirely, his own story of Jane's life and of their relationship, supplemented with a running account of his own present feelings about himself, his situation, and this new literary work. Soon he was compulsively at work on a very personal memoir in which past and present, other and self, became structurally and tonally inseparable.

What began as correction soon developed into creation, an act of love that soothed his spirit, a blessing of work that occupied his hours. Not that he thought of this as work in the ordinary sense. "Surely this is very idle work,—the rather if it is all to be burnt!"[89] But his usual distinction between real work for a public purpose and sham work for private ends had less force than his compelling need both to keep Jane alive through his daily writing about her and to occupy his time with some semblance of the kind of activity without which time itself lost all meaning.

During the hot days of early July, Carlyle resented whatever interruptions occurred. He was compelled to move back and forth between his ordinary social activities and those treasured hours when he could escape into the past. Mazzini, "kind and sad," made a condolence call. "No adoring son could have more faithfully watched a decrepit father" than did Tyndall in these months. Froude came to the house frequently, "almost the only man" he cared "to speak with, in these weeks."[90] Jack, at Cheyne Row through the early summer, was sympathetic but, for various reasons, he could express little compassion. Even now that Jane was dead, his judgment of her was qualified. "Though none of the rest of us except Mary ever got on well with her," he wrote to Alick, she "was really a most true-hearted and excellent woman."[91] But the brothers could not, of course, talk intimately about her. Except for occasional comments to Froude, Carlyle poured all his anguished memories and reflections onto the private, sacred sheets of her notebook; they were words of release, comfort, worship. At night, he often walked by himself, thinking of Jane and their life together. In the day, he returned to her notebook, as if to the comfort of the graveside.

For a few days at the end of the first week of July, he searched for all Jane's letters that had been saved and were now stored in various packets and drawers in Cheyne Row. Since very few of them had dates, they were "exceedingly difficult" to arrange. He spent a whole day "reading and arranging the *letters* of 1857." It was "such a day's *reading* as I perhaps never had in my life before. What a piercing radiancy of meaning to me in those dear records. . . . Oh, I was blind not to see how *brittle*" she was.[92] Deeply impressed by his own culpability and her great strength in adversity, he wondered if it were not his mission now to preserve Jane's letters and perhaps share them with others. In his eyes, their brilliance was unmistakable, clear demonstration that she actually had possessed the literary "genius" that he had claimed for her in the days of their courtship. Whatever inadequacy on his part the letters might imply, he had no fear for himself; whatever his contribution to her misery, which rose before him now more vividly through her letters than it ever had through her presence, he was deeply attracted to the possibility of setting the record straight and at the same time revealing his wife at her best. To do so would be a kind of penance. But, more than anything, it would be a way to encapsulate Jane's spirit in a text that would live into the future. There were many problems, however, particularly the courtesies and deference due to those who were still alive. Returning to writing his reminiscence of Jane, he put to the back of his mind for the time being the thought of editing her letters.

At the end of July, he felt as if he were taking "farewell of *Her* a second time"; but this was the more satisfying farewell, a sacred "devotional act," the closest thing to prayer of which he was capable. It softened his "bitterness" and calmed his spirit. But what he would actually do with this manuscript continued to perplex him. In the very act of storing it away, he insisted to himself that he "still mainly" meant "to *burn*" it before his own death. But at the same time he recognized that he would "always have a kind of grudge to do it, and an indolent excuse," torn between his desire for privacy and for a public memorial. As he would do numbers of times in the next fifteen years, he tried to compromise by expressing his strong hope that the parts of it which were not "*fit*" for public exposure would be eliminated by a wise editor and that the manuscript would reward only the "*worthy* curiosity" of "*friends*."[93] But he recognized not only his own ambivalent feelings but a more formidable practical problem: he and Jane were public figures whom the curiosity of the world, whether friendly or not, would never let alone.

Sometime in July Carlyle received timely evidence of this recognition in the form of a long biographical article that had recently appeared in *Unsere Zeit.* It was written by a friendly biographer, Friedrich Althaus, who, despite his good intentions, had included a substantial number of inaccuracies. Carlyle recognized that in the absence of an authoritative record he could expect unfriendly biographers not only to perpetuate but to distort inaccuracies of this kind. In August he brought Althaus' article with him to Ripple Court, near Dover, where he spent two weeks as Bromley Davenport's guest. After the strain of the past few months, the "hop-gardens, woods, clean verdant meadows, people all in the heart of their harvesting . . . was positively a kind of medicine" to his "sick, depressed and sorrowful heart."[94] He took to riding again, at a more somber, conservative pace. The guest and hostess read aloud to one another from Tennyson's *Idylls,* "with profound recognit*n* of the finely elaborated execut*n,* and also of the inward perfect*n* of *vacancy* . . . tho the lollipops were so superlative." Turning to Emerson's *English Traits,* they were thankful that there were "still Books for grown-up people too!"[95] But the very countryside that he now vacationed in was vivid with memories from long before. He remembered a Sunday "42 years ago" when he had wandered between Dover and Ripple Court "with Edward Irving and Mr. Strachey. What a flight of *time*!"[96] Reading Bryan Procter's book on Charles Lamb, "every page of it" recalled to him the "old Procter" whom he "used to talk with."[97]

Back at Cheyne Row in September, his memories were again stirred by reading Althaus, which, with pencil in shaking hand, he felt compelled to annotate, correcting errors of fact and interpretation. Unlike Geraldine, Althaus was so far off the emotional mark that he gradually felt less and less need to comment. But his final remark highlighted the overall problem:

> I now tie up this poor Article; put it away, amongst things of *Hers;* and shall, very possibly never see it again. . . . If I *don't* burn it, those that come after me are again charged to be cautious; & to consider well, in this case and in all others, *what* it will be useful to print, for such a public as ours, and what to withold. . . . Endless *silence* about us both,—that really would be my wish . . . but that is probably impossible or unattainable: and instead of hazy nonsense throughout, here and there a bit of certainty may have its advantages,—if they can be had cheap.[98]

Where he would deposit his aging body during the winter became a subject of concern. His inclination was to stay in London.[99] There was nothing physically the matter with him; and whatever the trials of a London winter, he was well used to them. But a number of friends, particularly Tyndall, urged him to accept an invitation from Louisa Ashburton to spend the winter with her at her villa in Mentone on the Riviera. He had never been to the Mediterranean. This might be a good opportunity to escape a confining English winter and let bright sunshine and vivid scenery minister to a depressed spirit. During the autumn, though, he refused to make up his mind; the problems seemed formidable, the simple getting there magnified to an almost insuperable obstacle. He felt that wherever he went he would carry his burden of sorrow and, moreover, that without some daily work to absorb him he would feel utterly useless.

Fifteen years before, when he had completed his life of John Sterling, he had for the moment thought of doing a brief biography of Edward Irving. However, the obsession that eventually produced *Frederick* had forced out of his mind the reminiscing mood. Now, for reasons that were mostly beyond his control, he was in that mood again, more intensely than ever before, and with few or no alternatives. While writing about Jane, he naturally revived his feelings about Irving. In September 1866 Carlyle desultorily began to write about his long-dead friend, uncertain whether or not he would make anything substantial of it. Still, it was something that would keep Jane alive in his imagination and on paper, a slightly less painful and more distanced way of reliving the subject that obsessed him. A memorial to this "very memorable man" was also a memorial to Jane. And the subject was really the only one that concerned him. For it was turning out "to be more about" himself than about Irving.[100]

5.

By late November 1866 Carlyle had actually decided to go to Mentone. Even he was startled by his decision. Eager to serve, Tyndall had exerted all his persuasive abilities to convince Carlyle that the trip was desirable and practical. He offered to arrange the details of the journey and accompany his mentor, though his professorial duties at the Royal Institution demanded that he return after only a half a day or so there. The offer seemed extravagantly generous. Carlyle "was shocked to hear of such a thing undertaken for my sake; but it was vain to remonstrate,—as well remonstrate with the wind. He is a strange, lean, ardent kind of soul."[101] Of course, he was not in the remonstrating mood, as Tyndall sensed. Through the late autumn, constant interruptions had kept him from finishing his reminiscence of Irving; he worked at it no more than one of every three days; and, if he had indeed finished, what had he then to do next? For "the writing of it *clears* my own insight into those past days; has *branches* and sections still dearer to me than Irving;—and calms and soothes me as I go on."[102]

Early in December, the nervous "uncertainty" and the preparatory details compelled him to put aside the manuscript for the time being. Stubbornly, he packed fifty of his favorite clay pipes in a manner that Tyndall assured him would result in most or all of them arriving broken. Arrangements were made to have his sister Jean and her son James stay at Cheyne Row from early December until he should return.[103] At the beginning of the fourth week of December, "rime . . . in the air, sucking the vital warmth out of every living thing," they left London. "A raw breeze blew" in their faces as they crossed the Channel. The daughter of the famous scientist Sir John Herschel must have recognized Carlyle; she helped him with his muffler.

After a restless night in a Paris hotel they sped southward by train through a "freezing mist." Tyndall, an intrepid Alpine climber, provided Carlyle with a wool-lined "sheepskin bag" that he wore through the day. At Lyons they purchased food and wine for the night; the two men discussed "the effects of synchronism in periodic motion" as they watched the water in a bottle vibrate with the motions of the train. They managed to sleep a little. In the morning, when they opened their eyes, they "found a deep-blue sky . . . and a genial sun shining on the world." At Marseilles, Carlyle for the first time saw the Mediterranean. He sat on "a bench in the shade of trees" and practiced his French with a "paralysed beggarboy," to whom he gave money. After a train ride from Marseilles to Nice, they took a carriage "over the hills. . . . The lights of Monaco shone below us. . . . From the summit we trotted down to Mentone, reaching it at two o'clock in the morning." It was the day before Christmas.[104]

At Villa Madonna, Louisa Ashburton greeted him lovingly, ensconcing him in Pavilion Madonna, a comfortable small guesthouse across a "mammoth-plastered parapeted terrace," with a view on the one side of olive and orange groves climbing into mountains, on the other, of the bright Mediterranean. On Christmas Day, which was hot and bright, Tyndall, Carlyle, and Lady Ashburton ascended "on asses by the rugged cliffs and sierras to a village and peak called St. Agnes . . . perched on the very point of the cliff." Tyndall continued to the summit of "the highest peak of the region."[105] The southern light lit the mountains, groves, and sea with an astounding clarity and brilliance that Carlyle had never seen before. "For bright sun and beauty of earth and sea and sky, we may challenge the whole world."[106] As they descended the mountain, a bright "blood-red" sunset illumined the promontories and the bays and shone on the three friends riding downward into the evening shadows. That night they dined with Lady Marion Alford, Louisa's only intimate among the English population of the area, and her son, Lord Brownlow, who was mortally ill with tuberculosis. From Monaco, Tyndall left by steamer via Nice for London.

Early in the afternoon of the second day of the new year, Carlyle, "looking towards the eastward Hills, bathed in sunshine, under a brisk west-wind," finished his reminiscence of Edward Irving. He was "sorry to end." It was "like bidding him farewell, for a second and the last time. He waits in the Eternities; *Another,* his brightest Scholar, has left me and gone thither."[107] Where the "Eternities" were he did not know; *that* was shrouded in mist more impenetrable than the London fog that Ruskin told him compelled candles at breakfast at nine. But what was absolutely unmistakable in the extraordinary clarity and warmth of Mentone was that the one person with whom he would have wanted to share this experience and whose health might have benefited from it was dead. Apparently he did not give thought to the possibility that her life might have been prolonged if he had proposed the benefit of a warm, dry climate. But, in good health despite his usual complaints, he was not unaware of the irony of the healthy widower finding solace on "this sunny Rivera" immediately after the death of his frail wife, who all her life had taken the punishment of English winters.

Not even the comforts of Pavilion Madonna and his daily routine could prevent such brooding.[108] Each day he sat at his desk until close to two, as if the posture of work, whatever the result, provided him with a sense of security and the satisfaction, sometimes recognizably hollow, of having done something useful. Lifelong habits and expectations were difficult to break. Each afternoon, except for one day when extraordinarily heavy rain kept him indoors for the first time in thirty years, he walked alone among the olive and orange groves, striking out, sometimes resolutely, other times aimlessly, hardly noticing his direction. First thing in the morning he went into the sun for a few moments to warm himself from the coldness of the night. In the hot afternoons, he found the coolness of the shaded groves refreshing.

Usually, as he walked, Jane was on his mind; and he soon realized that he had *more* to say about the past, especially since he had nothing else to write about. The day after he finished his memoir of Irving he began a reminiscence of Francis Jeffrey, who was dearer to him for Jane's sake than for his own, though all in all he was "a beautiful little man . . . and a bright island to me, and to mine, in the sea of things; of whom it is now again mournful and painful to take farewell."[109] The pain was in part a recognition that, once he had finished writing about Jeffrey, he must again face the problem of what to write next.

For a week he preoccupied himself unsatisfactorily with letters. The rich vein of the past was petering out. Of his intimates who were no longer alive only his mother remained unmemorialized; but it did not seem to occur to him to try to write about her now. Perhaps such an invocation demanded an emotional resoluteness and energy of which he did not feel capable. Still mourning for Jane, he did not have the will to mourn for his mother again.

At the end of January, he determined to have a go at "Reminiscences of Sundry," a potpourri of portraits of those literary and political personalities he had "met with" in his life. But, since "none of them" were "ever vitally interesting or consummately admirable" to him, he did it only "for want of something . . . better" to do.[110] After writing a brief sketch of Southey, whose kindness to him he remembered fondly, he found it difficult at the end of the first week of February to go on, among other reasons because he had caught a bad cold. He also had no deep interest in reminiscences about the famous; he could not engage himself emotionally with those whose emotions had never been intimately engaged with his. But there was still enough satisfaction in this kind of writing to motivate him to create in early March a brief, brilliant sketch of the Wordsworth he had known in London when, young and impoverished, he had first moved there. In his own judgment, the essay was a "rag" that was worth little, wearisome work that was of no use to himself or anyone else. It seemed trivial work to a man who lived "mostly alone; with vanished Shadows of the Past. . . . One is never long absent from me. Gone, gone, but very dear, very beautiful and dear! ETERNITY, which cannot be far off, is my one strong city."[111]

The daily routines that he created encouraged him to taste the pleasures and the pains of loneliness; but he found this self-imposed, continuous mourning, in its many aspects, a great help in dealing with Jane's death and in keeping his spirits calm. Tobacco helped also. Smoking more than ever, he reaped the temporary pain of his permanent stubbornness when all but three of the fifty clay pipes that he had packed arrived broken. Tyndall sent a new batch, every one of which arrived in perfect condition. In the evenings he often sat with Louisa; they read to one another, particularly from, of all things, *Frederick the Great.* When Gladstone visited for an afternoon in January on his way back to England, Carlyle did not let his detestation of this "stump-orator" interfere with his surface calm and "grandly silent sombre walks." At night, the stars seemed "ten times as *numerous* in the firmament."[112] To Caroline Fox, an old acquaintance, he allowed himself to complain, as if to assure her that he was still the same cantankerous but charming character, that he would "never have come but for Tyndall, who dragged me off by the hair of my head, and flung me down there, and then went on his way." He looked to her "thin and aged, and sad as Jeremiah . . . reading Shakespeare, in a long dressing-gown, a drab comforter wrapped round and round his neck."[113]

At the end of February the young Lord Brownlow died. Carlyle felt deeply sorry for his mother, and expected that the departure "of Lady A's chief friend and resource in this place" would now prompt Louisa to leave also. But Lady Ashburton remained, preferring Mentone and Carlyle to London. He soon begain to think of returning himself, however, and by the beginning of March, though his schedule was completely his to make, his mind was much on the desirability of going home. He had no possibility of doing any more work at

Mentone. And he undervalued what he had done, even the memoir of Jane that had been completely written in London and the memoir of Irving, part of which had been written in each place—it was all "a mockery of work."

But for a man who in February 1865, and then again in April 1866, had claimed that he could never again write anything, he had had an amazingly productive ten months or so of literary work since Jane's death. When, shortly after his own death, these two memoirs were published, along with his reminiscence of his father and some additional minor memoirs, including those on Jeffrey, Southey, and Wordsworth, they constituted two sizable volumes whose quality certainly belied his reservations. In January he had written to Emerson that he had "half or wholly the intention to burn . . . these things" before he died. But he had no other "employment" except that provided by assembling and reworking the facts and feelings of the past. The thought of doing some kind of edition of Jane's letters was still in his mind. For "to reduce matters to writing means that you shall know them, see them in their origins & sequences, in their essential lineaments, considerably better than you ever did before." Of course he would not write his own autobiography; the thought was "horrible" to him.[114] But, in effect, by indirection, he already had; the final touches to the self-portrait were to come in the next year in his extensive annotations to Jane's letters.

By March 1867 he had had enough of the Mediterranean; and though he made little of his social needs, certainly he acted as if he knew he had them, and knew they would be better fulfilled in Chelsea. Louisa urged a quick visit to Italy before he returned to London. From Mentone, it was no more than a few hours by carriage to San Remo. Would he not like to go to Genoa, or to Florence, or perhaps even Rome? The classical and modern culture of Italy was in easy reach. He refused. What he had prevented himself from seeing all his life there was now no need or point in seeing in old age. And, "while the days are, and any remnant of strength is, one ought not to wander in mere sadness of soul doing nothing."[115] He did think of stopping on the way back at Vichy, whose waters Jack recommended for his "acid, perpetually flatulent and miserable stomach."[116] But once he was on the road at the middle of the month he had no thought for anything but the direct route. At Avignon, he "wandered about the antique malodorous city." The next "grim grey morning" he was in Paris, enjoying an "hour's promenade on the old-known streets . . . strolling to various old places [he] had seen . . . years ago."[117] It seemed for a moment as if he were seeing them for the first time.

6.

For a man who bemoaned his inactivity Carlyle managed to be remarkably involved in literature and even politics for the four years that followed his wife's death. The extent to which his fallen spirit and his trembling right hand kept him from work, though very real, has been exaggerated; and certainly the reminiscences of Jane, Irving, Southey, Wordsworth, the Skirvings, John Wilson ("Christopher North"), and William Hamilton, the latter three done in the late winter of 1868, the annotations of Althaus, and the extensive annotations of Jane's letters, were among the most bold, vivid, and revealing writing he had ever done. In regard to public affairs he had claimed that " 'I don't wish to do anything, I only wish to say my say,' " and on the whole he had acted accordingly, but between 1866 and 1869 he was deeply involved in the major political controversy known as the Governor Eyre case—further proof that he was still capable of vigorous engagement.[118] In August 1867 he published in *Macmillan's Magazine* an essay, "Shooting Niagara: And After?" With scattered energy and in the authentic Carlylean voice of visionary rhetoric and personal despair, it spoke against the "leap in the dark," the Reform Bill of 1867. And in 1870, the outbreak of the Franco-Prussian War, whose issues touched directly on his lifelong concerns, stirred the rapidly aging "Sage of Chelsea" into a public statement of his views expressed with much of the vigor that had characterized his comments on social issues during his most active years.

Many of the critical public conflicts of Carlyle's life found their last focused expression in the Eyre case. In October 1865 Edward John Eyre, the English governor of Jamaica, assumed that an attack on the courthouse at Morant Bay by a few hundred black workers, who killed eighteen government employees including the chief magistrate, had been instigated and planned by the Baptist minister, George William Gordon, a black member of the House of Assembly who had been an active leader against Eyre and British rule. It seemed the first expression of a general insurrection. Eyre acted immediately. After declaring martial law, he vigorously suppressed the insurrection: "439 people were either shot without trial or hanged after court-martial; about 600 were flogged; and about 1000 dwellings were burned."[119] Under Eyre's orders, Gordon was arrested in Kingston, where martial law was not in effect, and transported to Morant Bay, where he was court-martialed, sentenced to death, and executed—all with Eyre's concurrence, though it was technically unnecessary. Apparently Gordon was guilty only in the broad sense that he was the vocal leader of the opposition to the British: some of his followers had committed crimes that could be interpreted as part of a larger conspiracy, a situation that permitted the abrogation of civil law. On the one hand, Eyre had acted decisively; on the other, his judgment and probably his motives were open to question. Martial law actually lasted one month; the troops met no resistance at all and "suffered no casualties."[120]

Eyre did have a reputation for personal courage and for reasonable fairness in his treatment of natives. But when the extent of these repressive actions became known in London, the governor's conduct and motivation seemed to many prominent people to demand full investigation and discussion. On the one hand, various missionary and philanthropic institutions immediately formed the Jamaica Committee "to demand punishment for actions attributable, in their eyes, solely to hostility to the Negro."[121] Liberals, particularly concerned about due process and democratic procedure, felt that principles of equity and individual rights were at issue. On the other hand, commercial interests believed that the governor's actions were a laudable effort to correct the widespread deterioration of colonial economies which had resulted from the attempt to transform a forced-labor economy into a free-labor market. And the conservative mind of the nation, from country gentry to cosmopolitan philosopher, maintained that the criticism of Eyre failed to give priority to the crucial importance of effective and decisive leadership in a time of threatening change. The collective spiritual order of the country was being undermined by a destructive insistence on the primacy of the individual. Some supporters of Eyre, of course, immediately blew the bugle of British patriotism; there was also some blatant, purposeful racism that was far less benign than the traditional English racism shared by many on both sides of the issue.

But much of the extraordinary passion that went into dramatizing the Eyre case had its origin not in the case itself but in the strong differences of opinion on the question of how England, not Jamaica, was to be governed. The country was in the first stages of the national debate that led to the Reform Bill of 1867. The Eyre case was an important minor step toward the Reform Bill, mainly because it harnessed energies and dramatized issues; the anti-Reform element basically had its way in the Eyre case, but the larger victory of 1867, the "leap in the dark," went to the democratic reformers. But even the initial victory won by Eyre's supporters was far from complete. A Royal Commission of Inquiry sent out in January 1866 praised Eyre's decisive response to the emergency. But it deplored the cruel, random, and excessive punishments, implying that they had been more vindictive than preventive. The government of course exonerated Eyre and declined to prosecute, but gradually it also made clear that his usefulness had ended. Furious at the administration's refusal to take any action beyond relieving him of his official position, the Jamaica Committee determined to prosecute the governor on its own.[122]

From London early in April 1866, four months after the details of the Jamaica insurrection had reached the capital, Jane had sent her husband, who was resting at Scotsbrig, an account of a dinner-table conversation she had had with William Hayward about the Eyre case.

> Hayward was raging against the Jamaica business—would have had Eyre cut into small pieces, and eaten raw. He told me *women* might patronize Eyre—that women were naturally cruel. . . . But no *man* living could stand up for Eyre now! 'I hope Mr. Carlyle does,' I said. 'I haven't had an opportunity of asking him; but I should be surprised and grieved if I found him sentimentalising over a pack of black brutes.' After staring at me a moment: 'Mr. Carlyle!' said Hayward. 'Oh, yes! Mr. *Carlyle!* one cannot indeed swear what he will *not* say! His great aim and philosophy of life being 'The smallest happiness of the fewest number!'[123]

But certainly any reader of Carlyle could have anticipated his response. Jane might call the rebels "black brutes" and Carlyle might express the thought that it would perhaps have been better "if Eyre had shot the whole Nigger population, and flung them into the sea," but his position was based neither on personal cruelty nor on virulent racial prejudice.[124] That blacks were innately inferior to whites seemed to him probable but irrelevant: despite his abhorrence of the Utilitarians, he had made clear as early as 1849 in his pamphlet "The Nigger Question" that white treatment of blacks in agricultural communities with large black populations demanded that the governing principle actually be the greatest good for the greatest number. In fact, he accused Abolitionists and liberals of attempting to impose, for their own narrow and selfish purposes, conditions of independence on blacks who were unprepared for them and who could not possibly function effectively either in their own interests or in the interests of the community. What was deemed emancipation was in reality desertion. In the interests of a stable economy and the humane treatment of dependents, blacks in Jamaica and America should be provided with a responsible structure that would support the greatest good for the greatest number rather than be cast into a competitive laissez-faire economy without the education and other advantages that would enable them to perform productively. Nothing, however, Carlyle believed, justified the mistreatment of slaves and dependents: the honest worker, whether contracted for by the day, the year, or the lifetime, had the inalienable right to personal dignity and a fair share in the rewards of his labor.

Carlyle was not in favor of slavery. "Work by compulsion is little good. You must carry man's volition along with you if you are to command to any purpose."[125] But it seemed to him sheer hypocrisy not to admit the desirability under certain conditions of lifetime contracts that were valid as long as both parties accepted the agreement and fulfilled its honorable terms. Such an agreement had more value than contracts by the hour, day, week, or year—contracts in which the employer (also sometimes known as a "master") shamelessly used his position of economic power to exploit his workers and in which a laissez-faire government perpetuated a surplus-labor market that inevitably made the worker a slave without dignity and fair reward. In Carlyle's eyes, the English "master" shamelessly exploited his workers. Was it not hypocritical to maintain that such exploitation was superior to labor arrangements in other parts of the world? He was convinced that this missionary and reforming obsession with foreign slavery was either unintended dereliction of duty or a purposeful attempt to divert attention from the miseries of the English working class.

During the American Civil War he supported the South: Carlyle believed that the North could not offer the Southern black as much as he already had, that in the American context emancipation was a self-serving deception. Of course, idealists like Emerson were not cruel; they were only deceived by sentiment into good intentions that would make matters worse. On the whole, it seemed to Carlyle that the industrial North wanted to make agricultural slaves into industrial slaves; and that, from all reports, the slaves in the South were treated with reasonable justice and compassion by a basically benevolent ruling class. Even Emerson and Moncure Conway, a welcome guest at Cheyne Row during these years, could not convince him to the contrary. As a native Southerner who had gone to New England and embraced the Abolitionist cause that he represented in England, Conway did his best to temper Carlyle's theoretical position with some facts about the treatment of blacks in the South. It took a long time for Carlyle to take seriously the claim that black slaves in the American South had been systematically deprived of their dignity and rewards as workers.[126] While the war raged, he felt anguish and anger at what seemed unnecessary slaughter. Toward the end of the war, both his sense of the complexity of the situation and his compassion for the victims dominated his feelings. "Poor old Lincoln, an innocent simple man, of considerably faculty . . . the very *best* man I have heard of in those American murderings . . . for no cause!"[127] After the war, he gradually admitted that he might have been wrong, not in principle but in fact. For whatever the reason, he allowed himself to become more aware of evidence that called into question the assumptions he had made about the equity and benevolence of the lifetime contracts between Southern blacks and their masters.

But Carlyle was still quite certain that an emancipation that was really a desertion of responsibility toward the worker and the economy was not in the best interest of the community as a whole. He shared the widely held belief that to emancipate the Jamaican blacks without having trained them to take responsibility for themselves as free laborers had been disastrous both for the Jamaicans and for the economy of the British Empire. Governor Eyre, then, had done his duty in attempting to restore order. If repressive measures were necessary, he was to be congratulated for his courage in doing what had to be done rather than condemned for acting decisively in a situation in which revolutionary pressures made careful evaluation of all the factors impossible.

Even Jane's death did not prevent him from translating his opinion on the matter into active engagement. In the late summer of 1866, when he had finished his reminiscence of Jane and not yet begun writing about Irving, the Eyre case also served a personal need. If providence had provided him with "some other little *work* to do" before he died, perhaps the challenge presented by the Eyre case might compose some portion of that mission. When the secretary of the newly formed "Eyre Defence Fund" wrote to him in August, Carlyle promptly replied that his name was at the disposal of the committee, for "whatever good it can do you." He had no doubt, he told Charles Kingsley, who had given a somewhat intemperate pro-Eyre speech at an Eyre benefit banquet in Southampton, that the governor's "conduct had been that of a faithful, valiant, wise and manful representative of the English Government."[128] On the next to the last day of August, he not only attended the committee meeting but let himself "be voted into the chair, such being the post of danger on the occasion."[129] His effort to strengthen the committee by persuading Kingsley and Froude to become members was unsuccessful. Kingsley angered some of his friends by vacillating. After consulting with his publisher, Froude found it professionally unwise for the editor of *Fraser's* to commit himself to a public position on a matter on which he might be called on to make nonpartisan editorial judgments. Two years later, after a visit to Jamaica, Froude apparently resolved any personal or professional scruples and supported Eyre unequivocably. Ruskin did not hesitate at all. Immediately committed to Eyre's case, he worked energetically with Carlyle (and much beyond Carlyle) to muster public opinion and raise funds.

In September 1866 Carlyle took the chair again, and during a series of meetings in the next months expressed himself vigorously, dominating some of the meetings with forceful and overbearing expressions of his feelings. Certainly he was angry, as he had been for a long time, at what seemed Britain's self-destructive commitment to mediocrity, inefficiency, and stupidity. Either directly before going to Mentone or just after his return in the spring, he seems even to have authored a petition to the House of Commons on Eyre's behalf. Whether or not it was actually submitted is unclear.[130] Eyre, increasingly worried about the activities of the "Jamaica Committee," thanked Carlyle, who assured him that "the insane uproar rising round such a man, as recompense for such service done, was summons to all sane citizens to stand forth as your vindicators."[131]

Though opposition to Eyre was formidable, Carlyle proved correct in predicting that its efforts would be frustrated. To the extent that this was a battle between great names, the most active of the anti-Eyre celebrities and eventually the chairman of the "Jamaica Committee," John Stuart Mill, enlisted the support of distinguished scientists and liberal writers such as Thomas Huxley, Charles Lyell, Alfred Wallace, Charles Darwin, Herbert Spencer, John Bright, Leslie Stephen, and James Fitzjames Stephen. They were opposed by Carlyle, Ruskin, and Tyndall, who also joined the "Defence" committee, which enjoyed the active blessings of Tennyson, Dickens, and all those who "instinctively" placed the highest value on the preservation of order and culture.[132]

In fact, this was not a struggle between intellectual titans; the issue was decided by the interaction between the legal system and the broader forces of popular sentiment, which in an increasingly democratic society tipped the balance clearly in favor of the rule of men rather than the rule of law or of intellectual analysis. In April 1867 the lord chief justice delivered a six-hour speech to a grand jury, charging it with his conclusion that by a legal definition of martial law "Governor Eyre and his subordinates were at fault. . . . The Grand Jury, ignoring the words of the Chief Justice, refused to allow the prosecution to continue."[133] The people had spoken, and, ironically, the conservative, not the liberal, position had been embraced; by the current standards of the community Eyre was *not* guilty of a crime.

Carlyle's work for the committee was almost at an end. Despite the committee's success in creating the climate of opinion that permitted the grand jury to decline to prosecute, he took little satisfaction in what seemed to him a minor tactical achievement. During the fall of 1867 and into 1868 he had urged the committee to adopt a more aggressive strategy, to "appeal" directly to the "people of England"; and once the grand jury's decision had been rendered, he urged that the question of Eyre's fitness to serve as a colonial administrator be raised in the most prominent and aggressive manner both in the press and in Parliament. He sensed that public sympathy for Eyre's position and values might be a valuable weapon in combating the larger enemies represented by the Reform Bill. But, apparently, the committee did not agree with him. At meetings, Carlyle's angry oratory, which ranged far beyond the Eyre case, was the price the committee paid for his active support. The committee, however, conceived its mission in narrow terms; it existed to help Eyre, not to tackle the failures of the nation as a whole.

As early as the fall of 1867, Carlyle sensed that his oratory was supportive, not persuasive. He soon doubted whether he "*ought* to go" to meetings "or indeed can with the least advantage either to Mr. Eyre or anybody,—myself included."[134] By early 1868 he was no longer an active member of the committee; he attended a meeting for the last time in 1869, and then only because the chairman could not be there. But the larger issue of which the Eyre case was a part still troubled him. It angered Carlyle that Eyre had to defend himself at all against such charges, that the government's support for its own colonial governor was so weak, and that almost at the same time as the charge was being dismissed the Reform Bill was being read in Parliament. And that anger gave him the energy for one final attempt to have his say on the most important problems of modern society.

At the request of David Masson, who edited *Macmillan's,* Carlyle began to write in the "violently hot" summer of 1867 what seemed to its author a "very fierce, exaggerative, ragged, unkempt, and defective" essay.[135] The writing was laborious and exhausting. The words did not come easily; his stomach bothered him; his hand moved more slowly than the words came.[136] What would happen after the passage of the Reform Bill, he asked, except an accelerated movement toward disaster? With a government committed not to long-range welfare but only to the immediately popular, even the sacred earth we live on was being destroyed, "regardless of gods and men and little fishes. Is Free Industry free to convert all our rivers into Acherontic sewers? . . . Are we all doomed to eat dust, as the Old Serpent was, and to breathe solutions of soot?"[137] Human beings were systematically destroying the very earth on which they depended for sustenance.[138] And each new generation was as self-destructive as those before.

> Tragical to think of: Every new generation is born to us direct out of Heaven; white as purest writing-paper, white as snow;—everything we please can be written on it;—and our pleasure and our negligence is, To begin blotching it, scrawling, smutching and smearing it, from the first day it sees the sun; towards such a consummation of ugliness, dirt and blackness . . . as is too often visible. Woe on us; there is no woe like this.[139]

The voice was far from completely Calvinist; this was man's doing, not God's. But the God-structure of the universe deplored anarchy and darkness. Such a state of affairs could not last. As he had maintained since 1837, the reawakening would come through the intensification of despair and the acceleration of disaster. The faster things were getting worse, the sooner they would get better. Late in July 1867 the Reform Bill passed its second reading. Early in August, "Shooting Niagara: And After?" appeared in *Macmillan's Magazine.* Soon it was published as a separate pamphlet, and by October over seven thousand copies of what Browning called "a grin through a horse-collar" had been purchased.[140]

Carlyle made one additional appearance on the activist stage, but it was briefer and less energy-consuming than his work on behalf of Eyre or the writing of "Shooting Niagara." In the summer of 1870, France, misled by Otto von Bismarck's designs and by the irresolute personal policies of Louis Napoleon, stumbled into the Franco-Prussian War without a realistic sense of its own vulnerability and Prussian strength. For Louis Napoleon, Carlyle had mostly contempt; having observed and even met Louis during his exile, Carlyle was certain that he was a comic actor on the European stage, vacillating between democratic shams and dictatorial illusions, a "Copper Captain" whose only aim was a personal glory that he had neither the intelligence nor the force of character to merit. Now he was the modern "stump-orator" dressed in emperor's clothes. Even the "great Napoleon," the "mountebanke's" uncle, had fallen considerably in Carlyle's opinion, contaminated by his nephew, by Carlyle's sour view of France, and by an honest sense that he had overvalued Napoleon's achievements, even as a soldier.[141] As a soldier, Louis Napoleon, of course, was a disaster. Carlyle's sympathy was entirely with Prussia. In his judgment, England and Germany were allied by the basic Teutonic virtues whose modern hallmark was the Reformation, whereas French culture on all levels embodied the false values of the Counter-Reformation, which unfortunately had not been removed by the Revolution.

By the end of the summer of 1870 the course of the war had been determined, though the armistice was not achieved until January 1871. Carlyle, "in good spirits about the victories of his own Prussians," found it repellent that the popular press in particular seemed to identify with France and lament its defeat, which he thought richly deserved.[142] Early in November he wrote a long letter, which the *Times* published on the 18th, arguing that in fact German territorial designs were merely an attempt to redress just grievances that had become embedded in German-French relations during the past four centuries. Alsace and Lorraine, originally German, should be German again. For "no nation ever had so bad a neighbor as Germany has had in France; . . . bad in all manner of ways; insolent, rapacious, insatiable, unappeaseable, continually aggressive." The author of *Frederick the Great* had little difficulty summarizing the facts and presenting his interpretation of "400 years of ill-usage" in which a fragmented Germany had been constantly cannibalized by a united and powerful France. "Germany, I do clearly believe, would be a foolish nation not to think of raising up some secure boundary-fence between herself and such a neighbor, now that she has had the chance."[143]

With the sincerity of someone whose misreading of the future was not inherent in the facts of the present and was partly the result of a lifetime of allegiances, Carlyle took Bismarck and Goethe as complementary sides of the same coin. "That noble, patient, deep, pious and solid Germany should be at length welded into a Nation, and become Queen of the Continent, instead of vapouring, vainglorious, gesticulating, quarrelsome, restless and over-sensitive France, seems to me the hopefulest public fact that has occurred in my time."[144] Meeting Browning one day in November 1870 in Green Park, Carlyle noticed that the Francophile poet seemed to get "nothing but damage out of my loud Germanism and me till our road parted."[145] Late in November, he received a telegram from a high German official, apparently Bismarck, who expressed "the thankfulness" of his countrymen for Carlyle's support.[146] Confident that "the Eternal rules above us, and that nothing finally *wrong* has happened or can happen, " Carlyle welcomed a united Germany's rise to power.[147]

7.

As the first anniversary of Jane's death approached, Carlyle relived the events of the previous April; he wrote to those who had been her intimates and to those who had some connection with her last hours. Soon he made it a practice to visit the spot in Hyde Park where she had died.[148] Remembering Johnson's penance for his injury to his father at the market at Uttoxeter, which he had written about tenderly thirty-five years before, Carlyle too bared his head in wind and rain.[149] Reduced to communing "with . . . loved ones, now unresponsive," he tried to strengthen himself with the courage of stoicism and the expressive force of literary examples. "Shakespeare sings . . . 'Fear no more'. . . . These tones go tinkling through me sometimes, like the pious chime of far-off church bells."[150] Occasionally he felt the need for but the impossibility of prayer. At times vague feelings that he had since his childhood associated with religious emotion momentarily spurred his latent hope that the governing power of the universe would ultimately resolve all human needs in forms consistent with the Christian structures of his parents' world. But still, it would be "sweet to rejoin, were it only in Eternal Sleep, those that are away."[151] On Jane's birthday, he sent a gift to Betty Braid.

Separation came both in final and in temporary forms. In the case of

Joseph Neuberg and Henry Chorley, it was the peaceful separation of the grave. Late in March 1867 Carlyle attended Neuberg's funeral. He had had "no kinder friend . . . in this world . . . so faithful, loyal, and willing a helper" for over twenty years.[152] Neuberg's sister now gave to him belatedly a meerschaum traveling pipe that Neuberg had intended to present to Carlyle before he left for Mentone. He kept it always on his desk. This unexpected death was "like a dull heavy weight; as a kind of corollary to that other, but with nothing of its poignancy; a dull broad blow following a stab into the heart."[153] Early one morning at the beginning of June he was one of only four mourners at the funeral of Henry Chorley. News from Thomas Erskine of the death of his sister and companion intensified Carlyle's sense of "this rapid and continual disappearance of friend after friend, since April gone a year!"[154]

Soon Ruskin and he were separated by a bitter misunderstanding that for a brief time threatened to be permanent. Shortly after Carlyle's return from Mentone, Ruskin had heard the "Sage of Chelsea" comment favorably on the manners of the French peasantry and the general sense of security he had felt in southern France. Whether or not he had also commented unfavorably on the safety of the London streets, Ruskin came away from the conversation with the clear impression that Carlyle had claimed that at least by comparison he had to fear for his safety on walks and rides about London. As he took his vigorous outdoor exercise over the years, Carlyle had undoubtedly seen enough of the variety of London street life, from posh Eaton Square to crime-infested Soho slums, to have no doubt that urban crime was a formidable reality, though London in the nineteenth century was becoming a better-policed and safer city than it had ever been. And certainly he had never hesitated to walk or ride wherever his fancy took him. But to serve a point or to express a mood Carlyle could use blunt and exaggerated rhetoric, leaving his listeners to draw the obvious conclusions. In this case, whatever the degree of Carlyle's directness on the point, Ruskin quite naturally concluded that he had been severely critical of the lawlessness of the English working class. In the middle of May 1867, Ruskin included a reference to this conversation with Carlyle in one of a series of letters he was writing to a workingman which were being published in the Manchester newspapers and which later appeared as *Time and Tide.* Carlyle was quoted as having told him "that he could not walk in the streets of Chelsea 'without being insulted, chiefly because he is a grey, old man; and also because he is cleanly dressed.' "[155] Soon the comment was being widely quoted and reprinted.

Carlyle felt compelled to set the record straight. In a letter, immediately made public, to a Rochdale workingman he flatly denied the truth of the report. Late in the month, he wrote to the *Pall Mall Gazette* that Ruskin's claim "disagrees with the fact throughout, and in essentials is curiously the reverse of the fact . . . erroneous, misfounded, and even absurd."[156] Apparently Carlyle chose to deny Ruskin the face-saving opportunity to initiate a public retraction or at least a correction of the first report; in his anger this alternative probably never occurred to him. And as a writer it was natural for Carlyle to raise his pen on his own behalf. But, of course, there was no text; the original conversation itself could not be consulted. A new but valued friend of both men had no doubt on the authority of "a person who was present" that Carlyle "did say . . . what Ruskin reported; but he said it in one of his wild moods of half-cynical, half-humorous exaggeration, very likely forgot his words as soon as uttered, and at least had no intention that they should be taken" literally, "or that he should be held responsible for them."

Furious and deeply hurt at what he felt to be an insult to his honor, Ruskin did his best to contain his anger. He could not possibly doubt Carlyle's sincerity; he was absolutely certain of his own. In an attempt at conciliation, he asked Carlyle for "a succinct statement of what you remember yourself to have said"; he would substitute that for his original report in the collected version of the letters. Deeply anguished, he could not understand why Carlyle had insisted on a public statement in the *Gazette,* but, recognizing the pain that would result from further public argument with the man he most admired in the world, he offered to take "no notice of the letter."[157] Carlyle tactlessly replied to Ruskin in private that nothing would change the fact that his original report was false. What could Ruskin do but insist that Carlyle either "justify the terms of that letter, or retract them?"[158]

Ruskin, of course, felt like a son publicly chastised by his father. He was being given no room to establish his personal credibility, to prove his honest intentions. Under great strain from various sources, he found both frustrating and infuriating an article in the *Times* which came down sympathetically on Carlyle's side. Increasingly aware that whatever his culpability Ruskin was being unwarrantedly pilloried in the public press, Carlyle relented sufficiently to write a conciliatory letter to the *Times* "for my own sake, and for a much-valued friend's." He had two points to make: first, he did not "join in heavily blaming Mr. Ruskin, and, indeed, [did] not blame him at all . . . except for the almost inconceivable practical blunder of printing my name, and then of carelessly hurling topsy-turvey into wild incredibility all he had to report of me, and indirectly of the whole vast multitude of harmless neighbors, whom I live with here"; second, "that in regard to the populace or *canaille* of London" he "substantially" agreed with "all that Mr. Ruskin has said of it."[159]

Having spent hours writing the note, Carlyle hoped that it would satisfy Ruskin and put an end to the matter. He assured his friend that his only fault had been to commit "an immense imprudence," which, once it had been done, only correction and contrition could ameliorate; and if he were still angry and refused to come to visit, then they should allow healing time to take its course. Carlyle thought his note to the *Times* a generous concession, and he recognized the special nature of Ruskin's anger. "Excuse me if I say, there is even something of amiable in *it* too (as there has uniformly been in all you have ever done, said or intended towards me); something generous and *filial;* like the poignant sorrow of a very good, but far too headlong *son,* getting his rebuke from *papa,* with the consciousness as yet of only having meant the just [?] papa too well and too kindly."[160] Insofar as he could "recollect those unlucky 10 minutes of loose talk," he had not referred to walking in public streets but only to riding through "unfrequented slums and wastelying outskirts of London." His discontinuation of his night walks had been "by order of the Doctor," not because of fear of attack. What he objected to in Ruskin's original report was not only that private words had been indiscreetly made public but that he had been depicted in a humiliating way, a "wretched dreary old Dotard . . . peering tremulously out of door at midnight, If he might now steal a little exercise,—and not substance enough left in him even to tell himself if he c^{d}n't alter such a state of matters."[161]

Carlyle felt justified in his revenge: the insult was so painfully personal both for itself and for being made publicly that Ruskin's chastisement seemed to him a deserved paternal corrective that the son should accept with humility and even thanks. If he did so, then they could be even more dear and loving than before, "much more humanly helpful to one another."[162] But it depended on Ruskin's willingness to accept his punishment and return to Cheyne Row without bitterness. It took the bewildered Ruskin some months to settle himself, for love to overcome resentment. He did not return to Cheyne Row through the late summer and autumn of 1867. "Ruskin and I are parted for the time being," Carlyle told Louisa Ashburton, "forever, if he like, the fool!"[163] But by the next spring the wound had healed. Over the next half-dozen years Ruskin's increasingly tender letters made the implied father-son relationship explicit—a relationship in which Carlyle's "loving disciple—son—I have almost now a right to say," asked his symbolic father to "accept my faithful love on all days."[164]

Fortunately, Carlyle found many companions and faithful friends in his old age. In the fall of 1867 he visited Addiscombe numbers of times, riding home one night "by moonlight and lamplight" through what once had been the "prettiest" road for driving, now polluted with "three railways" and innumerable excavations. But Louisa was the "brightest and strongest of shooting stars" and "Marykin" his adored favorite, though she apparently was frightened enough to "shriek" whenever she saw him.[165] In early November he spent a week at Belton at the "great" house of Louisa's friend, Lady Marion Alford, whom he had met at Mentone. But he was not comfortable. Despite Louisa's invitations, he declined to go to Mentone again, though Jack settled there for the winter. The Russian writer Ivan Turgenev, who was more often in Western Europe than at home and who had visited him earlier, came to visit again. In the winter of 1870 the two men walked in the park, Turgenev "plumper, taller, more stalwart than ever; only his head a little greyer. He was excellent company while we walked together; talking about English literature." The "sight of him" awakened "the saddest memories."[166] When Turgenev was a fellow guest at Louisa's Melchet Court home in Hampshire in the spring of 1871, Carlyle appreciated that the Russian writer's powers of conversation relieved him of the "labour of talking."[167]

With the help of David Masson, and with Froude and Forster acting as witnesses, he bequeathed Craigenputtoch to the University of Edinburgh for a scholarship fund for needy students. He felt "deeply moved," but held his "peace and shed no tears."[168] With the help of a new American friend, Charles Eliot Norton, who was living in Europe with his family for reasons of health, he gave to Harvard University all his books on Cromwell and Frederick. His sense of his indebtedness to America, particularly to New England, both for friends like the old Emerson and the young Norton and for practical benefits to him as a writer in his struggling days, was partially discharged. When Norton returned from Italy to live in England, Carlyle saw much of the young American, whom he liked considerably, before Norton finally returned with his family to America in 1873. These and other friendships were sustaining, to the extent that a life without work and in the shadow of his lost wife could be sustained at all.[169]

From Annandale also there came some human help in these difficult days. His family, the source of so much, sent messages and envoys. Jack was a constant visitor, moving between the Continent, London, and Scotland. With Maggie Welsh's departure in late 1867, he felt sufficiently alone, especially during the winter months, to welcome his sister Jean as a houseguest during much of the winter of 1868. It made the house seem "a little less lonesome."[170] Occasionally he remembered tender moments of his past in Scotland—how, for example, at Craigenputtoch close to forty years ago "on summer mornings after breakfast" Jane "used very often to come up to the little dressing-room where I was shaving . . . for the privilege of a little further talk."[171] Sometimes that "poor old Moorland *Home,* the obstructed but kindly Days" he had had there, shone out on him "from afar with a strange pathetic brightness in the vanished Long-ago."[172] But, on the whole, he hesitated to go to Scotland, though he had little else to do. It now seemed more than ever "a place of tombs, to the sad soul of me;—and to the weak wearied *skinless body,*" a place where he could "get—no certain *sleep* for one thing!"[173]

But in the summer of 1868 he returned to Scotland for the first time since Jane's funeral. For over a week he stayed in Edinburgh as the guest and patient of the surgeon James Syme, undergoing a minor procedure, probably to alleviate a hernia for which he had worn a truss for over ten years, an "apparatus" that had been "a complete" cure for a long time. He stayed with his sister Jean at Dumfries, finding that the advantages outweighed the difficulties; he felt more ghostly, more idle than ever. The family, however, had a gift for him in the person of his sister Jean Aitken's youngest daughter. At twenty years of age, Mary Aitken had time on her hands, energy in her young spirit. The small, slim, dark-haired, well-mannered and quite intelligent woman had to be provided with either a husband or some work of her own. During the summer, Carlyle found her attractive and companionable. She was not without some quietly expressed ambitions of her own, which at the minimum encouraged her to try some world other than Dumfriesshire. She "volunteered" to return to London with her uncle to see if she could be of some help to him.

Mary soon proved her value both as a companion and as a worker. On the train down from Scotland she attended to his comfort, and enjoyed the common bond of triumph when late in the day he "lit a cigar which he said was his signal of victory."[174] Froude and Ruskin immediately liked her. Never having been to London before, she explored its attractions eagerly, to Carlyle's delight, for she probably reminded him of his own first days in London long ago. Sometimes they walked together. She was as good a listener as her uncle had ever had, one "who will understand all you say, and except with her eyes answer nothing," "a kindly, well-mannered and well-looking 'Child of Nature.' "[175] Her fond uncle felt that her "cheery young face and voice" broke "the gloom" of a house whose absent mistress was always present.[176] She quietly began to take responsibility for the details of the household, and he did not hesitate to enlist her help in collecting and annotating Jane's letters.

Other than some occasional puttering and the overseeing of the Library Edition of his complete works, which Chapman was bringing out, this was his only emotionally sustaining work. He glanced at the proofs of the Library Edition, but not much more. Through the fall and

Mary Aitken and Jean Carlyle Aitken. Photograph, n.d. Courtesy of the Rare Book and Manuscript Library, Columbia University.

winter of 1868, he and Mary organized Jane's letters and contacted as many of her correspondents as seemed practical, requesting that they return whatever letters of hers they possessed. He began the difficult job of determining approximate dates, mainly by internal evidence, and placing them in chronological order. During the winter, he worked at the most painful task of all, writing the annotative material to serve as introductions to sections of letters, bridges between various groups of letters, and other explanatory comments: he had it in mind that this edition would be a kind of biography.

Unfortunately, his constantly shaking right hand shook even more when he tried to write. Despite Mary's eagerness and his willingness to try, dictation did not help; he could not feel, could not think, could not create concisely enough as a writer unless he actually did the writing himself. The work went slowly. Mary did mainly copying. By early spring 1869, however, much progress had been made on "this mournful, but pious, and ever interesting task" that he worked on "night after night, and month after month." It seemed as if it might be "*a blessing in disguise* . . . wholesome punishment, purification, and monition" of a kind that he had had in his life many times before. Perhaps, he thought, the task was a manifestation of "an actual particular Providence" guiding his steps.[177] By July, when he went to Addiscombe, where Mary and Jack stayed with him for most of his six-week visit, he had been at it for almost ten months; and by the beginning of August 1869 hard work had brought him almost to the end. The task had been as "sad and strange as a pilgrimage through Hades." With an irony that he did not recognize, "day and house altogether silent," he finally finished on August 5 "at Addiscombe in the room that was long 'Lady Harriet's.' "[178]

Though Lady Harriet had been dead for over a decade, she had not been forgotten. With unintended irony, Carlyle accepted an invitation to stay with Lord Northbrook, with whom he had a casual relationship from the golden days of the Grange, which would bring him to Stratton in Hampshire on the second anniversary of Jane's death. He would not be able to walk in Hyde Park on that sacred day. Fighting both guilt and sentimentality, he went to Hyde Park some days before the death date and found that "the place, which no stranger knows of," seemed "already quite changed." The main attraction of Stratton, of course, was its proximity to the Grange, for "a strange pathetic meaning lies in those old localities to me." Having accepted the invitation for the sake of the past, he made certain to ride "twice over" the familiar grounds. With Lord Northbrook and another companion, he visited Lady Harriet's gravesite in the church at Northington, which the dowager Lady Ashburton had had newly paneled and freshly decorated. In the late April weather, the parkland and the flower beds of the Grange were redolent with peaceful memories. But the living presences that had made it one of the centers of his life were gone, "all vacant, silent, strange like a dream; like reality become a dream." Perhaps he was remembering his favorite lines from Shakespeare's *The Tempest,* lines that he had first read on a placard in Annan over sixty years before. In the church he "sat in silence, looking and remembering." Guiding his horse over familiar turf, he felt as if he were riding "through a dream that once was so real." It was "not painfully sorrowful" but rather "solemnly soothing to have seen all this for probably the last time."[179]

In early March 1869 he was invited to have an interview with Queen Victoria, who was rapidly becoming the symbolic mother of England in this new age that was to take her name. Eight years before the queen had become a widow. But Carlyle had been twenty-four years old when she had been born, forty-two years old when the eighteen-year-old "little Queen Victory" had come to the throne. He was not in any way her child; his sensibility had been formed in an earlier time and in a different culture. In the year of her accession he had published *The French Revolution.* The queen certainly did not read Carlyle, though in honoring him she capped her culture's effort to make of the Carlyle who had authored *Cromwell* and *Frederick* a respectable "Sage." To Carlyle's relief, others were present at the interview, the historian George Grote and his wife, Charles Lyell and his wife, and Robert Browning. The perfunctory occasion went well. "Sacred Majesty was very good; thing altogether decidedly insignificant, ditto *tiresome.*" The queen knew little about the writers and less about their works. But it did not matter. She asked appropriate questions and did not express surprise when Carlyle politely insisted on sitting in deference to his age. "Little Queen Victory" still looked "plump and almost young . . . and sailed out as if moving on skates, and bending her head towards us with a smile."[180]

[17]

"A Monument of Mercy"
1870–1881

As Carlyle approached his seventy-fifth birthday, he recognized that he had reason to be thankful for his blessings in the present. While in Scotland during most of the summer of 1870, he had been reminded of the good fortune that had permitted him and so many of his brothers and sisters to "have all lived peaceably to be old men and women. . . . Many a time" he remembered "the old pious Annandale phrase, which every sinful man may well apply to himself, 'A Monument of Mercy.' "[1] During his last decade, his appreciation of such divine mercy softened his regrets and enabled him to wait for the inevitable with an emotional restraint greater than he had ever shown before. "If Spring would last," Ruskin wrote to him close to his eightieth birthday, "and one's strength, and one's time—What one could do!"[2] But the "Sage of Chelsea" genuinely felt that his own life had reached a natural and desirable end. "All your work is grandly done," Ruskin agreed, "and it is just time for coffee, & pipe, and peace."[3] With a bemused but sweet sense of the paradox, Carlyle almost welcomed his increasing weakness, as if he had been blessed with a final mild winter in which dying was no more difficult than going to sleep at the proper time. He good-humoredly commented to Allingham that he was literally shrinking. " 'I used to reckon myself six feet.' " Now he seemed no more than five-eleven.[4]

Had he known how long it would take him to shrink the rest of the way, his mood would probably have been very different, but at the beginning of 1872 he could in general agree with Emerson's injunction, "Happy man you should be, to whom the Heaven has allowed such masterly completion." Emerson had just received the last volume of the sumptuous library edition that Carlyle had slackly supervised through the press. It seemed an appropriate time for farewells and eulogies. Despite the differences between them over the years, Emerson generously reminded his friend of the sweet nature of real friendship. On the far edge of a tired life, Emerson himself still had sufficient rhetorical magic to transform his criticism into praise. For "I know well all your perversities, & give them a wide berth. They seriously annoy a great many worthy readers, nations of readers sometimes—but I heap them all as style, & read them as I read Rabelais's gigantic humors which astonish in order to force attention, & by & by are seen to be the rhetoric of a highly virtuous gentleman who *swears*."[5]

But swearing was now beyond Carlyle's desire and power; his right hand had become useless for any precise actions. "This *shaking of the right hand*" had become "the worst evil of all," and raising a teacup to his lips demanded an intense effort to keep the tea from spilling.[6] For a few years his voice still had some resonance, especially on issues he felt strongly about, but more often he bore mute witness to precious things from the past. Early in 1873, John Forster, in poor health and working hastily at his life of Dickens, wrote Carlyle's will, in which the critical clause, arrived at through a final correction by Carlyle, indicated that in the closing of his life he would complete the circle of his family world. "It is my express instruction that, since I cannot be laid in the grave at Haddington, I shall be placed beside or between my father and mother in the Churchyard of Ecclefechan."[7]

Far from an invalid, Carlyle entered the last decade of his life with a strong constitution that sometimes seemed an ironic insult to his real desires. He talked often with Froude about the nobility of the Roman style of suicide. For "a life without work in it, as mine now is, has less and less worth to me . . . sometimes a feeling of disgrace and blame. . . . Except for idle *reading*, I am pitifully idle. Shame, Shame! I say to myself, but cannot help it. Great and strange glimpses of thought come to me at intervals, but to prosecute and fix them down is denied me. Weak, too weak, the flesh, though the spirit is willing."[8] Despite such complaints, however, he was realistic enough to know that he had much for which to be thankful; "dying of old age" had its mercies. "This may be called an euthanasia,—and there are flaming glimpses and glories sometimes among the deepening clouds."[9]

2.

Emerson, across the Atlantic, expressed hope that the rumor that Carlyle would now finally visit America was true. Carlyle responded that some dreamy talk of his about the beneficial effects of "a long Sea-Voyage" must have been distorted into what he had not "the least shadow of intention to undertake."[10] When he returned from Scotland at the end of the summer of 1870, he made it clear that no foreign adventures would impinge upon his lifelong preference for traveling only the circuit between London and Scotland. Strange places had no interest for him; in his own mind he was already journeying toward the churchyard at Ecclefechan. During the summer he had fled the railway noises at Dumfries to spend five desolate, mournful days at Craigenputtoch where tokens of his past life, among them a wall built by his brother Alick, "firm every stone of it, a Memorial of affection," reminded him that he was a survivor.[11] He made "two pilgrimages," one to Ecclefechan, the other to Haddington. At each, the graves were peaceful, quiet, waiting. Back in London, the tumult of the Franco-Prussian War commanded his attention. Through the winter he was unusually active, even socially. In his own mind he spent much of his time "conversing with the Dead," but to Ruskin and others the old man at Cheyne Row was a fascinating "theatre of History—& Humanity."[12] By the spring he felt badly in need of his usual change and spent the summer of 1871, at the last moment declining an invitation to visit the Froudes in Wales, at Lady Ashburton's estate in the Highlands and then in Dumfries. He and Jack went by steamer to Aberdeen. Mary went directly to the Hill. By way of the Hebrides, Oban, and Greenock, the honored guest descended to Dumfries, where his bedroom had been newly "repapered and recarpeted."[13]

Mary Aitken did everything she could to make him comfortable, both in Dumfries and in Chelsea. When she abruptly returned to London with her mother in September, in response to the death of her older brother in an accident, Carlyle missed his dear niece and was "suddenly deprived of" his "*pen*."[14] He now wrote only by dictation. In that same summer the family was blessed with the first return of the Canadian exiles. Alick, like his brother, was too old and set in his ways to undertake the voyage. But his two sons, the eldest named after his uncle, the youngest after his father, created a "memorable day" for their uncle who "liked them both well." He remembered his nephew Thomas as a small boy in Scotland; his nephew Alexander impressed him "in the Scholarly or otherwise intellectual way."[15]

In London, at the end of September, Carlyle decided that he would make an effort to allow his niece to help him write something substantial. He had no illusion that he could make any further important contribution as an artist and an intellectual. But to be reduced to authoring only letters seemed a diminishment incompatible with the obvious fact that he was in good health for a man of his age and had long

Alexander Carlyle, Jr. Photograph, n.d. Courtesy of the Rare Book and Manuscript Library, Columbia University.

stretches of time to fill. With an irony that he hardly noticed, he returned to a literary activity that he had not practiced since his struggling youth, as if he were closing the circle of his literary life. His brother Jack, whose own best literary achievement was his translation of Dante, encouraged him in his plan to work with Mary to create a partial translation and partial recreation of the history of the early kings of Norway, using Snorro Sturleson's *Saga* and a modern *History of Denmark*. The interplay between history and myth in the Teutonic past seemed to Carlyle the source of much of the unconscious power of northern European culture, out of which the virtues of British character and civilization had sprung. Whatever the evidence, he could never dismiss his belief that the ancestors of his own Scots childhood had somehow been Teutonic rather than Celtic. Having chosen his subject and his task well, he was still only partly successful. As a narrative, the "Early Kings of Norway" has the merit of briskness and bright visual evocation; with his characteristic enthusiasm of style and vision, Carlyle found a rather bold and modern middle point between translation and recreation; and in his portraits and accounts of the lives of Olaf Tryggveson, King Olaf the Saint, and Magnus the Good, the powerful imagination that created *Heroes and Hero-Worship* flared again for a moment or two.

But, as he wrote through the "dark November and December days," he felt an "indolence and torpor" that had "now grown habitual."[16] The dictation went on into the new year. The composing was finished by the middle of February 1872, the tedious correcting by the end of the month. But dictation was not writing; the effort only proved to him "how impossible the problem is of writing anything in the least *like myself* by dictation; how the presence of a third party between my thoughts and me is fatal to any process of clear thought."[17] In his disgust, he condemned the result as "totally worthless." After allowing only Jack to read it, he locked away both the manuscript and his hope that he could ever write anything worthwhile again. In the spring, he told FitzGerald, with whom he exchanged twice-a-year reports of decrepitude, that "it is nearly impossible for any person on his feet to be more completely useless."[18]

For a short time it seemed as if one of the supports of his old age would be withdrawn. Mary's solicitude for her uncle had made her valuable but not indispensable, though in Carlyle's mind there seemed little reason why she should not continue to find a home with him. By temperament, Mary combined diffidence and assertiveness, pleased to be a part of the excitement of her uncle's literary world but also determined that there should be a fair return for personal services. In the early spring of 1871 Louisa Ashburton expressed the general high opinion in which Mary was held with the gift of a gold watch, "a shining testimony of that Lady's about her." "I think I could help to make you comfortable," Mary modestly told her uncle that summer.[19] But fairness also demanded that she be given the opportunity to fulfill her own ambitions. And Mary's hope that she might have a career of her own, if she did not marry, demanded that her uncle clarify what he expected of her now and in the future. In Carlyle's view, "the true and noble function of a woman" was to fulfill herself as "a wife and helpmate to a worthy man." However, it seemed "indubitable that if a woman miss this destiny or have renounced it, she has every right, before God and man, to take up whatever honest employment she can find open to her in the world."[20]

Unable to force a clarification of her expectations from her uncle, who had no sense of the urgency of the matter and assumed that everything would work out well in the end, Mary became increasingly sensitive in late 1871 to the need to do something. By early spring of 1872 she had moved out of Cheyne Row into London lodgings of her own in order to try to become a writer. Uncle and niece had not quarreled, but neither of them had been ready to make a full commitment to the other. Carlyle did not think of himself as completely dependent on Mary either as a housekeeper, a companion, or a nurse. Mary had not been ready to subordinate her ambition and her pride to an unresolved and unclarified dependency on a man who assured her that he desired her to stay only if she wanted to stay, at a point when she needed not free choice but helpful advice. She wanted to be urged to make a "sacrifice" by a man who did not want her to stay if it were indeed a "sacrifice."[21]

From her parents' home in Dumfries, during the summer of 1872, Mary tried to make arrangements for her future. She needed to support herself; her efforts to write had been unproductive. Her uncle did not urge her to return to Cheyne Row. In addition, she had had a tense altercation with Lady Ashburton, who apparently was critical of the young woman for her unwillingness to continue as her uncle's attendant. At Mary's departure in March 1872, Jack, "extremely shocked," had made it clear that the two brothers had "money enough—more than" they "know how to make a right use of" and he could not "see why she should go out to find a livelihood."[22] Actually, Mary's enthusiasm for making her own way in the world soon diminished, especially after she had been offered a position as a private secretary. Having demonstrated that she could find work for herself, she now offered to return "with pleasure and not look upon it as a 'sacrifice'." Carlyle responded ambiguously, unwilling to commit himself. Since she did "not like to fall between two stools and cast it aside on the bare chance of returning," Mary agreed to try the position.[23] In September 1872 Lady Ashburton, always outspoken, took the liberty of writing a letter critical of Mary to the young woman's mother. Furious, Mary appealed to her uncle, who, though he tried to calm troubled waters, basically agreed with Lady Ashburton's account of the situation. Jean Aitken discreetly supported her daughter. But Carlyle assured Louisa that the "letter you have written to my sister seems to me a condescension without parallel" on such an "inane and mad affair." Mary was wrong, not greedy or dishonorable; "only self-deception, and the facts as they really are must and will, one day, show themselves as *Facts!*"[24]

Though he had some misgivings, Carlyle did not withdraw his invitation to "poor luckless Mary" to stay with him for six weeks or so during the autumn, until Maggie Welsh were ready to come, to assist him in creating an appendix to his biography of Schiller. Mary, happy to be back at Cheyne Row, made herself helpful and agreeable, reserving her anger for Lady Ashburton, whose interference she could never forgive. Late in October, she returned the gold watch and in polite but caustic terms told Lady Ashburton that her letter to Mary's mother "contained an untruth, . . . in fact the sense of it was untrue."[25] By late December 1872 Maggie was at Cheyne Row; by the new year Mary began her work as a private secretary.

Fortunately, six additional months of separation, during which they increasingly recognized their mutual interests, soon brought uncle and niece together again. Carlyle speculated that "this separation" would "have good results for both of us, especially for her." He was struck "with the magnanimity and clear stoicism of her taking her departure." Close by, at Brighton, Mary kept in regular touch with her uncle. During the winter of 1873 she visited a number of times, aware of where her heart and her interests resided. Maggie Welsh performed competently as "ready writer and companion." But Carlyle's paternal affection for his niece increased with her absence—that "good little soul, whom I have a true love for after all!"[26] By June 1873 it had been agreed that Maggie would return to Liverpool in July and that the much younger Mary would accompany her uncle on a leisurely excursion through Norfolk to Scotland for much of the summer. They left London in a "blaze of July heat," sauntering comfortably through Norfolk for two weeks, visiting "the birthplace of Ann Boleyn," with its "spacious silences, fine old libraries, old trees, and breezy expanses," and "ancient Norwich itself," with its "grand Cathedral." The journey to Scotland tired him. But Mary was "his little Ariel ministering in all things." She even did not object to visiting Lady Ashburton at Skye. In Edinburgh for two days, Carlyle felt lonely, a survivor without friends in a familiar city; he went to Haddington to stand mournfully for a short while by Jane's grave. With his niece and his brother Jack, he went to Ecclefechan "to see the houses" in which the two old men had been born and to visit the graves of their parents. At his sister Jean's home in Dumfries he was surrounded by family comforts and attentions.[27] There it was decided that Mary, "very glad to be back with him again," would return to Chelsea, but not to the conditions that had created the previous tensions.[28] Though her obligations to her uncle would have priority, she would be granted sufficient time to work at her writing. Carlyle would provide his niece security for the future, the details to be settled at a later date. Having parted from his niece for a while, Carlyle had now regained her under circumstances in which his deep affection for her and his need to have loving companionship in old age could be better served. In mid-September 1873, in bright clear weather, with "brisk winds" and "spotted sunshine," they returned to London together.[29]

Despite Mary's literary ambitions, there was no thought in Carlyle's mind that his young, inexperienced niece could attend to his literary inheritance. Exhorted by his friends to write his own biography, he emphatically declined; it seemed "a frightful enterprise." There was not a shadow of a doubt, however, that others would insist on doing for him what he shrank from doing himself. The prospect repelled him, "the wish rising stronger and stronger" in him, "were it possible, not to have any Biography at all in a kind of world like this."[30] He had already determined that the problem of whether or not to publish Jane's letters, which he had annotated and placed in chronological sequence, must be confronted. He himself desired that they appear, and by 1871 he had decided that his most cherished younger companion, James Anthony Froude, should be made responsible for the final decision. In the middle of June 1871 he personally placed in the hands of "the valuablest Friend I now have in England" a "large parcel of papers" which contained all Jane's letters, with "an attempt at a preface, which had been abandoned," and the manuscript of the "reminiscence" of Jane which had been written directly after her death, "with a copy of the old direction of 1866, that it was not to be published." Froude to "take it simply and absolutely as my own . . . and to do with it as I pleased after he was gone. . . . Publish it, the whole, or part—or else destroy it all."[31]

Froude took the material with him to Wales for the summer. At Dumfries, "with a tremulous deep and almost painful feeling," Carlyle waited to hear his friend's judgment. "Be prepared to tell me, with all your candour, the *pros* and *contras* there."[32] With his deep admiration for Jane and an intense confessional instinct of his own, Froude shortly decided that, provided Carlyle consented to the publication of his memoir of Jane as a prefatory introduction to the collection, there was no reason why Jane's letters might not be published. Eager to have the letters in print, Carlyle immediately withdrew the prohibition against the publication of the memoir. In addition, he agreed that it made sense to modify his stipulation that the letters not be published until twenty years had passed; ten years from the present date would be sufficient. The grounds were purely practical: there could be no reason to assume that Froude himself would live long enough to honor a twenty-year prohibition. With his usual keen sense of practicalities, Forster, to whom Froude sent the manuscript, anticipated difficulties. "He would talk to Carlyle himself, and would tell him that he must make [Froude's] position prefectly clear in his will, or trouble would certainly arise about it."[33]

Busy lecturing in America during most of 1872, Froude put the problem of this future obligation to the back of his mind. But Carlyle, with much time on his hands and little to occupy him but reading and walking, was mulling over the related matter of his own biography. If he did not designate an official biographer and supply him with the documents that would ensure both emotional and literal truth, then would he not be subject to the friendly or unfriendly distortions of ignorant strangers? Again, reliance on Froude seemed the only sound alternative: there was no friend or relative who had the requisite literary skill; no one in whose loving good judgment Carlyle had such warm confidence, except perhaps Forster, who was disqualified by ill health and old age. In January 1873, while Froude was enroute home from America, Carlyle had still not made up his mind what to do and asked Forster to include in the will a stipulation that there was to be no biography. But his mind was far from closed on the matter. Within a short time, he had decided that he would not serve himself and the future well by such a prohibition. He did not want a biography but, if one were inevitable, he did not want to be ill treated by incompetent and uninformed biographers.

At the end of 1873 Carlyle sent Froude a huge collection of "his own and his wife's private papers, journals, correspondence, 'reminiscences,' and other fragments. . . . 'Take them,' he said to [Froude], 'and do what you can with them. All I can say to you is, Burn freely. If you have any affection for me, the more you burn the better.' " There were two separate tasks, the first an edition of Jane's letters and memorials, the second a biography of Carlyle: the first to appear approximately in 1881, the second to appear within whatever time after Carlyle's death seemed practical and appropriate to Froude. If "affection" was to be the censor, Froude had more than enough; but, like Carlyle, he also had an ultimate commitment to his vision of the truth. He "burnt nothing."[34] For the time being, he put all the material away. Early in the new year, his wife died. Carlyle saw "the most serious, rational and worthy of all [his] companions . . . sunk in boundless grief," though "he says little about his immense calamity."[35] Soon Froude, consoling himself with work, had accepted "an earnest mission from Lord Carnarvon" to go to the Cape of Good Hope to make a semiofficial report on the condition of the colonies, a journey that would be "only an attempt to give form to ideas" that he had "so often heard" Carlyle "express." Carlyle turned some additional papers over to him early in the summer "in case we should not meet again in this world," a possibility that Froude, who had a heightened sense of his own mortality, also anticipated. He urged his mentor to give him "directions about the sacred letters and Papers which you have trusted to my charge."[36] Froude, whom "nobody supplies the want of," was gone from the summer of 1874 through much of 1875; when he returned, Carlyle, approaching his eightieth birthday, was as glad to see him as to know that, however long he himself survived, his literary inheritance was safe in the hands of a distinguished friend.[37]

3.

In late September 1874, when Carlyle returned to London from Dumfries, he actually had a literary task almost in hand, the last essay of his life. It was fitting that it be "The Portraits of John Knox," for the Presbyterian Scotch reformer had been a powerful figure in Carlyle's imagination since childhood. But the widely accepted and long-established visual depiction of Knox, based on a sixteenth-century engraving done by Theodore Beza and then used as the basis for the "Torphichen Portrait," was, in Carlyle's view, an inadequate if not offensive representation that in no way fulfilled his assumptions about what "a heaven-inspired seer and heroic leader of men" ought to look like.

For Carlyle, external iconography and internal "spiritual endowment" could not be in conflict; when he himself looked into the mirror and when his contemporaries looked at his portraits and photographs, the visual appearance of the "Sage of Chelsea" did not contradict his image as a man of wisdom, genius, and "spiritual endowment." Carlyle believed that he *knew* intuitively what Knox looked like; and, in his essay, he created a portrait of Knox that was unwitting self-portraiture. For Knox, "the very choicest" Scotsman "we have known," had "utmost sharpness of discernment and discrimination, courage enough . . . a beautiful and simple but complete incompatibility with whatever is false in word or conduct; inexorable contempt and detestation of . . . *humbug* . . . a pure, and mainly silent, tenderness of affection. . . . Touches of genial humour are not wanting under his severe austerity; an occasional growl of sarcastic indignation against malfeasance, falsity, and stupidity . . . a most clear-cut, hardy, distinct, and effective man; fearing God and without any other fear."[38] Any alleged historical represen-

Thomas Carlyle. Photograph, 1874. By permission of the Trustees of the Pierpont Morgan Library, New York.

tation of the external Knox incompatible with Carlyle's notion of what such a man should look like was, in Carlyle's view, *ipso facto* not Knox.

Soon after he came to London in 1834, Carlyle had discovered an alternative to the Beza and Torphichen portraits which clearly met his personal needs, an engraving of Knox published in 1836 for the Society for the Diffusion of Useful Knowledge and reprinted in Charles Knight's *Pictorial History of England* in 1849. It was based on a portrait owned by the heirs of the Somerville family. In Scotland during the summer of 1873 Carlyle had been reminded of how inadequately Knox was memorialized in his native country. He and David Laing, his long-time friend and the librarian of the Signet Library in Edinburgh, agreed that the absence of a public monument to the great leader of the Reformation was a national shame. Late in 1873 Carlyle proposed that funds be raised to erect "a bronze statute of Knox . . . in the center of the College Square, Edinburgh," and that Knox's " 'dwellinghouse at the head of the Canongate' should be purchased by the city" and made into a Knox museum. The fulfillment of this memorial project soon became a sacred final mission for the old man who had "set [his] heart on seeing a real Monument set up to Knox, as probably the last thing" he would "meddle with in this world."[39] Only one problem existed. David Laing believed the Beza woodcut and the Torphichen portrait the only accurate representations of Knox done during the Reformer's lifetime; Carlyle believed only in the Somerville portrait. Without agreement between these two influential leaders, it was unlikely that any monument would be erected at all.

As if he were ten years younger, Carlyle exerted himself to prove the authenticity of the Somerville portrait. The attempt, both pathetic and admirable, was perfectly consistent with his lifelong efforts to coerce reality to fulfill his intuitive and ideological needs, as if an act of willful imagination could transform space and time into spirit and eternity. The facts *ought* to support his vision. First, he arranged to have the current owner of the Somerville portrait, Mrs. Ralph Smyth, bring it to London from her home in Ireland for examination by experts. Delays made him impatient; he finally saw the original in London in April. Various experts, some of them unwilling for personal reasons to challenge Carlyle's strong convictions, could not prevent him from making the premature claim that "the Portrait is universally accepted as genuine." Since there was no "external evidence" to support his position, he exerted his imagination to construct a historical provenance for the Somerville portrait, proposing that the sixteenth-century painter Francis Porbus had created the portrait from life.[40] Then he sent "autotype" likenesses, which he had made, to various experts, particularly to David Laing, "hoping . . . they might banish utterly the . . . other so-called 'Portraits of Knox.' "[41]

By May 1874, however, he had to make a minor strategic concession. His three experts and friends from the world of art, Samuel Laurence, Robert Tait, and Jacob Boehm, unanimously agreed that the Somerville portrait had been painted in the eighteenth century. Carlyle could not afford to contradict them. But they had no reason to argue with the position to which he now retreated: that the Somerville portrait was an eighteenth-century copy of Porbus' no longer extant sixteenth-century original. Before leaving for Scotland for the summer, not "the least shaken" in his "belief" in the Somerville portrait "as the one extant Portrait of the hero," he brought his campaign to a crescendo with a barrage of portrait copying and letter writing. His own mind was fully "made up" on the matter, as it had been from the beginning.[42]

In Scotland, Carlyle tried unsuccessfully to put the subject out of his mind. A gentle voyage on an Edinburgh steamer in "beautiful calm weather" had raised his spirits. With Mary, he briefly visited Lady Ashburton in the highlands before settling in Kirkcaldy for the month of September. Edinburgh, where he spent a week, seemed to have been "shorn of its old, grim beauty and . . . become a place of Highland shawls and railway shriekeries." In Dumfries and Annandale, among "the brooks and hills" that he had "first opened his eyes to in this astonishing world," he felt that he was becoming a ghost among ghostly presences, "worn weak as a cobweb but without bodily ailment."[43] At Kirkcaldy he enjoyed almost daily sea bathing and the companionship of his host, Peter Swan, a student of his when he had taught all those years ago in Kirkcaldy, "a pretty little black-eyed boy" who now had "several double chins."[44] In the Kirkwynd, he stood one day outside his "old lodging house" where Alick had once briefly stayed with him. But he did not enter. He "recoiled at the many memories it would have called up."[45]

In London in October 1874 he determined to make one final effort to resolve the Knox controversy by writing an essay on the subject. Allingham eagerly offered to publish it in *Fraser's*. The physical effort was excruciating, and he found dictation more emotionally trying than writing by hand. But the "pitiful" essay on that "unfortunate Knox" was finally finished by late January 1875. The enterprising Allingham had coaxed Carlyle to permit him also to publish "Early Kings of Norway" in three parts in the January, February, and March issues of *Fraser's*. In April, "The Portraits of John Knox" was published. There was never to be another new literary work by Carlyle. And, fittingly, the only essay he ever wrote to accomplish a specific practical aim did not succeed. Carlyle was wrong about the provenance of the Somerville portrait, as later research demonstrated, and David Laing correct about the Beza woodcut. The actual subject of the Somerville portrait turned out not to be Knox at all.[46] Though Knox's alleged house in the Canongate eventually became a Knox Museum, the bronze monument to the great Reformer was never built.

The process by which Carlyle himself was transformed into a public monument had been proceeding inexorably since the publication of *Frederick,* however, and now, as he approached his eightieth birthday, the unusual opportunity to petrify the victim while he was still alive gave additional impetus to his birthday celebration. Naturally, there could be no question about the legitimacy of the representation; but accuracy was another matter. What he had done to Knox others could do to him. Such a national monument by its very existence elicited, and even demanded, constant rechiseling to embody the angle of vision of the artist and the expectations of the society. In his personal portrait in prose, Althaus had captured the disciple's expectation that some new revelation was always about to emerge from the presence of the master. "I had never seen before so bushy, so venerable a head: the thick gray hair hung low over his forehead, the beard was brushed toward the face, the eyebrows fell thickly over the deep-set gray eyes. . . . Within . . . lay something solitary, withdrawn from the world, veiled. I often wished that he would throw off this shock of hair completely and let his face freely emerge: only then would he be seen as he is."[47]

But the history of Carlyle's portraits emphatically denies that there was a single Carlyle. In the same year as Althaus' word-portrait, George Watts painted an attenuated, murky, but elemental Carlyle that seemed to its subject an "insufferable picture" of a "delirious-looking mountebank full of violence, awkwardness, atrocity, and stupidity."[48] Four years later he sat for the finicky J. A. M. Whistler, who at first cajoled and then bullied him into cooperation until he "flatly rebelled" against "the most absurd creature on the face of the earth."[49] With the genius of his anti-Carlylean aestheticism, Whistler created a beautiful painting in which the representation of Carlyle the man was subordinated to the balance of formal arrangements and the muted harmony of shadowy colors. The Whistler portrait seemed to Carlyle "a fatuity . . . unfinished after many weary sittings . . . a Portrait not of my poor features, but of the clothes I had on; which and not the face seemed to occupy the strenuous attention and vigorous activity of my singular Artist all the while."[50] Carlyle accurately saw what Whistler had purposely painted. Though he insisted that it was the duty of the artist to paint with sincere conviction whatever his own eyes revealed to him, Carlyle nevertheless demanded that the moral, social, and representational elements of art take priority over aesthetic concerns. He did not misunderstand Whistler; he disapproved of him.

Thomas Carlyle. Painting by G. F. Watts, 1868. By permission of the National Portrait Gallery, London.

Arrangement in grey and black, no. 2: Thomas Carlyle. Painting by J. A. M. Whistler, 1873. By permission of the Glasgow Art Gallery and Museum.

Actually, of the three men of genius who tried their hand at Carlyle the best-known and most financially successful created the portrait that seemed to Carlyle most "strikingly like in every feature."[51] John Millais' portrait, begun in the spring of 1877 and never completed because of Millais' own dissatisfaction with it, delighted Froude, who had arranged to have it painted. After the sitting, Millais proudly showed Lady Ashburton and Carlyle his new "marble" mansion. She "hesitatingly returned to say that Mr. Carlyle wished her to inquire if all this magnificence was made 'out of his earnings as a painter.' . . . 'Tell Mr. Carlyle . . . that luckily my art is rewarded better than his.' " The portrait horrified Mary, for it seemed "an *interpretation* and is not strikingly like. It looks like an excited old gentleman about to burst into tears."[52] The idealistic and visionary Ruskin found what actually seemed to him a ready-made portrait of Carlyle in Assisi, near the grave of St. Francis. "My dearest Papa, there is the prettiest portrait of you here, close by me, in the lower-Church, as the leading Wise King, kissing the feet of Christ."[53] At the beginning of 1875, while Carlyle was sitting for a statuette by Boehm, Alphonse Legros did an etching of the "Sage of Chelsea" that particularly suited Mary's vision of her uncle, for "the expression is beautiful. It has not got that lachrymose look . . . but he is a hardy, hale prophet, looking out solemnly upon things; more in sorrow than in anger . . . as a little child . . . listening to the murmur of the 'sweet-winding Nith.' "[54] Boehm's statuette, commissioned by Lady Ashburton, anticipated the most frequently seen representation of Carlyle, the larger-than-life statue created and solemnly unveiled soon after his death which still stands at the foot of Cheyne Row on the Chelsea Embankment. Boehm's marbleizing hand also produced a life-size statue, a gold-medallion representation of Carlyle's face, and a curiously distorted death mask.

On his eightieth birthday, his contemporaries tried to draw the final lines of the portrait, to memorialize for the last time—other than the funeral occasion itself—the great man who had been among them for so long. From Harvard came a "big Doctor's Diploma and sublime little Letter from the President" which, despite his previous insistence on declining all such unearned degrees, Carlyle could not refuse.[55] Through Charles Eliot's letter spoke a series of friendly American voices that he had first heard in his Craigenputtoch obscurity over forty years before. To a gift of an expensive clock from twelve old friends, among them Lady Ashburton, he responded, " 'Eh, what have I got to do with Time any more?' "[56] From the Continent came a letter of congratulations which confused the occasion with his seventieth birthday. Gently correcting Bismarck, he assured him that, whatever the number, it was "probably enough" his "last Birthday." Bismarck

Thomas Carlyle. Painting by J. E. Millais, 1877. By permission of the National Portrait Gallery, London.

"very gracefully" turned back on Carlyle "the words" he "had used in the Hero as Man of Letters." Carlyle was "like the nightingale when the shepherd, who played so sweetly on the pipes, listened in silent rapture

Thomas Carlyle. Statue by Jacob Boehm, Cheyne Walk, Chelsea, 1881. Author's photograph.

to his song!" The contribution of *Frederick the Great* to German national mythography had earned Carlyle the appreciation of astute German nationalists. Still, Carlyle was perceptive enough to distinguish impersonal state purposes from personal affection, for the mistake about his actual age was "enough to quench any vanity one might have on a Missive from such a man."[57]

From more reliable friends at home came an unexpected honor, available only to someone who had outlived his time, the gold medallion created by Boehm, known as the "Edinburgh Medal," and a Testimonial letter. Just as over forty years before Carlyle had been instrumental in having a medallion engraved and a collective letter sent to Goethe on the "Sage of Weimar's" eightieth birthday, so his own friends, led mainly by David Masson, now did the same for him. The medal, also available in silver at a guinea and in bronze at five shillings, was a handsome representation of the Sage of Chelsea, and the Testimonial letter was signed by a roll call of 119 of the great and near-great of Victorian intellectual society: Browning, Darwin, George Eliot, FitzGerald, Forster, Huxley, Tennyson, Trollope, and Tyndall, but also Alexander Bain, Edwin Chadwick, Frederick Chapman, Frederick Harrison, R. C. Jebb, Samuel Laurence, W. E. H. Lecky, George Lewes, Harriet Martineau, John Morley, Margaret Oliphant, Richard Quain, Henry Sidgwick, and both James Fitzjames and Leslie Stephen. The medal was a "symbol" to Carlyle "of something still more *golden* than itself, on the part of my many dear and too generous friends."[58]

One of the most golden of his friends, whose ill health had become severe, insisted that on the evening of this eightieth birthday Carlyle dine with him as he had done for so many years on his birthday and at Christmas. The dinner at John Forster's was small, a welcome relief from the constant "racket" of a day that had begun in the "early morning." The only friend who had been admitted to Cheyne Row was Browning. Mary had exerted and exhausted herself to obey her uncle's order to " 'keep them all off him.' " But "everybody was very kind and on the whole he [seemed] pleased to see how much he is loved and honoured." Probably the most practical and most personally thoughtful gift came from his host at dinner, "the softest and easiest of easy chairs fitted up with a nice reading desk," the perfect waiting place for an aged man of letters. Even Mary, who found herself frequently irritated by Forster, repented "in sackcloth and ashes having made such illnatured remarks about him." Forster, who was constantly ill, noted in his diary in February 1875, that "Carlyle came—sat some time; grand, good old man, kindest & best—Described being blown down the Embankment, like an egg shell—so frail, yet so little susceptible of the bleak bitter cold"[59]

But such tokens of affection and respect did not deceive the old man into a complacency that the facts could not support. " 'They say I am a great man now . . . but not one of them believes my report; not one of them will do what I have bidden them do.' "[60] Admittedly his directions had been rather vague, but still he could perceive some considerable gap between the public honors lavished upon his name and the indifference to what he believed was his doctrine. He had brought a message to the world; when he had left Scotland and his parents' home, he had undertaken a mission, so he had assured his mother, a mission as much directed toward the good of mankind as those of Luther and Knox had been. To be an artist or even the hero as man of letters was not enough; he had wanted to make an active difference in the world, and in that he had certainly failed, though his own confusion about exactly what he had "bidden them do" encouraged him to be less then perceptive in understanding his own influence. But even in his old age neither public memorials nor disappointment about his spiritual "works" could prevent him from perceiving and expressing the constant battle with self-identity which had been one of the strongest forces of his life. One morning, getting out of his bath and drying himself, he looked into the mirror of self and exclaimed, " 'What the devil then am I, at all, at all? after all these eighty years I know nothing about it.' "[61]

4

In 1876 Benjamin Disraeli's aggressive pursuit of an alliance with the Ottoman Empire against Russia provoked Carlyle into the last words that he ever wrote for publication. During the Crimean War, despite his low opinion of Slavic character and culture, he had been outraged by what seemed a useless waste of English life and property in a struggle against a country with which he believed Britain would be better served by an alliance. Turkish customs and culture seemed to him barbaric; whatever his reservations about Slavic society, Russia at least belonged within the community of Europe. In the late spring of 1876 the Turkish slaughter of twelve thousand Bulgarian peasants (it was first reported and widely believed to be twice that number) intensified the division between the pro-Russian and the pro-Turkish forces in Britain. The Bulgarian atrocities became an international scandal. In addition, in Carlyle's judgment, Ottoman power was on the wane, whereas that of Russia was increasing. At some time in the future, he speculated, the two most powerful national forces with whom Britain would have to share world power would be Russia and the United States. With the United States there existed the natural alliance between a mother and its child, but any ties with Russia would have to be nurtured carefully. Disraeli's policy, which threated war with Russia in 1876 and 1877, appeared to Carlyle an actual disaster and a potential nightmare. Prompted by a friend and certainly encouraged by Lady Derby, the strongly pro-Russian wife of Disraeli's antiwar foreign minister, he dictated a letter expressing his opinion on English-Russian and English-Turkish relations, which was published in the *Times* in late

November 1876. The next spring, alerted by the rumor that Disraeli meant to provoke Russia "to declare war against England" and by a government-inspired inflammatory "newspaper outcry against Russia," he wrote immediately to the *Times* "lest in a few weeks the maddest and most criminal thing that a British Government could do should be done, and all Europe kindle into flames of war." Matthew Arnold, who visited Carlyle in May and found him "very easy to get on with, nevertheless thought "his letter to the *Times* is very mad. . . . He had not really anything but somebody's assurance that Dizzy wanted to do *something* in the East."[62] Whatever the validity of his conviction that he had been instrumental in restraining British "gun-fleet diplomacy," he took satisfaction in the fact that the threatened war was averted.

There were moments, however, when he muted his basically harsh opinion of Disraeli as a statesman and a man. Early in 1874 he had received the "order of Merit" from the German government in appreciation of *Frederick the Great,* an honor he found acceptable both because it honored the subject of his biography and because it recognized a specific accomplishment. To his surprise, late in the year he received a generous and fulsome letter from Disraeli on behalf of "a Government" that "should recognize intellect," informing him that the prime minister had decided to recommend that the queen confer upon him the Grand Cross of the Bath and provide a pension so that he should not "in the sunset" of his life "be disturbed by common cares." It was not Disraeli, however, who had initiated the idea but Edward Henry Stanley, the fifteenth earl of Derby and Disraeli's foreign minister, who suggested the award "partly because 'it would be a really good political investment,' since Carlyle was 'for whatever reason very vehement against Gladstone.' " Probably Lady Derby, who had become Carlyle's friend and supporter, had brought the advantage to her husband's attention. To Carlyle, the offer seemed "magnanimous of Dizzy," and Lady Derby reported that he "scarcely knew how to be grateful enough."[63]

His attitude soon changed, however. In fact, the "common cares" that Carlyle sufered from could not be attended to by money, of which he had more than enough anyway. He also had reservations about accepting a general honor that would inevitably force certain changes upon the way in which the world looked at him.[64] Becoming "Sir Thomas" would actually be an inconvenience; and at the age of eighty the son of Annandale peasants felt that it would be a betrayal of family pride and of some of the things that he had said and written throughout his life to accept an "elevation" that would remove him from his origins. He politely declined. Disraeli soon suggested that if he preferred a "Baronetcy" the queen would be happy to cooperate; the Grand Cross had been offered only on the assumption that since Carlyle was childless he would prefer a nonhereditary title. Despite some gentle pressure, communicated by Lady Derby, Carlyle declined what would be "an evident superfluity and impropriety."[65] He preferred to go to the grave with only the honor of his works.

That the offer came from Disraeli provided an uncomfortable but neat irony of which Carlyle could not help but be aware. Disraeli and Gladstone seemed to him the tweedledum and tweedledee of British political corruption and cultural decadence. Gladstone he thought an absurd fanatic who had deceived himself into a sincere belief that his self-serving corruption was indeed the highest self-sacrifice. Equally corrupt in values, Disraeli at least had the virtue of a steely self-awareness that refused to allow its possessor to deceive himself about either policies or personalities. Carlyle had said harsh things about both men, particularly about Disraeli, "the only man I almost never spoke of except with contempt, and if there is anything of scurrility anywhere chargeable against me, I am sorry to own he is the subject of it; and yet see, here he comes with a pan of hot coals for my guilty head!"[66] As a novelist, Disraeli was "worth little or nothing"; as a politician, he seemed to believe in "nothing whatever but success."[67] But Carlyle had a grudging respect for Disraeli's intelligence and disinterestedness; on a number of occasions he had even imagined that there had been a temporary communication of sympathy or at least agreement between them. But, of course, the special taint from which Disraeli could never escape was his Jewish ancestry.

Carlyle shared many of the anti-Semitic stereotypes of his age. Actually he had few contacts with Jews and no special interest in assigning Jewish stereotypes some prominent role in a cultural mythology. In the Scotland of his boyhood, Jews were almost without presence, except as looming religious antecedents to Christianity. In fact, the noble strength of the Old Testament patriarchs dominated the imagination of the Reformation in Scotland and of the Carlyle family household. All his life, Carlyle deeply admired those "thrice wonderful old Hebrews." But modern Jews were another matter. No more than most of his contemporaries, including Dickens, Tennyson, and Browning, could he avoid being contaminated by some of the crude stereotypes that pervaded Christian culture during the nineteenth century and that created a sharp division between respect for the Old Testament and popular prejudices about contemporary Jews. He unhesitatingly expressed his contempt for the liberal view of the civil rights of Jews when he sarcastically thanked Richard Milnes for his "Jew Bill. . . . By the very fact of their desiring admission" into Parliament they "*declare* themselves to be hypocritical men! A Jew is bad; but what is a sham-

Jew, a Quack-Jew? And how can a real Jew . . . try to be a Senator, or even citizen, of any country, except his own wretched Palestine, whither all his thoughts and steps and efforts tend,—where, in the Devil's name, let him arrive as soon as possible, and make us quit of him!"[68]

Carlyle's active anti-Semitism was based primarily upon his identification of Jews with materialism and with an anachronistic religious structure. He was repelled by those "old clothes" merchants on two levels: by "East End" orthodoxy, merchants who seemed to symbolize the dead hand of the past which was attempting to crush the efforts of fresh spirits to create a new religious vision for Western man, and by "West End" Jewish wealth, merchants clothed in new money who seemed to epitomize the intense material corruption of Western society. Though Carlyle's racism celebrated the Teutonic inheritance, it was not especially disparaging of the Jews; if Jews had a virtue, it was "toughness, the Jew quality"; if they had a vice, it was lack of humor.

As in so many other instances, Carlyle used some of his own qualities in creating his stereotypical "Jew." Thus "toughness" was primary among his own sustaining virtues, having brought him through desperate economic and emotional adversity. Much has been made of Carlyle's "laugh," but it was characterized by overbearingly satirical and sometimes bitter invective, qualities suggesting that Carlyle's notion of "humor" may have diverged considerably from the ordinary. And how would Carlyle have responded to the commonplace double stereotype that terms the Scots the "Jews of the North"? Clearly, Carlyle's blindness to the real nature of Jewish toughness and Jewish humor did not prevent him from loving individual Jews, such as Joseph Neuberg, nor did it prevent him from detesting a blatant Christian like Gladstone. He both detested and admired Disraeli for qualities and a performance that he could sometimes discuss completely independently of the man's Jewishness. Yet, pausing in front of the Rothschild mansion during one of his walks, the same Carlyle could draw on popular stereotypes to savor the just punishment that would one day be meted out to greedy materialism. Or he could, as he did in Hamburg, impose on the flowing white locks of a Jewish merchant the virtues of Lessing's "Nathan the Wise." In his most sarcastic, pessimistic moments, he thought it appropriate that Disraeli should be prime minister of this new England, not because he was unusually hostile toward Jews but because he believed England itself was coming to resemble the standardized image of the materialistic and anachronistic Jew. To the extent that he believed in or even used this stereotype, Carlyle was anti-Semitic. But his primary concern was with the condition of England, not the role of the Jews.

Quite consistently, Carlyle dissected new heresies as keenly as old orthodoxies. In general, modern literature and modern science seemed equally contemptible, though he still managed to separate individuals whom he liked from the doctrines they preached. And he was perfectly capable of changing his mind as new evidence presented itself. From Emerson in America he had in 1856 received a copy of *Leaves of Grass* "written & printed by a journeyman printer in Brooklyn, N.Y. named Walter Whitman." To Emerson, the book was "a nondescript monster which yet has terrible eyes & buffalo strength, & was indisputably American."[69] Apparently Carlyle read at least some of the poems. "If you could endow the parish bull with the faculty of human utterance and holding a pen between the halves of his hoof, *this* I imagine is much the thing *he* would write."[70] Though he found Whitman's gigantomania distasteful, an exemplification of what seemed a characteristic American boastfulness that he and other Englishmen of the time found repellent—"It all seems to be, 'I'm a big man because I live in a big country' "—he might have recognized some similarities in style and scope between himself and Whitman.[71] Ever since his first works appeared in print, less expansive personalities had implicitly compared him to a bull in a china shop who was, despite good intentions, badly damaging the crockery.

When, in 1872, he read *Democratic Vistas,* lent to him by Forster, he was pleased to discover the extensive influence that his own work, beginning with *Sartor,* had exerted on this American "buffalo" who detested the corruption of democratic government as intensely as he did. Of course, knowing nothing about the evolution of Whitman's political feelings, Carlyle was unaware that the American's hostile response to the antidemocratic positions of *Latter-Day Pamphlets* and particularly of "Shooting Niagara" had only gradually turned to grudging admiration, partly because of Whitman's respect for Carlyle's sincerity, mainly because of his growing awareness of the corruption of democratic government in post–Civil War America.[72] Actually, an earlier draft of *Democratic Vistas* had contained a sharp attack on Carlyle, which was omitted from the revised version because, having read "Shooting Niagara" again, Whitman concluded that it came "from an earnest soul" and contributed "certain sharp-cutting grains, which, if not gold or silver, may be good hard, honest iron." Carlyle certainly recognized the extent to which Whitman in his prophetic prescription for the renewal of American democracy sounded like an American version of the "Sage of Chelsea." Whitman wrote that the new world could be restored to its old promise only "by a sublime and serious Religious Democracy sternly taking command, dissolving the old, sloughing off surfaces, and from its own interior and vital principles, entirely reconstructing Society."[73]

Another intensely political poet, Algernon Charles Swinburne seemed to Carlyle more damagingly symptomatic than Whitman of the major corruption of modern literature, its disassociation from religious morality. Apparently a combination of distance and Carlyle's sympathy for Whitman's prophetic vision prevented him from discovering the personal traits that would have led him to condemn the American. But Swinburne walked the same London streets, and his flamboyant personal and literary immorality was part of a public self-definition that Carlyle could not help but notice. The relations between the two men were charged with the intensity of their differences and the volatile mixture of love and hate which the younger man felt for Carlyle. Apparently they met only once, around 1863, introduced at a party, probably by Richard Milnes, Swinburne's admirer and one of Carlyle's oldest friends.[74] An avid reader of Carlyle's works, Swinburne found his inventive use of language attractive, his radical contempt for defunct Western institutions such as the Christian churches admirable. In his poem "Les Noyades," published in the 1866 edition of *Poems and Ballads,* the young radical drew directly on Carlyle's dramatic description of the "Mariage Républicain" in *The French Revolution,* a book with which he was intimately familiar. Swinburne, aware that Carlyle's sensibility was basically Christian and his politics antiliberal, nevertheless found more to admire than to condemn. A deep residual respect for the older man's power as an artist and as a father figure outweighed his reservations.

By the time Carlyle published his opinions on the war between Turkey and Russia Swinburne had heard rumors that Carlyle disapproved of the moral content of his poetry and of his well-publicized personal improprieties. In his "Ballad of Bulgaria" Swinburne satirized Carlyle's support of Russia, but did so in a manner at once critical and gentle:

> Then out spoke old Sir Thomas the bold,
>   at Chelsea Knight was he;
> On earth no Knight was hardier wight,
>   no man had seen him flee;
> A stately sight of a grand old Knight
>   its men of old might see:—
> 'Lo, I will stand at thy quaking hand,
> And smite the Turk for thee.'[75]

But Swinburne reacted with savage anger when the full force of Carlyle's criticism—that Swinburne "sits in a cesspool and adds to it" and that he was "standing up to his neck in a cesspool"—reached him in the form of a newspaper interview with Emerson in which the

American had called him "a perfect leper and mere sodomite" and paraphrased Carlyle's hostile description. In a bitter letter to the *New York Daily Tribune,* the sensitive Swinburne countered with scatological invective of his own.[76] At about the same time, he vented his hysterical anger in a poem in Latin, "To a Filthy-Mouthed Old Man," in which he asked,

> Could the private parts even of a prostitute rotted with disease ever be fouler than your tongue, Carlyle? To think, you stinking fellow, that you should approach my Musas with your sour breath of a worn out old man? That you should defile with your breath the buttocks that you lick? That you should defoul them with your unchaste bites? . . . I have praised your genius and speech, eloquent old man, nor did I wish to be too bitter in fight . . . nor should I do so now but for the foul words that you spoke. Your stinking lips foul with their own filth-smell of dung.[77]

Carlyle was, of course, convinced that there was "not the least intellectual value in anything" Swinburne wrote.[78]

Carlyle had learned from the culture of his childhood the importance of looking ahead as well as of looking around. "As to Hell," Carlyle once said, "every man . . . must feel that he is a damned scoundrel, and therefore deserves it."[79] But this was a comment on his view of human nature rather than a statement of belief in Christian mythology. He certainly applauded the difference between his own demythologized religious dialectic and his father's literal belief that "after his death, he would have to face a judge who would lift him into everlasting bliss or doom him to eternal woe." It seemed to Carlyle "a great gain to have abolished this Terror."[80] But such freedom came at a high price. Among those who added to the inflation were scientists who attempted to explain the present as the material and evolutionary product of the past. It became increasingly difficult to look ahead to anything but a silent grave, to the loss of the individual self once the body ceased to exist. Carlyle had not needed the scientists to develop his conviction that the individual self did not survive the grave, however. As a young man, reading theology and Gibbon at the same time, he had come to the conclusion that "Christianity was not true." As an old man, he did "not in the least believe that *God* came down upon earth and was a joiner and made chairs and hog-troughs; or came down at any time more than He comes down now into the soul of every devout man." He dismissed literal interpretations of the Old and New Testaments. And the institutions that fattened on the "old religions" ate "mere putrid heaps of lies," just as the "English people at Christmas eat themselves as full as they can hold from a feeling of religious duty, and lay it all to Christ."[81] At times, however, the human dialectic between inborn sin and social corruption seemed to touch on frightening matters. To Carlyle, it seemed unbelievable, despite formidable evidence, that man could ever have arisen from complete bestiality or could ever return. In 1853 he had read "a strange pamphlet . . . children stolen by wolves . . . grown *wolfish* to the very soul—yet I perceive, tho' they bite, run on all fours . . . they are not *in*human altogether, only dreadfully misbred! Nothing can be more horrid than the thought all this gives rise to; yet there is a strange fascination to it."[82]

Still, the old religion contained a truth that, in Carlyle's view, the new science did not understand: God, as a commitment to the difference between right and wrong and as a permanent determining force in the universe, exists within each human being. "I know nothing whatever of God except what I find within myself."[83] *That* God, then, also existed in human history; and any attempt to explain the development of man which did not give priority to these nonmaterial forces and feelings must be inadequate. He felt that "it is impossible to believe otherwise than that this world is the work of an Intelligent Mind" and "that all things are governed by Eternal Goodness and Wisdom," though "we cannot see and never shall see *how* it is all managed."[84] The point was not simply, or even mainly, that Darwin and his followers were wrong; they were irrelevant. They did not deal with the crucial questions, which were sometimes personal, sometimes social, but *always* moral and spiritual. They provided a distorted view of a small part of a large mystery whose mysteriousness was inseparable from its power and its meaning. "Darwin & Co.'s hypothesis that I was once an oyster or an ape, and that Almighty God is mere Caloric does not seem a useful result!"[85] Man's mission was to create a dialectic between his aspirations and his limitations, between heaven and earth; and eliminating the primacy of the spiritual would be as disastrous a bit of self-destructiveness as leveling the dome of St. Paul's to the ground. He remembered, he told Allingham as they walked together along the Chelsea Embankment in the spring of 1874, that during his first visit to London he had caught "a glimpse from Cheapside of the huge Dome, its gold finger pointing to Heaven; human creatures creeping about (I one of them) on our petty errands. It was and is the grandest building I ever saw."[86]

The builder of the smaller house of evolution, however, turned out to be in person a delightful, attractive human being. In the summer of 1875 Carlyle and his niece stayed in Kent at Keston Lodge, "a charming hermitage" that Lady Derby put at his disposal for "two brilliant sunshiny months of the most perfect solitude and silence."[87] Fortunately, they were also "within three miles of Down," Charles Darwin's home.[88] "Seer" and "Scientist" had last seen one another over twenty years before. But for much of his lifetime Carlyle had enjoyed a warm connection with the closely allied Darwin and Wedgewood families through Charles's brother Erasmus. For years, Tyndall had urged on him Darwin's human as well as his intellectual merits. With Mary, Carlyle drove over to Down in August 1875, soon after coming to Kent; the entire Darwin family was at home. The perennially invalided scientist, whose own hypochondria rivaled Carlyle's, appeared delighted to receive the distinguished visitor. Believing that she had entered the lion's den, Mary was shocked to discover that the lion "looks such a fine good Patriarch, and has such a gentle voice it seems strange that he should be the founder of so revolting a faith."[89] Her uncle found Darwin delightful: personality was more important than doctrine, humanity more important than theory. Whatever Carlyle's opinion of modern science, Darwin had not been tainted by his association with it. He seemed "a pleasant *jolly*-minded man . . . with much observation and a clear way of expressing it." It had been a long time since he had "seen any brother mortal that had more of true sociability and human attraction" for him. Carlyle good-humoredly asked Darwin "if he thought there was a possibility of men turning to apes again. He laughed much at this, and came back to it over and over again."[90] Urged by the entire Darwin family, he visited Down a number of times in the next few weeks. In London, Tyndall was delighted at Carlyle's report that he had "never met . . . a more charming man."[91]

5.

All his life Carlyle had tried to maintain a bifocal vision that took in both heaven and earth, the dome of St. Paul's and the pavement of London. But the earth that is our final home dominated his vision during the 1870s as most of those who had accompanied him into the world or risen with him to prominence preceded him to the grave. The new decade had begun with a minor lament for the deaths of Thomas Spedding and Frederick Foxton, the latter his traveling companion in Germany in 1858. Thomas Erskine died in the early spring of 1870, nearly his "last Scotch friend, except [his] own kindred."[92] Shortly before he had learned of Erskine's death, he had had a "vision" of Erskine in which he had met him "face to face" in Princes Street in Edinburgh.

That he himself was a "Monument of Mercy," a survivor of other people's deaths, impressed itself on his consciousness with the news of the sudden death of the fifty-eight-year-old Dickens in June 1870. Five years before the novelist had "narrowly escaped *death*" in a railroad accident in "chase of still other thousands of pounds," which, in Carlyle's eyes, "he needed so little!" His relief that his friend had escaped that "tragical *mockery*" of dying in the service of an unnecessary materialism did not prevent him from noticing at a dinner party at Forster's early in the year that Dickens, despite his cheerfulness, seemed to have "some permanent nervous damage from that conquest of the £20,000 in Yankeeland and is himself rather anxious now and then about it;—a *foot* that goes occasionally wrong . . . and now latterly some fingers of a *hand* ditto:—but he has now *very* nearly done with these final London 'readings,' and promises to be all himself again. What a tragedy, a hideous nemesis were it otherwise!"[93]

The promise was beyond keeping, to Carlyle's unhappiness, to Forster's deep bereavement. Though his own feeling of loss was great, Forster's was overwhelming. The sense of what had been lost made Forster temporarily inconsolable. "I am profoundly sorry for *you*, and indeed for myself and for us all," Carlyle told him. "No death since 1866 has fallen on me with such a stroke, no literary man's hitherto ever did. . . . God be with you all, you at Gad's Hill in these sad hours." He pleaded ill health in declining to attend the funeral but opened his arms to Forster who came to Cheyne Row, "weeping every word," immediately after the "quite private Funeral in Westminster Abbey."[94] At the end of the month he and Mary dined with Forster, who had arranged to receive his one remaining oldest friend as an emotional tribute to the departed. From Dumfries, Carlyle thanked Georgina Hogarth, who had sent him one of Dickens' walking sticks as a "little memorial of the loved Friend."[95]

The family of the dead was rapidly becoming more numerous than the family of the living. Early in 1871 he went to say good-bye to Mazzini who was leaving England "for good." The eloquent Italian looked "very old and hoary," but his eyes were "still beautiful and genially bright." He suddenly seemed dearer for the sake of memories: "The look of his now aged face brought many thoughts . . . which were sad and strange, and, in some sort, even great." Like Carlyle, Mazzini "described himself as one dead all but the brain part . . . having rather the feeling of a *Revenant*."[96] In March 1872 Mazzini died in Rome. Led by Moncure Conway, his London friends held a memorial service to which Carlyle contributed the bemused admission that the wide-eyed idealist with his mad schemes had succeeded in some significant measure after all.[97] Stepping out of his house for a walk with Norton in May 1873, Carlyle was startled by the unexpected news that Mill had died in Avignon. "He had not even heard of his illness, and he was deeply moved at hearing thus without preparation of his death. 'What! John Mill dead! Dear me, Dear me! John Mill! how did he die and where? And it's so long since I've seen him, and he was the friendliest of men to me when I was in need of friends.' " Many "tragic memories" from the past "rushed down upon" him, all the aching early days when he and Mill had been young and hopeful together, when Jane had found Mill the favorite of their first friends in London.[98]

The intervening years had separated them, for reasons Carlyle never fully understood; and he thought of Mill now with gentle regret for a friendship that had been lost. When Mill's sister wrote to ask him to deny that her brother had been in any way irresponsible in regard to the destruction of the manuscript of the first volume of *The French Revolution,* as the newspapers were now claiming, he tactfully dismissed the issue as insignificant, suggesting that there was no blame to be cast, though it was his impression that the manuscript had been destroyed at Harriet Taylor's by "some trifling neglect."[99] To Norton, he expressed his conviction that the manuscript had indeed been burned by a careless "housemaid" at Harriet Taylor's "house on the riverside at Kingston."[100] Having been tactful, to the best of his ability, about Mill, *The French Revolution,* and Harriet Taylor while Mill lived, he was even more so now that Mill had joined, despite his years of self-imposed exile, the family that was gone. Yet, when Mill's *Autobiography* was published at the end of 1873, Carlyle could not help but be depressed, for the book seemed not the redemption but the reinforcement of a life fundamentally gone wrong: "It resembles more the autobiography of a logical Steam-engine, than any human creature's; and gives me, whenever I reflect on it, a peculiar, and dreary sense of desolation, disappointment," and "blighted pity."[101] The second and final loss of Mill was easier to bear than the first.

The month before Mill's death, Emerson arrived in London for a last visit on his way home from Egypt. A cruel irony now transcended the alternating currents of their friendship. There had been little correspondence between the two men during the late 1860s, primarily because of Emerson's increasing intolerance of the gap between his own rigid optimism about everything, including American democracy, and Carlyle's skeptical pessimism. By mid-1872 Emerson's mild aphasia had intensified; both his mental and physical health had declined with alarming rapidity, to the extent that, "bald, weak, and vague," he did not want his London friends to see him in his decline.[102] But, eager to see his son who was living in London and had been welcomed at Cheyne Row and Palace Gate, he allowed himself to be persuaded that he could tolerate a visit to London enroute to a winter in Egypt. In autumn 1872, he sailed for Liverpool with his daughter Ellen. In London, both men and their friends could not help but notice the contrast between the older man's good health and the younger man's infirmity. Saddest of all was the loss of memory. Emerson could not even find his way from his lodgings to Cheyne Row without detailed directions. The

Thomas Carlyle and Ralph Waldo Emerson's grandson. Photograph, n.d.
Courtesy of the Rare Book and Manuscript Library, Columbia University.

two old friends walked and talked together. It was a reception that seemed to Emerson's wife "most lovely and touching"; Carlyle "is as tender as he is savage."

In April 1873 Emerson returned to London, looking a great deal better for his winter voyage.[103] Aware of his friend's failing health, Carlyle attempted to be amiable and to increase Emerson's pleasure during the time they spent together. On April 24 Emerson made a final visit in order to say good-bye; the two men spent the afternoon together comfortably. Four days later, Allingham, who had called on Carlyle for a walk, found him about to go out to see Emerson one last time. "At Hyde Park Corner C. stopped and looked at the clock. 'You are going to Down St., sir?' 'No, it's too late.' 'The place is close at hand.' 'No, no, it's half-past five.' So he headed for Knightsbridge."[104] Actually, Emerson had left for Edinburgh and then Liverpool the day before. The two friends never saw one another again and direct communication soon ceased completely.

Soon after Carlyle's eightieth-birthday celebration one of the primary celebrants was gone. Having been ill so long that it had come to seem that illness was a natural part of his life, John Forster died at the beginning of Februray 1876. It was "the end of a chapter" in Carlyle's life "which had lasted, with unwearied kindness and helpfulness . . . for above forty years."[105] An indomitable host, friend, and business consultant, Forster had managed since Dickens' death to struggle with his own increasingly poor health and with his sacred commission to memorialize his friend in a biography. "Perpetual ill-health" did not prevent him publishing the first volume of his life of Dickens in late 1871; there was "a perfect rage or public famine" for what Carlyle thought a "true view" of Dickens.[106] To Forster, one year later, Carlyle enthusiastically praised the second volume, which "gives us . . . a complete Photograph of Dickens's existence." Carlyle eagerly anticipated the third, advising Forster to direct his "chief force of detail in making visual the *last* American voyage, which has to me always so tragical a character; and stands in such strange and mournful contrast to the first."

Despite "poor" Forster's struggles, Carlyle tried "to persuade" himself that there was "nothing deep gone wrong with him."[107] And while Forster still had a breath of life left, Christmas dinner at Palace Gate could not be avoided. In good health himself, Carlyle did not quite see the irony as the increasingly debilitated Forster not only drew up Carlyle's will but agreed to act as one of the executors. By the end of 1873, despite Forster's constant "heavy suffering," Carlyle worked hard to overcome his increasing conviction that he would never recover by persuading himself that his friend was "steadily, though slowly, getting better."[108] At the beginning of 1874, reading the third volume of Forster's *Dickens,* Carlyle proclaimed it a great triumph, "a wonderful Autobiography of Dickens." Through his letters that lost friend had been revived again in all his energetic cheerfulness, which was the richer for being now an inseparable part of the tragedy of a life that had ended prematurely. "Those two American Journies especially transcend in tragic interest to a thinking reader most things one has seen in writing."[109] Generously complimenting his friend, Carlyle considered "this Biography as taking rank, in essential respects, parallel to Boswell himself."[110] In the spring Forster became acutely ill; but, after a few days of "serious alarm" and a week recuperating at Hastings, Forster, who was an "*hexellent* cove no less than a *harbitrary,*" insisted on hosting a dinner for Carlyle at Palace Gate.[111] And where else could Carlyle dine on his eightieth birthday but at Forster's? It seemed almost as if ill health had made "Fuz" indestructible.

Forster's death came surprisingly quickly on Tuesday morning, Feburary 1, 1876. Carlyle, who had visited on Sunday, had been reassured by Dr. Quain that the patient was improving slightly; but the unexpected appearance of Quain at Cheyne Row on Tuesday about noon, "with considerable emotion of his own," soon made it clear to Carlyle that he had good cause for "very great grief." His closest friend other than his wife and blood kindred was dead. He actually went to the funeral. For Forster it had "clearly been an immense deliverance from long years of pain and distress."[112] For Carlyle, it marked another important step in the descent into his own grave. At Kensal Green cemetery, he found himself, along with two others, "leading the mournful procession," calmly, stoically listening to the service and watching the earth cover the coffin. Soon his old friend was "for ever hidden" from his eyes. Accompanied by Froude, he went home in the widow's carriage. During the next days images of Forster "in strangely new figure" constantly appeared to him, making the life of the living even more painful with loss, reminding him that he was "again . . . left alone."[113]

That among those he loved so many who were younger than he did not outlive him was one of the lessons that even his increasing stoicism found it hard to accept. He was sensible enough to grant that beyond a certain age the grave had been earned: his regret was not only that so many were dying but that Nature seemed to be making an exception to its usual pattern of taking the oldest first. The day before his eightieth birthday he received news from Canada intimating that in his "great frailty and constant suffering" his brother Alick probably did not have long to live.[114] Alick's photograph stood in his "dressing-closet, your

Alexander Carlyle and his wife, Janet. Photograph, n.d. Courtesy of the Rare Book and Manuscript Library, Columbia University.

true old face well known to me; among the shadows of my other Loved Ones who are far away."[115] The distance between them was now to be increased. A few weeks later he dictated a letter that he well knew might be his last to the favorite brother of his youth, a man whom he had not seen for almost thirty years. He gently protested that since he was the older he "by nature ought to be weaker; and certainly I am grown as weak almost as if I were a second time a baby."[116] The only resource was "patience" and "perfect submission."

Alick quickly slipped away, from weariness and old age, at the end of March 1875. Though the news took over a month to reach Cheyne Row, the eldest brother of the shrinking family had anticipated the event, quieting himself into the peace of acceptance. But he could not prevent his heart from being wrenched by the loss, especially when he learned that on his deathbed this "faithful, ingenious and valiant man," the "first human being" he had "ever" come "to friendship and familiarity with in this world," had leaped across time and space, his mind wandering to the old Annandale days when the two brothers had begun to part but were still brothers in their parents' home. The dying Alick had asked, " 'Is Tom coming from Edinburgh the morn?' " His "ever faithful" younger brother had "come back across wide oceans and long decades of time to the scenes of Brotherly companionship with me . . . going out of the world, as it were, with his hand in mine."[117] Again, Carlyle had been "left among the mourners, instead of being the mourned." Some months later, just as he had done for Jane, he wrote the inscription to be engraved on Alick's gravestone.

Of all the brothers, John had been most intimate with Carlyle, sharing his confidence, his company, and sometimes his daily cares. It seemed inconceivable that this moon-faced, argumentative, and deeply cherished younger brother would die before he did. When Jack had gone to medical school, his older brother had paid the bills. When the doctor needed emotional support and literary assistance, Thomas had provided them; and, in return, they had together reinforced the primacy of family, looked after the welfare of their aging mother, distributed largess to those members of the family who needed it, and argued long into the night and walked briskly together in the day both in Scotland and in England. Of all Carlyle's family members and friends Jack had been closest to the heartbeat of his relationship with Jane; and the impediments in the relationship between his brother and his wife, even between himself and his brother, did not in the least decrease the bond of fraternal love. He had found it necessary to reject Jack's suggestion that they attempt to live together in their widowed old age, but did so not out of selfishness but because he felt certain that it was in the best interests of both. The stubbornly ingrained personal habits of two rather opinionated elderly men could not readily be reconciled, and Jack had determined to spend his remaining days in Scotland, where he had recently been honored by a doctorate from the University of Edinburgh.

Thomas confidently assumed that Jack would outlast him. He was younger, despite his gray hair; he seemed stronger; he had never been

Dr. John Carlyle. Photograph, n.d. Courtesy of the Rare Book and Manuscript Library, Columbia University.

seriously ill. Other deaths might come, expectedly or unexpectedly. Betty Braid died in late 1874, removing Carlyle's last direct link to Jane's childhood. "Poor Twistleton," who had helped bury Jane, died in the same year. His older half-brother had died in his American exile shortly before. The deaths of Augusta Stanley, Harriet Martineau, his old friend and Knox adversary David Laing, and even Elizabeth Paulet,

Jane's Liverpool friend, seemed somehow abstract—the passing of a generation rather than deep personal losses. The sudden, unexpected death of Maggie Welsh in the summer of 1875, after a short illness and while making plans to visit again at Cheyne Row, did throw him off stride, but he soon felt better. Jack, in fact, was visiting at the time. The two men walked quietly, stoically together. His brother helped him pass his birthday the next year and stayed for a long visit through the spring of 1877.

By the next summer, however, Jack seemed seriously ill. And the next year what had seemed absolutely inconceivable to Carlyle became a fact. "As his condition grew hopeless, Carlyle was afraid every day that the end had come, and that the news had been kept back from him. 'Is my brother John dead?' " he asked Froude one day toward the middle of September 1879. "He was not actually dead then, but he suffered only for a few more days."[118] In the "last few years" he had lost "a great many of the people who called him *Carlyle* in addressing him," Mary wrote to FitzGerald.[119] He felt thoroughly alone, his only consolation his conviction that he too would die soon.

6.

But in his last years the survivor was hardly alone. He had the unusual good fortune not to be neglected by a younger generation of friends and family. Of his own literary generation (and, ironically, though old themselves they were younger still) only FitzGerald, Tennyson, and Browning were still alive. FitzGerald never left his country hermitage. On his increasingly infrequent visits to London, sometimes with his wife and sons, Tennyson usually called at Cheyne Row "on very good-natured terms. . . . A stout man . . . with only one deep . . . *crow* wrinkle just under the cheek bones."[120] Though in especially weak health herself, Mrs. Tennyson, whom Carlyle had always liked, called occasionally, accompanied by her two boys who listened eagerly to Carlyle's conversation. In the Tennyson family, he was one of the great men of history. Once, late in the decade, the two old friends were talking together. Tennyson remarked, "If I were a young man, I would head a colony out somewhere or other." Carlyle responded, "O, ay, so would I, to India or somewhere: but the scraggiest bit of heath in Scotland is more to me than all the forests of Brazil. I am just twinkling away."[121]

Of his old literary companions only Browning remained actively engaged in London life, a hungry social lion who had returned from Italy not long after his wife's death in order to make an Englishman out of his son and advance the young man's career as a painter. Browning had mixed success with both. Though Browning's new poems were no more pleasing to Carlyle than Tennyson's recent attempts at dramatic tragedy, Carlyle valued Browning's friendship while recognizing its limitations. The once young, sparkling poet now seemed "much hoarier, fatter," with the beginnings of "gout and a double-chin." Before Forster's death, they were often together at Palace Gate; and on Carlyle's eightieth birthday only Browning was admitted to Cheyne Row. Two years later, the poet dedicated his translation of *Agamemnon* to his old friend and the next year called on Carlyle on his birthday. The older man appreciated his company and conversation and in the next two years did his best to lend his support by going at least once, perhaps twice, to see the younger Browning's paintings.[122] But, like Carlyle, Browning and Tennyson were also becoming survivors, though they lagged over a decade behind the older man; still they were by and large unavailable for the kind of daily companionship that the younger generation generously provided.

Three men, Froude, Allingham, and James Fitzjames Stephen, were Carlyle's most constant companions outside the house; at home, Mary gradually took over most of the functions of daughter, wife, and mother to an old man who soon felt his second childhood coming on. Protecting him from the "conceited and half-crazed pilgrims" who frequently came to the door unannounced, she became more and more the good angel of the house and the guardian of the gate, intent on protecting her uncle's interests and her own as best she could understand them.[123] With Froude and Allingham, his favorite visitors, he took walks and carriage rides. Froude usually came twice a week, Allingham more sporadically. For years Fitzjames Stephen came almost every Sunday to walk with a man whose opinions he did not always share but whose achievements he deeply admired. Sometimes his younger brother visited. One day, close to Carlyle's eightieth birthday, while walking in the snow and dusk in Cromwell Road, the old man met Leslie Stephen, whose wife had died a few days before. "He turns and shakes hands, but does not speak. Carlyle says, 'I am very sorry for you, sir. My own loss did not come in so grievous a way.' S. departs without a word."[124] The very tall William Lecky, who disagreed with him about almost everything but did so tactfully, visited frequently. He towered noticeably over the old man when they walked together, solicitously stooping in order to hear and to be heard. Early in 1876, with other distinguished guests, Carlyle watched his friend Tyndall marry in Westminister Abbey. During the next years Carlyle occasionally went on Sunday to St. Paul's, since he found the "very grand and solemn" service unexpectedly moving and at the same time calming. He would sit for a while, quietly reflecting on all his loved ones who were gone.

But he needed personal companionship and exercise now more than he needed any kind of institutional comfort. In 1877 he took a sudden liking to riding on the omnibus, since he could no longer walk as far as he had used to and had not yet reconciled himself to the necessity of having a private carriage. "Amongst the faithful" who rode with him, usually to Regent Circus and back, were Froude, Allingham, Lecky, and Stephen. His favorite place to walk was the new Chelsea Embankment, "a really beautiful bit of public work . . . which has been a real godsend."[125] On the rare days on which none of his young men (most of whom qualified for that designation only by comparison) were available to accompany him, he always had Mary, "*faute de mieux,*" and never went "by himself."[126] Occasionally he burst into lively conversation, full of the old fire and prejudice. And he took some comfort in the fact that, though he was an unwilling survivor, his longevity had been blessed by weakness without pain and by the respect and love of younger companions. As he approached his eighty-fifth birthday, these young friends leaned even closer to hear his diminishing voice.

7.

While Carlyle's friends and family quietly waited for the inevitable, two people in particular had a special practical interest in his death. Neither Mary Aitken nor James Anthony Froude expected to profit in any way inconsistent with what they justly deserved; and certainly both of them felt the deepest compassion and respect for Carlyle. But Mary, who had devoted over ten of the most important years of her life to attending to her uncle, had no competence except that which her uncle would provide. And Froude had not only agreed to publish an edition of Jane's letters but had also begun working on an edition of Carlyle's reminiscences and a biography, together an immense investment of time and energy.

In his will of 1873, Carlyle appointed John Forster and John Carlyle executors; if Forster were to pre-decease him then Froude would be appointed; if John died, his youngest brother James would replace him. As to literary matters, Froude and John Carlyle were empowered to make all decisions in regard to the publication of heretofore unpublished personal materials. To each of his brothers and sisters he bequeathed one-fifth of the value of his estate other than manuscripts and private papers; but to Mary were to go the manuscripts of the reminiscences exclusive of the reminiscence of Jane as well as the sum of five hundred pounds "for the loving care and unwearied patience and helpfulness she has shown to me in these my last solitary and infirm years." All the other manuscripts and the personal possessions at

Cheyne Row were left to brother John, except the letters and memorials of Jane, with the introductory memoir, which were given to "my kind considerate and ever faithful friend James Anthony Froude."[127]

Between 1873 and 1875 Mary waged a gentle but firm struggle to persuade her uncle to provide her in explicit terms with the just reward for her years of service. Some of her uncle's autobiographical manuscripts and five-hundred pounds did not seem sufficient. She had two helpful allies, her uncle John and the Reverend Whitwell Elwin, the editor and biographer of Alexander Pope. One of Carlyle's female admirers had epitomized the extent of the world's concern for Mary when she exclaimed to her, "What a privilege yours is of waiting on and watching over such a grand creation of God's."[128] But John, who lived much of the year in Mary's parents' home in Dumfries, was sensitive to the practical awkwardness of her situation and took opportunities to urge his increasingly passive brother to act on his intention to provide a better inheritance for their niece.

At about this time, Whitwell Elwin established a paternal intimacy with Mary that enabled him to advise her as if she were one of his own daughters, a role that Mary sometimes found emotionally satisfying. Elwin's own literary achievements were minimal (Carlyle thought his biography of Pope a desecration, as if one could write a good biography of a man one basically disliked), but as the editor of Pope and the *Quarterly Review* he unquestionably had friends and some influence, though he is likely to be most remembered and regretted for his strict loyalty in executing Forster's wish that he burn Forster's "vast archive of correspondence." Undoubtedly, Mary found such loyalty a great virtue. He was attractive to her, in part because he embodied a rather stolid middle-class stability; his temperament, so different from her uncle's and from Ruskin's, expressed itself with paternal benevolence.[129] In Elwin's eyes, Carlyle had done his niece a "wrong."[130] For "you have devoted nine years of your young life to your uncle and . . . granted that he renders you present service as well as you do him, still the cases are not equal. Nothing that he can do for you is at the expense of his future life, whereas what you have done for him has been at the cost of *your* future unless he leaves you an independence."[131]

One morning, at the end of June 1875, Carlyle came into the dining room where Mary was writing and presented her with an unexpected gift, a satisfactory resolution of the problem.[132] He had recently purchased seven Russian bonds worth £1000 each; he gave one to Mary "as a present" and reminded her that he had in addition left her £500 in his will. But, beyond that, he had arranged with John, who was visiting at Cheyne Row, that all the possessions in the house which he had willed to his brother, including "his papers and his wife's jewelry," were by agreement between the two brothers to be left to Mary. That same day John expressed to her his approval of the new arrangement.[133] "The thing now is to see that the intentions are executed," Elwin soon urged her, "and endeavour that performance should follow resolution without delay."[134] But it was not until November 1878 that a codicil was added to the will. With the death of Forster, Froude was now made an executor; and James Fitzjames Stephen joined Froude and John Carlyle in that capacity, apparently with the intention of providing a second executor in anticipation of the unavailability of John. The main substantive change, however, put into writing the oral agreement of 1875. It bequeathed to Mary after John Carlyle's death all those things that had previously been left to John, including all the manuscripts and private papers, except the letters and memorials of Jane and the reminiscence of Jane which had been expressly designated for Froude.[135]

Much relieved, Mary found the new arrangement emotionally as well as financially liberating. Just as she looked after her uncle's bodily health, so she now thought it natural that she should look after his earthly reputation. When, in the early summer of 1877, a former clerk-secretary who had helped Carlyle in the research and in the preparation of the manuscript of *Frederick* published a biographical article about the "Sage of Chelsea" which inferred that it was based on authentic documents and had the approval of the subject, Mary immediately took up the pen on her uncle's behalf. Of the author, Frederick Martin, Mary scathingly demanded that his misstatements and misleading inferences be retracted; she would indeed have been even more than abrupt if she had known that Martin had stolen from Cheyne Row a valuable manuscript, the unpublished draft of "Wotton Reinfred," which Carlyle thought he had thrown into the fire thirty years before. To Martin's publisher, Mary admitted that she could "see that the article . . . is written in no malicious spirit, but there are statements in it that are inaccurate and misleading." She was "willing to look over the proofs of the subsequent chapters and to submit to Mr. Martin any corrections of statements of facts, as to which he may have been misinformed."[136] But her fullest wishes really would have been fulfilled only by the discontinuance of this serial biography; and certainly her uncle, who agreed with his niece, did not have to be strongly urged to dictate to her a brief note to the *Athenaeum* in which he flatly stated that "Mr. Frederick Martin has no authority to concern himself with my life, of which he knows nothing."[137]

But Froude did in fact have Carlyle's authority to "concern himself" with his life. By this time he already knew more about it than anyone else alive except the subject himself. When, in the summer of 1877,

Mary went yachting toward Ireland with the Froudes, in the hope of recovering from a series of minor illnesses under which she had been "threatening to break down," "the loved disciple" had already been hard at work on his literary inheritance.[138] Actually, all the parties understood that the codicil of 1878 did not override the widely acknowledged commitment that Carlyle had made to Froude as his literary executor. Unfortunately, however, there was still some room for misunderstanding, much of which resulted from a tired old man's indifference to (if not contempt for) the legal distinctions and forms that John Forster, when he was alive, had relieved him of. Only under pressure from Mary was the codicil formulated and written by a lawyer. Carlyle would have been content to leave it as an oral instruction or at most to have Mary herself put it into writing for his signature.[139] Probably, of course, the most important of the difficulties that arose after Carlyle's death in regard to his inheritance would have arisen even if he had been more careful in communicating his wishes to Mary and to Froude: ultimately, the disagreement had to do with broad differences of sensibility and attitude which transcended disagreements over particular stipulations in Carlyle's bequest.

By 1878 Carlyle had already turned over to Froude most of his literary papers, particularly the letters, for two express purposes—editing for publication the letters and memorials of Jane and writing his biography. *Letters and Memorials* itself, with Carlyle's biographical annotations, was ready for publication. In Froude's mind the only unanswered question was whether or not the volume should be prefaced with Carlyle's reminiscence of his wife, which was clearly Froude's property. The biography was still in its early stages. In the next two years Froude completed most of the first two volumes of what was to be a four-volume work, incorporating in part or in whole much of the material from the other letters and biographical writings. Whether or not a separate volume containing the various reminiscences of family, friends, and literary personalities should be published had been left to Froude's judgment, as had the decision whether such a volume should contain the memoir of Jane. These reminiscences, other than Jane's, were clearly understood to be Mary's property, but the decision whether or not to publish them was to be left to Froude.

But to whom did all the other papers belong? Carlyle had literally put them into Froude's hands, with the injunction that he do with them as he please, burning whatever he thought it best to destroy. Certainly Froude had good reason to believe that, except for express declarations to the contrary, whatever Carlyle had turned over to him was indeed his property. Yet Mary also had good reason to believe that her uncle's oral remarks and now his statement in the codicil indicating that everything at Cheyne Row was to be left to her meant that *all* the literary and private papers were to be her property. That the papers were not actually in Cheyne Row at the moment but were temporarily in Froude's possession seemed irrelevant to their ultimate disposition. And Carlyle had certainly left extremely vague the matter of how, if Froude decided to publish the reminiscences as a separate volume, the royalties would be divided. Probably it never came to mind at all.

Though initially under the impression that the papers turned over to him in 1871 and 1873 were to be his property, Froude by 1878 seems to have accepted the oral clarification that indicated that the bulk of the papers were to be Mary's. Somewhat disappointed that he had been unintentionally misled, he nevertheless took some satisfaction in the clear understanding that he was to have complete literary control over their use. Mary seems to have accepted this crucial distinction between legal ownership and literary use. In fact, in the last years of Carlyle's life neither his most cherished disciple nor his deeply loved niece felt or had any anticipation of contentiousness on the matter. At some level, of course, Mary may have felt that her own literary ambitions, diminished as they were, might have been attended to more sympathetically had her uncle and Froude extended her some nod of respect and responsibility. But certainly the paternal warmth that Froude felt toward Carlyle's niece and the familial regard that Mary had toward the Froude family were not in the least diminished by these minor complications for which, at this point, neither of them were responsible.[140]

Froude brought the problem of the appropriate vehicle for the publication of the memoir of Jane and whether or not to publish the other reminiscences at all directly to Carlyle in 1879. Though the very old man needed to be reminded of the contents of the memoirs, he seems to have told Froude that he did want them published directly after his death. When Froude suggested that Carlyle himself actually attempt to correct the proofsheets that could be set in type almost immediately, the old man thought that he indeed might try. But, in fact, it came to nothing; he was beyond that kind of activity now. Three months before his death the proposed volume of Jane's letters and memorials was on his mind. He asked Froude what he intended to do and reminded him that as literary executor he had the duty to publish them. To Froude, "the Letters implied the Memoir. . . . I decided, therefore, that the Memoir should be added to the volume of Reminiscences; the Letters to follow at an early date. I briefly told him this. He was entirely satisfied, and never spoke about it again."[141]

8.

Despite the weariness that had been accumulating gradually over the years, Carlyle still kept to his feet with surprising vigor, even after his eightieth birthday. That his lifelong complaints about his health were complaints of the spirit rather than of the body is implied in the claim of his "medical brother John" that "Scotland never sent forth a stronger man."[142] Ironically, at a time of life when illness usually dominates, it was clear to him and to all those around him that there was absolutely nothing wrong but old age. His eyes and limbs were sound; he could read, walk, talk, even travel; and if he occasionally seemed to be dozing at an inappropriate moment, between December 1876 and the spring of 1879 he showed no dramatic signs of imminent departure from this life. The one task that he still felt "a sense of incumbency as a thing yet to do" was a memoir of John Forster; but, though he recognized his obligation, he felt the impossibility of ever fulfilling it.[143] He gave up the idea without much of a struggle. To his relief, the anguish of remembering the past diminished considerably, both because his memory lost some of its power and because in advanced old age his interest in all aspects of life declined. "It is very curious," he said to Allingham, "the head is still the same, only the interest in things is nearly gone."[144] His young friends rode the omnibus with him and walked the Chelsea Embankment. They brought him books, aware not only of his need to keep himself occupied but also of his increasing inability to concentrate for very long on any one work. One day he spoke of his mother's death, but he had his own condition in mind. " 'It was like watching the moon fade away to the last pale sickle.' "[145]

In the spring of 1878 he and Mary decided to spend much of the summer in Scotland, first at a rented house near Dumfries and then visiting near Ecclefechan. There seemed good reason to go, beyond his usual desire to escape the oppressive London heat; it was reasonable to assume that this visit would be the last. One day, going out for a ride in a hired carriage, he said to Allingham, " 'I feel I may die at any time.' "[146] While he was still alive, let alone reasonably alert, his fondness for Scotland did not decline, for he sensed that ultimately Scotland had provided the sources of his life. Scotland still faintly glowed with the landscapes that he cherished, though in elegiac shadows. In addition, two of his sisters, one of them Mary's mother, still lived in the familiar places; they were now very old people too. And, most important, it was the summer in which his brother Jack, living with his sister, was showing signs of increasingly "poor health."[147]

In late July, he and Mary went to Dumfries. To the delight of both of them, two visitors from Canada appeared early in August after an absence of seven years. Alick's sons, Thomas and Alexander, were traveling together on their way from the Paris Exhibition and London to see "their native border country." Mary had probably met Alexander when he had visited her uncle in the summer of 1871. The cousins now found one another attractive. Within a half year they were engaged to be married. The wedding was to take place sometime during the next year, as soon as some practical matters could be attended to, including the couple's place of residence, Alexander's vocation, and Mary's responsibility to her uncle. When the two young men strode up to the park near Dumfries, they found not only Mary but the most distinguished member of their family eager to see them, delighted to be in touch with the future in this way. He usually spent the mornings reading, for a while his own *Frederick the Great;* but in the afternoons they went driving together in the countryside. Carlyle acted as guide; they "saw the house, with an archway running through it, where Uncle Carlyle was born."

Carlyle readily admitted to them that "it is a misfortune for a man to live so long. I should have been at rest long ago. I am getting like into second childhood again; my hands shake so that when drinking a cup of tea I am as likely to throw it in my face as anywhere." But he still had energy beyond his years. And he looked to these young cousins surprisingly vigorous. "He is tall and slightly stooped, but with a fresh colour in his cheeks. . . . He walks about a mile before breakfast every morning between 8 and 9 . . . reads a good part of the day . . . take[s] a carriage drive for a couple of hours . . . dines at 6 p.m. . . . sleeps . . . converses or reads for two or three hours . . . retires about 12 or 1 a.m."[148] By all accounts, when he returned to Chelsea at the end of September 1878 the change had done "him a great deal of good and a good many people remarked that they had not seen him looking so well for twenty years!"[149]

Carlyle passed much of the winter quietly, showing just the slightest increase of somnolence. To Mary it seemed an "unspeakable blessing that it is only his body that fails—his intellect is as clear as ever. And he is in general quite cheerful and contented."[150] Actually, as the dark months came on, he became increasingly anxious about his brother Jack, whose health rapidly declined for causes that could not be determined; Jack's vision was so impaired that he could not read. For Carlyle, the consolation that he offered himself and his brother was that the end to these wearinesses of the flesh and the spirit was an imminent and welcome one for which they must both wait patiently. "The final mercy of God . . . is, that He delivers us from a life which has become a task too hard for us."[151]

Early in the spring of 1879 Carlyle suddenly and alarmingly "broke down altogether" into lassitude and disinterestedness. For weeks he would not go out for a drive, though he continued to take very brief walks; but he "was very languid and slept much" during the day on the sofa; "he sometimes looked very sunken and low."[152] For a few days during March, in his alert moments, "he said continuously that he longed for the end." Distressed by his condition, Mary did not have the heart to wish against his wishes.[153] One day, when he seemed just a little more alert, Ruskin came to visit. His own illnesses were of a different kind, as he had explained to Carlyle: "It was utterly wonderful to me to find that I could go so heartily & headily mad; for you know I had been priding myself on my peculiar sanity!"[154] Ruskin's vision, however, was clear enough to understand accurately Carlyle's condition. After greeting one another warmly, "Ruskin knelt on the floor, leaning over Carlyle as they talked. Carlyle began to speak of Irish Saints," among them Saint Bridget. Allingham, who was with them, added that "Bridewell . . . had come to mean a prison. This seemed to interest Ruskin particularly, and he remarked, 'We make prisons of the holiest and most beautiful things!' He then took leave, very affectionately kissing Carlyle's hands."[155]

To everyone's surprise, Carlyle had so noticeably improved by early May that he was clearly out of imminent danger. In a short while he looked "so comfortable" that Mary hoped he might "be spared to us for a long time to come."[156] He had never been completely off his feet. But now he could again walk regularly, though shorter distances, and drive in the afternoons in his carriage. He had become unexpectedly active again, even eager to read and talk. In a little more than a month he reread all of Shakespeare. His rather shrewd doctor recommended that whether he were to live or to die in the next months he would be better off doing it in Scotland. By June, it had been decided that "if he is at all fit for the journey we mean to try for Dumfries this month." Though she felt "rather nervous about it," Mary "very much" wanted to go. "Uncle himself is anxious to try it."[157] He would be able to see his brothers and sisters again.

In a few weeks he was once more in familiar places, actually touring the countryside. For Alexander and Mary it was a honeymoon period. They were married at the Hill in August 1879. It had been agreed that, for as long as necessary, the married couple would live at Cheyne Row when they returned from Scotland. On his own merits and with the help of his uncle's influence, Alexander would attempt to find employment as a schoolmaster, for which he was trained, or as a civil servant. Carlyle was joined by his niece and her husband and by Allingham for a drive up through Nithsdale to Moffat. From the heights they could see far down into the Annandale where he had been born; and the route that he had traveled homeward many times from Edinburgh as a student was clearly visible. Quite animated, Carlyle that night interrupted Allingham's reading of Burns to read aloud a number of times some of his favorite Burns poems. From Moffat, on a fine early September afternoon, the four of them drove down to Ecclefechan. As they approached, Carlyle "pointed out the wooded hill called Woodcockair, and Repentance Tower."[158] Except at Lockerbie, where a farmer imposed himself on the party by asking to shake Carlyle's hand, the discreet local people kept their quiet distance, unwilling to intrude on this well-known "stranger" among them.

In Dumfries again, they prepared themselves for the inevitable. John Carlyle was unquestionably dying, ironically with "no belief" that the "medical skill" of any doctor could help him. Never one to linger over or even to confront direct good-byes, Thomas now purposely missed his brother's deathbed and his funeral. About September 10 he returned to Cheyne Row, with Mary and Alexander. Jack died on September 15, 1879.

Through the autumn Carlyle was in calm spirits. "Things might be worse," he said. On his eighty-fourth birthday, Browning and Ruskin visited; so too did the Leckys and Allingham. There were flowers on the table. The old man kept warm and quiet in his dressing gown and a "new purple and gold cap."[159] Though he made efforts to walk, suddenly his mobility decreased considerably, as if his legs were retiring after a lifetime of service. But each afternoon a carriage ride provided gentle exercise and some relief from the desultory reading that was his main amusement. By March 1880, however, he had almost lost interest even in looking out the carriage window. He lay "back crookedly in his corner, noticing nothing of the outer world." But there was "a dim fire still in his eyes, a dusky red in his cheeks."[160] His once-powerful voice was hard to hear, especially if there were any competing noise, but he occasionally talked about familiar topics and commented on his reading. Duffy, his companion in Ireland so many years before, came to visit in April. He found a "feeble" old man whose "chief trouble was to be so inordinately long in departing." Sipping brandy and puffing indifferently at a pipe, Carlyle confessed that though "he was content to consider his work at an end . . . much had been left altogether unspoken, because there was no fit audience discernible as yet, and a man's thoughts, though struggling for utterance, refused to utter themselves to the empty air."[161]

The fates had determined that in his case it would take "a long time to die." More and more he spent his hours on the sofa, though the spring awakened both his memory and some response to the London neighborhoods through which he drove. Shakespeare never failed him, as if the plays were the pages of life itself. "I read *Othello* yesterday all through," he told Allingham in April, "and it quite distressed me. . . . Honest Iago! I was once at this Play at Drury Lane . . . and when Emilia said—'O the more angel she / And you the blacker devil!'—a murmur swelled up from the whole audience into a passionate burst of approval, the voices of the men rising—in your imagination—like a red mountain, with the women's voices floating round it like a blue vapour."[162] In July 1880 "a very severe attack of Diarrhoea" left him "exceedingly weak, hardly able to walk fifty yards without help."[163] His strength did not return. Margaret Oliphant came to visit on a hot summer day. "Weary and irritated by the fatigue" of going downstairs to his carriage, he was warmly and heavily dressed "though the sun was blazing." He seemed so "worn and feeble."[164] But his exhaustion and irritation did not prevent him from celebrating with dignity and pride the birth of a son to Mary and Alexander, the only Carlyle ever born at Cheyne Row. They named him after his grand-uncle who "spoke of it with tender amusement and wonder."[165] In September, the long-ill Geraldine Jewsbury preceded him to the grave. When his doctor called one day in November, Carlyle mocked himself and the physician's impotence. "The only thing you could do, you must not do—that is, help me to make an end of this. We must go on as we are." On his eighty-fifth birthday, he actually seemed to be "better and easier; more himself."[166]

But it was clearly, as he repeated to all his visitors, death that he wanted. And it seemed finally about to arrive. Friends began to make what they sensed would be last visits. When James Stephen came, Carlyle, who was staring into the fire, mustered enough strength to ask, "How would it feel for a man to be put into a vast fire like that for all eternity?"—the fate his father had absolutely believed would be meted out to most human beings.[167] Late in December, when Allingham found him lying on the sofa, Carlyle reached out his hand to his friend but said nothing. His visitor doubted that Carlyle knew him. With the help of a servant, he carried the old man out to his carriage, wrapped in "his heavy seal-skin coat." He dozed during most of their drive through Hyde Park.[168] George Eliot had died the day before. But Carlyle, even if he had been alert, would not have been especially interested.

Tyndall came in one day and noticed that the old man had not touched some brandy and cigars that he had given him previously. Lighting one of the cigars, Tyndall put it into Carlyle's hand and was "astonished . . . at the vigour of his puffs. . . . After a time . . . he drank off the brandy-and-water, and with a smile gleaming in his eye, remarked 'That's well over.' " He shortly fell asleep. On New Year's Day 1881 he went out with Mary for his last drive, "a very sad one for he was suffering all the time and the shaking seemed to tire him out." Half a lifetime before he had remarked to his brother that "of *all* things there are only *so many times;* one time is the last."[169] For the next few weeks he kept slightly active, mainly by dressing in the morning and being pushed in a wheelchair from his bed, which had been moved downstairs to the sofa in the drawing room.

By the middle of January 1881 he was too weak to dress himself, even to move. His bed was brought into the drawing room, where he lay quietly, sleeping most of the time.[170] To remedy his increasing bed-sore discomfort and the incessant chill in his limbs Alexander attached a very large bedpan, constantly refilled with hot water, to the underside of the mattress. He seemed, awake or asleep, to toss around less. The cleverness of the device pleased him.[171] At the beginning of February he was sometimes delirious, though mostly quiet. Lucid moments were few and "his mind wandered back to the beginning. . . . He spoke often then about a baby sister who died when he was a little child, of his father, and he would put his arm round [Mary's] neck and often call [her] 'my dear Mother!' " It seemed, Mary thought, "as if time were indeed but a thing of one's imagination."[172]

He soon sank into "a deep heavy sleep." The constant ringing of the doorbell by newspaper reporters, eager to be timely with the news that the nation now momentarily expected, could not disturb him. "Bulletins pinned up" to the door "abated the nuisance." On Friday, February 4, Mary thought she heard him "saying to himself, 'So this is Death: well—. . . .' " Froude leaned over his unresponsive mentor and said, " 'Ours has been a long friendship; I will try to do what you wish.' "[173] That night the Allinghams sat for a while with Mary and Alexander by the bedside. At about 8:30 the next morning he quietly, almost imperceptibly, drifted off into the complete silence that he had for so long thought of as the highest blessing.

Now, finally, he was not to be the mourner but the mourned. Helen Allingham sat by the body and made two pencil sketches. Within an hour, Froude arrived and gazed for a while on "the large beautiful eyelids" that "were closed for ever." Toward noon the doorbell rang. A Scotchman, probably John Brown, had been sent by the queen to inquire about the condition of one of her most famous subjects. Allingham "told him of the death, asked him no questions."[174] Mary sent brief notes to friends and family. The undertaker prepared the body for viewing and for its final journey. Boehm asked to do a cast of Carlyle's head. Mary, who overcame her reluctance, gave permission to have a cast done only of the face, and was offended when Boehm's man not only took a cast of the whole head but "worked upon it for two hours and a half leaving everything so spotted with plaster and so disarranged" that another visit from the undertaker had to be endured.[175]

On February 9 the body was taken in the early evening to Euston Station to be conveyed on the overnight train to Scotland. Consistent

"Humilitate," Thomas Carlyle's bookplate and gravestone design. Author's photograph.

with their uncle's wishes, Mary and Alexander had declined Dean Stanley's persistent offers that this Scotsman be buried in Westminister Abbey. Leaving Carlyle's grand-nephew in the care of Froude's wife, they traveled on the same train, which stopped only at Lockerbie, where they spent the early morning hours. The body had to be brought to Ecclefechan. At dawn, from the railroad station waiting-room, Mary watched through smarting eyes the canopy of snow slowly falling from the gray sky.[176]

The small family of disciples, Froude, Tyndall, and Lecky, who had "journeyed together northwards," had stopped at Carlisle for the night. They now went on by local train to Ecclefechan. Moncure Conway, who had been visiting the sites associated with Carlyle's life since early in the week, arrived at Ecclefechan only after having found out from Mary Austen in Dumfries the day and the place of the funeral. True to the family wishes, none of the particulars had been published anywhere. Of his brothers, only the youngest was there to see the oldest brother into his grave. At the station, the hearse remained ready for its short procession, "powdered over by the frozen shower." The funeral was to be at noon. The disciples from London, who had necessarily arrived early, went their own way to pass the time. They walked through the snow to Mainhill, which seemed "narrow, cold, humid, uncomfortable."[177] Toward noontime, when the procession began to move from the station to the churchyard, "many of the villagers were off at the installation of a new minister in the neighboring church."[178]

On the hour, "the Presbyterian kirk bells tolled mournfully" and the hearse arrived, "followed by five funeral coaches," led by James Carlyle and about a hundred quiet, anonymous villagers. "The snow and rain now fell furiously." Carlyle's London friends stood silently. The flowers on the coffin were the only brightness in the gray scene; in the distance familiar landmarks were softly dressed in a white mist. Except for the tolling of the bells, there was silence. A momentary flicker of pale sun made the flowers suddenly brighter. Outside the churchyard gate, in her dark mourning, Mary remained in her carriage, looking out from "behind the curtain . . . and saw, or was seen by nobody." Some children from the local school were pressing curious "faces through the railing of the graveyard."[179] No one spoke. As was the custom, the coffin was lowered into the ground without a eulogy or a prayer.

Abbreviations

The following abbreviations and short titles are used in the notes:

Manuscripts

Berg	Henry W. and Albert A. Berg Collection, The New York Public Library, Astor, Lenox and Tilden Foundations
BM	British Museum, British Library, London
Chelsea	Carlyle House, Chelsea, The National Trust, London
Columbia	Rare Book and Manuscript Library, Columbia University
Edinburgh	Edinburgh University Library
Houghton	Houghton Library, Harvard University
Huntington	The Henry E. Huntington Library, San Marino, California
London	London Library
Morgan	Pierpont Morgan Library, New York
NLS	National Library of Scotland, Edinburgh
Northampton	Collection of the Marquess of Northampton, Castle Ashby, Northampton
Ray	Collection of Gordon N. Ray
Strouse	Strouse Collection, University of California, Santa Cruz
Trinity	Trinity College Library, Cambridge
V & A	Forster Collection, Victoria and Albert Museum, London
Yale	Beinecke Rare Book and Manuscript Library, Yale University

People

AC	Alexander Carlyle

Abbreviations

BB	Bingham Baring, Lord Ashburton
GJ	Geraldine Jewsbury
HB	Harriet Baring, Lady Ashburton
JC	Jean Carlyle (Aitken)
JAC	John Aitken Carlyle
JCH	Janet Carlyle (Hanning)
JF	John Forster
JR	John Ruskin
JS	John Sterling
JSM	John Stuart Mill
JW	Jeannie Welsh
JWC	Jane Welsh Carlyle
LA	Louisa Ashburton
MAC	Mary Aitken Carlyle (Mrs. Alexander Carlyle)
MC	Margaret Carlyle
MM	Richard Monckton Milnes
RB	Robert Browning
RWE	Ralph Waldo Emerson
TC	Thomas Carlyle

Books

a. Carlyle's Works

CE C	*The Centenary Edition of the Works of Thomas Carlyle.* Edited by H. D. Traill. 30 vols. London, 1896–1898. *Oliver Cromwell's Letters and Speeches* (1845).
CE CME	*Centenary Edition. Critical and Miscellaneous Essays.* 5 vols. (1827–1875).
CE FG	*Centenary Edition. History of Friedrich II. of Prussia Called Frederick the Great* (1858–1865)
CE FR	*Centenary Edition. The French Revolution* (1837).
CE GR	*Centenary Edition. German Romance* (1827).
JG	*Thomas Carlyle's Journey to Germany. Autumn, 1858.* Edited by Richard Brooks. New Haven, 1948.
Last Words	*Last Words of Thomas Carlyle.* London, 1892.
CE LDP	*Centenary Edition. Latter-Day Pamphlets* (1850).
"Netherlands"	"Notes of a Three-Day's Tour to the Netherlands, August 1842." Edited by Alexander Carlyle. *Cornhill Magazine* 126 (October 1922), 493–512; (November 1922), 626–640.
Notebooks	*Two Note Books of Thomas Carlyle.* Edited by C. E. Norton. New York, 1898.
CE PP	*Centenary Edition. Past and Present* (1843).
Rem	*Reminiscences.* Edited by C. E. Norton (Ian Campbell). London, 1932, 1972.
Report	*Report of the Commissioners Appointed to Inquire into the Constitu-*

	tion and Government of the British Museum with Minutes of Evidence. London, 1850 (29). Thursday, February 8, 1849, 272–285.
RIJ	*Reminiscences of My Irish Journey in 1849.* Edited by J. A. Froude. London, 1882.
CE S	*Centenary Edition. The Life of John Sterling* (1851).
CE Schiller	*Centenary Edition. The Life of Friedrich Schiller* (1825).
CE SR	*Centenary Edition. Sartor Resartus* (1834).
Two Rem	*Two Reminiscences of Thomas Carlyle.* Edited by John Clubbe. Durham, N.C., 1974.
CE WM	*Centenary Edition. Wilhelm Meister* (1824).

b. Letters

Bliss	*Thomas Carlyle, Letters to His Wife.* Edited by Trudy Bliss. London, 1953.
Browning	Charles Sanders. "The Carlyle-Browning Correspondence and Relationship." *Bulletin of the John Rylands University Library of Manchester* 57 (autumn 1974), 213–246; 57 (spring 1975), 430–462.
Calder	Grace J. Calder. "Erasmus A. Darwin, Friend of Thomas and Jane Carlyle." *Modern Language Quarterly* 20 (March 1959), 36–48.
Cate	*The Correspondence of Thomas Carlyle and John Ruskin.* Edited by George Allan Cate. Stanford, 1982.
CL	*The Collected Letters of Thomas and Jane Welsh Carlyle.* Duke-Edinburgh Edition. Edited by Charles Richard Sanders and Kenneth J. Fielding. 9 vols. Durham, N.C., 1970–1981.
Copeland	*Letters of Thomas Carlyle to His Youngest Sister.* Edited by Charles Townshend Copeland. New York, 1899.
Faulkner	Peter Faulkner. "Carlyle's Letters to Charles Redwood." *Yearbook of English Studies* 2 (1972), 139–180.
Graham	*Letters of Thomas Carlyle to William Graham.* Edited by John Graham. Princeton, 1950.
Huxley	*Jane Welsh Carlyle: Letters to Her family, 1839–1863.* Edited by Leonard Huxley. New York, 1924.
Ireland	*Selections from the Letters of Geraldine Endsor Jewsbury to Jane Welsh Carlyle.* Edited by Mrs. Alexander Ireland. London, 1892.
Larkin	Henry Larkin. "Carlyle and Mrs. Carlyle: A Ten-Year Reminiscence." *British Quarterly Review* 74 (July 1881), 15–45.
"Last Letters"	"Carlyle's Last Letters to Froude." Edited by Waldo H. Dunn. *Twentieth Century* 159 (1956), 44–53, 225–263, 591–597; 160 (1956), 240–246.
LM	*Letters and Memorials of Jane Welsh Carlyle.* Edited by J. A. Froude. London, 1883.

Marrs	*The Letters of Thomas Carlyle to His Brother Alexander.* Edited by Edwin W. Marrs. Cambridge, Mass., 1968.
Mineka	*The Earlier Letters of John Stuart Mill, 1812–1848.* Edited by Francis E. Mineka. Vols. 12–13 of *Collected Works of John Stuart Mill.* Toronto, 1963.
MSB	*Letters of Thomas Carlyle to John Stuart Mill, John Sterling and Robert Browning.* Edited by A. Carlyle. London, 1923.
Neuberg	Thomas Sadler. "Carlyle and Neuberg." *Macmillan's Magazine* 50 (August, 1884), 280–287.
NL	*New Letters of Thomas Carlyle.* Edited by A. Carlyle. London, 1904.
NLM	*New Letters and Memorials of Jane Welsh Carlyle.* Edited by A. Carlyle. London, 1903.
Norton	*Letters of Charles Eliot Norton.* Edited by Sara Norton and M. A. De Wolfe. Boston, 1913.
Pilgrim	*The Pilgrim Edition of the Letters of Charles Dickens.* Edited by Madeline House, Graham Storey, and Kathleen Tillotson. 5 vols. Oxford, 1968–1981.
Slater	*The Correspondence of Emerson and Carlyle.* Edited by Joseph Slater. New York, 1964.

c. Biographies

Archibald	Raymond Clare Archibald. *Carlyle's First Love: Margaret Gordon Lady Bannerman.* London, 1910.
Campbell	Ian Campbell. *Thomas Carlyle.* New York, 1974.
Froude	James Anthony Froude. *Thomas Carlyle: A History of the First Forty Years of His Life, 1795–1835; A History of His Life in London, 1834–1881.* 4 vols. London, 1882, 1884.
Hanson	Lawrence and Elizabeth Hanson. *Necessary Evil, The Life of Jane Welsh Carlyle.* New York, 1952.
Origo	Iris Origo. *A Measure of Love.* London, 1957.
Shepherd	Richard Herne Shepherd. *Memoirs of the Life and Writings of Thomas Carlyle.* 2 vols. London, 1881.
Wilson	David Alec Wilson and David Wilson MacArthur. *Carlyle.* 6 vols. London, 1923–1934.

d. Memoirs

Allingham	William Allingham. *A Diary.* Edited by Helen Allingham and D. Radford. London, 1907.
Conway	Moncure Conway. *Autobiography: Memories and Experiences.* 2 vols. Boston, 1904.
Duffy	Charles Gavin Duffy. *Conversations and Correspondence with Carlyle.* New York, 1892.

Espinasse — Francis Espinasse. *Literary Recollections and Sketches.* London, 1893.

Masson — David Masson. *Edinburgh Sketches and Memories.* Edinburgh, 1908.

Tyndall — John Tyndall. *New Fragments.* London, 1892.

e. Modern Collections

Clubbe — *Carlyle and His Contemporaries: Essays in Honor of Charles Richard Sanders.* Edited by John Clubbe. Durham, N.C., 1976.

Fielding — *Carlyle Past and Present.* Edited by K. J. Fielding and Rodger Tarr. London, 1976.

Sanders — Charles Richard Sanders. *Carlyle's Friendships and Other Studies.* Durham, N.C., 1977.

Siegel — *Thomas Carlyle: The Critical Heritage.* Edited by Jules Paul Siegel. New York, 1971.

Notes

In addition to the short titles and abbreviations indicated above, I have used some additional short titles in the notes. In such cases, the title is presented in full in the first reference to the work. For the sake of brevity, I have not used the abbreviation for page or pages. In citing both manuscript and published letters I have always provided the names of the correspondents and the date, to the extent ascertainable.

Chapter 1. The Pursuer

1. *CL* 3, 378. TC's notes (1868) to JWC/TC, 9/2/1825.
2. *Rem*, 21, 7.
3. *Two Rem*, 29–30.
4. *Rem*, 29.
5. Wilson 1, 18.
6. *Rem*, 26.
7. *CE LDP*, 313.
8. *CE CME* 5, 174.
9. Marjorie P. King, " 'Illudo Chartis': An Initial Study in Carlyle's Mode of Composition," *Modern Language Review* 49 (1954), 167.
10. *Rem*, 31.
11. *Rem*, 31; T. C. Smout, *A History of the Scottish People, 1560–1830* (London, 1969), 308.
12. Allingham, 289.
13. *Rem*, 28.
14. *CE FR* 1, 145.
15. Espinasse, 262.
16. *Rem*, 15–16.
17. *Rem*, 25.
18. *Rem*, 19.
19. *Rem*, 9; Conway, 88–89.
20. Conway, 88.
21. John Owen, *The Confessions of Faith* (London, 1676), chapter 15, sec. 4, 67.
22. John Owen, *The Grace and Duty of Being Spiritual Minded* (London, 1681), 349, 344, and *The Nature, Power, Deceit, and Prevelance of In-Dwelling Sin in Believers* (London, 1675), 120, 119, 123; *CE FR* 1, 183; *Notebooks*, 243. See *Works*, ed. T. Russell, 28 vols. (London, 1826).
23. *Two Rem*, 29–30.
24. *Last Words*, 13–15.
25. NLS. MC/TC, 7/19/1840.
26. *CL* 7, 105. TC/JAC, 2/25/1834.
27. *CL* 7, 60. TC/JAC, 12/24/1833.
28. NLS. JAC/TC, 2/20/1819.
29. Marrs, 556. TC/AC, 5/26/1843.

30. *Two Rem,* 30.
31. *Last Words,* 16–17.
32. *Last Words,* 16.
33. *Last Words,* 17.
34. Campbell, 5.
35. Moncure Conway, *Thomas Carlyle* (New York, 1881), 30; Conway, 2, 94–95; Wilson 1, 66.
36. Allingham, 247.
37. *Rem,* 30.
38. Marrs, 49. TC/AC, 12/5/1820.
39. *CL* 5, 120. TC's note, n.d., to TC/JAC, 6/29/1830.
40. *Rem,* 30.
41. Masson, 282.
42. *Rem,* 30.
43. *Rem,* 309.
44. *Rem,* 309.
45. Masson, 229; Campbell, 16.
46. *CE SR,* 88.
47. *Last Words,* 20.
48. *CE SR,* 88. Here and elsewhere I draw gingerly on the exaggerated accounts in *SR* of Carlyle's experiences at the University of Edinburgh. They are distorted accounts, to be taken with a grain of salt, but the only accounts available.
49. *CE SR,* 88.
50. *Last Words,* 21.
51. *Last Words,* 21–22.
52. *Rem,* 30.
53. Allingham, 253.
54. *Last Words,* 23.
55. *CL* 1, 3–4. TC/Thomas Murray, 6/24/1813, and editors' note.
56. Allingham, 219–220.
57. Carlisle Moore, "Carlyle: Mathematics and 'Mathesis,' " in Fielding, 64.
58. Fielding, 65.
59. *Two Rem,* 34.
60. *Last Words,* 22.
61. *Two Rem,* 33.
62. Conway 2, 90.
63. Swift, *Gulliver's Travels,* 2, 6.
64. *Two Rem,* 36.
65. *CL,* 1, 18. Thomas Murray/TC, 7/27/1814.
66. *CL* 1, 22. TC/Thomas Murray, 8/24/1814.
67. Wilson 1, 94.
68. *CL* 1, 58. TC/Thomas Murray, 8/22/1815.
69. *CL* 1, 63. Thomas Murray/TC, 12/8/1815.
70. *CL* 1, 32. TC/Robert Mitchell, 10/24/1814.
71. *CL* 1, 32. TC/Robert Mitchell, 10/24/1814.
72. *CL* 1, 48. TC/Robert Mitchell, 5/24/1815.
73. *CL* 1, 13–15. TC/Thomas Murray, 5/18/1814.
74. *CL* 1, 26. TC/Robert Mitchell, 10/18/1814.
75. For a brief discussion of Carlyle's student sermons, see G. B. Tennyson, *Sartor Called Resartus* (Princeton, 1965), 18–19, 332.
76. Wilson 1, 107–108.
77. *CL* 1, 36. TC/Robert Mitchell, 1/11/1815.
78. *Cl* 1, 30. TC/Robert Mitchell, 10/18/1814.
79. *CL* 1, 46. TC/Robert Mitchell, 5/24/1815.
80. *CL* 1, 52. TC/Thomas Murray, 6/21/1815.
81. *CL* 1, 55. TC/Thomas Murray, 6/21/1815.
82. *CL* 1, 52. TC/Thomas Murray, 6/21/1815.
83. *CL* 1, 54. TC/Thomas Murray, 6/21/1815.
84. *CL* 1, 61. TC/Thomas Murray, 11/28/1815.
85. Wilson 1, 71.
86. *CL* 1, 20–21.
87. *CL* 1, 20. Thomas Murray/TC, 6/27/1814; *CL* 1, 20–21. TC/Thomas Murray, 8/24/1814. Wilson 1, 93.
88. *CL* 1, 8–9, particularly editors' note 7, which quotes the *Dumfries Courier* of 2/15/1814, 3/15/1814, 3/8/1814, and 3/29/1814.
89. *CL* 1, 59. TC/Thomas Murray, 8/22/1815.
90. *CL* 1, 60. TC/Thomas Murray, 8/22/1815.
91. *CL* 1, 60. TC/Thomas Murray, 8/22/1815.

92. *CL* 1, 66. TC/Robert Mitchell, 12/11/1815.
93. *CL* 1, 69–71. TC/Robert Mitchell, 2/15/1816.
94. *Rem,* 183–184.
95. *Last Words,* 22.
96. *Last Words,* 23.
97. *CL* 1, 84. TC/Robert Mitchell, 8/3/1816.
98. *CL* 1, 78. TC/Robert Mitchell, 7/15/1816.
99. *CL* 1, 80. TC/Robert Mitchell, 7/15/1816.
100. *CL* 1, 68. TC/Robert Mitchell, 12/11/1815.

Chapter 2. The Heroic Self

1. *Rem,* 181–182.
2. *Rem,* 185; NLS. A. Christison/TC, 5/16/1816.
3. NLS. Kirkcaldy Town Minutes, 1816.
4. NLS. John Martin/TC, 6/14/1816.
5. *CL* 1, 81. TC/Robert Mitchell, 7/15/1816.
6. *Rem,* 185.
7. NLS. Kirkcaldy Town Minutes, 1816.
8. *Rem,* 10.
9. Wilson 1, 132.
10. Wilson 1, 139–140; NLS. JAC/TC, 9/16/1817.
11. NLS. JAC/TC, 9/16/1817.
12. *CL* 1, 93. TC/MC, 3/17/1817.
13. Wilson 1, 132, 139–141.
14. NLS. James Carlyle/TC, 2/20/1819.
15. NLS. JAC/AC, 1/7/1824.
16. *CL* 1, 88. TC/James Johnston, 12/10/1816.
17. *CL* 1, 89. TC/James Johnston, 12/10/1816.
18. *CL* 1, 125. TC/James Johnston, 4/30/1818.
19. *Last Words,* 29.
20. *Two Rem,* 38.
21. *Two Rem,* 38.
22. *Last Words,* 27.
23. *Cl* 1, 97. TC/Robert Mitchell, 3/31/1817; *Rem,* 193.
24. *CL* 1, 94. TC/MC, 3/17/1817.
25. *CL* 1, 103. TC/Robert Mitchell, 7/5/1817.
26. *CL* 1, 99. TC/Robert Mitchell, 3/31/1817.
27. *Rem,* 187–188.
28. *Rem,* 188–189.
29. *Rem,* 197.
30. *Rem,* 198.
31. *Rem,* 201.
32. Wilson 1, 139; *Rem,* 30.
33. *Rem,* 30.
34. *CL* 1, 112. TC/Robert Mitchell, 11/19/1817; *CL* 1, 127. TC/Robert Mitchell, 5/25/1818.
35. *CL* 1, 109–110. TC James Johnston, 9/25/1817; *Rem,* 9.
36. *CL* 1, 112. TC/Robert Mitchell, 11/19/1817.
37. *CL* 1, 42. TC/Robert Mitchell, 3/25/1815.
38. *CL* 1, 113. TC/Robert Mitchell, 11/19/1817.
39. *CL* 1, 128. TC/Robert Mitchell, 5/25/1818.
40. *CL* 1, 135. TC/Thomas Murray, 7/28/1818.
41. *CL* 1, 135–136. TC/Thomas Murray, 7/28/1818.
42. *CL* 1, 132. TC/James Johnston, 6/26/1818.
43. *CL* 1, 140. TC/JC, 9/2/1818.
44. *CL* 1, 176. TC/Thomas Murray, 4/14/1819.
45. *CL* 1, 141, TC/JC, 9/2/1818.
46. *CL* 1, 143. TC/Robert Mitchell, 11/6/1818.
47. *CL* 1, 149. TC/Robert Mitchell, 11/27/1818.
48. *CL* 1, 153. TC/MC, 12/17/1818; *CL* 1, 158. TC/James Johnston, 1/8/1819.
49. *CL* 1, 153. TC/MC, 12/17/1818.
50. *CL* 1, 161. TC/Robert Mitchell, 2/15/1819.
51. *CL* 1, 109. TC/James Johnston, 9/25/1817.
52. *CL* 1, 160. TC/Robert Mitchell, 2/15/1819.
53. *CL* 1, 174. TC/MC, 3/29/1819.
54. *CL* 1, 157. TC/James Johnston, 1/8/1819.

55. *CL* 1, 144. TC/Robert Mitchell, 11/6/1818.
56. *CL* 1, 158. TC/James Johnston, 1/8/1819.
57. *CL* 1, 217. Edward Irving/TC, 12/28/1819.
58. *Rem,* 205.
59. *CL* 1, 159. TC/James Johnston, 1/8/1819.
60. Archibald, 81.
61. *Rem,* 205
62. Archibald, 72–73.
63. Archibald, 75.
64. Archibald, 75–77.
65. Archibald, 68.
66. *CL* 1, 276. TC/ William Graham, 9/15/1820.
67. *CL* 1, 176–177. TC/Thomas Murray, 4/14/1819.
68. *CL* 1, 148. TC/Robert Mitchell, 11/27/1818.
69. *CL* 1, 177. TC/Thomas Murray, 4/14/1819.
70. *CL* 1, 182. TC/John Furgusson, 6/29/1819; *CL* 1, 190. TC/Robert Mitchell, 7/14/1819; *CL* 1, 192. TC/ John Fergusson, 8/25/1819.
71. *CL* 1, 183–184. TC/John Fergusson, 6/29/1819.
72. *CL* 1, 185. TC/John Fergusson, 6/29/1819.
73. *CL* 1, 193. TC/John Fergusson, 8/25/1819.
74. *Rem,* 208–209.
75. *CL* 1, 207–208. TC/Robert Mitchell, 11/18/1819.
76. *CL* 1, 226. TC/MC, 1/26/1820.
77. *CL* 1, 231–232. TC/Robert Mitchell, 3/18/1820.
78. *CL* 1, 252. TC/Matthew Allen, 5/19/1820.
79. *CL* 1, 252. TC/Matthew Allen, 5/19/1820.
80. *CL* 1, 251. TC/Matthew Allen, 5/19/1820.
81. *Rem,* 206.
82. *CL* 1, 231. TC/Robert Mitchell, 3/18/1820.
83. *CL* 1, 217. TC/Robert Mitchell, 12/30/1819.
84. Campbell, 40–41; *Rem,* 316.
85. *CL* 1, 223. TC/AC, 1/26/1820.
86. *Rem,* 316.
87. *CL* 1, 223. TC/AC, 1/26/1820.
88. *CL* 1, 229. TC/AC, 3/1/1820. See Tennyson, *Sartor Called Resartus* (Princeton, 1965), 25–32, for a discussion of these articles.
89. *CL* 1, 231. TC/Robert Mitchell, 3/18/1820; *CL* 1, 245. TC/James Johnston, 5/6/1820; Froude 1, 79. TC/JAC, 2/?/1820.
90. *Rem,* 214–215.
91. *Rem,* 225.
92. *Rem,* 226.
93. *CL* 1, 293. TC/MC, 12/6/1820; *CL* 1, 375. TC/MC, 6/21/1821.
94. *CL* 1, 293. TC/MC, 12/6/1820.
95. *CL* 1, 286. TC/John Fergusson, 10/22/1820.
96. *CL* 1, 318. TC/AC, 1/30/1821.
97. *CL* 1, 291–292. TC/AC, 12/5/1820; *CL* 1, 319. TC/AC, 1/30/1821.
98. Froude 1, 96.
99. Froude 1, 99–100. Irving/TC, 3/15/1821.
100. *CL* 1, 291. TC/AC, 12/5/1820.
101. *CL* 1, 295. TC/JAC, 12/7/1820.
102. *CL* 1, 325. TC/JAC, 2/10/1821.
103. *CL* 1, 327. TC/AC, 2/19/1821.
104. NLS. JAC/TC, 10/7/1823; *CL* 1, 313. TC/JAC, 1/25/1821.
105. *CL* 1, 326. TC/JAC, 1/25/1821.
106. *CL* 1, 330. TC/JC, 2/25/1821.

Chapter 3. The Phoenix

1. *CL* 1, 329–330. TC/James Carlyle, 2/25/1821; *CL* 1, 334. TC/MC, 3/2/1821; *CL* 1, 336–337. TC/AC, 3/6/1821.
2. *CL* 1, 316. TC/William Graham, 1/28/1821.
3. *CL* 1, 196. TC/John Fergusson, 9/25/1821.
4. *CL* 1, 268. TC/Thomas Murray, 8/24/1820.
5. *CE FG* 1, 325.
6. *CL* 1, 255. TC/Edward Irving, 6/3/1820.

7. *CL* 1, 255. TC/Edward Irving, 6/3/1820.
8. A. A. Adrian, "Dean Stanley's Report of Conversations with Carlyle," *Victorian Studies* 1, 1(1957), 74.
9. *CL* 1, 293. TC/MC, 12/6/1820.
10. *CL* 1, 255. TC/Edward Irving, 6/3/1820.
11. *CL* 1, 258. TC/John Fergusson, 6/3/1820.
12. *CL* 1, 224. TC/JAC, 1/26/1820.
13. Froude 1, 86. Edward Irving/TC, 4/15/1820; *Rem, 212.*
14. *CL* 1, 230. TC/AC, 3/1/1820.
15. *Rem,* 31.
16. *CL* 1, 230. TC/AC, 3/1/1820.
17. *CL* 1, 300. TC/AC, 1/2/1820 [1821].
18. *CL* 1, 304. TC/JAC, 1/9/1821.
19. *CL* 1, 297. TC/AC, 12/23/1820.
20. *CL* 1, 303. TC/JAC, 1/9/1821.
21. *CL* 1, 302. TC/AC, 1/2/1820 [1821].
22. *CL* 1, 342. TC/AC, 3/14/1821.
23. *CL* 1, 344. TC/Robert Mitchell, 3/16/1821.
24. *CL* 1, 349. TC/Robert Mitchell, 4/4/1821.
25. *CL* 1, 349. TC/Robert Mitchell, 4/4/1821.
26. *CL* 1, 356. TC/William Graham, 4/24/1821.
27. *CL* 1, 365. TC/William Graham, 6/12/1821; Froude 1, 100. Edward Irving/TC, 3/15/1821.
28. *Rem,* 98–99.
29. Froude 1, 129.
30. *CL* 2, 303. JWC/Eliza Stodart, 3/8/[1823].
31. *Rem,* 224.
32. *CL* 1, 362. TC/AC, 6/6/1821.
33. *CL* 1, 363. TC/AC, 6/6/1821; *CL* 1, 365. TC/William Graham, 6/12/1821.
34. *CL* 1, 361. TC/JWC, 6/4/1821.
35. *CL* 1, 361. TC/JWC, 6/4/1821.
36. *CL* 1, 360. TC/JWC, 6/4/1821.
37. *Cl* 1, 366–369. JWC/TC [late June 1821]; TC/JWC, 6/28/1821; TC/JWC, 7/16/1821.
38. *CL* 1, 370. JWC/TC, 7/18/1820.
39. *CL* 2, 17. JWC/Eliza Stodart [January 1822].
40. *CL* 1, 382. TC/JWC, 9/1/1821.
41. *CL* 1, 382–383. TC/JWC, 9/1/1821.
42. Hanson, 11, 17; *Rem,* 41, 52.
43. *CL* 3, 356–357. JWC/TC, 7/24/1825.
44. *CL* 3, 357. JWC/TC, 7/24/1825.
45. Hanson, 28.
46. *CL* 1, 201. JWC/Elizabeth Welsh, 10/5/1819.
47. *CL* 1, 380. TC/Edward Irving, 8/14/1821.
48. Froude 1, 134. Edward Irving/TC, 7/24/1821.
49. *CL* 1, 380. TC/Edward Irving, 8/14/1821.
50. *CL* 2, 38. JWC/Eliza Stodart, 2/12/1822.
51. *CL* 1, 420. JWC/TC, 12/29/1821.
52. *CL* 1, 420. JWC/TC, 12/29/1821.
53. *CL* 1, 421. JWC/TC, 12/29/1821.
54. *CL* 2, 21. JWC/TC, 1/17/1822.
55. *CL* 1, 389. TC/John Fergusson, 10/4/1821.
56. *CL* 1, 416–417. TC/AC, 12/25/1821.
57. *Rem,* 32.
58. *CL* 1, 394. TC/MC, 11/16/1821.
59. *CL* 1, 415. TC/AC, 12/19/1821.
60. *CL* 2, 64. Edward Irving/TC, n.d.
61. *CL* 1, 379. TC/Edward Irving, 8/14/1821.
62. *Rem,* 231.
63. *Rem,* 232.
64. *Rem,* 232.
65. *CL* 2, 7. TC/MC, 1/12/1822.
66. *CL* 2, 4. TC/James Carlyle, 1/12/1822.
67. *CL* 2, 14–15. TC/JWC, 1/14/1822.
68. *CL* 2, 20. JWC/TC, 1/17/1822.
69. Froude 1, 159. Edward Irving/JWC, 9/9/1822.
70. *Rem,* 234.
71. *Rem,* 235.
72. *CL* 2, 40. TC/JWC, 2/13/1822.
73. *CL* 2, 40. TC/JWC, 2/13/1822.
74. *CL* 2, 52. JWC/TC, 3/3/1822.
75. *CL* 2, 104. TC/JWC, 4/30/1822.
76. *CL* 2, 72. TC/David Hope, 3/23/1822.
77. *CL* 2, 138–139. TC/AC, 6/29/1822.
78. *CL* 2, 140. TC/AC, 6/29/1822.
79. *CL* 2, 107. TC/James Johnston, 4/30/1822.
80. *CL* 2, 30. TC/James Johnston, 2/4/1822.

81. *CL* 2, 70. TC/William Graham, 3/23/1822.
82. *CL* 2, 94. TC/AC, 4/27/1822; *Notebooks*, 27.
83. *CF SR*, 95–106; *CL* 2, 155. TC/JWC, 8/1/1822.
84. *CE SR*, 98.
85. *CE SR*, 99.
86. *CE SR*, 132.
87. *CE SR*, 135.
88. *CL* 2, 156. TC/JWC, 8/12/1822.
89. *CL* 2, 167. JWC/TC, 9/24/1822.
90. *CL* 2, 191. TC/William Graham, 10/30/1822; *CL* 2, 203. TC/MC, 11/14/1822.
91. *CL* 2, 196. JWC/TC, 11/11/1822.
92. *CL* 2, 219. TC/MC, 12/4/1822.
93. *CL* 2, 229–230. TC/JWC, 12/16/1822.
94. *CL* 2, 290. TC/JWC, 2/18/1823.
95. *CL* 2, 317. JWC/Eliza Stodart, 3/30/1823.
96. *CE Schiller*, 105–107; *Two Rem*, 52.
97. *CL* 2, 356. TC/JWC, 5/11/1823.
98. *CL* 2, 336. TC/MC, 4/16/1823.
99. *CL* 2, 342. TC/William Graham, 4/24/1823.
100. *CL* 2, 361. TC/AC, 5/24/1823.
101. *CL* 2, 381. TC/Thomas Murray, 6/17/1823.
102. *CL* 2, 368. TC/James Johnston, 6/3/1823; *Two Rem*, 52.
103. *CL* 2, 447. TC/JWC, 10/12/1823.
104. *CL* 2, 450. JWC/TC, 10/14/1823.
105. *CL* 2, 456. TC/JAC, 10/20/1823.
106. *CL* 2, 456. TC/JAC, 10/20/1823.
107. *CL* 2, 459–461. TC/JWC, 10/22/1823.
108. *CL* 2, 458. TC/JWC, 10/22/1823.
109. *CL* 2, 459. TC/JWC, 10/23/1823.
110. *CL* 2, 470. JWC/TC, 11/12/1823.
111. *CL* 2, 471. JWC/TC, 11/12/1823.
112. *CL* 2, 471. TC/JWC, 11/13/1823.
113. *CL* 2, 492. TC/MC, 12/23/1823.
114. *CL* 2, 492–493. TC/MC, 12/23/1823.
115. *CL* 3, 7. TC/George Boyd, 1/8/1824.
116. *Notebooks*, 55–56.
117. *Notebooks*, 56–58.
118. *CL* 2, 481. JWC/TC, 11/26/1823.
119. *CL* 3, 13. TC/AC, 1/13/1824.
120. Froude 1, 190; *CL* 3, 67. TC/JWC, 5/19/1824.
121. *CL* 3, 75. TC/JWC, 6/5/1824.
122. *CL* 3, 79. JWC/TC, 6/10/1824.

Chapter 4. "Society's Brazen Doors"

1. *CL* 3, 80. TC/MC, 6/10/1824.
2. *CL* 3, 79–82. TC/MC, 6/10/1824; *CL* 3, 82–84. TC/JWC, 6/23/1824.
3. *CL* 3, 89. TC/JAC, 6/24/1824.
4. *CL* 3, 84. TC/JWC, 6/23/1824.
5. *Rem*, 243.
6. C. R. Sanders, *The Strachey Family* (Durham, N.C., 1953), 121.
7. *Rem*, 246.
8. *CE SR*, 113, 116. See George Strachey, "Carlyle and the 'Rose-Goddess,'" *Nineteenth Century* 32 (1892), 470–486.
9. *Rem*, 248–251.
10. *CL* 3, 93. TC/AC, 6/25/1824.
11. *CL* 3, 93–94. TC/AC, 6/25/1824.
12. NLS. JAC/TC, 7/26/1824.
13. *CL* 3, 94. TC/AC, 6/25/1824.
14. *CL* 3, 94. TC/AC, 6/25/1824.
15. *CL* 3, 90. TC/JAC, 6/24/1824.
16. *CL* 3, 90. TC/JAC, 6/24/1824.
17. *CL* 3, 91. TC/JAC, 6/24/1824.
18. *CL* 3, 91. TC/JAC, 6/24/1824.
19. A. L. Drummond, *Edward Irving and His Circle* (London, n.d.), 66.
20. *CE S*, 53–54.
21. *CL* 3, 91. TC/JAC, 6/24/1824.
22. *CL* 3, 90. TC/JAC, 6/24/1824.
23. *CE S*, 56.
24. *CE S*, 57.
25. *CE S*, 61.
26. *CE S*, 58.
27. *CL* 3, 139. TC/Thomas Murray, 8/24/1824; *CL* 3, 233. TC/JWC, 12/20/1824; *CL* 3, 280. TC/JAC, 2/10/1825; *CL* 3, 199. TC/JWC, 11/15/1824; *CL* 3, 261. TC/JAC, 1/22/1825; *CL* 7, 249. TC/John Bradfute, 7/29/1834.
28. *CL* 3, 87. TC/Goethe, 6/24/1824.
29. *CL* 3, 88. TC/JAC, 6/24/1824.
30. *CL* 3, 86. TC/JWC, 6/23/1824.
31. *CL* 3, 88. TC/JAC, 6/24/1824.
32. *CL* 3, 100–101. TC/MC, 7/2/1824.
33. *CL* 3, 104. TC/MC, 7/6/1824.

34. *CL* 3, 104–105. TC/MC, 7/6/1824.
35. *CL* 3, 105. TC/MC, 7/6/1824.
36. Thomas A. Kirby, "Carlyle and Irving," *ELH* 13 (March 1946), 62.
37. *CL* 3, 94–95. TC/AC, 6/25/1824; *CL* 3, 106. TC/MC, 7/6/1824.
38. *CL* 3, 106. TC/MC, 7/6/1824.
39. *CL* 3, 115. TC/JWC, 7/24/1824; *CL* 3, 124. TC/AC, 8/11/1824; *CL* 3, 135. TC/JWC, 8/12/1824; *CL* 3, 143. TC/MC, 8/29/1824.
40. *CL* 3, 146. TC/JWC, 9/2/1824.
41. *CL* 3, 140, 142–143. TC/MC, 8/29/1824.
42. *CL* 3, 146. TC/JWC, 9/2/1824.
43. *CL* 3, 155. TC/JAC, 9/18/1824.
44. *Rem,* 262.
45. *CL* 3, 168–169. TC/James Carlyle, 10/4/1824; *CL* 3, 138. TC/Thomas Murray, 8/24/1824.
46. *CL* 3, 138. TC/Thomas Murray, 8/24/1824.
47. *CL* 3, 157. TC/JAC, 9/18/1824.
48. *CL* 3, 121. TC/JAC, 8/10/1824.
49. *CL* 3, 125–126. TC/AC, 8/11/1824.
50. *CL* 3, 156–157. TC/JAC, 9/18/1824; *Rem,* 264.
51. *CL* 3, 156. TC/JAC, 9/18/1824.
52. *CL* 3, 148. TC/JWC, 9/2/1824.
53. *CL* 3, 166. TC/James Carlyle, 10/4/1824.
54. *CL* 3, 169. TC/James Carlyle, 10/4/1824.
55. *CL* 3, 172. TC/JWC, 10/5/1824.
56. *CL* 3, 172. TC/JWC, 10/5/1824; *CL* 3, 178. JWC/TC, 10/14/1824.
57. *CL* 3, 171. TC/JWC, 10/5/1824.
58. *CL* 3, 171. TC/JWC, 10/5/1824.
59. *CL* 3, 171. TC/JWC, 10/5/1824.
60. Elizabeth Mercer, "Carlyle and the 'Blumine' of *Sartor Resartus,*" *Westminster Review* 142 (1894), 164–165, quoted by Sanders, 126; *CL* 3, 150. JWC/TC, 9/17/1824.
61. *CL* 3, 173. TC/JWC, 10/5/1824.
62. *CL* 3, 175. JWC/TC, 10/14/1824.
63. *CL* 3, 179. TC/JWC, 10/28/1824.
64. *Rem,* 268.
65. *Rem,* 268–269. For a later, caustically anti-French account of his 1824 visit, see William Knighton, "Conversations with Carlyle," *Contemporary Review* (June 1881), 904–920, 911.
66. *CL* 3, 180. TC/JWC, 10/28/1824; Knighton, 912.
67. *CL* 3, 181. TC/JWC, 10/28/1824.
68. *CL* 3, 186. TC/JAC, 11/7/1824.
69. *CL* 3, 180. TC/JWC, 10/28/1824.
70. *Rem,* 271–272.
71. *Rem,* 272; *CL* 3, 187. TC/JAC, 11/7/1824.
72. *CL* 3, 188. TC/JAC, 11/7/1824.
73. *Rem,* 271.
74. *CL* 3, 187. TC/JAC, 11/7/1824.
75. *Notebooks,* 98.
76. *CL* 3, 185. TC/JAC, 11/7/1824.
77. *CL* 3, 219. TC/AC, 12/14/1824.
78. *CL* 3, 213. TC/JWC, 12/4/1824; *CL* 3, 240. TC/AC, 1/8/1825.
79. *Rem,* 274.
80. *CL* 3, 233–234. TC/JWC, 12/20/1824.
81. *CL* 3, 240. TC/AC, 1/8/1825.
82. *CL* 3, 272. TC/JWC, 1/31/1825; NLS. JAC/TC, 1/25/1825.
83. *CL* 3, 244. TC/JWC, 1/9/1825.
84. *CL* 3, 246. TC/JWC, 1/9/1825.
85. *CL* 3, 231. JWC/TC, 12/19/1824.
86. *CL* 3, 244. TC/JWC, 1/9/1825.
87. *CL* 3, 247. TC/JWC, 1/9/1825; *CL* 3, 249. JWC/TC, 1/13/1825.
88. *CL* 3, 250. JWC/TC, 1/13/1825.
89. *CL* 3, 245. TC/JWC, 1/9/1825.
90. *CL* 3, 264. JWC/TC, 1/29/1825.
91. *CL* 3, 266. JWC/TC, 1/29/1825.
92. *CL* 3, 281. JWC/TC, 2/14/1825.
93. *CL* 3, 277–278. TC/JAC, 2/10/1825.
94. *CL* 3, 291–292. TC/AC, 3/4/1825, and 292n; NLS. JAC/TC, 4/25/1825.
95. *CL* 3, 293. TC/AC, 3/4/1825.
96. *CL* 3, 289. TC/JWC, 2/28/1825.
97. *CL* 3, 302. TC/JAC, 3/21/1825.
98. *CL* 3, 330. TC/JWC, 5/22/1825.
99. *CL* 3, 307. TC/JWC, 3/23/1825.
100. *CL* 3, 399. TC/James Johnston, 10/26/1825.
101. *CL* 3, 349. TC/Anna D. B. Montagu, 7/18/1825.
102. *CL* 3, 347. TC/JWC, 7/4/1825.
103. *CL* 3, 349. TC/Anna D. B. Montagu, 7/18/1825.
104. *CL* 3, 427. TC/JWC, 12/11/1825.

105. *CL* 3, 407. TC/JWC, 11/4/1825.
106. *Rem,* 282; *CL* 3, 378–379. TC's notes to JWC/TC, 9/2/1825.
107. *CL* 3, 379. TC's notes to JWC/TC, 9/2/1825.
108. *CL* 3, 343. JWC/TC, 7/3/1825; *CL* 3, 378. TC's notes to JWC/TC, 9/2/1825.
109. *Rem,* 281.
110. *Rem,* 282.
111. *Rem,* 282.
112. *Rem,* 282.
113. *CL* 3, 356. Anna D. B. Montagu/JWC, 7/20/1825.
114. *CL* 3, 357. JWC/TC, 7/24/1825.
115. *CL* 3, 357. TC/JWC, 7/29/1825.
116. *CL* 3, 360. TC/JWC, 7/29/1825.
117. *CL* 3, 359. TC/JWC, 7/29/1825.
118. *CL* 3, 361. JWC/TC, 8/4/1825.
119. *CL* 4, 59–60. JWC/TC, 3/16/1826.
120. *CL* 4, 47. JWC/TC, 3/4/1826.
121. *CL* 4, 60. JWC/TC, 3/16/1826.
122. *CL* 4, 35. TC/JWC, 2/5/1826.
123. *CL* 4, 70. TC/JWC, 4/2/1826.
124. *CL* 4, 69. TC/JWC, 4/2/1826.
125. *CL* 4, 94. TC/JWC, 5/13 and 16/1826.
126. *CL* 4, 94. TC/JWC, 5/13 and 16/1826.
127. *CL* 4, 93. TC/JWC, 5/13 and 16/1826.
128. *CL* 4, 72–73. Grace Welsh/TC, 4/10/1826.
129. *CL* 4, 143. TC's notes to JWC/George Welsh, 10/1/1826.
130. *CL* 4, 150–151. TC/JWC, 10/9/1826.
131. *CL* 4, 153. TC/MC, 10/19/1826.

Chapter 5. "Jenny Spinner"

1. *CL* 4, 152. TC/MC, 10/19/1824.
2. *CL* 4, 153. TC/MC, 10/19/1826.
3. *CL* 4, 153. TC/MC, 10/19/1826.
4. *CL* 4, 154. TC/JAC, 10/24/1826.
5. *CL* 4, 53. TC/JWC, 3/7/1826; *CL* 4, 213. JWC/TC, 4/16/1827; *CL* 4, 217. TC/JWC and Grace Welsh, 4/19/1827; *CL* 4, 438. JWC/TC, 12/30/1828.
6. *CL* 4, 152. TC/MC, 10/19/1826.
7. *CL* 4, 155. TC/JAC, 10/24/1826.
8. *CL* 4, 154–155. TC/JAC, 10/24/1826.
9. *CL* 4, 155. TC/JAC, 10/24/1826.
10. *CL* 4, 155. TC/JAC, 10/24/1826.
11. *CL* 4, 155. TC/JAC, 10/24/1826.
12. *CL* 4, 157. TC/MC, 11/16/1826.
13. *CL* 4, 156. TC/MC, 11/16/1826.
14. *CL* 4, 155. TC/JAC, 10/24/1826.
15. *CL* 4, 156–157. TC/MC, 11/16/1826.
16. *CL* 4, 159. TC and JWC/MC, 11/16/1826.
17. *Notebooks,* 67.
18. *Notebooks,* 81.
19. *Notebooks,* 81–82.
20. *CL* 4, 164. TC/MC, 12/9/1826.
21. *CL* 4, 172. TC/Anna D. B. Montagu, 12/25/1826.
22. *CL* 4, 177. TC/AC, 1/1/1827.
23. *CL* 4, 167–168. TC and JWC/MC, 12/9/1826.
25. *CL* 4, 181. TC/MC, 1/2/1827.
26. *Notebooks,* 78–81.
27. *CL* 4, 166. TC/MC, 12/9/1826.
28. *CL* 4, 173. TC/Anna D. B. Montagu, 12/25/1826.
29. *CL* 4, 184. TC/AC, 2/3/1827.
30. *CL* 4, 180. TC/MC, 1/2/1827.
31. *CL* 4, 191. JWC and TC/MC, 2/17/1827.
32. *CL* 4, 200. TC/AC, 3/29/1827; *CL* 4, 193. TC/Hunt and Clarke, 3/16/1827.
33. *CL* 4, 222–223. TC/AC, 5/10/1827; *CL* 4, 228. TC/JAC, 6/4/1827.
34. *CL* 4, 231. TC and JWC/JAC, 6/4/1827.
35. *Last Words,* 148.
36. *CL* 4, 196. TC/James Carlyle, 3/?/1827.
37. *CL* 4, 200. TC/AC, 3/29/1827.
38. *CL* 4, 198. TC/AC, 3/29/1827.
39. *CL* 4, 214. Grace Welsh/TC ?/1827.
40. *CL* 4, 218. TC/Grace Welsh and JWC, 4/19/1827.
41. *Rem,* 317; *Two Rem,* 53.
42. *CL* 4, 24. TC/Thomas Murray, 8/24/1814.
43. *CL* 4, 190. JWC and TC/MC, 2/17/1827.
44. *Rem,* 317.
45. *CL* 4, 190. JWC and TC/MC, 2/17/1827.

46. *CL* 4, 190. JWC and TC/MC, 2/17/1827.
47. *CL* 4, 222. JWC and TC/Anna D. B. Montagu, 5/7/1827.
48. *Rem,* 317.
49. *CL* 4, 228. TC/JAC, 6/4/1827.
50. *CL* 4, 252. JWC/Anna D. B. Montagu, 9/2/1827.
51. *CL* 4, 228. TC/JAC, 6/4/1827.
52. *CE CME* 1, 20. "John Paul Richter."
53. *CE CME* 1, 21.
54. *CL* 4, 230. TC/JAC, 6/4/1827.
55. *CE CME* 1, 7.
56. *CE CME* 1, 25.
57. *Rem,* 319.
58. *Rem,* 320.
59. *Rem,* 320.
60. *Rem,* 368.
61. *Rem,* 370.
62. *Rem,* 370.
63. *CL* 4, 238. TC/JAC, 7/?/1827, and 238n1.
64. *Rem,* 377.
65. *Rem,* 380.
66. *CL* 4, 291. TC/JAC, 11/29/1827; *Rem,* 265.
67. *CL* 4, 291. TC/JAC, 11/29/1827.
68. *CL* 4, 282. TC/Anna D. B. Montagu, 11/20/1827; *CL* 4, 291. TC/JAC, 11/29/1827.
69. *CL* 4, 249. TC/JAC, 8/27/1827.
70. *Notebooks,* 114.
71. *CL* 4, 250. JWC/Anna D. B. Montagu, 9/2/1827.
72. *CL* 4, 251. JWC/Anna D. B. Montagu, 9/2/1827.
73. *CL* 4, 256. TC/AC, 9/11/1827.
74. *CL* 4, 256. Henry Duncan/TC, 9/13 and 9/19/1827.
75. Wilson 2, 30. Jeffrey/TC, 9/6/1827.
76. *CE CME* 1, 72–73. "State of German Literature."
77. *CL* 4, 270. TC/JAC, 10/25/1827.
78. *CL* 4, 296. TC/David Hope, 12/12/1827.
79. *CL* 4, 290. TC/JAC, 11/29/1827.
80. *CE CME* 1, 210. "Goethe."
81. *CL* 4, 318. TC/JAC, 2/1/1828.
82. *CL* 4, 376. TC/Thomas Murray, 5/31/1828.
83. *CL* 4, 301. TC/Goethe, 1/17/1828.
84. *CL* 4, 314. TC/AC, 1/29/1828.
85. *CL* 4, 325*n*6. Goethe, 3/14/1827.
86. *CL* 4, 324. TC/AC, 2/19/1828; Wilson, 2, 42. Jeffrey/TC, 12/24/1827.
87. *CL* 4, 337–338. TC/JAC, 3/7/1828.
88. *CL* 4, 355. TC/AC, 4/15/1828.
89. *CL* 4, 369, 371. TC/MC, 4/20/1828.
90. *CL* 4, 359. TC/JAC, 4/16/1828.

Chapter 6. "My Wild Moorland Home"

1. *Two Rem,* 65.
2. Wilson, 2, 63. Jeffrey/TC, 9(?)/?/1828.
3. Wilson, 2, 62. Jeffrey/JWC, 8/23/1828.
4. *CL* 4, 385. JWC/Eliza Stodart, 7/28/1828.
5. *CL* 4, 399. TC/JAC, 8/25/1828.
6. *CL* 4, 417. JWC/Eliza Stodart, 11/21/1828.
7. *CL* 4, 414–415. TC/JAC, 10/10(?)/1828.
8. *Rem,* 23–24.
9. *CL* 4, 381. TC/JAC, 6/10/1828.
10. *CL* 4, 416. TC and JWC/JAC, 10/10(?)/1828.
11. NLS. JAC/JWC, 12/16/1828; JAC/MC, 10/19/1828.
12. *CL* 4, 419–420. TC/JAC, 11/26/1828.
13. *Notebooks,* 161.
14. *CL* 4, 427–428. TC/Eckermann, 12/9/1828.
15. *Rem,* 324.
16. Wilson 2, 65–66. Jeffrey/TC, 9/22/1828.
17. *CL* 4, 413–414. TC/JAC, 10/10(?)/1828.
18. *CL* 4, 428. TC/Eckermann, 12/9/1828.
19. *CL* 4, 421. TC/JAC, 11/26/1828.
20. *CL* 4, 433. TC/Thomas De Quincey, 12/11/1828.
21. *CL* 4, 433. TC/Thomas De Quincey, 12/11/1828.
22. *CL* 4, 437–438. JWC/TC, 12/30/1828; *CL* 5, 11. TC/JAC, 3/5/1829.
23. *CL* 5, 6. Jeffrey/TC, 1/4/1829.

24. *CE CME* 2, 75, 79.
25. *CE CME* 2, 80.
26. *CL* 5, 81. TC/JAC, 3/19/1830, and 81n14.
27. *CL* 4, 382. TC/JAC, 6/10/1828.
28. Wilson 2, 99.
29. *CL* 4, 400. TC/JAC, 8/25/1828, and 400n17.
30. *Rem*, 286.
31. *CL* 5, 20. TC/JAC, 8/11/1829.
32. *Rem*, 328.
33. *Rem*, 328.
34. *CL* 5, 30. JWC/Eliza Stodart, 11/11/1829.
35. *CL* 5, 70. JWC/Eliza Stodart, 2/5/1830.
36. *CL* 5, 52. TC/An Editor, 1/1830.
37. *CL* 5, 66. TC/MAC, 1/29/1830; *CL* 5, 71. TC/JAC, 2/11/1830.
38. *CL* 5, 24. Anna D. B. Montgu/JWC, 7/3/1829.
39. *CL* 5, 111. TC/MC, 6/4 or 11/1830; *CL* 5, 116–117. TC/JAC, 6/29/1830.
40. *Notebooks*, 157.
41. *CL* 5, 120. TC's note to TC/JAC, 6/29/1830.
42. *CL* 5, 121. TC/JAC, 7/14/1830.
43. *CL* 5, 98. TC/JAC, 5/1/1830.
44. *Notebooks*, 136.
45. Wilson 2, 116. Jeffrey/TC, 11/3/1829.
46. Wilson 2, 138. Jeffrey/TC, 3/9/1830.
47. *Notebooks*, 155.
48. *CL* 4, 408. TC/Goethe, 9/25/1828.
49. *CL* 5, 91. TC/JAC, 4/10/1830.
50. *CL* 5, 102. TC/G. R. Gleig, 5/21/1830.
51. *CL* 5, 109. TC/Anna D. B. Montagu, 6/3/1830.
52. *CL* 5, 153. TC/Goethe, 8/31/1830.
53. *CL* 5, 153. TC/Goethe, 8/31/1830.
54. *Notebooks*, 171.
55. *CL* 5, 145–146. TC/JAC, 8/21/1830.
56. *CL* 5, 136. TC/Gustave D'Eichthal, 8/9/1830.
57. *CL* 5, 136–137. TC/Gustave D'Eichthal, 8/9/1830.
58. *CL* 5, 278. TC/Gustave D'Eichthal, 5/17/1831.
59. Wilson 2, 186. Jeffrey/TC, 11/13/1830.
60. *CL* 5, 144–145. TC/JAC, 8/21/1830.
61. *CL* 5, 145. TC/JAC, 8/21/1830.
62. *CL* 5, 145. TC/JAC, 8/21/1830.
63. *Notebooks*, 179.
64. *CL* 5, 204. TC/JAC, 12/19/1830.
65. *CL* 5, 175. TC/JAC, 10/19/1830.
66. *CL* 5, 184. TC/Anna D. B. Montagu, 10/27/1830.
67. *CL* 5, 184–185. TC/Anna D. B. Montagu, 10/27/1830.
68. *CL* 5, 175. TC/JAC, 10/19/1830; *CL* 5, 185. TC/Anna D. B. Montagu, 10/27/1830.
69. *Notebooks*, 100; *CL* 5, 212. TC/Macvey Napier, 1/20/1831.
70. *CL* 5, 213. TC/JAC, 1/21/1831.
71. *CL* 5, 215, 217. TC/JAC, 1/21/1831.
72. *CL* 5, 229. JAC/TC, 1/10/1831; *CL* 5, 233. JAC/TC, 2/12/1831.
73. *CL* 5, 233. JAC/TC, 2/12/1831.
74. *CL* 5, 233–234. JAC/TC, 2/12/1831.
75. *CL* 5, 247. TC/MC, 3/15/1831.
76. *CL* 5, 248. JAC/TC, 3/10/1831.
77. *CL* 5, 250. TC/JAC, 3/17/1831.
78. *CL* 5, 258. TC/MC, 3/29/1831.
79. *CL* 5, 275. TC/MC, 5/17/1831.
80. *CL* 5, 283. TC/JAC, 6/6/1831.
81. *CL* 5, 297–98. TC/JAC, 7/7/1831.
82. *CL* 5, 305. TC/JAC, 7/17/1831.
83. *CL* 5, 309. TC/MC, 7/19/1831; *CL* 5, 312. JWC/TC, 8/6–9/1831.
84. *Notebooks*, 192.
85. *CL* 5, 90. TC/JAC, 4/10/1830.
86. *CL* 5, 318–319. TC/JWC, 8/11/1831.
87. *Notebooks*, 194.
88. *CL* 5, 310. Macvey Napier/TC, 7/28/1831.
89. *CL* 5, 327. TC/Goethe, 8/13/1831.
90. *CL* 5, 339. TC/JWC, 8/17/1831.
91. *CL* 5, 341. TC/JWC, 8/17/1831.
92. *CL* 5, 353. TC/JWC, 8/22/1831.
93. *CL* 5, 353. TC/JWC, 8/22/1831.
94. *CL* 5, 354. TC/JWC, 8/22/1831.
95. *CL* 5, 354. TC/JWC, 8/22/1831.
96. *CL* 5, 362. TC/JWC, 8/24/1831.
97. *CL* 5, 376. TC/JWC, 8/29/1831.
98. *CL* 5, 343. TC/AC, 8/18/1831, and 343n2.
99. *CL* 5, 399. TC/JWC, 9/4/1831.
100. *CL* 5, 403–404. TC/John Murray, 9/6/1831.

101. *CL* 5, 429. TC/JWC, 9/14/1831.
102. *CL* 5, 417. TC/JWC, 9/11/1831.
103. *CL* 5, 417–418. TC/JWC, 9/11/1831.
104. *CL* 5, 442. TC/John Murray, 9/19/1831.
105. *CL* 5, 444. TC/JWC, 9/23/1831.
106. *CL* 5, 446. TC/John Murray, 9/24/1831.
107. *CL* 5, 444. TC/JWC, 9/23/1831.
108. *CL* 5, 447. TC/John Murray, 9/24/1831.
109. *CL* 6, 6. John Murray/TC, 10/6/1831, and 6n1.
110. *CL* 6, 9. JWC and TC/MC, 10/6/1831.
111. *CL* 6, 17. TC/AC, 10/15/1831.

Chapter 7. London Doubts

1. *Notebooks,* 32.
2. *CL* 5, 286. TC/Goethe, 6/10/1831.
3. *Rem,* 13.
4. *CE CME* 2, 377. "Death of Goethe."
5. *CE CME* 1, 203. "Goethe."
6. *CE CME* 1, 67–68. "State of German Literature."
7. *CL* 4, 354. TC/Walter Scott, 4/13/1828.
8. *Notebooks,* 214–215.
9. *CL* 5, 305–308. Fifteen English Friends to the Poet Goethe, 7/17/1831; *CL* 5, 325, 327. TC/Goethe, 8/13/1831.
10. *CE CME* 3, 41. "Characteristics."
11. Morgan. JAC/TC, 6/29/1831.
12. *CL* 6, 65. TC/James Carlyle, 12/13/1831; *CL* 5, 323. JWC/TC, 8/11–14/1831.
13. *CL* 5, 437. TC/MC, 9/19/1831.
14. *CL* 6, 25. TC/MC, 10/20/1831.
15. *Notebooks,* 197; *CL* 5, 379. TC/JWC, 8/29/1831.
16. *Notebooks,* 197.
17. *CL* 5, 379. TC/JWC, 8/29/1831.
18. Morgan. JAC/TC, 12/27/1834.
19. *CL* 6, 24–25. TC/MC, 10/20/1831.
20. *CL* 6, 25. TC/MC, 10/20/1831.
21. *CL* 6, 25. TC/MC, 10/20/1831.
22. *CL* 5, 375. TC/JWC, 8/29/1831; *Notebooks,* 217–218.
23. *Notebooks,* 218–219.
24. *Notebooks,* 199.
25. *CL* 5, 362–363. TC/JWC, 8/24/1831.
26. *Notebooks,* 205–206.
27. *Notebooks,* 208–209.
28. *CL* 5, 369. TC/MC, 8/26/1831.
29. *CL* 5, 382. TC/JWC, 8/30/1831.
30. *CL* 5, 423. JWC/TC, 9/11/1831.
31. *CL* 5, 423. JWC/TC, 9/11/1831.
32. Marrs, 516. TC/AC, 3/21/1841.
33. *CL* 5, 364. TC/JWC, 8/24/1831; *Notebooks,* 200.
34. *CL* 5, 413. TC/JWC, 9/11/1831.
35. *CL* 5, 349. TC/JWC, 8/22/1831.
36. *CL* 5, 349. TC/JWC, 8/22/1831.
37. *CL* 5, 433. TC/JWC, 9/14/1831.
38. *CL* 6, 8. JWC and TC/MC, 10/6/1831.
39. *CL* 6, 10. JWC and TC/MC, 10/6/1831.
40. *CL* 6, 8. Anna D. B. Montagu/JWC, 9/30/1831.
41. *CL* 6, 36. JWC/Helen Welsh, 10/26/1831; *CL* 6, 44. JWC/MC, 11/1831.
42. *CL* 5, 398. TC/JWC, 9/4/1831.
43. *CL* 5, 387. TC/JWC, 8/30/1831.
44. *CL* 5, 398. TC/JWC, 9/14/1831.
45. Mineka 1, 85–86. JSM/JS, 10/20–22/1831.
46. *Notebooks,* 205.
47. *CL* 6, 47. TC/JAC, 11/13/1831.
48. *CL* 6, 65. TC/James Carlyle, 12/13/1831.
49. *CL* 6, 126. TC/JAC, 2/16/1832.
50. *CL* 6, 24. TC/MC, 10/20/1831.
51. *CL* 6, 33. TC/JAC, 10/21/1831.
52. *CL* 6, 57. TC/AC, 11/24/1831.
53. *CL* 6, 32. TC/JAC, 10/21/1831.
54. *CL* 6, 13. TC/Macvey Napier, 10/8/1831.
55. *CL* 6, 12. TC/Macvey Napier, 10/8/1831.
56. *CL* 6, 13. TC/Macvey Napier, 10/8/1831.
57. *CL* 6, 58. TC/Macvey Napier, 11/26/1831.
58. *CL* 6, 62. TC/AC, 12/4/1831.
59. *CL* 6, 58. TC/Macvey Napier, 11/26/1831; *CL* 6, 85. TC/JAC, 1/10/1832.

60. *CL* 6, 52. TC/JAC, 11/13/1831.
61. *CL* 6, 52. TC/JAC, 11/13/1831.
62. *CE CME* 3, 1–2. "Characteristics."
63. *CE CME* 3, 10.
64. *CE CME* 3, 27.
65. *CE CME* 3, 3–5
66. *CE CME* 3, 27.
67. *CE CME* 3, 28.
68. *CE CME* 3, 37, 41.
69. *CE CME* 3, 40.
70. *CE CME* 3, 23, 43.
71. *CL* 6, 79. TC/JC, 12/25/1831.
72. *CL* 6, 92. TC/AC, 1/14/1832.
73. *CL* 6, 72. TC/JAC, 12/20/1831.
74. *CE CME* 3, 55–56.
75. *CL* 6, 96. TC/MC, 1/22/1832.
76. *CL* 6, 95, 98. TC/MC, 1/22/1832.
77. *CL* 6, 114–115. TC/James Carlyle the Younger, 1/30/1832.
78. *CL* 6, 103. TC/MC, 1/24/1832.
79. *CL* 6, 103. TC/MC, 1/24/1832.
80. NLS. JAC/TC, 2/20/1832.
81. NLS. JAC/MC, 3/29/1832.
82. *Rem,* 19.
83. *Rem,* 1.

Chapter 8. "My China Row Chelsea"

1. *CL* 6, 134. TC/AC, 2/19/1832.
2. *CL* 6, 141. TC/James Carlyle, 3/23/1832.
3. *CL* 6, 131. TC/MC, 2/18/1832.
4. *Notebooks,* 246.
5. *CL* 6, 132. TC/MC, 2/18/1832.
6. *CL* 6, 131. TC/MC, 2/18/1832.
7. *Notebooks,* 257.
8. *NLM* 1, 35. TC's note (1868) to JWC/MC, 10/6/1831.
9. *CL* 6, 143. TC/AC, 4/7/1832; *CL* 6, 146. TC/Macvey Napier, 4/8/1832.
10. Froude 2, 280.
11. *CL* 6, 182–183. TC/JAC, 7/2/1832.
12. *CL* 6, 171. JWC/Eliza Miles, 6/16/1832.
13. Froude 2, 284.
14. *CL* 6, 270. TC/JAC, 12/2/1832.
15. *CL* 6, 210. JSM/TC, 7/7/1832.
16. *CL* 6, 265. TC/Leigh Hunt, 11/20/1832.
17. *CL* 6, 236. JWC/Eliza Stodart, 10/10/1832.
18. Froude 2, 308–309.
19. Froude 2, 310.
20. *CL* 6, 235. JWC/Eliza Stodart, 10/10/1832.
21. *CL* 6, 242. TC/JSM, 10/16/1832.
22. *CL* 6, 288. TC/JAC, 1/8/1833.
23. *CL* 6, 290. TC/JAC, 1/8/1833.
24. *CL* 6, 372. TC/JSM, 4/18/1833.
25. *CL* 6, 373. TC/JSM, 4/18/1833.
26. Froude 2, 329.
27. *Rem,* 384.
28. Wilson 2, 318.
29. *CL* 6, 366. TC/JAC, 3/29/1833.
30. *CL* 6, 346. TC/MC, 3/16/1833.
31. Froude 2, 330.
32. Froude 2, 338–339.
33. *CL* 6, 393. JWC/Eliza Stodart, 5/24/1833.
34. Froude 2, 353.
35. Froude 2, 370–371.*CL* 7, 7. TC/JAC, 10/1/1833.
36. Froude 2, 372.
37. Froude 2, 356–357; Ralph Waldo Emerson, *English Traits,* in *Works* 2 (Boston, 1903–1904), 165.
38. *CL* 6, 438. TC/JSM, 9/10/1833.
39. *CL* 6, 446–449. TC/JSM, 9/24/1833.
40. *CL* 7, 83–84. TC/Sarah Austin, 1/21/1834.
41. *CL* 7, 83. TC/Sarah Austin, 1/21/1834.
42. *CL* 7, 280. TC/AC, 8/28/1834.
43. *CL* 7, 101. TC/JSM, 2/22/1834.
44. *CL* 7, 104. TC/JAC, 2/25/1834.
45. *CL* 7, 103. TC/JAC, 2/25/1834.
46. *CL* 7, 105. TC/JAC, 2/25/1834.
47. Froude 2, 407–408.
48. *CL* 7, 221. TC/AC, 6/27/1834.
49. *Rem,* 68.
50. *CL* 7, 60. TC/JAC, 12/24/1833.
51. *CL* 7, 124. TC/JAC, 3/27/1834.
52. *CL* 7, 112. TC/John Welsh, 3/4/1834.
53. *CL* 7, 209. TC/MC, 6/12/1834.
54. *CL* 7, 211. TC/MC, 6/12/1834.
55. Froude 2, 468.
56. *CL* 6, 414. TC/JSM, 7/18/1833.
57. *CL* 6, 414. TC/JSM, 7/18/1833.
58. *CE FR* 1, 6.
59. *CE FR* 2, 38.

60. *CL* 7, 25. TC/JSM, 10/28/1833.
61. *CL* 7, 81. TC/JAC, 1/21/1834.
62. *CL* 7, 23. TC/JSM, 10/28/1833.
63. *CL* 7, 54. TC/JSM, 12/17/1833.
64. *CL* 7, 55. TC/JSM, 12/17/1833.
65. *CE FR* 3, 322–323.

Chapter 9. Fire and Friends

1. *Pilgrim* 1, 380. Charles Dickens/Daniel Maclise, 2/24/1838, and n2.
2. NLS. TC/MC, 2/11/1840.
3. *CL* 7, 269. TC/JAC, 8/15/1834.
4. *CL* 7, 269. TC/JAC, 8/15/1834.
5. *CL* 7, 269. TC/JAC, 8/15/1834.
6. NLS. TC/JC, 1/28/1835.
7. *CL* 7, 272. TC/JAC, 8/15/1834.
8. *CL* 7, 78. TC/JAC, 1/21/1834.
9. *CL* 7, 273. TC/JAC, 8/15/1834.
10. *CL* 7, 322. TC/MC, 10/25/1834.
11. *CL* 7, 340–341. TC's note (1868) to JWC/MC, 11/21/1834.
12. *Graham,* 72; *CL* 8, 5. TC/William Graham, 1/10/1835.
13. *CL* 7, 344. TC/David Hope, 12/19/1834.
14. Froude 3, 18.
15. *CL* 7, 305. TC/JAC, 9/21/1834.
16. Huntington, HM 7244. TC/JAC, 3/23/1835; *CL* 8, 177–178.
17. *CL* 7, 307. TC/JAC, 9/21/1834.
18. *CL* 7, 269–270. TC/JAC, 8/15/1834.
19. *CL* 7, 285. TC/MC, 9/1/1834.
20. *CL* 7, 306. TC/JAC, 9/21/1834.
21. *CL* 7, 317–318. TC/JC, 10/24/1834.
22. *CL* 7, 323. JAC/TC, 10/4/1834.
23. Graham, 73; *CL* 8, 5. TC/William Graham, 1/10/1835.
24. Graham, 73. *CL* 8, 5. TC/William Graham, 1/10/1835.
25. NLS. TC/MC, 2/17/1835; *CL* 8, 55.
26. Duffy, 167.
27. Duffy, 168.
28. Huntington, HM 7244. TC/JAC, 3/23/1835; *CL* 8, 75–76.
29. NLS. TC/Harriet Mill, 5/17/1873.
30. NLS. Harriet Mill/TC, 5/15/1873.
31. NLS. MC/TC, 4/13/1835.
32. Froude 3, 28.
33. Froude 3, 28.
34. Huntington, HM 7244. TC/JAC, 3/23/1835; *CL* 8, 76.
35. Mineka 1, 253. JSM/TC, 3/7/1835, 3/10/1835.
36. NLS. TC/JAC, 4/30/1835; *CL 8, 103.*
37. NLS. JC/TC, 4/4/1835; *LM,* 1, 10.
38. Slater, 135. TC/RWE, 6/27/1835.
39. NLS. TC/MC, 4/20/1835; *CL* 8, 96.
40. NLS. TC/JAC, 6/15/1835; *CL* 8, 147.
41. NLS. TC/MC, 7/1/1835; *CL* 8, 164; NLS. TC/MC, 7/19/1835; *CL* 8, 177–178.
42. NLS. TC/MC, 9/9/1835; *CL* 8, 200.
43. Graham, 75–76; *CL* 8, 215. TC/William Graham, 9/25/1835.
44. *CL* 8, 279. TC/MC, 12/24/1835.
45. *NL* 1, 3. TC/JAC, 3/31/1836.
46. *NL* 1, 37. TC/JS, 10/3/1836.
47. *NL* 1, 40. TC/MC, 11/20/1836.
48. *NL* 1, 50. TC/JS, 1/17/1837.
49. Slater, 166. TC/RWE, 6/1/1837.
50. NLS. TC/JAC, 7/6/1838; Marrs, 426. TC/MC, 5/27/1837.
51. Froude 3, 110. TC/JS, 7/28/1837.
52. Marrs, 379. TC/AC, 2/29/1835.
53. *Rem,* 348; Huntington, HM 7244. TC/JAC, 3/23/1835; *CL* 8, 80.
54. *Rem,* 347–348.
55. *Rem,* 354.
56. *Rem,* 356.
57. Huntington, HM 7244. TC/JAC, 3/23/1835; *CL* 8, 81.
58. Slater, 133; Froude 3, 31; *CL* 8, 80–81. TC/JAC, 3/23/1835.
59. Froude 3, 31; *CL* 8, 80–81. TC/JAC, 3/23/1835.
60. Huntington, HM 7244. TC/JAC, 3/23/1835; *CL* 8, 81.
61. Froude 3, 31–32. *CL* 8, 80–81. TC/JAC, 3/23/1835; *CL* 8, 87–88. TC/JSM, 3/27/1835; *CL* 8, 123–124. TC/RWE, 5/13/1835.
62. *Rem,* 359.
63. *Rem,* 360–361, 364.
64. Espinasse, 213.
65. NLS. TC/MC, 4/20/1835; *CL* 8, 97–99.
66. Froude 3, 74; *CL* 9, 20. TC/JWC, 7/24/1836.
67. *CE S,* 105, 262.
68. *CE S,* 106.

69. *CE S*, 95.
70. NLS. TC/MC, 6/4/1835; *CL* 8, 130.
71. Slater, 146. TC/RWE, 4/29/1836.
72. NLS. TC/MC, 6/4/1835. *CL* 8, 130.
73. *MSB*, 245–247. TC/JS, 8/4/1841.
74. *CL* 7, 53n6.
75. Hanson, 212. JWC/Susan Hunter, 9/12/1836; *CL* 9, 56–57, 9/11/1836.
76. *MSB*, 125–126. TC/JSM, 5/2/1836.
77. *Rem*, 76.
78. *Rem*, 76.
79. See F. W. Hilles, "The Hero as Revolutionary: Godefroy Cavaignac," Clubbe, 74–90.
80. *NL* 1, 12–13. TC/JAC, 6/?/1836; *CL* 8, 362. TC/JAC, 6/25/1836.
81. *CL* 9, 88. TC/MC, 11/20/1836.
82. Joseph Slater, "George Ripley and Thomas Carlyle," *PMLA* 67 (1952), 346.
83. *CL* 9, 102. TC/JAC, 12/2/1836.
84. *CL* 9, 102. TC/JAC, 12/2/1836.
85. *Rem*, 117–118.
86. Slater, "Ripley," 343–344.
87. Slater, 110. RWE/TC, 11/20/1834.
88. Slater, 117. TC/RWE, 2/3/1835.
89. Marrs, 389. TC/AC, 6/31/1835.
90. *CL* 8, 288. TC/JAC, 1/26/1836.
91. Slater, 18.
92. Slater, 238–239. TC/RWE, 6/24/1839.
93. *NL* 1, 145–146. TC/MC, 12/29/1838.
94. "Carlyle's Unpublished Letters to Miss Wilson," *The Nineteenth Century* 89 (May 1921), 808. TC/Jane Wilson, 5/1/1840.
95. Slater, 183. TC/RWE, 3/16/1838.
96. Slater, 277. RWE/TC, 8/30/1840.
97. NLS. TC/JC, 3/27/1839.
98. Copeland, 70. TC/JCH, 1/19/1837.
99. Froude, 3, 70.
100. Froude 3, 70.
101. NLS. TC/MC, 1/22/1837; *CL* 9, 125.
102. Slater, 151. TC/RWE, 11/5/1836.
103. *MSB*, 167. TC/JSM, 3/23/1839.
104. *LM* 1, 50. JWC/JS, 2/1/1837.
105. *CE S*, 103.
106. Marrs, 396. TC/AC, 2/18/1836.
107. NLS. TC/MC, 3/22/1836; *CL* 8, 322.
108. *MSB*, 46. TC/JSM, 4/18/1833; *CL* 6, 369.
109. *MSB*, 173. TC/JSM, 2/24/1841.
110. *NL* 1, 38. TC/JS, 10/3/1836; *CL* 9, 68.
111. *LM* 1, 95. JWC/Mrs. Sterling, 1/8/1841.
112. *LM* 1, 96. JWC/Mrs. Sterling, 1/8/1841.
113. Graham, 77; *CL* 8, 215. TC/William Graham, 9/25/1835.
114. Slater, 241. TC/RWE, 6/24/1839.
115. NLS. TC/MC, 5/1/1840.
116. *NL* 1, 63. TC/JAC, 3/21/1837; *NL* 1, 67. TC/MC, 3/27/1837; *NL* 1, 71. TC/JAC, 4/23/1837; *LM* 1, 49. JWC/JS, 2/1/1837; *CL* 9, 176, 178, 190, 133.
117. *NL* 1, 71. TC/JAC, 1/23/1837; *CL* 9, 191.
118. *LM* 1, 78. JWC/TC, 9/10/1838.
119. NLS. TC/JAC, 6/29/1836; *CL* 8, 363.
120. Slater, 188. TC/RWE, 6/15/1838.
121. Froude 3, 111. TC/JWC, 7/22/1837; *CL* 9, 259.

Chapter 10. A Public Man

1. *NL* 1, 48. TC/JC, 12/29/1836; *CL* 9, 110.
2. *NL* 1, 40–41. TC/MC, 11/20/1836; *CL* 9, 87.
3. Copeland, 71. TC/JCH, 1/19/1837.
4. NLS. TC/MC, 2/18/1837; *CL* 9, 153–154.
5. Marrs, 418. TC/AC, 3/5/1837.
6. Calder, 39.
7. R. P. Karkaria, *Carlyle's Unpublished Lectures . . . On The History of Literature* (Bombay and London, 1892), ix.
8. *Times* May 9, 1837; Berg. TC/James Fraser, 5/2/1837; *CL* 9, 201–202.
9. Berg. TC/James Fraser, 5/2/1837; *CL* 9, 202.
10. NLS. MC/TC, 5/23/1837.
11. "Mr. Thomas Carlyle's Lectures," *Spectator*, May 6, 1837, 422.
12. *Spectator*, 422.
13. Froude 3, 120.
14. *MSB*, 201. TC/JS, 6/9/1837; *CL* 9, 226.
15. Siegel, 52, 67–68.

16. *CL* 9, 288. TC/JAC, 8/12/1837.
17. *CL* 9, 271. JWC/TC, 8/3/1837.
18. *CL* 9, 293. TC/JWC, 8/18/1837.
19. *NLM* 1, 67. JWC/TC, 8/29/1837; *CL* 9, 302.
20. *NL* 1, 94. TC/MC, 10/9/1837; *CL* 9, 328.
21. *NL* 1, 91. JWC/MC, 9/21/1837; *CL* 9, 316–317. 9/22/1837.
22. NLS. TC/MC, 12/7/1837; *CL* 9, 357.
23. NLS. TC/JAC, 12/3/1840; Trinity. TC/MM, 11/19/1841.
24. *NL* 1, 87. TC/JAC, 9/21/1837; *CL* 9, 311.
25. NLS. TC/MC, 12/23/1837; *CL* 9, 375; NLS. TC/MC, 11/9/1837; *CL* 9, 347.
26. NLS. TC/MC, 3/30/1838.
27. *NL* 1, 107. TC/AC, 1/10/1838.
28. NLS. TC/MC, 1/21/1838; NLS. TC/MC, 2/15/1838.
29. NLS. TC/MC, 2/15/1838.
30. Graham, 78. TC/William Graham, 5/10/1838.
31. *NLM* 1, 68. JWC/JC, 5/1/1838.
32. Graham, 79. TC/William Graham, 5/10/1838. Karkaria, ix.
33. Karkaria, x.
34. *NL* 1, 126. TC/AC, 5/10/1838.
35. Karkaria, x.
36. *The Examiner,* May 6, 1838, 278.
37. *NL* 1, 121. TC/JC, 5/1/1838.
38. *NL* 1, 131. TC/JC, 7/6/1838.
39. Slater, 222–223. TC/RWE, 4/13/1839.
40. *MSB,* 215. TC/JS, 12/7/1838.
41. Slater, 198. TC/RWE, 11/7/1838.
42. Slater, 233–234. RWE/TC, 5/15/1839.
43. *NLM* 1, 79. JWC/Grace Welsh, 5/17/1839.
44. NLS. TC/JC, 5/27/1839.
45. *MSB,* 223. TC/JS, 9/29/1839; *NLM* 1, 83–85. JWC/TC, 8/19/1839.
46. Slater, 249. TC/RWE, 9/4/1839.
47. NLS. TC/MC, 3/17/1840.
48. *NL* 1, 155. TC/MC, 3/8/1839.
49. *NL* 1, 155. TC/MC, 3/8/1839.
50. NLS. TC/JC, 5/27/1839.
51. Trinity. TC/MM, 7/13/1838.
52. *NL* 1, 167. TC/JAC, 6/20/1839.
53. Trinity. TC/MM, 4/?/1841(?).
54. Trinity. TC/MM, 7/19/1841.
55. NLS. TC/JAC, 11/9/1840. For Carlyle's own attempts to write poetry, see G. B. Tennyson, "Carlyle's Poetry to 1840," *Victorian Poetry* 1 (1962), 161–181.
56. Allingham, 240.
57. Browning, 222.
58. *NL* 1, 225. TC/JS, 1/12/1841.
59. Browning, 461.
60. Browning, 462.
61. Slater, 363. TC/RWE, 8/5/1844.
62. Sanders, 195.
63. Slater, 552–553. TC/RWE, 1/27/1867.
64. Sanders, 208.
65. *MSB,* 250. TC/JS, 10/31/1841.
66. Edgar Johnson, *Charles Dickens, His Tragedy and Triumph* (New York, 1952) 2, 799.
67. *MSB,* 155. TC/JSM, 7/18/1837; *CL* 9, 256.
68. *MSB,* 206–207. TC/JS, 7/28/1837; *CL* 9, 268.
69. John Forster, *Life of Charles Dickens* (1872) 1, 109.
70. Froude 1, 177–178. TC/JAC, 3/17/1840.
71. *MSB,* 240. TC/JS, 12/7/1840.
72. NLS. TC/MC, 6/16/1841.
73. V & A. TC/JF, 8/26/1870.
74. *MSB,* 223; TC/JS, 9/29/1839; NLS. TC/JAC, 9/13/1839.
75. *NL* 1, 168. TC/JAC, 7/27/1839.
76. Ray. TC/F. D. Maurice, n.d. (1840?).
77. Morgan. TC/W. D. Christie, spring 1840.
78. *Two Rem,* 98–99.
79. Marrs, 495. TC/AC, 5/12/1840.
80. NLS. TC/MC, 5/9/1840.
81. *NL* 1, 195. TC/AC, 5/12/1840.
82. Berg. TC/Chapman, 5/14/1840.
83. NLS. TC/MC, 5/20/1840.
84. *NL* 1, 194. TC/Thomas Ballantyne, 5/11/1840; *NL* 1, 196. TC/JC, 6/15/1840.
85. *NL* 1, 197. TC/JC, 6/15/1840.
86. Slater, 273. TC/RWE, 7/2/1840.
87. Ray. TC/Julius Hare, 8/1/1840.
88. *NL* 1, 207–208. TC/JC, 8/25/1840.

89. NLS. TC/MC, 9/12/1840; Marrs, 504. TC/AC, 9/10/1840.
90. Trinity. TC/MM, 9/14/1840.
91. *NL* 1, 220–221. TC/JAC, 10/29/1840.
92. *MSB*, 173. TC/JSM, 10/7/1840.
93. NLS. TC/MC, 11/14/1840.
94. Marrs, 508. TC/AC, 11/18/1840.
95. NLS. TC/MC, 1/21/1841.
96. V & A. TC/JF, 1/11/1841.
97. *MSB*, 243. TC/JS, 3/2/1841.
98. Slater, 293. TC/RWE, 5/8/1841.
99. Marrs, 515. TC/AC, 3/21/1841.
100. Miss Wilson, 809. TC/Jane Wilson, 3/10/1841.
101. Marrs, 512. TC/AC, 1/7/1841.
102. Bliss, 125. TC/JWC, 4/7/1841.
103. NLS. TC/JWC, 4/20/1841.
104. Trinity. TC/JWC, 4/10/1841.
105. *LM* 1, 99. JWC/JS, 4/29/1841.
106. NLS. JWC/JAC, 4/23/1841.
107. NLS. JWC/JAC, 4/23/1841.
108. Slater, 292–293. RWC/TC, 4/30/1841.
109. NLS. JWC/TC (July 1841?).
110. *NL* 1, 236–237. TC/JS, 7/14/1841; Slater, 292–293. RWE/TC, 4/30/1841.
111. NLS. TC/MC, 9/28/1841.
112. NLS. Harriet Martineau/JWC, 7/7/1840 (?).
113. Bliss, 130. TC/JWC, 9/1/1841.
114. Froude 3, 218. TC/JAC, 7/28/1841.
115. Froude 3, 221. TC/JAC, 8/20/1841.
116. NLS. TC/MC, 10/12/1841; NLS. TC/MC, 11/5/1841.
117. Marrs, 531. TC/AC, 12/27/1841.
118. Trinity. TC/MM, 12/2/1841.
119. Trinity. TC/MM, 4/25/1841.

Chapter 11. Revolutions (1)

1. NLS. TC/MC, 3/30/1844.
2. Froude 3, 167. TC/JAC, 9/13/1839.
3. *MSB*, 244. TC/JS, 8/4/1841.
4. Yale. TC/MM, 12/31/1839.
5. NLS. George Hobson (?)/TC, 11/22/1843.
6. London. TC/Victor Marshall, 10/27/1841.
7. *CE CME* 4, 135. *Chartism.*
8. London. TC/Victor Marshall, 12/21/1841.
9. Trinity. TC/MM, 12/2/1841.
10. London. TC/Victor Marshall, 12/7/1841.
11. NLS. TC/JC, 2/21/1842.
12. Yale. TC/Henry Cole, 4/25/1840.
13. G. Mazzini, "The French Revolution," *Monthly Chronicle*, January 1840, 73.
14. Mazzini, 74; Siegel, 257.
15. Mazzini, 74.
16. Siegel, 260.
17. Froude 3, 454.
18. *Rem*, 75.
19. Siegel, 260.
20. Huxley, 34. JWC/JW, 10/22/1842.
21. Susanne H. Nobbe, "Four Unpublished Letters of Thomas Carlyle," *PMLA* 70 (1955), 876–884. TC/GJ, 4/26/1840, 6/15/1840, 10/21/1840, 12/1/1849.
22. Nobbe, 882–883. TC/GJ, 10/21/1840.
23. Nobbe, 884. TC/GJ, 10/21/1840.
24. NLS. TC/JC, n.d. (March 1841?).
25. NLS. JWC/TC, n.d. (4/15/1841?).
26. Ireland, 5–6.
27. Ireland, 15–16. GJ/JWC, 5/6/1841, 6/15/1841.
28. Froude 3, 216. TC/JWC, 7/?/1841.
29. Edinburgh. JWC/Eliz. Aitken, n.d. (1842).
30. Slater, 317. RWE/TC, 2/28/1842.
31. *LM* 1, 105. TC's note (1867?) to JWC/JS, 1 or 2/1842.
32. *LM* 1, 105. TC's note (1867?) to JWC/JS, 1 or 2/1842.
33. NLS. Thomas Erskine/JWC, 9/17/1849.
34. Bliss, 131–132. TC/JWC, 3/1/1842.
35. Edinburgh. JWC/Eliz. Aitken, n.d. (1842?).
36. Trinity. TC/MM, 4/10/1842.
37. NLS. TC/MC, 3/6/1842 (?).
38. *NL* 1, 262–263. TC/J.G. Lockhart, 4/5/1842.
39. Bliss, 143. TC/JWC, 4/14/1842.
40. Bliss, 146–147. TC/JWC, 4/25/1842, 4/27/1842.
41. *NL* 1, 265–266. TC/AC, 7/1/1842.

42. *LM* 1, 110. JWC/Mary Russell, 4/?/1842.
43. Bliss, 145–146. TC/JWC, 4/19/1842.
44. London. TC/Victor Marshall, 11/18/1841.
45. Slater, 325. TC/RWE, 7/19/1842. See also "A Preface by Carlyle and by the Editors," Fielding, 14–23, for a recently discovered fragment by Carlyle on Cromwell and contemporary cultural problems.
46. NLS. TC/MC, 5/6/1842 (?).
47. Trinity. TC/MM, 5/23/1842.
48. Marrs, 539. TC/AC, 7/1/1842.
49. Slater, 328. TC/RWE, 8/29/1842.
50. Yale. TC/ Edwin Chadwick, 8/1/1842.
51. London. TC/Victor Marshall, 12/7/1841.
52. Berg. TC/A. J. Scott, 1/27/1843.
53. Slater, 329–330. TC/RWE, 8/29/1842.
54. Ray. TC/Spring Rice, 8/5/1842.
55. Ray. TC/Spring Rice, 8/5/1842.
56. "Netherlands," 500.
57. "Netherlands," 502, 510, 632.
58. "Netherlands," 633–635.
59. "Netherlands," 639–640.
60. *LM* 1, 126. JWC/TC, 8/20/1842.
61. Bliss, 154. TC/JWC, 8/20/1842.
62. Bliss, 154. TC/JWC, 8/20/1842. It may have been the fragment referred to in note 45.
63. Slater, 328. TC/RWE, 8/29/1842.
64. Bliss, 154. TC/JWC, 8/20/1842.
65. Trinity. TC/MM, 8/17/1842.
66. Huxley, 15. JWC/JW, 9/2/1842.
67. Huxley, 17. JWC/JW, 9/7/1842.
68. *NL* 1, 267–268. TC/JS, 9/6/1842.
69. Copeland, 132–136. TC/MC, 7/7/1842.
70. Huxley, 22. JWC/JW, 9/9/1842.
71. Trinity. TC/FitzGerald, 9/18/1842. On the manuscript, FitzGerald has written, "About middle of September 1842, Wm. Thackeray took me to tea with Carlyle, whom I had not previously known." FitzGerald's error is corrected in *The Letters of Edward FitzGerald,* ed. A. M. and A. B. Terhune (Princeton, 1980), 1, 339–342.
72. Copeland, 141. FitzGerald/Bernard Barton, 9/22/1842.
73. Copeland, 140. FitzGerald/Bernard Barton, 9/22/1842; Copeland, 143. TC/FitzGerald, 9/24/1842.
74. NLS. TC/MC, 9/29/1842.
75. Froude 3, 279.
76. *MSB,* 260. TC/JS, 11/2/1842.
77. Miss Wilson, 810. TC/Jane Wilson, 12/9/1842.
78. Huxley, 63. JWC/JW, 12/8/1842.
79. Marrs, 543. TC/AC, 11/13/1842.
80. Froude 3, 280.
81. Huxley, 79. JWC/JW, 1/9/1843.
82. Berg. TC/A. J. Scott, 1/27/1843.
82. Yale. TC/James Marshall, 2/7/1843.
84. *NL* 1, 281–282. TC/JS, 2/23/1843.
85. Slater, 337. TC/RWE, 3/11/1843.
86. Huxley, 98. JWC/JW, 3/12/1843.
87. Slater, 350. TC/RWE, 10/31/1843.
88. Graham, 83. TC/William Graham, 11/8/43; *NLM* 1, 135. JWC/Mary Russell, 12/30/1843.
89. *NL* 1, 303. TC/JC, 12/26/1843.

Chapter 12. Revolutions (2)

1. Huxley, 57, 66. JWC/JW, 11/?/1842, 12/25/1842.
2. Huxley, 61. JWC/JW, 12/8/1842.
3. Ireland, 38–39. GJ/JWC, 10/29/1841.
4. Huxley, 83. JWC/JW, 1/18/1843.
5. Wilson, 5, 5. TC/HB, 8/9/1842.
6. Huxley, 80–83. JWC/JW, 1/18/1843.
7. Huxley, 97. JWC/JW, 3/12/1843.
8. Huxley, 112–114. JWC/JW, 4/2/1843.
9. Huxley, 120. JWC/JW, 4/18/1843.
10. Huxley, 134–135. JWC/JW, 6/21/1843.
11. Huxley, 128–129. JWC/JW, 5/28/1843.
12. NLS. TC/Spring Rice, 9/30/1843.
13. Huxley, 226. JWC/JW, 10/21/1844.
14. *LM* 1, 202. JWC/John Welsh, 11/28/1843.
15. Huxley, 278. JWC/Helen Welsh, 6/26/1846.
16. Huxley, 189. JWC/JW, 2/15/1844.
17. Huxley, 202. JWC/JW, 5/6/1844.

18. *MSB,* 274. TC/JS, 6/9/1844.
19. Huxley, 206. JWC/JW, 6/?/1844.
20. *LM* 1, 214.
21. *NLM* 1, 142–143. JWC/TC, 7/12/1844; *NLM* 1, 146. 7/15/1844.
22. NLS. TC/JWC, 7/17/1844.
23. Huxley, 209–210. JWC/JW, 7/26/1844.
24. Huxley, 211. JWC/JW, 8/1/1844.
25. NLS. TC/MC, 8/14/1844.
26. Huxley, 222. JWC/JW, 9/12(?)/1844.
27. Huxley, 235. JWC/JW, 2/6/1845, 2/21/1845.
28. Northhampton. TC/HB, 2/20/1845.
29. Huxley, 246–247. JWC/John Welsh, 6/28/1845.
30. Bliss, 210–211. TC/JWC, 8/26/1845; Marrs, 618–620. TC/AC, 8/31/1845.
31. NLS. TC/JWC, 10/8/1845.
32. Northampton. TC/HB, 9/13/1845.
33. Huxley, 278. JWC/Helen Welsh, 6/26/1846.
34. Huxley, 257. JWC/JW, 11/16/1845.
35. *NLM* 1, 177. JWC/TC, 9/28/1845.
36. Huxley, 255–256. JWC/JW, 11/16/1845; NLS. TC/JC, 11/26/1845.
37. Huxley, 256–257. JWC/JW, 11/16/1845.
38. Huxley, 258. JWC/JW, 12/4/1845.
39. Huxley, 259. JWC/JW, 12/4/1845.
40. Northampton. TC/HB, 11/4/1845.
41. NLS. TC/MC, 12/4/1845.
42. Huxley, 264. JWC/JW, 3/5/1846.
43. Huxley, 268. JWC/JW, 3/10/1846.
44. *NLM* 1, 185. JWC/MC, 3/28/1846.
45. Huxley, 274–275. JWC/JW, 5/19/1846.
46. Bliss, 222–223. TC/JWC, 7/6/1846.
47. Bliss, 224. TC/JWC, 7/13/1846.
48. *NLM* 1, 190–191. JWC/TC, 7/6/1846.
49. *LM* 1, 273. JWC/TC, 7/14/1846.
50. NLS. TC/JWC, 7/15/1846.
51. Bliss, 225. JC/JWC, 7/14/1846.
52. Northampton. TC/HB, 7/28/1846.
53. Northampton. TC/HB, 8/9/1846.
54. Huxley, 281. JWC/Helen Welsh, 8/19/1846; *LM* 1, 275. JWC/TC, 8/23/1846.
55. *NLM* 1, 204. JWC/TC, 8/17/1846.
56. Bliss, 233. TC/JWC, 8/20/1846.
57. *NLM* 1, 207. HB/JWC, 8/18/1846.
58. Slater, 399. RWE/TC, 5/14/1846.
59. *NL* 1, 274. TC/JC, 10/17/1842.
60. Huxley, 26. JWC/JW, 10/17/1842.
61. Marrs, 542. TC/AC, 11/13/1842.
62. *NL* 1, 287. TC/MC, 3/24/1843.
63. Froude 3, 339.
64. Slater, 348. TC/RWE, 10/31/1843.
65. Marrs, 551. JAC/AC, 3/22/1843.
66. Marrs, 557. TC/AC, 5/31/1843.
67. NLS. TC/MC, 6/23/1843.
68. Marrs, 555–556. TC/AC, 5/26/1843.
69. Marrs, 565–568. TC/AC, 6/19/1843.
70. Marrs, 571. TC/AC, 6/23/1843.
71. *NL* 1, 277. TC/JAC, 11/2/1842.
72. Marrs, 543. TC/AC, 11/13/1842.
73. Huxley, 315. JWC/JW, 12/23 or 30/1848; Marrs, 668. TC/AC, 12/8?/1848.
74. *MSB,* 268. TC/JS, 5/5/1843.
75. Slater, 357. TC/RWE, 1/31/1844.
76. *MSB,* 272. TC/JS, 6/9/1844.
77. *NL* 1, 318–319. TC/JS, 8/27/1844.
78. *MSB,* 276–277. "To Thomas Carlyle (By John Sterling—four days before his death). September 14th, 1844."
79. Slater, 365–366. TC/RWE, 9/29/1844.
80. Trinity. TC/FitzGerald, 10/26/1844; V & A. TC/JF, n.d. (1844?).
81. *Pilgrim* 4, 33. Dickens/JWC, 1/27/1844.
82. V & A. TC/JF, 6/6/1844.
83. NLS. TC/JWC, 7/4/1844.
84. NLS. TC/? 9/18/1846; NLS. TC/MC, 7/19/1843.
85. Bliss, 178.
86. Slater, 426. RWE/TC, 7/31/1847.
87. Slater, 427. TC/RWE, 8/31/1847.
88. Slater, 427. TC/RWE, 8/31/1847.
89. Slater, 420. RWE/TC, 4/30/1847.
90. Yale. TC/HB, 10/26/1844.
91. Slater, 434. TC/RWE, 11/13/1847.
92. *NL* 2, 58. TC/JC, 3/26/1848.
93. Trinity. TC/MM, 3/10/1848.
94. NLS. TC/JC, 7/19/1848.
95. Froude 3, 440.
96. Bliss, 246. TC/JWC, 7/7/1848.
97. NLS. TC/JC, 7/19/1848.
98. Slater, 443. TC/RWE, 12/6/1848.
99. Froude 3, 423.

100. Calder, 43.
101. See Carlyle's annotated copy of George Bancroft, *History of the Colonization of the United States* (Boston & London, 1837), in the Carlyle House, Chelsea.
102. Froude 4, 46.
103. Froude 3, 258.
104. NLS. TC/MC, 5/31/1844.
105. *NL* 2, 12. TC/Alexander Scott, 12/5/1845.
106. Slater, 391. TC/RWE, 2/3/1846.
107. Yale. TC/John Grey, 6/20/1846.
108. BM. TC/Robert Peel, 6/19/1846.
109. BM. TC/Robert Peel, 6/22/1846.
110. Yale. TC/John Grey, 6/20/1846.
111. Yale. TC/J. C. Symons, 11/28/1848.
112. See Steven Marcus, *Engels, Manchester, and the Working Class* (New York, 1974).
113. Yale. TC/J. C. Symons, 11/28/1848.
114. NLS. TC/MC, 3/14/1847.
115. NLS. TC/MC, 3/22/1848.
116. Slater, 453. TC/RWE, 4/19/1849.
117. *NL* 2, 99. TC/JAC, 7/3/1850.
118. Froude 4, 48.
119. *NL* 2, 46. TC/MC, 8/29/1847.
120. Berg. TC/Bridges Adams, 3/7/1848.
121. Slater, 439. TC/RWE, 2/28/1848; "Louis-Philippe," *Examiner* March 4, 1858. Reprinted in Shepherd 2, 265–369.
122. Yale. TC/Mrs. Rich, 3/24/1848.
123. NLS. TC/JC, 7/19/1848.
124. Froude 3, 454–455.
125. Froude 3, 448.
126. Froude 3, 429.
127. Froude 3, 423; BM. Gladstone Papers. Add Ms. 44776. f. 196.
128. See Carlyle's annotated copy of *Ranthorpe* (London, 1847) in the Carlyle House, Chelsea, and his annotated copy of *Rose, Blanche and Violet* (London, 1848) in the Berg.
129. The manuscript of Carlyle's unpublished essay on "Phallus-worship" is in the Hilles Collection in the Beinecke Library, Yale University. See Fred Kaplan, " 'Phallus-Worship' (1848): An Unpublished Carlylean Response to the Revolution of 1848," *Carlyle Newsletter,* no. 2 (March 1980), 19–23.

Chapter 13. "Fierce Rage"

1. Duffy, 46.
2. *RIJ,* 13.
3. *RIJ,* 16.
4. *RIJ,* 25.
5. *RIJ,* 29.
6. *RIJ,* 39.
7. *CE CME* 4, 138. *Chartism.*
8. NLS. TC/MC, 4/28/1845.
9. NLS. TC/MC, 4/28/1845.
10. Marrs, 637. TC/AC, 10/3/1846.
11. NLS. TC/MC, 6/19/1847.
12. Northampton. TC/HB, 3/24/1847.
13. Marrs, 644. TC/AC, 3/18/1847.
14. NLS. TC/MC, 4/16/1847.
15. Yale. TC/John Grey, 4/17/1847.
16. NLS. TC/MC, 3/8/1847.
17. Marrs, 648. TC/AC, 4/19/1847.
18. Northampton. TC/HB, 10/17/1848.
19. *RIJ,* 51.
20. *RIJ,* 56–57.
21. *RIJ,* 64.
22. *NL* 2, 72. TC/JWC, 7/11/1849.
23. *RIJ,* 103–104.
24. See L. P. Curtis, Jr., *Anglo-Saxons and Celts: A Study of Anti-Irish Prejudice in Victorian England* (Bridgeport, Conn., 1968), and Reginald Horseman, "Origins of Racial Anglo-Saxonism in Great Britain Before 1850," *Journal of the History of Ideas* (1976), 387–410.
25. *RIJ,* 166–167.
26. Trinity. TC/FitzGerald, 7/10/1849.
27. *RIJ,* 122, 188.
28. *RIJ,* 175–176.
29. *RIJ,* 104; Bliss, 250. TC/JWC, 7/17/1849.
30. Duffy, 112–113.
31. Duffy, 100.
32. NL 2, 77–78. TC/JWC, 7/29/1849.
33. Morgan. TC/JWC, 8/4/1849.
34. *RIJ,* 211.
35. Morgan. TC/James C. Cork, 7/17/1849.
36. *RIJ,* 219–220.

37. *RIJ*, 226.
38. *RIJ*, 226.
39. *LM* 1, 331–332. JWC/TC, 7/26/1849 and TC's note (1868) to JWC's narrative.
40. *LM* 1, 336–337. JWC's narrative.
41. *LM* 1, 345. JWC's narrative.
42. *LM* 1, 348. JWC's narrative.
43. *NL* 2, 78. TC/JWC, 7/29/1849.
44. Bliss, 258. TC/JWC, 9/2/1849.
45. NLS. HB/JWC, 9/14/1849.
46. NLS. JWC/JC, 10/6/1849.
47. *LM* 1, 356. JWC/MC, 10/?/1849.
48. NLS. JWC/JC, 10/6/1849.
49. NLS. JWC/TC, 9/21/1849.
50. Yale. TC/Aubrey de Vere, 9/29/1849.
51. V & A. TC/JF, 10/2/1849.
52. Froude 3, 320. TC/JWC, 8/2/1843.
53. Froude 4, 22.
54. Northampton. TC/HB, n.d.; Huxley, 326.
55. *RIJ*, 6.
56. *NL* 2, 82–83. TC/JC, 11/21/1849.
57. Faulkner, 169. TC/Charles Redwood, 12/23/1849.
58. *NL* 2, 85. TC/JAC, 1/9/1850.
59. *NL* 2, 86–87. TC/JC, 1/26/1850.
60. Faulkner, 170. TC/Charles Redwood, 2/16/1850, 7/20/1850.
61. Northampton. TC/HB, 1/18/1850.
62. *NL* 1, 86. TC/JC, 1/26/1850.
63. NLS. TC/JC, 1/26/1850.
64. Calder, 43. See Ruth apRoberts, "Carlyle and Trollope," Clubbe, 213–214.
65. *NL* 2, 87. TC/JC, 2/19/1850.
66. *NL* 2, 88. TC/JC, 2/19/1850.
67. NLS. TC/JAC, 4/1850.
68. *NL* 2, 93. TC/JC, 4/25/1850.
69. Northampton. TC/HB, 5/14/1850.
70. NLS. TC/JC, 5/28/1850.
71. NLS. TC/MC, 5/11/1850.
72. NLS. TC/MC, 6/27/1850.
73. NLS. TC/MC, 7/17/1850.
74. NLS. TC/MC, 7/17/1850.
75. Shepherd 2, 272.
76. *CE LDP*, 240–241.
77. *CE LDP*, 158.
78. *CE LDP*, 316.
79. *CE LDP*, *336–337*.
80. *CE LDP*, 76–78.

Chapter 14. "Imperfect Sleep"

1. Bliss, 262. TC/JWC, 8/2/1850.
2. Ireland, 427. GJ/JWC, 10/6/1851.
3. *LM* 1, 374–375. JWC/TC, 8/4/1850.
4. Bliss, 266. TC/JWC, 8/28/1850.
5. *LM* 1, 391–392. JWC/TC, 9/23/1850.
6. Bliss, 268. TC/JWC, 9/16/850.
7. Trinity. TC/FitzGerald, 12/17/1850.
8. Huxley, 346. JWC/Helen Welsh (?), 11 or 12/1850.
9. Trinity. TC/FitzGerald, 12/17/1850.
10. Marrs, 680–681. TC/AC, 11/15/1850.
11. Marrs, 682. TC/AC, 11/15/1850.
12. Slater, 466. TC/RWE, 11/14/1850.
13. Faulkner, 175. TC/Charles Redwood, 12/23/1850.
14. NLS. TC/MC, 10/26/1850.
15. NLS. TC/JC, 11/30/1850.
16. George G. Worth, "Three Carlyle Documents," *PMLA* 71 (June 1956), 543.
17. NLS. TC/JAC, 5/8/1851.
18. Slater, 474. Harriet Martineau/RWE, 2/25/1852.
19. NLS. TC/JAC, 2/2(?)/1851.
20. Marrs, 688. TC/AC, 10/24/1851.
21. Elizabeth Jenkins, *Tennyson and Dr. Gully* (Lincoln, England, 1974), 5.
22. *MSB*, 286. TC/RB, 8/21/1851.
23. Northampton. TC/HB, 9/11/1851.
24. NLS. TC/JC, 2/8/1853.
25. NLS. TC/MC, 3/12/1853.
26. Slater, 494. TC/RWE, 9/9/1853.
27. Northampton. TC/HB, 6/1/1854.
28. Bliss, 260. TC/JWC, 1/29/1850.
29. Siegel, 244.
30. Slater, 300. RWE/TC, 5/30/1841.
31. Siegel, 280, 283, 300.
32. Siegel, 302–303.
33. Siegel, 304, 307–308.
34. Siegel, 317.
35. NLS. TC/MC, 12/11/1850.
36. NLS. TC/MC, 12/11/1850.
37. *NL* 2, 107. TC/JAC, 3/29/1851; See William Blackburn, "Carlyle and the Composition of the *Life of Sterling*," *Studies in Philology* 44 (1947), 672–687.
38. Neuberg, 286. TC/Neuberg, 7/25/1851.

39. Siegel, 379.
40. *CE S*, 124.
41. *CE S*, 174.
42. *CE S*, 103.
43. *CE S*, 103.
44. *CE S*, 61.
45. *CE S*, 259.
46. Ireland, 333–334. GJ/JWC, n.d. (1850?).
47. Ireland, 347. GJ/JWC, n.d. (1849?).
48. Chelsea. JWC/Kate Sterling, 8/?/1851.
49. Ireland, 371. GJ/JWC, 10/22/1850.
50. NLS. TC/MC, 10/26/1850.
51. Northampton. TC/HB, 11/22/1851.
52. *Last Words*, 156.
53. William Irvine and Park Honan, *The Book, The Ring, & The Poet: A Biography of Robert Browning* (New York, 1974), 278.
54. *Last Words*, 161.
55. *NL* 2, 113. TC/JAC, 10/7/1851.
56. Bliss, 276. TC/JWC, 9/28/1851.
57. Neuberg, 291–292. TC/Neuberg, 4/18/1852.
58. *NL* 2, 112. TC/JAC, 10/3/1851.
59. Northampton. TC/HB, 10/27/1851.
60. "Excursion (Futile Enough) to Paris; *Autumn* 1851," in *Last Words*, 149–191.
61. *MSB*, 289–290. TC/RB, 10/28/1851.
62. Huxley, 352. TC/JW, 10/15/1851.
63. Northampton. TC/HB, 11/14/1851.
64. *NL* 2, 120. TC/JAC, 12/20/1851.
65. Faulkner, 176. TC/Charles Redwood, 12/26/1851.
66. *NL* 2, 121–122. TC/JAC, 1/3/1852; Northampton. TC/HB, 2/10/1852.
67. *CE CME* 4, 7. "Parliamentary History of the French Revolution."
68. *Report*, 273–275.
69. NLS. TC/MC, 2/10/1849; Espinasse, 190; Shepherd 2, 136–143.
70. *Rem*, 131.
71. *CL* 5, 102. TC/G. R. Gleig, 5/21/1830.
72. *CL* 2, 288. TC/James Johnston, 2/18/1823.
73. *NL* 2, 7. TC/JWC, 10/8/1845; *CL* 6, 187–188. TC/Eckermann, 7/27/1832; J. D. E. Preuss, *Friedrich der Grosse* (Berlin, 1836), and *Die Lebengeschichte des grossen Konig Friedrich von Preussen* (Berlin, 1837).
74. *Last Words*, 253. TC/Varnhagen von Ense, 11/5/1847.
75. *Last Words*, 263–264. TC/Varnhagen von Ense, 10/29/1851.
76. *NL* 2, 117. TC/JAC, 11/20/1851.
77. *Last Words*, 266. TC/Varnhagen von Ense, 6/6/1852.
78. *NL* 2, 124. TC/JAC, 2/23/1852.
79. *NL* 2, 124. TC/JAC, 2/23/1852.
80. NLS. TC/JC, 2/12/1852.
81. Northampton. TC/HB, 7/21/1852.
82. *NLM* 2, 42. JWC/TC, 2/3/1852.
83. Bliss, 280. TC/JWC, 8/13/1852; Neuberg, 281. TC/Neuberg, 11/10/1849; NLS. TC/JAC, 8/22/1856.
84. Bliss, 284. TC/JWC, 8/27/1852.
85. *NL* 2, 134. TC/JAC, 9/1/1852.
86. Northampton. TC/BB, 10/7/1852.
87. Bliss, 290. TC/JWC, 9/9/1852, 9/15/1852.
88. Slater, 490. TC/RWE, 5/13/1853.
89. Bliss, 291. TC/JWC, 9/15/1852.
90. Bliss, 288–289, 293, 298. TC/JWC, 9/9/1852, 9/15/1852, 10/1/1852.
91. BM. TC/John Marshall, 3/13/1853.
92. Bliss, 295. TC/JWC, 9/20/1852.
93. NLS. TC/MC, 9/18/1852; Bliss, 292. TC/JWC, 9/15/1852.
94. Bliss, 299. TC/JWC, 10/1/1852.
95. NLS. TC/MC, 9/19/1852.
96. *NL* 1, 152. TC/MC, 6/29/1853.
97. *NL* 2, 153. TC/MC, 6/29/1853.
98. Marrs, 695. TC/AC, 1/6/1853.
99. NLS. TC/MC, 11/8/1852.
100. *LM* 2, 8. JWC/TC, 7/8/1853.
101. *NLM* 2, 46. JWC/JAC, 9/15/1852.
102. *LM* 2, 11–13. JWC/TC, 7/20/1853.
103. Chelsea. JWC/Kate Sterling, 9/?/1853.
104. NLS. TC/JAC, 8/15/1853.
105. BM. TC/John Marshall, 9/19/1853.
106. NLS. TC/MC, 12/4/1853.
107. BM. TC/John Marshall, 12/11/1853.
108. Northampton. TC/HB, 12/23/1853.
109. Marrs, 703. TC/AC, 12/28/1853.
110. Northampton. TC/HB, 12/25/1853.
111. Bliss, 309. TC/JWC, 12/27/1853.
112. Bliss, 310. TC/JWC, 12/27/1853.
113. Bliss, 311. TC/JWC, 1/1/1854.

114. Northampton. TC/HB, 12/31/1853.
115. Northampton. TC/HB, 1/3/1854.
116. Northampton. TC/HB, 1/11/1854.
117. Slater, 483–484. TC/RWE, 6/25/1852.
118. NLS. TC/Neuberg, 11/5/1852.
119. Faulkner, 178. TC/Charles Redwood, 12/23/1852.
120. Bliss, 306. TC/JWC, 7/23/1853.
121. NLS. TC/JC, 4/10/1854.
122. Yale. TC/Spring Rice, 7/4/1854.
123. BM. TC/F. Madden, 7/10/1854.
124. NLS. TC/JAC, 12/16/1854.
125. BM. TC/John Marshall, 4/29/1855.
126. Slater, 505–506. TC/RWE, 5/13/1855.
127. NLS. TC/JAC, 7/28/1855.
128. Cate, 184. TC/JR, 3/5/1856.
129. Houghton. TC/JAC, 8(?)/22/1856; Northampton. TC/HB, 4/3/1856.
130. *NL* 2, 178. TC/JC, 5/5/1856.
131. Yale. TC/FitzGerald, 10/18/1856.
132. NLS. TC/JC, 3/5/1857.
133. Northampton. TC/HB, 1/14/1857.
134. Northampton, TC/BB, 9/15/1857.
135. NLS. TC/JC, 12/9/1857.
136. *LM* 2, 92. JWC/TC, 8/24/1857.
137. Marrs, 708–709. TC/AC, 4/8/1854.
138. Marrs, 711–712. TC/AC, 9/6/1854.
139. NLS. JAC/Alexander Glen, 10/19/1854.
140. *NLM* 2, 78. JWC/Mary Russell, autumn 1854.
141. Marrs, 712. TC/AC, 9/6/1854.
142. NLS. TC/JAC, 9/5/1854.
143. Northampton. TC/HB, 2/8/1855.
144. Northampton. TC/HB, 10/11/1855.
145. Froude 4, 154–155.
146. Northampton. TC/HB, 11/13/1855.
147. Northampton. TC/HB, 12/15/1855.
148. Northampton. TC/HB, 1/19/1856.
149. Northampton. TC/HB, 8/7/1856.
150. Northampton. TC/HB, 8/7/1856.
151. Northampton. TC/HB, 8/20/1856.
152. Northampton. TC/HB, 2/23/1857.
153. Northampton. TC/HB, 3/9/1857.
154. *NLM* 2, 136. JWC/Mary Russell, 5/?/1857.

Chapter 15. A Victorian Sage

1. Neuberg, 285. TC/Neuberg, 1/16/1851, 7/25/1851.
2. *NL* 2, 166–167. TC/JAC, 10/13/1854.
3. Northampton. TC/BB, 9/30/1854.
4. Northampton. TC/BB, 11/4/1854.
5. *LM* 2, 152. JWC/Susan Stirling, 10/21/1859.
6. Yale. TC/Ford Maddox Brown, 5/5/1859; for an account of the trip to South Kensington, see Conway, 393. "Maurice consented to sit, but Carlyle refused and could barely be persuaded to accompany the artist to South Kensington and stand against a rail while the photographer took the full length figure needed. Carlyle made a sort of grimace, and said plaintively, 'Can I go now?' Something like that grimace appeared in the photograph, and Maddox Brown found in it a valuable suggestion for a portrayal of the characteristic laughter."
7. Origo, 181.
8. BM. TC/John Marshall, 2/25/1855.
9. Copeland, 217. TC/JCH, 4/8/1855. Marrs, 713. TC/AC, 4/8/1855.
10. NLS. TC/JC, 3/5/1857.
11. NLS. TC/JC, 3/5/1857.
12. NLS. TC/JAC, 3/21/1857.
13. Marrs, 725. TC/AC, 8/13/1857.
14. *LM* 2, 97. JWC/TC, 8/30/1857.
15. *LM* 2, 104. JWC/TC, 6/25/1858.
16. *NLM* 2, 166. JWC/Mary Russell, 11/20/1857.
17. *NLM* 2, 166–167. JWC/Mary Russell, 11/20/1857.
18. *NLM* 2, 166–167. JWC/Mary Russell, 11/20/1857.
19. Cate, 188–190. JR/JWC, 11/?/1857.
20. Mrs. Kelton, "History of Frederick II," *North British Review* 30 (1859), 12.
21. Siegel, 431, 427.
22. William Stigand, "Carlyle's Frederic the Great," *Edinburgh Review* 110 (1859), 409.
23. "History of Frederick the Second," *The Athenaeum,* no. 1612 (September 18, 1858), 354.
24. Siegel, 440.
25. Siegel, 430.
26. Siegel, 454.

27. Siegel, 410, 413.
28. G. H. Lewes, "Carlyle's Frederick the Great," *Fraser's Magazine* 58 (December 1858), 633–635.
29. James Fitzjames Stephen, "Mr. Carlyle," *The Saturday Review* 5 (June 1858), 638–640.
30. Allingham, 206.
31. Allingham, 119; Wilson 5, 582.
32. Slater, 511–512. TC/RWE, 6/20/1856.
33. Wilson 5, 258.
34. Larkin, 17–18. TC/Larkin, 1/30/1857.
35. Larkin, 25. TC/Larkin, 1/8/1858.
36. Cate, 213. TC/John Ruskin, Sr., 11/30/1861.
37. Larkin, 40, 43.
38. *NLM* 2, 188. JWC/TC, 7/30/1858.
39. Bliss, 329. TC/JWC, 7/5/1858.
40. *JG*, 1.
41. *JG*, 9.
42. *JG*, 10–14.
43. *JG*, 46; Bliss, 340. TC/JWC, 9/5/1858.
44. Neuberg, 287. TC/Neuberg (?), 8/?/1852; Shepherd 2, 169.
45. *JG*, 84; Bliss, 343–344. TC/JWC, 9/14/1858.
46. Bliss, 345–346. TC/JWC, 9/15/1858; *JG*, 97.
47. *JG*, 108–109.
48. *JG*, 114.
49. *JG*, 115.
50. *JG*, 119–120.
51. *NLM* 2, 199. JWC/TC, 9/22/1858.
52. *LM* 2, 131. JWC/Mary Russell, 10/1/1858.
53. Larkin, 32. JWC/Larkin, 9/11/1858.
53. *NLM* 2, 198–199. JWC/TC, 9/22/1858.
55. Larkin, 32. JWC/Larkin, 9/22/1858.
56. *LM* 2, 133. JWC/J. G. Cooke, 10/?/1858.
57. *JG*, 120.
58. Marrs, 730. TC/AC, 10/15/1858.
59. *NLM* 2, 201. JWC/Mary Russell, 1 or 2/1859(?).
60. *NLM* 2, 212. TC/JAC, 4/14/1859.
61. *LM* 2, 136–137. JWC/Mary Russell, 12/30/1858.
62. BM. TC/Mrs. Cameron, 12/3(?)/1858.
63. Copeland, 223. TC/JCH, 1/17/1859.
64. Northampton. TC/BB, 1/30/1859.
65. NLS. TC/JAC, 4/14/1859.
66. Larkin, 35. TC/Larkin, 7/28/1859.
67. *LM* 2, 139. TC's note (1868) to JWC/J. G. Cooke, summer 1859.
68. *LM* 2, 143. JWC/George Cooke, summer 1859.
69. *LM* 2, 142. JWC/Miss Barnes, 8/24/1859.
70. Marrs, 733. TC/AC, 10/7/1859,
71. Larkin, 35. TC/Larkin, 7/28/1859.
72. *LM* 2, 154. TC's note (1868) to JWC/Mary Russell, 1/28/1860.
73. BM. TC/James Marshall, 11/28/1859.
74. NLS. TC/JC, 12/10/1859.
75. *NLM* 2, 226. JWC/Mary Russell, 6/6/1860.
76. *LM* 2, 159. TC's note (1868) to JWC/George Sinclair, 8/1/1860.
77. *NLM* 2, 227. JWC/JC, 8/11/1860.
78. NLS. TC/JAC, 10/30/1861.
79. Bliss, 351. TC/JWC, 8/22/1860.
80. *LM* 1, 162. JWC/TC, 8/10/1860.
81. *LM* 2, 179–180. JWC/TC, 9/3/1860.
82. Bliss, 352–353. TC/JWC, 8/28/1860.
83. *LM* 1, 180. JWC/Mary Russell, 9/7/1860.
84. Strouse. TC/Frederick Chapman, 9/5/1860.
85. Shepherd 2, 175–176.
86. *LM* 2, 186. JWC/TC, 9/17/1860.
87. Bliss, 354. TC/JWC, 9/5/1860.
88. Froude 4, 242. TC/Thomas Erskine, 10/12/1860.
89. *NL* 2, 209–210. TC/JAC, 11/19/1860; Trinity. JWC/MM, ?/1860.
90. George J. Worth, "Three Carlyle Documents," *PMLA* 71(1956), 544.
91. Trinity. JWC/MM, ?/1860.
92. Browning, 444. TC/RB, 12/4/1855.
93. Browning, 446. TC/RB, 1/27/1856.
94. Browning, 446–447. TC/RB, 1/27/1856, 4/25/1856.
95. Browning, 448. JWC/TC(?), 7/4/1856; Hanson, p. 447.
96. Slater, 512. TC/RWE, 7/20/1856.
97. Browning, 450.
98. Browning, 451. TC/JAC, 8/9/1861;

TC/JF, 8/17/1861; NLS. TC/JAC, 8/9/1861.
99. Browning, 451. TC/JAC, 8/9/1861; TC/JF, 8/17/1861.
100. Browning, 452.
101. *MSB,* 180. TC/Mrs. Harriet Taylor, 7/13/1842.
102. NLS. TC/MC, 4/24/1851.
103. *MSB,* 183. TC/JSM, 4/30/1852.
104. Larkin, 39; *NL* 2, 196. TC/JAC, 5/4/1859.
105. NLS. JWC/Allingham, n.d.
106. Trinity. TC/MM, 10/29/1855.
107. Trinity. TC/MM, 6/15/1857.
108. Trinity. TC/MM, 8/7/1860.
109. Trinity. JWC/MM, n.d. (1861?).
110. Trinity. TC/MM, 8/11/1864.
111. Sanders, 212–213.
112. Sanders, 215. JWC/Emily Tennyson, 10/4/1862.
113. NLS. TC/JAC, 10/6/1849.
114. *LM* 1, 385. JWC/TC, 9/2/1850.
115. *NL* 2, 127. TC/MC, 4/10/1852.
116. V & A. TC/JF, 4/17/1851.
117. Slater, 523. TC/RWE, 6/2/1858.
118. *NL* 2, 205. TC/JF, 10/26/1859.
119. Wilson 5, 505; Copeland, 228–229. TC/JCH, 4/29/1863.
120. Copeland, 228–229. TC/JCH, 4/29/1863.
121. *NLM* 2, 333. JWC/TC, 8/2/1865.
122. *NL* 2, 155. TC/JF, 9/29/1853.
123. *NL* 2, 198. TC/JF, 7/10/1859.
124. *LM* 2, 318. JWC/Mary Russell, 12/27/1864.
125. Wilson 5, 532. TC/MM, 12/29/1863.
126. Slater, 496. TC/RWE, 9/9/1853.
127. Northampton. TC/HB, 10/11/1855.
128. Berg. TC/A. J. Scott, 6/30/1858.
129. *NLM.* 2, 245. JWC/Mary Russell, 4/14/1862.
130. Gordon S. Haight, "The Carlyles and the Leweses," Clubbe, 183–185.
131. Clubbe, 188–190.
132. Strouse. TC/G. H. Lewes, 10/18/1839.
133. See Carlyle's annotated copy of *Ranthorpe* (London, 1847) in the Carlyle House, Chelsea, and his annotated copy of *Rose, Blanche and Violet* (London, 1848) in the Berg.
134. Clubbe, 188.
135. Huxley, 319–320. JWC/JW, 2/5/1849.
136. *NL* 2, 90–91. TC/JAC, 3/5/1850; *NL* 2, 93–94. TC/JC, 4/25/1850; Huxley. JWC/JW, 4/1/1849.
137. Ray. TC/James Marshall, 7/14/1854.
138. Duffy, 222.
139. Clubbe, 181. TC/RB, 10/10/1851.
140. Clubbe, 191. G. H. Lewes/TC, 10/19/1854.
141. Clubbe, 192. TC/JAC, 11/2/1854.
142. *NL* 2, 190. TC/W. Lattimer, 3/3/1858.
143. Clubbe, 196–198. JWC/George Eliot, 1/22/1858, 2/20/1859.
144. Duffy, 223.
145. Clubbe, 196.
146. Clubbe, 202. JWC/Alexander Gilchrist, 7/31/1861.
147. Yale. TC/Spring Rice, 4/16/1854.
148. Northampton. TC/LA, 2/23/1870; Allingham, 202.
149. Chelsea. TC/John Downes, 1/26/1862.
150. Froude 3, 440.
151. *NL* 2, 59. TC/JF, spring 1848.
152. *NL* 2, 59. TC/JF, spring 1848.
153. Froude 3, 459.
154. Ireland, 292. GJ/JWC, 8/20/1849.
155. Northampton. TC/HB, 11/28/1853.
156. Espinasse, 218.
157. Froude 4, 254–255.
158. Yale. TC/Froude, 10/23/1860.
159. Cate, 2.
160. Cate, 61–62. TC/JR, 3/9/1851.
161. Chelsea. John Ruskin, Sr./W. H. Harrison, 1/28/1851.
162. *NLM* 2, 76–77. JWC/JAC, 5/9/1854.
163. Chelsea. JWC/Kate Sterling, 5/14/1846.
164. Cate, 83–84. JR/TC, 12/?/1859.
165. Cate, 72–73. TC/JR, 1/18/1856.
166. Cate, 89–90. TC/JR, 10/29/1860.
167. Cate, 91–92. TC/John Ruskin, Sr., 4/23/1861.
168. Cate, 92–93. JR/TC, 8/28/1861.
169. Ray. TC/Froude, 4/14(?)/1862.
170. Cate, 98–99. JR/TC and JWC, 12/?/1861.
171. Cate, 103–104. TC/JR, 4/?/1863.

172. Cate, 105–106. JR/TC, 2/26/1864.
173. Cate, 106. JR/TC, 3/12/1864.
174. *NL* 2, 225. TC/JAC, 3/1/1865.
175. Bliss, 381. TC/JWC, 7/27/1865.
176. NLS. TC/MC, 4/1/1853.
177. NLS. TC/MC, 4/1/1853.
178. *LM* 2, 205–206. TC's note to JWC/Miss Barnes, 9/22/1861.
179. Wilson 5, 451. TC/Lady Sandwich, 2/1/1862.
180. Northampton. TC/BB, 9/15/1857.
181. *NL* 2, 191. TC/JC, 5/5/1858.
182. Northampton. TC/BB, 10/23/1858.
183. *NLM* 2, 222. JWC/Mary Austin, 1/1860.
184. *NLM* 2, 224–225. JWC/Mary Russell, 2/24/1860.
185. *LM* 2, 191. JWC/Maggie Welsh, 12/8/1860.
186. Origo, 173–174.
187. Origo, 174.
188. Northampton. TC/BB, 4/27/1861.
189. Northampton. TC/LA, 9/19/1862.
190. Berg. JWC/Mrs. Ruden, 11/2/1862.
191. *LM* 2, 239–240. JWC/Mary Austin, 10/23/1862.
192. *LM* 2, 241–242. JWC/Mary Russell, 11/21/1862.
193. Northampton. TC/LA, 12/20/1862.
194. *LM* 2, 248. JWC/Betty Braid, 12/25/1862.
195. NLS. LA/JWC, n.d. (March 1864?).
196. Northampton. TC/LA, 4/11/1864.
197. Bliss, 362. TC/JWC, 4/1/1864.
198. *NLM* 2, 259. JWC/TC, 8/24/1862.
199. Berg. JWC/Mrs. Jameson, n.d.
200. *CL* 7, 337. JWC/MC, 11/21/1834, and *NLM* 2, 75; Yale. TC/JAC, 6/5/1863; *LM* 2, 264–265. JWC/Mary Russell, 6/3/1863.
201. *LM* 2, 265. JWC/Mary Russell, 6/3/1863.
202. *LM* 1, 266. JWC/Mary Austin, 7/5/1863.
203. *LM* 2, 271. TC's note (1867?) to JWC/Mary Russell, 9/16/1863.
204. *LM* 2, 271. TC's note (1867?) to JWC/Mary Russell, 9/16/1863.
205. Northampton. TC/LA, 9/30/1863.
206. Northampton. TC/BB, 10/1/1863.
207. Northampton. TC/LA, 12/4/1863.
208. *Rem*, 147; Northampton. TC/LA, 12/21/1863. See Fred Kaplan, *Dickens and Mesmerism: The Hidden Springs of Fiction* (Princeton, 1975), 17, 26. Espinasse (231) writes: "I remember to have seen him . . . listening during the best part of an hour, to what the late Dr. John Elliotson had to say of Animal Magnetism, for his devotion to the practice of which he sacrificed a fine medical practice."
209. NLS. TC/JAC, 12/29/1863.
210. *LM* 2, 274. TC's note (1867?) to JWC/Mary Russell, 9/16/1863.
211. *LM* 2, 274. TC's note (1867?) to JWC/Mary Russell, 9/16/1863.
212. *LM* 2, 283. TC's note (1867?) to JWC/TC, 4/8/1864.
213. Northampton. Maggie Welsh/LA, n.d. [1/?/1864].
214. Larkin, 41.
215. Larkin, 41.
216. Larkin, 41–42; *NL* 2, 219. TC/JC, 1/10/1864.
217. *LM* 2, 286. JWC/Maggie Welsh, 4/?/1864.
218. Northampton. TC/LA, 4/11/1864.
219. *LM* 2, 285. JWC/TC, 4/19/1864; NLS. JWC/JF, 4/25/1864.
220. *LM* 2, 286. JWC/TC, 4/25/1864.
221. *NLM* 2, 294. JWC/TC, 4/29/1864.
222. Northampton. Maggie Welsh/LA, n.d.
223. Northampton. Maggie Welsh/LA, n.d.
224. *LM* 2, 292. JWC/TC, 7/23/1864.
225. Bliss, 369–370. TC/JWC, 7/25/1864.
226. "Last Letters," 46. TC/Froude, 8/16/1864.
227. Trinity. TC/MM, 8/11/1864.
228. Northampton. TC/LA, 8/21/1864.
229. *NLM* 2, 296. JWC/TC, 8/19/1864.
230. Bliss, 375. TC/JWC, 9/29/1864.
231. Morgan. TC/Froude, 9/4/1864.
232. *NLM* 2, 303. TC/Mary Austin, 10/9/1864.
233. *NLM* 2, 305. JWC/Mary Russell, 10/20/1864.
234. *LM* 2, 307. JWC/JF, 10/?/1864; *LM* 2, 316–317. JWC/Mary Russell, 12/20/1864.

235. Wilson 5, 561.
236. *NL* 2, 226. TC/JAC, 3/1/1865.
237. "Last Letters," 46. TC/Froude, 8/6/1864.
238. *CE FG* 8, 290–291; also see Morse Peckham, *Victorian Revolutionaries* (New York, 1970), 44–46.
239. *NL* 2, 225–226. TC/JAC, 3/1/1865.
240. *Rem*, 132.

Chapter 16. "My One Strong City"

1. *NL* 2, 232–233. TC/JAC, 12/5/1865.
2. Cate, 113–114. TC/JR, 12/20/1865.
3. *NL* 2, 225–226. TC/JAC, 3/1/1865.
4. *NLM* 2, 321–323. JWC/Betty Braid, 3/12/1865; JWC/Mrs. Oliphant, 3/29/1865.
5. *LM* 2, 334. JWC/TC, 6/3/1865.
6. Strouse. TC/Cunningham, 3/13/1865; *LM* 2, 324.
7. *LM* 2, 328. JWC/TC, 5/24/1865; Yale. TC/William Maccall, 5/17/1865.
8. Marrs, 741. TC/AC, 8/6/1865.
9. *LM* 2, 339. JWC/TC, 6/28/1865.
10. *LM* 2, 338. TC's note (1868) to JWC/TC, 6/28/1865.
11. Bliss, 382. TC/JWC, 7/31/1865.
12. Cate, 110–111. JR/JWC, 7/13/1865.
13. *LM* 2, 342. TC's note (1868) to JWC/TC, 7/27/1865.
14. *LM* 2, 352–353. JWC/Mary Russell, 8/23/1865.
15. Froude, 4, 289. TC/JWC, 7/1865.
16. Strouse. TC/B. C. Trench, 10/24/1865.
17. Froude 4, 294–298; Shepherd 2, 188–189.
18. Froude 4, 295–296.
19. Shepherd 2, 188–189.
20. Chelsea. TC/P. Kelland, 11/29/1865; Berg. TC/P. Kelland, 12/8/1865.
21. *NLM* 2, 343. JWC/Betty Braid, 12/28/1865.
22. Trinity. TC/MM, 3/10/1866.
23. Trinity. JWC/MM, 3/?/1866.
24. Yale. JWC/Mrs. Simpson, 3/23/1866.
25. Tyndall, 350–352.
26. Tyndall, 358–362.
27. NLS. JWC/?, 3/?/1866.
28. Bliss, 384. TC/JWC, 4/1/1866.
29. Tyndall, 362.
30. Shepherd 2, 212; Tyndall, 363.
31. Tyndall, 363; Shepherd 2, 207.
32. Tyndall, 363; *CE CME* 4, 449, 451.
33. *CE CME* 4, 451, 472.
34. *CE CME* 4, 478–481.
35. *CE CME* 4, 481–482.
36. Tyndall, 364.
37. Bliss, 386. TC/JWC, 4/3/1866.
38. *LM* 2, 382. JWC/Susan Stirling, 4/11/1866; Tyndall, 364.
39. Shepherd 2, 230–231; Forster 3, 276–277.
40. Shepherd 2, 231.
41. Conway, 97.
42. NLS. T. Erskine/JWC, 4/3/1866.
43. Bliss, 387. TC/JWC, 4/4/1866.
44. Bliss, 387. TC/JWC, 4/4/1866; Conway, 88–92; Tyndall, 365.
45. Froude 4, 306.
46. Bliss, 388–389. TC/JWC, 4/11/1866; *LM* 2, 378. JWC/TC, 4/4/1866.
47. Bliss, 392–393. TC/JWC, 4/19/1866.
48. Bliss, 388. TC/JWC, 4/11/1866.
49. Edinburgh. Maggie Welsh/JC, n.d. Bliss, 389. TC/JWC, 4/11/1866.
50. Bliss, 390–392. TC/JWC, 4/15/1866.
51. *NL* 2, 235. TC/JC, 4/28/1866; *LM* 2, 388. JWC/TC, 4/21/1866.
52. Bliss, 394. TC/JWC, 4/20/1866.
53. *LM* 2, 388. TC's note (1869) to JWC/TC, 4/21/1866.
54. Marrs, 751–752. TC/AC, 5/3/1866; V & A. TC/JF, 4/22/1866.
55. NLS. GJ/Betty Braid, 4/22/1866.
56. V & A. TC/JF, 4/22/1866.
57. NLS. TC/W. Dods, 4/22/1866.
58. V & A. TC/JF, 4/22/1866.
59. Berg. GJ/Constance, Marchioness of Lothian, 4/22/1866.
60. NLS. GJ/Betty Braid, 4/22/1866.
61. Tyndall, 368–369; NLS. GJ/Betty Braid, 4/22/1866.
62. *NL* 2, 236. TC/JC, 4/28/1866.
63. Edinburgh. Maggie Welsh/JC, n.d. (April 1866?).
64. NLS. GJ/Betty Braid, 4/22/1866.
65. Marrs, 751. TC/AC, 5/3/1866; *LM* 2, 391. GJ/TC, 5/26/1866.
66. *LM* 2, 391. GJ/TC, 5/26/1866.

67. Froude 4, 315; Marrs, 752. TC/AC, 5/3/1866.
68. NLS. JAC/W. Dods, 4/24/1866.
69. *LM* 2, 390. JWC/TC, 4/21/1866.
70. Conway, 99.
71. *NL* 2, 235. TC/JC, 4/28/1866.
72. NLS. JAC/W. Dods, 4/24/1866; *Rem*, 166.
73. NLS. JAC/W. Dods, 4/24/1866.
74. *Rem*, 166; Froude 4, 315.
75. Berg. GJ/Constance, Marchioness of Lothian, n.d.; Marrs, 752. TC/AC, 5/3/1866.
76. Northampton. TC/LA, 4/28/1866.
77. Northampton. TC/LA, 4/28/1866.
78. NLS. TC/Betty Braid, 5/2/1866.
79. NLS. Dickens/TC, 5/13/1866.
80. NLS. GJ/?, 5/1/1866.
81. Slater, 549–550. RWE/TC, 5/16/1866.
82. Froude 4, 318. TC/Thomas Erskine, 5/1/1866.
83. Cate, 246. JR/TC, 10/1/1866.
84. NLS. GJ/Lady Ambereley, 6/12/1866.
85. Duffy, 231.
86. Cate, 240. TC/JR, 5/10/1866.
87. *Rem*, 156–157.
88. "Last Letters," 48–49. TC/Froude, 8/2/1866.
89. *Rem*, 49, 79.
90. *Rem*, 69, 139, 162; Froude 4, 301.
91. Marrs, 754. JAC/TC, 7/4/1866.
92. *Rem*, 137–138.
93. *Rem*, 169; see Anne M. Skabarnicki, "The MSS. of Carlyle's *Reminiscences* in the NLS," *Carlyle Newsletter*, no. 1 (March 1979), 12–15.
94. NLS. TC/JAC, 8/13/1866.
95. Slater, 552–553. TC/RWE, 1/27/1867.
96. Froude 4, 327.
97. Trinity. TC/Brian Procter, 8/17/1866.
98. *Two Rem*, 121–122.
99. Marrs, 757–758. TC/AC, 10/20/1866.
100. *Rem*, 307.
101. *NL* 2, 240. TC/JAC, 11/28/1866.
102. *Rem*, 307.
103. Strouse. TC/James Aitken, 12/5/1866.
104. Tyndall, 371–374.
105. Froude 4, 334; Tyndall, 374.
106. Neuberg, 296. TC/Neuberg, 2/10/1867.
107. *Rem*, 307.
108. Slater, 551. TC/RWE, 1/27/1867.
109. *Rem*, 341.
110. *Rem*, 343.
111. *Rem*, 364–365.
112. Froude 4, 335; "Last Letters," 50–51. TC/Froude, 2/10/1867.
113. Origo, 181.
114. Slater, 552. TC/RWE, 1/27/1867.
115. Cate, 125–126. TC/JR, 2/15/1867.
116. NLS. TC/JAC, 3/10/1867.
117. Northampton. TC/LA, 3/18/1867.
118. Espinasse, 185.
119. Gillian Workman, "Thomas Carlyle and the Governor Eyre Controversy," *Victorian Studies* 18 (September 1974), 79.
120. Workman, 78–79; George H. Ford, "The Governor Eyre Case in England," *University of Toronto Quarterly* 17 (1947–1948), 220–221.
121. Workman, 79.
122. Workman, 80.
123. *LM* 2, 380–381. JWC/TC, 4/10/1866.
124. Bliss, 388. TC/JWC, 4/11/1866.
125. Allingham, 209.
126. Conway, 364–367, 357–358.
127. NLS. TC/JAC, 5/1/1865.
128. Workman, 92–93.
129. Froude 4, 329. TC/Davenport Bromley, 8/30/1866.
130. Workman, 98–100.
131. Workman, 96–97.
132. Ford, 233.
133. Ford, 233.
134. Strouse. TC/"Dear Sir," 8/9/1867.
135. Froude 4, 353.
136. Northampton. TC/LA, 5/8/1867; NLS. TC/JAC, 5/11/1867.
137. *CE CME* 5, 47.
138. *CE CME* 5, 16.
139. *CE CME* 5, 40.
140. Froude 4, 356; Browning, 453; Conway, 412.
141. Shepherd 2, 281–282.
142. Northampton. TC/LA, n.d./1870.
143. *CE CME* 5, 52.
144. *CE CME* 5, 59.
145. Browning, 455. TC/JF, 11/2/1870.
146. Froude 4, 405.
147. Marrs, 774. TC/AC, 1/28/1871.

148. Allingham, 172.
149. Allingham, 171–172.
150. Shepherd 2, 244–245.
151. Froude 4, 356.
152. Neuberg, 297.
153. Northampton. TC/LA, 4/20/1867.
154. *NL* 2, 246. TC/JAC, 7/5/1867.
155. Cate, 131. JR/TC, 5/30/1867.
156. Cate, 131. JR/TC, 5/30/1867; TC/The Editor, 5/28/1867.
157. *Norton* 1, 362. Charles Eliot Norton/G. W. Curtis, 7/22/1869; Cate, 131. JR/TC, 5/30/1867.
158. Cate, 132. JR/TC, 6/1/1867.
159. Cate, 133–134. TC/*London Times,* 6/8/1867.
160. Cate, 133–134. TC/JR, 6/8/1867.
161. Cate, 136–140. TC/JR, 6/13/1867.
162. Cate, 136–140. TC/JR, 6/13/1867.
163. Northampton. TC/LA, 8/27/1867.
164. Cate, 176–177. JR/TC, 12/3/1873.
165. Froude 4, 353–354; Northampton. TC/LA, 10/7/1867.
166. NLS. TC/JAC, 11/26/1870.
167. *NL* 2, 279. TC/JAC, 5/13/1871.
168. Froude 4, 346.
169. Shepherd 2, 256.
170. Yale. TC/JCH, 2/14/1868.
171. Froude 4, 359.
172. *NL* 2, 256. TC/JAC, 7/15/1869.
173. NLS. TC/JC, 5/18/1868.
174. NLS. MAC/JC, 9/30/1868; *NL* 2, 256. TC/JC, 3/11/1869; NLS. TC/JAC, 5/1/1857.
175. Chelsea. TC/C. A. Ward, 10/21/1868.
176. Northampton. TC/LA, 10/18/1868.
177. Froude 4, 381.
178. *LM* 2, 388. TC's note (1869) to JWC/TC, 4/21/1866.
179. Froude 4, 367–368; Rodger L. Tarr, " 'A Sentimental Journey': Carlyle's Final Visit to the Grange," *Notes and Queries,* January 1970, 21–22.
180. NLS. TC/JAC, 3/6/1869; *NL* 2, 254–255. TC/JC, 3/11/1869.

Chapter 17. "A Monument of Mercy"

1. Marrs, 768. TC/AC, 10/6/1870.
2. Cate, 226. JR/TC, 7/12/1875.
3. Cate, 166. JR/TC, 12/?/1871.
4. Allingham, 233.
5. Slater, 585. RWE/TC, 1/5/1872.
6. NLS. TC/JAC, 6/10/1870.
7. V & A. TC/probably dictated to JF, January 1873.
8. Froude 4, 424.
9. Allingham, 228.
10. Slater, 573. TC/RWE, 9/28/1870.
11. Marrs, 769. TC/AC, 10/6/1870.
12. Marrs, 771. TC/AC, 2/28/1871; Cate, 154. JR/TC, 10/?/1870.
13. NLS. MAC/TC, 7/17/1871.
14. "Last Letters," 261–262. TC/Froude, 9/26/1871.
15. Marrs, 776. TC/AC, 12/16/1871.
16. Duffy, 242.
17. Froude 4, 417; *NL* 2, 284. TC/JAC, 2/24/1872.
18. Trinity. TC/FitzGerald, 6/15/1872.
19. *NL* 2, 278. TC/JAC, 3/25/1871; NLS. MAC/TC, 7/17/1871.
20. Shepherd 2, 297–299.
21. NLS. JAC/TC, 9/24/1872.
22. NLS. JAC/TC, 3/31/1872.
23. NLS. MAC/TC, 5/22/1872.
24. Northampton. TC/LA, 9/12/1872, 9/16/1872.
25. Northampton. MAC/LA, 10/29/1872.
26. Northampton. TC/LA, 1/10/1873, 2/11/1873.
27. Houghton. TC/Norton, 11/3/1873; Copeland, 244–246. MAC/JCH, 2/3/1874.
28. Copeland, 247. MAC/JCH, 2/3/1874.
29. *NL* 2, 299. TC/JAC, 9/20/1873.
30. NLS. TC/JAC, 3/25/1870; Houghton. TC/Norton, 1/29/1874.
31. Froude 4, 408–409.
32. "Last Letters," 263. TC/Froude, 9/26/1871.
33. Froude 4, 413.
34. Froude 4, 414.
35. NLS. TC/JAC, 3/7/1874.
36. Cate, 202–205, 208–210. TC/JR, 7/15/1874, 7/30/1874; *Froude's Life of Carlyle,* abridged and edited by John Clubbe (Columbus, Ohio, 1979), 37–38: Froude/TC, 7/10/1874.
37. NLS. TC/JAC, 11/6/1874; Houghton. MAC/Norton, 1/3/1875.

38. *CE CME* 5, 319.
39. NL. 2, 304. TC/JAC, 1/1/1874.
40. *CE CME* 5, 364–367; BM. TC/Mrs. Ralph Smith, April/1874; BM. TC/ Lady Derby, 3/23/1874.
41. Houghton. TC/Norton, 4/23/1874.
42. "Last Letters," 245. TC/Froude, 7/18/1874.
43. Trinity. TC/FitzGerald, 11/6/1874.
44. Houghton. MAC/Norton, 1/3/1875.
45. Marrs, 784. TC/AC, 3/4/1875.
46. For an account of Laing, see Gilbert Goudie, *David Laing* (Edinburgh, 1913). Laing's authority as a Knox scholar is attested to by his edition of Knox's complete works (Edinburgh, 1848–1864). Also, see Jasper Ridley, *John Knox* (Oxford, 1968).
47. *Two Rem,* 10.
48. Froude 4, 380.
49. Allingham, 226–227.
50. Houghton. TC/Norton, 4/1/1875.
51. Wilson 6, 406.
52. Houghton. MAC/Norton, 6/11/1877; Walter Sichel, *The Sands of Time, Recollections and Reflections* (London, 1924), 45.
53. Cate, 193. JR/TC, 6/27/1874.
54. Houghton. MAC/Norton, 7/15/1875.
55. *NL* 2, 318. TC/JAC, 11/20/1875.
56. Origo, 185.
57. Houghton. MAC/Norton, 12/8/1875; *NL* 2, 320.
58. *NL* 2, 324. "To Thomas Carlyle," 12/4/1875; Shepherd 2, 306–307.
59. Houghton. MAC/Norton, 12/8/1875; Huntington. "Forster Collection: 1882 Mrs. Forster Private."
60. Froude 4, 435–436.
61. Allingham, 248.
62. Shepherd 2, 307–313; Robert Blake, *Disraeli* (New York, 1967), 439, 570–654; *Letters of Matthew Arnold,* ed. George W. E. Russell (London, 1895), 2, 139.
63. Blake, 552; Froude 4, 429–432. Disraeli/TC, 12/27/1874; TC/Disraeli, 12/29/1874; Allingham, 236.
64. Allingham, 236; Froude 4, 432.
65. Froude 4, 433–434. TC/JAC, 1/1/1875.
66. *NL* 2, 310–312. TC/JAC, 1/1/1875.
67. Allingham, 234.
68. Cate, 202–205. TC/JR, 7/15/1874; Trinity. TC/MM, 12/30/1847.
69. Slater, 509. RWE/TC, 5/6/1856.
70. Houghton. TC/Norton, 12/2/1875.
71. Moncure Conway, *Thomas Carlyle* (London, 1881), 100.
72. Allingham, 212; Wilson 6, 261.
73. Gregory Paine, "The Literary Relations of Whitman and Carlyle with Special Reference to Their Contrasting Views of Democracy," *Studies in Philology* 36 (July 1939), 557–559; also see Fred Manning Smith, "Whitman's Poet-Prophet and Carlyle's Hero," *PMLA* 55 (1940), 1146–1164.
74. Wilson 6, 137–138; Philip Henderson, *Swinburne: The Portrait of a Poet* (London, 1974), 53.
75. BM, 43949. f. 37; see Samuel Chew, *Swinburne* (Boston, 1929), 162, and Henderson, 199–200.
76. Wilson 6, 138; *Swinburne, The Critical Heritage,* ed. Clyde K. Hyder (New York, 1970), 118–119.
77. Berg. Swinburne, "Poems in Latin to Thomas Carlyle," three holograph drafts of one poem.
78. Allingham, 258. In his sonnet "On the Deaths of Thomas Carlyle and George Eliot," Swinburne reserved all his praise for George Eliot, and in another sonnet, "After Looking into Carlyle's Reminiscences," his oral-anal vehemence demanded that "These deathless names by this dead snake defiled / Bid memory spit upon him for their sake."
79. Espinasse, 187.
80. Tyndall, 377.
81. Allingham, 232, 238, 261; Neuberg, 289. Neuberg/Miss Neuberg, 12/27/1852.
82. Allingham, 238. Northampton. TC/ HB, 6/8/1853.
83. Allingham, 256.
84. Allingham, 264, 268.
85. NLS. TC/JAC, 12/9/1873.
86. Allingham, 233.
87. Houghton. TC/Norton, 12/2/1875.
88. Northampton. TC/LA, 9/1/1875.

89. Houghton. MAC/Norton, 11/20/1875. See K. J. Fielding, "Froude's Second Revenge: The Carlyles and the Wedgwoods," *Prose Studies* (London, December 1981), 301–316, and Barbara Wedgwood, " 'Mrs Wedgwood—Address Forgotten' ": The Neglected Friendship of Jane Welsh Carlyle and Frances Mackintosh Wedgwood," *Carlyle Newsletter,* no. 3 (October 1982), 18–25.
90. *NL* 2, 314–315; TC/JAC, 9/2/1875; Allingham, 239.
91. Tyndall, 388.
92. *NL* 2, 264. TC/JAC, 3/19/1870; Froude 4, 392.
93. *NL* 2, 256–257. TC/JAC, 4/28/1869; NLS. TC/JAC, 1/28/1870.
94. V & A. TC/JF, 6/11/1870; NLS. TC/JAC, 6/15/1870.
95. Northampton. MAC/LA, n.d. (1870); Berg. TC/Georgina Hogarth, 7/4/1870.
96. NLS. TC/JAC, 2/10/1871.
97. Conway, 60.
98. *Norton* 1, 495. *Journal,* April 20–May 10, 1873; *NL* 2, 298. TC/JAC, 9/20/1873.
99. NLS. TC/Harriet Mill, 5/17/1873.
100. *Norton* 1, 496. *Journal,* April 20–May 10, 1873.
101. Houghton. TC/Norton, 11/3/1873.
102. Slater, 53.
103. *NL* 2, 296. TC/JAC, 3/22/1873; Slater, 55.
104. Allingham, 223–224.
105. *NL* 2, 325. TC/JAC, 2/5/1876.
106. Duffy, 245.
107. C. R. Sanders, "Carlyle's Letters," *Bulletin of the John Rylands Library* 38 (September 1955), 223; Northampton. TC/LA, 1/10/1873.
108. Houghton. TC/Norton, 11/3/1873.
109. NLS. TC/JAC, 2/4/1874; V & A. TC/JF, 2/10/1874.
110. Shepherd 2, 303; Allingham, 231–232.
111. "Last Letters," 242. TC/Froude, 6/20/1874.
112. *NL* 2, 325–326; TC/JAC, 2/5/1876; Houghton. MAC/Norton, 2/2/1876.
113. Northampton. TC/LA, 3/21/1876.
114. *NL* 2, 321. TC/JAC, 12/4/1875.
115. Marrs, 760. TC/AC, 1/12/1870.
116. Marrs, 787. TC/AC, 2/15/1876.
117. *NL* 2, 328. TC/JAC, 4/22/1876; Marrs, 788. TC/Thomas Carlyle (nephew), 5/4/1876.
118. Froude 4, 464.
119. Houghton. MAC/FitzGerald, 6/2/1879.
120. *NL* 2, 266. TC/JAC, 4/2/1870.
121. *Alfred Lord Tennyson: A Memoir by His Son* (London, 1895), 2, 236–237.
122. Browning, 457–458. RB/TC, 3/26/1878, 3/27/1878; Houghton. MAC/Norton, 12/8/1875.
123. NLS. Whitwell Elwin/MAC, 6/22/1876.
124. Allingham, 241.
125. Houghton. TC/Norton, 4/1/1875.
126. Houghton. MAC/Norton, 10/7/1876.
127. James Anthony Froude, *My Relations with Carlyle* (London, 1903), 71–77.
128. NLS. Annie Munro/MAC, 5/24/187?.
129. Cate, 216–217. JR/MAC, 8/28/1874. See Anthony Burton, "The Forster Library as a Dickens Collection," *Dickens Studies Newsletter* 9 (June 1978), 36.
130. NLS. Whitwell Elwin/MAC, 2/1/1877.
131. NLS. Whitwell Elwin/MAC, 12/24/1876.
132. Mary's own attempt to solve the "problem" did produce an anthology: Mary Aitken (Mary Aitken Carlyle), *Scottish Songs* (London and Glasgow, 1874).
133. James Crichton Brown and Alexander Carlyle, *The Nemesis of Froude* (London, 1903), 136–137.
134. NLS. Whitwell Elwin/MAC, 12/31/1876.
135. Froude, *My Relations with Carlyle,* 77–80.
136. NLS. MAC/Trubner, 6/7/1877; Wilson 6, 250–251, claims that Martin also stole some letters and "abstracted . . . hundreds of old letters and other papers."
137. Wilson 6, 412.
138. Houghton. MAC/Norton, 11/6/1877.
139. K. J. Fielding, "Froude and Carlyle:

Some New Considerations," Fielding, 245.

140. There is no indication of anything other than good feelings between Mary and Froude until after Carlyle's death. Their subsequent conflict and its consequences for Carlyle's reputation have produced a large body of secondary literature whose citations are available in Rodger L. Tarr, *Thomas Carlyle, A Bibliography of English-Language Criticism, 1824–1974* (Charlottesville, Va., 1976).
141. Froude 4, 466–467.
142. Espinasse, 71.
142. *NL* 2, 333. TC/JAC, 5/29/1877.
144. Allingham, 262.
145. Houghton. MAC/Norton, 9/22/1878.
146. Allingham, 267.
147. "Reminiscences of a Visit with Carlyle in 1878 by His Nephew and Namesake," ed. E. W. Marrs, *Thoth* 8 (1967), 75.
148. *Thoth,* 75, 80, 69.
149. Houghton. MAC/Norton, 9/22/1878.
150. Houghton. MAC/Norton, 9/22/1878.
151. Froude 4, 463; *NL* 2, 341–342. TC/JAC, 2/8/1879.
152. Allingham, 275.
153. Houghton. MAC/Norton, 5/11/1879.
154. Cate, 400. JR/TC, 6/23/1878.
155. Allingham, 275.
156. Houghton. MAC/Norton, 5/11/1879.
157. NLS. MAC/? n.d. (1878).
158. Allingham, 280.
159. Allingham, 284.
160. Allingham, 285.
161. Duffy, 252–254.
162. Allingham, 286.
163. Copeland, 254. MAC/JCH, 7/18/1880.
164. Margaret W. Oliphant, "Thomas Carlyle," *Macmillan's Magazine* 43 (April 1881), 494.
165. Oliphant, 494–495.
166. Froude 4, 468–469; Allingham, 306.
167. Conway, 153.
168. Allingham, 306.
169. Tyndall, 390; *CL* 7, 121. TC/JAC, 3/27/1824; Houghton. MAC/Norton, 3/26/1881.
170. Houghton. MAC/Norton, 3/26/1881.
171. C. F. Harrold, "Remembering Carlyle: A Visit with His Nephew," *South Atlantic Quarterly* (1937), 382.
172. Houghton. MAC/Norton, 3/26/1881.
173. Allingham, 308–309; Froude 4, 469.
174. Allingham, 309.
175. Yale. MAC/J. Boehm, 2/7/1881.
176. Harrold, 382; Marrs, 793. Alexander Carlyle (nephew)/Thomas Carlyle (nephew), 2/11/1881.
177. Tyndall, 390–391.
178. Conway, 191.
179. Conway, 191; Copeland, 258–261. MAC/JCH, 2/11/1881, 3/3/1881.

Index